For the Love of a Highland Home

For my husband, Malcolm,
our son and daughter, Daniel and Mary,
and our daughter-in-law, Sarah.

For the Love of a Highland Home

The Fraser brothers' Indian quest

Kathy Fraser

ISBN: 9780992486549 (paperback)

ISBN: 9780992486556 (hardback)

Front cover image: 'Source of the River Jumna' by James Baillie Fraser.
Back cover image: Inverness, Scotland in 1821 by William Daniell for Voyage Round Britain, R. Ayton. Courtesy *Inverness Courier*, Old Inverness, Robt Carruthers & Sons 1967 and Am Baile/Highland Libraries.

Published by:
Grey Thrush Publishing
13 Marlton Crescent
St Kilda 3182
Australia
email: oryxpublishing@bigpond.com

Reprinted with alterations in February 2017 by Bell and Bain, Glasgow.

Copies of this book can be ordered from:
Reelig House,
Kirkhill,
Inverness-shire IV5 7PP
United Kingdom
email: kreelig@aol.com.

Foreword

'Would you suppose it?' wrote Aleck Fraser from Delhi in 1811. 'We usually sit down 16 or 18 at the Residency table, of whom nearly half, sometimes more, are always Scotchmen – about a quarter Irish, the rest English. The Irish do not always maintain their proportion – the Scotch seldom fail.'

The Scots were slow starters in the field of Empire building. Early attempts to set up a Scottish East India Company in 1695 and found a colony at Darien in Panama three years later both proved humiliating failures. But by the end of the 18th century the Scots were making up for lost time. Well connected but financially embarrassed Scots gentry queued up to take their chance in the great Indian lottery, flooding first into the East India Company, then into the successor institutions of the Victorian Raj and the wider Empire. As the 19th century progressed, the Scots diaspora filled a disproportionate and ever-growing number of imperial positions across the globe.

If the Scots diaspora played a major role in Imperial projects from Vancouver to Mandalay it was particularly in South Asia that they came to prominence. 'It was India,' writes Linda Colley in *Britons*, 'that the Scots made their own.' In most fields of life – political, economic, agricultural, commercial, industrial, in the building of infrastructure, from the combat of disease to the birth of the cup of chai – Scots played a surprisingly central role in the birth of modern India.

Throughout the history of the British in India, it always seemed as if the Scots were better than the English at adapting to India, making lives there, and not infrequently falling in love with it. The Scots always seemed to volunteer to take positions in the more remote outposts, so putting themselves in a position more open to cultural and economic interaction, friendship and even love.

There is no more outstanding example of this Scottish tendency than the Frasers of Reelig. The first of the family who headed eastwards was James Fraser (1713–54) who by 1740 had managed to build a significant body of Persian texts on history, poetry and other subjects while working in Surat and the surrounding country, where he learned fluent Persian from a certain Mullah Fakhr-ud-Din. As well as writing a history of the Persian adventurer Nadir Shah he also published in 1742 *A Catalogue of Manuscripts in the Persic, Arabic and Sanskerrit Languages Collected in the East by James Fraser.* The collection was probably the largest of its day, and now forms the core of the Bodleian Oriental collection.

On the 6th of March 1799, James Fraser's grandson, James Baillie Fraser set off in the opposite direction, westwards first to St Vincent and to Guyana, in an attempt to make his fortune in the volatile and often brutal world of the cotton plantations. Here he was soon joined by his younger brother Edward. But the member of the family to leave the most interesting imprint on imperial history was James's younger brother William, who in March 1801 set off on the first stage of his journey from Reelig towards India.

William immediately took to his new home, and before long had mastered Persian, Bengali and Hindustani, winning the gold medal of the new Fort William College. In 1805 his outstanding abilities led to him being promoted above all his contemporaries and he was sent up country from Calcutta. His destination was the Mughal capital of Shahjehanabad, or as it was known by its many of its inhabitants, Delhi. Before long Fraser had became intimate with several leading cultural figures of 19th century Delhi, including Shah 'abd al-Aziz of the Madrasa i-Rahimiyya, with whom William read Persian, and Mufti Sadr al-Din Azurda, who held weekly poetic mushairas and who later became an important figure in the Delhi College. William was also close to Urdu's greatest and most complex poet Ghalib, who later wrote that when Fraser died, he 'felt afresh the grief of a father's death'.

A few years later, in 1815, William was joined in Delhi by his artist brother, James, who had already heard many rumours of William's fondness for Indian customs. Not only did William frequently wear Mughal clothes -- James found him 'in the usual morning dress of the country – a pair of loose drawers & a sort of morning gown cut in the native fashion and called the ungurca; nothing on his neck, a purple foraging hat on his head; large whiskers'. His house too was thoroughly Indianised: 'tygres skins, caps of tygres heads, saddle cloths of ditto, quantities of saddlery, matchlocks, bows and arrows, quivers, belts, armours, guncases ... Persian books and Indian curiosities of all sorts filled up the place.' James concluded that 'his knowledge of the country and the natives [is such], and his habits are so assimilated that he can do what no other man would think of attempting'.

These two Fraser brothers are now recognised as extremely important figures in several fields of history: their commissions and patronage are celebrated by art and literary historians, and the surviving pictures of the Fraser Album would be enough on their own to immortalize William and James Baillie Fraser as some of the greatest and most inspired of all patrons of Indian art. For the Fraser Album is an unparalleled and extraordinarily vivid exploration of urban Delhi and its rural environs, at a particular moment in its history. What Rajaraja Chola was to Indian art in the 11th century, or Shah Jahan in the 17th, the Fraser brothers are to Indian painting in the 19th. They were partly responsible for bringing about its final flowering before British Colonial influence snuffed out many of its great traditions forever.

But this is not all. The journey of James to the source of the Ganges is recognised as a landmark in exploration; William's period of rule in Delhi is now regarded as central to understanding the politics of the last days of joint Company-Mughal rule in the capital; James's paintings, etchings and novels are still eagerly read and admired and collected; while William's recruiting of Gurkha soldiers changed the face of British military history. All these aspects of the adventures of a single generation of brothers from Inverness have been celebrated and written about at some length.

Yet in this book, Kathy Fraser has written the most substantial and sensitive account of the Fraser brothers yet published. She pulls together all the correspondence of all the Reelig Frasers, not just the more famous ones, deftly knitting it together with a light touch and elegant turn of phrase, as she paints a series of penetrating and sympathetic psychological portraits of this extraordinary band of brothers. It's a wonderful story, beautifully told, and as well as containing much new material missed by earlier researchers, she succeeds in bringing this extraordinary family to life in a group portrait that is as entertaining as it is wholly convincing. It is a remarkable achievement and deserves the widest possible audience.

William Dalrymple
Mira Singh Farm
New Delhi
11 November 2015

Contents

Prologue

Our house stands drowsing in the low winter sunshine, its pink sandstone glowing against the darkness of the cedar trees behind. In front, the wide circular lawn merges into the field beyond. A magnificent beechwood provides the backdrop; the trees, of cathedral height, clamber up a steep slope; from the top the view extends north, back to the house, over the garden and fields, away across the firth to the far distance where the great humpback of Ben Wyvis guards the way to the west.

The burn starts its journey high up in the hills to the south, flowing quietly, like an English stream, over moorland, gathering momentum through fields, down into a deep narrow glen. Here it slices its way through a gorge, tumbles down steep waterfalls, calms itself through woodland, flows past the house and out, peacefully again, to the firth and the sea.

In the history of the place this house is relatively young, the original part a mere 270 years old. To the west, an untidy half-buried heap of boulders, mossy host to snowdrops, daffodils, bluebells, forget-me-nots and daisies in due season, bears witness to an earlier dwelling. There have been many other changes over the years to the house, in the garden, the grounds and the glen, but the essence survives – of a place that tugs at your hand, pulling you back. Whatever changes you meet when you return, the spirit of the place is still as it was, and the burn flows on, tumbling, drifting, dancing, through the glen to the sea.

When I came first to the house, in 1970, I was intrigued by a set of sepia photographs, skilfully framed in gilt scrolling and mahogany, hanging in the hall. Five young men, really no more than boys, gazed out at me, their names and dates of birth carefully written on the back: James, 1783, William, 1784, Edward, 1786, Alexander, 1789 and George, 1800. Edward, glamorous in his tartan coat, looked friendly and relaxed; William's hair was falling over his face; Aleck seemed nervous and lost. Their father, Edward Satchwell Fraser, was there, too, along with a pretty sister. 'Who are they?' I asked my husband of a few weeks. 'Not sure. I think they were ancestors who all went to India,' was all I could get out of him. Further investigation revealed them to be photographs of portraits painted by Henry Raeburn in the early nineteenth century and sold in 1897 (see Plates II and III). With that I had to be content.

Some years later, a battered old trunk in the basement revealed a secret: a rich archive of journals and letters between the Fraser boys and their parents and sister as, one by one, they were sent to Guyana or India, in search of the fortune that would save their father's tottering estate. Little by little I untangled their story and set about trying to bring them to life as their letters, full of excitement and adventure, love for one another, nostalgia, heartache and longing for home, took me on a journey across the world and back again.

For the most part their writing is legible, at least when compared with their mother's, and I was fortunate in their father's letter-books, into which he meticulously copied their letters, in his clear and elegant hand. I have only altered their spelling and punctuation when necessary for the sake of clarity of meaning. Above all, I have tried, as far as possible, to let them, in their own words, tell their remarkable story.

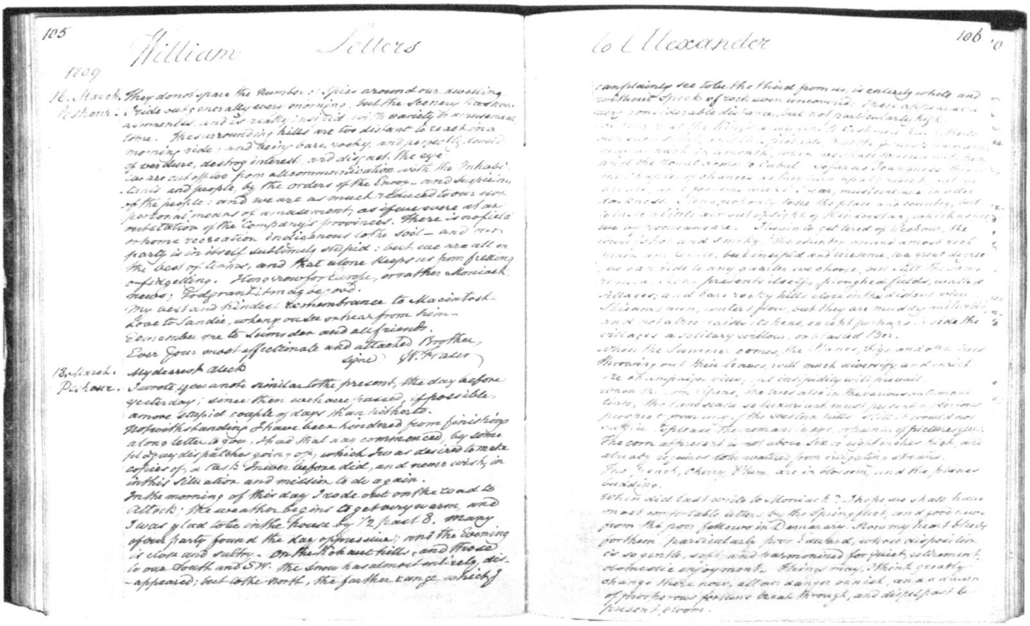

One of Edward Satchwell Fraser's 'letter-books' in which he meticulously copied the family's letters.

Private collection

INTRODUCTION

Edward Satchwell Fraser, the paterfamilias with whom the story starts, was born in 1751, five years after the battle of Culloden and four years after his clan chief lost his head at Tyburn. It was the beginning of half a century of economic turbulence and social change for the Highlands of Scotland. The atrocities, proscription, discord and misery following the Duke of Cumberland's bloody victory at Culloden are well known. When the furore died down there was an attempt to impose some sort of order on the Highlanders, who were considered by the Lowlanders and English as lawless barbarians. This opened the way to new ideas. Those who upheld the old traditions and values of Gaeldom gradually gave way to the promulgators of fresh ways of thinking. Commerce, considered a tool of civilisation, could be used to hone the wild clans into shape. The cattle trade to the Lowlands was extended and drovers herded their small black cattle south to the great markets at Crieff, Falkirk and beyond. There was also increased demand for wool, fish, kelp and wood from the Highlands. The wealth brought to the Lowlands and England by the rapid development of industry during the late seventeenth and eighteenth centuries was not shared by the north of Scotland; naturally, Highland landowners wanted to catch up with their wealthier neighbours in the south. There was a general mood of optimism as they set about enclosing their lands, 'improving' their farms and building villages to house and employ the tenants they had had to displace.

In the eastern and southern Highlands their hopes were in some measure realised, but in the north and west the expected change did not materialise and conditions, for tenants at least, slowly deteriorated. The prices of cattle, kelp and herring fell, leaving only wool profitable. Sheep farmers, mainly wealthy Lowlanders, soon saw off the peasant population of the northern Highlands as men were replaced with sheep.

In 1801 and 1802, six ships sailed from Fort William taking over a thousand people to Nova Scotia. Watching the exodus, both eastward and westward, Edward Satchwell Fraser felt moved to write a treatise on emigration[1]. He understood the causes, especially the lure of the New World, with its rich resources and absence of landlord, factor and sheep, very beguiling to the romantic and adventurous Highlander. He also knew well the fierce loyalty that his countrymen had for one another. He wrote:

1 National Library of Scotland, MS 9646.

> When Highlanders are removed from their native Glen or Tribe it becomes very immaterial to them whether they move across a mountain, to a strange Glen or across the Atlantic to a foreign clime. If their tribe or kindred are in the latter, their decision will be for it.

Despite the failure of their estates to benefit from the winds of change, Highland lairds and their ladies were inevitably affected by new ideas. Gone, apparently, was the old loyalty between clansmen and chieftain. The family estates continued to be run on feudal lines, but chieftains had become landlords, who now looked on their properties as commercial enterprises. Some of them pocketed the rents, gave nothing back to their estates and went to live in Edinburgh. By no means all abandoned their patrimony in this way, but most began spending money on comforts and even luxuries.

As the world beyond the Highlands became more accessible the landed gentry began to pick up the extravagant ways of their richer southern contemporaries. Teenage sons at school in Edinburgh or in London, bound for India, were given commissions ranging from fashionable hats for mothers and ball gowns for sisters to modern fittings for fathers' estate cottages – all to be bought at the very best shops. Other sons trained for careers in the law in Edinburgh and were thereby introduced to urban attitudes and habits.

The culture of militarism still survived in the Highlands and in the mid-eighteenth century was rekindled by the Government's need for regiments, first to support the growth of empire and then to fight the American War of Independence and keep Napoleon at bay. Many younger sons from large impoverished Highland families joined the army, where the spending habits of the richest were the norm. Officers were expected to equip themselves with uniforms and horses and frequently began their commissions already in debt. Those who returned were often bankrupt.

At home, although Highland hospitality was legendary, in the post-Culloden zeal for order and civilised behaviour the rules of hospitality became more sophisticated. Elaborate preparations to accommodate important visitors were made: rooms were painted and furniture borrowed to make the right impression. All this was expensive.

The piper, who had traditionally entertained guests after dinner, was to some extent replaced by the women of the family playing the piano and singing. The standard of performance was high, the instruments and tuition costly, but it all went to show that the laird and his family were embracing the new polite life. Daughters returning home from schools in the south were much admired, especially if their accomplishments included an English accent. The more sophisticated the laird's wife and daughters became the more likely they were to pester him for a townhouse in Edinburgh, Perth or even Inverness. Fortunate and few were the Highland wives and daughters who had neighbouring gentry within walking distance.

The town of Inverness is strategically placed, but in the eighteenth century the only roads possible for coaches were those built by General Wade to the south and east; those to the north and west were no more than rough tracks. The Highlands was therefore something of a social desert, its people still burdened with lingering memories of country, clans and families split by civil war. In June 1788 thirteen Highland gentlemen, among them Edward Satchwell Fraser, met to discuss what could be done to add some merrymaking to the social life of the Highlands, hoping that by bringing people together, old breaches might be healed. The result was the Northern Meeting in Inverness – an annual week of balls, parties, games, riding to hounds, horse-racing and, eventually, piping competitions.

Its object was 'Pleasure and Innocent Amusement'. Members were forbidden to discuss politics or business and there was to be no quarrelling. Membership was wide and reflected differences in clan loyalties, religion and politics. A sharp eye was kept on the latest fashions in dancing and dress in Edinburgh and London, and efforts were made to ensure civilised conduct. Inevitably, there were problems and dramas, and over the years there have been many changes but, remarkably, a shortened form of the Northern Meeting continues to this day with the same aim.

Many gentlemen's residences were built in the eighteenth century in the Highlands. Some were vast, built on the proceeds of Caribbean slave plantations. Others were more modest, built simply to replace a former tumbledown dwelling but along modern lines. A drawing room, dining room and sometimes even a library, lined with costly books, became essentials of civilised living.

As the roads south gradually improved, the expense of travel grew, with regular expeditions to Edinburgh or London. Once the battle of Waterloo was won and Bonaparte safely imprisoned on St Helena, people became curious about Europe, and France in particular, since living there was extremely cheap.

It is estimated that in 1814 fewer than 10,000 people travelled to the Continent; by 1820 that number had doubled.[1] The young Romantic poets, especially Byron, had aroused excitement about the Continent, it was considered important to learn fluent French and there were also reasons of health: now that Europe was open to all, the lure of the sun and the numerous spas was beguiling, especially to those used to the short dark days of the long winters in the north of Scotland. For many reasons, therefore, the first decades of the nineteenth century were years of financial crisis for almost all Highland lairds, and many long-held properties were sold as a result.

One tradition, however, survived, albeit in a different mode. Despite the apparent demise of the old clan system, the ties between members, of whatever status, were too strong to disappear completely. There were close relationships, often intermarriages, between families of the same clan, resulting in the existence of a supportive network. The clan system meant that there were many families of the same name in one area, hence the custom of referring to families by the names of their estates to avoid confusion: Edward Satchwell Fraser, for example, was known as 'Reelig'. A strong Highland identity survived, and however far a clansman travelled, the bond with his homeland was never quite broken.

Many of the boys who joined the East India Company found themselves deep in debt, unable to send home the fortune they sought or indeed to see their homes again. Others spent uncomfortable years in the West Indies in the hope of wealth from sugar and cotton

1 *The Smell of the Continent*, Richard Mullen and James Munson (2009, p. 56), Pan.

plantations. During the last decades of the eighteenth century Guyana was reputed to be the greatest cotton producer in the world and fortunes were certainly made there. James Fraser of Belladrum near Inverness was said to have returned from Guyana with £40,000 in his pocket, and the magnificent house he built bore witness to this. Others reached Guyana after the boom and returned empty-handed.[2] The Guyanan territory where numerous Highlanders endured the appalling climate and the horrors of slavery was Berbice.

Guyana

On the north-east coast of South America, bordered to the west and south by Venezuela and Brazil, lie the three territories of Guyana – Demerara, Essequibo and Berbice – finally taken from the Dutch by the British in 1796. The territories stretch along the coast, each punctuated by a mighty river flowing from Brazil over savannahs and through impenetrable jungle. The plantations, each around 600 yards wide, were long narrow allotments stretching back from the coastline as far as their owners had the energy to penetrate the jungle and separated by dead straight roads. It was an unattractive part of the world, having an unreliable climate with very high rainfall, a considerable incidence of fatal disease and, being completely flat, a great deal of mud.

In the early nineteenth century, the British outnumbered the rest of the white population by something like two to one, while in Berbice by 1810 there were a great many black or coloured slaves to every white man. The names of the various estates, Belladrum, Cromarty, Inverness, Seafield, Dunrobin, and slaves given names like Dingwall and Inverness, are testimony to the fact that Scots were far more numerous that the English, most of them coming from the three Highland counties of Inverness-shire, Ross-shire and Sutherland.

There were at least two reasons for this: it was an age of patronage and the Highland network of clan connections was used not only to find openings abroad but also to ensure welcome and care on arrival. There were few permanent settlers in Berbice, most adventurers being there for what they hoped was a very short time before returning home with their pockets full. Thus it was important to start the adventure where there were family or neighbourly contacts to ease one into the strange, unfamiliar and uncomfortable years ahead.

Some of these adventurers were the sons of impoverished Highland gentry. It was very tempting for a father with an estate to maintain and a large family (often ten or more children) to support, regaled at dinner with stories of unimagined success, to follow the trend and persuade a planter cousin or neighbour to take on his son as a trainee overseer. He might even be moved to speculate himself. In 1801 Lord Seaforth bought ten lots of land and a tract of 3,000 acres, a project in which Fraser of Reelig was involved along with several others, seeing it as an investment for his sons.

For a young man it was indeed an unpleasant life. As no one planned to be there for very long there were no social institutions; there was little to do and few comforts.

2 The slump was the result of various effects of the Napoleonic Wars and the competition of cheap cotton from the US.

Berbice – 'abominably ugly, perfectly flat' – there was nowhere to walk except along a dead straight road bordered by stinking ditches or in a mosquito-infested wood.

Social life centred mainly round gambling and drinking, the regular topics of conversation being the price of cotton, the likelihood of slave rebellion, the gossip of the colony and the chances of getting home. The only women were the wives of the estate owners, and it was perfectly acceptable for a young bachelor planter to choose a comely female slave to keep house for him and share his bed. 'Countess', for example, the chosen companion of William Macpherson, bore him three children, all of whom eventually returned to Scotland.[3]

The economy rested on the exploitation of black slaves, whose numbers had more than tripled since Britain gained control of the colony. Most came from the Gold Coast and many died within three years of arrival: cholera, yellow fever, smallpox, dysentery and malaria were rife, but often death was simply from malnutrition and unremitting overwork in appalling conditions.

The Scots were reputed to be harder taskmasters and more ruthless than other Europeans. Whatever the reason, during the eighteenth century the majority of Scottish slave overseers embraced the system wholeheartedly and efficiently. Yet in Edinburgh different views were abroad, voiced by some of the great names of the Enlightenment. People like Adam Smith,[4] his student, John Millar,[5] and James Beattie,[6] all argued passionately against slavery.

3 *A Private Empire*, Stephen Foster (2010), Pier 9, Murdoch Books, Australia.
4 *The Theory of Moral Sentiments* (1804).
5 *Observations concerning the Distinctions of Ranks* (1771).
6 *Elements of Moral Science* (1790).

But, with one or two exceptions, there is little evidence that any of this influenced young men intent on making money and getting home as fast as possible.

However, the views of the Edinburgh intelligentsia, along with the experiences of a few young men who had worked in the West Indies, later providing William Wilberforce with first hand information,[7] laid the foundations first for the abolition of the trade in 1807 and then for final emancipation in 1834.

Evangelicalism

The vision and passion of William Wilberforce had gathered momentum from gentle beginnings at the end of the eighteenth century to become an immense reform movement in the nineteenth. The burning desire to tackle the decadence, corruption and moral collapse of eighteenth century England needed a leader of calibre to take it forward. It also needed the support of the ruling class, who to a large extent set the moral tone of the country, and it had to be seen to be free of any whiff of liberalism or radicalism.

After the horrors of the French Revolution the British Government was terrified by any idea of political reform; this was to be a reform of morality alone. Wilberforce accordingly collected a band of prominent men around him, mostly big landowners, several members of Parliament, all wealthy, influential, conservative and mostly evangelical. One of these was Charles Grant, born in 1746, who entered Parliament in 1802 to represent Inverness-shire in 1802. The Highlands were thus lapped by the tide of Evangelicalism flowing through the country, and many families came under the influence of the deeply evangelical Charles Grant (see Plate V) and his wife Jane, few more so than the Frasers of Reelig.

India

In 1821 Sir Walter Scott referred to India as 'the cornchest for Scotland where we poor gentry must send our younger sons as we send our black cattle to the south'.[8] This was nothing new. There are Scots in the seventeenth century records of the East India Company, and the number increased in the eighteenth, when in return for electoral and political support the sons of Scottish gentry were offered positions in the Company. Such was the need for employment that this bribery was accepted gratefully. Besides, during the first half of the eighteenth century, when fortunes really were made, the effect of this patronage was the investment in Scotland of large amounts of money.

They went out as doctors, soldiers, clerks, mercenaries, adventurers, administrators and, later, missionaries. Often they went in their mid-teens with no training or any knowledge of the languages, religions and cultures they would find at the end of their six-month voyage. Few of the sons of the landed gentry, if any, went out with lofty ideals of imperial service; they went each with two aims: to make the fortune needed to support their father's estate and their numerous siblings and to get home again. The European burial grounds bear witness to the many who died within a few years,

7 Notably James Stephen (1758–1832) and Zachary Macaulay (1768–1838).
8 *The Cornchest for Scotland: Scots in India* Alex M. Cain (1986) National Library of Scotland

sometimes months, of arrival. Some lived long enough to come home, but once most of the dubious ways of amassing fortunes had disappeared, they rarely had enough money to support themselves in Scotland.

The India in which so many young Scots, including the five sons of Fraser of Reelig, found themselves at the dawn of the nineteenth century was nearing the end of a period known as the 'Great Anarchy'. The mighty Mughal Empire which, since the great Akbar's death in 1605, had been slowly disintegrating, was entering its twilight years. During the second half of the eighteenth century powerful tribes – the Marathas, Rajputs and Sikhs – vied for supremacy with each other and with the British, French and Dutch. After Clive's victory at the Battle of Plassey in 1757, the first steps were taken towards changing the British presence in India from that of a commercial body with a few scattered trading posts to a political power with Calcutta as the seat of government. The East India Company was thus to become the greatest company the world has ever known.

All contenders had their eye on the ultimate prize – the imperial city of Delhi, famed throughout the world for its fabulous treasures, magnificent court, great mosques and colleges and brilliant literary and artistic traditions. Although it continued to dazzle – its opulence embodied in processions of elephants, magnificently adorned, splendid ceremonial dress and all the myriad trappings of power – the actual position was very different. Its wealth had diminished, its territories shrunk and its puppet Emperor, Shah Alam, blinded by a tribal chief, cowered in his palace.

In 1803 Lord Arthur Wellesley[9] defeated the great Maratha chief, Scindia, and claimed Delhi. Shah Alam was taken under British protection, given a generous personal allowance and kept in material comfort with respect paid to his imperial dignity. He would be all-powerful within the Red Fort and protocol would be maintained. But this was outward show; in reality the British Resident was now in charge and would supervise Mughal affairs.

Britain, with a growing confidence in her moral and racial superiority, was now in control of most of India apart from the princely states. The more enlightened of the East India Company servants still accorded the Emperor the dignity and respect due to the symbol of a mighty empire, but as the nineteenth century progressed the romantic interest in all things Indian and the regard for Indian sentiment slowly gave way to the ideals of utilitarianism and evangelicalism sweeping through Britain. Shiploads of missionaries docked alongside the 'fishing fleet', the name given to the ships bringing the young women designed to divert the Company servants from the delights of their Indian mistresses. Little by little, the respect and honours paid to the Emperor diminished. Until the death of the last Mughal Emperor in 1857, however, the fading light of pomp and circumstance still glimmered around the Peacock Throne.[10]

9 1st Duke of Wellington (1769–1852), brother of Lord Richard Wellesley, Governor General of India, 1797–1805.

10 The original Peacock Throne was commissioned in the early seventeenth century by Shah Jahan and stolen by the Persian Nadir Shah in 1739. Its replacement was in the Red Fort until 1857.

India – early nineteenth century

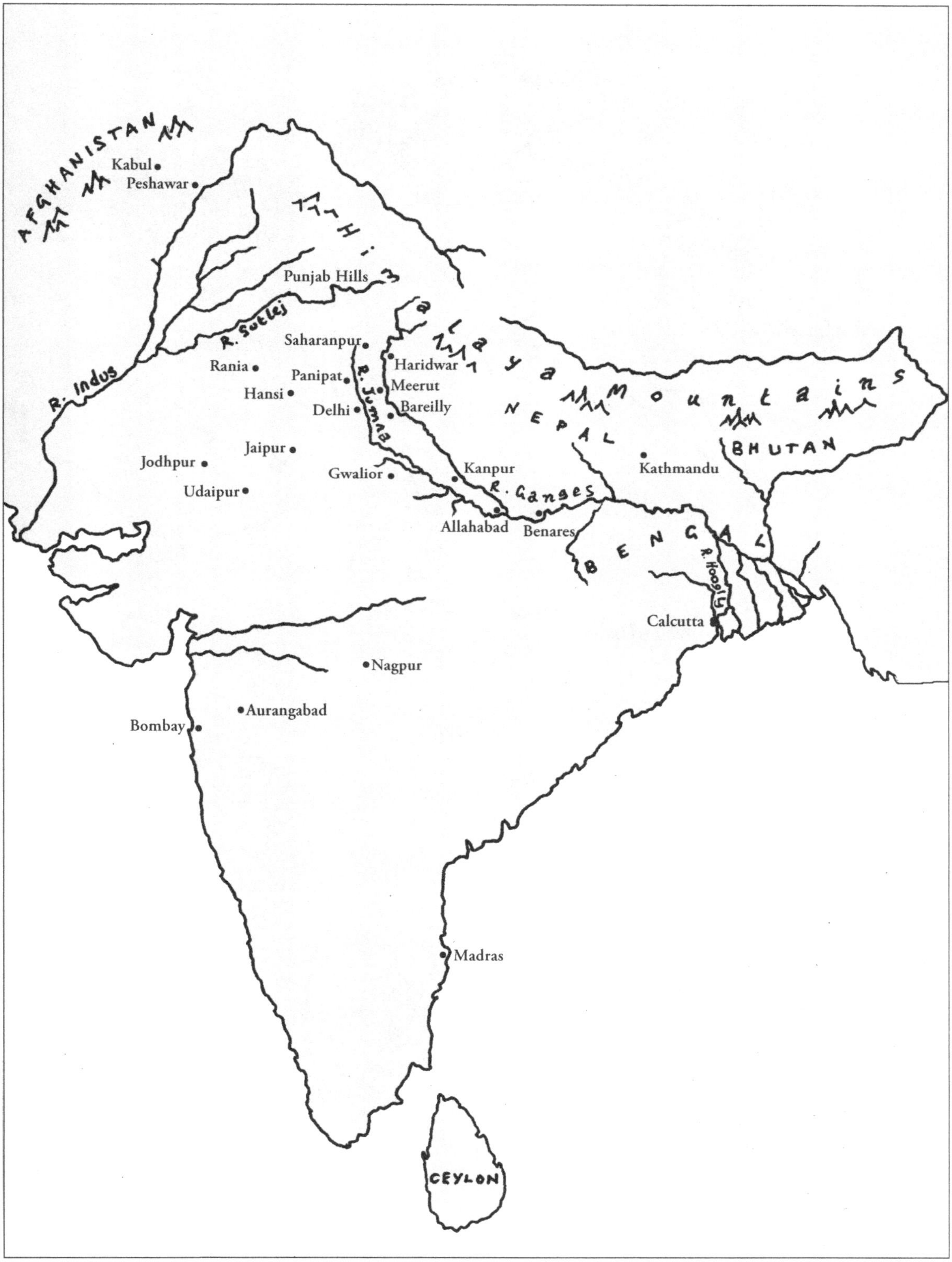

Neighbouring houses – some still standing – that play a part in the story.

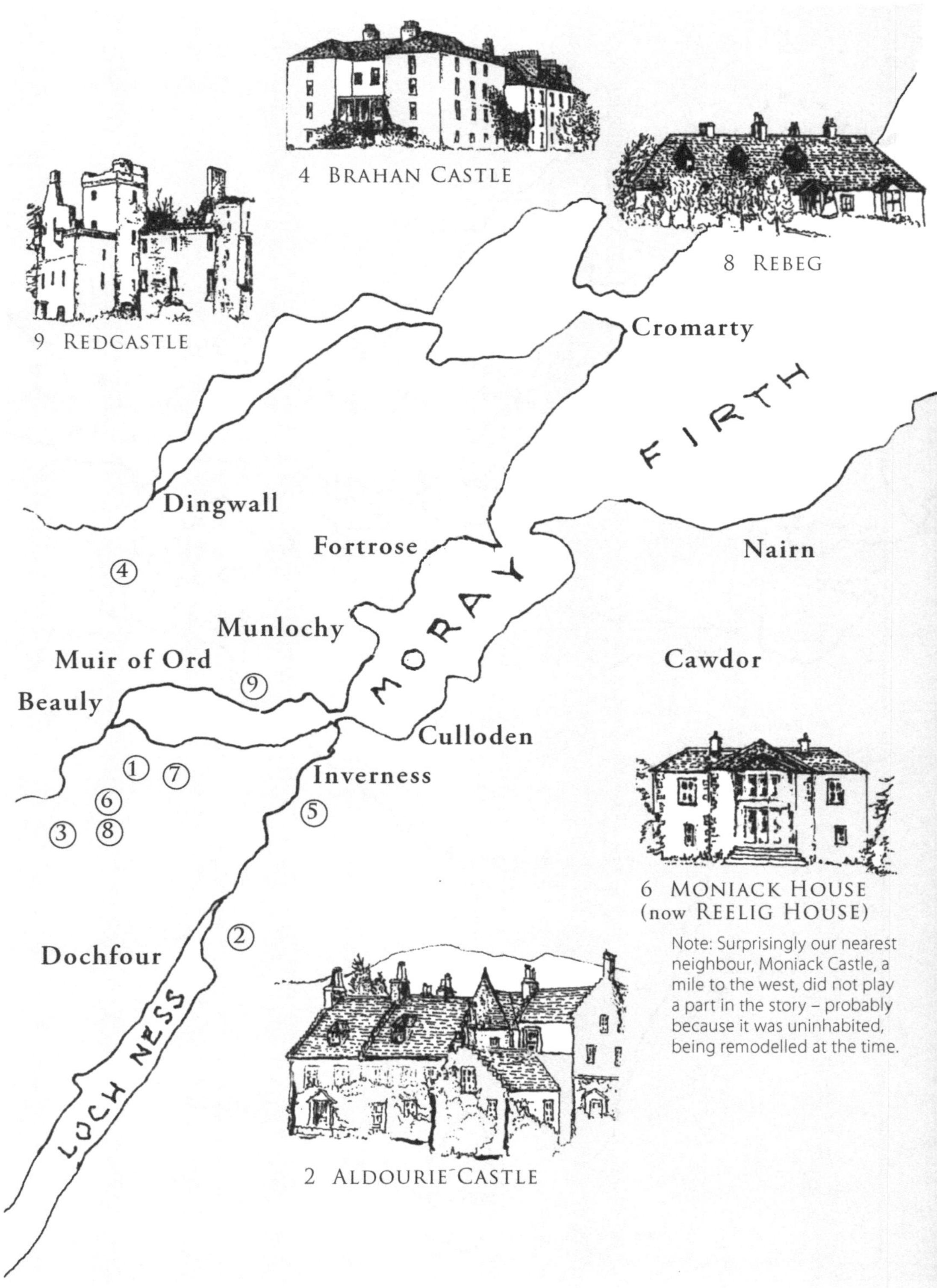

Note: Surprisingly our nearest neighbour, Moniack Castle, a mile to the west, did not play a part in the story – probably because it was uninhabited, being remodelled at the time.

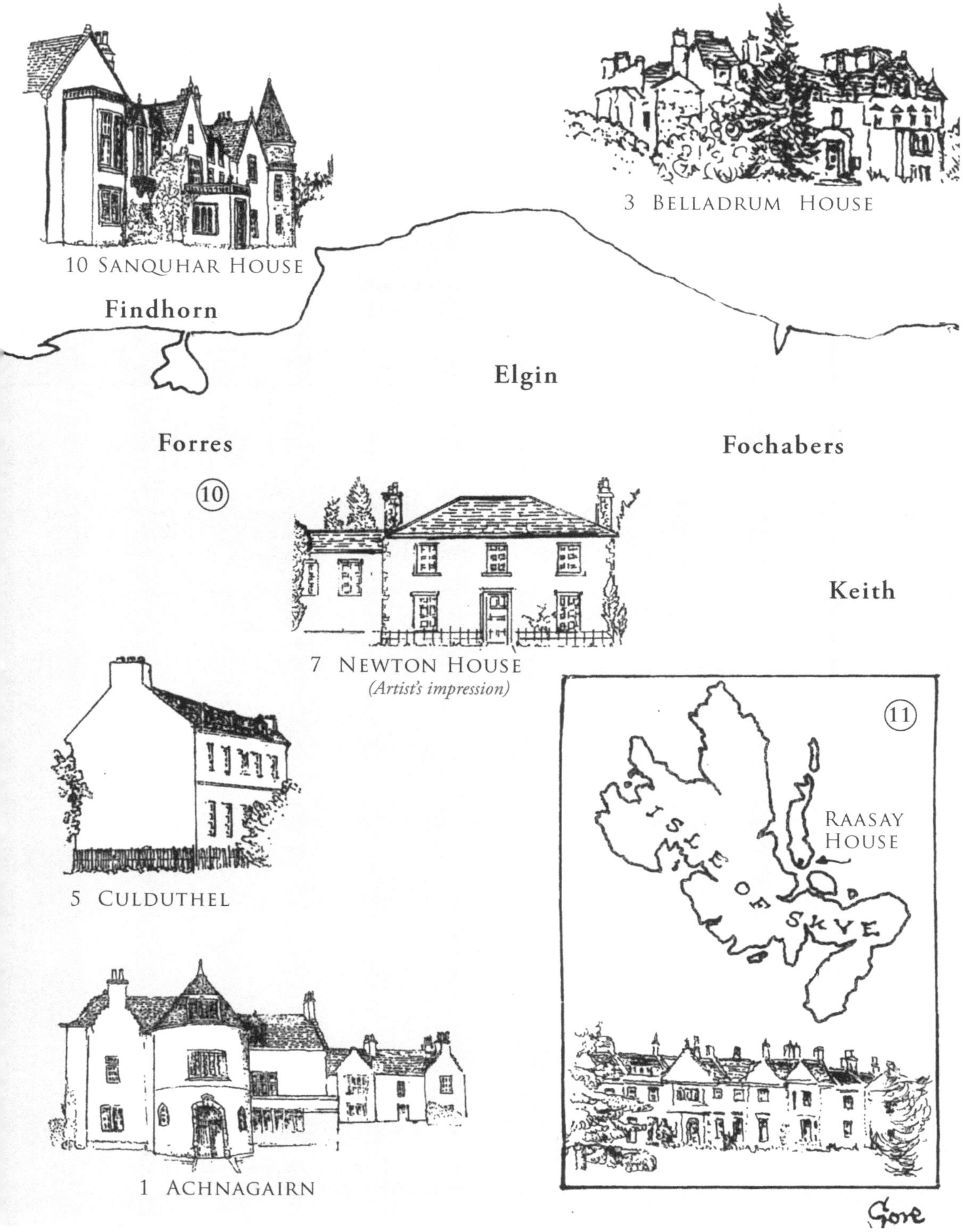
10 Sanquhar House
3 Belladrum House
Findhorn
Elgin
Forres
Fochabers
10
Keith
7 Newton House
(Artist's impression)
11
Raasay House
Isle of Skye
5 Culduthel
1 Achnagairn
Gore

Family Tree

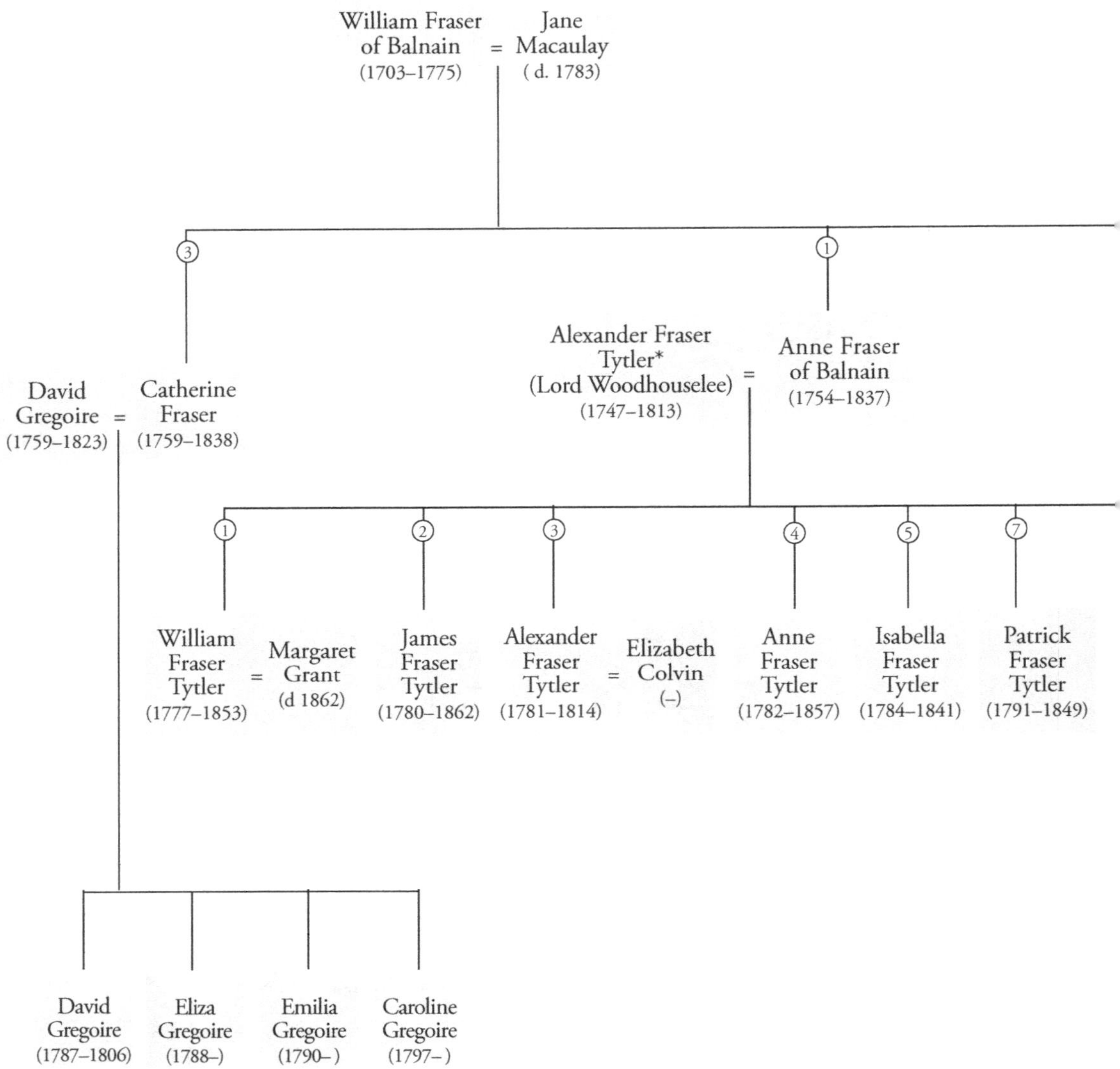

*Note: Through his marriage to Anne Fraser of Balnain, Alexander Tytler, Lord Woodhouselee, added Fraser to his name. For the sake of brevity, I have omitted the Fraser part throughout the text.

- James Fraser, *12th of Reelig* (1713–1754) = Mary Satchwell, *13th Lady of Reelig* (1726–1795)
  - (1) Edward Satchwell Fraser, *14th of Reelig* (1751–1835) = Jane Fraser (1757–1847) [(2), line continuing from the left]
    - (1) James Baillie Fraser, *15th of Reelig* (1783–1856) = Jane (Jeanie) Fraser Tytler, *16th Lady of Reelig* (1786–1861) [(6), line continuing from the left]
    - (2) William Fraser (1784–1835)
    - (3) Edward Fraser (1786–1813)
    - (4) Alexander (Aleck) Fraser (1789–1816)
    - (5) Mary Fraser (1791–1806)
    - (6) Jane b & d 1793
    - (7) Jane Catherine Fraser (1794–1797)
    - (8) Jane Anne Fraser, *17th Lady of Reelig* (1797–1881) = Philip Affleck Fraser of Culduthel (1787–1862)
      - (1) James Fraser (1817–1818)
      - (2) Jane Fraser (1819–1879)
      - (3) James Fraser (1820–1888)
      - (4) Edward Fraser (1822–1849)
      - (5) Millicent Fraser (1823–1878)
      - (6) Mary Fraser (1825–1901)
      - (7) Affleck Fraser (1827–1870)
      - (8) William Fraser (1828–1850)
      - (9) Alister Fraser (1830–1870)
      - (10) Georgina Fraser (1832–1907)
      - (11) Frances Elizabeth Fraser (1834–1852)
      - (12) John Donald Fraser (b & d 1838)
      - (13) Catherine Amelia Fraser (1840–1906)
    - (9) George Fraser (1800–1842) = Wilhelmina Moore (–)
  - (2) Catherine Fraser (1752–1783) = Thomas Henry Abbot (–)

The Lairds of Reelig

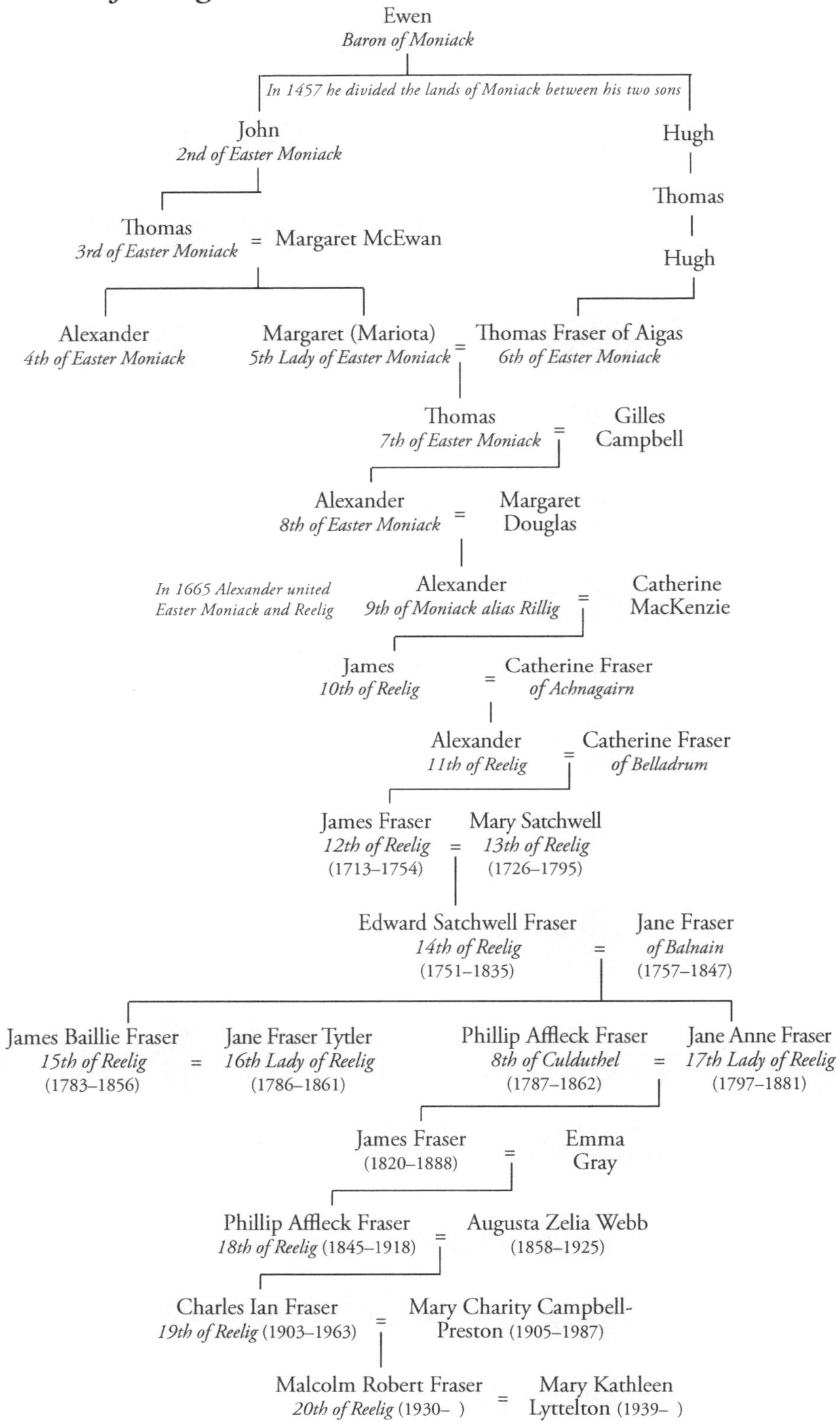

1

1751–1801

An English childhood

The house was too small. This was the decision of James Fraser, 12th of Reelig, when, in 1749, he and his young wife, Mary, arrived home at Moniack in Inverness-shire. During seven years in the service of the East India Company he had collected, not only some important Sanskrit manuscripts[1], but also a large number of 'Oriental articles of great value and curiosity'. He needed the space to display these treasures to their best advantage and also more comfortable accommodation for the family and friends who flocked to admire them. Mary, who was a capable hostess, had recently managed to accommodate eight Highland chieftains to dinner at one sitting but it had been an undignified crush and 'they assuredly were not very fastidious' wrote her son, Edward, in his memoir, years later. Accordingly, with the help of 'the elder Adam, architect' and the less useful advice of family and friends, James built a bigger house, 'a pretty box' (see Plate I).

He could trace his ancestry to Ewen, Baron of Moniack,[2] and the early fifteenth century. Mary was English, from an old Worcestershire family, and had married James when she was sixteen. Edward described her as small, beautiful and 'exquisitely neat'. She was also …

> … of most kind and benevolent nature; most scrupulously honest and honourable; rather vain of her English blood and yet popular among those who had not very agreeable recollections of the troubles of 1745 and the savage conduct of the English royal commander at Culloden.

Two of her four children survived infancy: Edward Satchwell, named after his English grandfather, was born in 1751 and his sister, Catherine[3], followed in 1752.

Two years later James Fraser was dead and the children's English grandfather, Squire Satchwell, who had never ventured north of Worcestershire, undertook the arduous ride from Cheshunt in Hertfordshire, to Moniack to assess his daughter's situation.

---

1 Reputedly the first collection of its kind to come to Europe. Now in the Bodleian Library, Oxford. A gifted linguist, Fraser also wrote The History of Nadir Shah, 1742.

2 He divided his land between his two sons. Six generations later the lands were united by Alexander who called himself '9th of Moniack alias Riligg'. Hence the confusion of the two names, the house, Moniack and the lands, Reelig.

3 She married Lieutenant Thomas Abbott and followed him to the American War but in 1783 was drowned, with her baby son, off Florida.

Horrified by the wild and poverty-stricken Highlands, he immediately arranged for the place to be let, sent the little family south by sea and galloped home to prepare their welcome at the 'most agreeable compact property', leased on the estate of Theobalds, former site of the magnificent Theobalds Palace[4]. Here Edward with his mother and sister spent a comfortable but rather lonely childhood.

The children were taught by 'an ancient infirm Lady', the eccentric Mrs Jarvis, who kept a mute but alarmingly free-ranging parrot which swooped and swung over the heads of her pupils.

> We assembled at her Bedside on our knees to receive rudimental instruction in Latin and Greek, and even in Hebrew ... she was very infirm but very good, kind and anxious to make the teaching palatable to us; but it was necessary in return, to gratify her by loving her Parrott.[5]

The eight-year-old Edward was then sent to the Charterhouse, in the City of London (see Plate IV), an endowment for 'Eighty Pensioners, who ought to be Decayed Merchants, and Forty Boys, who ought to be Decayed Merchants Sons'. It was a shock. He was bullied unmercifully by two monitors – supposedly his 'protectors'.

> I contributed to their favourite recreation of swinging me, one by the arms, the other by the legs ... from the top to the bottom of the Garden Slopes ... If my head came unluckily against a Clod, a Stump or a Stone, that I could not refrain from crying out, I was swung down again, as a poor soft fellow. And if I could contain myself, and did not complain, why! I was a stubborn and sullen Scotsman and sent down flying again.

Despite this harsh treatment, customary in boarding schools at the time, Edward cheerfully accepted school life and understood the value of the classical education he received. Mrs Jarvis's soothing tuition also stood him in good stead, and soon after his arrival he was moved up two classes. There were various events to relieve the monotony of school life, such as the great fire at Cornhill[6] and a holiday in 1760 when King George II died. On this occasion the boys were allowed into Charterhouse Square where they met some other holidaymakers, 'a School of young Ladies'. If Edward's memory, around seventy years later, was accurate, this was an enjoyable experience for the nine-year-old: 'A gallant rencontre of mirth, and gentle romping ... showed me my duties to the Ladies'.

✻

Holidays were spent at Theobalds. The Squire included his grandson in many of his daily activities – riding out to greyhounds or hawks and playing bowls or backgammon – and he kept an excellent table:

---

4 Completed c. 1585 and demolished c. 1650. Built by Lord Burghley to accommodate Elizabeth I who visited often. James 1 gave Hatfield House to the Earl of Salisbury in exchange for Theobalds where he died in 1625.

5 Memoir completed 3 May 1832 and presented to his daughter, Jane Anne Fraser of Culduthel.

6 It started in a 'Peruke maker's' shop in Bishopsgate on 9 November 1765 and spread between Cornhill and Threadneedle Street.

> Venison in the season of Buck, Doe and Fawn, with Cygnet, Peafowl or Bittern ... Carp, Tench, Perch and Pike in plenty – Turbot and Sturgeon occasionally. I recollect well that pipes and tobacco and Punch, fine wines and old Ales were brought in after dinner.

It was a far cry from the Highlands, and if the boy ever asked about Scotland the subject was swiftly changed, his grandfather having 'a sort of John Bullish aversion' to the place. Long after, however, Edward was to write:

> I do not think that in the course of all my family losses, I ever so acutely felt grief, as when my Grandfather died. I loved him beyond measure, as did my sister ... so attached were my sister and myself to his memory, that we both used to steal, in the evenings, into the room where he lay, to contemplate him.

Edward was fourteen when he lost his grandfather, and a year later his pretty mother married again. Her new husband was a sailor, John Delamotte. Although he had manners that his stepson considered not quite polished, he was very goodhearted and kind to the children.

For the next few years the family lived in Woolwich, where Delamotte had a job in the Dockyard. After leaving Charterhouse, Edward tried his hand at various employments, including the Navy and four very happy years in the commercial house of a Swiss silk merchant. In 1771, however, his life changed forever: when his cousin James Baillie[7], recently home from the West Indies, announced that he needed a travelling companion to Scotland, the twenty-year-old Edward readily agreed to go with him.

SCOTTISH INHERITANCE

The cousins spent Christmas in Edinburgh in a whirl of social activity:

> We were visited and invited by many interesting persons, who knew more of us, and of our connections and family than we ourselves knew. For my part, I knew nobody, my Grandfather Satchwell never having encouraged, and still less satisfied, my enquiries relative to Scotland, or my Scottish kindred

Edward enjoyed the concerts, assemblies and excitement of eighteenth century Edinburgh and was impressed by the good looks of almost everyone he met, especially the young ladies. It was a pleasant interlude but the Highlands beckoned and in the New Year he and James set off for Inverness.

There they based themselves at the winter house of James's elder brother, Alexander Baillie, laird of Dochfour. News of strangers travelled fast and, soon after their arrival, a stream of visitors appeared, through deep snow, from all corners of Inverness-shire to welcome the newcomer, often claiming kinship and overwhelming Edward with offers of hospitality. Seeing this warm reception as a mark of affection and respect for 'those

7 Son of Edward's aunt Emilia Fraser who had married Hugh Baillie of Dochfour.

who had preceded me', he looked forward to accepting these invitations; but first he had to see Moniack.

It was a bright, frosty day when, with two companions, he set off to walk the nine miles over the hill from Dochfour, on Loch Ness-side, down to the lands of Reelig. He could not contain his excitement, constantly asking whether they were nearly there, and his friends goodnaturedly played a trick on him; when he asked, yet again, when he would see the house, they pointed to …

> … a poor dwelling, on a bare muir, amid a multitude of poor earthern huts, as the house and place of my Family. I was humbled and disappointed, but never doubted.

Taking pity on his gullibility, they indicated another house, 'in a snug recess ... under the hill' and asked if that would please him better. It was love at first sight:

> I own I was powerfully and delightfully astonished, with all I saw. The extensive Birch woods with their rich red racemose branches and weeping twigs, supported by the silver stems a beautiful Background to the House and offices. The House though not large, of pleasing symmetrical architecture, and chaste design, by the Adams's. It is a *morceau de bijouterie*, but injudiciously abridged, by scale, from their original designs ... on the well meant suggestions of my Father's friends in Inverness.

From that moment, Edward's ambition was to return one day to settle at Moniack. Meanwhile, he had to learn how to be a Highland gentleman and '*Fear na Reelick*' (the Goodman of Reelick). He understood the delicacy of his situation, having had an English education 'very hostile in many respects to my Countrymen, since the years 1715 and 1745'. It was, after all, less than thirty years since the brutal slaughter and suppression of Highland culture after the Jacobite defeat at Culloden, and Highland memories are long. He had to tread very cannily in order to reconcile the local people to his English accent and 'southern manners'. He met nothing, however, but natural courtesy and respect, apart from Hutcheon Dubh (Black Hugh) Fraser, a redoubtable nonagenarian: on hearing Edward's name, he growled, 'a Sassenach name, fitting only for a dog'.

For the next few months Edward travelled around the Highlands meeting old friends and kinsmen of his father. He rode deep into the straths and glens on either side of Loch Ness where he was entertained by Fraser family after Fraser family, as well as a scattering of Grants and a sprinkling of Chisholms. Unaware of the clan system, he was amazed by his welcome from so many people claiming cousinship as he had, from childhood, been led to understand that he was more or less alone in the world. He loved talking to the local people and was frustrated at not having a word of Gaelic to allow him the courtesy of using their own language.

> It was now that I took into my heart that attachment to these, my country and people, my kindred and my property, which never can be displaced from it; and which has rooted me in Scotland – and probably will determine the Bias of my children.

Reelig[8] (this, the name of his lands, was how he was known to Highlanders and henceforward how he considered himself when in Scotland) wrote a journal of his travels and the people who had taken him to their hearts. It is a colourful account, punctuated with descriptions of flora and fauna, food and drink, eccentric characters, country customs and even a 'tumultous' Highland funeral.

By now he had been away about a year and it was time to return to England. James Baillie offered to rent Moniack. Happy to have come to such a satisfactory arrangement, Reelig planted forty acres of high hillside with fir to mark his return to his patrimonial property and set off south on horseback.

Marriage

The question was what to do next. Edward now knew that one day he would make his life in the Highlands, but meanwhile he was a healthy, well-educated, energetic twenty-one-year-old with no money but, as he was discovering, an adventurous spirit. He based himself with his mother and stepfather in Woolwich, home of the Royal Artillery, and enrolled in the Foot Guards, keeping an eye open for an exciting project.

The name of Captain Cook[9] was on everyone's lips. He had recently returned from Botany Bay and laying claim to New South Wales, and was now planning to circumnavigate the globe in search of a great land mass believed to lie in the Southern Ocean. Edward's imagination was set alight by this project and he 'asked the King's leave to embark with Captain Cook'. But he was too late: the volunteer crew was complete. Luckily another chance of adventure was just around the corner.

Across the Atlantic there were rumblings of revolution which would result in the War of American Independence. In April 1778 Edward was given an Ensigncy in the Regiment raised by his kinsman, Major General Simon Fraser of Lovat, whose ADC he eventually became. He was promoted to Lieutenant in 1780 and, a year later, to Captain. Throughout his service in America he kept a detailed journal and wrote to his mother as often as events would allow. His plan, on leaving the Army, was to live in Scotland, where she, now a widow, would join him. But events took a slightly different turn: in 1782 he met and married Jane Fraser.

Family, hearth and home were very important to the Georgians. For both men and women it was essential to marry, although for different reasons: men needed a cheerful companion who could run their house; women needed the status and security of marriage. Eighteenth and nineteenth century literature is littered with tales of tragic single women; two of them tiptoe humbly into a later part of this story.

All authority rested with the husband, whom his wife had to obey; but this did not imply weakness, a featherbrain or total submission. Highlanders sought wives who were strong

8 To distinguish between the large number of Frasers in the Highlands, landowners tended to be known by the name of their estate – hence Belladrum, Newton, etc.

9 British explorer (1728–1779). Completed the outlines of Australia and New Zealand and depicted accurately the north-west coast of America.

enough to bear children, accomplished enough to be entertaining companions in the long winter evenings, artistic enough to decorate and furnish the house according to the demands of the time, educated enough to hold an interesting conversation on serious topics and, above all, competent and intelligent enough to run the house, family and servants. In Jane Fraser of Balnain Edward found such a wife.

Six years younger than Edward, Jane was the youngest of three daughters of William Fraser of Balnain, an estate on the eastern side of Loch Ness, about fifteen miles from Moniack. He was a Writer to the Signet,[10] married to the daughter of Archibald Macaulay, three times Lord Provost of Edinburgh. The girls were brought up in Edinburgh with holidays at Aldourie, their father's house at Balnain (see Plate IV).

We know little of Jane's early years, although she undoubtedly would have had an interesting and stimulating upbringing. The Edinburgh of her childhood was a cramped jumble of towering tenements, murky wynds, raucous street markets and steamy taverns jostling for elbow room and clinging to a steeply sloping rock. While Jane was growing up the concept of a new town to the north was still on the drawing board of a young architect, James Craig, and the city was bordered northwards by the drained valley of the Nor' Loch. When she was six the foundation stone of a bridge across the valley was laid, a project which was to result in the splendid proportions and spaciousness of the streets and squares of the New Town.

Jane's childhood surroundings were the small, dark panelled rooms and narrow alleys of the Old Town, from which she must have welcomed the summer escape to the space and riverside of Aldourie. There were compensations, however, to life in Edinburgh during the excitement of the Enlightenment. She lived in a household where intellectual discussion would have been the norm and where poets, philosophers, clerics, doctors, professors, lawyers and judges were regular visitors.

Edward Topham,[11] an English visitor to Edinburgh in 1774/5, was struck by the difference between the young ladies of Edinburgh and those in England. The Scottish girls seemed on a more equal footing with the opposite sex and were consequently more open and less affected. Their education appeared more thorough than that provided in London at a fashionable Bloomsbury boarding school, where needlework and a smattering of French were the heights of ambition. A girl at a school in Edinburgh would emerge versed in 'the precepts of morality, virtue and honour', well informed through wide and deep reading, confident, entertaining in conversation and full of good sense.

Young ladies in Edinburgh, according to Topham, were no followers of fashion but, like the French, dressed sensibly according to the climate and season as well as to their age. They were fortunate in that 'Nature [had] been as liberal to them in decorating their external parts, as in ornamenting their minds'. Their complexions did not need the assistance of paint, nor did they add artificial height to their heels or hair. Topham

10 Senior Scottish solicitor conducting cases in the Court of Session.
11 *Letters from Edinburgh, 1774–5*, Edward Topham, facsimile James Thin (1971).

reckoned that Edinburgh men paid too little attention to the fairer sex but attributed this to their association on equal terms.

Eighteenth century Edinburgh was above all sociable. 'Scotch Ladies', revealed Topham, 'drink more wine than an English woman could well bear; but the climate requires it ... and you will allow that a certain degree of wine adds great life to conversation.' After supper there was singing which lasted far into the night. Jane would have also enjoyed the dancing assemblies, concerts and plays and her lessons on the new fashionable instrument, the pianoforte.

At some point Jane's father, William Fraser, acquired Gardener's Hall,[12] just outside the town, an elegant house where Edward and Jane were married on 11 September 1782. He was thirty-one and she was twenty-five. He announced the event thus to his mother:

> Madam,
> You and I acquired yesterday a new relation – it is not for me to say of what value – and I think that next year, after that you & she & I have passed some short time together, I shall have little occasion to give my own opinion of her worth but by appeal to you.

Jane's portrait, by an unknown artist, shows a pretty, fairly determined face framed in brown curls. With one hand she clutches a fur tippet around her shoulders, and her expression is one of slight impatience to be up and doing (see Plate I).

Family Matters

Just under a year later Jane was back at Gardener's Hall for the birth of her first child, James. Soon afterwards the young couple set up home at Moniack and concentrated on enjoying their increasing family. William appeared in 1784, followed by Edward in 1786; in 1789 Alexander (Aleck) was born and then, after the four boys, came four daughters: Mary in 1791, Jane, who only lived a few weeks, in 1793, another Jane born in 1794, who was swiftly followed, when she died of whooping cough, by Jane Anne in 1797 and finally George, in 1800. Reelig's mother, Mary Delamotte, completed the family, living at Moniack until her death in 1795.

So what exactly had Reelig inherited? A 'very pretty box' of a house of moderate size and with grounds to match; a smaller house, Rebeg, in very bad condition; some tenanted farmland with little productive ground; one or two small hill farms; around 900 acres of moorland rising to 1300 feet above sea level; and about two picturesque miles of burn flowing down through a dramatic rocky gorge into the Beauly Firth – nothing, in fact, that could be relied on for a good income. Rents, which tenants could rarely pay, were low, and there was no lucrative sport to speak of on the estate. Reelig had nothing but an Army pension and so, from the start of his married life, there loomed the question – how was Moniack to pay its way?

12 Gardeners Hall was built c.1723 by the Society and Fraternity of Gardeners, a group of prominent businessmen. It was demolished in the early 1820s. The present Gardners Crescent marks the spot.

Jane set to with a will to make the most of Highland life. She was a diligent, economical housewife, bottling and preserving the garden produce, keeping bees, making cheese. The children's clothes were mended and passed down, the repairs being done mainly by the devoted Nanny Rose, sewing, or 'work' as it was called, not being one of Jane's talents. Music was her passion, followed closely by entertaining her numerous friends and large family; this was her main extravagance. She was a competent hostess and never happier than when her house was full to the brim, especially with the young.

Jane and Reelig adored their children and he, especially, rejoiced in his large, affectionate family. Having had a relatively lonely childhood himself, he relished the fact that his children never wanted for companions and had all the freedom they could want. Moniack was an idyllic place to grow up in: the tumbling burn where children could fish and bathe, trees to climb, gorges, caves and cliffs to explore, woodland walks, dogs to play with, ponies to ride and summer fruit and honey to harvest. There were seaside holidays at Nairn and constant exchanges with the rumbustious cousins at Aldourie; they also frequently mixed with other families, mostly other Frasers, in the neighbouring houses of the local area known as the Aird[13] – Belladrum, Newton, Achnagairn and others further afield.[14] The memory of their secure childhood, the close companionship of each other and the love of their parents in such beautiful surroundings would in years to come support and nourish all the children in an era when partings were frequent and separations long.

After the deaths of two daughters, one in infancy and the other, aged three, at whose bedside he stayed alone till the end, Reelig was terrified by the slightest sign of illness in his remaining children. Long years later, Aleck, reviewing his upbringing, admitted that he had been extremely spoilt on account of suffering more childhood ailments than normal. His father cosseted him and forbade any undue exertion. While his brothers were out in the woods, fishing the burn, climbing trees and fighting, Aleck was kept close by his father's side. This favouritism did not endear him to his elder brothers, who simply ignored him. Much later he wrote that he was 'proud and pusillanimous; irritable and cowardly, weak in Body, enervated in Mind'. He had a lifelong terror of physical fights although he was always capable of winning a verbal altercation.

When, in the summers of 1797 and 1798, the seven cousins from Aldourie came to stay, no one had time to worry about nine-year-old Aleck. For the first time in his life he was free to wander through the woods at will with his bow and arrows. He longed to distinguish himself by bravery and had thoughts of seeking the 'glittering attractions of a military life'. He was still, however, outside the circle. 'My only resource was Solitude, and rambling with my dogs, through the woods.'

---

13 Area between the River Beauly and Glenurquhart, traditional heart of Clan Fraser territory.

14 It is surprising that our nearest neighbour, Moniack Castle, did not play a part. This is probably because it was being remodelled, and therefore uninhabitable, during the early 19th century.

Reelig, passionate about education, was determined that his sons would have the best schooling he could afford. At the age of around fourteen the three elder boys were sent to Edinburgh to be tutored under the watchful eye of their Uncle Alexander Tytler, later Lord Woodhouselee,[15] husband of Jane's eldest sister, Anne.[16] The Tytler family lived in one of the fine new houses in Princes Street and 'Uncle Woodhouselee' was a significant figure in academic and literary circles, with many interesting and influential friends. These included Walter Scott, who as a young man lived near Woodhouselee, the Tytler country house 'romantically seated on the eastern slope of the Pentland Hills',[17] six miles south of Edinburgh (see Plate VI).

The Tytler cousins (and, occasionally, the Fraser boys) would often be taken on walks by Scott. Pied Piper-like, he would lead the enchanted band to the top of a hill where he would weave his magic with story after story. 'It was a beautiful feature in his character that he required no audience of the learned or the great to draw out the charm of his conversation,' wrote Anne Tytler.[18] In the evenings there were ghost stories by firelight, followed by his Lordship's favourite activities – a good game of Blind Man's Buff or a musical evening with his children, to whom he was a most indulgent father.

James and William, the first to leave home, aged fifteen and fourteen, were very happy in Edinburgh, enjoying plays, bands, the circus, parties, skating and shooting. In the holidays their tutor, Mr Thom, took them on fishing trips and expeditions and sent occasional reports to their father:

> I have only to say, dear Sir, in addition to Willie's letter that we are all well – still continuing by our good conduct to merit your and Mrs Fraser's approbation – George [school friend] and Willie are still using at times some vulgar expressions picked up in the streets or from some of their companions ... with respectfull compliments to Mrs Fraser and all the Children, I am dear Sir, your oblig. &c John Thom.

At the end of 1798 the kindly Mr Thom gave way to the stricter Mr Fenwick. Despite his severity he was liked by the boys who asked their mother to send him a cask of butter, as it was very expensive in Edinburgh.

The boys had their noses in books from 8.00 am to 8.00 pm daily; compared to the classical syllabus at Charterhouse their education was broad, including Book Keeping, Mathematics, Arithmetic, Writing, Natural Philosophy, Universal History and Languages. Reelig wanted his children to learn to draw, but with such a timetable Mr Thom decreed, 'an hour cannot be given to drawing'. William grumbled, 'I have only one hour in the day that I can call my own.' He found time, however, for reading and pleased his father with his preference for books of travel and adventure.

15 1747–1813. Judge in the Court of Session and Professor of Universal History at Edinburgh University. Created Lord Woodhouselee in 1802.

16 On her father's death Anne had inherited Balnain and now added the name Fraser to Tytler but for simplicity the single name Tytler is used in this story.

17 *Ordnance Gazeteer of Scotland,* ed. Francis H. Groome.

18 *A Memoir of Patrick Fraser Tytler*, John W Burgon (1859) John Murray, London.

As the boys grew up, the question of what they were to do in life became pressing. There was scant opportunity for employment in the Highlands and, after much deliberation and advice, Reelig accepted the offer of an apprenticeship for James on a cotton plantation in St Vincent,[19] where he would be indentured to the firm of James Brown and William Matheson. For William, Reelig would seek a career in the East India Company, of which their close friend and Jane's cousin, Charles Grant, was a director.

On 6 March 1799 James, aged sixteen, set sail to seek his fortune in St Vincent and was replaced in Edinburgh by thirteen-year-old Edward, who immediately flourished. William proudly reported to their father that there were ninety in Edward's class at the High School and he was around twenty-sixth. Edward, somewhat ambiguously, claimed that he attended the High School 'as regularly as William does the College'. He was fortunate to coincide with the rectorship of Alexander Adam,[20] although he and the Rector did not always see eye to eye:

> Mr Adam and me [have been] disagreeing very much ... he lickt me twice telling at the same time that the next time he would take the assistance of the Janitor which I really believe if I tease any more.

A little later, he asked his father for permission to skip the examinations 'for I do not think myself entirely fit for answering all the questions which he [Dr Adam] asks'.

Holidays were often spent at Woodhouselee where there was always plenty going on. The cousins, Anne (Annie), Isabella, Jane (Jeanie), William, James, Alexander (Sandie) and Patrick (Peter) Tytler, more or less matched the Fraser children in age and over the years the two families became very close. The idle charmer, happy-go-lucky Edward, was a great favourite with everyone: his aunt called him 'dear Teddy Boy' and his cousin Anne wrote to his mother, 'I do not know how we can ever give you back Edward – he is such a favourite'.

'If ever a father was idolized by a band of amiable and intelligent children, that man was Lord Woodhouselee. He was the sun and centre round which they moved.'[21] He turned a blind eye to any unruly behaviour, remaining unperturbed by his sons' frequent participation in the 'bickers', the street fights which were commonplace all over Edinburgh. The steep, narrow, dimly lit alleys, murky doorways and nooks and crannies threaded daily by the boys on their way to and from school provided the perfect arena for this popular form of gang warfare.

The youngest of the four Tytler sons, Patrick,[22] loved the sport of the bicker above all else. His sister Anne describes him tearing into the house in Princes Street with 'his face all bruised and streaming with blood' demanding to be cleaned up and allowed back to

19 In the Caribbean Windward Islands.
20 'An accomplished scholar, a courtly gentleman, and an ideal Rector' (*The Royal High School Edinburgh*, J. J. Trotter, Pitman, 1911).
21 *A Memoir of Patrick Fraser Tytler*, John W Burgon (1859) John Murray, London.
22 1791–1849. Known as Peter.

the fray that instant.[23] He was the exact contemporary of William's tomboy sister, Mary, and they no doubt encouraged each other in wild escapades at Aldourie and Moniack.

There is a glimpse of another cousin, David Gregoire. Catherine, the younger of Jane's sisters had, misguidedly as it turned out, married a Frenchman, M. Gregoire, and their only son, David, the same age as Edward, had spent much of his childhood at Moniack, where he was considered as an extra brother. Later he went to school in Boulogne near his family in Dunkirk, and William heard that he was 'quite metamorphosed into [a] buck with his hair curled & neckcloths & expecting a pair of boots'. A year later the boys were shocked by the news that David had been removed from his French school for bad behaviour.

However happy and busy the boys were, there was still time to think longingly of home. Early in his schooldays, William declared, 'I would not give up one walk up the burn for every one that is in Edinburgh'. He was concerned, too, about the happenings at home, especially his parents' move to a small house in Castle Street in Inverness; Reelig had found employment as a Customs Officer and had let Moniack for two years. Jane explained it was far easier to economise in Castle Street, where there was little room to entertain and they would have to live 'very savingly' for some years, as 'your Father's money engagements are serious'. For Jane, with her love of country life, entertaining and the bustle and merriment of a house full of children, the move was very hard.

⁂

There are many references to the boys' writing: handwriting in the early nineteenth century was an essential part of a boy's education; jobs depended on a good hand. William's New Year letter to James in 1801 was beautifully written with just a hint of the flamboyant flourishes that characterise his later hand and, perversely, make it so difficult to decipher. His mother commented hopefully to James:

> I am sure you will see a great improvement in Willie's handwriting – from nothing but writing slow & taking pains – it is still time for you by attention & writing slow to amend your own which it still requires greatly.

Reelig advised William …

> … *never to scribble*, but even were it a washerwoman's list of your linen, write it with equal care as any other thing – scribbling never saves time & ruins a hand – & in India a fine hand is most essential even to fortune.

Reelig's own writing is beautiful, easily legible, while Jane's wild and erratic hand, with its constant fierce underlinings and disregard for punctuation, apart from a dusting of dashes, brought occasional complaints from her sons. Her spelling was also fairly unpredictable but this did not stop her from pointing out to William that his last letter had contained fifteen mistakes.

23 *A Memoir of Patrick Fraser Tytler*, John W Burgon (1859) John Murray, London. Ch. 2.

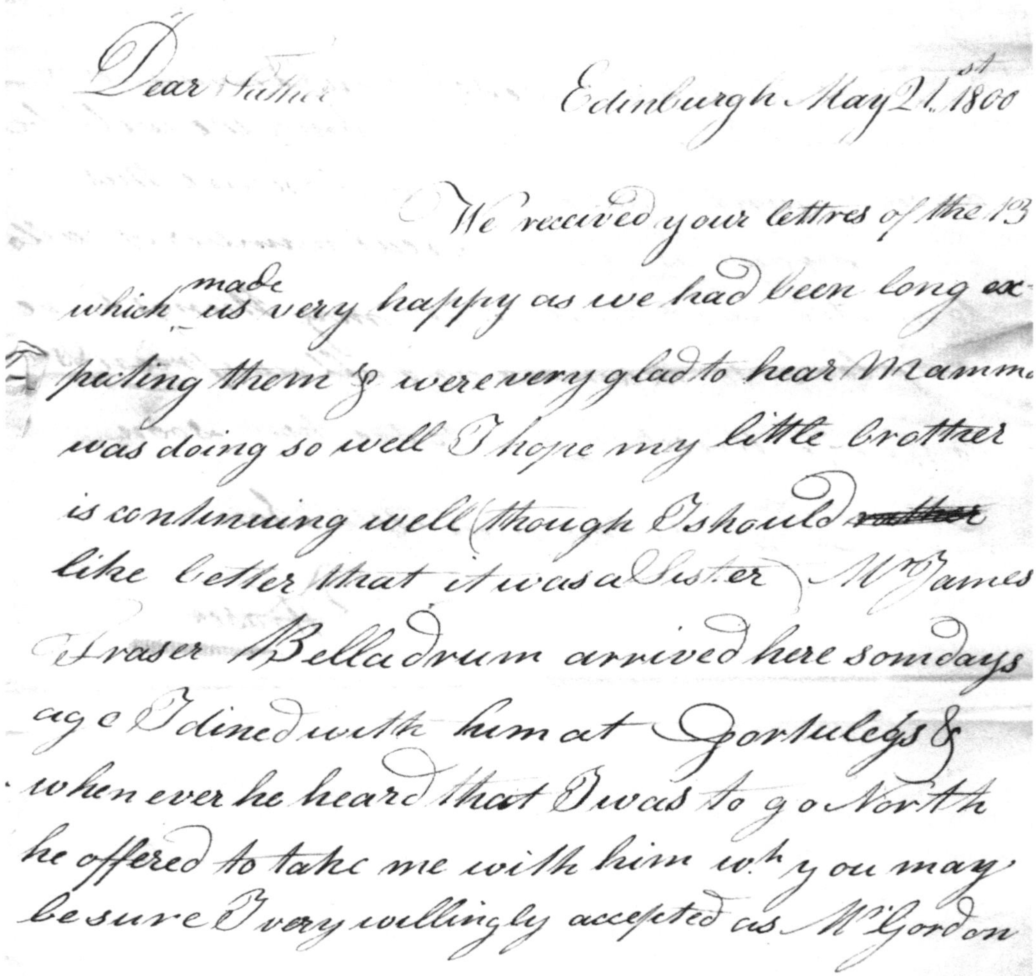

Dear Father Edinburgh May 21st 1800

We received your letters of the 13 which made us very happy as we had been long expecting them & were very glad to hear Mamma was doing so well I hope my little brother is continuing well (though I should ~~rather~~ like better that it was a Sister) Mr James Fraser Belladrum arrived here somdays ago I dined with him at Fortules's & when ever he heard that I was to go North he offered to take me with him wh you may be sure I very willingly accepted as Mr Gordon

Private collection

William's letter of 21 May 1800 to his father.

Mr Grant's handsome gift

A year after James sailed to St Vincent, George was born, on 13 May 1800, to complete the family. William, by now fifteen, was hoping for an appointment as a Writer (civil servant) to the East India Company in Calcutta. He arrived home at Castle Street in fine spirits and soon set about a long letter to James:

> I rode out to Belladrum yesterday – there are a great number of improvements going on there – young Belladrum[24] is building two wings to the house which will make it very handsome; he is also going to build new offices ... I wish very much that Pappa could get me out to the West Indies that I might be in some situation near you ... I am dear James your affect Brother *but a very idle Dog* [added by Papa] William Fraser

24 William's second cousin, James Fraser younger of Belladrum, son of his father's first cousin, Hannah Baillie, who married James Fraser of Belladrum.

James, however, would be happy to hear that the idle dog promised to be 'a manly sagacious candid Lad', from whom his father expected great satisfaction.

It seemed to Reelig that if he was to invest in the West Indies he should go and see the place for himself; he accordingly applied for leave from the Board of Customs. In late September William wrote again to James:

> Pappa had some thoughts of going out to the West Indies with Lord Seaforth to Barbadoes I am affraid it is to true the only thing that may prevent him is that he has not as yet received any letters from the Board of Customs giving him leave to go. I am I believe to stay in Inverness and to be at Baillie Inglis's Bank to learn Business to prepare me for going to the East Indies where Pappa hopes to get me ... but I must conclude supper being on the table.

The following month William's appointment to the East India Company was confirmed and Reelig's leave of absence to go to the West Indies was refused. He was, however, already in London and he stayed there for three months, his first long absence from the family, investigating investment in Guyana; all around the Highlands, notably next door at Belladrum, there was evidence of the fortunes to be made there.

The Frasers of Belladrum owned three Guyana plantations, so far very productive. James of Belladrum, about to buy more land with another neighbour, Lord Seaforth and others, offered Reelig a partnership. It was too tempting for Reelig, in deep financial trouble, to refuse; he saw it as a kind of insurance and optimistically thought it would 'enable me to assist any of my Children in their outfit, and adventure in Life – and should any be unsuccessful, it may give me the means of assisting them essentially, and repairing their disappointments'. The deal was concluded in March 1801.

⁂

The next letter to James was much treasured, dog-eared, often read and refolded; it reveals how much the family had felt Papa's long absence in London. William started the letter and then left 'the rest of the paper to Mamma who I dare say has a great deal more to say than I have'.

Mama, still in bed recovering from George's birth, always had a great deal to say and finished the letter in her usual style, scrawling her news in every spare space, often sideways or upside down and sometimes almost obliterating William's writing. Much of the content of her letters was what the family termed 'chitchat', but she rarely missed a chance to get in some moral precepts or advice:

> George's Nurse playing with him at the window was the first who perceived the carriage stop & gave the joyful cry that 'Papa was come'! – Jane Anne immediately started up crying 'Let me run Let me run to him! for my heart is just coming out'! ... & Willie & Aleck seeing the carriage took to their heels & in a moment the whole group were at Mamma's bedside and a more joyful group I believe not ...

> He is in perfect health and since his return we have all got well ... Your Papa was much struck with Willie's improvement ... he is indeed quite a young man – & attending with the utmost vigilance to improve himself at Mr Inglis's – we must soon lose him I am much afraid & tho certainly Mr. Grant's[25] handsome Gift of an appointment to India is the object ... severely shall we feel parting with him to such a distance ... Mary ... is still a wild little creature but I make no doubt will turn out well ... Pray have you any place for Publick worship on your Island – or is there any respect or attention paid to Sunday?

Charles Grant, his wife and family were already playing a significant part in the lives of the Fraser family. They were both of Highland stock, Charles's wife, confusingly another Jane, being a Balnain Fraser, thus a cousin. Immediately after marriage in 1773, the couple had embarked for India. There Grant was appointed secretary to the Board of Trade in Calcutta[26] and immersed himself in the amusements on offer, spending long hours and huge fortunes at the gambling table. While in India they had seven children, the first two of whom died of smallpox in infancy within nine days of each other in 1776. This double tragedy changed the lives of the Grants forever: Charles regarded it as a wake-up call from God and, with the support of his young wife, abandoned the gaming tables and committed himself to evangelical Christianity.

After nearly twenty years and a successful career, Grant and his wife, both alight with missionary fervour, returned to England with their five surviving children: Maria, Charles,[27] Robert,[28] Charity Emilia ('Charemile', a year older than William) and Sibylla. Two further children were born in England. In 1794 Grant was elected unopposed as Director of the East India Company and along with another Director, Reelig's neighbour James Grant of Redcastle, was instrumental in obtaining a Writership in the Company for William.

Soon after his return to England Grant met and became close friends with William Wilberforce and Henry Thornton, both members of a brotherhood known then, somewhat derisively, as the Clapham Sect or 'The Saints'. They were wealthy and prominent individuals, many of whom were members of Parliament,[29] committed to practical Christianity and opposition to slavery. They also worked tirelessly for improvements in education and public morality, the establishment of Christian missions and provision for the poor.

The Thorntons, Grants and Wilberforces, generally recognised as the leaders of the Clapham Sect, lived in close community at Battersea Rise, an estate in Clapham, then a

25 Charles Grant (1746–1823), Director of the East India Company.

26 *The Life of Charles Grant: sometime member of Parliament for Inverness-shire and Director of the East India Company*, Henry Morris.

27 Member of Clapham Sect, MP for Inverness-shire, created Baron Glenelg in 1835.

28 Member of Clapham Sect, MP for Elgin, 1834 Governor of Bombay, composer of hymns, notably 'O Worship the king all glorious above'.

29 They were nearly all Tories but they followed an independent line and the Government was often anxious to secure their support *The Clapham Sect*, Margaret Bryant (2004) Clapham Society.

village in Surrey, where they worshipped at Holy Trinity Church. Other regular visitors to Battersea Rise included John Shore, later Lord Teignmouth, William Chambers, a doctor, who married Grant's sister-in-law, Charity Fraser, and Thomas Gisborne, a noted poet, whose house in Staffordshire was a country centre for the group.

Mrs Ogg's school

Mary, 'a wild little creature' of nine, had accompanied her father to London in 1800. When she was born, on 18 February 1791, there was great rejoicing in the family. Not only was she the first daughter, after four sons, but from the start she was 'funny and frisky', brimful of character. Everyone immediately fell in love with her and, being the baby of the family, she naturally became somewhat spoiled.

Mary's early years were spent sharing her brothers' idyllic childhood at Moniack, running wild in the woods, splashing in and out of the burn, riding her pony, helping her father plan the new walks through the trees, tending her menagerie of animals and birds, playing hide-and-seek with the roe and fallow deer that haunted the glen, running in and out of the estate workers' houses and 'romping' over gates and stiles. By the time she was nine her wild behaviour was causing her parents such anxiety that they decided to investigate boarding schools.

In their search for a school her parents consulted Charles Grant's wife. She considered Mary much too young to be sent away and recommended keeping her at home, at least until she was twelve. Mary's parents, however, were adamant and so the obliging Jane Grant went to work and sent particulars of 'the only school I am at all acquainted with, and can recommend'.

> It is not in the country indeed, but in a very good situation in London, & if ever you can part with Mary to such a distance, in point of care of health, morals & accomplishments you can hardly fix upon a better – but wherever you send her, you need hardly any assurance that every attention we can pay, we shall most gladly offer.

She enclosed with her letter the terms of Mrs Caroline Ogg's school in Queen Square, Bloomsbury. This may be the school with a limited curriculum mentioned by Edward Topham in his *Letters from Edinburgh* – 'a fashionable girls' school, known as the ladies' Eton'. The entrance fee was twelve guineas and forty-eight guineas a year would be charged for Board and Teaching. The curriculum, certainly extended since Topham's description, included English, French, Writing, Arithmetic, Needlework, Dancing and Geography. Music and Drawing would be extra at six guineas a year each, while washing would cost an annual five guineas. The advantage was that the school was just round the corner from the Grants' house in Russell Square; they would have Mary for days out and holidays.

Mary and her father set off for London in November 1800; she was not quite ten years old. Although she was not the first to leave home, it was a big step for her and her mother who, according to Edward, was exhausted by the preparations:

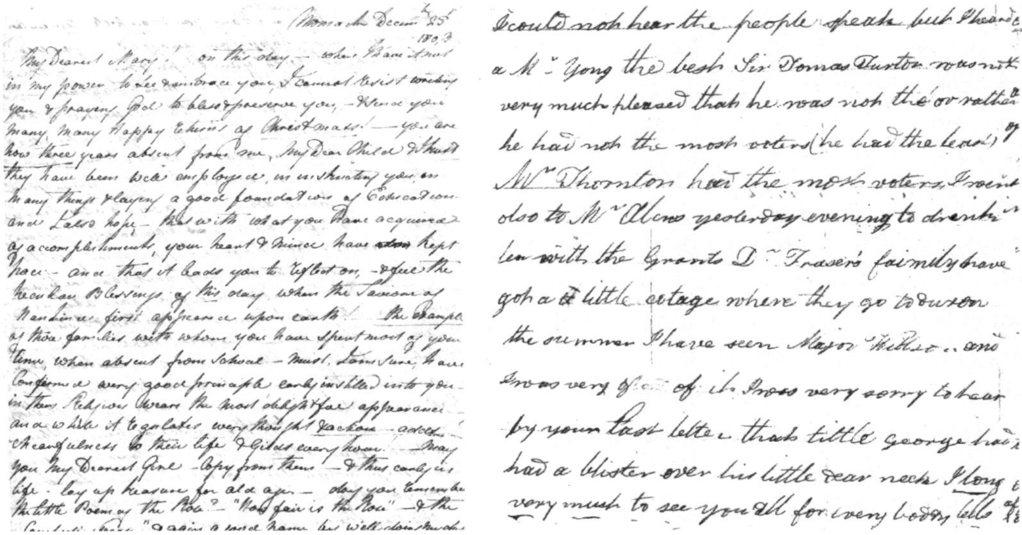

Monach Decemr 25th
1803

My Dearest Mary! on this day — when I have it not in my power to see & embrace you, I cannot resist wishing you & praying God to bless & preserve you, — & send you many, many Happy returns of Christmas! — you are now three years absent from me, my Dear Child & I trust they have been well employed, in instructing you in many things & laying a good foundation of Education — and I also hope — that with what you have acquired of accomplishments, your heart & mind have kept pace — and that it leads you to reflect on, — & feel the peculiar Blessings of this day when the Saviour of Mankind first appeared upon earth! The Example of those families with whom you have spent most of your time, when absent from School — must, I am sure, have confirmed a very good principle early instilled into you in their Religious [illegible] the most delightful appearance and while it [illegible] every thought & action — adds cheerfulness to their life & Gilds every hour. — May you my Dearest Girl — copy from them — & thus early in life — lay up treasure for old age — Do you remember the little Poem of the Rose — "How fair is the Rose" — & the [illegible] ...

I could not hear the people speak but I heard a Mr Yong the best Sir Thomas Turton was not very much pleased that he was not the or rather he had not the most voters (he had the least) Mr Thornton had the most voters, I went also to Mr Allens yesterday evening to drink tea with the Grants Dr Fraser's family have got a little cottage where they go to during the summer I have seen Major Withers .. and I was very glad of it. I was very sorry to hear by your last letter that little George has had a blister over his little dear neck I long very much to see you all for every body tells ...

Private collection

Mary wrote home carefully when Mrs Ogg was peering over her shoulder, in contrast to her writing when 'romping' on holiday with the Grants or Fraser families.

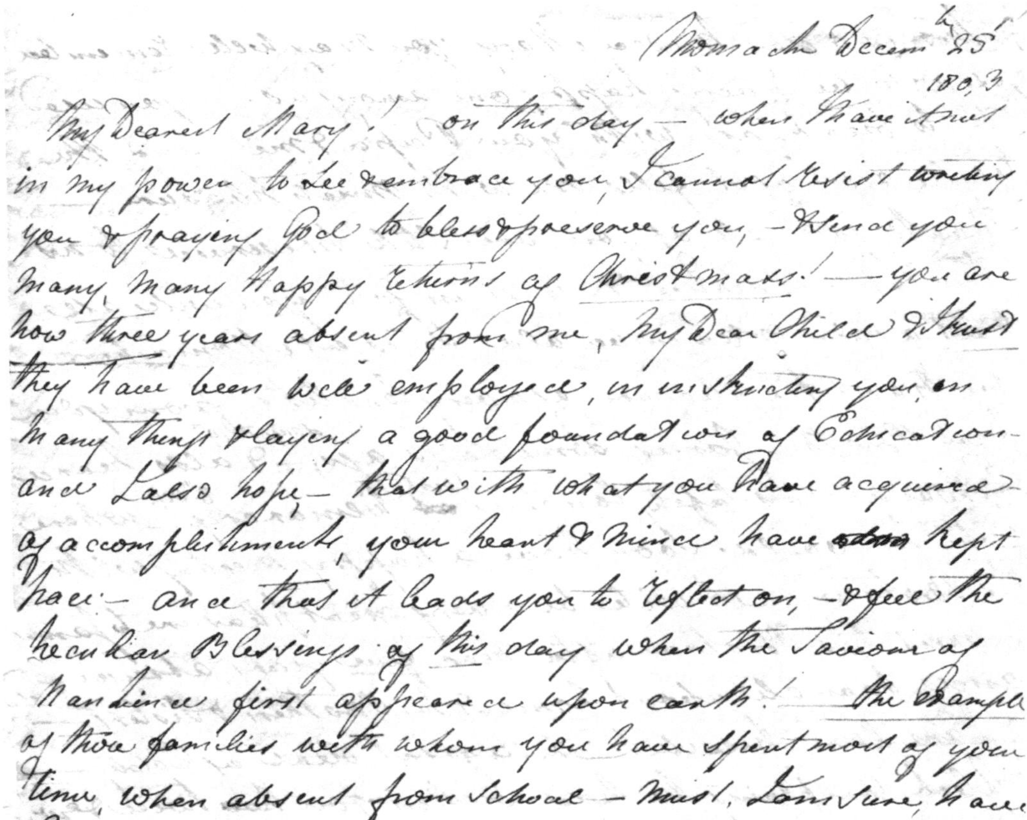

Monach Decemr 25th
1803

My Dearest Mary! on this day — when I have it not in my power to see & embrace you, I cannot resist wishing you & praying God to bless & preserve you, — & send you many, many Happy returns of Christmas! — you are now three years absent from me, my Dear Child & I trust they have been well employed, in instructing you in many things & laying a good foundation of Education — and I also hope — that with what you have acquired of accomplishments, your heart & mind have kept pace — and that it leads you to reflect on, — & feel the peculiar Blessings of this day when the Saviour of Mankind first appeared upon earth! The Example of those families with whom you have spent most of your time, when absent from School — must, I am sure, have

Private collection

Jane's writing was a constant source of annoyance to her sons who complained of her 'pothooks and hangers'.

> My dear Mother I was exceedingly sorry to hear that you were so far from well ... I am sure if I had been with you, you should not have fatigued yourself so much as I would have taken a great deal of the packing off your hands at which I am very famous.

Father and daughter stopped in Edinburgh long enough for Reelig to be painted by Raeburn (see Plate I).[30] He chose for the event a dark blue coat with a deep velvet collar. His greying hair and slightly increasing chins bear witness to his forty-nine years, but there is at the same time an energy about him.

The first reports of Mary, via Jane Grant,[31] were good: '[she] promises to be a clever little Creature'. Mrs Ogg's first letter to Jane was also positive:

> Those traits of disposition which you allude to I certainly observe. But ... she is open to reproach and so much ingenuous ... that at the very moment of reproaching I feel delighted by her strict adherence to truth – she was highly delighted by your letter which I read to her & purposes writing herself – she has already sent a note to her papa.

Mary followed the note to her papa ('the first I have ever written to you') with regular letters home, thirty-two in all, mostly written on lines in huge, beautiful, copperplate script, with Mrs Ogg clearly looking over her shoulder, censoring, suggesting and correcting punctuation. They ended more or less consistently, 'Believe me to be, my dear Papa, your ever affectionate and dutiful little Girl, Mary Fraser'. On the few occasions when she wrote from the Grants or the Fraser cousins, while on holiday, her letters were much more natural, scribbly, misspelt and badly punctuated, but they all, unprompted, declared her love for Mrs Ogg and appreciation of her kindness.

'I AM ON BOARD MY SHIP'

At the end of March 1801 William set off on the first stage of his journey to India. Just before he left he sent James pen portraits of Aleck and the two younger children:

> Aleck is a very curious fellow indeed & I think will be good for nothing but a Lawyer as he is very fond of reading & is always disputing and arguing with everybody he meets ... stoping people in the streets for the sake of argueing with them. Jane Anne is a most delightful chearful little thing & is always singing & speaking to herself. George is a delightful little fellow & whenever we ask where is James he looks to your picture which hangs above the fire.

His last day at home was spent with his father who, to distract him, took him off to the woods with Noble, the gardener, to plant the remaining trees of the spring. There was no

30 Sir Henry Raeburn (1756–1823), the renowned society portrait painter of the day.

31 Jane Grant is referred to by E M Forster in his biography: *Marianne Thornton* (1956) Edward Arnold Ltd, London. Marianne, granddaughter of the founder of the Clapham Sect, describes Mrs Grant as 'the loveliest sweetest type of an Indian mother, I mean of a woman who had married in India and had a large family around her, every one of whom leant upon her for comfort and advice and sympathy ... Their house was always open to us, and every event of joy or sorrow that occurred in ours brought her to us ... so soft, so gentle, so unwearied.'

preaching or last minute advice – just a companionable day's digging. Years later, he was to look back at this moment, remembering the exact place 'and even the directions you gave Noble' and wondering how the trees were growing.

Once in Edinburgh with his Tytler cousins, despite a heavy cold and cough, William had a happy week paying calls, advertising in coffee houses for a travelling companion to London (on his father's instructions) and, most importantly, sitting to Raeburn (see Plate II). The first day he had 'a standing of about 2 hours & a ½', and on the last day before he left 'my Picture was finished yesterday and Uncle thinks it very like but you will be best judge when you see it'.

Raeburn himself considered the result a better picture than the one of Reelig. When the two portraits eventually arrived at Moniack they were immediately hung and considered to be very good likenesses. William's picture[32] reveals a good-looking fellow with a fresh complexion, a confident, intelligent expression and dark tousled hair, a couple of locks of which fall over his face. He has large slightly heavy-lidded eyes and there is the hint of an impatient smile about his lips.

No travelling companion having appeared, William disregarded his father's advice to take a postchaise (the more or less standard vehicle for respectable families) and set off for London on the mail coach. Edward saw him off; William had been 'very much affected at parting with this family but [he] behaved in a very manly manner. Uncle and I went with him to the Mail and saw him set off he had greatly got the better of his cold and looking very well'. On hearing about the coach, a frustrated Reelig, permanently edgy about his children's health, loosed off a reproachful letter to William in London:

> I cannot conceive why you ... went by the Mail ... It is not your pleasure but your Health I consult. I am sorry to find you was not well when you arrived at Edinburgh & not quite well when you sett out for London ... I could see no reason for your staying so long beyond the time I prescribed at Edinb. unless for Health or for the Picture. If I understand Edward right you did not sit often enough to have justice done your picture ... Now unless you were unable from illness I cannot conceive why in a week you did not sit often enough – & if you was ill, why did you not stay till quite well. Your Health is my greatest object, next to your Virtue.[33]

Jane, longing to hear every detail of William's adventure, was as frantic as her husband:

> You may believe we are uneasy on account of your *cough* ... I fear sleeping in the Mail was not favourable for it – I am quite provoked at (poor) Eddy who says not one word *particular* but that you went in the Mail & did not look at all well the *first* days you were in Edinbh.

32 Now in the Metropolitan Museum, New York.

33 Health was a major concern in the early nineteenth century; disease and death lurked round every corner so that a cold or cough was regarded with dread. People were beginning to survive smallpox owing to the development of inoculation by Edward Jenner (1749–1823), but measles and whooping cough were often fatal. The usual 'remedies' were bleeding by the application of leeches (a process used for centuries to treat almost every disease and which only fell into disfavour in the second half of the 1800s), blistering (in the belief that the blisters formed by a burn would force the original illness from the body) and medications such as calomel (mercury chloride), a dangerous compound used since the sixteenth century as a diuretic and laxative. Laudanum (tincture of opium, and highly addictive) was also widely used for sleeplessness, the relief of pain and many other complaints.

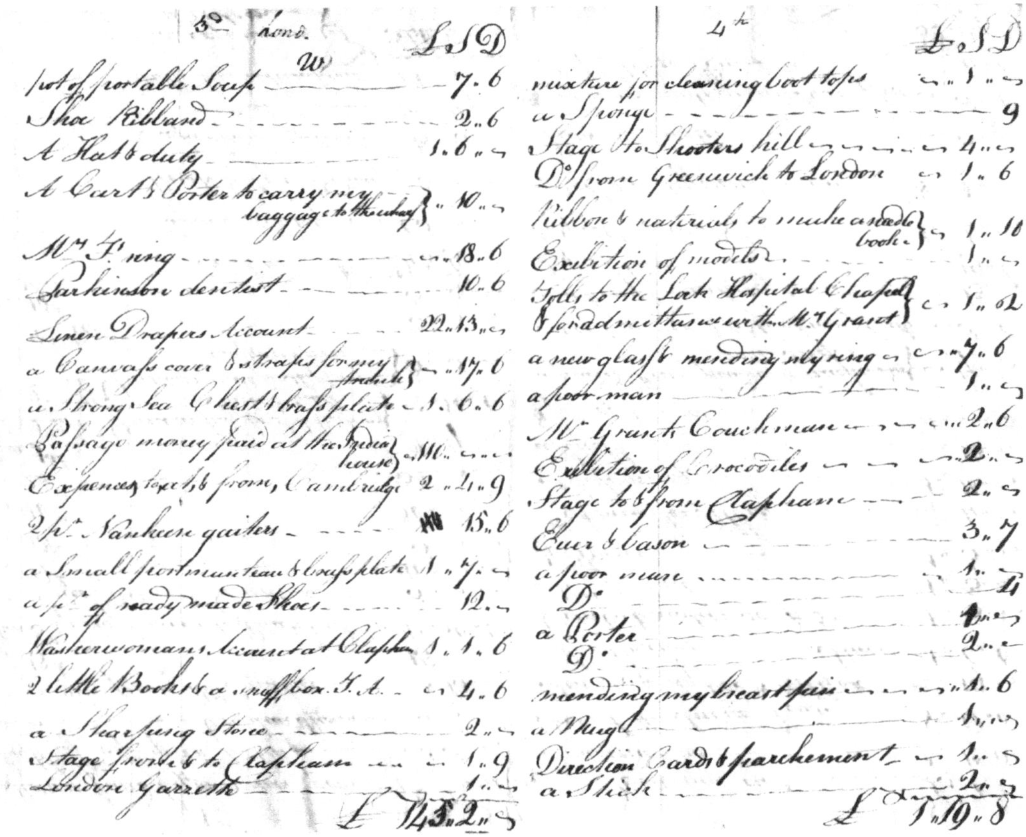

3d Lond.	£ S D	4th	£ S D
pot of portable Soup	7.6	mixture for cleaning boot tops	0.1.0
Shoe Ribband	2.6	a Sponge	9
A Hatt & duty	1.6.0	Stage to Shooters hill	4.0
A Cart & Porter to carry my baggage to the wharf	10.0	Do. from Greenwich to London	1.6
Mr F. ning	0.18.6	Ribbon & materials to make a saddle book	1.10
Parkinson dentist	10.6	Exibition of models	1.0
Linen Drapers Account	22.13.0	Toll to the Lock Hospital Chapel & for a dinner that was with Mr Grant	1.2
a Canvass cover & straps for my trunk	0.17.6	a new glass & mending my ring	0.7.6
a Strong Sea Chest & brass plate	1.6.6	a poor man	1.0
Passage money paid at the India house	110.0.0	Mr Grant's Coachman	2.6
Expences to & from Cambridge	2.4.9	Exibition of Crocodiles	2.0
2 pr. Nankeen gaiters	15.6	Stage to & from Clapham	2.0
a Small portmanteau & brass plate	1.7.0	Ewer & bason	3.7
a pr. of ready made Shoes	12.0	a poor man	1.4
Washerwomans Account at Clapham	1.1.6	Do.	
2 little Books & a snuffbox T.A.	0.4.6	a Porter	1.0
a Sharping Stone	2.0	Do.	2.0
Stage from & to Clapham	1.9	mending my breast pin	0.1.6
London Gazette	1.0	a Mug	1.0
		Direction Cards & parchment	1.5
		a Stick	2.0
	£ 143.2.0		£ 1.19.8

William's detailed account of some of his expenses in London.

Private collection

Then a week later:

> How did you like Cousin William's wife? And how does she look as a married lady? – you will say I give you too many *queries to answer – but just take this letter* – & *answer* it line for line the moment you receive it even tho you may have wrote the part before – it is what you think & feel that we wish to know – as well as yr expences – & where you go.

All went well, however, in the mail coach till Doncaster, when William was unlucky in his companions, one of whom was 'eternally sick & dirtying the coach most abominably the rest being all dull stupid country fellows'. Four days later he arrived in London.

William sent his father a detailed account of his expenses from Edinburgh to London – mostly fares but including items like '… my portrait by Raeburn ... 21.10.6, liquorice ... 1/- and a pair of gloves at Doncaster ... 3/-.'

His father, copying it into his letterbook, noted in the margin that 10/6 unaccounted for was 'probably a present to two young ladies'.

After a couple of days spent with his patron, the kindly James Grant of Redcastle, who took him to the Opera and to Astleys Circus, William visited the Grant family in Clapham, where he found Mary. She had grown taller, 'speaks very well & is much improved'. Kind as the Grants were, the next months were frustrating and difficult for William; constantly expecting news of a passage, in which case he would have to hurry to Portsmouth, he could not plan more than a day or two ahead. Quite apart from all the shopping to equip himself for the voyage and for India, he was also laden with lists.

There were lists of articles that his parents considered essential, of people who might provide him with letters of introduction for India and of commissions to send home. Among these were whin seed, a ring, shoes and stockings, a veil, cabbage seed, a pruning knife, larch seed, a lock for the door (from Bramah in Piccadilly) and a tea urn 'of the best construction, quite plain, no silver ornaments'. In July his mother wrote:

> Your Papa gave you a commission for a *tea urn* I believe I must give you one more for a *Riding Hat* – you must go to Breach No 46 New Bond Street & look at the *black* beaver ... hat – & enquire the price – see if that is the most fashionable (they fall down at the sides & tie under the chin) & write me the price & if any colour but black is worn.

William did his best. Ten days later he reported that he had seen the hat she mentioned, that black was indeed the fashionable colour and that the cost with postage and packing would be around 30/-. But he needed to know the size, and the helpful shopkeeper had given him a 'card of directions how to take the measure... a string passed tight round the *outside*, & close to the bottom of the Crown of a Hat in present use, will prove a tolerable correct measure for a new hat'.Then there was the urn:

> Tell Papa that I have got an Urn, that the price of it will be I suppose about £3.8/- or 10/- & that as I know he likes to have everything of the best quality, I took one with a particular kind of cock which prevents any water droping out, that by screwing of a kind of nut below the part that turns you find [a] screw which by tightening it a little effectually prevents the water coming out, that you must also sometimes take out the part that turns (which is done by unfastening the screw altogether) & put a little grease on it that it may not become stiff on turning & it only makes a few shillings difference.

'Everything of the best quality' was indeed what Reelig and Jane aimed at. Breach and Criddle later described themselves as 'HATTERS to her MAJESTY & the PRINCESSES', and Bramah, established at 124 Piccadilly in 1784 and still selling locks today, is London's oldest security company.

Jane had second thoughts about the hat, wondering if she would prefer a 'white Hatt if much worn'; she eventually concluded that 'for *aged* Ladies *black* is better' but felt unequal to the task of measuring with string. 'Just choose a small size,' she advised William. Two weeks later she decided that she would really rather have a straw hat; but it was too late, the black hat was bought. In early September 'My Hatt arrived yesterday & I like it much & am just going to put it on – the *Urn* came also safe & is very handsome'.

While he was finding his way around London and coping with all these demands William divided his time between the Grant family in Clapham and his cousins, Dr Fraser, his wife Isabel and their family, in Lower Grosvenor Street. He was lucky in his hostesses: the motherly Mrs Grant, with experience of two teenage student sons, 'has taken it upon herself to get all my Linnens[34] which is a great Burthen of my hands'; of Isabel Fraser, Reelig said he had 'seldom met any person I could have compared to your own mother but her'. Jane was always worrying that one family would be offended by William's residence with the other but he managed it all very well. He was, nevertheless, badly missing his father's support: 'I indeed feel the want of your advice in everything I do as Mr Grant is not able & would never think on every little thing that is necessary as you would.' Unfortunately, Charles Grant had fallen seriously ill soon after William's arrival.[35]

The Grant family was a source of great interest to William. 'Charemile,' he teased James, 'is grown tall & very handsome & they sometimes ask her questions about you which always makes her blush & angry. The two young men [Charles and Robert] are going to be lawyers, are excellent scholars & carried off all the prizes at Cambridge this year.' To his mother he admitted he had fallen for Charemile: 'I like her by far the best ... she is so funny, goodnatured & sensible & I'm sure would make any man happy'.[36]

William also enjoyed his time with Dr Fraser and his family. The two Fraser sons, Thomas and William, were at Eton, and in July Mrs Fraser took William with her 'to see a famous cricket match between the Westminster & Eton Schools which I thought a very fine thing.[37] I saw all Windsor when I was at Eton they join one another.'

Reelig wrote constantly to William, and his letters followed a certain pattern: criticism of both content and writing of William's letters, worries about health and advice on how to pack for the voyage. He sent recommendations for books and subjects worthy of study. He provided useful information on how much to tip servants; comments on current affairs; news of neighbours, cousins and the family; and, more often than not, what he called 'a preaching':

> You will, I am sure, reflect, when you arrive in India, that it is upon your Honor, and expected by all who love you, that you will devote all the time you comfortably can, to Study & Improvement. It is a duty every man owes to Society, to render himself as capable as possible, of being both useful & agreeable.

---

34 Underclothes.

35 This was an inflammation of the pleura, accompanied by loss of voice.

36 The Grants' house in Russell Square was a welcoming port of call for many Scottish travellers to London. In *Memoirs & Correspondence of Mrs Grant of Laggan* (1844) Longman, the author describes a later visit when she was also charmed by the attractive Charemile: 'There is one girl called Charamile, who is ... witty, lively, and extremely entertaining ... the rest seem sensible, affectionate and natural.' (Vol 1 p.159). Marianne Thornton (see Note 22) wrote that Charemile 'exercised a sort of witchery over me ... there were few people so gifted ... she captivated everyone that she wished to please'.

37 The score was apparently so discouraging to Westminster that they did not play Eton again for many years thereafter (Eton College Archivist).

Next month, June, the topic was economy:

> Whatever your income may be from the hour you arrive progressively as it increases ... lay by a small part, say one fourth, one third, or one half, according as it increases; the interest of money is so great, that a fortune speedily accumulates.

Then came hopes for William's financial independence:

> When you have once left Britain – you are to stand wholly on your own feet ... except you should meet with misfortune on your voyage – in which case *only* you will draw on me.

✽

In the chinks between sightseeing, social life, expeditions, dutiful calls, commissions for his parents, writing letters and visits to the hairdresser and dentist, William tried to concentrate on finalising the paperwork for his appointment at East India House[38] (see Plate VIII) and booking a passage:

> I said in my last that I was to pass at the India House last Wednesday the 29th I accordingly went there ... you may be sure I was a little alarmed at first, but there was no questions asked. I walked up to the President & heard my petition read he then asked me if it was *my writing* 'it is Sir' – 'you may retire Sir' & that was all. I am to go there next Wednesday to get my appointment & orders for embarking & then all will be finished.

To reassure his father in case 'we are taken by the French or if we are lost at Sea none of which I hope will come to pass' he told him the name of his ship, *Comet*,[39] and the Captain, Larkins. Captain Larkins proved hard to pin down when it came to the cost of the passage; it started as £120, which William considered steep enough. A few days later, William received a note from the Jerusalem Coffee House:[40] it had quite slipped the Captain's memory that civilian passengers had to pay £15 more than cadets. Then there was the question of a single cabin:

> If you have not a Cabin to yourself you are obliged to sit up as late & to gett up as early as the other people do because the place where you sleep is where we all mess & must be very uncomfortable. Now the convenience of one is very great in it you can do anything you like nobody disturbs you & if you are sick can have everything your own way. I daresay you will think me very extravagant to go in this way ... the difference tho is something not above the comfort £30 which makes the passage £175.

38 HQ of the East India Company in Leadenhall Street, demolished in the 1860s to make way for the offices of Lloyd's.

39 *Comet*, the second ship of the name, had been recently launched. She was 120ft long and 32ft wide with three decks (*Comet* Journal, 10 Apr 1801–10 Feb 1803, British Library L/MAR/B/302B).

40 One of the City's oldest coffee houses or newsrooms, frequented by merchants and captains involved with voyages to China, India and Australia and displaying shipping lists, arrivals, departures, casualties etc.

Reelig was suspicious that Larkins was taking advantage of William's youth but, after much enquiry, William established that 'the Captain of the *Comet* ... is by far the most genteel man of any of [the] Captains'. Larkins was, in fact, a member of a famous seafaring family which had been associated with the East India Company's ships for seventy years. Larkins Lane in Calcutta is a relic.[41]

Now all William needed was the estimated date of departure, aware that he would have to get himself to Portsmouth at a moment's notice if the wind was right. His father warned him against 'the abominable corruption and profligacy' of Portsmouth where 'you cannot walk the streets without risque of being drawn aside by the most dangerous of bad company of all sexes'. He was to avoid inns ('horribly extravagant and noisy, and seductive'), billiard tables and gambling. His mother lamented the 'disipation & corruption of that place' and 'the dreadful and melancholy scenes ... of young men – ruining their fortunes before going on board ship'.

William started packing in mid-June. Everyone had made sure he had enough books for the voyage:

> Richardson's Asiatic Dictionary, Gil Blas, Pope's Workes, Milton's ditto, the Rambler, the Guardian, Asiatic Annual Register, Asiatic Researches, Digest of Hindu Law, Robertson's History of Scotland, Buchanan's ditto, Hume's History of England with Smollett's continuation, Bibliotheque de Campagne, Johnson's Dictionary & Jones's Persian Grammar.

Dr Fraser had presented him with the *Works of Shakespeare*; his mother advised him to take the *History of India* 'that you may neither be – nor appear ignorant to those you converse with'. She felt reassured that, after all this, 'you are well provided in Books & they will be a great resource to you in your little Cabbin'.

The hot days dawdled along in London and William became increasingly unsettled, his thoughts constantly at home with his beloved dog, Buchan:

> Poor Buchan ... I am affraid I shall never see [her] again but I am sure she will be taken care off ... tell Mamma that I beg & intreat of her & Edward & Aleck that they will take the greatest care of her, for nothing would grieve me so much as to hear that she was lost or any way ill used or ill taken care of.

It was now August and Inverness-shire would be alive with friends and cousins for shooting parties. On 12 August he wrote to Edward of his frustration: he could have spent the last four months at home and was missing the Glorious Twelfth[42] –'one of the happiest that I spent was last year, when we were all together ... & in the highest spirits ... it makes

41 *East Indiamen*, Cotton and Fawcett (1949) The Batchworth Press.
42 First day of the grouse shooting season.

me quite in low spirits & in a rage at the worthy People that have detained us so long (the Directors I mean) my honoured Masters'.

Two days later it was Edward who broke the news to William of Buchan's accident. On her way to the moors she had jumped out of the window of the carriage and injured her legs so badly that Reelig despaired of her. However, Kate Martin, poultry keeper at Moniack, came to the rescue and nursed her back to health. Back in the confinement of Castle Street, however, she escaped again and headed across the river towards Moniack. Edward tore after her 'crying to everybody in the street to stop her'. Tying his handkerchief round her neck he dragged her home.

❊

At last there was news: Captain Larkins had left for Portsmouth and any moment the passengers would be summoned. But now William's courage was deserting him: he worried about seasickness and the cramped conditions on board, not to mention the other passengers, none of whom he had yet met, although he tried to be optimistic – at least he had his six-foot-square 'hole' and his books for company. Into this space he had to fit a bed, a table, a chair, a washstand, a trunk, a small bookcase, two portmanteaux and a large box.

On 18 August the sailing was postponed yet again; William was in despair:

> How much better it would have been in every way if I had waited till the next fleet which sails in January. I should have spent another happy year with all of you ... There was a report (but I believe unfounded) that the Ships were not to sail ... you don't know how it affected me when I heard it, thinking how much longer I might be near you & have the pleasure of hearing from you so often as I do now, & perhaps that I might even again see Scotland & home.

At this point the family doctor, Dr Robertson, appeared to see him off. William was relieved to have such a close friend to share his last couple of days and loaded the doctor with things to take back to Inverness:

> A few trifles to my Brothers & Sisters & likewise a snuff box & snuff for Kate Martin which I will be obliged to you if you will give it to her with your own hand & tell her it is from me for having saved the life of my poor Buchan. You must excuse the badness and shortness of this letter as I am in the greatest hurry in getting everything settled before going, as I am affraid I go tomorrow.

His father worried that he would, after all, miss the sailing, but William was more organised than he thought; he also sensibly ignored his mother's sudden notion that he might find time to call on the old and dear friend she had just remembered lived at Andover, en route to Portsmouth; he declared himself 'perfectly ready to set off at an hour's notice'.

At last, on 29 August, the urgent message came – the Pursers had left for Portsmouth 'and the Ships are to sail tomorrow if the wind is fair (which it is not now)'. He was to leave that evening at five o'clock, hoping to be in Portsmouth by seven in the morning.

Now William wrote almost daily. In return there was last-minute 'preaching', chitchat and advice from the family before the long silence of the voyage.

> 31st August 1801. My dearest Father,
> Here I am, with no prospect of sailing, the wind being direct against us & I fear with no great prospect of its changing. Dr Robertson saw me off & I assure [you] that it was a great comfort to me (as I was in very low spirits) to have him with me at that time & to see one of my greatest & best friends with me on leaving the last place that I had any in.
>
> 2nd September 1801. My dearest Edward,
> I have just finished my solitary dinner consisting of a tough old hen & French beans &c. I write you just now in one of the boxes of the Coffee House where I dine surrounded by a parcel of noisy fellows who are calling for, & swearing at the waiter, & for what? Because he can't serve them all at once ... I this day went on board my Ship & spoke to the Capt as to whether or not I was to go on board just now ... & said that if it was equally the same to him, I would come on board tomorrow, which he agreed to ... it will be much more agreeable, as I can read & write as much as I like in my own Cabin ... I have now I believe seen most of my fellow passengers, & I daresay they will turn out well.
>
> 7th September 1801. My dearest Father,
> I am now living quietly on board tho when the sea is rough rather sickish & not able to keep below or in my own Cabin ... There are about 15 or 16 passengers altogether ... in the first place there is Dr Stacey his wife & 8 children. He is perhaps one of the cleverest men you can meet with ... I went on Saturday last out with him to shoot partridges on the Isle of Wight ... he was most agreeable during our walk & his conversation rather intelligent ... there are two more writers on board ... both of them are very genteel young men, indeed so are all of the passengers & I don't think there are any of them as far as I have seen that you could call the least of a blackguard.

On 9 September at half past eight, with a breeze from the south-east, *Comet* weighed anchor and 'made sail in company with the honourable Company's Extra Ships [of which there were eleven] with several others bound to the Coast of Africa and the Cape of Good Hope, the whole consisting of Twenty sails under Convoy of His Majesty's Frigate *Sea Horse*'.[43]

43 *Comet* Journal 10 Apr 1801–10 Feb 1803, British Library L/MAR/B/302B.

> 9th September 1801 [To James]
> My dearest Brother, I am on Board my Ship – but that is not all – I am underweigh & I have but a very short time to write this as the Pilot who takes us thro the Needles & who carries this is going off almost directly ... Farewell for the present

He stood on the deck in the early autumn sunshine. Facing south, he watched the Isle of Wight slide past as *Comet* made her way through the Solent, past the Needles and out to the wider world. Suddenly, unaccountably, the misty morning hills of the island reminded him of home. He was diverted by a call for all letters to go ashore on the pilot boat. Remembering the half-written letter to his mother on his cabin table, he scrambled below and, for once unmindful of his parents' opinion of bad writing, blots and misspellings, scribbled his last instructions:

> The other [request] is to take the greatest care of Buchan and not to let her race be extinct & if ever she is again a happy Mother & if Papa thinks her Children worthy to see the daylight that you may preserve them with the greatest care for I expect in a few years hence to be sending home for some of her offspring ... Remember me kindly to all our friends ... to all my young friends at the Academy *of both Sexes*. My love to Pappa Aleck & Edward & all of you – always my dearest mother your most affect & Dutiful Son Willm Fraser.

It was 10 September 1801, over five months since he had left home. Four days earlier, William had turned seventeen years old.

2

1801–1806

Schooldays

When William set sail, Edward and Aleck, fifteen and twelve, were studying at Inverness Academy. Edward, released from Edinburgh, had lost no time in throwing himself headlong into the social whirl and enlivened all the parties, teaching everyone to play the exciting new game, Blind Man's Buff, which he had learnt at William Tytler's wedding. Confined in the small house in Inverness, however, he and Aleck dreaded having to 'mope in the town' all summer long. Jane was as disconsolate as her sons, finding 'the Town *dull* and like a Prison'.

The school day was too short for all that Edward had to do, and 'one thing that I dislike here is attending Willie's class for it is such a one as I never did see before so hot and uncomfortable and besides the most of the Boys are so dirty that it is very unpleasant'. The academic Aleck, however, oblivious to conditions around him, worked so hard that 'he is almost constantly *Dead*'. Exhausted after a year's hard study, he went off to stay with the Mackenzies[1] at Knockbain Manse for a restful fortnight.

⁂

Meanwhile, Mary, still exiled at school in London, littered her letters with longings for home:

> I assure you I long to see you so much that I can do no longer without you or dearest Papa even if you would send me a bit of your hair I should be very happy for then I could kiss it ... I long to return to my mountains to see you all again for I am quite tired of England but not of its inhabitants.

She asked for pictures of her parents, but Jane replied that they would be too expensive to send. Desperate to hear of Mary's 'improvement', she had pestered William, then still in London, for news of how she looked and behaved. He had reported Mary well, in good spirits. His mother needed more than this: 'I wish you had said where and how she ... received you – if she ran to you *at once* or behaved ... well & under constraint.'

William's next letter gave more brotherly information, not all of it welcome:

1 Revd Roderick Mackenzie married Charles Grant's sister, May.

> She is much improved in her looks but allways romps when she can get her full scope ... She is not near so great a romp as she was nor so rude but perhaps as I see her so little I am not a proper judge ... I forgot to say that Mary gets 1/- a week she says she buys books with it ... I was obliged to buy her a doll.

Mary's animals were never far from her thoughts:

> I hope you keep Bobby for my sake for I assure you I do not forget any boddy or beast in my *dear country*_... I hope you will find me improved in everything when you see me next ... I love you all dearly to my heart ... I hope my cat is in good health.

The considerate Dr Fraser and his wife provided various livestock for Mary and their daughter Annie, during the holidays at their country house at Snaresbrook.[2] During one long summer holiday:

> Polly the cow has got a little calf and Annie and me have named him Primrose and Polly is hers and Primrose is mine and I have got a hen and four such pretty little chickings you cannot think.

✲

Jane's dilemma was when to allow Mary to come home for good. Mrs Ogg hinted darkly that she needed more time to turn Mary into 'an accomplished & a *good* young woman' although she had faith in her 'real goodness and affectionate heart'. In the spring of 1802, however, Mary fell ill; she spent her convalescence with the Frasers and then the Grants:

> I wold have written you a longer letter from Dr Fraser's only the post was just going off when I thot of it ... Charles [Grant] has brought me a new dol he is very good to me I am going to school tomorrow morning and am glad for one reason and that is that the more I learn the soner I shall leave school and spend my time with my dearest Mama and hope to be a comfort to her and devote my hole time in striveing to make you and dear Papa happy I assure you I shall never forget the kindness that Mrs Grant showes to me I am sure that if she had not been in England I would have been very unhappy for [all] I have to comfort me is that I have such a kind friend when I am so far frome my dear Papa and Mama.

Staying as often as she did with two families in the swing of political affairs, Mary was privy to much topical talk and rumour and always relayed her gleanings to her family, inaccurate though they often were. She sent Aleck some 'very good news ... which I hope is all true but I fear it is too good to be true and that is that Bonaparte is dead and that it was all a report [rumour] about the Duke of Kent being taken'.

Both were indeed rumours: the Duke was safe and the ogre Boney was still disturbing the nights of terrified children. Mary, however, was not letting him worry her: 'I do not think there is much likelihood of his coming as far as London.'

2 Now part of north-east Greater London.

Calcutta but no Dromedaries or Camels

William arrived in Calcutta in February 1802 after a voyage blessed with excellent weather. His climbing skills, honed on the rocky outcrops bordering the Moniack burn, had proved useful:

> The way I passed my time was mostly in reading, and in exercising myself, by going all over the ship; and as I daresay you remember, I was a great climber, there was not a part of the ship or rigging that I was not on.

The small part of his journal that survives proves that he made the best of what must have been, for an active seventeen-year-old, long trying months. He meticulously divided his day into various activities: reading the classics; delving into Dow's *History of Indostan*; playing backgammon and learning picquet. He spotted whales from his vantage point on the rigging; he invented a new oil lamp to replace a broken one and made a trap for the mouse that shared his cabin; he daily visited his fellow passengers to join them for a drink or a delicacy like raisins stolen from the gunroom by Mr Keith who, at Christmas, was discovered drunkenly singing 'Galick songs' to the bemused messmates.

When, on 28 January 1802, the faint misty outline that was India appeared on the horizon, William, with his spyglass, was as high as possible in the rigging. His initial impression of India was not favourable: he was disappointed not to see 'Elephants, Dromedaries and Camels pacing the streets' and considered 'this country is as much inferior to Britain as it is possible to be'.

⁂

The usual system for newly arrived boys was to stay for a week or two with one of their introductions, in William's case a cousin, Major Charles Fraser, and then to move into Writers' Buildings[3] (see Plate X). This institution dated back to the end of the seventeenth century and accommodated the junior servants, or Writers, of the Company – a hostel, in fact, where the thirty-eight youngest were housed.

The boys had to furnish their 'three large comfortable rooms', employ about twelve servants and buy at least one horse; unless they had arrived with money in their pockets, they immediately had to borrow from Indian moneylenders, from whose clutches it was almost impossible to escape. By the end of his first two weeks William owed Rs1100. His salary was Rs246 a month, a rupee then equalling about twelve pence.

The number of servants was dictated by the strict demarcations of the caste system: six bearers for the palanquin[4] (see Plate XVI) as well as a *hircarrah* (courier) to run ahead and carry messages; a *mussaulchee* (torch bearer) to carry the lantern at night; a *kitmutgar* to wait at table; a tailor, a *khansama* (steward), a waterman, a sweeper and a *hooka-burdar* to take charge of your hookah. This establishment cost William around Rs80 a month and his servants were, in his opinion 'indolent, lazy dogs':

---

3 A fine example of classical European architecture but replaced towards the end of the nineteenth century by a gigantic Gothic structure, today the Secretariat of the West Bengal Government.

4 A covered litter consisting of a large box carried on two horizontal poles by four to six bearers.

> [The] one who runs before your palanquin to clear the way of people, will not carry a lantern by the side of it ... one who brings your water in a goblet or bottle for drinking, will not bring you a glass.

All, he reckoned, 'very vexing and troublesome'.

Luxuries at home were considered necessities in India: according to Fanny Parkes, the redoubtable wife of an East India Company Servant, it was essential for a man 'to have everything good about him – a good house, good furniture, good carriages, good horses, good wine ... good humour; good servants and a good quantity of them, good credit and a good appointment'.[5] Small wonder, then, that seventeen-year-old William, straight from the impoverished Highlands, should have fallen instantly and irrevocably into debt.

His 'chum' or room-mate was a good-natured fellow but they had little in common: 'he would not give sixpence for a horse or a dog and would much rather be with himself than with the Ladies. Now I like all three and could scarcely live without them though I can also pay attention to other things'.

For young men, Calcutta in the early nineteenth century was a very attractive place. Not only was it the seat of Government, the place to catch the eye of the right person when it came to finding a job, but there were also fancy dress balls, race meetings, hunting expeditions, river trips and sightseeing, not to mention the *nautches*[6] and religious festivals – and all this half the world away from the parental eye.

Not surprisingly, William found it hard to concentrate on his studies. To start with he found the work difficult as he only attended Fort William College[7] twice a week and needed self-discipline to study at home. After four months, however, he began to enjoy his classes – primarily Hindustani, with some Classics, Chemistry and a bit of Natural History. Arabic and Persian would come in year two. It was too late, however, to catch up and his first year was something of an academic disaster.

He was constantly calculating how long before he went home: 'I am almost reconciled to 20 years,' he told his father a month or two after arriving, and two months later:

> I find my condition here becomes more and more comfortable every day; and though this country is in no way to be compared to Britain, I think a man may live very happily in it for some years, always enjoying the prospect of a speedy return to Britain.

Well aware of the importance of making his mark, he worked hard at following up his introductions. He was a popular dinner guest and made friends among the married couples. From the boys of his own age he found no one with similar 'inclinations, desires, passions', but keeping his contemporaries at arm's length was also a way of avoiding the numerous expensive temptations of Calcutta. He had, by now, moved out of Writers' Buildings and was

---

5 *Begums, Thugs & Englishmen, the journals of Fanny Parkes, selected and introduced by William Dalrymple* (2002), UK Sickle Moon Books, Eland Publishing.

6 An entertainment given by professional dancing girls.

7 Established in 1799 in Calcutta by the Marquis Wellesley (1760–1842), Governor General – his 'University of the East' to provide an education for young Company Writers.

lodging again with the Frasers. It was far cheaper to have dinner with them, some interesting conversation wreathed in smoke from the hookah, a little music from his hostess and an early bed, than to frequent the town's gambling and drinking dens with a group of teenagers.

Going home to the Frasers' house in Barrackpur, which was by the river and 'airy, pleasant and cool', from 'hot, stinking and dusty' Calcutta, reminded him of going home to Moniack from Inverness. He was fond of the Major but less so of his talkative wife, dreading the evenings spent à deux hearing about Mrs Fraser's travels, romantic intrigues and illnesses. She was 'very broad and fat and not at all handsome' but definitely accomplished, singing delightfully, playing the piano, drawing and painting skilfully and speaking several languages. 'She does very well for the Major', said William, 'but keep me from such a wife'.

Marriage was never far from his thoughts although he had little confidence in the prospect. By the time he was out of debt he would be old, with probably no fortune and 'a broken constitution … and this is what you have to offer a young, accomplished, good and handsome woman'. Most of his female acquaintances seemed affected and silly; the endless social round was tolerable but too ceremonious:

> The Ladies of the Gentlemen in the highest stations have here what they call public nights; where you walk into a room, make a bow to the Lady of the house, perhaps are asked to supper; if not, you may walk out again as soon as you please.

William preferred evenings with five or six friends, rational conversation and a little music. He was discovering stimulating companions among the more educated Indians: some of the senior of the Company's servants were 'among the cleverest men that I have ever seen, and who, to me who am so young in the world, present a most useful and advantageous conversation.'

His greatest hardship was that for ten months he had no letters; during this time he wrote fairly regularly and grew more homesick. He longed for details of home and asked for maps of Scotland and a lock of hair from each member of the family. He also wanted the Scottish newspapers, some tartan and, if possible some whisky 'not for the pleasure of drinking it, but of being able to say I have it – these little things give a true Scotsman great pleasure'. He often daydreamed about the day when they would all meet again at Moniack. One day he imagined them all at breakfast:

> With a fine appetite (such as I am seldom blessed with here) enjoying all the prospect of a fine day, and walk together after dinner up the burn, looking out for Roes or Hares with Fun, Frolic and Glee, and perhaps poor Buchan, with you. You will I think hold me foolish for running on in this way ... but I am still a boy, when on the subject of Moniack, and ever will be.

He longed to have enough money to send home presents: Jane Anne must wait for her gold and silver gown 'until I have gold and silver to buy it with'. He also wanted to be able to contribute to the improvements at Rebeg, the house on the hill below the moor on which he had spent many happy hours with his brothers and Buchan (see Plate III):

> I remember you and me going to the Muir alone and spending without exception the happiest days of my life. Poor Buchan is now dead! I really (though ashamed to say so) when reading it in Papa's last letter could not refrain from dropping tears for her. Poor as I am just now, I would give 20 guineas for either a son, or a daughter of hers.

Five dogs, however, were keeping him company: three terriers, a spaniel and a pointer. They were naturally enough named after the Moniack dogs, Fun, Frolic and Glee, Buchan of course, and Aikendrum, after Lord Woodhouselee's beloved old dog.

❊

William's second year of hard work at College was rewarded with a Medal of Merit for his progress in Arabic and good conduct. He had found Arabic hard but Persian he thought intensely beautiful, and he sent home some Persian songs written in 'the English character that any of you may be able to sing it'. He quoted a favourite poem, which 'alone would tempt a man to learn Persian':

> Sweet maid, if thou wouldst charm my sight,
> And these arms thy neck enfold,
> That rosy cheek, that lily hand,
> Would give thy Poet more delight,
> Than all Bokhara's vaunted gold,
> Than all the gems of Samarkand.[8]

It was around now that William borrowed £500 and sent it home, along with his Medal of Merit, hoping that it would make James's life more comfortable or go towards equipping Edward for the start of his career. Otherwise it might help towards the improvements projected at Moniack which would certainly make it 'the prettiest place in the Aird'.

Needing someone with whom he could talk about home, he anxiously scanned the passenger list of each ship for the arrival of the Mackenzie cousins from Knockbain in Ross-shire. When they eventually appeared William found the younger, Charles, very congenial. Charlie's temperament suited William – 'a warm heart, a good temper, a cheerful and excellent disposition'.

Both Mackenzie boys, however, fell prey to the temptations of Calcutta and William did his best to guide them to a safer way of life. It may have been this apparent bossiness that caused a rift between him and Charlie in the summer of 1804. Whatever it was, there was no reconciliation before Charlie caught a fever and died, leaving William 'completely unhinged and unfitted for the smallest business'. He was alerted in time to be with Charlie and performed the necessary deathbed duties, including cutting a lock of hair.

Charlie's death stopped William in his tracks. He was not yet twenty and had never before wholly confronted death but now mused about it in his letters home. He had only

8 Translated by Sir William Jones (1746–94), judge, linguist, poet, historian, philologist and naturalist. 'Unquestionably the greatest scholar England ever sent to India'. *The Great Arc* John Keay (2000) Harper Collins.

three simple ambitions: first to acquit himself in India 'well and honourably'; second to go home one day 'with a moderate income'; and third to be reunited with his family who he would meet again:

> ... all joyously in the world that is prepared for us by the founder of our religion ... All that I aspire to, is that it may be truly said at my death 'he was a good man, injured none, and did what good was in his power'.

Once he had made his fortune he would be perfectly happy to live 'in a cottage such as Rebeg with a little wife and a brace of pointers'.

⁂

Aware that anyone with good exam results 'has the ball at his foot and may drive it wherever he likes', he enrolled for another year at College. At the same time, he moved into a house of his own, ostensibly the better to study (out of earshot of the garrulous Mrs Fraser), along with Mr Lumsden, a tutor in Persian and Arabic. In reality he wanted to be out of range of the Major, who thought that William was spending too much on horses. Young Writers certainly needed at least two or three horses, but William's interest was fast developing beyond mere need.

Living with the academic Lumsden did the trick: William worked from 10.00 am to 6.00 pm, during which time 'the pen is never out of my hand' speedily translating Persian, Arabic, Hindustani and Bengali. His father complained that his handwriting had deteriorated; was it surprising, retorted William, when he had to write so much and so fast? In any case, his letter writing had to wait until after dinner when 'I am so blessed with an overplus of sleepiness that I cannot generally hold up my head after the 9th hour'. He was showing signs of becoming something of a loner, remarking to James that there was no one in Calcutta whose companionship he preferred to a good book.

In the November exams he was disappointed to find himself, overall, third rather than first, with only two prizes – Arabic and Bengali. His parents, however, were perfectly content with this result and with the prospect of an appointment. In June 1805 he heard that the Residency in Delhi was to be his destination. He reminded Edward of the old family playing cards at Moniack, adorned with the head of the great Moghul.[9] It was to his Court that he was going, as Second Assistant to the Resident.

A salary of Rs760 per month seemed a wonderful prospect and William felt optimistic again about the chance of getting home early. If he spent only Rs260 a month, he calculated he would be out of debt in a couple of years. The six months of unemployment gave him a chance to indulge his passion for sport, and it was at this point that the spark of his interest in horses was finally fanned into flame. He now had a stableful of Arabs who, he wrote, were the only friends he had: 'Sweet beautiful animals. I am grown so fond of horses that I cannot live without them'.

9 Probably the Emperor Akbar, known as 'the Great' (1542–1605).

Guyana – 'Abominably Ugly, Perfectly Flat'

In 1803 the family moved back to Moniack; during that spring and early summer the house was brimming with Aleck and Edward's friends and Tytler cousins. Jane was, as always, happy with a full house, especially as she was bracing herself for two more partings: Edward, now seventeen, was destined for Berbice in Guyana, to join James, and the fourteen-year-old Aleck was off to Revd Henry Jowett's school in Norfolk.

Edward set off in July 1803, via the studio of Henry Raeburn (see Plate II). In London he stayed with the Grants. As both Charemile and Maria were away, however, he found Russell Square rather tedious until Mary's arrival; life could never be dull with Mary around. She was 'greatly improved in everything – her language is perfect English, her manners are very good, her carriage also very good'. She clearly had something of her old spirit left, however, as she had decided to cut her own hair 'and such a figure as she has made of herself you never saw'.

Mary, delighted with her glamorous brother, enthused to her mother:

> I think I should not have known him he is so much improved had it not been for his great likeness to both you and I and I also think that he is the most charming boy that ever was ... PS I hope you will send for me soon.

✻

Edward arrived in Starbroek[10] at the beginning of October 1803 to start life as overseer on a cotton plantation. His first impressions of his new surroundings were not good:

> There are no streets ... between each row of houses there is a large broad canal of stagnated stinking water ... The houses are all made of wood, none of them have chimneys, which looks strange to a newcomer, as well as the country in general ... all around as far as you can see which is not very far, you see nothing but cotton fields, and a few scattered trees.

He was no more impressed with New Amsterdam – 'the shabbiest thing to call a town that ever I saw'. He was shocked by 'a parcel of drunk men – I can scarce call them gentlemen – smoking tobacco, drinking gin and playing at Billiards'; but above all he was disappointed that he had not yet found James, who was employed on Novar plantation. This was only twenty miles from the Welldaad Estate, where Edward was staying temporarily with Simon Fraser Belladrum, but with no transport available there was no way he could walk there in the heat. All he could do was write to James and wait.

It was a difficult time: he had nothing to do, was very homesick and longed for letters. He wrote to his parents regularly, but the post depended on the goodwill of someone travelling to the only Post Office – in Starbroek. He was badly missing his piano and had to whistle in compensation. Mrs Simon Fraser had a very fine grand piano but half the notes were silent and the other half out of tune. There was nowhere to walk except along a dead straight road bordered by stinking ditches or in a mosquito-infested wood.

10 Later Georgetown, capital and main port of Guyana.

At last, after three long weeks, the brothers were reunited. They recognised each other immediately. James, Edward reported, had not changed except in colour; he was as handsome as William Tytler ('You must not tell him so though'). James had been living with the Novar manager, Arthur Limson, reputedly a very good planter but 'a harsh disagreeable vulgar little creature', who kept the house abominably dirty which deeply shocked Edward:

> James never tasted wine at his house, never had a candle to go to bed, and often not a drop of water to wash his face ... He will now be somewhat more his own master ... all this I have yet to go through.

Now it was Edward's turn at Novar. Apart from when he and James met, at best every three weeks, he was stuck with no one but Limson for company. The owner of the plantation, the 'growling' Dr Munro, had his own house. James was only fourteen miles away, a good walk there one day and back the next, but Edward only had Sundays off and was determined not to ask Limson for any favours.

His salary was £50 a year. He made his little room as comfortable as he could afford, with a small bed and a washstand. Apart from these, 'a table and 2 chairs, my writing desk and books constitute the furniture of my apartment'. The most expensive item had been the essential mosquito net.

Where food was concerned, he assured his mother, they were not badly off: fresh mutton twice a week, plenty of good butter and milk, but the fruit was disappointing – just pineapples, melons and coconuts; none of it compared with the strawberries, pears, plums and greengages of Moniack summers. Vegetables were limited and yams were a substitute for the expensive potatoes 'which the parsimony of Mr Arthur would be frightened at!'

From the start he deplored slave labour. The Negroes' diet was scanty in the extreme, and he wondered how contented the slaves really were, although they seemed to like him: 'Most people put no value on that but I think it is better than to be hated by them'. He was deeply affected by his visit to the mother of a four-day-old Negro child who died of lockjaw: 'It made me quite melancholy all the evening for which I daresay I was laughed at by Arthur'.

In his constant letters home he mused on the delights of Moniack:

> I cannot think on Moniack without being melancholy ... I hope you sometimes remember me in your walks by the burn. Since I cannot enjoy those myself it always makes me happy to think you do ... are all the new seats in the new walks finished? There was one half done when I left you ... I mean the second by Mr Tytler's bridge where there is a beautiful caskade. It would do my heart good to see the semblance of a hill or valley now. The more I think of this the more provoking it is to see the eternal ugly level in this country

He shared with his mother his memory of the day he left home:

> I recollect so well what I felt on losing sight of the house and the tops of the woods and last of all the hills. I compare myself standing with the workmen up the burn to standing over the Negroes of 28 obliged to keep on stern sour looks and scolding

every moment (don't shew this letter to my father if you can avoid it for I know it would vex him).

Ever since the successful Haitian revolt[11] apprehensive planters everywhere had lived in perpetual fear of rebellion by their slaves, who heavily outnumbered them. Christmas was a particularly dangerous time:

> Here every person is on the watch very closely on cristmas day for fear of disturbances among the negroes instead of being merry and careless. In short it is distinguished by nothing but the negroes having holiday and by their hideous dancing and discordant songs. James spent cristmas at Welldaad. I was asked to meet him but I could not go. The Doctor was far from home so that Mr Arthur and I were left alone to make the best of it.

New Year was just as dull: social life was almost non-existent. 'People meet to get drunk and talk about cotton planting and play cards'. Even at smart Welldaad nothing more interesting happened. The talk about cotton crops and prices started well before dinner, even in the company of the wives; at dinner the conversation revolved drearily around food and drink.

At last, in September 1804, Edward was able to take leave of Arthur Limson and start work at their father's property, two lots away from Mr and Mrs Simon Fraser and her piano. Although there were still considerable frustrations – the house was thatched and only half built, with Edward's bedroom open to the elements – things now took a turn for the better with a visit from James every second day and, meanwhile, the Frasers' company.

By the time James joined him, Edward was more or less settled on his father's estate. A box had arrived from home containing a book of poems, sheets, tablecloths, towels, cake, cheese, smoked tongue and newspapers – all in good condition except the cake, which was slightly mouldy. Edward was getting nervous about James's grand ideas:

> James is just beginning to keep house – I foresee he will at a great expence and I fear will be obliged to get into debt to be able to keep a decent house ... what do you think of £300 or £440 for a set of mahogany tables not so good as yours at Moniack?

He was also finding his brother less of a companion than he had hoped. James was totally preoccupied with the plantation and had, in any case, been away from home for over five years. When Edward wanted to talk about home James changed the subject to 'a new plantain walk or planting sweet potatoes'. A conversation with the workaholic James might go thus:

> Edward: Would you have more tea, James?
> James: Edward, how much was there packed yesterday?

11 Toussaint Louverture (1743–1803) led enslaved Africans and Afro-Haitians in a struggle for independence from France 1791–4. He fought off a British attack, abolished slavery and secured native control over Haiti. The effect of this was to shake the institution of slavery throughout the New World and, indirectly, to hasten the end of slavery in the British Empire.

> Edward: *Laughs*
> James: For God's sake, Edward, what are you laughing at?

But Edward conceded admiringly, 'my head would never be able to contain half of what he has to think of'.

A year later Union Plantation, lots 28, 29 and 30, hitherto shared with Belladrum and others and very inefficiently run, was divided. James was to manage his father's share with Edward as his overseer. While both boys were nervous about how they would cope with this 'mighty charge', Reelig was optimistic. At last he would be …

> … fixed finally on my own Base – without partners and with all accounts settled – *I shall find my way easy* – and I trust a good income to us at home and a good opening to independence for the Lads.

To encourage them he had sent off from Greenock, along with Donald Noble, the second son of the Moniack gardener:

> … a grand eating & drinking & furniture cargo ... value about £200 – and a Box of Linen and clothing & table & bed linen & silver spoons assorted and a multitude of other things to the amount of £80 more from this House ... & a good pipe of Madeira.

Mr Black and Mr Jowett

After Edward's departure in July 1803 Moniack seemed unnaturally quiet. Aleck, and cousin Sandie Tytler, did their best to fill the gap, but not for long as Fate, in the shape of Aunt Woodhouselee, intervened. She had secured one of the best tutors in Edinburgh, Revd John Black, to supplement the High School education of her sons and suggested that Aleck should share the lessons, en route to Norfolk, to prepare him for the rigours of Mr Jowett's classical training. It seemed too good an opportunity to miss.

So, in early August, Jane was thrown into yet another frenzy of packing and last minute instructions; if only Edward had been at home his famous packing skills would have come in handy; he would have had some notion of what Aleck would need at school, his brother being a disorganised scatterbrained creature with little idea of his belongings and less idea of how to control them. Aleck and Sandie, both fourteen, set off in early August.

In Edinburgh they visited to Raeburn's studio to see Edward's portrait; Aleck considered it 'so like that I could have spoken to it; it is dressed in a Tartan jacket'. Aleck was also painted by Raeburn, sitting, or rather standing, six times ('tiresome enough' – see Plate II). The resulting portrait was not the instant success that those of his brothers had been: Uncle and Aunt Woodhouselee marched Aleck straight back to Raeburn's studio and told the Master in no uncertain terms how to put the mouth right. Aleck had to stand another two hours while Raeburn made considerable alterations, although his parents were 'quite vexed that Raeburn attempted to improve your mouth & spoil your likeness'.

No other portraits or miniatures of Aleck have come to light so it is hard to tell just how 'like' it is. It depicts an intelligent boy with an oval face, long nose and large wide-set eyes.

His fine dark straight hair falls over his forehead and his full lips are slightly parted. Being only fourteen, he has none of the confidence of William or the poise of Edward, who were sixteen and seventeen when they were painted, but rather seems hesitant and apprehensive. His white shirt, open at the neck, gives him a youthful look, while the good-looking Edward, resplendent in neckcloth and beautiful tartan coat, has a more sophisticated air.

Jane thought Aleck's portrait 'not so strikingly like as Edward's' and:

> We think also, the picture is languid – wants animation & really as you had been fatigued or distressed when it was taken – notwithstanding all these defects – we are still much pleased with it ...George indeed thinks it has none ... for from the moment it was set upon the sopha – he ... would not suffer anyone to approach it or to look at it! – saying it was *his* – 'My own Brother Alecky'.[12]

One might wonder how Reelig, with his huge debts, could have decided to have his boys painted by a leading artist. But a good portrait was the only means of capturing the true likeness of a son about to depart, perhaps forever, to the other side of the world, so it would have been a wholly justifiable expense and an indication of paternal pride.

Aleck was delighted to be reunited with the Tytler girls whom he preferred to their boisterous brothers. He wrote to Edward:

> Jeanie Tytler is a charming creature, Isabella still more so. She is, I think, beautiful and interesting, particularly when playing on her harp ... it puts me in mind of former happy days at Moniack ... Edward! When shall we fish again in the Burn together? Perhaps never! This reflexion often makes me melancholy for though we may meet, and I trust we shall, we will not then be Boys.

Aunt Woodhouselee secretly hoped that Aleck's parents would let him continue his education with Sandie but, once the decision had been made for him to go south to the Norfolk Rectory, she wrote reassuringly:

> You are really blessed in the hearts and dispositions of your children. Aleck has all the good points of the others; and so far as I can judge excellent talents; he has a most retentive memory and great command of expression. In their exercises of translation, his has often the air of an original composition; and uniformly better English than the others ... I feel my heart as heavy as parting with him, as if he were my own child. Thank heavens the cousins have always been like one family; and through life, I trust, and believe it will be even so.

She did not consider him the right material for India and felt he should stay at home; she also seemed somewhat suspicious of the Grants and their Evangelical circle:

> You are right in wishing him to be a week or two at Mr Ch Grant's before he goes into Norfolk. Everything there is so different from the ways of ordinary people and Mr Jowett, I suppose, exactly one of his own and Mr Wilberforce's School.

12 Raeburn's portrait of Aleck is the only one that has not come to light.

Why did the Frasers send Aleck so far when Scottish education was so good and there were tutors like Mr Black nearer at hand? The answer lies in their involvement with Charles Grant; on returning from India he had sent his extremely able sons to Jowett's predecessor, the evangelical John Venn, then Rector of Little Dunham, subsequently of Clapham. They had flourished in his care and went on to achieve high honours at Magdalene College, Cambridge. This was testimony enough for the Frasers; they could, with peace of mind entrust their clever Aleck to Mr Jowett's care, where all his future schoolmates were sons or nephews of members of the Clapham Sect.

⁂

But for now the adventure of school was safely in the future and Aleck was at Woodhouselee being taught by Revd Black. He later wrote that he got more out of the two months with Mr Black than from the whole of the rest of his education.

The lessons took place in Lord Woodhouselee's library, a wonderfully romantic room at the top of the tower with a view towards Edinburgh.[13] Here Mr Black, slender, stooping and Spanish-looking 'with his black hair hanging carelessly on his neck'[14] worked his magic on Aleck, Sandie and the girls. When the large celestial and terrestrial globes had stopped spinning and the books were closed for the day, they would gather round the schoolroom fire to hear the latest part of his pastoral poem – 'The Falls of Clyde or the Farewell of the Fairies to the Earth'; he knew a great many fairy tales. His extraordinary shyness made it impossible for him to walk straight into a room; the family accommodated this in the evening by leaving the door slightly open to ease his entrance and placing a chair nearby on to which he would sink 'with his frightened look'. He then played a private game of Grandmother's Footsteps, slipping through the shadows from one chair to the next while no one was looking 'till he had attained a tolerably near proximity to my father, to whom he looked up with the profoundest admiration'.[15]

All too soon Aleck was on his way to London in a post chaise, rumbling past the military camps[16] guarding the East Lothian coast, so close to them that he could see the soldiers on parade. In London he found his way to the Fraser cousins where, he had persuaded himself, life would be all 'strictness and severity', but the easy-going family put his mind at rest. He was, however, at a loss how to behave with these new, relaxed, teasing, cousins whose 'every jest offended, every frown intimidated'.

Dr and Mrs Fraser thoughtfully invited Mary out from school on Aleck's first weekend. 'I never was happier, or so happy, to meet anybody after a long absence as Mary, unless it was Papa when he returned from London'. His progress report was comforting: she had lost her Inverness-shire accent and was still just as lively 'but not in the least riotous, as she used to

13 Here, when their father was late walking home from the town, his daughters would place a candle in the window. When his Lordship caught sight of this twinkling beacon through the dark trees of the avenue he always felt immense gratitude 'for the many blessings by which he was surrounded, and the happy home to which he was returning'. *A Memoir of Patrick Fraser Tytler*, John W Burgon (1859) John Murray, London.

14 Ibid.

15 Ibid.

16 In 1803/4 a French invasion was expected daily and a vast network of coastal defences was constructed.

be at Moniack ... I think she is rather fond of dress; and she made me go and dress myself; for, she said, she liked to see people in the fashion.'

After a few visits to Mary at Mrs Ogg's Aleck developed a lifelong antipathy to girls' boarding schools. He was furious that he had not been allowed to see his sister unchaperoned: 'a stiff governess' sat tight-lipped and steely-eyed beside them – a perfectly normal practice according to Reelig. It seems that later, during their holidays with the Grants, the high-spirited Mary sometimes managed to persuade Aleck to help her outwit the authorities. These adventures she sometimes ingenuously reported to their father, who expostulated to Aleck:

> Mary tells me that you used to do very dangerous things even in Russell Square – walking on the top of garden walls – and sitting on the ledge of a deep place below the skylights where, if you fell, you would fall 3 stories down to where the Plate Chest was kept. Is this right? Is it kind to us?

⁂

Still only fourteen 'and more awkward, more timid, more ignorant, more prejudiced, than most children at 10 or 12', Aleck arrived at the Rectory at Little Dunham, a tiny hamlet five miles north-east of Swaffham in Norfolk (see Plate VII).

A letter from his father was waiting for him packed with the usual instructions, hopes and precepts: surely there would be no comparison between Reelig's own tough experiences at Charterhouse and what Aleck would meet at a Rectory school where the six other boys were all related to highly respected members of the Clapham Brotherhood, friends of Charles Grant and 'all I believe Englishmen – and of respectable Families – I mean not only of respectable rank & station, but of exemplary Character'.

It is difficult to imagine what it must have been like for Aleck coming from a sheltered, loving and comfortable upbringing in the Highlands to a draughty Rectory in the wilds of Norfolk. An intellectual boy, loftily fond of ideas and debate, slightly on the priggish side and very young for his age, he was extremely absentminded with little idea of how to look after himself. His first letters home are full of practical problems: he desperately needs a new coat as the current one 'is so totally worn out it is good for nothing'. How is he to get his washing done when he has no money to pay the washerwoman? In fact, he has no money for anything as he had to part with his last penny to buy some apples with the other boys – for fear of being called stingy. The other six seem to have had plenty of pocket money, all being the sons of wealthy men. He needs a writing desk with a lock to keep his letters safe but not a 'very handsome one' which would undoubtedly be scratched by his schoolfellows. He has had to buy a new hat as his old one was used as a football and the crown kicked out. How is he to keep himself equipped with paper, ink and quills? The boys have all been invited to a ball but he is determined not to go as he doesn't have the right clothes.

He was also being bullied, especially by the Gisborne brothers, sons of Revd Thomas, renowned poet and respected member of the Clapham Sect, who made it their business 'to mortify and oppress me'. After trying to cope with it himself he appealed to Mr Jowett, 'one of the most agreeable and kindest men I ever met with', who did his best to sort it out. His parents answered his miserable letters bracingly: it was common for boys, even young men, to bully newcomers. Edward had gone through it in Edinburgh and James, under 'a harsh severe master' in St Vincent. His mother, with wisdom and foresight as it turns out, felt that Gisborne (the name fiercely crossed out by Aleck in case her letter was read) would probably become one of Aleck's best friends.

Reelig trusted that Aleck could take a joke and was capable of self-defence. He must:

> … consider this as a specimen 'in parvo' of what you are to meet with in struggling through the world.

Being the youngest of the seven boys, with a Scottish accent, a desire to work hard, peculiar old-fashioned clothes, and no money, Aleck was clearly a target for teasing. The six other boys detested 'everything that savoured of meanness or effeminacy' and were 'ignorant of everything out of their own walk of life'. In despair, he was sometimes tempted 'to fly to the nearest seaport and go to sea'.

Letters flew regularly between Moniack and Little Dunham. Jane's are full of the usual family news, chitchat or local births, marriages and deaths, demands for more detailed information from Aleck (is Mr Jowett married and, if so, what is she like? Which boys has he made friends with? Who is doing his mending?), gratitude to Almighty God for keeping them all safe, news of the animals and birds, a few moral precepts and details of various illnesses and medications. From his father Aleck needed news of what was going on at home:

> Desire Papa to tell me more about home ... Last night I thought to have been with Edward, fishing. I think I never was so unhappy as when I woke.

That year, 1803, England was braced for an invasion from France and Reelig was anxious: what were Mr Jowett's plans for his pupils should the enemy land near Norfolk? Aleck was reassuring: the Norfolk shores were extremely inhospitable and, in any case, the Norwich Volunteers would protect them. He hoped, however, that Papa was preparing Rebeg as a fortress; on its rock, with uninterrupted views, it would make an excellent stronghold.

The school curriculum consisted of Greek and Latin. Aleck was astonished: 'No Arithmetic, French or anything else. Is this not curious?' The boys were kept hard at it during the day which, being a natural student, Aleck enjoyed. Reelig was equally surprised: trusting in Charles Grant's judgement, he had not researched the curriculum beforehand. He sent Aleck an irritable questionnaire:

> I am desirous to know what is to be learned there in the course of three years ... Is there any study of Mathematics ... What is done towards religious & moral instruction & government of Temper, Disposition & manner & the fixing sound religious, moral & political principles ... is any Hebrew, or Oriental Tongue taught? Are French, Italian, German or any European language taught? I conclude Fencing, Broadsword, Cudgelling, Boxing, Riding, Dancing out of question ... Music, Drawing &c or the study of Natural History I suppose must be deferred. History, Geography,

> Poetry & Drama may come in among your lighter studies ... Have the rudiments of principles of Natural or Moral Philosophy been ever touched on to his pupils?

Totally bemused by all this, Aleck simply reiterated his daily timetable: up at seven o'clock, Greek till prayers, breakfast, Greek for two hours, Latin till twelve thirty, exercise and dinner, Latin four till six, more Latin in the evening. 'This is the *sum totum* of *my* studies with Mr J ... Except Babington, I do not think anyone here studies in the least in private; indeed the idea is laughed at.' There were no classes. Mr Jowett told each boy individually what to do every morning and, for the rest of the day, they just got on with it.

He shared a small room with Gisborne and Stephen.[17] The only fire in the house was in the parlour, where the boys congregated to study, but Aleck, thankful to be on his own, worked in his room, often so cold that he could hardly write. One day, taking refuge there, he discovered that the elder Gisborne had poured water on his bed and 'aqua fortis'[18] on his coat so that 'the skirt burned off'. He could not see how he could ever be intimate with any of the other boys and was still terrified of being involved in a fight. He liked the Jowetts although he felt that they were somewhat lax in their care of the boys; their four children, the church and parish work kept them too busy to pay much attention to their pupils.

Aleck was deeply shocked by the behaviour of the other boys during the weekly church service: the moment Mr Jowett left his seat to mount the pulpit, with his back to the boys in the choir stalls, they laughed, threw stones and 'kick at me & each other, so that I cannot attend to the service'.

Reelig was astonished: he had had first-hand experience of the brutality of English schools but:

> I did not expect at so private a Seminary, and so worthy a man, that the sons of such excellent men, should be so illiberal and so ill-trained at their age.

It was a hard winter in East Anglia that year, fine for skating; but even that now held little charm for Aleck. He needed 'a William, or an Edward' to share his pleasure. The ice itself did not seem as good as at home. Reelig was nervous, foreseeing all sorts of icy practical jokes, undoubtedly dangerous, but Jane remembered the happy skating of the last years vividly:

> ... the delightful remembrance of dear Eddy & you – last winter, as our *solace* and most dear companions ... I do not allow myself to dwell on the remembrance of this – as *never* to return – but on the contrary – hope very soon again – to see two – or three – of you together at Moniack.

Apart from loneliness, Aleck's main worry was money. The other boys thought nothing of the extras that daily cropped up, like a collection to start a library. Aleck was less put out by the money demanded than by the lack of consultation beforehand. What was worse for the absentminded Aleck was the scheme for stocking the library by a system of fines – sixpence for being late or for burning a candle after eleven at night. Less than a week after

17 Sir James Stephen (1789–1859); instrumental in implementing the slavery abolition act.
18 Nitric acid.

this scheme was implemented Aleck was already the poorer by two shillings and sixpence. His father thought fines 'not a bad plan – they teach punctuality, a point very often deeply essential in life – & often wanting'. What he was more concerned about was that, in view of the relatively high fees (£26.5.0 per quarter) Aleck had not got a room of his own.

Another worry for Aleck was how to keep his belongings, always liable to escape his control, private and safe. Knowing that his letters were being read by the other boys, and having lost the key to his trunk, he had asked for a writing desk with a lock. In early February, he wrote with triumphant news:

> I have received my desk ... which has greatly exceeded my expectations; it is the most compleat I ever saw ... I only fear it will be too expensive, for it is of very fine Mahogany; I have got with it a canvas cover, which is very necessary, to keep it from damage, scratches &c.

Things were suddenly looking up. As well as the excitement of the desk, Aleck reported that, without knowing how it happened, 'I found my company solicited by the others and they began asking me why I spent my time altogether alone, in my own room'. Although Babington was still unfriendly, Stephen, Wilberforce's nephew, was becoming more communicative: he told Aleck about his famous uncle, who was apparently 'not at all a grave man, but very affable and cheerful, and extremely entertaining'. Aleck had at last learnt 'to stand the brunt of ridicule; and to answer it in kind; to mix with my own comrades ... and, joining in their sports, to endure buffets like the rest'.

The school holidays were spent in London with the Grants, according to Aleck 'the most intelligent and exemplary family perhaps in England'. His first daunting experience of them was etched on his memory:

> [I] well recollect being ushered into a Brilliant Drawing room ... at 10 o'clock at night; having travelled that day 100 miles. The glare of the lights dazzled, the brilliance of the company abashed me; and I fancy my friends conceived no very high idea of me on my first appearance. I still kept on my Boys dress; was slovenly in my apparel, awkward in my address, and in short, drowned in mauvaise-honte ... Every eye I thought was turned on me, and my uncouth appearance of which I was sensible. I fancied a sneer on every face; and when I rose next morning, it was long before I had the courage to go downstairs to meet the Family ... Mr Grant's Family is the most accomplished of any I have had an opportunity of knowing ... I never saw any one of its members idle for a moment. The Mind was in continual activity; Knowledge in incessant progression. The conversation in that house was really an intellectual Feast. Continual occupation produced continual cheerfulness. Good humour uniformly prevailed.

The result was that Aleck became less self-confident and more awkward than ever. Although well above average intelligence himself, he felt there was no way he could hold his own in such a family. Even the daughters, who were younger, seemed his intellectual superiors. He took to leaving the house whenever he could and wandering aimlessly through the streets, narrowly observing the men of fashion and striving to emulate them. In his own words, he became 'an awkward fop whose happiness lay in a pair of new boots'. His plunging self-esteem made him apathetic, and the Grants gave up trying to interest him in their many activities. Once again he was outside the circle. At the end of the three months, 'dejected and miserable', he was almost glad to get back to Little Dunham, where at least he was better than anyone else at Latin and Greek.

HOMECOMINGS: 'THE HOUSE IS ONCE MORE LIVELY'.

The Peace of Amiens, signed in 1802, during which people flocked extravagantly to Paris, was now in tatters and the war resumed with Napoleon as self-declared Emperor. Three years later, Nelson's navy made sure that France and her allies would never again challenge the British at sea.[19] Reelig was optimistic about the prospects for Guyana:

> Our immortal Nelson has ruined the combined fleets. Our colonies and commerce will be secure and our manufacturers have full vent in Europe. This must do us cotton planters good service.

Trying to keep alight William's concern for home affairs, Reelig gave him news of the beautiful houses being built in the Aird as estate owners returned from the West Indies or India with bulging pockets: at Belladrum 'a palace', at Phoineas 'a nice house', a charming house at Eskadale and a 'massy mansion' at Fingask. A little further afield, Drynie, New Hall and Mountgerald were equally splendid houses.

Reelig also sent William copies of the Parliamentary reports on the great new canal[20] planned for the Highlands. He was apprehensive, rightly as it turned out, about the cost of the canal and whether the tolls would pay for repairs. By the time the canal eventually opened in 1822, it had taken nineteen instead of seven years to build, was too shallow for the increasingly large steamships and had cost almost double the original estimate of £474,000.

Meanwhile, the family at Moniack were anticipating Mary's return. There were reports that she had shone at the School Ball and that Mrs Ogg considered her remarkably gifted musically. Aleck confirmed that she had a good figure and had become very pretty, but Jane could not quite believe that the wild, troublesome nine-year-old she had parted with four years previously had grown into an accomplished teenager. In any event, she would certainly need a governess, who would probably also need an escort, to control Mary on the journey home.

In June 1804 the obliging Mrs Grant found a suitable governess in the person of Miss Phoebe Chipps, who held that the skill of education was 'to blend amusement

19 Battle of Trafalgar (21 October 1805).
20 The Caledonian Canal, 62 miles long, crossing Scotland from north-east to south-west.

& instruction'. She was also clearly intrepid, being prepared to travel so far from her elderly mother, to whom she was deeply attached; there were, after all, plenty of governess positions to be had around London. Perhaps it was the charm and challenge of Mary which drew her. A family friend, Miss Murray,[21] agreed to escort Miss Chipps, and the trio arrived at Moniack in early July.

No one need have worried: Mary was an instant success. Reelig was thrilled with her and Jane wrote to Aleck:

> [She is] in most perfect health & tho certainly not tall of her age, not so 'intolerably' [short] as from yr account ... She is delighted with home and everybody & everything – thinks Moniack infinitely improved and *more beautiful* than before – Jane Anne is delighted with her! ... if [only] we had a sight of you or dear Eddy Boy – but you must fag a little before that I fear.

Mary was affectionate to both her parents and attentive to Miss Chipps, setting an excellent example to Jane Anne, 'who is as wild as a roe & has not an idea of doing anything *she does not like*! – Miss C is much amused with her!' The two little ones doted on her and the fickle four-year-old George forsook Jane Anne, his faithful playmate, for Mary. Jane briefly worried about this treachery, but Jane Anne was of such a sunny disposition that she probably had not noticed.

Mary revelled in her freedom and was a lively companion to Reelig in his woodland excursions. Her fourteenth birthday treat on 18 February 1805 was a long walk with her father to name all the new paths through the glen on either side of the burn. They named them for each boy, for Jane Anne, for Mary (who had the 'wild walk'), and for cousin David Gregoire. There was one left, the newest, romantic and beautiful 'and this we named Mamma's'. One warm summer evening, Mary and her parents were wandering along the burn when they came across the strange white deer that haunted the woodland.

The first we hear from Mary herself after her return is from her September letter to Aleck:

> My dearest Aleck,
> I received yours of the 1st of this month this moment and am according to your desires sat down to write your Lordship ... you express a great wish to know how I like Miss Chipps, I like her pretty well ... I ride on Bobby every day now and he behaves extremely well and I hope to be able by the time you come home to ride with you as far as you like if it be 40 miles. I am sorry to say that both Papa and Mama are laid up the one with the gout and the other with bad eyes but I hope in God they will be soon well for it makes me quite unhappy to see them in such a condition and we are all so dull you know when they are not well ... adieu yet I remain your affectionate and loving Sister, Mary Fraser.

21 An unmarried and homeless friend of the family who, in the tradition of the nineteenth century, divided her time between various Highland households, supporting, caring and generally befriending.

In the Norfolk Rectory that winter things were going better. By now Aleck was something of a hero to his schoolmates: not the slightest impressed by his intellect or hard work, they greatly admired his prowess on the frozen ponds of Little Dunham. 'The fellows here are not superfine skaiters,' he boasted to Edward. 'I am one of the chief and it is my element.' Often now he had to choose between study and his friends pestering him to go skating. He liked James Stephen, who was his companion on his daily walk, but he doubted that any would be lifelong friends because of their different prospects.

He considered the English, though 'more polished than their Northern neighbours', less warm-hearted, and he now appreciated the value of family relationships:

> Before I left dear Scotland, I knew not how to estimate the friendship of Brothers and relations; no sooner was I set down among people ... who would not go a quarter of a mile out of their way to save me from hanging, than I saw my folly, in not cultivating with more care and attention, my friends at home.

Mr Jowett, aware of Aleck's potential as a scholar, was leading him deeper and deeper into the classics. At the end of each day he had to learn sixty-six lines of 'this plaguy Horace' but tried to rise to the challenge:

> Livy and Xenophon alone are my constant companions ... Latin themes and verses are what I come off worst in ... I found not the way strewn with flowers but with thorns ... I cannot *think* in Latin which is the only way.

Letters were a great consolation; he took trouble over them and was frustrated when shortage of time meant sending what his father called a 'watergruel' letter. Isabella Tytler's long letters to him were 'interesting and clever' and Mary's, when they came, were 'excellent fun'. To Aleck's accusation of laziness she replied that she had been 'realy unwell for some time back with a pain in my breast ... I am sure you will be delighted with your walk for it is so beautiful and mine too for it is so wild'.

❊

Worrying about his lack of success with the opposite sex, Aleck confided in Edward:

> I have always found that you are a favourite with the Ladies, an advantage I have not been able to obtain. There is something in manner and address which I have not been able to acquire and is necessary. They are capricious beings. I always like Girls that are not clever best; they have no right to being clever; and I always look foolish, or at least <u>feel</u> so, in the company of a clever woman ... Mrs Simon Fraser, I suppose, from what I have heard of her is so. You are much in her society, I suppose, the only Lady you know on that inhospitable shore ... I do not see a Lady from one end of the year to the other. Mrs Jowett I do not count one; she is not a demi Lady neither.

He was also anxious about his future, aware that his father had Cambridge in mind for him, followed by a legal career. This all sounded very expensive and protracted. He was impatient to prove his mettle and contribute something to Moniack. After all, William was surely well on the way to becoming independent, and he mistakenly assumed Edward was 'in a fair way for making a fortune'. He wanted to join the 'foreign adventurers' in the family and sought independence 'in preference to riches, Power or anything'. Still lacking in self-confidence, however, he expressed his feelings in metaphor:

> Ambition would tempt me to emerge from obscurity, and sail on the Sea of Fame; but my bark not being properly equipped, not sufficiently strengthened to encounter the blasts of adversity, I must content myself to sail down the Stream of Security, in a Wherry.[22]

To Mary he confided that what he would like, eventually, was to return home and farm:

> I shall never be as happy anywhere else as I have been there and I shall take some of James's children to my care and instruct them after my own method. I shall spend Christmas at Moniack and dine there on Sunday. There are my castles in the air and when I walk out alone, even if I am reading, I forget my book often and sit down and ruminate on them.

One of the highlights of that year for Aleck was his spring holiday in London, for once released from the Grants. Uncle Woodhouselee was in London with Sandie, who was about to embark for India. Sandie and Aleck took long walks together talking about the delights of Moniack and Woodhouselee; Sandie reported to William:

> I saw your brother Aleck when in London, he will certainly be the greatest genius in the family, and I have no doubt will make an eminent lawyer for which his father intends him.

Sandie's departure was made more difficult for his family and friends because several of his contemporaries had recently gone down with the *Earl of Abergavenny*[23] (along with several letters from Reelig and Jane to William). Sandie, however, set off cheerfully, taking for William some tartan, a bundle of newspapers and the longed-for whisky.

Holidays in London were expensive. Reelig had constantly asked Aleck for regular accounts; these had not been forthcoming and things were getting out of control. Aleck had permission to apply for money to Mr Jowett and to the family agent, Dunbar, (who was as vague as Aleck and never answered Reelig's increasingly irritated letters). Could Aleck, therefore, send an up to date account of his income from all these helpful sources and of his expenditure?

A month later nothing had happened and Reelig loosed off an infuriated letter. Still no answer. Back at school, Aleck's excuse for not writing was that he had left many of his

22 A light rowing boat.

23 A large East Indiaman which sank on 4 Feb 1805 two miles off Weymouth with the loss of 263 lives. Her captain was John Wordsworth, brother of William, who wrote *Elegiac Verses in Memory of my Brother, John Wordsworth* ('Sea-Ship-Drowned-Shipwreck-so it came/ The meek, the brave, the good, was gone;/ He who had been our living John/ Was nothing but a name').

belongings in London. His father's letter had 'made me quite melancholy'; he was frightened of facing the accounts but he would try to make time to write home once a week while he was still at school which he was hoping might not be for much longer. He longed for a forgiving letter and, above all, 'a summons to quit this place':

> I am conscious, my dear Father, of being much too expensive ... allow me to set out from this place as soon as the holydays come ... I am willing to be anything you please; anything will please me most ... that will cost you least ... I have *not* made use of any subterfuge or evasion to conceal my extravagance ... I hope you will put an end to it by removing me.

His parents decided to take his plea seriously and to bring him home in September. Mr Jowett agreed and took Aleck for a walk. 'Well, Sir, I am sorry to find I am to lose you too in the crowd of my departing pupils,' he said, and the subject was closed.

Much as he had ached for this decision, Aleck was beginning to have mixed feelings. He was longing for home and his father's company 'but I know if he is writing for Mr Grant or in the Custom House you might as well draw the sun from his course as him from his desk'. He would, however, miss his school companions, and his studies would no doubt suffer. His fear that he would be forced into the legal profession was still nagging away; his father must realise that he might not have the necessary steadiness to be a lawyer.

All in all, he concluded, it was a pity that his father had thrown away a good education 'on such a useless fellow', who would have been better employed digging a trench. 'If I had a son like me I would not be so patient as you are and I hope still will be'.

He left Little Dunham on 28 August 1805, escorted as far as Swaffham by a group of his friends bearing farewell presents. Mr Jowett, who was in Norwich visiting the Bishop, had earlier refused Aleck's offer of a present (his *Rollins History*), so Aleck left his copy of Herodotus on Mr Jowett's table with a note – the least he could do. He was amazed at the regret he felt at leaving the school and was surprised and touched by the affectionate send-off. Two weeks later, a thin and healthy sixteen-year-old, he arrived home.

Edinburgh and 'a New World of Science'.

At home Aleck immersed himself in the familiar activities: fishing the burn, stocking a pond in the deer park, advising on Reelig's plan for flooding the shrubbery, exploring all the new paths through the woods with his father and Mary, and capturing a large trout to inhabit his pool in the poultry yard. He had also scrambled with William Baillie, his oldest friend and schoolfellow, 'into the most romantic and tremendous recesses of the channel' in the glen.

Although Charles Grant had been consulted about Aleck's future, no decision had yet been made, and all too soon he had to turn his back once more on home to continue his education in Edinburgh on a course designed for him by William Tytler, now in his father's shoes as Professor of Universal History. The programme involved private tutors for Greek, Mathematics and French. Aleck was thrilled by Maths: 'It opens a new world of Science to my view ... at every new proposition I am as much delighted as Archimedes when he ran naked thro Syracuse.'[24]

He was also glad to be learning French. His tutor, M Dufresne, was 'entertaining, gay, sensible ... French from head to foot'; he abused his country unmercifully and showed 'considerable glee at the battle of Trafalgar'. More importantly, he had met Edward and enquired affectionately after him. Nobody forgot meeting Edward.

At home, Mary, longing for her turn to experience the bright lights of Edinburgh, was hoping in vain for interesting accounts of the plays, concerts and balls Aleck would presumably be attending. To her disappointment, he refused an invitation to a ball, preferring to remain snug at home 'and while the rest of the family were figuring away at a rout and a ball I amused myself with a philippic against the dissipation of the town in a letter to one of my friends'. When an invitation came from Mr Blair, the Solicitor General, Aleck was just writing his refusal 'when Aunt came thundering into the room' and made him write an acceptance, for Peter as well.[25] He had no pleasure in the prospect of 'walking a couple of miles thro dirty streets to a stiff dinner with a little Jackanapes for my companion'.

This Jackanapes, who had so delighted in the thrills of the 'bicker', was 'a terrible thorn' in Aleck's side. He was always hovering at Aleck's elbow just when he was deep in 'the close reasoning of Euclid' He was 'the most insufferably inquisitive boy imaginable', constantly provoking his interesting older cousin, asking questions and interrupting his studies; he was clearly going to go far.

Although he had moments of homesickness Aleck would look back on this period as one of the happiest of his life. Despite Aunt Woodhouselee's 'overstrained and useless frugality' which made her grudge every expense, Aleck managed to remain on good terms with his aunt, taking care not to contradict her 'which she cannot bear'. It was quite hard to study in a crowded house with people constantly coming and going, but 'I improved my intellectual powers considerably in the short space that I was permitted to remain'. He felt, at last, equal to his Tytler cousins and appreciated being in a family 'of the most perfect social happiness'.

Without Aleck at home, Mary was missing her two best friends from London: Isabella Fraser and Sibylla Grant. They were faithful correspondents and their charming letters, in nineteenth century teenage terminology and full of titillating encounters to make Mary's heart beat faster, arrived regularly, if not often. Sibylla Grant described an expedition to Ramsgate which Mary, with her 'partiality for sailors', would have enjoyed:

> I think them the nicest set of men I ever saw ... one of the little sailor boys was very pretty & would have quite delighted you ... perhaps you have not heard that we landed at 9 o'clock at night in a rough sea and then had to walk over a great deal of seaweed. We must certainly have slipped down if the sailors had not helped us.

24 Greek philosopher (287–212 BC) who, when in the public baths in Syracuse, discovered that a body must displace its own bulk of water when immersed. Immensely excited, and without waiting to dress, he ran home to continue the experiment.

25 Patrick Fraser Tytler (1791–1849) was two years younger than Aleck and known to his family as Peter. He was a historian, his major work being the nine volume History of Scotland.

In Clapham the Grants' next-door neighbour was Mr Wilberforce; Sibylla found his children a great trial ('so noisy & rough, I really was afraid to play with them'). Mr Wilberforce, however, was 'so entertaining & agreeable I am quite fond of him & so are we all'.

Isabella Fraser wrote from Mottingham, the country house where she and her family were spending the summer; there had been an exciting attempted burglary:

> We were a little alarmed certainly at our nightly visitants and had the pleasing reflection that one had been hid in the house some time before we went to bed, Mama was quite a heroine upon the occasion, I had not the least claims to that appellation, for though wide awake, I did not think fit to come out of my room till someone else did so lay very quietly till Mama came out, we mustered a most forlorn troop, one man about four feet high, our sole defender, his arms consisted in the kitchen poker, there being no gun or anything else in the house; our dresses delightfully varied, some in the height of the fashion, striving to equal their mother Eve, others more cool had dressed themselves decently, Annie excelled everybody as she dressed herself completely on the stairs not daring to stay in her room.

The household then, as one, clutching candles and each other, bravely moved on tiptoe throughout the dark house, searching every corner, even venturing down to the cellars where they found evidence that someone had been lying there on the straw. But the birds had flown, and after shutting all the doors they went back to bed, where the excitement continued:

> Mama, Annie & I got into *not* a very large one [bed]; 6 persons got into the nursery where one moderate sized bed and two cribs contained them *all*, think what fun we had!

There is a chilling end to Isabella's story:

> But the *best* of all is 2 of our friends were hung, almost within sight of our windows, yesterday, they had committed numerous depredations upon all the neighbourhood.

She stuck this letter in the pocket of Aleck's greatcoat, which he had left behind, along with other belongings, at Lower Grosvenor Street. The coat was 'to take a seat in the Mail to Edinburgh where I hope it will find him in perfect health'.

Up river to the court of the Great Mughal

In July 1805 William had set off to Delhi up the Hoogly River and into the Ganges. His vessel was a 'budgerow', described by Emily Metcalfe[26] as a covered barge 'built of wood, painted green and very comfortably furnished and divided into two rooms each – for sleeping and sitting rooms'; a separate budgerow was fitted up for kitchen and servants' use; yet another accommodated chickens and goats, William's horses and the dogs; this small flotilla kept company together and proceeded along the great rivers, sometimes towed by men walking on the river bank, sometimes rowed by boatmen on board, sometimes sailing with the wind.

26 *The Golden Calm*, ed. M M Kaye (1980) Webb & Bower Ltd.

His journal of the river voyage, which his father laboriously copied into a letterbook,[27] was very detailed. He recorded his intense interest in everything and everyone he saw and tried hard to convey some of the excitement of these new experiences to his parents.

The river first wound past cloth factories and through indigo[28] plantations, passing the fine European-style houses of the owners and managers. He knew some of the occupants of these grand houses and dined or breakfasted with them but was just as intrigued by the teeming local life on the banks of the great river.

There were difficulties. Sometimes the livestock boat would be blown too far across the river for the goats to be accessible and William had to drink milkless tea. Sometimes the cook boat would get left behind and he went to bed 'very surly' after supping on dry bread and water. At other times the boat had to be pulled by the boatmen by means of a rope attached to the mast. It was a slow, primitive and tedious business and there was constant danger of the high riverbanks falling in and swamping the boat.

William tried to bring the ever-changing landscape alive for his parents by comparing it with something familiar. The river at one point was like 'our River Ness at opposite Fraser's Hotel'. In the villages the beautiful groupings of trees and distant pagodas made William think of the English villages along the Thames. When he became frustrated by high banks obstructing his view he found that 'on the topmast of the boat you have an enchanting prospect all around probably to the extent of 4, 5 or 6 miles'. Sometimes the twists and turns of the river were such that 'you see sails and boats masts in every direction, without seeing the water ... it reminded me of the view from Stirling Castle, where you see sloops and boats winding all manner of ways with the serpentine turnings of the River Forth'.

One evening, he prevailed upon two local men to guide him to the top of a hill to watch the sunset and view the mountain range east of the river. This was his first sight of mountains since leaving home and he imagined them covered with heather and harbouring grouse, although he knew in reality they would be the haunt of 'the Tyger and Rhinoceros'. He was reminded of the view of Ben Wyvis from Moniack.

In Murshidabad[29] he was impressed with the lifestyle of the Company servants:

> The style in which the Gentlemen live is most luxurious; they have the best wines that Europe produces. Their tables are furnished not only with beef, mutton, veal, lamb, kid and all sorts of Poultry in abundance, but excellent game, wild duck, teal, partridge, wild boar, venison, hares, and in season, snipes; most of the gentlemen keep 1 or 2 riding horses, a close carriage, phaeton, or curricle and a buggy for their visiting friends. I wish I could do this in Scotland.

At last, on 20 September, the Kanpur skyline came into view and that evening William rode into the town. He made for the Post Office, where he was informed that all his letters, the first he had had for a year, had been sent to a Captain Rose. This hospitable

27 Volume 29.
28 The plant *Indigo feratinctoria* and the dark blue dye made from it (*Hobson Jobson, The Anglo Indian Dictionary*).
29 Mughal capital of Bengal and seat of British administration until 1790.

character, a total stranger, had been expecting William for some time and offered him 'a home, a bed and a dinner'. William brought his river journal to a close that night:

> This day I received a packet from Delhi containing letters from dear Inverness; and as it is best now to close this strange diary, I shall do so by beginning a regular letter. I wrote the above to amuse myself, and perhaps my friends ... my further journey hence to Delhi may perhaps be given in a continued journal.

His further journey was, however, delayed by fever, which kept him at Captain Rose's house for nearly two months. The kind Captain, the son of a neighbour of Reelig,[30] 'behaved more like a brother than one whom I had only known for a fortnight', attending him day and night and administering calomel[31] with his own hand. On recovering, William declared himself to be so slim 'that I might pass for a lady with a fine waist'.

For the final part of the journey he rode an elephant. It was gradually getting cooler and the countryside was becoming less interesting, although there was no shortage of ruins, especially those of 'Canouge [Kannauj] one of the greatest Hindoo cities that ever existed'. Shocked by the dilapidated state of these monuments he felt that 'every Judge and Magistrate of a district should pay attention to the repair and preservation of them'.

The Taj Mahal was the highlight. Despite feeling ill, he managed to explore every corner and wrote a two-page description packed with superlatives:

> There exists not a more elegant, more exquisite, more chaste, more superb monument of Eastern taste, Grandeur, Cost or Magnificence ... it is the richness and the beauty united, with the exquisite delicacy, perfection of workmanship, and immense value of materials ... that constitute this place a magnet to draw travellers from all quarters.

He was especially impressed with the flowers portrayed in inlaid stones and gems:

> Some of the flowers which I examined resembled the Tulip, the colours of which are beautifully blended or shaded into each other, and the inlaying was so exquisite, the various hues so well adapted, that I could believe that I held the flower in my hand. The different tints of a fading or insect-bitten leaf or petal were most nicely or naturally shown ... I could have devoted a week to the examination and contemplation of them.

In mid-December he reached Aligarh, where he stayed over Christmas with Mr Russell, the Collector, in order to regain his strength, 'having pleasant society, nothing to do, and gaining strength fast'.

He arrived in Delhi a month later to find five more letters from home awaiting him. 'This morning ended my journey by breakfasting with Colonel Ochterlony in Delhi, six months and a day since I left Calcutta.'

---

30 Rose of Holm.

31 Mercurous chloride.

3

1806

Plantation life

In Guyana, life was not improving for Edward. He wrote constantly to his parents, his letters sometimes spanning six closely written foolscap pages. There were long periods of silence from home owing to ships being taken by pirates, various embargoes to do with the war and, sometimes, because James had no money. His mother found it incomprehensible that he could not borrow a guilder or two to pay the Post Office. Edward explained:

> A man in this country is readier to give anything than cash. James's being so well-known is nothing. Nobody in town would give him or anyone a gilder without receiving a bill or produce first.

James was still poor company:

> He reads all the time at breakfast and dinner and when candles are lighted he goes to Simon's ... I have little of his conversation ... it looks to other people as if he did not like my company – however, I know it is not *that*.

James disliked it when Edward resorted to his newly acquired flute, and he was mostly either monosyllabic or else short-tempered, using language that shocked his younger brother. Jane naïvely hoped that James never got in a passion or swore at the slaves; Edward, however, knew well that 'having to do with negroes would make the most *patient* persons do both':

> But I never have seen him forget himself so far as to strike a negro – which I think is most shocking and coward like because it betrays your weakness to the negro and because the poor creature must have his arm cut off if he attempts to return a white man's blow.

Alexander Fraser from Clunes, a house near Moniack, struck a slave so hard on the temple that he died. The horrified Attorney organised a search, but Alex Fraser had disappeared. Edward reckoned that he would probably not hang, if caught, but would be publicly whipped and banished from the colony, adding that nobody pitied him since he was always cruel to Negroes.

The conduct of Simon Fraser's mother-in-law, Mrs van Batenburg, the wife of the Governor, was currently enlivening dinner parties: she had eloped with a Major Hardiman. Simon Fraser challenged the Major and a harmless duel was fought. To provide dinner parties with topics of conversation other than the price of cotton, the Governor obligingly remarried swiftly, a woman who was not only a milliner but thirty years younger – 'the same age with my father – only think of it, the old fool – they are all love and affectionate', wrote Edward.

Gradually, Edward was invited to one or two social gatherings, especially on Sundays when there was nothing else to do. Jane anxiously enquired about Sunday observance, which Edward admitted was non-existent. Sunday for the slaves meant work all morning and a free afternoon, in which they visited friends, worked in their gardens and slept, followed by an evening of dancing.

Edward had become a favourite with Mrs Simon Fraser, a strong-minded woman whose husband was firmly under her thumb. They were building what would be one of the best houses in the colony which Mrs Fraser had planned and directed, her husband realising, just too late, how expensive it was going to be. Edward remembered his mother's comments on Mrs Simon Fraser's extravagant outfits at Belladrum: those were plain compared to what she now wore to dinner – 'lace, jewels and all those things'. Yet he was fascinated by her – 'being the only woman almost I ever see she will run in my head'.

He was wondering about a wife for James; so was his mother. Four of Jane's five sons, all good-looking and intelligent, but penniless, were now far from her watchful eye, and it mattered very much whom they chose as wives, especially as the girls would be facing life abroad. They needed to be robust enough to survive long voyages, lonely postings and extremes of temperature. What Jane had in mind for each was a sweet-natured, rosy-cheeked Highland lass of good family who could sing, play the piano and dance. She needed to be plump, even 'stout' (not the derogatory word it is today) – a fragile, skinny miss was not considered a good investment as she might not last the course of constant childbearing. If she had a little money, so much the better.

All Jane could do was keep the subject alive, with what tact she could muster, and from time to time send the boys the names of suitably enticing girls among the pretty young hopefuls of 'the fishing fleet'[1] on the high seas. Reelig tried his best, too, losing no opportunity to recommend marriage as the most comfortable way of life; it was all a question of finding the 'Congenial Personage'.

*

With no Congenial Personage at hand to help, Edward gradually settled into housekeeping and, with more pleasure, gardening. He planted orange trees, potatoes and pineapples, which, although a poor substitute for strawberries and cream, were perfectly acceptable. Guavas, mangoes, apples, melons, bananas, limes, pumpkins and figs were to follow. He made marmalade, which James laughed at but was happy to eat. Soon a cow was bought,

1 The name given to the shiploads of single young women who sailed to India in search of a husband.

to be joined by hens, ducks and a couple of geese. Later, ten sheep, a few lambs, three young hogs and some pigeons joined the menagerie. Edward badly needed the advice and support of a Kate Martin, the cheerful poultry girl at home, to help him keep it all under control.

Someone, however, did arrive from Moniack: Donald Noble, the gardener's son, came out as an overseer, bringing letters and the box of goodies from Reelig. Among other things Jane had packed a teapot, black and green tea, hams, mutton, candles, some muslin, a shawl and two presents from Mary: a 'very elegant' purse she had made for Mrs Simon Fraser, and a chess set for her brothers. Edward feared the workaholic James would never have the patience for the game:

> ... he is too much on the *fidgits* for it ... he is such a *prude* that I fear he would think it too great a relaxation even when business is done.

Nor was he sure how to cope with Donald, who clearly did not know his place:

> He calls for the servants – for his lemonade & for a candle or anything he wants with much more freedom than I do ... he even reads the newspapers at breakfast which all proceeds from ignorance and not sufficient understanding what an overseer is. It is not from forwardness ... he seems to think whatever I do he may do ... James has given him the broadest hints which he never takes to himself.

Edward remembered his own first weeks at Novar Estate, when he would eat his meals without a word and fade into the background as fast as possible. Not so Donald: when callers arrived he sat at table and entered freely into the conversation. Worst of all, he kept his hat on at breakfast.

Writing fewer personal letters home than his brothers, James was, at this point, a fairly shadowy character but Edward, still struggling to understand this elder brother, often described him. He was like Aleck in many ways, handsome but so unconcerned about his dress that he often appeared eccentric in company. Edward was never really relaxed with his brother, needing to humour him – 'He must have his own way in everything'.

In return for the presents that arrived with Donald Noble, Edward packed up a box to send home; twelve small pots of preserves, seeds of castor oil and cotton and cayenne pepper prepared by their Negro cook, Jacoba, who asked for a present from Scotland:

> I told her it was going to you. She said 'Missy must send her something for it' so ... you would do Jacoba great favour if you would send her any gaudy cheap piece of calico print enough to make a petticoat or a pair of the most gaudy common gilt ear-rings such as one gets for 5 shillings. Jacoba's a very good woman and our head driver's wife.

He also asked for 'a good many strings of the commonest beads and the cheapest only. Let them be gaudy. I want them to give them away to the negro children'.

Edward made vinegar from bananas and churned milk into fresh butter. He asked his mother to send a recipe for curry and a cookery book 'as our cook knows nothing but the

Dutch Creole way of cooking which is bad and expensive'. Poor Jacoba! Her delicious-sounding aromatic cabbage, chopped up like 'spinnatch with pounds of butter', was rejected in favour of the plain boiled variety, and her nourishing soup, the only one she knew, 'of salt pork, salt beef, salt fish, plantain and pease all muddled together in one pot', was also pushed aside.

At last the estate carpenter finished the new house. Though neither large nor elegant, it was neat, convenient and dry. Downstairs there was a dining room, James's bedroom and a porch, where they breakfasted and sat in the evening; upstairs, Edward and Donald each had a comfortable and airy attic.

⁂

The work of an overseer was unremitting: up at dawn to set the slaves to work with the crack of a whip and out in the field, with only occasional breaks, till sundown. Edward also had to supervise the milking of the cow and check the food supplies. He spent the middle of the day in the house writing up the plantation journal, reading, writing letters home and playing his flute, and was in bed by eight or nine. He was happiest when working with the slaves: 'I am fond of the negroes. James sometimes charges me with being too familiar with some of them but I have never found them to disobey my order.'

The first whispers of abolishing the slave trade were rustling through the banana plantations in 1805, although the Bill was not passed until 1807. Naturally enough, the rumour 'occasioned universal disgust among the inhabitants here', and Edward reckoned that the planters would soon find ways of smuggling slaves into the colony.

In July 1805 the welcome news came that Reelig had been allotted the same plantation as before. James and Edward could now settle down for four or five years with the community of slaves they had got to know during the last eighteen months. They had looked after them so well that there had not been one death or even a 'skulker'[2] under their management.

Aleck, at home, was delighted to hear that his brothers 'have proof of the affection of their negroes as therein is proof of the lenity of their treatment and the care of their masters'. The whole question of slavery concerned Aleck, knowing as he did several of the sons of Wilberforce's circle. He hoped that 'the poor slaves will feel their burthen lightened' under his brothers' administration and that no use was made of the whip:

> Be kind to your poor negroes and reflect on their situation ... If a West Indian planter was to figure to himself how miserable he should be to be enslaved in Africa and worked as the Negroes are, he would, if not destitute of every particle of humanity, ameliorate the condition of his slaves. I do not see why they should not be free; they would work, for the experiment has been tried; and, if not so hard, that would ... be compensated by ... better health, the less frequency of desertion and lessened numbers of deaths ... Gratitude they are undoubtedly not destitute of; for Stephen has often told me that when Mr Wilberforce's name was mentioned to

2 A shirker.

> the Blacks, they gave every demonstration of love, gratitude and joy ... I heartily wish for the Abolition of the Trade which, I am sure, would be for your interest, and that of Planters in general as well as of the Negroes.

Edward told him in no uncertain terms that he disagreed:

> It is morally impossible to keep negroes ... in proper order without very severe punishments occasionally and on reflection it always occurs to me what right have we to inflict such punishment ... You are certainly mistaken in thinking that the negroes could be free and could still be made to work. The abolition of the slave trade must be the loss of the colonies ... the more I see of their treatment the more shocking I think the trade ... It's no use to say as some people have done that their situation is better than many of the poor in Europe – at least I can never think so.

Nevertheless, he took every opportunity to improve his slaves' lives: when James's back was turned on a Saturday Edward would give the slaves permission to dance, even though this involved drumming, singing and merrymaking from early evening till dawn, rendering sleep impossible for everyone else.

Hertford Castle, East India Company College

The year 1806 started well for the family at Moniack and their scattered sons. James and Edward were settled in their new house running their father's plantation, and William had fallen in love with Delhi the moment he got there; this was partly due to the character of the Resident to whom he was Assistant.

David Ochterlony, scion of an old Scottish family, had been brought up in Massachusetts He joined the army of the East India Company in 1777 and fought in several successful campaigns. Becoming Resident in Delhi in 1803, he lived magnificently in the style of a Mughal nobleman. His thirteen wives, legend has it, were led in procession round Delhi every evening, each on her own elephant. He dressed in Indian costume and liked to be called by his full Mughal title, *Nasir-ud-daula* (Defender of the State). Although he was old enough to be William's father, and was soon replaced as Resident by Archy Seton, he impressed his eager new Assistant and the two remained lifelong friends. Much later, William was to acknowledge his good fortune in having served under four 'of the most distinguished characters of the Bengal Service in General Ochterlony, Mr Seton, Mr Elphinstone and Mr Metcalfe', three of whom were Scots (see Plate XI).

Ochterlony was equally impressed by his enthusiastic and linguistically brilliant Assistant, and William's reputation was such that Charles Grant and James Grant of Redcastle swiftly offered brother Aleck a Writership. In preparation, Aleck would spend a year at the new East India Company College in Hertford (see Plate V). Reelig was ecstatic: William's 'behaviour and promise has encouraged these two valuable friends to try another of my sons'. Jane, while she rejoiced at Aleck's good fortune, hoped he would be home again before he set off on his Indian adventure. Mary was loath to part with another brother but wrote:

> I do it most willingly ... for surely it is the thing in the world that you most wished for ... Alas! Your poor large trout is dead. Remember me to all the Grants not forgetting Mr Grant whom I really think I love best in the world next to my Family.

⁂

Once Reelig had got over his excitement he inevitably started to worry; knowing Aleck well, and aware of the temptations of life in India, he hoped that William would keep a brotherly eye on him. He sent William a pen portrait of Aleck:

> He is clever and a very capital classic ... he is not without considerable failings – he is proud – I hope not conceited. He is wholly careless in money matters but not addicted to any improper expenses. Thoughtless and lavish – you must be his brother and temper advice and authority with affection and indulgence. His Heart is Excellent ... he has, I think, very virtuous tendencies but God knows the strengths of the temptations which must assail in India ... Heaven guide ye and preserve ye right.

He then bombarded Aleck with advice: instructions about how to get to London, where, before anything else, he was to see Mr Grant; how to get his trunk repaired; how to pack his belongings and his books and transport them to Hertford.

⁂

Hertford Castle[3] was the temporary home of the new East India College, and Charles Grant, Chair of the Court of Directors, was influential in planning its curriculum: 'Maths, accountancy, law, political economy, philosophy and history were essential additions and a basic introduction to Oriental Languages was deemed to be valuable.'[4] The students were to be 'imbued with a reverence and love for Religion, the Constitution, and Laws of their own Country'.[5] Typically, Grant hoped that this would enable them to uphold British values and impose them on the Indians. In his desire to make his College as much like a university as possible, he recruited the teaching staff – a prestigious group – from Oxford and Cambridge. The other subjects offered were Humanity and Philology, Mathematics and Natural Philosophy, Classics, Sanskrit, Hindustani, Law, French, Drawing, Fencing and Dancing. In October 1805 the East India Company bought an estate of sixty acres called Hailey Bury on which to build their College. Meanwhile, the Castle was prepared for a temporary intake of twenty-three students.

In early February 1806 the first students, Aleck among them, arrived at Hertford Castle. The accommodation was not comfortable and Aleck considered it distinctly spooky: 'If you saw me winding along one of the long passages in the dusk, you might easily imagine you were in the monastery of the Black Penitents.' The bedrooms, divided

3 Originally a Norman castle on the River Lea. Now home to the Town Council and a wedding and corporate venue.
4 *The East India College at Haileybury 1806–1857*, Andrew Hambling, Noble Books, 2005.
5 Ibid.

by temporary wooden partitions 'just holding a very small bed and a chair' were badly lit. Having arrived early with another student, Holt Mackenzie (universally well-spoken of, according to Jane, and a great favourite with the Grants), Aleck managed to find a room for two. 'Behold me and Mackenzie, sitting and each writing at his table, Euclid on the right hand; Tacitus on the left'.

⁂

Letters arrived regularly from Moniack. Reelig pointed out the huge expense of Aleck's education and urged economy, observing, as he often did, that 'the Union of Trifles is not Trifling'. He advised on curriculum and preparatory reading and how to spend leisure time; he wanted to know what the food was like, whether the Professors dined with the students, whether the beds were comfortable. Aleck should not be taken in by the 'fascinating manners' of his companions and must remember that the first set of friends of any young man was the most important. He worried about Aleck's carelessness and the belongings which lay scattered in his wake: 'Were all your friends to return you your wandering goods, you would be well furnished indeed.' He concluded, 'I have reason to fear ... that you will prove more expensive to me than all my children put together. I have now done.'

Aleck replied to all this mildly and concisely with as much information as he could muster. He listed all his expenses, including a fishing rod 'to amuse myself now and then on the River Lea'. He described his curriculum and his tutors, who included William Dealtry, Professor of Mathematics ('a man of extraordinary talents, and an universal favourite at Cambridge'), and Malthus,[6] Professor of History and Political Economy, 'a pleasing man, gentle and very diffident in his manner'. He was affectionately known by his students as 'Pop' or 'Old Pop', an abbreviation of 'Population' Malthus.

Reelig was delighted to hear that Aleck had discovered the River Lea, which was:

> ... one of my earliest acquaintances. Many a day have I deprived it of its Dace, Roach, Chub, Gudgeon &c in vast numbers. I have much attachment to Hertfordshire'.

He was also pleased about Aleck's tutors; his clever son would at last be among equals:

> I think Malthus a very superior man indeed – you should cultivate him ... you will I hope have it in your power to attend closely to Malthus's lectures.

Rising seventeen, Aleck expected to be treated like an undergraduate and soon expressed irritation with the rules, 'a great many so trifling that I cannot remember them'. Beyond two miles from the College was out of bounds, and leaving the gardens after 7.00 pm was forbidden.

6 Revd (Thomas) Robert Malthus, 1766–1834, renowned and highly influential economist whose *Essay on the Principle of Population* (1798) argued that population would eventually outstrip adequate food production. In 1817 his pamphlet in defence of the East India College saved it from closure.

> We are prohibited from running accounts, with tradesmen or servants; or from entering an Inn, except in company of a Professor or a Parent, or from taking any meals in our rooms. There are Penalties against being late at meals or at Prayers or being out of bed with any light after Eleven of the Clock (a great thwart to study).

Jane considered the rules perfectly reasonable; it might be better if Aleck rose earlier to get his studying done. Nothing, she was sure, would distress Charles Grant more than disregard for the rules.

Aleck was delighted, however, with his Professors. Of Malthus, whose introductory lecture he attended, he wrote:

> Nothing has pleased me so much for a long time ... he has an impediment in his speech[7] ... but nevertheless I was so taken up with the matter of his lecture that the disagreeable effect soon wore off.

Another tutor, Bridge, could make even Euclid appealing, and Aleck appreciated being invited to spend an evening or two in Bridge's room, especially as a coolness had developed with his room-mate, Holt Mackenzie. They were, in fact, hardly on speaking terms in a room twelve feet square, a situation that dragged on for a year and a half. Holt possessed all the self-confidence and application that Aleck lacked: like Aleck, he loved arguing but only argued 'for victory'. He was 'both arrogant and overbearing ... He displayed his powers only in mortifying others, by exposing their ignorance'. They managed a coldly civil co-existence, but Aleck long harboured resentment and dislike of him.

⁂

In May 1806 the students joined in the excitement of the laying of the foundation stone of Haileybury.[8] Aleck, however, thought things could have been done better:

> We are to have the whole College committee down here to lay the foundation stone of the College. They transmit to posterity on a golden plate the names of the Planners and Architects of the College. I think they certainly should have inscribed the names of the original members.

Much as he appreciated the attractions of Hertfordshire, Aleck felt it was 'Beauty without Sublimity' and missed his Highland hills. He sometimes spent the evening wandering along the riverbank watching the fishermen and thinking of his father: 'Your early acquaintance with Hertfordshire endears it to me, when I recollect that you have often trodden the ground I tread.' In his dreams he was often at the Moniack fireside, but was 'torn very disagreeably from it by an old fellow, as stern as Charon',[9] who woke him up at half past six.

In time Aleck seemed to be working hard and was more or less content, although his letters were littered with complaints: there was no library; Persian classes had not yet

7 A cleft lip and palate.
8 The present day Haileybury College, well-known co-educational public school.
9 In Greek mythology the old man who ferried the souls of the dead across the rivers Styx and Acheron to Hades.

started; other languages were taking precedence over the beloved Classics; and the Principal had forbidden a visit to the theatre. Although his old friends James Stephen and Thomas Gisborne, now studying in Cambridge, had visited him, he was making few friends and was critical of both students and Professors. His father had clear views on this:

> I do seriously caution you not to proclaim your opinions of people – and particularly of their personal and mental defects. Most men can better bear to be termed irreligious or immoral, nay, even dishonest or dishonourable rather than wanting in manners, fashion, rank, opulence or wit or talent. You have hitherto had collision with only a few youths in a sister nation.

Once again the approaching holidays posed a problem; Aleck was hoping against hope that he would not again have to spend the summer with the Grants:

> I must confess that I should wish extremely to see home ... I have much to say to you, that I could not say on paper. Indeed I know nowhere I can go except Inverness, and no way but by Ship. The vessels, I hear, keep too close to shore, to be in danger of capture, and the south wind would soon waft us down.

His father wrote back testily:

> I gave you Mr Grant's decision sometime since viz 'I would not have you take him home this year' now that must in Gratitude and in Propriety be Law to me. I also gave you my detailed objections as to the sea – even had you been to come home – & very grave these were.

Finally, Dr Fraser and his family came to the rescue, and Aleck was invited to stay at Mottingham, 'their charming place in Kent'.

Early years in Delhi and a horse fair

Despite Aleck's 'growling', as the family termed it, there was certainly much to be happy about at Moniack in the springtime of 1806. The three youngest were giving pleasure and satisfaction: Jane Anne, now nine, was, according to her father's letter to William:

> ... just as good a little Girl, and as fine a creature as ever you knew & I think will be a capital musician and a charming companion by the time you return however soon. Indeed if you protract it too long you may be an uncle!

Mary, almost fifteen, was likely to 'add greatly to the comfort of us all ... She promises good open comely looks – a tolerable Height & stout'. George at six was 'another thin small-boned spirit of a thing as you was – with much action – & will probably resemble you in figure, as he does wonderfully in face and manner'.

Reelig, who was in the pink, 'as brisk as a roe', sprinkled his letters with happy vignettes of family life:

> At this moment while I am writing to you Miss Murray and Miss Chipps are working,[10] Mamma and Jane Anne at chess, Mary at the Piano and George scribbling. All well. Thank God.

He was comforted that, when Aleck reached India, each of the four abroad would then have the companionship of a brother and wrote that 'Mary and Jane Anne will, I hope, be very happy together. I think Jane Anne's temper so fine and so amiable that Mary cannot but love and cherish her – and George is the idol of us all.'

He took especial delight in the 'love of home' manifested by all his children and in their affection for one another, as he told William:

> It is my duty to provide for a continuance among ye all of that Love and Harmony ... which I have so happily succeeded in producing among ye all from Infancy to this day. No source of happiness more sure than that which is in the Union of Brothers and Sisters ... I trust that my 2 East Indians and my 2 West Indians will live in brotherly affection abroad and eventually aid each other to Fame Wealth and Honor and above all to virtuous constancy ... It is not every person who knows the blessing of a Brother – I had none. I stalked through life alone.

*

When the news of Aleck's appointment eventually reached him, William was as excited as anyone: he had high hopes of a sparkling future for his clever brother and envisaged him, in a couple of years, taking over his own job as Second Assistant to the Resident while he moved further up the ladder. He wanted to know as soon as he could the name of his ship and date of sailing: 'I must positively be in Calcutta on his arrival.'

Embarrassed by his debts, he hoped that Aleck might succeed in supporting the family where he had failed. He agonised about the difference between his lifestyle and that of his 'West Indian' brothers: they were living on 'salt beef and pease, [calling] a few poultry and a single milch cow a luxury', while he sat down 'every day to a luxurious table' waited on hand and foot. However, by borrowing he could send home £500 a year or more. Far better to sink deeper into debt through helping members of his family than through extravagance on himself. He urged his parents to accept that he was no longer 'a giddy boy' but 'a man, who having once determined is well known for his obstinacy'.

He was in a fog where the family finances were concerned: it was nearly five years since he had left home and as far as he could ascertain 'there appears no break in the clouds' over Guyana. But was this the case? His parents' letters left him in confusion: his father sent him 'delightful accounts of our paradise' while his mother 'talks in so desponding a tone that I know not what to think'.

He was never happier or healthier than when roaming the countryside and sleeping under canvas. His curiosity about the varied characters who peopled his surroundings

10 Sewing

was never satisfied, and he was spending much of his spare time perfecting the various languages he needed. He was hoping to start a collection of oriental manuscripts, following in the footsteps of his grandfather, 'but, alas they cost money and money is scarce; and debts are heavy, and payments must be made'. Meanwhile, he was constantly horrified in his rambles by the state of historic monuments reduced to 'a heap of desolation'.

Delhi at the beginning of the nineteenth century bore witness to the ravages of the previous forty years when invaders and marauders had vied to win control of the Mughal capital and its famed wealth. Surrounding the city was desolate country strewn with magnificent buildings in varying stages of dereliction – houses, palaces, mosques and tombs. Deeper in the countryside lay the ruins of villages deserted through famine, drought or fear of invaders; the few still inhabited were small fortresses surrounded by high mud walls, each under a headman or mini-warlord, who resisted all authority and lived by banditry, plunder and cattle-lifting. The efficient local administration and revenue collection of the first half of the eighteenth century had long since fallen into disuse, along with the irrigation canals. William had arrived in Delhi in 1806, three years after the young Lord Arthur Wellesley's decisive victory at the Battle of Assaye over the great Maratha chief Scindia and his triumphant entry into the city. For some years the Marathas remained quiet,[11] but wild tribesmen still roamed the ruins.

The job of the Second Assistant to the Resident was to ride out into the tribal areas around Delhi, to win the confidence of the tribes and establish a tax collection system. William was well suited to this kind of work: he loved adventure, the freedom of working independently far from the rules and regulations of Calcutta, and living in a tent, often alone. His linguistic brilliance, his passion for investigating how people lived and thought and his total fearlessness helped him tame the wild tribesmen, many of whom served him loyally (in Aleck's eyes 'faithful and attentive servants, but, I fear, only so, when Willie's'). Throughout his life his physical courage led him into many a scrape, but in the villages of the untamed regions it stood him in good stead.

Much later, Aleck was to write:

> In the district of Mewat, which he was stationed in, to civilise it, he built a Fort, and called it Fraser-Ghur in which he maintained a thousand sepoys of his own raising and disciplining, out of the Mewatees themselves, who formerly were the Banditti of that wild country – but by his going unarmed, and unaccompanied, into the heart of their country and fastnesses, hunting and living with them, and gaining their confidence and esteem, and admiration of his excellent Horsemanship and perfect use of their arms, the Sword and Spear, and all their exercises, he made those Barbarians honour his courtesy and manners, and his warlike discipline, and his peaceful and social habits with themselves – and he thus induced them to range under his Government and to control themselves under his regulations. There he lived like a Nawab, being absolute in his domain, as Bonaparte in France.

11 They were finally brought to heel in 1818.

Sometimes there were ceremonial events that demanded William's presence. When Lake's army arrived in Delhi, which meant 'a whirl of bustle, hurry and dissipation', William was on duty, and when the General (who remembered Reelig from their service together in the War of American Independence) went to pay his respects to the King of the World, or Shah Alam II,[12] William went along too. Shah Alam had reigned for over forty years, during which his city had been invaded and plundered by one marauding tribe after another. Brutally blinded by the insane Afghan, Ghulam Qadir, one of his ministers, he was now back on his illusion of a throne, powerless but under the protection of the British, who afforded him a generous allowance and the respect due to his position as the descendant of Akbar, the Great Mughal. To William he presented 'one of the most affecting and afflicting sights I ever beheld':

> The poor old, blind King, a most venerable figure, received his Lordship, with an embrace ... we were presented one after another; offering our gifts, as is always the custom, which were received by the King's own hand. This ceremony being over, we retired to an adjacent chamber, to receive our dresses of honor, each according to his rank ... The Emperor placed with his own hands the Turban on the head of Lord Lake, the greatest honor that can be conferred.

At one of the springtime Muslim festivals William accompanied the King to the Mosque and was again impressed by 'the extreme nobility in his gait, aspect, and mien. The loss of his eyes does not at all disfigure his countenance ... on his death, and not till then, we may say that the line of Timoor[13] is extinct as a dynasty; beginning with the lame and ending with the blind'.

*

Haridwar, north-east of Delhi, near the sacred spot where the Ganges emerges from the Himalayas, is an ancient place of Hindu pilgrimage and the site of an annual horse fair to which people travelled from all over India, an irresistible expedition for William. He set off in March 1806, with elephants and horses for riding, camels and bullocks for baggage, some regular sepoys and a dozen troopers for protection.

Everything enchanted him: camping under the scented blossom of mango trees; strolling into the villages, snug behind their high mud walls, to talk with the locals; admiring the women 'most beautiful but poorly dressed'; watching the sun rise behind the Siwalik mountains[14] and the moon sail over the Ganges. It 'threw its silver beams over the mountains, and danced them on the water'. He sent home a detailed account of the landscape, agriculture, flora and fauna. The peaceful and serene appearance of the inhabitants especially impressed him; he got somewhat carried away in reflecting on how

12 Emperor of India, 1759–1806.

13 Timur the Great (1336–1405), conqueror of much of western and central Asia. Great-great-grandfather of Babur (1483–1531), who founded the Mughal Dynasty. Lamed in battle.

14 Southernmost mountain chain of the Himalayan system, rising abruptly from the plains of the Indus and Ganges to 2,000m and extending 1,600km from Sikkim through Nepal into Kashmir and N. Pakistan.

British rule had brought peace to these remote areas, so long a battleground for warring tribes and cruel tyrants:

> See it now; the plains of Hindoostan from Hurdwar to the sea, enjoying a state of security and tranquillity, unknown even in Europe, and which India never knew before; governed by the mildest laws, and by men of a nation so famed for humanity, justice and mercy ... who now see the Widow unoppressed, the Orphan protected, the rustic happy, the landowner secure, the religious unpersecuted, and every individual confiding in the faith of the Government.

He described some of the characters he met. A blind fiddler reduced him to tears with his 'wild yet pleasing and simple tunes'; William left him two rupees which he said he would take home to his mother ('his heart is not blind'). A Hindu hermit who worshipped a black stone and lived in a small hole, accessible only by ladder, regarded William and his companion without the slightest surprise, although 'our dress and appearance was such as he had probably never seen before'. He answered their questions without moving his eyes or a muscle of his face; he had lived in his hole for over twenty years.

As before, on his journey up the Ganges, William was bewitched by the holy river. Where, in its lower reaches, it had stretched to the horizon and beyond, 'an immense rolling tide ... conveying on its waters the wealth and produce of many countries', now he was gazing at 'a pure purling stream' reminiscent of a Highland burn. Camping beside the river with the chill night air blowing from the snows made William glad of his gloves. The next day, they crossed the river, looking down on the town below, and he fervently wished he could draw.

The scene so captured his imagination that he climbed higher for a better view. Now the houses, tents, horses, cattle, elephants, camels 'seem floating on the surface of the earth ... in constant motion'. There was endless noise, like 'the continued rush of falling torrent rather than the busy hum of man'. Sometimes the sound of a drum, a shrill trumpet, the roar of a refractory elephant or the cry of a loading camel would shake itself free of the cacophony. Looking carefully, one might make out the distinctive dress of the huge variety of people attending the fair:

> ... the loose robe and round Turban of the Northern Mogul; the unbound cloak, and fur cap of the northern Persian; the Tartar girl, with sword, bow, and arrows from the banks of the Caspian; the Thibetian, and northern Chinese and Chinese Tartar with woollen caps; the bareheaded Hindu and naked mendicant; the painted priest, and tattered Pilgrim, Jews, and Christians; Musslemen and Hindoos; pagans and fire worshippers.

Later that day, he witnessed the magnificent spectacle of a forest fire, which, like a river, seemed to flow down the mountain – an Etna or a Vesuvius; even the full moon, rising from behind the hills, seemed in danger from the conflagration. He watched her ascent and 'in melancholy musing mood' was reminded of a song he had learnt as a child:

> The moon had climbed the highest hill,
> Which rises o'er the source of Dee.

Remembering where he was, far from the Dee and from home, brought tears:

> God knows how or whence – from the heart I believe ... leaving the moon to shine; the fire to burn, and the Ganges to run, I hoped for future happiness elsewhere, and tried to forget in social friendship, my regrets and my melancholy; it was as weakness to repine.

The Fair was all William could wish for. Horses were brought from all parts of India and from countries far beyond, with names that breathed mystery and adventure:

> ... from Cabul; the Punjab; Candahar; and the banks of the Caspian Sea, that is Tartary; from Balkh, Bokhara, and from Summurkund.

There were crafts from all over the world: the broadcloth of Europe, silks of China, carpets from Persia and Turkey, furs from Siberia and assorted manufactures from Bengal, Madras, the Punjab and Kashmir.

Pilgrims were everywhere, and William attempted to explain to his parents the power of Ganges water; a nail paring from St James was not more precious to a Roman Catholic than a drop of Ganges water to a Hindu:

> This water is carried, from hence even to Cape Comorin[15] and there sold at a high price; just as a Priest sells absolution, and with just as much efficacy ... Thus, my dearest Father, I have given you a long tedious account of a little journey; if it amuses you, I shall be content.

THE HAPPIEST OF SUMMERS

At home, spring turned into the long days of a Highland summer and some of the family moved up to Rebeg. Jane had been 'bustling to clear the House for Painters' because Charles Grant, now an MP, and his family were taking nearby Achnagairn for the Parliamentary recess; Reelig envisaged entertaining them 'and thought it right to furbish up our House in compliment ... the Expense is not trifling – the inconvenience great – but we shall be at Rebeg probably for two months comfortable enough'. The painters moved into the hall, drawing room and dining room. Mary wrote to James:

> I am delighted with the thoughts of seeing the Grants ... we begin to enjoy the summer very much and Papa and me take long evening walks almost always up your walk. I often wish you were with us that you might partake of our pleasure. I hope you will soon if not this season at least next but I would rather it was this both on account of its being the nearest and likewise that you would renew acquaintance with our old friend Charemile who is a very delightful young woman

15 The southernmost tip of India.

and very beautiful ... You have been so long away that you will scarcely remember me or even Aleck – you never saw Jane Anne but on the breast and sweet little Georgy not at all ... Mama and Papa are now beside me very busy packing up a little parcel for you of threads – tapes – needles – silks etc and a few other articles which may prove useful to you as Eddy tells us that anything will be of some use to you in your country ... Kate Martin is still alive and healthy and Papa has built her a new house and a poultry square which is called Martin Place ... it is a very nice little place and a black cock and partridge which I have are to have one of the partitions ... I am [getting] this week a magpie ... a very droll bird – I have canary birds ... and besides them two bullfinches, a Goldfinch and a linnet all of which are my own and at present I have the care of an old canary bird 14 years ... I daresay you will not be much amused with this letter but I am not good at writing and so I have given you such a letter as I could which at least may serve to shew you that I have not forgotten you – Goodbye – your affectionate sister Mary Fraser.

After a bad bout of Guyanan fever, Edward arrived at Moniack on convalescent leave in mid-July to a rapturous welcome. Mary was among the first to embrace him, followed closely by the nine-year-old Jane Anne 'tearing from Miss Brown[16] and W. Tytler's children to greet me'. He found his father working in the shrubbery: 'The recollection of that day will always be a delight to me ... I look back on my last sojourning there with more pleasure and satisfaction than any time of my life.' The first few weeks were almost too good to be true: 'I always have a kind of notion that I am in a dream and am presently to be waked.'

He could not bear to think of going back to the West Indies and was missing Aleck:

> *Meet we must* in some way or other before I quit Britain ... the thought of leaving James alone in that country distresses me beyond measure and I have not yet dared to think of quitting Moniack.'

To Jane's delight the house was full to the brim – 'all bustle & confusion'. It was one of the happiest of summers: Edward was home and Jane Anne and George were growing up satisfactorily; the teenage Mary shared her parents' passion for gardening and was an entertaining companion to her father in his various projects. Now fifteen, she was progressing well at the piano under the supervision of Mr Thomson, who considered her 'a superior musician'; at his annual concert she excelled and as a reward was allowed to see a play at the New Theatre.[17] Her mother wrote a few months later to William:

> She was then in high health and really beautiful – that beauty at least which ever captivated – & pure unaffected nature – an animated expression and such a fairness of skin & glow of colour ... made everyone at once say 'What a lovely Girl!' Indeed I was afraid she would have been spoilt by the admiration.

16 The Aldourie governess.
17 *Douglas*, a romantic tragedy by John Home (1722–1808).

Though still fondly called 'Gipsy Mary' by her father, Mary's increasing maturity was a joy to her parents. She was a vivacious, entertaining companion for Edward and she adored this handsome, funny, easy-going elder brother, who filled the gap left by Aleck.

The shadows cast over this sunny domestic scene were Aleck's absence, the continuing lack of success in the West Indian enterprise, silence from James and worries over William – his passion for dangerous sport, his total inability to save money, his marriage prospects.

His mother had taken the liberty of sending him the name of a 'Mrs Dyer', already in Calcutta and William had something to say:

> Certainly a lovely woman but I fear, in other respects, very faulty. I know her but never liked her ... have been frightened once or twice and a burnt child dreads the fire ... the fact is, that in many respects, I am more changeable than the wind; and I write seriously, and say seriously at one time, what at another I laugh at myself for having done.

He was far too cautious to rush into any arrangement without 'weighing and examining all the bays and creeks, sounds, shoals, rocks, which might be concealed under the placid appearance of immediate momentary happiness'. In any case, Charemile Grant was still unattached and he compared every woman with her – unfavourably.

As far as dangerous sport went, his father was 'falsely alarmed', which his new boss, Archibald Seton, would corroborate. He never exposed himself to the sun, his passions, hunting wild hogs and hawking, being early morning activities. Seton, 'a most excellent, worthy and well-known character', with whom William was getting on admirably, was a fellow Scot:

> Extremely kind, and most friendly to me... he is the man of most others I would prefer being under ... strict, upright and virtuous, moral, enlightened, and unaffected; such is the man I have the happiness to be under; and the boast to call friend.

Part of the mutual attraction between the two men was their similar background. Seton, aged forty-eight, was the owner of Touch, an estate in Stirlingshire, which he had left in the care of his brother-in-law, Sir Henry Steuart of Allanton. He and William talked about 'Stirling and Inverness, Touch and Reelick', and William daydreamed about one day introducing Seton to Moniack. He gradually took Seton into his confidence, letting him read all the family letters, so that Seton 'became acquainted, intimately and pleasingly acquainted, with every member of the respectable family at Moniack' and also, more significantly, with their disastrous financial situation. He was particularly taken with Reelig's letters, which revealed to him a man of 'high endowment, elegant acquirement, knowledge of the world and strong affection which I never saw equalled'. He felt he already knew Reelig and was very pleased to hear that he had actually been to Touch.

Stuck in the terrible summer heat of Delhi, William was looking forward to the cold weather, when he would be able to get out into the districts and 'thus business and pleasure will go hand in hand'. At the moment there was little to suit William's taste for adventure: 'India is again quiet for a time ... no power dare now molest us.' There was now little to fear from the Maratha tribes, and most of his daily work was dispensing justice in Delhi. He was not finding the job too arduous although, inexperienced as he was, he asked his father to 'pray that I may judge aright'. There was plenty of time to think of home and daydream to his mother:

> All your descriptions of walks, improvements &c are to me most interesting; I think, however, it would be a great improvement to have a nice little house on the Knockbain side of the river (Burn, I mean, but always talking of a river here, the Jumna, it came out unawares) where one of us might live. Now, when James comes home, he will require the Big House, Edward and his wife another, say Rebeg, and I intend the first money I have, to send it home, and have a snug box, on the Knockbain side in the field that the Hares used to skip about in, in the summer's evenings. I think the plan excellent, and we shall want another house for Aleck; which I do not know where to place ... When all assembled in that delightful spot, which by that time will rival the most elegant Nobleman's seat, time shall, alas! too quickly fly; we will count the moments by the Clock of pleasure; and say, this truly is happiness.

⁂

Once Moniack was painted and shipshape, the family awaited the arrival of Charles and Jane Grant, their four daughters and son Robert. Entertaining them would be small recompense for all that Charles Grant had done for William and Aleck.

Earlier in the year, Sibylla, one of the daughters and Mary's great friend, had written to her from Russell Square in high excitement:

> As soon as your note came we ran downstairs to look at the map where we found Achnagairn close to Moniack. How delightful! I hope you will not be tired of me for I intend to make you go everywhere & shew me everything ... We are continually building castles in the air of all that we are to do and see. How we shall ramble 'over hill and dale'. I am sure I shall never be tired of walking ... I really must not say any more about Scotland or I shall grow quite silly ... I remain ever your affect friend Sibylla Grant

Hard on the heels of this came a long, chatty update from Mary's other close friend and cousin from London days, Isabella Fraser, full of banter and teenage activities. She had been banished from town to remove her from 'scenes of dissipation ... & to my sorrow left town the first of May leaving five invitations to balls unenjoyed'. She was therefore extremely glad that Aleck had come to spend his holidays at Mottingham, especially as she was having a problem controlling her younger siblings in her parents' absence.

The serious-minded Aleck was initially astonished at the 'savage manners' of the children, scolded poor Isabella roundly for her lack of control and declared '*his sister Mary* was politeness itself in comparison'. The others soon disillusioned him: if Mary were there, she would enjoy 'romping over gates & stiles' as much as the rest of them. He gradually began to thaw and join in, eventually performing 'various feats even beyond our barbarous ability such as riding the Poneys without saddle'. They were all sad when the time came for him to leave.

Isabella's brother John, who had long admired Mary from a distance, sent his best respects to her or 'his love if you will accept it from him as he is a very timid youth'; they were all hoping that she would not 'grow too prim nor object to the sports of the field such as playing in the hay jumping over hedges & ditches &c', adding finally:

> I suppose you have read the Lay of the Last Minstrel[18] can you not say it all by heart? If you cannot I advise you by all means instantly to sit down with it in your hand & never take off your eyes nor eat drink nor sleep till it is finished.

Perhaps Isabella encouraged Aleck to read it during that summer holiday at Mottingham. He at any rate thought well enough of it to include it later in the year in a parcel of books – mostly classics – that he was sending to James via Mrs Fraser Belladrum.

The general excitement about the Grants' arrival was growing daily, and Edward was heartily tired of the endless preparations, growling, 'I wish they would come and then there would be less fuss here – papa and mamma think of nothing but getting necessaries for them'. They finally arrived on 24 August, especially delighted to be reunited with their favourite, Mary. She was equally glad to see them although she had not been able to ride to meet them as she was unwell; because of this she also refused most of the later invitations to dine at Achnagairn, much to the vexation of Robert Grant, who was one of her most faithful admirers.

So, in typical Highland fashion, Moniack was full to brimming in August: six Frasers and five Tytlers, overflowing from Aldourie across the loch, seven Grants in and out all day, not to mention Miss Murray, Nanny Rose and the servants. Miss Chipps had left to look after her mother, to everyone's regret, and the hunt for a successor had not begun. The beginning of September was only slightly quieter, as Reelig reported to Aleck:

> The Tytlers are here and Culduthel and his brother Roderick from India. They are all murdering partridges for the Grants' larder. I must now go & dress for Dinner – a Crowd to be here – your mother stands it all perfectly.

It was an especially happy season for Reelig and Jane: Edward was home to help organise the shooting parties and Mary, her mother's right-hand, coped with all the duties of running, in Jane's words, a 'merry abode', or, in Edward's, the calm 'I take to be the forerunner of a storm'.

18 Sir Walter Scott's first important original work published 1805, a poem in six cantos.

Gipsy Mary

One morning, halfway through September, when Edward and William Tytler were just mounting their horses to ride to Aldourie, Mary flew out of the house waving a letter from James. The boys dismounted at once while the letter, dated 7 July, was read and re-read: Plantation No 23 had been sold for £7,000 and, moreover, the son of Aleck's old nurse, David Shaw, had reached Berbice and was working very well:

> … James now has a good overseer – and only one Estate to manage – a good House – plenty of sheep and poultry, fruit & Garden stuff – and his Business much lessened by all the old Union concern being closed.

This was the news that they had been waiting for: everything now seemed set fair. There was also, at last, an excellent letter from William of 16 February from Delhi. When Edward and William Tytler eventually rode off, the household, 'all of us in high health and happiness', settled happily back to normal, looking forward to a peaceful family autumn round the Moniack hearth.

❀

A few days later, Edward received a message from his father that Mary was not well; he immediately rode home. She had woken her parents at four o'clock in the morning two nights before in agony and had been bled and blistered by Dr Robertson. When Edward got home she was considerably better; he wrote to Aleck:

> I write in the next room to where Mary is, she is easy at present and quiet … I trust that her danger is not so great as our father and mother seem to apprehend.

The following day, having satisfied himself that she was out of danger, he rode back to Aldourie.

Charles Grant was away at Waternish, his estate in Skye, but his wife Jane walked the mile and a half each day from Achnagairn to enquire after Mary. To Edward's scorn the younger Grants took no interest in Mary's illness and, through fear of infection, had forbidden Annie Tytler, staying at Achnagairn, to visit her sick cousin. Annie, however, climbed out at one o'clock in the morning and crept through the dark fields to Moniack. A couple of days later, Edward was again summoned home to find Mary no better: the fever had to reach a crisis, and there was no knowing when that would be.

For a week Mary fought her illness until one morning she 'fell into a sweet sleep and sweat'; it seemed that the turning point had perhaps been reached. The doctor was hopeful and left at eight in the evening promising to return in the morning. Reelig went to bed, leaving Jane and Edward watching by Mary's bed. At midnight Reelig took over the watch from Jane; at two o'clock there was a turn for the worse. Edward continues the story for William.

> We immediately sent for Robertson tho I was convinced it was all over with my darling angel. My mother heard me coming downstairs in a hurry, and came out of her room, and with a look that I shall never forget, asked me Is she gone? I told her not, and begged her if she could, to compose herself and go once more to see her child – she did go, and took a last look at her expiring Daughter; Mary spoke to her as long as she staid in the room. I waited till my mother came down for I was aware that I could not stand the sight – I could bear to see my sister in her last moments; but I could not behold with composure her Mother. In a few minutes she came down and met me on the stairs, begged of me to go up to my sister; 'I cannot' said she, 'stand the scene but you perhaps may be able'. Thank heaven! I *was* able.

Edward and his father stayed with Mary for the next two hours. At five the doctor returned and said he could be of no further use. Edward told his mother, waiting alone in her room, then went back to Mary, who knew him and spoke to him. At half past five Dr Robertson thought it best that Reelig should leave, while Edward and two maidservants remained with Mary.

> I then knelt down by her bed and she *then* mentioned my name, and cast a look on me that pierced my heart; the bare remembrance of it agitates me to a degree that I cannot express; I hope in God my dear Willie you may never experience such a feeling as I did at that moment ... my darling Mary never took her eyes from off me after that moment till a few minutes past six; she was then gone forever from me.

Edward's letter ends with a despairing eulogy:

> Mary was to me what I fear no other person can ever be again ... she was the sweetest creature, the most affectionate endearing girl that ever lived and she is now an angel ... God has deprived me of the person in the world that I loved the most dearly – but he knows what is most for our good ... Religion it is true affords the greatest consolation to many ... but religion will not restore Mary to me. My mother bears her loss with the most exemplary resignation – she is indeed a pattern of everything that is virtuous.

Jane added a disjointed couple of pages to Edward's account. She had been worried about Mary's health ever since the middle of July. The rest of the family had laughed at her worries; Mary, after all, joined in all the family rambles, scrambles and rides and was apparently fit and well.

❈

The day Mary died, Reelig wrote to William:

> This day it has pleased God to remove from us our dear child your sister, Mary, in all the Bloom, in all the engaging properties, & in all the innocence & sweetness of Fifteen. A purer mind never was – is that not Consolation – we have more –

> we have that exceeding proportion of human happiness, which the excellent & promising conduct of all our surviving children gives us ... we are humbled & resigned but greatly supported ... ought we not to be deeply thankfull, for what we enjoy in possession & in prospect and to bless the hand which chastises.

He sent it with a covering letter to the agent in Calcutta so that the news could be broken gently to William – in six months' time.

William, meanwhile, had also been ill and was sailing down the Ganges on a recuperative voyage to Calcutta. With time on his hands he was writing a letter to his father about Mary, the sister he had not seen since she was nine. He hoped that she was mature enough to enjoy herself 'in her closet'[19] with no companion but 'a volume of Cowper, Dryden ... or a volume of Shakespeare'. He trusted that she would turn into 'an accomplished lady instructing Jane Anne ... able to converse in French and in Italian ... Tell her I expect great things and that I shall feel happy only when I see her refined and elegant'. This letter reached Moniack early the following year.

Charles Grant, when he came home from Skye to the news of Mary, 'was so shocked and overcome that he was obliged to retire to his own room', after which he wrote 'a most kind friendly & pious letter' to Reelig, visited the family with his wife and lent them some 'consolatory books'.

Jane wrote, 'my heart sinks beneath the stroke – nor do I find hitherto the smallest lessening of my grief – on the contrary – I think I bore up better in the first week or 10 days than now'. But Jane was a woman of her times with a strong Evangelical belief in the Almighty's plan for his creation and a conviction that all would be for the best:

> Oh! How wonderfully are our joys and sorrows mingled in this world! Perhaps the Almighty saw it would have been too much for us to have retained every Blessing – he restored Edward to us to be a comfort under the impending affliction ... [Edward] is everything the fondest parent could wish – our solace & comfort & companion.

A few days later, a letter arrived for Mary from Aleck marked firmly 'On pain of never seeing my handwriting again shew this to no-one whatever'; in it, among other matters, he expressed his opinion of the Grants. It was otherwise full of homesick questions about the family and their doings. Edward replied, on 10 October, with another long description of Mary's death and a warning of the effects of grief:

> After such an affliction as we have had the mind does not easily settle, or compose itself so as to write or do anything else. This my dear Aleck you will experience; I daresay you will find it a hard matter to apply to anything, even writing a letter ... Oh how I feel for you and our absent brother but more for you who knew her as

19 A Georgian woman's private space.

> a companion and a friend – James and William knew her only as a child but you and I have seen her an amiable engaging and affectionate creature. Jane Anne sweet child is as fine a creature as can be, but I can never love her as I did Mary.

There is a slip of paper in Reelig's writing preserved with this letter:

> Edward Moniack 10 October 1806. A simple production of pure affection – that which exalts the author above Philosophers and Poets.

⁂

The news had been broken to Aleck by his tutor, Dealtry – Robert Grant had thoughtfully organised this; luckily, his friend from Dunham days, James Stephen, was with him at the time and stayed to support him. Aleck managed to write a letter to his father on 6 October but did not know how to write to his mother. He mourned Mary, his 'earliest friend' and 'Guardian Angel' as the companion nearest to him in age, with whom he had shared many experiences when far from home. He dreaded his next visit home because all his plans had included her:

> My fondest hopes were to see that sister happily settled in the world, who is now forever removed from my sight ... it is an event which disheartens me from placing attachment on any one again ... Looking into my drawer, my eye caught ... one of those letters which she had written in all that flow of spirits which was natural to her; the thought that the hand was cold, which had written them, struck like Ice on my heart.

At this point the family were alone apart from the faithful Annie Tytler and Miss Murray, who had arrived just too late to see Mary. She stayed to comfort the bereaved, and Edward paid tribute to her:

> She is cheerful without being too much so and really raises one's spirits without one's being sensible of it, and God knows it must be with violence to her own feelings, for she *has* felt bitterly on this occasion, only think my dear Aleck of her coming only a few hours too late to see her dear child in life – and *how* she loved Mary and my darling loved her God knows.

About a month later, Reelig wrote a black-bordered letter to Aleck urging him to concentrate more than ever on his studies:

> I never repel the image of your angel sister ... I still make her my companion when I walk or think – and am cheered by the illusion ... You too, my dearest Aleck, must be strong in mind ... and remind yourself that it must be the lot of those who live longest, to suffer the most in domestic stresses.

⁂

As was the custom of the time, Mary's funeral, four days after her death, was attended mainly by contemporaries of her father. James Grant of Redcastle, Jane reported, 'has been much affected'. Although very incapacitated, he walked 'close to her side the whole way' with tears in his eyes, according to Edward. There were others similarly distressed 'beyond what you could imagine'. 'Gipsy Mary' had clearly danced her way into the hearts of many.

During the weeks after Mary's death, letters of condolence flooded into Moniack. Lord Woodhouselee mourned 'the death of a beloved and promising child at the period when she was about to enter the world' and ended with a thoughtful and practical suggestion to his brother-in-law:

> Might not you arrange matters so that you and Jane could come up in the end of this season and pass a month or two with us? ... I am confident you would both be much the better for it. Try if you can arrange matters so – it would be a great comfort for the sisters to be together.

The letters to Jane from her two sisters, Anne Woodhouselee and Catherine Gregoire, reveal their different personalities: Anne, like many others, spoke of Heavenly Inheritance and Divine Providence and declared there was much to be thankful for, especially Edward's homecoming. Mary, moreover, had had two years at home and was at home when she died. At this point Anne's feelings overcame her and she laid down her pen. The following day, she resumed, only to be interrupted by her husband, who said she was writing far too much and was merely adding to her sister's afflictions.

Catherine Gregoire's letter was a very different matter, not without reason. Her only son, the wayward David, had been wounded fighting for Napoleon on 15 September and died of his wounds on 1 October, two days after Mary. When this news reached Moniack is not clear but Jane, in any case, delayed until 22 October before reporting Mary's death. Her sister's response duly arrived in the form of four long pages of tiny writing, heavily underlined and scattered with countless exclamation marks. Always in a delicate nervous state, Catherine was 'entirely unhinged' by the news from Moniack and had fallen prey to 'a Black impenetrable Cloud'. The letter rambles incoherently, only occasionally recalling its purpose:

> I *tremble* for you my beloved sister during the course of the ensuing winter – I know how *dreary* a season you found the last – and now when *every object around* you will unceasingly present to your afflicted mind and *maternal* heart the Angel you have lost.

But most of the time Catherine bewails her own situation and that of her children, threatening to bring all her problems to Moniack. Her daughter Eliza, a difficult child, was at this point seventeen; Emilia, a year younger, was teaching the nine-year-old Caroline and running the household while coping with her mother's mental fragility:

> I am incapable of *application* to anything – I sit whole hours in my Closet alone – I dare not often ask for my Emilia's company ... Alas poor child she has enough to do

> ... I am not often able to go down to our common dining, and *sitting* room, which is a mere *thoroughfare* – can I *expose* myself, even to our only Servant ... in fits of *trembling*, *starting*, almost to convulsions?

Lady Woodhouselee was contributing financially to the French family, but it was not enough. M Gregoire, a shadowy figure who, apart from references to his 'terrible tempers', does not feature much in the correspondence, was making some sort of an effort to support his family but survival seemed to depend on the whim of a certain 'Great Man' who had been very fond of David 'and ... would I am fully convinced have protected, and advanced him'. Whether this Great Man would now transfer his favours to the rest of the family Catherine could not tell. Towards the end of the letter Catherine's attention once again momentarily focuses on her sister and promises to 'unceasingly *tremble* for you all'. But then her own troubles resume:

> My mind is so *weak* ... the *falling of a pin* makes me start! ... my life – oh pardon me the expression my dearest Jaisy! is become almost a *burthen* to me, heavier than I can bear!

She manages to end, albeit tremblingly, with a practical suggestion. David's favourite cousin had always been Edward, the boy nearest to him in age:

> Let my dear Edward *plant* a *yew* tree (you know that is the badge of the Clan Fraser) in my poor Boy's *walk* at Moniack – he always talked to me of some *new* walk there, that was *his favourite* one – they are in Heaven! – *our children* are there together!

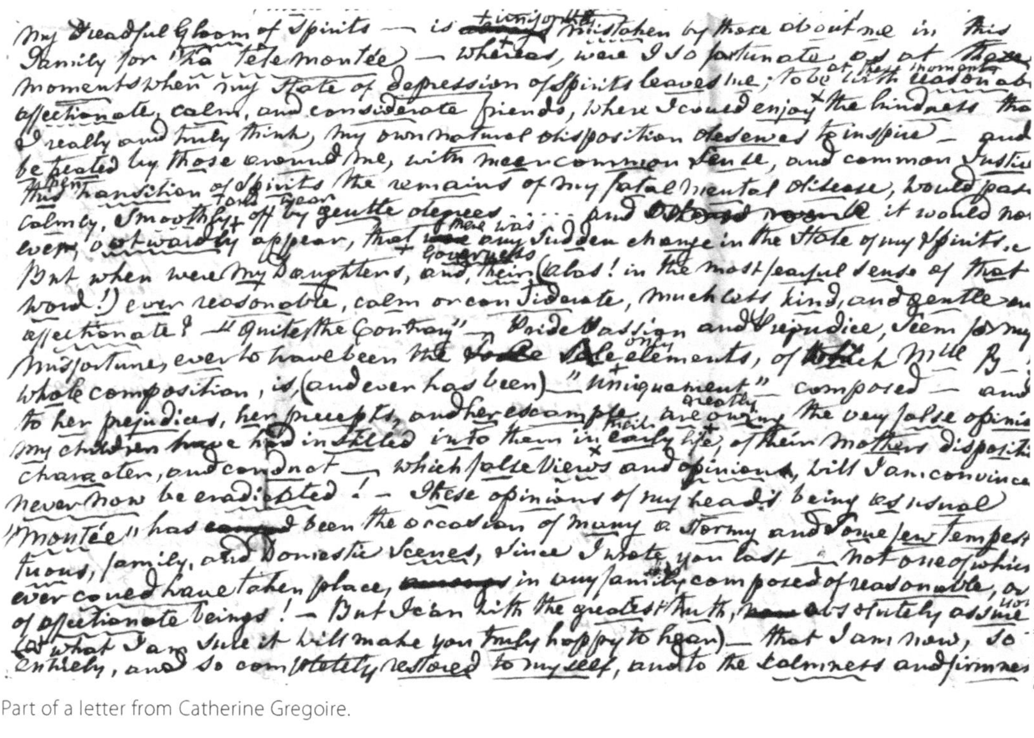
my Dreadful Gloom of Spirits — is ~~[illegible]~~ mistaken by those about me in this
Family for tête montée — whereas, were I so fortunate as at those
moments when my State of depression of Spirits leaves me; to be with reasonab
affectionate, calm, and considerate friends, where I could enjoy the kindness tha
I really and truly think, my own natural disposition deserves to inspire — and
be treated by those around me, with mere common sense, and common Justic
this transition of Spirits the remains of my fatal mental disease, would pas
calmly, smoothly off by gentle degrees ... and ~~[illegible]~~ it would no
ever, outwardly appear, that there was any sudden change in the State of my Spirits.
But when were my Daughters, and their Governess (alas! in the most fearful sense of that
word!) ever reasonable, calm or considerate, much less kind, and gentle an
affectionate? "Quite the Contrary" — Pride Passion and Prejudice, seem for my
misfortune, ever to have been the ~~[illegible]~~ only elements, of which Mlle B—
whole composition, is (and ever has been) "uniquement" composed — and
to her prejudices, her precepts, and her example, are greatly owing the very false opinio
my children have had instilled into them in their early life, of their mothers disposit
character, and conduct — which false views and opinions, will I am convince
never now be eradicated! — These opinions of my head's being as usual
"montée" has ~~[illegible]~~ been the occasion of many a stormy and some few tempes
tuous, family, and Domestic Scenes, since I wrote you last — not one of whic
ever could have taken place, ~~[illegible]~~ in any family composed of reasonable, or
of affectionate beings! — But I can with the greatest truth, ~~[illegible]~~ absolutely assure you
(& what I am sure it will make you truly happy to hear) — that I am now, so
entirely, and so completely restored to myself, and to the calmness and firmnes

Part of a letter from Catherine Gregoire.

Private collection

Groves of sturdy yews punctuate the soaring conifers of Reelig Glen on either side of the burn. There is one yew, however, that, to this day, stands alone, just at the entrance of the Glen, beside the burn by the path that is known as 'David's Walk'.

Exam fever

Time wore on and Christmas approached: for the Grant family December meant the election in Inverness, in which Charles Grant turned out to be unopposed. The family accordingly packed up Achnagairn and set off for Christmas and New Year in Russell Square.

For Edward, December meant pondering his future: Charles Grant offered him a cadetship in India, while James Grant of Redcastle, along with Reelig and, rather more reluctantly, Jane, thought he should return to Berbice so that James could come home. Meanwhile, Edward was enjoying the company of cousin Tom Fraser who, Reelig hoped, would help him 'by example by rousing his powers from their torpor – Edward would willingly slide through life'.

For Aleck, December meant examinations. Like many a student before and since, he warned his parents that he was unlikely to do well. He had a handful of excuses: he was suffering from 'listlessness and melancholy reflection' and the Classical prize would surely go to the single-minded Bird. His parents must not expect a good Mathematics result: the other four had studied the subject thoroughly before coming to College. Political Economy, History and Law depended on study and memory and 'My memory is wretched, and without that qualification, the former avails not'.

He was astonished at the examination method (which does not seem to have changed much over the years):

> We are turned into a large room at separate tables; pens, paper, ink, and a List of Questions is given to each. Nothing else but pen and ink allowed ... seriously I have no hopes.

He longed to be allowed home for Christmas, but it was decreed that, once again, he would be thrown upon the hospitality of either the Frasers or the Grants. This brought forth a tirade:

> However worthy the families I suppose I am to live with at Christmas, I see little in them to interest me ... I am far from wishing to meet Mr G's eye, after the approaching examination, at which I expect not to make a good appearance. I could give you sufficient reason, were we together.

Once the exams got under way Aleck could not sleep. He was finding the whole thing 'inconceivably fatiguing' and was irritated that Holt Mackenzie had answered '*every one* of the Mathematical questions, except one trifling one which he forgot'. The Classical exam had focussed on the History, Laws and Manners of the ancient civilisations with little demand for the languages in which Aleck excelled. He had 'bungled abominably' the piece of unseen Latin that he had to construe and wished that his parents 'had Mackenzie as your son: he would fulfil expectations, that deserve a better fate than they will most assuredly meet with.' In short, he 'never was so completely disgusted, fatigued, and miserable, on all accounts, as at present'.

Then the results came out. His two weeks of hard work had paid off: he had won the Classics and General Literature Prize, was second in Maths, third in History and Law, fourth in Political Economy and eighth equal in Persian. Reelig waxed lyrical:

> I congratulate you from my heart on your very brilliant successes ... you will love classical learning & general literature now more deeply than ever and will, as long as you live, delight in the Ancients ... whether you lie in the bustle of business or in the Retreats of the Country – whether you have to speak in public or to write in private – the liveliest & loveliest tints will be thrown over your life, your words & your works.

Aleck managed to avoid the Grants that Christmas; he stoutly made his own plans, spending it at Cambridge with a school friend, staying in rooms at Trinity College and dining in Hall with the Fellows. He braved the Grants in the New Year and, although he found it difficult being an outsider in a close family at a time of celebration, he reckoned their stay in Scotland had done them good:

> Charemile has divested herself of a load of affectation and the cold climate of Scotland seems to have had the opposite effect of warming the frigid heart of Maria. The younger ones are less ridiculously reserved than before and improved in personal accomplishments. Mr Grant seems to have contracted somewhat of our Northern hospitable familiarity, and they all please me greatly with their attachment to Scotland, Scotch people, Scotch servants, Scotch scenery, and Scotch affability of manner.

The family did their best to help Aleck and he was rarely left alone, but he felt very isolated, having moments 'when the remembrance of misfortune comes bitter upon me'. A letter from Tom Fraser, still keeping Edward company at Moniack, enclosing a lock of Mary's hair, 'completely for the moment deprived me of firmness ... I felt as if I was a second time deprived of my beloved, my dearest treasure'. The following year, Edward, writing to Aleck, remembered the summer of 1806 as a time when 'one of the great sources of the happiness of both of us ... dried up'.

4

1807–1811

Aftermath

During the following winter Reelig found consolation in pursuing his creative work in the woods. Edward took refuge in exercise 'like a Highlander at the expence of Hares & Partridges, Muirfowl & Woodcock'. Jane found it less easy to rise above her depression. The winter weather did not help – February's snowdrifts made visits to Inverness impossible. The grounds of the house, although facing south, are a frost pocket where snow and ice can last for depressing weeks on end, but Jane wrote that even the prospect of spring 'brings no joy to me'.

In Hertford, Aleck was also suffering from low spirits and the monotony of College life:

> The routine of lectures so much confounds one day with another that I actually suffered your birthday, Edward's, Jane Anne's and my own to pass without thinking in the least of either of you.'

New rules had been introduced at the College: owing to 'punch parties & debauchery', candles had to be extinguished at 11.00 pm – very trying to Aleck, who liked reading into the small hours. He reckoned he was in the middle of his set, somewhere 'between the totally idle and the outrageously studious'. One of the latter was Holt Mackenzie, still his uncomfortable room-mate. Aleck admired Holt's application and his financial acumen and wrote sadly to his father, 'Often do I wish you had him for your son, instead of me'. Reelig testily replied, 'I have no desire to change any of my sons for any sons I know.'

Aleck's admiration, however, was still tempered with dislike; he could never be friends with Mackenzie 'because I am not disposed to be obsequious enough'. If, however, his parents ever met him they would no doubt be most impressed by his manners and conversation. Aleck was convinced that Mackenzie 'would be a Great Man,[1] were it not for a certain caution and selfishness that would, I should think, damp enterprise. Self ... appears the sole moving principle of his every action.'

1 Holt Mackenzie (1787–1876) went on to have a very successful career in India. He was President of the Council of the College of Fort William and is best remembered for his work as a settlement officer. Convinced that the village was an important social institution in North Indian society which needed to be preserved, he devised a much fairer system of revenue (Mahalwari settlement) for the villages.

Holt's father, Henry,[2] a friend of Lord Woodhouselee, was a lawyer, essayist and poet, who wrote *The Man of Feeling*, the most popular novel of its decade, published anonymously in 1771. Reelig hoped that a boy from such a background would become a lifelong friend for Aleck and tactlessly suggested that Aleck might try to emulate Holt in economy and application to his studies. The infuriated Aleck shot back:

> There is no necessity for imitation to attain excellence, I can form in my own mind a standard infinitely superior to what can be expected in any mortal ... Then, surely, you cannot blame me for not imitating Mackenzie or anyone else. If my strength of mind were competent to it ... I would practise Economy without meanness, I would be firm without harshness and arrogance ... studious without being morose ... religious without superstition, and rational without scepticism. But if I could not have these virtues of Mackenzie, without the analogous vices, I would as soon, on the whole, remain as I am.

Aleck wondered whether he had written 'in a style of freedom too much like impertinence', but Reelig replied that, although he certainly seemed to be at fault where fastidiousness, pride and carelessness of pecuniary matters were concerned, 'you need never fear to write to me with freedom ... I expect it'.

Aleck was, as ever, worried about money. In the continuing absence of a College Library, he had had to buy numerous expensive books, including the essential Persian Dictionary. He hoped, however, that his 'very considerable collection, more than most here' would enhance his father's little library at Moniack.[3] Clothes were another problem: two black suits were necessary to accord with mourning conventions, and he had certainly become more fashion conscious. After all, 'were I to be shabbily dressed the blame would fall ... on my Father'.

Reelig was less anxious about Aleck's clothes than about his over-lofty ideals and his tendency towards quick criticism of others:

> Are people never to see their faults & repent? Many of these may prove good & great men ... Meekness of comportment – not indignant expression of voice or feature is the Christian corrective ... if disgusted unavoidably never express it ... bear & forebear ... never revolt the faulty by their own picture but attract them to the right by a more pleasing picture.

Soon the summer vacation would be a welcome release for Aleck. Edward, still at home but destined soon to return to Berbice, was delighted that he and Aleck would be together again 'possibly, I may say probably, the last time in our lives'.

---

2 Henry Holt MacKenzie (1745–1832).
3 Quite a number of Aleck's books are still in the Moniack library

William arrived in Calcutta in mid-November 1806. On the long voyage he had renewed old friendships and met acquaintances along the way; most of these were making their fortunes in commerce. Their enticing offers of positions in their enterprises, which would make him richer sooner, 'almost shook my constancy'. But in Delhi he had his foot on a ladder that he had set his heart on climbing. If he had not been in debt, he wrote, he would have certainly gone straight home from Calcutta 'and brought out Aleck with me and a Scotch lass. What a happiness would this have been.' At this stage he neither wanted to remain a bachelor, nor did he want the responsibility of having to provide for 'children unfortunately born of Indian mothers – look to Baillie and Edmonstone, both with families of countryborn children. What a care is that to provide for, and if they are Girls, how much more difficult to bring them up in the paths of virtue and honor!' Future events were to prove this pronouncement somewhat prophetic.

Fully restored to health, he returned to Delhi in August 1807 to find a packet of letters, among them several, written almost a year before, bringing the news of Mary's death. When he opened his father's he was at the Qutub Minar,[4] nine miles south-west of Delhi, escorting the King to the tomb of a saint. He scribbled a quick reply:

> With regard to your letters and those from the different members of our family, all I shall say in reply to them, is that I have received them ... read them, and draw a veil over the contents – for ever – Cherish Jane Anne and George; keep them always with you; the other brothers will take care of them.

What he longed for more than ever now was diversion, but there was nothing in Delhi to satisfy his thirst for adventure. He was aware that his situation was 'just worth double in comfort and emolument that of most of my contemporaries' and that it was a matter of waiting patiently for a 'trump card'. Meanwhile, every letter from home:

> ... works on me to labor for a return. I have no thoughts but for it, and labor only for Moniack. Thank God I am now ... saving every rupee to spend in Inverness-shire.

THE PAIN OF SEPARATION

Once the summer holidays were clearly in sight, Aleck's spirits rose. The weather that May was unseasonably warm, he was swimming every day – 'I cannot live without bathing' – and the cool, deep pools of the Moniack burn beckoned. He arrived home in late June 1807 and for two happy months he and Edward were together again.

Aleck's meeting with his parents, the first for over eighteen months, was depressing: both were in low spirits, partly owing to the situation in Berbice, where the rise in fortune after the sale of No 23 had not materialised. They were also leaden-hearted at the thought of saying farewell again to the boys, especially to Aleck, knowing that it might well be forever. William entreated his father 'not to think of the time and distance he will be removed from

4 The highest tower in India, built outside Delhi between 1193 and 1386. 73m high, its base diameter is 14.3m and its top 2.75m. Now a World Heritage Site.

you; consider his affections as in your trust till he return home ... I thank God his father lives and will I trust long live after his return. If you, in parting with him, believe it is to be forever, in this world, the trial will be insupportable.'

Aleck, however, soon stopped worrying and threw himself into the old pastimes with Edward, fishing and shooting day after day. Far too soon, the moment came to leave home again.

⁂

Six weeks later, Aleck, his mother and Edward were on their way to Edinburgh. Reelig followed later. At Woodhouselee Aleck met the Gregoire girls for the first time and was enchanted, especially with Emilia:

> These new Cousins of ours have taken, I know not how, a terrible hold on my affections; I cannot get them out of my thoughts; although I know I must endeavour to think of more sordid things, and exert myself to shake off those romantic ideas, with which they have inspired me.

Hardly had he met them than he had to tear himself away. He managed to scribble a letter to his father during an hour's stop in Newcastle:

> I slept quite well last night, but that I was continually imagining myself at Woodhouselee ... I cannot avoid thinking to a degree of certainty that I never shall return, but do not imagine that these ideas can emasculate me, or render my efforts for a speedy return less vigorous.

There was no time for more, the horn was sounding and he had to climb back into the mail coach bound for York. There he dipped into a book of poems, *The Pleasures of Memory*,[5] a leaving present from his mother. He learned by heart the description of Mary Queen of Scots' last look at her native France, as she 'gaz'd her soul away', and scribbled another letter:

> Now that I am a little recollected from the confusion of ideas occasioned by parting, thousands of things crowd into my mind, which I would give worlds to be able to say to you; for I cannot write my mind ... I think of you all, waking, and dream of you, sleeping.

⁂

Late back for College, Aleck received dirty looks from Charles Grant. There were now sixty-four students in residence, but Aleck was still very much at odds with his colleagues:

> Oh! That I had the satirical pen of a Johnson, to paint the depth of brutality, into which this College is sunk. The mean extravagance, the spiritless profligacy, the witless prophaneness, and total absence of everything pleasant or desireable.

5 By Samuel Rogers, published 1792.

Again Reelig wrote bracingly: he expected more broadminded views from Aleck. It was hopeless using 'the assemblage of well-disposed and happy people as at Woodhouselee' as a yardstick to measure everyone else:

> Assure yourself there are scintilla of fine fire in the rudest & most irregular flints. Keep your Heart warm, your Head cool – judgement is Gold, Genius is Gilding, Knowledge is Power. Drink deep then – let your only avarice be of Time – misspend not one moment.

Meanwhile, Reelig was consoling himself with building castles in the air in the shape of a timetable for the homecoming of his boys. He reckoned they might all be home for good by 1822:

> However, to know & hear of your welfare & welldoing is Happiness to us ... how deep my cause for thankfulness when I think on my Children & on all my Domestic comfort.

⁂

At Woodhouselee it was now Edward's turn to take his leave; knowing how he would be feeling, Aleck wrote to him 'as merrily as I could':

> I had just put off my clothes to go to bed, when looking at my watch, which has taken a strange whim to go correctly, I find it just wanted twenty minutes of One, and being quite awakened by a dish of Moniack tea, which I drank with Papa and Isabella Tytler, thought I might as well spend the remaining twenty minutes, and dish of tea, with you. I fear Papa and Mama (I love the old words) are no longer with you ... I will not begin to prose on the pains of separation &c for there are things which I think we should keep to oneself.

A letter from Isabella, diverting him from the delectable Emilia, had moved him to tears; after re-reading it he resorted to his studies and 'buried among triangles and spheres, among tenses and Dialects &c I tried, for a moment, to forget you all.'

Edward agreed that parting from Papa and Mama ('I love the old names as well') had been traumatic. Nothing, however, could exceed the Tytlers' kindness to him. Best of all, Aunt Tytler had given him 'a very nice pianoforte which as you know was a very great present to me'.

At Moniack, although there were draughty spaces left by Edward and Aleck, the house was suddenly overflowing with '6 female cousins, 3 male, four aunts & 2 uncles – a party rarely to be met with'. The Gregoires and Tytlers had arrived. Reelig and Jane were rather apprehensive about the French invasion, Aunt Gregoire being 'strange indeed', but Aleck was relieved that the autumn and winter would be brightened for his parents by a house full of cousins.

⁂

On 5 September 1807 the civilian casualties at the second Battle of Copenhagen[6] caused controversy throughout Britain; at Hertford College the Professors debated it heatedly. Aleck was fortunate enough to be invited to dinner by the great Malthus where he encountered Professor Hamilton socially for the first time. Hamilton, a Francophile and 'prodigious admirer of Bonaparte and French genius and valour', denounced the government for this 'flagrant piece of injustice'. Aleck was almost persuaded: he was doubtful 'of the necessity of this expedition; and if not necessary, it was not justifiable'.

The yearly examination was looming, and Aleck's customary pessimism returned. He knew that there was no time now to catch up: the Professors were piling on the work in order to get to the end of the syllabus. Spherical Trigonometry and Astronomy; Statistics; Political Economy and History; Herodotus and Tacitus; Sanskrit and 'Hindustanee'; Chemistry and French – all were being crammed in and, with still few books, everything had to be transcribed.

There were also few indications as to what form the exam would take, except that it would be different from last time. The Principal would not delegate to the Professors, yet was unable to take decisions himself, and Aleck had definite ideas of what should be happening:

> Had one simple sensible man had the conduct of the institution of this college, it would have been ... a residence of real improvement, in Morals, and Knowledge. It would have supplied India, not as now, with a set of ignorant, indolent, pernicious servants, whose sole and professed intention is to make money, as soon, and in whatever way they can; but with a series of useful intelligent conscientious administrators who would not postpone the happiness of a numerous and respectable, at least a harmless people, for their own emolument and shortlived gratification.

Rumour had it that twenty-one students would sail to India in March 1808. Aleck was determined not to repeat William's long dreary wait in London; surely it would be cheaper to go home for a few months than to stay in London until his voyage? For once, Charles Grant was not consulted; Reelig and Jane gave Aleck their blessing, along with the inevitable list of travel instructions and directions about coping with his possessions.

Aleck was right about the exam results – 'partly by misfortune; partly by former idleness' he was placed lower than last year in all the important exams; predictably, he considered the exam was not fair 'or judicious in some respects'. Half the students had got prizes, which seemed excessive. Mr Grant 'spoke two words to me, expressing his half-disapprobation but acquiescence in my Northern jaunt'. But who cared? 'We have, however, done with the College'.

6 The British bombarded Copenhagen Aug/Sept 1807 to force the surrender of the Danish fleet and save the Baltic from Napoleon's blockade.

Rain

Edward returned to Berbice and to a great welcome from his slaves. Now at least he had Aunt Woodhouselee's piano to keep him company. It had arrived safely with, miraculously, not even one string broken. In that damp climate, however, he had to tune it every day.

The day Mary died, Jane had closed the lid of her piano; now at last she had apparently been persuaded to open it and was slowly getting into her old stride. Edward wished she had resumed sooner 'that I might have once more heard you. I used often, often, to long for it yet never liked to ask.'

In Berbice, his next door neighbour, Mrs Fraser, 'who pines for home most terribly', gradually induced the soft-hearted Edward to lend her his piano: 'I am glad I lent it to her because she really began to forget a little & it is a great pleasure to me to hear her play when I go there'. Her playing of his favourite Scotch airs, however, left much to be desired; he was surprised that she did not know *The Flowers of the Forest* or *Highland Laddie* but he trusted that one day he would again hear his mother play these old favourites.

Without the piano time hung even more heavily on Edward's hands and letters to his mother became more frequent. He talked to her often of James: it was high time that his brother, now twenty-four, came under the civilising influence of home. Standards were slipping and his manners and 'neatness in dress' left a lot to be desired. There were not enough women around to keep him up to the mark; he could do with 'the discipline of the Tytlers & Gregoires'.

Social life was now restricted to evenings with the Frasers. On Sundays Mrs Fraser would not open the piano, which Edward felt 'fastidious in this country'; on other days he listened to her playing while 'the two Jameses sleepily nod at one another. Indeed Mr Fraser often snores so loud that it disturbs the music.' Evenings spent at home were generally pretty short: a single game of chess (which Edward disliked and only played to amuse James) and then, thank goodness, bed.

On Sundays, when conversation replaced music, there were often long, noisy discussions round the table about the slave trade. Edward had a lot to say about its evils but confronted with the others 'all trying who can drown the others voice & on the same side of the question' he remained silent: 'If I say anything against it James rates [scolds] me to such a degree that I am glad to hold my tongue'.

Occasionally there were balls at Government House: both brothers were invited to the Queen's Birthday Ball, to which James went, leaving Edward in charge on the plantation. Not being much of a dancer, James was relieved to find that there was no need for him to participate as there were about fifteen ladies to a hundred gentlemen.

✻

That year was marred by incessant rain: 'it is most wearing to see the cotton hanging on the trees & yet not being able to pick it for the wet ... most uncomfortable to ourselves & the poor negroes who can bear anything better than cold'. Edward's mind was constantly on home, how soon he was likely to see it again and what to send when James went back: a rattlesnake skin perhaps, some feathers, cashew nuts or some fruit syrups. He would, however, exchange every pineapple, melon, grape and fig for a bowl of Moniack strawberries, raspberries or gooseberries.

When he got home hot, exhausted and often soaking wet, James, his mind constantly on cotton, would greet him with 'Well, how are the people coming on?' or 'Are there many pods on the trees?', questions he sometimes could not answer having spent the day in a daydream of home:

> For I very often walk from the house to the feild & the feild to the house again without looking at the cotton or (if I look) without observing & then when he asks how it looks I am confounded – & resolve to look better the next time & perhaps the next time I go out the same thing happens'.

The remorseless rain continued. All over the colony the crop failed, and the brothers succumbed to fever; Edward recovered quickly, but James was very ill. He was prescribed mercury, with disastrous effects: he could neither talk nor eat. Edward acted as nurse, tempting him with soup and milk, although 'he will not be able to eat with ease for weeks to come'. As he recovered, for once he provided Edward with 'very agreeable company at all times – this I know is put on, not natural to him, but it answers the same purpose as if it were'.

It was now imperative for James to go home for a few months to recuperate. He was desperate to see Moniack again: the family finances were such that the old home might not be there if he delayed another year. Edward was very apprehensive about being left in charge; he had 'terrible foreboding' at the thought of his loneliness without either James or the Frasers, who would also be leaving soon.

Worse than that was the thought that he could not go home until James returned and, if things continued badly, it might then be too late; he might have taken his 'everlasting leave' of Moniack.

Christmas 1808 at No. 29 with the Frasers was a quiet affair, although as usual the slaves were 'a little unruly from the quantity of spirits they had drunk'. The white population were still in continual dread of rebellion and likely to remain so 'as long as we live in a slave country'. Edward, however, was proud of his Negroes, who always seemed to him cheerful. They had plenty to eat and drink 'and as to punishment (which of course they now and then must have) they seem to consider that as a matter of course – & I really believe they think less of it than we do'. He thought they would not want to change to another master but was still convinced that if there seemed any benefit to them in such a change their loyalty would vanish: 'Not one of them would care a pin if we were both dead tomorrow'. Suicide and murder were commonplace. 'There must surely be something radically wrong in a thing that is the source of so many miseries and crimes'.

Just after Christmas, they heard that Reelig had finally mortgaged Moniack. Edward was ambivalent: he disliked the thought that the place was 'in the power of the Bank, or anyone' but clearly it was the only way to save the estate '& now everything depends on what 28 does to liquidate that heavy debt'. Then at the turn of the year 1809 he wrote to his mother full of excitement about the continuation of the American Embargo of 1807,[7] which would ensure high prices for cotton:

> [James] can talk of nothing else ... he heard this news & when he came home he made such a racket about ginning, cleaning, baling, picking, shipping etc. that anyone but myself would have thought he had gone mad ... he sent for all the Drivers, gave them such charges about picking plenty of cotton & changed all the work he had ordered the day before – all the time walking up & down the room as fast as his legs could carry him tho he had come in from a very long hot ride ... at last I ventured to ask the reason for all this & then by degrees he let out that the American embargo was to continue till November – & cotton rising in price & a ship of Gladstone's[8] arrived to carry away our crop by the 1st February & he has never rested a moment since – I rejoice heartily at it & only wish we had more cotton to send home to such a good market.

Setting Sail on the Sea of Life

Aleck's final days at home were fewer than anticipated. He had made the best of them, however, having 'visited some, rode some, shot some, read none'. He had been persuaded reluctantly to go to the Queen's Birthday Ball in Inverness and bargained with the steward 'for the prettiest lass in the room'. This turned out to be Miss Jane Kennedy, who, according to his friends at Cambridge, was the toast of the University; he also bumped into an old friend, Caroline Shaw. So while James was standing around at the ball in Berbice, wondering how soon he could go home, Aleck was uncharacteristically dancing every dance with 'incomparably the most lovely girls in the room'. He arrived home in the early hours, to the unsettling news that his passage in the East Indiaman *Calcutta* was confirmed and he must leave home in two days.

The whole household rushed into action: Reelig wrote lists of equipment and the French cousins set to 'working hard with the rest at my Linnens and Stores'. He set off at the beginning of February 1808.

In Edinburgh he was dismayed to find that he was just in time for a ball being given by the Tytler girls. The three girls, all in their early twenties, were now deeply

7 This resulted in a wider market for the cotton trade.

8 Sir John Gladstone (1764–1851), Scottish merchant, philanthropist and MP, who made his vast fortune in Liverpool in grain, tobacco and shipping. He was Reelig's agent and adviser for the import of cotton from Guyana. He married Anne Robertson, daughter of a Provost of Dingwall, and their fifth child was William Ewart Gladstone, the future Prime Minister.

entrenched in the Edinburgh social scene and Aleck thought they needed a good blast of Northern fresh air to restore the roses to their cheeks. He knew none of their friends, felt out of place and missed the cousinly companionship of former days; Annie, Jeanie and Isabella could talk of nothing but parties and partners, beaux and balls. An evening at home was passed 'in yawning and discontent'. Their father was threatening to take the whole family to Woodhouselee for a rest – he was completely worn out by parties and junketings and longed nostalgically 'for his children's evening society'.

Boarding the southbound coach, Aleck was hurt by the seeming indifference of the girls' hasty farewells, focussed as they were on that evening's party. It seemed that he 'was expelled by frivolous amusement from the few hearts, where I had thought I held a place'. But this, he reflected, was probably one of the lessons in humility that he could expect to meet in life. Later, he could not resist telling the Tytlers that the Grants had postponed a party in order to see him off to Portsmouth.

In London he desperately needed advice on all fronts and had been hoping to meet Redcastle or Charles Grant. The former, however, was failing in health, and the latter was far too busy until Aleck's last night, when he gave him letters of introduction and advice about behaviour. Worrying about clothes, Aleck tried the agent Dunbar, who was 'almost as much at a loss as myself'. In desperation, Aleck showed his father's list of essential articles to a friend of Dunbar, well used to fitting out young men. This helpful fellow roared with laughter and cut it down by a third. Aleck's final list included: one black hat, two white hats, one Opera hat, three waistcoats, twelve pairs of cotton drawers, two coats, one pair of cord pantaloons, one pair of dark nanqueen (cotton) trousers, one pair of dress breeches and some expensive hosiery.

By 2 March 1808 he was in Portsmouth, 'that sink of all abomination'. On board *Calcutta* there was more chaos than usual as there were many more passengers than ever before – a total of 400. Eventually, Aleck and his room-mate, Smalley, were given the choice of a tiny cabin for two or a larger and better one for three. They chose the latter and Scott as their companion – 'a quiet sort of fellow and pleasant'.

Meeting two Scottish college mates, David Ruthven and his cousin William Leslie-Melville,[9] he felt somewhat forlorn when he found that their elder brothers, the Lords Ruthven and Balgonie, had come to see them off. For diversion he went on a tour of the Docks and was much impressed by the Stores and Foundries and the 'particularly stupendous' anchors. Like William before him he found the prospect from the hill above Portsmouth breathtaking: the view of the town laid out below, all the shipping beyond and the Isle of Wight in the distance.

He was in an unusually optimistic mood as he set off, and there were no backward glances or tears. All the ship's personnel seemed helpful; the crew were happy and contented; his cabin-mates promised calm, quiet and a good supply of books; if his first meal was anything to go by, the food would be excellent. He was in good form physically. The wind was set fair. Things boded well. His last letter to his father is full of enthusiasm and excitement:

9 (1788-1856); son of the 9th Earl of Leven, known at school simply as Melville.

> Here is a gay scene of confusion; heaving anchor, hoisting sails &c ... I never saw so pleasant a scene of confusion ... yet, I must leave the poop and the rigging, where I have been amusing myself, and just write two lines, to send by the Pilot. Although the ship rolls and pitches (I have not yet the correct phrases) she yet permits me to hold the pen ... We are twelve sail and this, for her size, one of the finest ... I must conclude this letter, for the Pilot is just going off and indeed my hand can scarcely hold my pen for cold.

At last Aleck was on his way, sailing, in his words, on his own bark towards the Sea of Life with the helm in his hands, headed for independence, a career, a salary and, God willing, a fortune to bring home; and William would be there to meet him.

⁂

The voyage, under Captain Maxwell, 'reckoned ... the best seaman in the service', was relatively uneventful. Aleck had been looking forward to long days of serious study but found this almost impossible: his cabin was often full of boisterous Hertfordians playing cards for stakes well beyond his means. The five ladies on board were off to look for husbands or, as Aleck decorously put it, 'seem prudently to have taken an Easterly course, finding no port in a Westerly direction'.

He was interested in the communication system between the fleet of twelve ships: ten coloured flags, each corresponded to a number which, in turn, referred to a word. Then 'whether 1, 23, 46 or any number, you have only to turn to the vocabulary, and see what word it answers'.

A short stop in South Africa provided welcome relief. He was enchanted by the sight of the vast horseshoe bay sparkling in the sunshine and alive with the ships entering, colours flying, to join the Indiamen, merchantmen and men of war already riding at anchor. The journey from Simonstown to Cape Town, 'singularly adapted to break bones', reminded him of the childhood trips from Moniack to Nairn in 'our old covered cart'. It was twenty miles of appalling, boulder-strewn track along which slaves, carrying huge burdens of provisions to the ships, struggled several times a day.

In Cape Town he had nowhere to stay, but the resourceful Melville produced a letter of introduction to a Mr Anderson, who supplied all their needs, including an outing to the theatre, where 'all the beauties of Capetown were on display'. Dutch women were very handsome but rather free in their conversation and conduct: 'A lady's reputation here is not the delicate vulnerable thing it is in Britain'. Most of his shipmates accepted invitations to the King's Birthday Ball but Aleck refused: it would be a late night and he might miss the ship. He likewise turned down an invitation to dinner with a Highland Regiment, the 72nd, because 'they drink too hard ... it is impossible to avoid getting rather jolly among so many countrymen'.

Smoothing the way for Aleck

William was both excited and apprehensive about Aleck's arrival. He was still only twenty-three and could well remember his own first days, the numerous temptations of Calcutta and the inevitability of serious debt. Small wonder that he was worried about the less robust Aleck. He was well aware by now that some East India Company servants were chained by debt to a life in India, with no hope of ever going home. He remembered Aleck as a sensitive, spoilt and delicate boy of eleven, his father's favourite, highly intellectual but less outgoing than his extrovert older brothers. Aleck had already proved himself to be somewhat disorganised, especially where money was concerned. He seemed to be exactly the kind of young man likely to be led astray by the wealthier, wilder members of Calcutta society.

The obvious answer was for William to return to Calcutta to meet Aleck off the ship. But he was in 'a Whirlpool of Business' and also on tenterhooks about the possibility of joining an important mission to Kabul, which could well turn out to be the adventure he had been looking for. He hoped to solve the problem of Aleck's initiation into Calcutta life by planning for it from Delhi as meticulously as his father would have done and enlisting the help of friends.

He arranged to fit Aleck up with everything from horses and a buggy to silver plate for his table. He also organised his accommodation and provided introductions to all the right people, including Neil Edmonstone, Secretary to Government and 'my best and earliest friend'. He asked Mr Downie, the Fraser agent in Calcutta, not only to act as 'a constant adviser and most careful friend' but also to keep a sharp eye on Aleck's spending: 'Take him by the hand, my dear Downie, and tell him frankly, when he goes wrong, that he is ruining me, and breaking his father's heart, who has ever looked upon him as his favourite son.' He followed up this letter with one to Aleck himself:

> My happiness, my comfort, my earthly bliss is in your hands, for in yours is that of my father's; you ever was his most beloved son, and on you rest his hopes, and his fears ... it is my duty to communicate with you by constant letters, and to express to you my ideas and belief on the manner and conduct which is to secure to you health, happiness and independence.

He then turned to more practical matters. Servants would swarm about Aleck the moment he set foot on dry land. He advised about clothes and the best tailors. Then there was money: 'Whatever you may want, Downie will give you on my account. Take not a farthing from a black man.' Finally, essential for civil and military life in nineteenth century India, there was the matter of horses. Since the Haridwar Fair, William had been supplementing his income by horse dealing, one of his closest friends and trading partner being Nawab Ahmad Baksh Khan of Firozpur. He had already sent Aleck a couple of horses and 'in a few days I will send off for you my own buggy or curricle, which has never been used ... I had forgotten a Palanqueen, which you may either purchase readymade, or order a new one to be built for you, at any of the coachmakers in Calcutta'.

He left the most important piece of advice almost to the end: Aleck was to exercise moderation:

> Women, wine, and play ... are all dangerous, and in excess, death to mind and body; ruin to fortune, reputation, peace and health ... again and again, I repeat it, avoid, at the utmost, exposure to the Sun.

Finally, he promised to write daily; in return he needed regular letters with details of every part of Aleck's new life: 'your wishes, your wants and desires; how you feel yourself in health and situation, how you have been received, where you first rested, and every particular concerning you'.

Inevitably, Aleck did not receive this letter until some days after his arrival and so was unaware of the preparations made for him. When it caught up with him, however, he replied to William, 'my favourite of all my brothers', announcing his safe arrival and that of the horses, his residence with Aeneas Mackintosh, a prominent Calcutta businessman whose family came from Raigmore, just outside Inverness, and his firm refusal any of the money or presents offered. William urged him to reconsider: what was his was Aleck's ...

> ... for, I conceive, there exists as little difference between your funds and my funds, as there does between my right-hand and left-hand ... you talk of taking presents from me, that is nonsense; I cannot give you presents; there is a physical impossibility in the way; we were born Brothers.

William also suspected that the diffident Aleck was unlikely to elbow his way into the right areas of Calcutta society. He tried to smooth the path by sending a long list of people that Aleck should cultivate, adding optimistically:

> I have no doubt your own engaging manners and propriety of conduct will ensure you an honourable reception into every house, and all the genteel society in Calcutta.

At this point William's letter was interrupted by the exciting news that he was to leave immediately with the Mission to Kabul. This was 'another small part in the global conflict between Britain and France' and, as Aleck told his parents, 'an Embassy deemed of very high importance'.

In 1807 Napoleon had signed the Treaty of Tilsit with Tsar Alexander 1, which, for the moment, ended the war between Russia and the French empire. The Treaty was signed on a raft in the middle of the Nieman River,[10] under which, it was rumoured, a British spy was clinging. Word reached the ear of Lord Minto, then Governor-General, that the two emperors were plotting to divide British India between them, starting with invasion through Persia and Afghanistan. Whatever the source of the leak, Lord Minto took the

10 In present-day Lithuania.

threat seriously and, in the hope of blocking the invaders' path, planned to send missions to the various rulers between British India and Napoleon – to the Sikh leader, Ranjit Singh, in Lahore, to the Amir of Sind, to Shah Shuja in Kabul and to Fath Ali Shah in Teheran.

The Hon. Mountstuart Elphinstone was the man chosen to approach Shah Shuja (see Plate XII). Elphinstone was 'the most romantic of the empire builders',[11] a young man of thirty who had been in India since he was sixteen and already embarked on a brilliant political career. Aleck was convinced that his brother was perfect for Elphinstone's team:

> I have no doubt of William being particularly distinguished by him, as their qualities and dispositions are precisely similar, both being bold dashing characters with acute powers of mind, well fitted for conducting a negociation with a powerful, independent, and barbarous nation ... I need not say anything of Elphinstone as he is precisely William in, I believe, all points.

Enchanted by the prospect of adventure, William was only sorry that it would delay his reunion with Aleck. He repeated his caveat about excess of all kinds and exposure to the sun, but also carefully drew up a daily timetable for Aleck to follow. There was no excuse now. Aleck had at his fingertips all that was necessary for a young man seeking a successful career in the East India Company. But Aleck was already encountering distractions, as he wrote to his father:

> It is difficult to study here, every impediment that an enervating climate and general example can throw in your way, obstructs your progress. It requires no small fortitude to suppress all temptations, and to force all barriers to success.

From West to East

While William, in Delhi, was preparing for the journey to Kabul and Aleck was fending off temptation in Calcutta, James and Edward were finding life in Berbice even more of a struggle. The excitement of the American embargo and the hope of higher cotton prices had soon evaporated. Throughout 1809 the disastrous weather continued – heavy and incessant rain for weeks, followed by short bursts of intolerably hot and dry conditions. All over the colony spirits were low and tempers frayed. The slaves were miserably disheartened in the rain and cold, and whenever James turned his back Edward let them have a good long sleep.

Now that James's plan to return home was made, he was impatient to be gone and very irritable. Provokingly, he listed for Edward all the aspects of Berbice life that he would miss – especially the walks round the plantation, far more interesting, he declared, than any walk at Moniack could ever be. Edward with difficulty held his tongue; it was important to keep on good terms with James at all costs. 'This country,' he told his mother, 'must have some hidden charm in it which I never could yet discover.'

Although he was nearly twenty-three – old enough to stand on his own feet as a manager – he felt unprepared for it. To take his mind off all this he threw himself into preparations

11 *The Cornchest for Scotland: Scots in India* Alex M. Cain (1986) National Library of Scotland

for James's departure, writing to Jane Anne telling her what James would be bringing: some red and black beads, 'some very pretty feathers and seeds of flowers and a nest of a humming bird'. He worried that Caroline Gregoire would be offended at having no feathers, but perhaps James would share out the beads. There were also some tunes:

> They are very pretty but they are too difficult for poor me to play but I suppose you will think them quite easy ... you know you used to be so ignorant as to laugh at my fingering and I assure you, you would laugh still more now. I often wish, my dear 'Catty' that I had you here to put me into good spirits now and make me laugh as you used to do.

She would be amused by the black children, 'just like little monkeys'. There was his friend Cuffy, nearly three, who 'comes every day to breakfast to beg for a bone or a crust of bread ... indeed he is hardly ever out of the house at meals when he fights with the dogs (of whom we have a plentiful stock)'. He was including in James's luggage the skin of the neck of a flamingo, the skin of a rattlesnake, some sweetmeats including Guyana jelly, ginger and chocolate. There were also several copies of pieces of music, mainly Haydn, for his mother, and, for Miss Murray, a copy of *Paddy O'Rafferty*, her favourite Irish jig. The music would be rolled up in a piece of bamboo 'which will be a curiosity in itself'. The rest James was planning to pack in a bale of cotton, the only way to avoid the prohibitive duty.

Edward needed boots and shoes, which were expensive in Berbice and, because of the wet and mud, lasted no time. If only he could depend on James's 'memory and attention' he would ask him to send some things from Liverpool or Glasgow, 'but he would either forget altogether or do it in a slovenly sort of way by trusting somebody else to get it done'.

James had decided to take home with him two slaves, Black John and Toby. Knowing James's inability to look after himself, Edward agreed that they were an essential part of the venture: 'James will be the most helpless being in the world without [them] for the servants at home are not accustomed to serve in the way the blacks do.' Jane Anne must be good to the black boys for they had attended both Edward and James through several illnesses; she was not to laugh at their funny English or Toby's face 'all cut and marked after the fashion of his country in Africa'.

Knowing the uncivilised way that James behaved in Berbice, Edward worried that his parents would be offended by his habits: James might want to read a book at dinner or take his boots off in the drawing-room and throw himself full length on the sofa. He would undoubtedly find life at Moniack very correct and the neighbours, and even his parents, 'stiff formal beings'. He did not trust James to give his parents the right impression of life in Berbice – they were to believe 'half what James tells you of Berbice and half what I tell you and you may be near the truth'. James would, however, certainly want to hear his mother play the piano again and she had better start practising James's favourite Scottish airs: *The Land of the Leal* and *The Flowers of the Forest.*

Towards the end of March Edward wrote:

> … my spirits begin to fail – the day after tomorrow he leaves me – tho I daresay he will not sail for a week or more … this is a dismal day in all respects – James's going away and pouring down torrents of rain destroying everything.

Soon James, Toby and Black John were on their way, in a 'running ship',[12] James being too impatient to wait for the next fleet. In late May 1809 they arrived at Port Glasgow and James arranged an indenture for Toby:

> Toby Fraser of his own free will and accord hereby becomes bound as an Apprentice and servant to the said James Baillie Fraser … to serve as a footman or servant or any other lawfull employment … at all reasonable hours by night and day, honestly faithfully and obediently.

He was to abstain from gaming and vice and every species of immorality, while James was bound to feed him clothe him, pay medicines, doctors and surgeon's fees and provide 'all other necessaries suited to his station'. James signed the Deed and Toby put his X.

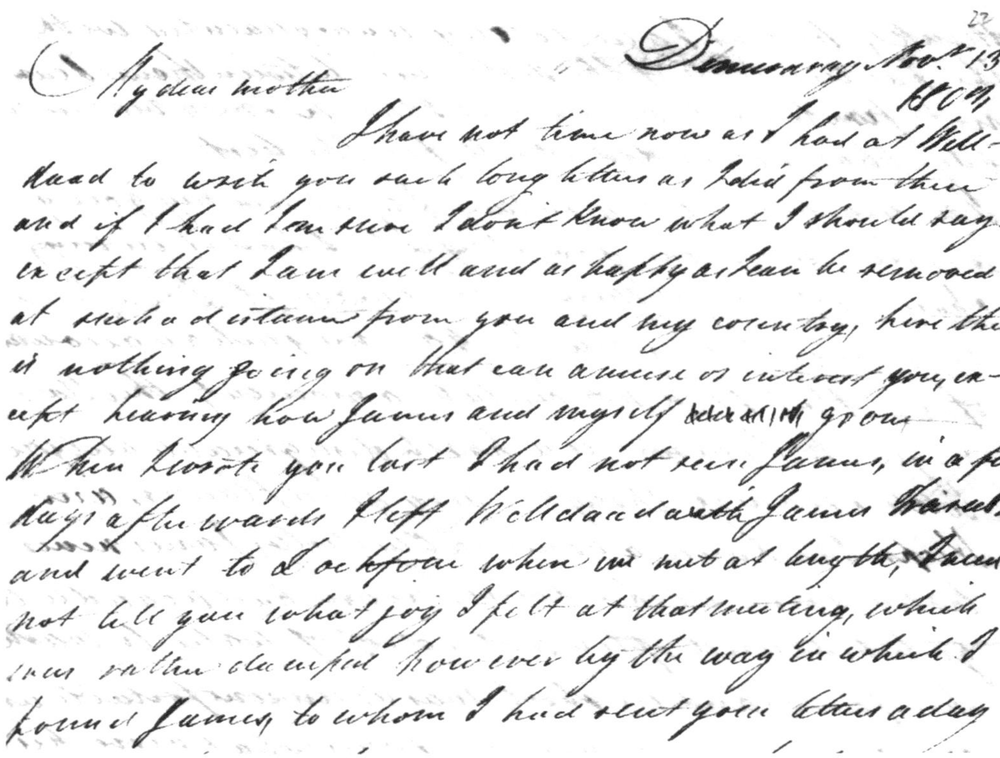

Demerary Novr 13th 1809

My dear mother

I have not time now as I had at Wellhead to write you such long letters as I did from there and if I had I am sure I don't know what I should say except that I am well and as happy as I can be removed at such a distance from you and my country, here there is nothing going on that can amuse or interest you except hearing how James and myself [illegible] grow. When I wrote you last I had not seen James, in a few days afterwards I left Wellclose with James Baird and went to Dochfour when we met at length, I can not tell you what joy I felt at that meeting, which was rather damped however by the way in which I found James, to whom I had sent your letters a day

A letter home from Edward.

Private collection

12 A ship sailing in time of war without a convoy.

Without James around the evenings dragged and Edward longed for his piano. Although Mrs Fraser allowed him to play it a little, she always quickly resumed the keys herself, mostly to play Haydn. She was 'such a critic and talks so much of having been taught by one of Haydn's scholars that she thinks nobody can play decently that has not had that advantage'. Perhaps Mrs Fraser would return it to him when she left. 'I have more pleasure in music and the study of it than anything in the world almost – I intend to make myself master of it wherever I have the opportunity – if I live.'

He was flattered to receive an early letter from James, sent at the first opportunity from Grenada, 'full of kindness and anxiety about my health'. Although he was missing his brother, the work was proving more interesting. As manager he no longer had to stand for hours watching the slaves at work. He could now take a daily ride or walk round the plantations, including No 27, whose manager he had suddenly become in a very bizarre fashion.

The former manager of No 27, a Mr Maynard, had had a dream in which he was visited by two bats, a good genius and a bad genius, fighting over his soul. The good genius, having won the battle, told Mr Maynard 'to go and make some alterations in the Christian religion'. Maynard thereupon arranged to go 'to propagate new doctrines in America' and offered his job to Edward; he wanted the best for his slaves and reckoned Edward would care well for them.

Edward was now finding it hard to keep track of all the 'separate and distinct things' he had to attend to. The inevitable book-keeping was 'a great Bore' which got in the way of his letter writing. He constantly fretted that he was not keeping up James's standards; he knew that he was not getting as much work out of the slaves. He felt, however, that they were behaving well for him:

> I have rarely to punish them, that is to flogg them – thanks to James's good discipline ... in which I am afraid he will find a falling off when he returns – but I cannot help it.

He always gave the slaves a morning in bed if they had had a very hard day previously and, unlike other managers, he let them have Sunday mornings off.

In June, Mrs Fraser finally departed for Scotland and Edward got his piano back. Music was his only comfort amid the general gloom of the colony during that disastrous year. The tiny crop from No 27 had not shipped in time for the good prices and there was no chance of picking more for six months – 'everything here [is] so gloomy and everyone in such low spirits at the misfortunes of this country ... if we have made no second crop we are ruined'.

The rain eventually stopped, only to be succeeded by drought and extreme heat, encouraging the mosquitoes, from which there was little respite. After dinner, the swarms made it impossible to sit reading or play the piano. How different from his memories of walks at Moniack, when it was:

> ... delightfull in returning from James's or William's walk to observe the setting sun and then when darkness drives you home, how pleasant the inside of the house and a little cheerful chat or music before supper.

By now he was resigned to loneliness: the only way to save money was neither to accept nor issue invitations, when people's only desire was 'to be filled as full of wine as they can hold'. He had not met anyone local 'whose pursuits or whose dispositions was at all similar to my own'. His contemporary William Macpherson from Blairgowrie was too far away for regular contact.

Edward Shaw, son of the Moniack old retainer, was still helping, but Donald Noble had gone elsewhere; this in many ways was a relief as he was not good with the slaves. Edward still stuck to his theory that however well one treated them they owed their masters nothing:

> I do not believe that there ever exists any sincere ... attachment between negroes and their masters, nor do I think that the negroes owe that attachment even to the kindest of masters ... nobody will agree with me – both James and James Fraser have argued the point with me – but you know I am as obstinate as a mule in matters of opinion and do not easily give up my own.

James, en route for Moniack, stopped off in Edinburgh; he spoke rapturously of his cousins and it was apparent that the musical Jeanie Tytler had won his favour. Edward was cynical: 'he seems all of a sudden to have grown fond of music'. Later he admitted that Jeanie had 'all the softness and feminine manners that a woman ought to have ... and is withal clever, spirited and animated as much as any female should be – and not a bit too much'.

Once home, after the obligatory social visits, James posted all over the country consulting his father's advisers and finding out for himself the true extent of the financial disaster that seemed about to engulf Moniack. Having, as he thought, got to the bottom of the story, he spent another week at home, sat to Raeburn in Edinburgh (see Plate II) and then raced to Liverpool, shouting instructions over his shoulder to his parents about 'retrenchment'. He probably also dropped hints that his parents might point the Gregoires tactfully in the direction of France; four fewer mouths to feed would help. He had, however, touched the heart of Eliza, who burst into tears when he said goodbye. She wrote from Moniack that she constantly wore the necklace he had brought her and trusted that 'it will prove a talisman that will make us meet once more in this land of kindness'.

Despite Edward's fears, Reelig seemed satisfied with the way James had turned out:

> His mind is elegantly and nobly tuned. His manners are mild and pleasing tho not courtly and his disposition is sweet and ingratiating ... he will be a popular character but deservedly so. He has been to his parents tractable, obedient, attentive and dutiful ... he has no feeling of separate interest – he considers ... all of us as one ... this will bind ye all in true fraternity.

Armed at last with the true facts of the financial situation at Moniack, James arrived back in Berbice early in 1810, prepared to give Guyana one more year before going home, probably for good. He was full of energy, optimism and plans for a new business – making hemp from plantain. It was clear that his father needed an assistant from among his sons; if he could leave everything in Guyana on such a footing that Edward could run it easily, he could be that assistant. Edward was not convinced by this plan, but there was no gainsaying his brother: 'He has set his heart on it and it is wonderfull how one finds ways and means and excuses to do a thing they have at heart'. Nor was Edward optimistic about hemp: many people had tried it and all had given it up as a bad job. John Gladstone, who had been consulted in Liverpool, was also discouraging.

James certainly had reservations about Edward's ability to run the plantations. Discipline had become very lax and Edward 'has no idea of anything but conducts the Estate in the plainest way possible, and, if allowed to draw for every sum he wants, and to keep only in order what can be done without exertion to himself or the negroes, he would do very well, but this neither would do nor can it be done'. James was finding Edward more assertive and argumentative, and prepared to ask his father for money rather than to get into debt. 'I tell him that resource is Dry & cannot be reckoned one', to which Edward would answer that, in that case, they should give up the unequal struggle.

Since James's return, however, he had become, as far as Edward was concerned, 'an arrant scrub' (skinflint) when it came to catering: he refused to spend money on even 'eatables of the commonest kind', and Edward, for once, looked forward to dinner invitations; at home they had nothing but 'fish, salt beef, not a ham or a bit of poultry or sheep or anything or pease or barley to make soup'.

The piano had been sold. Edward was, once again, lost without 'the greatest source of amusement after writing [home]' but he had sold it well. He sometimes played the flute with James but was frustrated by James's impatience and lack of ear for music. 'James will never play well for he does not blow clean or equally and will not practise ... he begins a tune in one key and ends it in another or if I begin to whistle a tune he will accompany me in another key without seeming to hear the discord.' Eliza had hastily copied out some music for James to bring back, but mostly it was wrongly transcribed. Edward could, however, more easily identify the notes from her inaccurate copies than from James's attempt to sing the songs!

Toby, who had returned with James, had been a great success at Moniack, making himself very useful about the house. He enjoyed the family musical evenings, and Jane admired his dancing and his voice. Black John, however, had been left at Moniack, and Jane reported that he was very much missing his master and must therefore be very attached to James. Edward disagreed:

> I have no doubt that he likes his master better than he does most people ... but, if he was to return to this country with his master ... and if there was an insurrection among the negroes here I am sure he would just as soon see his master and me killed as not.'

He was, however, full of praise for the way that James cared for his slaves: 'It would do you good to see the care he takes of the sick and old people – and his tenderness even to the children'.

With James back, Edward had more time; whenever James was away he tried to create a little flower garden round the house. It was mostly grass and weeds 'and it is unpardonable in this country to have it so because the flowers grow so fast that you have to keep down the weeds for a very short time', but 'I think it is [right] when one has the prospect of remaining several years in a place to make it as comfortable as one can.' Behind James's back, he could steal slave labour from the fields to help him, but James grudged the time spent on such a frivolity, unless the slaves used their precious Sunday mornings.

By now the hemp project had, predictably, failed and James had got hold of a new idea, the possibility of growing a plant that produced a valuable dye selling for 4/6 a pound in England from 'Cayan' (Cayenne), down the coast in French Guiana. He was very restless, and Edward was finding him hard to live with: 'He seldom lets me rest long enough to write a letter except by pieces'. It was something of a relief to Edward when he went off to consult friends on the Corentyne coast.

In April the welcome news came that William had sent £2,000 as a 'stopgap as you call it', which removed for a year the prospect of losing Moniack. The Gregoire family, moreover, were planning to return to France in the autumn which would lessen the domestic outgoings. Their departure was sad, though, for Jane Anne, who would miss Governess Emilia, and for Jane, who would miss the bustle of a full house. What was more, George, now aged ten, was being detached from his mother's and Nanny's apron strings. He was sent to Achnagairn, all of two miles away, to join the children there for some kind of schooling and discipline while future plans for his education were considered.

In May all plans in Berbice went awry. James again became seriously ill with fever and Edward, not trusting anyone else to administer the medicines correctly, sat up with him night after night. He wrote to his mother from the bedside 'to keep my attention more alive during the long dreary hours of the night'. Although James recovered fairly soon from that bout, the fever returned from time to time, and in the autumn the two brothers took time off on the coast to recuperate.

❧

By November 1810 it seemed, once more, that there was no hope for Moniack: John Gladstone in Liverpool was 'pushing for his money'. Edward had privately been preparing himself for this news. He was amazed at James's optimism in the face of disaster. 'James says he will never give up hope of purchasing it ... this idea keeps up his spirits a little ... [but I] am almost broken-hearted about it'. Could his parents not let it for six or seven years and live somewhere else where there might be the chance of a better job for his father?

James finally forced himself to face facts: there was no point in pretending that Moniack could be saved as things stood, since £8,000 was needed by February and 'where are two to come from?' Nothing but the direct intervention of God could save it. Meanwhile, they would stay in Berbice awaiting the better times that must surely come.

⁂

But the 'better times' were not just around the corner; by the beginning of 1811 Edward was writing, 'I do believe James begins to be as heartily tired of this country as ever I was.' In fact, he was wrong. After Edward eventually went home, leaving James alone, James's letters were full of unhappiness at the thought of leaving – 'the negroes I suppose,' commented Edward, 'for to the soil or the country he surely can have no attachment'. This was an understatement. James had tried so hard to make it work for his father and felt bitter disappointment at its failure. He was reluctant to abandon all his schemes but 'matters here are now too desperate to hesitate ... I have advised my father and will again to sell', but not yet. Eight estates were coming up for sale in the next six months and would most likely go for only a quarter of their value.

Charles Grant advised Reelig 'to [wash] our hands of the slave trade'; plans were made for Edward to return home in the spring while James stayed to hand over control of the estate and put things in order for an eventual sale. He would then join Edward at Moniack for a long holiday before they sailed to India together.

When Edward left James missed him deeply – 'my only society, my chief comfort'. Before he, too, could go home there was, however, 'a most unpleasant sett of difficulties' to be faced. He would sell all he could – a few sheep, a cow or two, a horse, some furniture, 'but oh what teasing I shall have to pay actual debts'. He derived comfort, however, from the thought that the four brothers would soon be together in India and before that there would be a happy winter at Moniack with 'readings & talkings & tellings of all we heard & all we saw'.

He was also looking forward to visiting the Tytlers. He had been excited to get a recent letter from Jeanie 'but ere I had got on two sentences my wonder ceased'. Jeanie only had her mother's permission to write to James on condition that it was between 'affectionate cousins'. Although there was no possibility of a future with Jeanie on account of the family misfortunes, James was resolved to continue the correspondence.

As Edward guessed, James was desperately worried about the fate of his slaves: few plantation owners who would care for them as he and Edward had. He confided to his journal:

> It will cost me more than one pang to say to myself 'No 28 – habitation where I have passed seven years ... I shall see you no more – negroes whom I love & consider as my children & friends ... who all look up to me for redress or happiness – no more shall I see ye do so – I bid you a long farewell – and when we 'meet at compt' will you then acknowledge me and ... testify for me.

He was right to be worried. His attorney, Lewis Cameron, had appointed a manager, James McDougall, to run the estate when James eventually left. McDougall was a man of 'violent passions', only engaged because he was a knowledgeable planter. Trouble was taken to train him in the ways of slaves and to warn him to control his temper and, for a time, all went well. But in a letter to Reelig in June 1812, Cameron described what happened one day when he was away on business. McDougall took the opportunity '(from motives which I can only conjecture) to ill-treat two invalid negroes, Willitick & his wife Dobie together with their three children (one a girl about 12 or 13) in a most Wanton and Cruel manner'. Willitick was beaten to the ground and flogged. Dobie was tied on the ground between two poles and left there for two hours (according to McDougall; eyewitnesses maintained it was four). She was then flogged and put in the stocks. Two days later both received this treatment again. Their terrified daughter left her work to plead on their behalf, whereupon she was flogged, along with her two younger brothers. McDougall's excuse for this barbarity was the insolence of Willitick and Dobie 'which all the Negroes present contradict & very improbable it is, because very inconsistent with the character of the helpless man with whom this treatment commenced'.

McDougall was dismissed and Cameron resigned. Perhaps, he thought, he should have brought the matter before the Fiscal:

> ... but the man is punished more than I could wish by a dismissal as he will not find it easy to procure another employ. I am very sensible how necessary it is to support proper order & discipline amongst negroes but the facts that I have related are very wide of my ideas on that subject.

Whether Reelig recounted this story to James is not clear, but as James never referred to it in letters or his Journal, he was probably spared the agony of knowing.

Three years later, James looked back on the morning he left the plantation just as the sun was rising over the cotton fields:

> I have not yet forgot the pain of it; when I stole away from my own house, secretly through the plantain walk, that I might not have any more painfull farewells for my unfortunate negroes and old servants.

5

1808–1810

Mission to Kabul

When Aleck arrived in Calcutta 'the cold North East wind of this season blowing off the snowy mountains of Thibet and Tartary' made the air delightfully cool. Before starting his studies, he bravely made contact with William's friends the Fultons, who took him on a river excursion. In the country he attended a *nautch*, but this was second-rate compared to the expensive ones in Calcutta: 'It is not uncommon for a Native to give one or two thousand rupees to a dancing Girl for exhibiting one night. This almost equals Madame Catalanie.'[1]

Back in Calcutta, eager to send presents home, he was beguiled by the rich assortment of fabrics to be haggled over at every corner. Mrs Fulton helped him choose shawls for his mother and Miss Murray and muslins for his sisters. Knowing about colour and quality, she laughed at his choice of thin white material for his mother – 'I thought ... that thinness was a good quality, but was assured that they were valued according to their thickness'. They eventually settled on a thick plain black one and another, scarlet and flowery.

Some months later, however, he wrote:

> I fear that the little parcel, which I sent you by the *Calcutta,* containing two shawls, and a few pieces of muslin, is *lost* as that ship (my own as it bore me to India) is not heard of. Much do I regret poor Maxwell. It was to be his last voyage after a rough life.

On 14 March 1809 *Calcutta*, with Captain Maxwell on his final command, went down off Mauritius along with three other East Indiamen, all lost without trace.[2]

Inevitably, Aleck was soon deeply in debt and after some months the amusements of Calcutta, especially the balls, were losing their charm. He had never been one for dances 'but here, I think, they are superlatively stupid'. There were too many people and 'indeed I feel no enjoyment in a dance unless I have some regard for the girls I dance with which I think will never be the case here, at least while the memory of the Scotch lasses continues as fresh in my mind as it is at present'.

Aware of the temptations around him and his own weaknesses, he wrote touchingly to his father a few months after his arrival:

1 Angelica Catalani (1780–1849), renowned Italian opera singer.
2 *East Indiamen*, Cotton and Fawcett, The Batchworth Press, 1949.

> All I can promise you as yet is my Endeavour not to disgrace your name; and to justify your kindness, and liberality in my education. At the same time, it is no easy task to undertake; and I fear people will sometimes ask, with some surprise, if this is a son of Reelick's? Indeed, it is the only title, which as ever, as yet, procured me a kind, or a pleasant reception; and I am perhaps more pleased with it, than if it were for my own sake.

Elphinstone's Mission to Kabul set off in mid-October 1808. Accompanying him were a Secretary, two Assistants, one of whom was William, a Surgeon, two Surveyors and eight Officers in charge of the escort of four hundred men. The colourful, chaotic column of elephants, camels, horses and men stretched for two miles.

Once embarked on the long trek, William had hoped to write to Aleck daily, but as they normally made camp late at night after an early morning start, he had 'neither the means, nor the power of writing to anyone'. However, he told Aleck he was writing a daily journal but 'you must never expect very accurate or detailed accounts, in long flowing sentences, and finely tuned periods'. Even when they stopped for a few days, William's writing was constantly interrupted; he always made himself completely available to the local people and sometimes let them sit in his tent from dusk till dawn. Moreover, the postal system,[3] the *dawk* or *dak*, was not secure, and the further they travelled the more it deteriorated. One packet for William was stuffed with straw, the next was torn to pieces and in the third there was only 'the envelope of a letter ... the *dawks* are constantly rifled and nothing now is safe'.

Despite all these hazards, Aleck received around sixty letters from William during the year or so of the expedition. Aleck's letters to William have not survived. In March 1809 William complained he had had no word for nearly two months. If Aleck were ill he would have heard from Downie, so he mistakenly attributed Aleck's silence to serious application to his studies.

Aleck certainly did write to William, and to his parents, but owing to his absent-mindedness things often went wrong. Sometimes he folded his letters '*broad* and in the European way' instead of rolling them up. Sometimes he wrote on the spur of the moment and put the letter away until it could be sent, but then forgot it. Another letter 'owing to some unaccountable neglect ... was not even finished; and, a few days ago, happening to open a large Blotting Paper book, I found it, sheet by sheet, safe in its folds'. There was also censorship to contend with and, for letters home, the ever-present risk of ships disappearing en route, victims of French privateers or shipwreck.

Aleck was considered the luckiest of all the young men who were 'on thorns whilst the fleet is momentarily expected ... People here live on Europe letters'. When a ship arrived the constant refrain was 'How many letters have you?' Aleck almost always won this competition and was also confident that 'in interest of matter and subject, none could compare with mine. The arrival of a fleet here, seems to revive the whole settlement ... every one is wrapt up in his letters.'

3 Originating in the fourteenth century, this consisted of relays (usually ten miles apart) of men on foot or horseback with the mail in leather bags.

Often Reelig would enclose his correspondence in a bundle of newspapers, and the letters that most pleased Aleck were those containing chitchat, tiny domestic details and news of his parents' health. Like Edward, he found writing home one of his greatest joys:

> I have been so completely at home, since I took my pen to write to you, that I have baffled the rage of the mosquitoes, who are generally intolerable at this late hour ... My lights (which are here all of Oyl made from the Cocoanut) are now warning me to leave off by their failure, and my old favourite Highland terrier, yclept[4] 'Smeorach' by me, and by the vulgar, 'Murphy' is retired to his box of *Sunn*, or Hemp which I provide for him in the cold weather.

He was constantly frustrated by the six-month time lag in correspondence 'for there are a thousand remarks and queries and observations which I could wish to answer instantly'. Letters from India were passed eagerly from hand to hand, first among the family and then to friends and neighbours. Aleck usually ended his letters with an account of the health and progress of the many 'Invernessmen' whose paths he crossed.

His letters reveal the same easy, confident, open but respectful relationship with his parents as had all his brothers and sisters:

> I know people who when they write their parents, think it necessary to buckram their whole letters with copious phrases of respect and veneration; and not to write a sentence or a word, without previous cautious study. But I am of opinion, that where real affection is, respect will come of course and I had rather you should see my sentiments in their naked undisguised state, than assume those that I have not, though they might be graver and more correct.

He periodically forwarded William's letters to his parents, although as the letters became longer this became more difficult. At Aeneas Mackintosh's request he also passed them to the local Calcutta newspaper, but William remonstrated: 'It would be very disagreeable and disadvantageous to me, if a report was spread that I conveyed to public papers any particulars relative to the mission or to the country through which we passed'.

❊

The previous year, William had hatched a plan to take over half his father's debts. Meanwhile, Aleck was instructed to remit £50 to Scotland every three months from William's salary, until he was in a position to make his own contribution. William reckoned 'the struggle will be nothing, when got the better of; and the Sacrifice will be a feast of enjoyments'.

Aleck feared his father would never accept such a scheme. William was determined:

> Next to my Parents, my brothers and sisters, and my near relations, *that Property* is the dearest tie to me upon earth – and to preserve which, I would spend my heart's blood. If my Father were to lose that property, he would be most wretched ... To save Moniack ... is what I wish to do; what I ought to do; and what must be done.

4 'called' – Middle English and obsolete.

He still owed large sums but was confident that another year would see him in the clear. The debt hanging over Moniack was in the region of £30,000 and as far as William could see, 'the only chance of salvation is from our exertions in this country. Let me tell you, that two persons determined to make that sum, would very soon accomplish the task'. Waiting to cross the Indus, he allowed himself a moment to daydream:

> How I should enjoy now one year of home! Thank God the prospect though distant is distinct to both of us. My dearest Aleck, were we two to go home with fortunes and James and Edward also to retire with the usual Demerary success, what a place we would make Moniack! It must be wonderfully improved since I left it, now just 8 years, and at that time, who would have believed I should now be some thousand pounds in debt or otherwise than independent. We used to talk of ten years residence in the East and West and of then returning with a fortune. What illusion!

Sending this letter home, Aleck added a comforting postscript:

> Is it not pleasing to see him on the banks of the Indus recurring still continually to home? And in the bustle of business constantly revolving in his mind the means of making his relations and himself finally comfortable in our own dear country.

Meanwhile, as William's march took him further westward, he wanted a picture of Aleck. He recommended Middleton, a miniaturist in Calcutta:

> To him you must go immediately, I entreat you, and sit for your miniature; that I may have a good copy of the *fair* original, before the bloom of Scotland's mountains be supplanted by the brown of Bengal.

He periodically reminded Aleck of this request, but there is no record that Mr Middleton ever had the pleasure of painting Aleck's 'Fraser face', as a family friend later called it. Meanwhile, Aleck was not to entrust to the *dawk* the family miniatures painted for William in Edinburgh. Aleck confessed to his mother, however, that in the rush of leaving London he had left these behind in Russell Square. Mrs Grant had kindly packed them up and entrusted them to the 'more careful hand' of Aleck's old rival, Holt Mackenzie, who brought them safely as far as Ceylon, but there they were stolen. Aleck, considering them extremely bad, was greatly relieved.

William warned Aleck that his own appearance had changed:

> At present I am certain you could never recognise me so altered am I in face, colour and person, which with the addition of a very respectable pair of whiskers on the upper lip, gives me more the appearance of a Turk than of a Highlander ... one or two of our party have gone the length of preserving their beards also. This is however, a step too far and I condemn it.

Two later portraits of William show him with a very respectable beard.

Absolute Monarch of the North

The march to Afghanistan was everything William could have wished: it was uncomfortable, adventurous and dangerous. The first part, across the desert and plains to the Indus river, was familiar; once across the Indus, however, in unknown territory he was entranced with the scenery: roaring torrents, snowy mountains, fertile plains, primitive villages. There were many setbacks – regular attacks from brigands, camels with precious loads tumbling off narrow mountain paths and, nearing Peshawar, the winter capital of Shah Shuja, torrential rain.

Quite early on, the progress of the Mission was slowed down by the fact that the expected *mehmendhar*,[5] the escort from Shah Shuja, had not yet arrived, and William was disappointed that they would not reach Peshawar until the spring: 'I wished to pass the month of January 1809, midst the snow and frost and *skating* of Cabool.'

In the New Year, encamped for several weeks at Dera Ismael Khan, about 100 miles south of Peshawar, there was time for letter writing. Sometimes William loosed off five a week, frustrated in his longing for details of Aleck's life:

> Do you ever see Edmonstone? Are you intimate with Matthew Lumsden and his brother? Do you go much about in the evening to those hateful public routs? Are you a great Philander? And how many times have you been in love since your arrival in Calcutta? Are you fond of riding? Are you fond of idleness? ... At what family houses are you most intimate? In short, what is your life in Calcutta? And what do you think of a Calcutta life? Of Indian society, customs and manners?

He mused to Aleck on the subject of marriage in general and on Charemile Grant in particular:

> What do you think of Charemile? And would not she make me a good wife? And marry me? Not that I think that can or is ever likely to happen ... but she is the only woman, of whom I have a recollection, to whom I would unseen & unknown unite myself ... I would not marry a woman, of whose mental endowments I had not the best opinion; and this I had of the lady in question.

He worried about Aleck's progress and reiterated his three precepts: learn the Oriental languages, get to know the local population and take every chance to associate with the 'most intelligent, well informed, respectable members of your Calcutta society'. There was little evidence, however, that Aleck was attending to any of these.

At last the escort arrived, and once again William was reminded of home:

> We were met by a hundred of the King's Cavalry, the commander of which bore a letter from His Majesty, to our Envoy ... the man who bore the letter dismounted as did also the Envoy ... Mr Elphinstone, having received it ... stuck it in his hatband

5 An official courier appointed to escort an important traveller.

> [and] carried it thus into Camp, as our Burgesses, you recollect it, when they receive the freedom of the Royal Burgh of Inverness.

Passing Kohat as they approached Peshawar, they travelled through a welcoming fertile valley where William was delighted to find 'European' trees, shrubs and flowers:

> Plane, sycamore, plumb, apricot, willow, palm willow, water cresses ... clover, plaintain grass and some others. The stream ... flows through several Gardens and its sides are decked with these English trees and plants, which put us all so much in mind of home.

Escorted thus in splendour by the *mehmendhar*, on 25 February 1809 the Mission arrived in Peshawar. Three days later, however, 'we are still in confinement in our house, as we have not as yet been introduced to the King; and the time is not yet settled, as the ceremonies have not been quite adjusted'. Apparently, no envoy had ever sat down in the presence of the King of Kabul; it was pointed out to him that sitting was acceptable in all European and most Asiatic courts, 'but His Majesty does not seem to be of the same opinion, and the matter is still in suspence'.

The matter remained in suspense for two weeks until one night they were woken and told to be up by six, ready to go to the Palace at eight. Inevitably, however, it started to rain again:

> ... after waiting *in armour* until eleven o'clock, a messenger arrived from His Majesty saying that since the forenoon had turned out to unpropitious, our introduction would be postponed until another day.

William, meanwhile, was impressed by neither their accommodation nor the town:

> The house is miserable in appearance, and reality, and either fire or water would destroy us ... nothing more than a jumble of mud walls dancing in all directions ... and not a street, or stone building to be seen. For mere exercise we are obliged to walk up and down on the roof, morning and evening; and the tops of all the neighbouring houses, walls, and trees, are crowded with people gazing at us.

But when the rain stopped, there was the compensation of a view:

> From the roof of our house the hills looked this evening most sublime; magnified by the still floating mists; and joining in with rich fantastic clouds gilded by the setting sun; their rough outline and the successive ranges displayed a magnificence I have not frequently seen equalled.

The discussions on protocol dragged tediously on. There was 'no amusement', and William, who had brought with him more books than anyone but Elphinstone, had finished them all. Totally unused to inactivity, he was thankful that he had his journal and letters to write. He had mostly stopped attending meals, since among the fifteen or sixteen people he reckoned that there was only one intelligent and well informed individual – the Envoy himself, with whom he was not getting on: '[we] are now like poker and tongs on opposite sides of the fireplace'.

Eventually, some sort of compromise was reached and the members of the Mission received detailed instructions on how they were to conduct themselves – they were allowed to wear their boots provided they covered them on entering the Palace – and how to behave in the presence:

> We take off our hats three times with a bow, and then joining our hands, as if to catch or take water, hold them up before the lower part of the face; say silently a short prayer for the King; and make the show of stroking our beards; after which we walk up into the hall, and stand almost on a level with the King, in a line down the room: the Envoy being close to him; the King is then to ask a few questions of our country, and the King of England, to which, I daresay, he will receive ready coined answers. He is then to look at his presents, of which he is to express his approval, and shortly after we retire. The Envoy is then to be admitted to a private audience when he is to be permitted to sit in the presence of his Majesty; and then the Ceremony will end.

On 6 March the huge procession, sepoys, rocket boys, flag bearers, macebearers, *hircarrahs*[6] followed by the Envoy and the 'gentlemen of the embassy', the cavalry and fifty irregular horsemen and finally, bringing up the rear, the presents, proceeded through the narrow, muddy streets crowded with spectators. At the entrance to the great fortress, the Bala Hisar, they passed Shah Shuja's armed troops, 'a miserable rabble, no two armed or dressed alike', sitting on the ground and, beyond a vacant stare, paying no attention to the spectacle passing them. They eventually reached the hall of audience, a long court with fish tanks down the middle and fountains playing. At the end there were two storeys open to the air, with a pavilion on the upper floor. A dome covered the pavilion marking 'the seat of Majesty' and under it, on an elevated throne of gilt wood, sat the King, magnificently clothed and laden with jewels. He was, according to Elphinstone, 'a handsome man, about thirty years of age, of an olive complexion, with a thick black beard'.[7]

The embassy lined up at the end of the court and, as rehearsed, removed their hats three times, raised their hands to their faces, 'muttered something supposed to be a prayer' and stroked their beards. They were then introduced by one of the King's officers: 'This is Mr E Furingee,[8] the ambassador, God bless him', and so on down the line. Some of the names – Cunningham, McCartney, Fitzgerald – were too much for him and he was soon blurting out 'any sound that struck him'. Dead silence fell for a long minute broken by the stentorian voice of the King:

> *Khosh Amuded* ... you are welcome. On receiving this satisfactory assurance, we were again directed to lift our hands in humble prayer for the health of the monarch.

They then moved ten paces forward and, after another long silence, the King shouted '*killu*' – an order for honorary dresses. Off came their hats again and they all proceeded to

6 Courier, spy.

7 *An Account of the Kingdom of Caubul*, The Hon Mountstuart Elphinstone, (1815) London & (1998) Munshiram Manoharlal, New Delhi.

8 European or foreigner.

another part of the court, where more prayers were said. Another silence. Then the King asked after the health of His British Majesty and how long the mission had been on the road. The next lengthy silence was broken by the King's assertion that the British and his nation had always been on the best terms, which he trusted would endure.

Hats off again, and everyone but Elphinstone and his Secretary were ushered away. The Governor General's letter was then delivered to which the King 'was pleased to give the most gracious replies and flattering assurances'. They all then put on their honorary dresses and rode home.

⁂

During the audience William never took his eyes off the King. His excitement about coming face to face with the 'Absolute Monarch of the North' rings out from the twelve pages he wrote to Aleck the next day, later carefully copied into his father's letterbook with the significant episodes proudly marked, before it went the rounds of neighbours and friends.

It was extraordinarily detailed; the King's eyelashes and eyelids were 'blackened with antimony' and he sat erect, legs doubled under him, hands resting on his thighs and elbows sticking out. 'This is the posture which fierce independent fellows assume generally ... such as I have seen [Charles James] Fox assume in the House of Commons when preparing to rise and thunder his invective against corrupt ministers'. The spot they were standing on was 'where public demands are executed and where justice receives his sanction ... My eyes rested at the ground by my feet ... it was stained with blood.'

The King's hexagonal crown was adorned with black heron's feathers – the 'mark of God's chosen upon earth'. It was smothered in enormous emeralds, rubies and pearls, as were his collar, bracelets and clothes – so much so that he seemed rather 'stout and squat; but this probably arose from the nature of this dress which was thick and heavy, with the superadded bulk of a load of jewels'.

The account continues with descriptions of the honorary dress and gifts presented to Elphinstone, the courtiers' appearance, dress and weapons. Shah Shuja had insisted on full ceremony, and William was 'particularly struck with 'the dignity of his appearance and romantic Oriental awe which his situation, person and Majesty impressed on me'.

Writers' buildings

Meanwhile, Aleck had left the safe haven provided by Aeneas Mackintosh for which he was extremely grateful:

> His house is the resort of all the young men in Calcutta, that are worth associating with ... and I do assure you, it raised my spirits, associating with the Heroes to whom we owe the half of Hindostan, the Officers who served in Lord Lake's victorious army ... in short, had it not been for my acquaintance with him, I might have gone to the Devil long ago.

He now felt he needed more freedom and followed William's footsteps to Writers' Buildings, optimistic that he could at last start working hard and save some money. William flatly disagreed:

> The buildings are a very bad place for the restless and impatient, the unsteady or animated ... there is dissipation, idleness, frivolity, waste of time, lounging, unsteadiness, temptation to idleness, constant interruption, the breaking in of wild and idle young men, making others idle ... The moment I came into Buildings, I became a vagabond and wild ... I would press you to leave the Buildings notwithstanding the addition of expense.

He was right to be concerned. Aleck moved in with a shipmate from *Calcutta,* the Eurasian James Curtis, an Inverness alderman's nephew, who already had a considerable establishment, the cost of which Aleck had to share:

> My chum ... and myself have between us upward of sixty people ... I have before mentioned no one of these Gentlemen will, on any consideration, do the work of another. A Bearer will rather die than carry away an empty tumbler, after you have drank the water he brought you in it ... I'd rather have gawky Sandy our stable boy than the whole set of them.

William would have preferred Aleck to chum with someone more his equal in intellect: why not Holt Mackenzie, who had now caught up with Aleck in Calcutta and had, inevitably, come top in the recent exam? 'Who is James Curtis?' he asked crossly. 'If he is good and quiet it seems all that can be said of him; his class rank speaks not for him; and I fear his praise must be negative'.

Much later, the disillusioned Aleck confessed the expense of his stay in Writers' Buildings. It turned out to be a trap from which he could not easily extricate himself without letting down his companion, in whose confused affairs he became inevitably involved.

⁂

James Curtis did his best to initiate Aleck into all that was on offer in the Buildings, but without much success. He introduced him to a set of hearty sportsmen: 'never did I see such low shameless and disgusting profligacy less graced by any redeeming or tolerable qualification'. Their principal conversation was 'Horses and Hounds', punctuated with smutty jokes and 'details of their many valiant exploits in beating their servants &c'.

One of the drawbacks of having rooms in the Buildings was the arrival of young men who needed a friendly sofa while they waited for a room of their own. One such was James Fraser from Achnagairn and Aleck's less than encouraging report of him was presumably heavily edited by Jane before being delivered across the fields to his mother:

> James Fraser Achnagairn is I fear, in no very good course of conduct, or Circle of Society. He is ambitious of being considered a Buck, and becomes ridiculous to all parties ... His health has been pretty good and had he been less careless, would have been excellent, but his frequent unnecessary and indeed almost willful exposure to the sun, has lately subjected him to an attack of Bile, which a smart application of purgatives has now repelled.

Aleck could not refuse James the use of his sofa but, with a year's experience of Calcutta behind him, explained why he could in no way influence the new arrival:

> Your young friend James Fraser is sleeping on his couch beside me while I am writing this ... in supposing that *my* advice or guidance could be of any service to him you mistook both of us. In the first place, when a young man arrives here, he is so entirely his own Master ... that he ... spurns any advice or counsel, especially from an equal ... you mistake in supposing me capable to be anywise an advisor to him. He has really much more prudence than I have, and I think likely to get on better in every way. I do not indeed think he will study or distinguish himself in college but he will fully avail himself of the very numerous introductions he has to the first people here, and get into excellent society which is everything.

James stayed for two weeks – 'no slight annoyance on my quiet grave habits'. Aleck then introduced him to Aeneas Mackintosh, 'as the best service I could render him'. Experienced in the ways of teenagers released into the temptations of Calcutta, Mackintosh was far more optimistic than Aleck about the prospects of young Achnagairn.

Excursions on the river and sport, especially hoghunting, provided Aleck with welcome diversions. William had given him Eclipse, a horse which 'has not his parallel in India for viciousness, and goodness' (see Plate X), along with a favourite servant who kept Aleck entertained with anecdotes about William. Eclipse accompanied Aleck on most of his travels in India and was several times wounded while hoghunting. He was painted by a Calcutta artist in 1814, and the watercolour is inscribed:

> Eclipse purchased for me at Haridwar in April 1808 ... has since then twice accompanied me to Delhi, and twice back to Calcutta. Killed in two successive mornings, with his assistance, ten wild boars, in March 1812. He was severely wounded by a boar in January 1814. Since which time I have not rode him.

William knew that Aleck would be unlikely to resist the attractions of hunting, although he naïvely hoped that Aleck had 'neither Dog nor Gun':

> Did I hear you mention the word 'snipe'? I should not have a moment's peace, till I saw you; and I am afraid to write 'hoghunting' lest the word should put the desire into your head.

Faint hope indeed, for in the spring of that year Aleck described an adventure on a shooting expedition which threw William into a paroxysm of rage; he snatched up his pen:

> I cannot say that I have ever felt equal uneasiness or distress, to that which the perusal of your last letter gave me ... the single fact of your having been out in the sun, in *jeel*,[9] or one of the banks of the river, snipe and duck shooting, and that

9 Stagnant water.

> too in the middle of the day, has given me greater pain, than had I learnt you had been expelled the College and sent home.

Ironically, in the light of future events, he asked how Aleck would feel if 'I was unnecessarily, and with inconsiderate rashness, to place myself in the way of certain and positive danger, and probable death'.

> What in God's name could have tempted you, or inclined you to be a whole day out in the sun ... I have misspent time, I have run into all manner of extravagance and folly ... but I always had sufficient control over my desires and passions, to resist the allurements of every amusement, which might endanger my health, and by doing so the permanent happiness of my family ... You say there was no danger in the amusement although you was out from morning to night ... Was there no danger when you got into the quicksand? What in God's name led you to shoot on the banks of the river?

To pacify William, Aleck enthusiastically but misguidedly described the other, less hazardous, activities he was enjoying. This brought on another tirade:

> You talk of lounging at a Billiard table, an auction room and shops – this I call, positively not only lost time, but misspent time. At the first you can learn nothing, but an idle and unprofitable game, and besides generally see bad company, loose manners and men debased to the lowest state of humanity. At the two last you waste time, without obtaining the least information, and generally throw away some money ... I am at a loss to conceive how you, with such a mind, and talents ... can lounge about in shops, billiard rooms and auctions.

Peshawar

Still confined in cramped steamy muddy quarters in Peshawar, the crotchety William had very little else to do but write lengthy letters. Negotiations were continuing and a treaty with the King was on the point of completion when the news came that Kandahar had fallen to the King's half-brother and arch rival, Shah Mahmoud Khan. A month later, Kabul also fell to the rebels, who then prepared an attack on Shah Shuja in Peshawar.

Who was now King, and whether the treaty just signed with Shah Shuja held good, were matters of dispute. Shah Shuja was anxious for British protection but it daily became clearer how tenuous was his hold on the throne. Meanwhile, the members of the mission divided their time between research and relaxing in the King's pleasure gardens. Never much one for the company of his peers, William longed to get out among the villages to investigate the lives 'of the mass of the common people'. For the moment, however, this had to be suppressed while he waited for the next move in the uncomfortable, crowded house in Peshawar, where the rain continued most days and even if it stopped, the hottest season of the year was approaching. William realised that there was now little hope of seeing Kabul but daydreamed about a springtime trip to 'Cashgar ... and coming back by the hills to the north of Cashmeer'. The very word 'Cashgar'[10] took him straight home to Moniack and the stories from *The Arabian Nights* that had so stimulated his childhood fancy. He shared this with Aleck:

> Do you not recollect the purveyor to the Sooltan of Cashgar, being mentioned in the Arabian Nights; how often does that book come into my mind now, and the days of bliss in which I read it.

As assistant to the Envoy, William had to cope with routine clerical jobs; he found copying letters and dispatches the worst 'of all the torments ever invented ... I never was one for a drawling sleepy assistant', and his relationship with the Envoy was worse than ever. Forwarding this letter to his parents, Aleck, just twenty, commented:

> You will see he is not quite happy with his superior; this I am vexed at, as Elphinstone is a remarkably fine young man; and very much of Willie's temper and disposition but I think little of it ... two minds so much alike, as I know Elphinstone's and William's to be, must ere long coalesce.

The two minds were far from coalescing, and later William gave Aleck his version of the relationship. Before William was chosen to accompany the Mission and they were still equals, Elphinstone was 'open, free and familiar'; but once he was made leader of the expedition, his manner changed 'and this so palpably, that I became immediately disgusted, and we have ever been since that, cool and indifferent ... I do not pay him any attention, and he is nettled ... if there is anything to do he sends it, and I do it; he never speaks to me on any sort of business; I never ask him a question ... thus we go on, and shall go on'.

❈

At last, however, William managed to wangle an invitation to breakfast in one of the tribal villages. He and his companion were welcomed by the headman and conducted to a circle of mats in a grove of mulberry trees beside a stream. An excited crowd had gathered and conversation flowed easily for an hour. When it began to flag, the schoolmaster and the priest took over, alternately reciting verses and odes of Hafiz[11] – all 'most interesting, novel and amusing'. After a breakfast of pilau and fresh milk they rode back to the town, very pleased with themselves. William did not divulge the adventure to Elphinstone but an account appeared in the Calcutta newspapers (possibly via Aleck) and subsequently also in *An Account of the Kingdom of Caubul*, Elphinstone's masterly report of his Mission, annotated thus:

> The following account ... appeared in the Calcutta newspapers, and is evidently written by some gentleman of the mission.

❈

10 Kashgar – westernmost city in China, of strategic importance on the Silk Route between China, the Middle East and Europe.
11 Fourteenth century Persian poet.

The weather at last changed, and William described for Aleck the now green but totally dry landscape, contrasting it with 'our own country, and sweet England and we may traverse the Globe and not meet its match':

> I hope, my dearest Aleck, we may see it together, and in health and happiness. What would I not at this moment give for an hour's conversation with you! When I recollect the boy I left in his bed asleep, on the morning when I set out from Inverness, the picture of my grief at that moment is so fresh in my memory, it unmans me even now; and when I recall the winter we passed together, you at the Academy, me at poor Inglis's, it comes over me as a sweet and melancholy dream, from which I have just awakened.

Although fidgety and impatiently longing for something to happen, William was so interested in everything going on around him, and so intent on describing every detail, that he forgot to worry about Aleck except in a paragraph or two at the end of each letter. Then he repeated his usual warnings about the need for abstinence in all things, the desirability of keeping in touch with the right people and the dangers of the heat. He complained with a touch of asperity that as he hardly ever heard from Aleck, he would have to get news from other sources.

By now he was harbouring a very unwelcome suspicion that Aleck was not working as hard as he should at his Oriental languages. In an effort to stiffen Aleck's resolve he implored him to 'set your whole soul to Persian and Arabic and, for a year, make them your hobby'. His suspicions were correct. Aleck was definitely not enjoying his studies. Unlike his linguistically brilliant elder brother, he found the Oriental languages extremely difficult: 'OH! what a contrast are my present studies to my Hertford ones! With what rapture, now I know their value, would I return to them.' As always, he worried about the approaching quarterly examination. He managed to pass, but William, with an eagle eye on the results, commented that there were six people above him, both in Persian and in Hindustani, four of whom at least he should have overtaken.

Debt and depression

After five months in Writers' Buildings, Aleck was on the move again. He and James Curtis let their apartment in the Buildings and rented a house in the village of Ballygunge, now a smart residential area of South Kolkata, then about four miles outside the city, where he hoped to be far enough from temptations, particularly the auctions; there were two or three of these enticing events every day:

> … people having such a rage for buying, and selling here, that they cannot change from one house and much less from one Station to another, without selling their whole goods and Chattels by auction; or as it is called expressively here 'Outcry'.

His daily routine, in which study did not feature highly, remained more or less the same: he usually rode out before breakfast and then studied:

> … sometimes until tiffin[12] or 2 o'clock, sometimes not above an hour, sometimes not at all. After tiffin, I am so heavy and dull, in this enervating climate, I cannot do anything scarcely but read English; and that generally very light books.

Then another ride, dinner, chat and bed. William thought little of this, calculating that:

> … thus you pass out of the 24 hours – 10 hours in sleep, 11 in eating and idleness and three only in doing yourself good.

He emphasised the importance of a high place in the final exams if Aleck was to get a job suited to his undoubted ability and stressed the need to attract attention to himself: 'seek the society of men famed for mental cultivation; distinguish yourself by research; write on worthy subjects; do something!'

In April 1810 Aleck received a rare, and extremely long, letter from James, written during his short visit home the previous year. It made worrying reading: nothing 'but much superior luck' would get the family out of debt. Any profit made in cotton had disappeared into the bottomless pit of their father's debts. It was therefore the turn of 'our Indian Boys' to provide what was needed. James was perfectly aware of the 'almost Boundless Extravagance' into which young men launched the moment they arrived in India but trusted …

> … that the opposite may be the case with my two brothers – that the same yearning after our native home, the same '*maladie du pays*' that we feel in the West may inspire them with a wish to be soon home.

Knowing that his father was 'not so open on the subject of his embarrassment as I could wish him to be' and that William and Aleck were known not to be 'of dispositions to hoard or even make money', he felt compelled to impress on them the critical situation of Moniack:

> By the lapse of the next eighteen months we shall be aware of our fate. We have great sums to pay in that time seven or eight thousand pounds at least – and whether we shall be able to compass that sum God knows – I have hopes but many fears.

Whatever Aleck felt about this, William remained, as ever, optimistic. He was confident that, as things improved in Europe, so they would in the family's affairs. He was pretty sure that things would soon 'greatly change … all our danger vanish, and a dawn of prosperous fortune break through'.

⁂

William was by now something of an ascetic, verging on vegetarianism and self-disciplined where alcohol was concerned; he wondered whether Aleck's lethargy could be attributed to drinking in the middle of the day. He himself never touched wine or meat in the hot season.

12 Midday meal in Anglo-India.

Realising that the anti-social Aleck would have made few of the right friends, he racked his brains for people who might appeal to him. Given his interest in religion, perhaps he might have something in common with William Carey, the great missionary.[13] Then there was John Leyden,[14] the poet, easily approached as he had visited Moniack and even composed two or three of his poems there. He realised that Aleck might not find many kindred spirits in 'the higher circles of Calcutta but ... it is only by mingling there that you find the jewel of intelligence, learning and information'.

The 'teasing rigmarole lecture' continued and the advice went on, often repetitively, but it shows real concern and an imaginative attempt to use every means of persuasion available to get Aleck on to the path to success.

⁂

By now, however, Aleck seemed to be suffering from depression, which may have accounted for the lack of reply to William's letters. There had been a silence of nearly three months when William announced that he had seen the next exam results in the Calcutta Gazette 'and I am writing a letter in consequence'. Luckily for Aleck, it was probably one of the letters that vanished somewhere between Peshawar and Calcutta. His final place was ninth, disappointing indeed for William, who had won so many prizes during his College years. It was no surprise to Aleck who was convinced not only of the partiality of the President but also of the absurdity of the marking system: in the language papers every wrong word was marked with an x 'and he who has the fewest [errors] is first ... every error being equal, a man who writes a cow for an oyster, is as sensible as one who puts, by inadvertence, a mule for an ass'.

His state of mind was probably due to a combination of factors. Highly sensitive, shy, idealistic, introspective, something of a perfectionist and extremely intellectual, the product of a rigorous classical education, he had none of William's resilience, self-confidence or energy although he did share his brother's arrogance. Too high-minded and fastidious to join in the rumbustious and somewhat immoral life of his contemporaries, unfulfilled by the course on offer at the College and distrustful of the morals of those in authority, he felt isolated and diminished.

⁂

He was, however, always cheered by news from home. Jane Anne was now a pretty, affectionate girl of twelve 'of the sweetest nature' and George an intelligent, high-spirited, fairly indulged nine-year-old. Aleck felt that Jane Anne should be kept from anything that would wrongly stimulate her imagination and, remembering the library at Moniack, wrote to his mother:

> As to Jane Anne, I believe you were perfectly right, when you shut up the little Poetical Library, *from* her: for with the Gold of our Poetry, too much dross is intermixed. When she shall have learned by your instructions to separate them, they will be a Fund to her of innocent delight.

13 (1761–1834). Founder member of Baptist Missionary Society, the first evangelical missionary society in India. Orientalist and Professor of Sanskrit, Marathi and Bengali in Calcutta.

14 (1775–1811). Scottish poet and orientalist. Professor of Hindustani in Calcutta.

The welfare of this only sister was important to him and he had strong views on boarding schools for girls. His mother, who had seen nothing but 'the best side of the World and its inhabitants' and in whose presence 'vice and impudence are alike repressed', could not possibly know what went on at boarding schools. He, however, did and, in Calcutta, had come across the typical product of such places:

> A single Girl of lax principle, and lively seducing manners, [who] may corrupt and undermine the strict purity of a hundred in a place where romantic friendships are formed and the tie of those is secrecy. Secrecy or concealment of sentiments is the most ruinous of all things to a young Girl.

The four closely packed pages on this subject show his passionate belief that Jane Anne should be kept at home. A mother, after all:

> ... has all the experience and authority, without the invidious Office of Mistress; and has all the power with more tenderness for, and interest in, the Child ... Never suffer her to be removed from your own immediate inspection, from the same roof.

All the accomplishments necessary could be learnt at home, mostly from her mother, in whom Aleck had great faith as a teacher, especially of music:

> I think hearing you play is the best school she could have ...Would I not rather traverse the Globe to hear you play Lochiel's march, than move my foot to attend at Catalanie's most scientific, and tasteful squalling ... As to drawing ... I would give the world for a Drawing of Moniack fireside ... or the image of a well remembered scene in the Burn; nay the picture of a favourite tree, or even Flower from Jane Anne's pencil; but I would not give a fig for her drawing of the death of Wolfe.

For a wife he would choose a 'woman who has never been out of her Mother's house, and the immediate Circle of Domestic Society' and if his wife should die he would marry again to make sure his daughters were not packed off to school.

The End of the Mission

In steamy Peshawar, time for William was standing still. The town was in confusion and the King's situation was worsening:

> Everything seems to go against him, an empty treasury, sordid mean cowardly servants quarrelling with one another, without troops, without means of raising any, without country, and obliged to pawn the few remaining Crown Jewels he possesses to make the show of resistance.

Elphinstone was known to have plans which, for the moment, he was keeping to himself, but the rumour was that the Mission would probably retire to the safety of nearby Attock in order not to appear to take sides. If the fast-approaching rebel army took Peshawar the

Mission would either be recalled to Delhi or else would 'purchase [Shah Mahmoud's] friendship by a large present'.

If, on the other hand, Shah Shuja retained power, then they had already done all that was necessary in obtaining his friendship and agreement to prevent any French advance through his territories. William summed up the situation for Aleck:

> Mahmood, as a King, is detested for his cruelty and vices; but his Vizier or head Sirdar[15] is beloved by all for his liberality, affability and profusion. Shah Shooja is beloved as a Sovereign, for his mellowness, leniency and liberality; but his Minister Ukrum Khan is detested for his avarice, haughtiness and severity ... Mahmood has a little, and is likely to get, more, money. Shah Shooja has none, nor prospect of any. There is not as yet a ray to catch at for conjecturing on which side fortune may shine.

Everything was therefore up in the air and rumour was rife. Troops were approaching from all sides as the rebels closed in. The King had no idea whom he could trust, and the surrounding 'Clans and Chiefs relieved from the slight control which did exist, plunder, quarrel and fight with others, and with one another'.

With no hope of further adventure, William turned his gaze on Calcutta and wrote to Edmonstone, now Secretary to the Government, to ask for leave to visit Aleck and to point out respectfully that he himself would soon be in need of a job. It was also time to start thinking of employment for Aleck and he needed to know what job Aleck would like in order 'to sett all my engines of interest to work and open the road to success'. He urged Aleck to get in touch immediately with Seton 'particularly, as I fear you have no friends in Calcutta, who are sufficiently interested about you, to exert their mind of influence in your favour'.

During William's absence, the Resident in Delhi, Archy Seton, forwarded his letters to Aleck and, eager to get to know William's brother, struck up his own correspondence with Aleck, very pleasing to both. Seton wrote with characteristic ebullience and underlinings:

> I *cannot* tell you – I *really* cannot, how much and how strongly my heart enters into all the concerns of your family. I consider them in fact as interwoven with those of *my own* and I swear to you ... that, at my return to our native land, I will regard it as a point, a most *pleasing* point – of my duty to pay the same attention to your excellent parents that I could pay to my own.

By now it was June and the Mission had been in Peshawar since 25 February. The heat was becoming daily more oppressive, the town more unpleasant and the situation more dangerous. William and his colleagues sat all day in a deep, damp cellar then climbed on to the roof to sleep in the open air. He was missing Delhi, and even if Shah Shuja was victorious and returned to Kabul, that would now hold no attraction for William. No welcoming job offers, however, arrived, and he became daily more despondent.

15 Commander

In his darker moments he felt he had been foolish to be lured, against advice, into this adventure, when he could have been furthering his career in Delhi.

At last things started to move. Shah Shuja set off westwards for Kabul to confront Shah Mahmoud's army, while the Mission headed south-east to safety beyond the Indus. Five days later, in searing, late June, pre-monsoon temperatures, they camped beneath the walls of the great fort of Attock.

Now came news of Shah Shuja's defeat at the battle of Nimla: many of his army were dead, others had been won over by bribes to change sides and the rest deserted, leaving Shah Shuja once more a lone fugitive, eventually to seek asylum in India. The report of the Shah's reversal was followed by the order for immediate return to Delhi, a journey that would last well into the autumn.

There were adventures and encounters on the long march, including a visit to Shah Shuja's elder brother, Shah Zaman, former ruler of the Durrani Empire in Afghanistan, blinded by rivals to render him powerless. and now a refugee in Rawalpindi,

The blind Shah received them in a tent spread with carpets and they went through the same performance to show their respect as with Shah Shuja. Once again, the fascinated William took in every detail and everyone present was moved 'at this picture of royalty in misery'. Shah Zaman spoke of the plight of his brother but, enumerating the fortunes of various ancestors, said such reverses were the common portion of Kings. 'Had he gone over all the history of Asia,' wrote Elphinstone, 'he could scarcely have discovered a more remarkable instance of the mutability of fortune than he himself presented; blind, dethroned, and exiled.'[16]

⁂

Between William and Delhi there were three great rivers to cross including the *fabulosus Hydaspes* (modern Jhelum), from where he wrote to Aleck. How excited Aleck, with his great love of ancient history, would be, to stand at the site of the Battle of the Hydaspes, won by Alexander the Great in 326 BC. It would take about five days to get the Mission across this mighty river, since it was a mile and a quarter wide and there were but five boats available. Once across, there was still the Chenab river to negotiate. After that, a more straightforward march keeping north of Lahore would take them to Amritsar and on, across the river Sutlej, to Ludhiana and Delhi.

Receiving no news of his future employment from Seton, William grew daily more convinced that there would be no job for him in Delhi. Although he took comfort in the thought of his consequent freedom and the prospect of a reunion with Aleck, he could not help musing on the Mission and its frustrating outcome:

> I am certain I could have done more good had I remained at Dihlee ... nothing could be pleasanter than travelling about as we have done, were it not for the idea ... that a life of mere personal gratification must always be fruitless of comfort on retrospection ... I have not done one atom of good since I left Dihlee, and therefore

16 *An Account of the Kingdom of Caubul*, The Hon Mountstuart Elphinstone, (1815) London & (1998) Munshiram Manoharlal, New Delhi.

> cannot look back on my trip with patience, or comfort; yet I have always the satisfaction to remember, that the primary intention, and first prospect was not only natural, and correct, but proper and honourable.

At long last, having just crossed the last river before home and after a silence of four months, William received letters from Aleck; he was well but divulged no ideas for his future career; furthermore, he regretted he was not on sufficiently intimate terms with Edmonstone to enhance William's prospects. William now swung wildly between hope that his job would still be there for him and certainty that it would not. He persuaded himself that Seton must have regarded his impetuous acceptance of a place on the Mission as 'ungrateful and improper'. But 'what was the temptation? Could any man resist? I am now punished, and must console myself for what I have lost, with what I have seen'. Henceforward he would hover on the side-lines being useful wherever he could; it was now Aleck's career that mattered.

⁂

Two days later, everything changed: the *dawk* brought an affectionate letter from Seton dispelling all William's fears and welcoming him home. Seton had already expressed amazement to Aleck that William had any doubts about his place in the Residency family:

> God forbid it should be otherwise. I am much, very much, attached to Delhi But were I deprived of the sweetly interesting prospect of once more having him for my fellow labourer in this vineyard I should think Delhi a most melancholy Residency ... he was only *lent* to the Caubul Mission ... dearly, *most* dearly does Delhi love him.

Suddenly there was nothing for it for William but to leap on his horse and ride as fast as he could for Delhi – he could be there in three days' time 'that is if my horses stand it out'. At Ludhiana he discovered more letters, including one from Aleck reporting a riding accident, and took a minute to scribble him a note on the risk to health from the sun. Then silence for two months – William had thrown himself heart and soul into his new job.

It suited him very well; he was once more under canvas, busy with useful employment in the unsettled areas 'making a triennial settlement for the land revenue, establishing a police and arranging the country' and, in the middle of all this, snatching moments to write to Aleck. He did not, however, find time to write to his parents. Aleck loyally explained the position to Reelig and Jane: William was healthy, happy and being well paid for the important work that he was doing. He was so busy that he was relying on Aleck to write 'copiously':

> and you must not think from his thus writing by proxy that his relish for home correspondence is in the least lessened, but he dislikes sitting down to write short unsatisfactory lines ... and therefore waits, from day to day, for an hour to two of leisure, which I really believe he has not had since his return from Peishour.

A few months later, he reported that he was trying to make head or tail of William's wonderful Journal of the Mission: it was 'utterly illegible, consisting of notes chiefly written on Horseback, and in Pencil'.

William was becoming daily more embroiled in the intricate and intensely interesting life in and around Delhi. His domestic routine was also becoming more eccentric. He ate little but 'boiled pease and scones ... flour cakes and *dal* and never had breakfast, dinner or tiffin except when he dined out. He called himself 'as hardy as a Spartan ... In living and diet I am a perfect hermit; and in work, a horse or a Hercules'.

But William could enjoy society, too: as the end of the year approached, the weather became 'delightful, and quite English, and the sun pleasant all day', and William, camped near a cantonment, was leading a much more sociable life than for several years:

> I have not only found many Scotch, but many Invernessmen ... both the Battalions have messes, and I generally dine at either the one or the other, and I sometimes give a party in camp. How comfortable we both could be here!

He continued to send Aleck last minute advice:

> Unless you distinguish yourself, you cannot claim the right of choosing from among the vacant appointments. Think of this my dearest brother, and the disappointment we shall both feel, and Seton too, unless you fit yourself to come to Delhi.

He promised that he would give him as much 'Tyger' hunting and deer and partridge shooting as he could possibly want, provided Aleck would as faithfully promise to forbear, for the present, to use his guns and dogs. He himself was having to give up riding for the moment 'by the consequences of Bazaar imprudence, which never shall hereafter happen'; he hoped Aleck was managing to avoid such indiscretions.

Aleck was still not meeting the right people, such as William's contemporary, Charles Metcalfe.[17] It would benefit both of them if only Aleck could be persuaded to get to know him while he was in Calcutta. Metcalfe was a brilliant linguist and, like William, enjoyed negotiating with the local population. It was Metcalfe who much later wrote of William:

> He is masterly and selfwilled to so great a degree that no power can be entrusted to him without some risk of its being abused, and he might drag the Government into mischief before they had the means of avoiding it.[18]

But that was far in the future. For the moment William was doing more or less as he was told.

---

17 Resident in Delhi 1811–1819 and 1825–27. In Calcutta as political/private secretary to the Governor 1819. Resident in Hyderabad 1820.

18 *The Cornchest for Scotland: Scots in India,* Alex M. Cain (1986), National Library of Scotland.

6

1810–1812

Third Assistant

> I tell you a piece of news: I am at last freed from the bondage of College; and at length have a speedy prospect of not only seeing, but acting publickly with William, having every prospect of being appointed to Dehli.

It was January 1810, but Aleck was in no hurry to leave Calcutta on account of his friend, Dr Simon Nicolson, from Inverness.

This doctor, 'incomparably the ablest practitioner here', had known Aleck since he was a child. His marriage, to a Eurasian, had caused a disagreement between Aleck and his parents, but in Mary Nicolson there was no 'more valuable wife or mother ... solely delighting evidently in her Husband and two uncommon fine children'. Mary Nicolson had recently died, and Simon had asked Aleck to keep him company for a few months. He accordingly moved into the doctor's quarters in the General Hospital after New Year 1810.

Seton had offered Aleck the position of Third Assistant:

> ... if you would but condescend to accept this situation ... how inexpressibly happy you would make me. I *do* long to be introduced to the personal acquaintance of the brother of William Fraser.

The three of them could have 'such nice *cracks*[1] about the Land of Cakes'; Aleck was just as happy: 'To be with Willie is everything; but in addition to be under such a man ... would really make me esteem myself indeed a favourite of fortune.' Seton had described William to his sister as 'a most superior man' and Aleck as '*the* young eaglet of a valiant nest'. He wrote:

> How I should like to dedicate part of some summer after my return to visiting the amiable family in Inverness-shire. Their younger son Alexander is lately come out to this country on the civil establishment and as there is a vacancy at Dehli I have offered the situation to young Fraser of whom, though I have not yet seen him, I have formed the most exalted idea.

✻

1 Scots: conversation, gossip.

To the west and south-west of Delhi roamed hordes of lawless bandits. William had demanded to be allowed to deal with this menace, and Seton's account of his achievements was glowing:

> Unattended and unarmed he went into the fastnesses of these savages, and by ... sound judgement animated by personal intrepidity, and tempered by address and persuasion he without shedding one drop of blood, so far gained a sweet, mild, but a firm and lasting victory over their minds that they are now under the [British] protection ... in every respect become good subjects of the State.

In fact, continued Seton, half a dozen of the wild children of these erstwhile warlords were at that moment romping round his room. The 'saucy little rogues' were intrigued with a picture of his home, Touch, hanging above his desk; they pestered him with questions about it while he searched for words to describe its 'unequalled loveliness' to the little ragamuffins.

His description of William's character and talents was enough to make any parent burst with pride: he was sagacious, intrepid, well educated and perfectly au fait with the languages, customs and character of the natives. His excursions into the fearsome strongholds of the brigands had gained him ...

> ... immortal honour, and procured from Lord Minto the recorded approbation of Government expressed in the strongest Terms ... such is my young friend William Fraser. His parents must be Super Excellent.

This paragon, often alone in his tent at night, found time for thoughts of home.

For some time there had been rumours concerning James and Jeanie Tytler. William shared his mixed feelings with Aleck:

> I scarce know whether or not to desire his union with Jane Tytler, but I suspect he would find it difficult to find another to equal her – and the family alliance has already been productive of so much real happiness to both, that a closer union could but strengthen and augment it.

Then he touched on his own castle in the air – the hope of communication with Charemile Grant. Knowing Aleck's elegant command of English, he asked him to compose a letter to Charemile on his behalf. 'I dare not do it myself for fear of criticism and satire'. He called this speculation, however, 'a dream of bliss as I may call myself wedded to India'.

❁

The news of Aleck's appointment threw William into a perfect whirlwind of travel plans, reminiscent of his father: Aleck could come by road 'to Lucknow, and stay with Baillie, and then to Kanpur, and stay with Rose, then to Futtygurh and Coel, where I would meet you'. Or maybe he could get leave to go to Calcutta and accompany Aleck

Touch House, 'of unequalled loveliness', was Archy Seton's beloved home. He left it in the care of his brother-in-law, Sir Henry Steuart of Allanton.

all the way: 'I see so many delights in this plan that I really would press it. Our journey up would be delightful'. Or how about meeting somewhere on the river? So as not to miss each other, he would fly a square red flag while Aleck should fly an oblong blue one. Or what about marching? This would take two months, but might be preferable to palanquin or boat, and William could send Aleck his elephants and camels.

What Aleck made of all these breathless suggestions is unknown, since he remained silent. He found a suitable travelling companion, a Mr Forrester, and left Calcutta on 7 April 1810, proceeding in leisurely fashion by boat.

He is all in all here

Aleck found his mother's demand for a Journal of his river trip very taxing:

> My observations can be but few ... but you say 'Send a Journal' and I will send one ... I have seen nought yet. From the Boat nothing appears but on one side a steep perpendicular 20 to 40 feet high, of mud, and on the other, dry sand without a speck of vegetation, extending sometimes half a mile inland.

They had come at the only season 'when a traveller is prevented from enjoying himself on the river'. Aleck therefore resorted to thoughts of home:

> The glittering prospects, with which my Imagination was filled, in setting out for India, are long vanished. My sole ambition now is to see you once more in comfort and peace, and to pass the latter end of my life, if it please God to lengthen my days, in my own Country.

At the end of May, assuming that Aleck must have set off, William wrote:

> I cannot in any way account for your silence, nor create excuses for you, as it is

> considerably more than two months since you have written ... You must certainly by this time have reached Benares or Ghazeepore; and I hope the weather has become cool and favourable, the river full and the wind fair. Today I have written to Calcutta through Seton for a month's leave of absence, from Dihlee ... I hope to meet you at Cawnpore [now Kanpur].

Then he started planning further: they would spend every afternoon in the country and always keep weekends free for leisure. He ended huffily:

> As you have commenced your trip, without saying how or when, I think it is probable you will persevere in silence so that I may content myself, or rather endeavour to do so, and smooth my uneasiness, and hug my distress, probably until your worship may reach Cawnpore, when perhaps you may condescend to write.

⁂

If Aleck had expected William to meet him at Kanpur with fresh horses for the final 200 miles or so, he was disappointed. Eighty miles further on, at Fatehgarh, still no William and no horses. When they were about 70 miles from Delhi, one of William's servants galloped up: William was apparently still 140 miles away at Kurnal and he himself would accompany Aleck on the rest of the journey. So, once more Aleck mounted Eclipse and rode another thirty miles. By this time he and his companion, 'overpowered with sleep', rolled themselves in blankets and slept beside the road. They rose while it was still dark and, as dawn broke, they reached Sekundara, where dimly through torrential rain they made out a group of horsemen cantering towards them. Aleck recognised William instantly:

> He is wonderfully stout and was not fatigued by his ride of near 110 miles: though I was with mine of 70. We rode the last 25 or 30 miles under the heaviest rain I ever saw ... but his presence was better to me than the strength of Samson; by his care, and that of a fine fellow, an Irishman (Macartney) who lives with him, I was as well at ease, and felt not the slightest fatigue by the next morning.

Aleck joined William at the Residency with Seton and no sooner was it known that William's 'little brother' had arrived than the house was seething with 'natives Great and Small' to welcome him. He was instantly struck by the difference from Bengal of 'the whole character of this place and people, their manners, pursuits and dispositions'. Many of these faithful servants were once bandits, perhaps murderers, whom William had won over; they slept by his bed and would risk their lives for him.

> He is All in All here ... with Willie, I feel my inferiority, without being galled. I am content to rest my reputation on being his Brother.

Once he had recovered from this extraordinary welcome, Aleck set about another more detailed description of William; all his parents had to remember him by was the portrait by Raeburn painted when he was sixteen and a watercolour, attributed to Robert Home, painted in Calcutta around 1806 (see Plate IX and also Plate XIII), which had revealed, to his mother's consternation, a fellow 'wearing a quirky mixture of Indian and Scottish costume' .[2] Now Aleck updated his father:

> His countenance is certainly materially altered, very full and round ... he is grown extremely grave; and I could almost suppose him annoyed by my occasional levity ... I think he is often like you in expression, little gestures and habits; a way of indulging a little in reverie, and smiling when awakened from it. Sometimes, nay very frequently in the sound of his voice ... he brings you before me, every hour and minute ... Noble, generous, affectionate, but proud, fiery and impetuous, perfectly mild and gentle with his real friends, and unassuming with those who assume not; but perfect touchwood on a hint of disrespect, or premature familiarity ... his only fault, if a fault it can be called, because it terrifies and distresses me, is that he is too fond of exposing himself to danger ... I trust now that I am with him, his wish to preserve me from danger may induce him to risk less.

He described William's vast army of servants. Along with the ferocious Gujars whom William had tamed there were Hindus of high caste in charge of horses, hunting and shooting, the post etc; Muslim table servants; ten Hindu bearers for the palanquins who also cleaned shoes and pitched tents; the Klassses, responsible for maintaining the tents and marching equipment; they also punished delinquents and acted as messengers. Each horse, of which there were at least six, was assigned a Groom and a Grasscutter, and the dogs had a keeper of their own. Elephants had a driver each plus assistants, and two or three servants were assigned to each of the seven camels. There was a cook and assistant, water carriers, two washermen, one or two tailors and a barber; a company of sepoys acted as escort whenever Willie journeyed out of Delhi.

A LAWYER AFTER ALL

To begin with, William turned his back on business and devoted every day to Aleck. They spent the time ...

> ... chatting of you and Mamma and the ever dear scenes & Inhabitants of Moniack. No person, no place, no walk, no Tree is forgotten. Willie could still point out the old Crabtree; and we can still regret the fall of the old roddin [3] at the Mill.

Aleck proudly embellished Seton's account of William's work among the lawless tribes:

> He went alone, & unarmed, among the most ferocious; this confidence instantly reassured the minds of many powerful families, who had suffered shamefully

2 *India Revealed*, Falk & Archer, 1989.
3 Rowan.

> from the cruel treachery of the French in the time of Perron, the French Marhatta General. They saw now that they might depend on English honour ... Stations of Police were erected and guarded in the recesses which formerly were the scenes of Rapine and Bloodshed, now changed into flourishing villages – and cheerful cultivation took place of unwholesome swamps & dreary Jungles ... Were the detail in my hands, I could tell of many hairbreadth scrapes and perilous accidents in which our Hero was engaged ... Often was he alone in the huts of Barbarians, and gained the confidence of these savage mortals, by familiarity and kindness ... his rule, never to betray confidence, or by indirect or unworthy means to deceive, or to circumvent, gained wonderfully on the minds and hearts of those uncivilised Beings.

His father was not to criticise 'the bad Grammar' of this letter; it had been written ...

> ... as fast as the pen could run; and in a room like a thoroughfare; a dozen people and half a dozen languages resounding in my ear all the time – & frequently talking and writing at once and a continual change of visitors and voices.

William was still in debt but, optimistic as ever, felt he would be solvent in a few months. Aleck was in far more troubled waters; he was confident, however, that now he was employed, he would be able to begin to clear his obligations, and there was a real prospect of William soon being appointed Resident. Seton was about to become Governor of Prince of Wales Island,[4] William had friends in high places and, in any case, 'there is no man in India so well fitted for the situation'. The Resident at Delhi had to be 'Judge, a Magistrate, a Politician, a Linguist and a man of elegant deport ment, dignified and easy manners'. He must be bold and decisive, regardless of personal danger, firm and intrepid. 'Above all, he should be intimately acquainted with the customs, manners and dispositions of the natives, of the districts, under his command.'

Aleck was full of excuses to his parents for William's inability to pick up a pen: from morning to night he was constantly at the beck and call of natives who appeared on business or just 'to congratulate him on the arrival of my noble Lordship'. That very morning he had just persuaded William to sit down to write home 'when a vile packet of Persian letters came in and interrupted him – it is a question whether I can get him so seated again'.

Soon, however, there was little time for Aleck to write letters. After breakfast and half an hour with his hookah he spent the day at Court. 'All the business of Civil Law is in my Department, for Seton has, since my serious attention to business has begun, almost given up his attendance, except on very important Cases'. He was in Court until 3 o'clock, 'when I go home and refresh myself with a *piece*,[5] as we used to call it'. Then another hookah and another three hours at Court before dinner with Seton 'or a dish of Tea at home' and a last hookah.

---

4 Penang
5 A snack (Scots)

Although he did not find his work particularly stimulating, various local events were interesting, especially the arrival home of a renegade Prince, Mirza Jehangir. Rebelling against the British restrictions on the Imperial Family of Delhi, this lively and spirited fellow had contrived to make friends with some young Europeans and his 'youthful excesses' had brought a reprimand. Incensed, he barred the Resident from the Palace, which was instantly surrounded by troops. Seton tried to reason with him 'but ... the Prince seized a Gun ... and fired at Seton. The ball went through the Hat of a soldier at his side. At this outrage the Gates were instantly blown open – the Palace stormed – but happily with little bloodshed.' The Prince was then imprisoned in Allahabad, where he remained until, at the entreaty of Shah Alam, he was recalled to Delhi.

According to Aleck, in his homecoming this recalcitrant Prince appeared 'more like a triumphant General than as a Penitent'; all his brothers, including the Heir Apparent, and an escort of troops rode to meet him as he approached. They were followed by Seton and Aleck on elephants, with royal salutes at every halt until, cheered on by an immense crowd of spectators, the procession reached the Palace.

Although he was intrigued by this extraordinary spectacle, the rational Aleck was irritated by Seton's attitude to the Royal Family which he considered servile in the extreme. Like his predecessors and most of his contemporaries, including William, Seton was influenced by 'romantic veneration for the unfortunate descendants of the Moghul Kings' and had forgiven his would-be assassin. Aleck reacted by obtaining leave to go to Kurnal for two weeks 'half in sulks, half from desire to see Willie'.

On Christmas Day in Delhi that year, 1810, Aleck wrote letters by a roaring fire. He alarmed his father by describing how William had shot a lion:[6] 'To attack an animal of this description on horseback, with small shot in a fowling piece, seems to a rational man, little short of madness'. Concerned by William's disregard for his personal safety, Aleck asked his mother to add her pleas: 'I am confident that one word from you would at once put an end to these unnecessarily dangerous Exploits'.

William's 'fondness for the natives and for their customs' was also hard to accept; surely William was demeaning himself in adopting some of the Hindu customs of his servants who 'feel some respect for us if we adhere as religiously to *our* customs, as they do to *theirs*; but if we concede, they regard us with contempt, as mere time servers'. There was also another reason for Aleck's discomfiture: he was finding, as Edward had in Guyana, that he was less interesting to his elder brother than was comfortable: William seemed to prefer the company of the wild ragamuffins who thronged loyally about him.

William also wrote at Christmas, admitting that he had not written a proper letter home for five years and that now it was difficult to catch up. 'Yet it does not matter; I have but

6 Owing to years of trophy hunting by William and his like the population of the Asiatic lion fell to around fifteen in the early twentieth century. There is now a single 'endangered' population in the Gir Forest National Park and Wildlife Sanctuary in Gujerat, where in 2010 there were 411 lions, an increase of 52 since 2005.

two objects on Earth: to make home comfortable – and then to get to it!' But that could not be until every debt was paid off. Once more he talked of sending money home: 'You will, I think, say here's William been promising and promising for the last 3 or 4 years, and after all done nothing. This is certainly true.' But he would be out of debt by the end of the year, and eight months more would put him 'above the world' and able to contribute to Moniack.

By now the brothers had moved out of the Residency and had their own bungalow[7] by the river Jumna. Aleck described the surroundings to his mother:

> It is now 9 in the evening and I am sitting by a fine fire, in our house, on a bank of a branch of the Jumna. The main branch is within sight of the windows ... A little down the river ... lies the grand Palace of Shah Jehan and across the stream connected by a Bridge (a very fine one) the frowning Bastille of Dehli now nearly uninhabited ... All along the stream on which our Mansion is built, lie prostrate the remnants of Indian magnificence. Viewing Dehli from an eminence near this spot, you might fancy yourself in Fairyland. Far as the Eye can reach nothing meets your view, but an extended waste of barren rocks, mixed with splendid ruins: Mosques, Palaces, Mausoleums, Temples, and broken Towers, lie before you in the wildest confusion. In the midst, modern Dehli relieves the Desolation of the scene, by a mixture of splendid houses, and more modern Mosques and public buildings of the Hindoos and Mussulmen.

⁂

By April 1811 Archy Seton had left Delhi and William was made Acting Resident. At this point there arrived a long letter of reproof to Aleck from his father: first, he had not become acquainted with the right people in Calcutta; second, he had spent too much money; and third, he had not learnt the requisite languages while at College. To all this Aleck gave a spirited and reasoned response: he had no regret for not having met 'the right people' in Calcutta; admirable and amiable as Lumsden and Edmonstone were, their wives and associates, in Aleck's opinion, left much to be desired. He had delivered all his letters of introduction from Charles Grant, to no avail and, being Aleck and not William, had pursued it no further. He was admittedly deeply in debt because he shared with Curtis and because of 'the confusion of his affairs' in Writers' Buildings.

As to his lack of fluency in the languages, his working knowledge was adequate for his job; his father should cease to regard him as an idle, irresponsible student and start to take him seriously. He now had a good position at which he was working hard and he also had the approval of Seton; only four or five of over a hundred cases that he had dealt with had gone to appeal. Without any legal training to speak of, he was doing his best and keeping his duty to his father in the forefront of his mind.

---

7 The most usual class of (one-storey) house occupied by Europeans in the interior of India (*Hobson Jobson*).

From West to East

Meanwhile, Edward had landed at Liverpool at the end of May. All he now wanted to do was get to Moniack as soon as possible and wait for James. Then, together, they would set sail for India:

> My dearest Mother, my anxiety to be with you exceeds everything. You cannot, I think, estimate the happiness I feel on reflecting on my having bid adieu to Berbice and the West Indies ... I grudge extremely every hour I am away from you ... I cannot express the Happiness I feel in the prospect of meeting you all once more, though it is meeting to Part again.

While he awaited instructions from his father he lodged with the Gladstones and 'their charming group of children'[8] and used the time to write a letter of thanks to Charles Grant, who had secured for him a general posting to the East India Company. He felt diffident about addressing 'so *awful* a man but gratitude told me it was a duty. I can never be sufficiently thankfull to him.'

Impatient to get home, he set off for Edinburgh, where a letter from his father threw him into confusion: a passage had been booked for him on *Baring*, and he needed to be in London by 20 June. This would give him almost no time at Moniack: 'I confess I feel it very hard to be packed off the moment I arrive – and when I consider that I may never see you more, I should think that a little longer than even a month might have been allowed for us to be together.'

The reason for this sudden panic was Jane's discovery that Sir George Nugent, the new Commander in Chief in India (see Plate XIV), his wife and their entourage were to be passengers on *Baring*. It could clearly be advantageous for Edward, who had a passage but no specific job in view, to sail with them. He thought otherwise:

> Nothing can make up to me for the deprivation of not seeing you – I am determined to go north at all events – and then, you and my mother shall do with me as you please. I go to Woodhouselee this evening. When I left my dear James both he and I indulged hopes of meeting in Scotland, before either of us embarked for India. This hope supported me at parting from him – I have lived on it ever since.

In the event, he managed almost two weeks at home before setting off south. His feelings were in turmoil: he had not got used to being home again and there had been no time to see all his old friends, including Nanny Rose and William's old nurse. He was also acutely aware that, in view of his parents' age, it might well turn out to be a final goodbye. Yet, once on his way, he was relieved to be going.

Arriving in Edinburgh too late for the evening mail to London, he bravely made a surprise visit to Woodhouselee, where he found the family at dinner but nonetheless pleased

8 Including William, the future Prime Minister , then aged two.

to see him, especially Isabella. She slipped a tiny folded message[9] into his pocket, addressed to 'Alex C. Fraser Esq', which read:

> My Dearest Aleck I send you by Edward a ring set with my hair. Will you wear it for my sake? I have put on it no sentimental inscription, your Cipher and mine ingraved on the back without any device, you may remember you used sometimes to laugh at me for being a little addicted to sentiment but I am quite cured of all my romantic visions, and am become a sober steady little body ... Good Night my Dearest Aleck I must go and sing to poor Eddy to keep up his spirits. This is a melancholy visit. God Bless you my very dear friend. Most affectionately yours Isabella Tytler.

In London Edward lodged with the Grants, with whom, he reassured his mother, he was now quite at home, even with Charles Grant 'though he is rather terrible to young people but I think there is no good in being afraid of those sort of people'. Aleck, hearing of this successful visit, was full of admiration for his 'uncommon' brother, who seemed so unaware of his own qualities:

> It is thus that his mild unassuming manners, and unaffected amiableness of temper have invariably attached to him the affections of those with whom he consorted even for a short time. Even the Grants, hard as they are to please, stiff and fastidious as they unquestionably are, and rarely attracted but by the more brilliant and obtrusive qualities – yet, when Edward came among them, he won their hearts in a week ... Willie they liked – they had a little cold regard for me – but Edward they truly loved – and he deserved the distinction.

There were musical evenings in Russell Square at which Edward produced his flute, Charemile played 'astonishingly well' and Sophia sang charmingly. Used, however, to the ample fare at Moniack, he was always hungry. 'We hardly have enough to eat sometimes,' he told his mother, 'the shabbiest dinners ever I saw. One of your dinners would serve them four days.'

He managed to see Miss Chipps and deliver some money from his parents, but the encounter awoke 'painful recollections' of Mary and home. He also met a Miss Clarke, who was off on the 'fishing fleet' to Delhi. He reassured his mother that she need not fear for Willie as she was 'neither pretty nor accomplished' and added,' I should think the native women ... may be just as much subjects of your alarm'.

Charemile introduced Edward to the flamboyant Lady Hood (see Plate XII), later to become a close friend of William. Edward was less than impressed: 'Lady Hood is reckoned handsome ... I think her a downright fright ... immense in size and color and she was ill dressed'.

9 This tiny folded message, less than an inch square, was found at the back of a drawer at Moniack House in 2000. It had survived the journey to London and the six-month voyage to India in Edward's pocket, five more years in Aleck's keeping and then a return voyage and journey north.

On his last Sunday in London ...

> ... just as I was getting into bed Mr Grant sent for me and gave me a *screed of advice* as Jeanie Tytler calls it. He told me, that as in all human probability, he might never again see me, that he wished to say a few words of advice to me at parting ... I think I shall remember his few words as long as I live, or have recollection.

He bade a sad farewell to the Grants, all nine of them – 'you will rarely see a finer family'. It reminded him of his first departure from their house, exactly eight years previously, when the twelve-year-old Mary had been one of the group waving him off. On a very hot day, 12 July, he set off for Portsmouth and from there to Ryde on the Isle of Wight.

Ryde was the home of a friend of Jane's – a Mrs Gregory, who was prepared to accommodate Edward while he waited to sail. A cheerful, homely person, she had three sons and one daughter, Kate, 'very handsome, very tall, on a large scale, black hair, brilliant colour, fine teeth, fine features. They received me like an old friend, with a shake of the hand and hearty welcome'.

Armed with his note of introduction from Charles Grant, Edward hoped to bump into the Nugents, also staying in Ryde. First, however, he had to find his cabin and shipmate. Joining the ship at such short notice meant no hope of a cabin of his own or a servant. He had, however, managed to share with his cousin, the handsome John Fraser,[10] nephew and ADC to Sir George Nugent, for £75.

> We found the *Baring* a scene of complete confusion but she seems a fine vessel and the apartments fitted up for Sir George and Lady Nugent are very pretty (at a cost of £3200 for Sir George and his wife, two aide de camps, one gentleman and six servants). Our Cabin is 8 feet square ... The *Baring* is very crowded; I suppose there are not less than 25 or 26 at the Captain's table.

Evenings in the Gregory family were spent with music and singing. The attractive Kate, flashing her dark eyes, played the piano well but, irritatingly, her singing wandered in and out of tune. Edward was flattered that the three Gregory boys (one very like Aleck 'in having no patience with anyone and not being able to conceal any feelings regarding other people') kept him company on his frequent trips to Portsmouth.

Baring's Captain Templar seemed 'rather a shuffling fellow ... he looks rather ill-tempered'. The Purser was 'an obliging man and rather gentlemanly ' and he played the fiddle. There were seventy crew members, fifty soldiers, cows, sheep, a pack of hounds and forty-five passengers, several of whom were returning to India and knew William and Aleck; one recognised Edward by his family likeness and they all thought Edward lucky to have the chance to join his brothers.

10 This was Dr Fraser's third son, the 'timid youth' who had had a schoolboy crush on Mary during her friendship with his sister Isabella.

Sir George Nugent, however, proved elusive, and Lady Nugent never rose before 1.00 pm, so Edward's morning visits to their quarters achieved little. Charles Grant's letter of introduction produced an invitation to dinner, and Edward sat next to Lady Nugent 'and spoke a little to her'. Sir George, however, only 'took a little notice of me'.

He liked his cabin-mate and they agreed what was needed to make their cabin habitable, all in a space 8ft square: 'washhandstand, a small table, 2 chairs and a chest of drawers between us ... and we have a Floor cloth, too, cost £2, a great comfort'. Luckily, they made friends with two other passengers who had paid more for their cabins and who had sensibly removed the partition between them:

> In the daytime they remove their cots and have their Trunks covered with cushions and flounces like a sopha – these being secured by cleats make good seats. Here they propose, if we are all good friends, to sit sometimes and play chess or cards, or read, or do as we like.

Next door were Captain and Mrs Midwinter, who had 'a Pianoforte – she plays and sings and he plays the Flute'. So, what with this and the fiddling Purser, music at sea was a possibility.

The wind, however, was as fickle as ever, and after three days aboard everyone was ordered off the ship. Edward had to throw himself once more on the hospitality of Mrs Gregory; the passengers with families seeing them off had to endure the agony of a second parting:

> Poor Lady Nugent was much to be felt for, the day she came on board, after parting with her children. She walked down to the Beach, and seemed quite unable to walk by herself. I felt for her much but a great deal more for old Colonel Murray, who came on board with his son. I never saw such a picture of Grief when he shook hands with his only Son and only Child.

Lady Nugent, who had dreaded the posting in India and the separation from her children, the youngest of whom was only six weeks old, felt the parting so poignantly that she wrote a passionate poem about it which ended:

> And never more I'll quit my home,
> For India's glory, India's pride ...[11]

As he watched these scenes of heartbreak, Edward's feelings were once more in turmoil: he had spent three days among strangers 'in an uncomfortable ship, bad rainy weather and nobody to care a pin about me' and was feeling in lower spirits than ever before.

He was also worried about James: fearful that his brother would get home to find Moniack let and also concerned about his health, he longed for a reassuring letter. He would have set off 'cheerfully comparatively speaking if I had a letter from his own hand. The only pleasure I can now look forward to is that of meeting my Brothers.'

11 *Anglophone Poetry in Colonial India 1780–1913: A Critical Anthology* ed. Mary Ellis Gibson, 2011.

He did not have much hope of further acquaintance with Sir George, who was to eat separately and he was not likely to be 'among those chosen to dine at his Table'. When the Nugents took the air on deck they were surrounded by others hoping to catch their eye.

It was now 25 July, nearly two weeks since he had arrived in Portsmouth, and he was viewing the coming six months with some trepidation:

> I wish the voyage was over and I in India ... I fear our cabin is a wet one and will be very hot. However, when I left Moniack I bade farewell to all comfort and happiness for a good while to come ... I shall always be happy in having left the West Indies – that reflexion always cheers me – at the same time it leads me to my dear James whom I fear I shall not now hear of.

Next day, the wind changed and he was woken at 4.00 am and told to return on board as quickly as possible where he found letters from his father but not a word of James. A day later they sailed, and there was still time, while *Baring* passed the Needles with a fair wind and lovely weather, to write a final letter to his mother. The table seating plans were at last pinned up and 'I am sorry to tell you that I am not of Sir Geo's party at dinner'. In other respects, it was a better arrangement: John Fraser, as ADC, was naturally in attendance at the Nugents' table, and Edward would thus have the tiny cabin to himself for a while. His only bitter regret was that there was now no hope of hearing from James.

Retrenchment

In Delhi, Charles Metcalfe (see plate XIV), not William, had been appointed Resident to replace Seton. William was to continue as Acting Resident until Metcalfe arrived. Aleck was outraged:

> I think if Lumsden and Edmonstone were real and warm friends of Willie, they might have procured the Residency of Delhi for him ... Willie has had but the empty honor of having charge of the Residency for a few months: and lost 360 rupees per month, which he had in the Country, while he is acting Resident. Our consolation is, that in 5 or 6 years, Metcalfe, the new Resident, will in all probability, go home and then, Government cannot, without manifest injustice, place anyone but Willie in this situation.

Reelig, unaware as yet of this news, was looking forward to having all four sons in the same country. He sent some hints to William and Aleck as to what to expect of James and Edward. They would find Edward ...

> ... a most satisfactory brother – affectionate, prudent, mild and well principled. His shades are preferring present comfort to present exertion – tenaciousness of opinion and I think of prejudice – with all his gentleness, very silently obstinate and if prejudiced, secretly, deeply and permanently inveterate.

James was quite different:

> … but like Edward, most virtuous and honourable. He is very sanguine, very positive and far too much attached to argument in ordinary society. He is restless and bustling, deficient in method and order – but full of life and energy.

His father reckoned that in the right place, with his energy channelled in the right direction, he would go far – 'I think he will be ultimately a man of deep and extensive knowledge'. He was extremely proud of all four and rejoiced that they would support and cherish one another.

Metcalfe arrived in July and made a good impression on Aleck, although 'I can never however I think, love him so much as Seton, who was really almost a faultless character'. William then departed to his tent again.

Aleck was now more or less settled in his job. Given his earlier reluctance to become a lawyer, it is ironic that his day consisted of deciding lawsuits – 'assuredly a most disgusting employ'. He was 'Judge & Jury & Counsel, with no Law to guide me further than that of Common Sense and Justice'. He was finding Indians most litigious and capable of making the simplest affair inextricably tangled. A backlog of court cases had accumulated which would take at least another year to clear, but often Aleck found himself with a 'half ludicrous, half melancholy task to be told on reading the names of the suers, that such a one was dead, such another not heard of. In some both parties were dead.' In other cases the disputants, tired of waiting to be heard, had settled their differences themselves.

At last, though, he seemed to have achieved something like contentment with his lot. He liked routine and preferred not to miss a day's work. The worst he had to endure was 'that the noise of quarrelling and argumentation in the day, pursues me at night; and often I am kept awake during the whole night by the recurrence of the day to my mind'.

He was also happy with the small social circle of the Residency: Metcalfe, Stuart, the Persian Translator and 'a man of Talents and information', and Gardner, the Second Assistant, 'a most gentlemanly well informed man'. There was also a Surgeon, 'an excellent Scotchman, named McWherter'. There were always people coming and going through Delhi, and often sixteen to eighteen sat down to dinner, of whom at least half were Scots.

At home, the difficult decision had been taken: Moniack was to be let and Reelig and Jane would move to Inverness, thereby saving money on servants' wages. They had found a suitable house in Castle Street with a view westward over the river towards the hills beyond. Aleck was dismayed: his father would surely miss Moniack; after all, Reelig's whole way of life consisted 'in his improvements, the healthiness of the spot, and the thousand ties of endearment by which you are bound to it'. What kindred spirits would he find in Inverness?

Despite this move, in September that year Aleck and William received a packet of letters from their parents, written at the beginning of 1811,'almost extinguishing the hope of saving Moniack'. The news that the old home might really have to go threw Aleck first of all into a storm of remorse for past profligacy and then into a passionate resolve to retrench. He dismissed as many servants as possible and hoped that William might follow suit but, as his brother lived a very frugal life and all his extravagance was directed towards 'the unthankful and evil', he was not optimistic.

Two days later, he received no fewer than sixteen letters at once from his father and mother; it was a nerve-racking business opening them as the next might well bear the terrible news that 'the little Paradise of my Father's forming' was no longer theirs. However, although they all contained the same gloomy prediction – that Moniack must go – the worst had not yet come to pass. But the last letter was written six months earlier. All Aleck could do was reply in the same vein:

> Moniack, I fear, is gone. But do not allow your whole happiness to center there. Place some in the hopes of seeing your Children once more in your family, if it be in another place. If the scene of all our early joys and childish sports, of your happiest days ... be torn from us, yet they cannot separate our mutual affections from each other. They cannot render you less the object of our love and reverence; nor us less the object of your tenderness and hope.

It was at this point, receiving word of the real danger to Moniack, that Seton wrote to Reelig imploring him not to make any hasty decisions for a year. He expressed 'the warmest and sincerest interest in the welfare and prosperity of your family' which he had long considered as half his own and asked that Reelig would 'suspend for the present your purpose'. He had a plan.

Sailing in the wake of the Nugents

Once the trauma and uncertainty of departure were over, Edward found life at sea on the whole to his liking. The day started around 7.00 am with a walk until breakfast, followed by reading until dinner at 1.00 pm. There was a variety of books on board, 200 of them provided by the obliging Lieutenant Caulfield, with whom Edward was making friends.

While John Fraser studied Persian, Edward reluctantly tried to learn some Hindustani. After the study hour, more walking followed, on the trail of the Nugents. When John Fraser went to dinner at 4.00 pm, Edward, with the cabin to himself, played the flute. Then it was time to dress for the activities, usually chess or whist, which filled the rest of the evening until bed at 11.00 pm. He was getting on very well with John Fraser but was as far from Sir George's notice as ever:

> I am quite excluded from Sir Geo's society, except meeting on deck by chance – and it is evident he does not mean to pay me even any trifling attention – for he had numberless ways of shewing distinction between me and others, if he chuses it ...

> he has several persons at his Table whom he never saw before – and who had no introduction to him.

On the endless walks on the quarterdeck there were always at least half a dozen pushier passengers elbowing themselves between him and Sir George. Lady Nugent, however, conscious of her duty as the Governor General's wife, was doing her best to entertain the passengers. She twice mentioned in her diary that she had invited 'all the gentlemen and ladies on board to our cabin', where they lunched off grapes, cake and malmsey.[12] She also provided hot chocolate for the two ADCs when they came off watch during the night ('not only a treat, but nourishment to them, as growing boys'), prevailed upon her *ayah*[13] to cook a curry for the numerous Indian servants on board and provided albatross soup and albatross pie for everyone.[14]

Edward was still worrying about James, for whom he was keeping an account of the voyage, highlighting 'everything that I think can be usefull to him':

> Had I taken my Cabin from the Captain, instead of from John Fraser, I should have been at Sir Geo's Table instead of the Cadets' table – and had I applied early for a Cabin a Servant and a whole Cabin would not have cost me more than my half cabin and no servant. It is nothing to me now. But I would not like that James suffered discomfort and disquiet.

James must bring Black John with him – he would be 'a treasure of no small value'. The thought of Black John reminded him of the likely plight of his slaves under a new master – 'Indeed it is so painfull a subject that when it comes across me I instantly go in search of someone to talk to and divert my attention in other ways.'

His fear that they might not stop at the Cape – 'if we do not my linen will be short although I have 60 changes' – was unfounded. On 22 October 1811, in weather cold enough to make him don his woollen stockings, they arrived in Table Bay.

Luckily, he stayed with a Dutch family who looked after him when he fell ill and spent several days 'lying in a room ... with open windows while in the hot fit of the ague – my old West Indian enemy – I got so bad a sore throat that I have hardly yet got rid of it'.

Back on board, Edward, spurred on by John Fraser, summoned up the courage to ask Sir George if he could move to his table. Impossible, said Sir George: it was much too crowded anyway, and if anyone was to join, it must be an Ensign in the King's service.

The seating plan of the Nugents' table was, at this point, reorganised to accommodate Lady Nugent, who declared it was 'injurious to her eyes' to sit facing the glare of the sun on the sails. The new arrangement, however, enraged Captain Midwinter, Edward's flute-playing neighbour, who refused to change his seat and stamped off to his cabin with orders that his meals be served there for the rest of the voyage. Lady Nugent noted in her diary:

12 *A Journal from the year 1811 till the year 1815*, Maria Lady Nugent, British Library ORW 1986 A2764/1&2, pp.17 & 32.
13 A native lady's maid or nursemaid.
14 Lady Nugent's journal.

> ... it seems Captain Midwinter is a West Indian and suspected of being party-coloured and these people are always very furious in all their passions.[15]

Edward, by this time, had made friends with another clansman, the penniless Archibald Fraser, son of an Inverness-shire minister and a neighbour of Moniack. Archy provided him with another opportunity to approach the Nugents; he needed help with transport from Bengal to his job in Bombay. Edward braved Lady Nugent and obtained for Archy a promise of a passage to Bombay and a recommendation to the Governor there. 'This shewed a goodness of heart in Lady N and I also took it as a mark of kindness towards myself".

Baring was now within a few weeks of Calcutta. Edward was apprehensive about his arrival but trusted that Aeneas Mackintosh would come to his rescue. He was also concerned about parting from his shipboard friends, especially John Fraser. Another friend, Major Brown, who was returning to India and knew William, had been helpful, and probably realistic, about Edward's prospects.

> He recommends to me not to be sanguine in my expectations. God knows I am not ... All I expect is ... for some years, to have a decent lively hood – to get into some mercantile House in a subordinate situation. I shewed Major Brown Raigmore's[16] letter ... regarding me. He shook his head and told me not to depend on anything of that sort.

As the long journey neared its end, so did the supply of provisions; there was now little fresh meat and certainly no luxuries. 'The Table is very scanty, so much so that I was obliged to tell the Captain so'. Edward was not at all sorry to be parting company with the Captain, about whom he could think of nothing good to say:

> He has quarrelled with several of our passengers seriously and is now on speaking terms with only one or two ... he has behaved all along very ill to the young cadets and to many of the other Passengers. Still, we have had a very pleasant passage.

This was certainly partly due to the good health that he had sustained throughout, apart from the fever at the Cape and a resulting troublesome cough.

Towards the end of the voyage, tempers inevitably started to fray; there was an incident between the bad-tempered Captain Templar and John Fraser ADC after the latter interfered with Templar's rough treatment of a soldier and 'Templar pulled Fraser by the nose to the astonishment and horror of all of us.' Although Fraser remained perfectly calm, he demanded satisfaction and there was a general boycott of Captain Templar's table.[17] The Captain was so ashamed that he offered to dine in his own cabin

15 Ibid., p. 51.
16 Aeneas Mackintosh's brother and a neighbour of Moniack.
17 Lady Nugent's Journal, p. 64.

for the rest of the voyage. 'In short,' recorded Lady Nugent, 'all was unhappiness and I have never left my cabin since.'[18]

The affair was resolved on dry land at Saugar Island, at the mouth of the Hoogly river:

> Templar after receiving Fraser's fire (which was ineffectual), without returning it, expressed his sorrow and contrition for what he had done ... thus the affair was settled without Bloodshed.

Edward was concerned that John Fraser's mother, who was Lady Nugent's sister, would hear a false account of the incident. His mother must put the gossips right and reassure John's mother that 'everyone approves his conduct and admires his spirit'.

The Toast of Calcutta

Aleck was also on a boat, sailing down the Ganges to Calcutta; he had been ill with fever and had been recommended to take a river trip. With time to write letters, he admitted to his father that things were not especially happy between the brothers:

> William's outward manner to me has, ever since we met, from the 10th or 12th day at least, been inflexibly cold and repulsive ... when alone, he scarcely ever speaks to me ... In short, he has never made me a companion, and constantly repelled every endeavour at familiar or cheerful Intercourse. Yet I believe firmly that he has a rooted regard for me, as I have for him; but I believe it to be for me, from his recollection of home, and that association of pleasant remembrances with my name and existence, not from any value for me as a Man, as possessing any qualities that excite Esteem.

Aleck reassured his father, however, that this attitude of William's was but another eccentricity and that in matters relating to the family, or matters of real importance, 'perfect confidence prevails'.

Having worked such long hours since arriving in Delhi, Aleck found it hard to conquer boredom during the lonely, idle hours of convalescence on the river. Like William he was frustrated that he had not learnt to draw…

> … for often have I passed beautiful spots or remarkable old buildings, and regretted I could not sketch them, especially at Dehli, where every 100 yards for miles around presents objects worthy of the Pencil.

He was, however, renewing his acquaintance with his beloved Classical authors, Sallust, Caesar, Livy and Tacitus. When he ran out of Latin texts he had Dr Johnson for company: 'I do not read a page of Johnson without either acquiring new ideas, or having new light thrown on old ones.' He particularly relished Johnson's biography of Sir Francis Drake and considered Drake 'one of the finest models for emulation I have met with' and Johnson unrivalled as a biographer:

18 Ibid.

> I have scarce been so much delighted with any sort of reading as these lives of old Johnson and may add that, bigoted Scotsman that I am, I read his *Tour to the Hebrides* with great pleasure and in it could not find a syllable that could, or at least ought, to offend Scotland.

He was worrying about Edward's imminent arrival in India and pessimistic about Edward's prospects, but 'such disappointments are to be looked for, and the remedy found not in useless regret, but in vigorous exertion and patient perseverance'. After all, he had just read that Sir Francis Drake had started life as a 'friendless Cabin Boy'. James, however, must not put a foot in the direction of India until Aleck and William gave the go-ahead; there were no longer any real openings except for people with capital at their disposal.

Midway between Delhi and Calcutta lies Allahabad …

> … situated at the confluence of the two Holy rivers, the Jumna and Ganges. Hence it is a place of immemorial and extreme sanctity. Those who bathe there are supposed to be absolved for their past sins ... Pilgrims resort to it from the farther parts of India.

The Emperor Akbar's great fort guarding the union of the sacred rivers much impressed Aleck, as did the confluence itself, where …

> … the different colour of the two rivers is discernible ... and distinct for above half a mile ... the Jumna perfectly transparent, the Ganges excessively muddy.

Two of Aleck's servants paid a rupee each for the privilege of a dip in the holy rivers; one of them shaved his head and 'presented his hair to the river as a propitiation' in order to free his father from his sins. The other, 'a perfect savage, although faithfull and brave (one of William's proteges)' was ecstatic at being able to visit the holy place.

At Benares – another sacred spot for Hindus – Aleck stayed an extra day in order to allow the servants 'to gratify their piety or curiosity by traversing the City and paying their devotions'. Meanwhile, he went to the Post Office and found to his delight a packet of letters from his parents, two of which, written in March and June that year, brought news of Jane's good health and of George's general progress.

> The picture you give of George is highly pleasing ... I never doubted his promise of mental excellence. As a Child, his disposition was always singularly sweet, and his understanding of great promise; but bodily strength and robustness of Constitution, I feared would not have been his.

There follows in this letter home a long dissertation on Despair and Hope, sprinkled with literary and classical allusions and Latin quotations, very much in his old style and concluding:

> To what purpose all this trite and general, and uninteresting discussion, will perhaps be your enquiry, if you ever get this letter, and ... if you ever read thus far in it. Why the truth is, I write more to amuse myself perhaps, than my correspondent. I am alone; and have read till tired, and by natural progression, fall to the only other resource, writing ... such a mixty maxty, as you would call it.

On went the letters and on went Aleck's voyage, through Ghazipur to the mouth of the Gogra, on whose banks the scenery 'is said to be *sublime* beyond anything known; for it rushes through rocks, and over immense precipices, forming beautiful cataracts, and with solemn woods covering the surrounding mountains'. Like William before him, Aleck was enticed by such scenery, born as he was into the dawn of Romanticism, with its fascination for the Sublime and Picturesque. He had, however, neither time nor energy to explore 'these Romantic Regions'. After a tediously slow final leg, owing to the sluggish current and an easterly wind, he reached Calcutta towards the end of January 1812.

Edward had reached Calcutta earlier that same month to a warm welcome from Aeneas Mackintosh and was soon engulfed in a social whirl. Feted by William's and Aleck's friends, with his good looks and outgoing personality, he was instantly popular and on every guest list. He loved every minute of it and wrote home excitedly:

> Since I arrived I have been doing nothing but going about, in visiting and dining about Calcutta ... when I got to Mackintosh's the first thing he told me was that he expected Aleck in a few days in Calcutta. I instantly guessed that he had been ill, which I find too true – but Aeneas assures me he is quite recovered ... Aeneas Mackintosh is as friendly as it is possible to be ... Aleck I believe is his favourite of us three but I believe he would do any of us every kind act in his power. If he ever goes home I am sure you will like him very much.

At last, one evening a couple of weeks later, the brothers met after a separation of four years, and Edward handed over to Aleck the carefully preserved message and ring from cousin Isabella:

> I learnt on my arrival [wrote Aleck] that Edward ... had that morning gone 16 miles from Calcutta to see some racing at Barrackpore. In the Evening, however, after having passed a day of restlessness and expectation, I was gladdened by a sight of him. He knew me immediately, and we retired to our room (at Mackintosh's) and enjoyed a long chat upon past events and future prospects, for we were too happy to allow the present to encroach on our thoughts.

The Eldest Son Returns

James, meanwhile, had at last shaken the mud of Guyana from his boots and was in Scotland. He arrived in mid-October 1811 and threw himself into the week-long celebration of the Northern Meeting in Inverness. His father was delighted – what a chance to find a wife:

> The Gentry of seven counties, and many strangers, ought to give him a view of Northern society ... he has seen little of Society, except West Indians, and a narrow circle at Edinburgh and Liverpool.

He was very pleased with his eldest son – 'a fine manly fellow'.

Aleck treasured the letter that gave him an account of James's arrival home:

> When I read that little account, I felt myself at Moniack ... and rejoiced in the superior interest of an Eldest Son returning after a twelve years' absence ... in short, I became a spectator of the whole scene, partook of your and James's delight, and forgot, for a time, that I was in the sultry plains of Bengal, and conceived myself breathing the refreshing gales from our heath covered Mountain.

By this time, the news that William had not secured the Residency had reached Moniack. Reelig felt that William should have remained in Delhi instead of adventuring off to Peshawar. He had written, as Aleck had requested, to William on the subject of 'Tygers and Lions', and they were, he added, all drinking tea from the urn on which William had spent so much time and trouble all those years ago in London.

❊

In the Highlands, 1812 was ushered in by the most glorious weather, with roses and violets blooming together on New Year's Day. Despite not securing a tenant for Moniack, the family were settled in the small house in Castle Street in Inverness, where George was now doing well at the Academy. His parents were finding life far cheaper in town as 'we neither give nor accept entertainment'. James, 'a restless bird, not fond of a cage', was rarely at home. There were still hopes of selling Plantation No.28 in Berbice and of letting Moniack, but the future was more uncertain than ever. Reelig had to turn to William again:

> I shall write Willy soon. I fear that if he does not succeed in a loan for me, so as that the bills reach me before August 1812, the Bank will force Moniack to sale in which case my crisis, or rather our family's crisis, is complete. If he succeeds in a loan, I shall fear little.

William did succeed, with a loan of £2,000 supplemented by £500 from Aleck, and everyone was able to breathe again. Reelig hoped that cutting down on servants did not deprive Aleck of 'necessary ease and comfort' or of 'necessary appearance for your station'. He and Jane were managing with 'Old George' and Black John as manservants. Otherwise 'our sole reliance is Mary McGillivray and one of the Nurses and one maidservant'. Jane, at least according to Reelig, was bearing up well under this. Jane Anne was doing her best to help her parents and George was proving quite a handyman. A month later, Moniack was let to a Mr Mackenzie of Flowerburn for £180 sterling per annum for three years – another sigh of relief all round.

Reunion

In Calcutta there followed a month of non-stop activity for Aleck, whose friends wanted to catch up with him, and Edward, who continued to charm Calcutta society as Aleck had never done. They dined out every night, including with the Nugents, whom Aleck found 'very pleasant and far removed from any affectation of supercilious dignity, or pride of station'. Edward even persuaded his brother, a reluctant dancer, to accompany him to a 'grand masked Ball'. Aleck wrote reassuringly to his father:

> Edward has quickly made his way into the best society. Coming out with our really pleasant Commander in Chief was undoubtedly an advantage ... but his own temper and manners are of themselves sufficient to secure him a welcome wherever he goes.

Seton, now back in Calcutta with a seat on the Supreme Court, was thrilled with Edward and reported to Reelig that he was …

> … without even a single exception the most interesting youth I ever saw. His amiable appearance of manner and his uncommon intelligence make their way to the heart at once.

He would be delighted to be considered as Edward's banker and he was working on his plan to save Moniack.

Edward made numerous friends and lost no time in introducing Aleck to some of the people so often recommended by William. But he had come to the same conclusions as Aleck about Calcutta women:

> Vulgarity indeed seems rather a common failing among the Calcutta ladies – Mrs Hall is ladylike – and one or two more that I saw – but as for the rest, they are very much below par.

The one exception to this was the wife of cousin Sandie Tytler. She was 'a charming little woman – she met us with all the frankness that one of Sandie's sisters would have done – she is said to be very sensible and she certainly is very engaging without being in the least handsome.' Sandie had been singularly fortunate in finding such a 'Congenial Personage'.

After a month of Calcutta society, Aleck was heartily tired of parties and expensive frivolity and longing to get back to Delhi and his 'Courthouse and causes'. As William was mostly away from Delhi and not at all agreeable company when he was at home,

Aleck was eager to take his newfound brother home with him. Edward, on the other hand, thoroughly enjoying life in Calcutta, wanted to stay until James arrived. There seemed, however, to be slightly more hope of an opening for Edward in Delhi, and after much discussion and advice from friends, he was persuaded to go. Aleck began to indulge in all sorts of delightful plans:

> I mean, on returning, to get a small cottage, outside of the City, where we can pass the Evening, night and morning ... When in Delhi before, solitude (Willie being almost always absent) made me indifferent to all the little comforts of life; but now I have one to talk to, and consult, and who will help me and partake the enjoyment; I shall have resources of comfort, and innocent enjoyment unknown to me before.

The brothers set off for Delhi in early March 1812 and, realising that his parents would by now have had a surfeit of descriptions of the river between Calcutta and Delhi, Edward confined his account to a few enthusiastic details. He was very pleased with the boat, this time a pinnace.[19] It was very comfortable, with ample room for essential furniture, Edward's piano, Aleck's hunting kit and toolbox and 'about a hundred and fifty volumes of books – scattered about in all directions'. There were two additional boats, one a cookboat and the other for Eclipse and the luggage ('no small matter'), a greyhound, a terrier and two pointer pups. 'The servants ... I think only 15 – are stowed in all three boats.' The boats reminded Aleck of Noah's Ark – three thatched houses sitting on flat-bottomed vessels – and 'with this equipage we go on about 10 or 12 miles a day'.

Their routine in this cosy home was fairly constant: up in the cool of dawn for a walk with their guns; after breakfast they read or worked 'at something or other' until dinner at 3.00; then another walk to watch the sun go down, followed by tea and a game of backgammon. Both enjoyed themselves, Aleck because he was feeling well again and at last had company, and Edward because it was so different from his life in Berbice; he now had 'nothing to do but amuse myself & to study how to do so most agreeably – instead of being continually obliged to do what I had no pleasure in doing'.

Conversation aboard often turned to James and his prospects. Edward was worried that 'James, at his time of life, and after twelve years lost in a warm climate, should be in such a situation as not to be in some degree independent'. Nevertheless, he could not conceive of his admired eldest brother being unemployed for long. Aleck agreed:

> If my voice be aught [I] would strongly recommend James to come out immediately. He has here at least a comfortable home comparatively, where he can await, & (probably would not have long to wait) some independent employ; or at least some step to independence.

Edward, finding the long time lag in correspondence difficult, was eager for letters from home:

19 A small boat with sails and/or oars.

> What a melancholy difference there is between hearing from you almost every fortnight as we did in Berbice and here! It will soon be a twelvemonth since I left you and I know nothing of any of you ... but in every other respect there is no comparison. Berbice compared to Bengal seems like the most savage part of Cornwal compared to Devonshire – better tho it be, however I do not think the most splendid fortune, added to long habit, could make this country obliterate Scotland ... I feel attached to the very soil and I shall I trust be so as long as I am your most affectionate son.

At Kanpur they found a packet of letters waiting for them, including the longed-for news of James's homecoming. Edward had his heart in his mouth every time he opened a letter from home in case it bore news of the sale of Moniack, and he was worrying again about the fate of his slaves:

> I shall now be impatient to hear from James and to know how he has disposed of the Boat, and what is become of Ben the Captain, who was one of the best Negroes in the country. But it grieves me so much to think of what hands they may fall into ... often often I think of them and the reflexions they will make on our deserting them when they find themselves in the hands of harsher masters.

They arrived in Delhi in mid-July 1812 and were joined by William four days later. Edward was amazed by his appearance:

> He is very much altered so much so that I could not have known him – yet he looks very well and healthy – very stout and broad chested ... but the increased size of his face altogether and the fierce look which the whiskers and Moustachios give – entirely alter the expression of face that I remember.

Their talk on that first evening together ranged from memories of home and James's future to lucrative openings for Edward, but always came back to the question nearest to all three hearts – how to save Moniack.

Seton's plan

The plan proposed by Seton and explained by Edward to his father with characteristic clarity, was 'a sum of money £20,000 to be raised on your behalf'. Of this Seton would provide a third, their friend in Lucknow, Major John Baillie, another third, and the final third would come from Mr Walter Munro, head of the medical board in Calcutta; he, so far, was unaware of the scheme and his part in it. This, along with the possible sale of the remaining plantation in Berbice, the rents from Moniack, the Customs House salary and £1,000 annually from William and Aleck, might, after the interest had been paid, provide their father with an income of £1,000 a year. Could he live on £500 a year, the other £500 going to reduce the £8,000 owing to different people?

The question was, however, academic as Mr Munro, although reputedly liberal and very rich, had not replied and was discovered to have many poor relations. The plan was therefore' all fudge', as Reelig wrote in red in his letterbook. Seton, however, had already instructed his agents to put £6,000 at Reelig's disposal. 'So tranquillize your mind', he wrote, 'banish all Gloomy ideas' and look forward to many happy days together 'in the Land of Cakes'.

Reelig was ecstatic: Seton's contribution and remittances from William and Aleck 'have done wonders. They have not only paid off pressures but they have, whilst diminishing debt, given a confidence that procures me time.' October was also brightened by the news of a good crop in Berbice 'to quiet Mr Gladstone and liquidate a considerable debt'.

Inevitably, Reelig could not resist spending some of Seton's money on improvements. He demolished the old ruin of Rebeg and used the materials to build a good new stable; the old stable he converted into living quarters for the family. He then turned his attention to the garden:

> I have taken some pains to nourish the great *old Ash tree* and have built an hexagonal seat round it and seated it with the great ancient cupple and roof trees of the old family House which with the venerable tree it surrounds I mentally dedicate to Mr Seton, whose friendship cherishes my sons and may save our Estate.

Seton was delighted:

> Had you but seen the interest excited by your account of the seat placed round the favourite Ash tree, could you but have heard the nice comfortable craik[20] about domestic matters to which it gave rise, you would have thought that not only William and Alexander but I also had been born at Moniack.

He was looking forward to 1816, when he would have the pleasure of ...

> ... paying my respects to Mrs F and you and, while seated perhaps under the shade of the venerable ash tree at Rebeg, tell you all about our dear friends in India, how well I left them, and when you may expect their return.

Archy Seton's extraordinary desire to save an estate he had never seen for a man he had never met, was, however, causing problems back home at Touch. From the correspondence[21] between Archy and his brother-in-law, Sir Henry Steuart, there emerges a tussle of wills. Sir Henry, longing to be rid of responsibility for Touch, constantly demanded his brother-in-law's presence at home. When, in 1811, he heard that Archy was leaving the Delhi Residency for Penang, he once again urged him to come home, to no avail. Archy had other ideas: after a year in Penang there was not only an attractive job in Calcutta on offer but also another reason for staying in India – nothing more or less than his desire to save Moniack. He had decided to spend another year in India expressly 'for the purpose

20 Gossip, chat (Scots)
21 National Library of Scotland, MS 19208, 126–295.

of enabling myself to make a salutary exertion in favour of this worthy family – the pecuniary distress of which affects me almost as much as if they related to our own family'.

He admitted that he had already contributed £6,000, which, with contributions from William and Aleck, he hoped would free the estate. Aware that Sir Henry might well not see it his way, he added that, although the finances of Touch could not be called flourishing, at least the estate was safe and now he wanted 'to give equal safety to that of a *friend*'.[22]

Why was Seton was so intent on saving Moniack? It seems that he was simply a philanthropist in need of a cause. As one by one the young Fraser brothers gathered in Delhi, all with the aim of restoring their family fortunes, the cause, as it were, landed on his doorstep.

Sir Henry, meanwhile, had recently produced what he hoped was his trump card; his wife, Archy's sister, needed him home. She was extremely fragile, both physically and mentally, and the news had ...

> ... seemed quite to overpower her spirits ... the idea that her beloved brother, in whom her whole heart and soul are wrapped up, should ... now delay his return, after an absence of more than three and thirty years, was more than she could support.[23]

But it was all in vain. Her brother remained in India for several more years. Meanwhile he opened his house, and his heart, to anyone needy. Something of an eccentric, he lived very frugally:

> My house and everything about me are quite simple ... Most persons in my situation have half a dozen carriage horses – as many saddle horses, and a variety of carriages while I have only a simple chaise and pair, and not a single saddle horse. In a word, I have neither show nor *dash*; and do not expend a Rupee unnecessarily.[24]

His house, however, was often so full that people overflowed into tents in his garden while 'he himself is cooped up with his books and papers into one room and that one the smallest'. Much later, James stumbled on a story relating to Seton's past. It seemed that his father, Hugh, had been a man of a 'dangerous speculative turn' who had been declared bankrupt, leaving his son with debts of £300,000. A court order reduced the debt to £60,000 and Hugh disappeared to India as a private soldier and died in Bombay. Archy never knew of his father's life in India until after his death. 'How natural' mused James was 'Seton's fear of speculation, his dislike of all adventure in the mercantile line'. How natural, too, was his desire to help four boys burdened by the debts of their father and striving to hold on to their family home.

22 Ibid.
23 Ibid.
24 Ibid.

At the same time there was good news from that home. Jane was in fine health and spirits and thought nothing of walking the ten miles from Inverness to Rebeg. Life in Inverness, however, was tedious, and she missed the 'bustle' and country pursuits of Moniack. No opportunity was lost to visit friends 'to divert her mind and keep up her present good health which depends much on cheerful and active occupation'. Jane Anne was now 'tall, stout and comely ... she is merry and reckless, but always guarded, discreet, reserved and judicious'. She was discriminating in her companions and had a fine powerful voice. She was a good French scholar, had a great desire for knowledge, was inquisitive, observant and intrigued by science. On the practical side, she was a good mantua[25] maker 'but would prefer other persons darned her stockings'.

In June 1812 James set off on a Highland walking tour with a dog and Black John on horseback. His father approved of his 'making acquaintance with his native country and countrymen and [catching] the last view of the Highland manners'. What the future held for James was still a mystery. Both William and Aleck had taken the brave step of writing to Charles Grant asking him to discourage James from India. The great man himself seemed perplexed: he threw cold water on the Indian adventure to start with but 'I know not what he can pursue if he go not to India.' James's frustrated father complained, 'I am wholly in the dark as to his future destination.'

Then the news that Belladrum was up for sale, advertised for £70–80,000, rocked the Highlands and the Fraser clan in particular. 'Who next?' the clansmen wondered, and Reelig was especially shaken. The Belladrum Frasers, neighbours and cousins, had been there from the moment he arrived at Moniack; so many scenes of his bachelor days and of his children's childhood had been played out at that beautiful place. But then the Belladrum Frasers had no children, and that made all the difference. All he prayed for was the health of his children, the reduction of his debt and a future for James. He was now receiving about £702 yearly in rent from Moniack, and with that and 'the aid I receive from you and William' he reckoned he might save the old place . James must do his bit too. He could not 'comfortably possess Moniack' unless he repaid his brothers.

Trio in Delhi

Soon after arriving back in Delhi, Aleck was promoted; he was now in the Court of Criminal Jurisdiction, his job being to 'try the Prisoners, and report each case, with an abstract of the Evidence, and the impression made on my mind'. William's employment was much the same as ever – 'settling the different quotas of the several districts under Delhi &c and also ... travelling about arresting Criminals and sending them with Evidences into Delhi for trial'. There was now a possible opening for Edward 'in an excellent house of agency', but Aleck was doubtful about his suitability for a position

25 A loose gown.

which demanded 'a bustling Energy and restlessness', quite the opposite of Edward's nature. James would suit them better.

Edward, however, was hopeful. He had been promised money from friends, John Baillie and Hugh Rose, to enable him to join a house of agency and reckoned he could muster some 'bustling Energy' if need be. He would give James half his share in the business; the agency would thus get two Fraser brothers for the price of one. If none of this succeeded, then, despite William's pride, Edward was perfectly prepared to apply for one of the 'small appointments'; he would take any job to avoid being a burden on his brothers.

William was enjoying the company of Edward, who was finding his eccentric brother 'less austere and starched than expected. He is very far from it and is cheerful and droll.' Edward was also making the most of his social life despite the shortage of female company. He was very pleased with their house, with its view of a fine old bridge over a branch of the Jumna, especially as there was a garden 'which gives us grass, vegetables and fruit'. He was intrigued with William's menagerie – a full grown lion, two tigers three quarters grown and another about the size of a fox – and admired the twenty or thirty skins of tiger, lion and leopard, all killed by William: 'They would make beautiful sopha covers for winter.'

William and Aleck swam in the Jumna every morning at sunrise and sometimes again in the evening. Edward, still bothered by his cough, was, for the moment forbidden to take part in these excursions, but 'I am picking up again – the cold weather will bring me round again quite'. He had settled down happily in the comfortable company of his brothers and the rest of the Residency staff, looking forward to contributing towards his keep and, in the far-off future, to sending remittances home. The three brothers were shaking down together pretty well; now all that was needed was the arrival of James.

7

1812–1813

HIGHLAND FAREWELL

In the summer of 1812 James and Black John explored the West Highlands, Raasay and Skye, Black John riding and James walking alongside, with 'a stout highlander as a porter'. Wherever possible, James accepted the hospitality of local lairds; otherwise they stayed in inns of varying comfort and cleanliness. At Cluanie, where they arrived at dead of night, the landlady, wakened by their knocking, was 'very much frightened at my servant's black face' but managed to provide a supper of cream, eggs, cheese, barley bread and a chicken. James then retired to a dirty but comfortable bed where, he noted in his diary, he much missed the comfort of a companion. Where Black John slept is almost always a mystery.

In Skye, at dinner in Portree with the local lairds, the talk stretched late into the night on the engaging subject of second sight. James, who had previously associated second sight with superstition among the illiterate, was astounded by the members of the company 'of the most undoubted integrity and the . . . most acute sense and observation' who declared firsthand experience of second sight but, alas, there was not time to record all their stories.

The next highlight was a visit to the Macleods on the island of Raasay with strawberries and cream for dinner. James enjoyed the company of the Macleod family, especially a niece, Miss Ross, who sang some Gaelic airs, including 'one of the sweetest lullabies I ever heard'. Her sister, just back from education down south, impressed him with her new accent, speaking 'like a native of England'.

Back on the mainland they often covered nearly thirty miles a day. Whenever he could, James sketched and all the way he fished. Arriving at the inn at Lochcarron, they found 'the whole clergy of the county assembled in Synod' fortifying themselves well for their deliberations. James, cold and wet, declined their invitation to join them.

It rained nearly every day but at Loch Maree there was a spectacular sunset followed by an almost equally breathtaking sunrise, balm to James's artist's eye:

> The lake appeared in the distance one sheet of living gold, the hills variously tinted with brilliant hues ... till ... they were lost in purple glory. The morning was sweet beyond expression and there was a charm, a languid loveliness breathed over the face of nature ... so hot, so still that the leaves seemed afraid of moving.

The final week of the tour took them into Sutherland, where, short of lairds, they found accommodation in shepherds' cottages and dined on 'curds, cream and bread and cheese'. Then, on 1 August, home to Inverness, where to James's consternation a letter from Charles Grant offered an opportunity to sail for India forthwith. James suffered a sleepless night. He was certainly not ready to go anywhere immediately and not sure that he wanted to go to India at all. He had various plans for the rest of the year and needed to consider his options: should he take the risk and go to India, or would he be more use at home?

Needing objective advice, he rode off to breakfast with cousin Evan Baillie who had no hesitation in recommending that he immediately proceed to India. His next consultant was William Tytler at Aldourie, now Sherriff of Inverness. He agreed with Evan: creditors would look much more kindly on the family's problems if they saw all four brothers 'in situations of respectability'. Convinced by these arguments, James rode home to accept Grant's offer.

As it happened, his departure was not as immediate as he had feared; there was some difficulty in finding a passage, and he now embarked on a social whirl, accepting every invitation and seeing as many friends as possible. His family, meanwhile, made lists and assembled his belongings.

He spent many pleasant evenings with his cousins at Aldourie, with music, dancing and songs from 'the sweet voice of Jeanie Tytler' (Plate IX), until the moment came for the family to return to Edinburgh for the winter. On their final evening James reflected that this …

> … is the last night I might ever be in company with J. Tytler, the girl I loved & the Friend I now feel the truest attachment to & who has evinced the same to me.

He was suddenly deeply pessimistic: this might be …

> … a last adieu … I do think and feel as if any hopes of Domestick Settlement or happiness in this life were quite destroyed – for little prospect appears of anything of the sort taking place while I am yet of an age to enjoy it much.

The autumn, however, brought diversions: from the Mackenzies at Brahan he collected letters of introduction to Lord Moira, the new Governor General of India; one of the numerous Misses MacKenzie helpfully approached her friend, sister of Captain Maxwell of the frigate *Daedalus,* about a possible passage for James. There were musical evenings at home in Castle Street, although the singers were invariably judged 'very far inferior to Jeanie Tytler'. Sometimes, when there were no guests, the family would gather round the fire and James would read from one of Miss Burney's latest novels or from Jeanie Tytler's farewell present to him, a volume of Southey's[1] latest poetry.

⁂

That October, the fifteen-year-old Jane Anne was allowed to go to the Election Ball in Inverness. She 'danced every dance & every reel almost – & looked very well,' reported James with rare brotherly pride. She also performed at a concert given by her music teacher, Mr Thomson:

1 Robert Southey (1774–1843), Poet Laureate 1813–43.

> My sister played a duet with Betsy Kerr which was very well done & went off admirably – she also played a little Rondeau – which was very brilliant ... she made only one little slip but certainly played extremely well – she trembled exceedingly all the time.

Jane Anne, despite her concert nerves and her late bedtime, was so buoyed up with her success that the next day she played for a whole hour to Mr Proby, the local fiddle master, and a day later she 'performed pretty well' at Farraline.[2]

There were also expeditions further afield: Reelig, who had customs business in Cromarty concerning hemp from Riga, took James along for the freezing three-and-a-half-hour journey. James was delighted with Cromarty and especially its firth:

> ... that finest of all Bays – Cromarty – with its entrance between the noble and majestic suitors[3] rearing themselves as guardians of the spacious harbour which runs up for many miles affording anchorage for all the navies of the world.

Squeezed into the cracks between visits, sport and entertaining at home was letter-writing. Jeanie Tytler had written 'a very interesting one on a most deeply engaging subject'. He confided to his diary, 'my answer was equally serious & grave & I think such as the letter most naturally demanded – the letter and the answer will I think not readily be lost to my remembrance'.

By the end of November James began to make preparations for India in earnest. On 10 December 1812 he was present 'at the Baptism of poor [Black] John (at his own request) in the great Church [the Old High Church in Inverness] by Parson Thomas Fraser'. Another, more delicate, matter on James's conscience was his responsibility for 'poor Betsey and little Edward'. Whoever they were, and it seems fair to assume the reference is to an illicit liaison, he summoned the courage to ask his father to look after them in his absence, giving him 'my ideas of how to treat them'.

Then came the long-dreaded last day, 15 December, his mother's birthday. The family made a determined effort to be cheerful, but James was especially sad to say goodbye to Jane Anne, his precious only sister, reflecting that he would miss out on her most interesting years and would return to find her 'perhaps lost to me – married perhaps'. He found his father 'much affected' but still in control enough to tell James to bear in mind two things: 'to keep in view a most early return and secondly to write fully and frequently'. James had been dreading his mother's emotions as she sent yet another son to an uncertain life in the East but he found her very composed.

> She never hinted a sorrowful word till the moment I bid her adieu and even then seemed held up by a cheery presentiment as if we should meet soon ... I have a similar presentiment that I shall see each & every member of my family alive & well on my return.

2 Another Fraser house on the eastern side of Loch Ness.
3 The Sutors, the two headlands at the entrance to the Cromarty Firth.

Thirteen-year-old George was most indignant at seeing the last of his brothers disappear to the other side of the world but generously marked the occasion by presenting James with one of his favourite books, *The Farmer Boy*. His mother gave him her usual parting present – *The Pleasures of Memory* by Samuel Rogers – which James gracefully accepted, though 'God knows there is not need for any remembrance between my mother & myself'.

Two o'clock and the mail coach was at the door. Dr Robertson was tactfully waiting in the street; he shook hands with James, promising him that he would let him know if his father's health should fail.

> I quitted Inverness then this day for my second long absence in life and to the other side of the globe from that I have spent 12 years of my life in ... can I help feeling the difference of our quiet fireside enlivened by the unreserved social intercourse of familiar conversation and the cheering musick of my sister. No, it must be bitterly missed.

Man o' War

James reached Edinburgh in time to hear the Castle guns heralding the Russian victory over Bonaparte.[4] In the Tytler house in Princes Street much of his time was spent sorting out a rumour flitting round the family: his mother apparently disapproved of the correspondence between James and Jeanie on the grounds that she was keeping James 'hanging on'. Everyone agreed that there was no impropriety in the correspondence and that James, who was furious, should write to his mother about her 'most erroneous opinion of Jeanie':

> Now hear me ... when I explicitly pointedly and most unreservedly declare, that no change of circumstances in her life or mine *can ever create a possibility of Jane Tytler being my wife* ... My warmest friendship, my most animated admiration and sisterly love she always shall have thro life ... but no nearer connexion *can* ever take place ... you will restore her to that place in your love & esteem she *once* possessed ... Thus it is settled – the correspondence will go on.

He then took leave of all his cousins, kissed the children, boarded the telegraph coach for Glasgow and had a pleasant enough journey to the Talbot Inn in Liverpool which provided a 'a cold sorry bed in a cold sorry room'. Nevertheless, he slept late the next day, Christmas Eve, which he spent with the Gladstone family.

Christmas Day saw everyone celebrating the news of 'The Disastered State of the Army of France', and on New Year's Day 1813 James set off for London. His first impressions of the capital compared unfavourably with the glories of Georgian Edinburgh – 'the streets are narrow and poor and far inferior to Edinburgh in Beauty, regularity or splendour'.

4 Napoleon's retreat from Moscow, October 1812.

He fetched his luggage from the Docks, ordered some necessary articles of clothing, including some pairs of 'inexpressibles',[5] then made for the Theatre Royal, Drury Lane, where he saw John Braham[6] in a performance of *The Castle of Andalusia*.[7] He was entranced by the whole evening: the superb saloon with its marble columns filled after the show with all sorts of people, including crowds of 'women of the town of all appearances, some very beautiful', the 'soft sweet light' from 'the fine wax candles in their glass shades', the gold carving ornamentation of the boxes, the stage contained between two immense green marbled columns' and, of course, the opera and the afterpiece, *The Prince of the Dwarfs*.

Another night it was *The Jealous Wife*[8] performed by Mr and Mrs Kemble.[9] This event was made more interesting by a '*fille de loge*' who came and sat next to James and 'sighed so deeply & seemed so full of sorrow that I could not help asking her what was the matter ... I asked her place of abode which she told me. I shall call on her merely to see what she really is & if she is less abandoned than most of her sisterhood – they are wonderfully handsome & inviting'. This encounter he did not mention to his mother.

He was often invited out to dinner; on other evenings it was something of a relief to order in soup and a steak before taking himself off to the theatre. There were also more mundane affairs to attend to, like a visit to the shoemakers and to Mr Smith to have his hair 'put in order', and then the inevitable round of visits to Miss Chipps, the Grants and the Chambers family.

By now he was not feeling well, having developed a swollen testicle and a high fever. After medication, leeches, the attentions of several friends and the welcome news that he had secured a passage on *Daedalus*,[10] he felt recovered enough to take the overnight coach for Portsmouth on 26 January with Black John and two large trunks.

James's first impression of the frigate which was to be his home for at least five months was good: dinner with Captain Maxwell the first evening revealed him to be 'a pleasant man enough', while the other two passengers, Mr Stewart and Mr Uthoff, and the officers were reassuringly friendly.

A frigate was, however, considerably less comfortable than an East Indiaman. The three passengers were each accommodated with a hammock or 'cot' in the gunroom on the second or lower deck, where the eight officers, who slept in the surrounding cabins, spent the day. The gunroom was about 15ft wide, 22ft long and 5ft 6ins high, with the mizzenmast at one end and a long table taking up nearly all the room. At night the three passengers' hammocks were slung above the table; there was no privacy whatsoever, and the discomfort was compounded by heat and airlessness; the only source of air was a skylight, which had to be closed when it rained. James, however, remained cheerful.

5 Underpants.
6 One of Europe's leading tenors (1774–1856).
7 A comic opera by Irish playwright John O'Keeffe (1747–1833).
8 Comedy (1761) by George Colman the Elder (1732–94).
9 Charles Kemble (1775–1854) and his wife Maria Theresa (1774–1838).
10 A 38-gun frigate. Originally a French ship, *Corona*, captured by the British in 1811.

Unanimous verdict

In India, Aleck and Edward were also at the start of a sea voyage. During the heat of the Delhi summer Aleck had become aware that Edward was very unlike himself, listless and with little desire to go out. Aleck was not especially worried by these symptoms, ascribing them to the heat and concern about the situation at Moniack. It could not be lack of employment that was depressing Edward, as at last 'the most flattering prospects' were in view. Despite his impatience with medical men, however, Edward was persuaded to consult Dr Ludlow, the Residency surgeon, who prescribed a simple diet and some medicine.

One day in early September, things took a turn for the worse. Aleck was in the riverside bungalow working on a legal case, William had gone out to bathe in the river and Edward was pruning the orange trees in the garden. Aleck was suddenly summoned by a servant: Edward was spitting blood, and a surgeon was sent for. 'Mr Crichton ... told us not to be alarmed, that there was nothing dangerous in the symptom, and said it would only require care and rest'. He prescribed digitalis and abstinence from wine and red meats. Edward soon felt better enough to join a breakfast party given by the Commanding Officer of the Palace guard and then a tour of the Palace to view 'the Curiosities' which, to Aleck's alarm, involved a lot of walking and several staircases.

On his return home Edward had two recurrences of the attack; William demanded another opinion from Crichton, who repeated that there was no cause for concern and recommended a river trip to Calcutta and a sea voyage. Edward put his foot firmly down: that would be far too expensive and would involve a lot of unnecessary trouble. In any case, he was far more likely to recover in a comfortable house than at sea; he had had his fill of travelling.

A week later, however, he had been persuaded to accept Aleck's companionship on the three-month voyage downriver to Calcutta. Refusing to believe that anything much was wrong with him, he continued to eat what he pleased; mild tempered as he was, 'if his obstinacy were once provoked; if his temper were ruffled, nothing could be done'. They arrived in Calcutta on 27 October and were welcomed by their doctor friend, Simon Nicholson.

Nicholson was so struck by the change in Edward that, along with two other medics, McWhirter, a close friend of the brothers, and Skoolbred, 'considered the best Physician in Calcutta', he immediately prescribed a sea voyage to St Helena. 'Three of the ablest men in Calcutta,' Aleck told his mother, 'were unanimous in declaring it a measure of the most absolute necessity'. They also agreed on diet: vegetables and a meat broth. Edward, who was feeling better, 'seeing friends, talking and laughing', sleeping well and daily regaining his energy, vigorously opposed all this.

Nor would he hear of Aleck's accompanying him, on the grounds that absence would damage his brother's career. Aleck, however, suspected it was because he would insist on the medication prescribed which Edward considered 'little better than Quackery'. Eventually, he agreed to accept Aleck's company, but nothing could persuade him that he was really ill; his answer to anxious enquirers was that he was 'as well as they'll allow me to be'.

How they were to manage financially was one of Aleck's major concerns. His own salary of Rs500 per month was cut to Rs300, and Edward was earning nothing. Rs300 a month was not going to go far towards two passages, two outfits for the voyage and living expenses on St Helena. His own debt amounted at this point to near Rs30,000, and creditors were not keen to help people leaving the country. Aeneas Mackintosh came to the rescue, along with the head of another trading house, offering Rs6,000 and Rs5,000 respectively, while Seton's fulsome note to Aleck offered support of all kinds:

> The truth is, my dear Alec, that I have so long been in the habit of considering our families as *one* that I cannot (thank God, I cannot) now bring myself to regard their interests, their comforts, or their happiness as separate ... if, in a word, you do not consider all that I have, as at your command you will wrong me, *cruelly* wrong me.

St Helena was prescribed on account of its mild weather, 'the finest Climate in the world for Phthisical Patients'. *Surrey* was chosen because her sailing was imminent and because of the good reputation of Captain Beadle. On hearing of Edward's illness, he had reduced the price considerably. They also knew some of the passengers, including an old friend, Mr Wilton, an indigo merchant from Patna, who over the years had played host to all three brothers. The others included three women, eight children under the age of six, various soldiers, a handful of servants, some prisoners of war and 'an invalid' who died on the way and was buried at sea. Edward did not allow himself to be classed as an invalid.

The moment the brothers left Nicholson's house, however, Edward's spirits began to droop. He detested the idea of the voyage, maintaining that it was 'needless to talk of comfort at sea'. They sailed on 29 November 1812.[11] Aleck had racked his brains for anything that would make the voyage more bearable, including 'a comfortable large Couch ... medicines, Flannels, and all the necessaries normally provided for an invalid'. Two goats were taken on board in case Edward wanted milk. They took two servants, one a Negro, the other a Bengali, 'who by their attention and zeal are of great assistance'.

The last-minute booking on *Surrey* meant that their cabin was small (13½ft by 6ft), uncomfortable, noisy and unsuitable for a patient. Edward, however, liked the racket being 'rather cheered than disturbed by bustle'. It was also on the windward side and there was no way of controlling the temperature. The weather for the first month was cold and wet; rain poured through the crevices round the porthole and streamed through the cabin. Edward could not endure the closeness of the cabin with the windows shut, and the ensuing damp and cold worsened his cough.

The ship's surgeon, Mr Daun, son of an Aberdeenshire minister, was consulted. He recommended blisters, which Edward refused, saying that 'everything was expected from the sea, and that he could not endure more harassment'. As the pain in his chest and difficulty in breathing worsened, however, he was forced to accept the treatment. This, together with a change of diet, helped, but only temporarily. Soon all the symptoms

11 Log book of the *Surrey*, British Library IOR.L/MAR/B/191D.

returned and he reverted to a diet of milk, sago, sweet biscuits and raspberry jam. The kind Mr Wilton, himself in bad health, thoughtfully supplied the biscuits and jam and paid Edward daily visits.

The weather continued to deteriorate: the ship's log records a heavy swell, hard squalls of rain and constant showers; for four weeks Sunday's Divine Service on deck was cancelled. Edward's spirits were very low and it was hard to know how best to get him through the day; he no longer wanted to read or to be read to, spending the day reclining on his couch 'occupied in thought, neither speaking nor reading much'. The evenings were his best time, when 'he would come out, and talk and laugh cheerfully with the Ladies, or join in a Whist party'.

On the last day of January they sighted land. It is hard to imagine Aleck's feelings as the tiny speck on the horizon grew slowly into the towering, jagged, inhospitable rock that is St Helena. How was he to cope with Edward in such a place? Edward, on the other hand, was only thankful that at last they would reach dry land, where he was sure he would feel better.

At sea

Aboard *Daedalus,* James also had to contend with a stormy start to his journey. A few days into the voyage, the sea rose through the scuttles, flooding the officers' cabins and the gunroom where the heat was almost unbearable.

Occasional dinners with the Captain helped to ease the monotony. James got on very well with Maxwell's wife and sister and relished the Scottish gossip. They lent each other books, Byron's *Childe Harolde's Pilgrimage* in exchange for *Rokeby,*[12] Sir Walter Scott's new narrative poem, which James considered very inferior to *Lay of the Last Minstrel* and *The Lady of the Lake*: the poem had none of Scott's 'exquisite pathos and vivid description ... Oh I fear his falling off sadly'.

He was intensely interested in the workings of the ship and made daily records of wind, weather, latitude and longitude. He also attempted to learn Persian, aided by a huge dictionary lent to him by his fellow passenger, Mr Uthoff. Soon, however, the others complained that his books were taking too much room on the table and the draught funnelling down the mizzen mast blew all his papers about.

There was continual uproar, not only from the flapping of the sails, the moaning of the wind and the creaking of the timbers but also from the other ten members of the gunroom: 'one is playing the fiddle – another the flute to different tunes and another preparing another flute'. Others were arguing, laughing or singing. Even if they were quiet, there was 'constant roaring from morn till night' from the thirty midshipmen in steerage. James wished he had his father's powers of concentration: *he* could read and write whatever was going on around him 'particularly when a romping fit seizes Jane Anne & little George'.

Despite all this, James managed to keep up a regular correspondence with his parents and Jane Anne. Squashed at the only dry corner of the table, hardly able to think for

12 1813. In Scott's own words, a 'pseudo romance of pseudo chivalry'. Its poor reception convinced him that Byron had replaced him as the nation's favourite poet, and he turned to novels instead.

the racket and trying to keep the papers from blowing away, he wrote his letters and journal. Given these circumstances, they are surprisingly legible, albeit in unusually tiny writing in order to eke out his precious supply of paper. His apprehension increased as the voyage dragged on:

> When I think that my three brothers are in the continent that I am approaching, two of whom I haven't seen for so very long – and one of whom I look on as part of myself, I cannot repress a restlessness, the child of uncertainty – shall I see them at all?

He had no idea where Edward would be. Would he get on with Aleck and William, almost strangers to him? It might well be that whatever job he got would be far from where they were settled. What, in any case, was this job to be?

> What am I to do when I arrive? Am I to run through the plain plodding course of Asst Clerk, junior & senior Partner in a house of business ... or am I to try a speculation, many have succeeded in, many have been ruined by, and attempt a quick arrival at fortune ... or am I to be kindly helped over the style by some kind able friend?

He would not be at home to watch Jane Anne and George growing up and help them become 'amiable lovely & worthy' beings. What kept him going was the feeling that, at least, he was doing his duty to Moniack; that and the happy prospect of finding Edward, 'the Brother of my best love'.

As the weather improved, walking on deck became a regular pastime, and one beautiful early morning evoked nostalgia for Guyana and for the people he had known, especially one:

> This morning put me in mind of a fine Dewy morning in the dry weather in Berbice ... I traced this morning every little act of my daily work & pleasure on a fine day there ... my walk to the waterside viewing the different cotton pieces on the way tracing the different dayly improvements & measures on the young plants or the increasing harvest of Blossoms & Pods – then my meeting my dear Brother Edward ... My return, to Breakfast, the log work weighing cotton etc. overlooking my poor negroes & all the routine of the plantation which now seems so delightfull to me then hated and despised – my placid tranquil evenings ... my Brother's music and oh! the infinite succession of trifling but now interesting incidents, I pause on & review with bitter regret ... should I not miss many many whom I depended on for portions of comfort – and none more than the good creature who lived with me and made my life comfortable so long.[13]

'Well,' he concluded, 'all may be for the Best – I hope it is.'

⁂

13 Presumably a reference to a slave mistress.

A few days later, on the slow progress towards the South Atlantic and St Helena, James contracted mumps. He was grateful for the Doctor's cabin for daytime rest and escape from the nonstop chaos of the gunroom and, by the end of February, was recovered enough to take a conciliatory role in a row that had developed in the Mess: his fellow passenger, Stewart, was complaining about Mess fees.

Thereafter, shipboard life resumed its tedious routine. There were a few diversions to break the monotony:

> This evening a signal was made from the *Rose* Indiaman that there was a man overboard – and unfortunately the Boats sent to pick him up from two ships were unsuccessful – he rose no more – & the Boats returned without him.

Another tragedy occurred when a boy was missing at muster on *Daedalus*. The ship was searched high and low but no trace was found; it was concluded that he had most probably jumped overboard – 'he having been heard to threaten as much on being promised a flogging'.

Flogging was common. According to the ship's log, on one 'Day of Punishment' sentences ranging from eleven to forty lashes were carried out on six men whose crimes were contempt, theft and disobedience, and James, an observer *par excellence*, witnessed the event. A dispassionate note in his journal compared it with the punishment inflicted on his slaves in Guyana, judging it 'certainly severer than that we inflict on the negroes, tho less Blood is drawn – the Back is all Black & Blue and completely Bruised'.

Dinner parties aboard other ships of the convoy were a regular occurrence and, in some fairly unsettled weather, the company on *Daedalus* were invited on board *Aquilon* to see a play:

> The theatre was fitted up on the larboard side of the half deck and the proscenium ornamented with Painted canvas Pillars & curtains as usual. The Band sat in front of a Green Cloth hung by way of separating the stage from the audience – there were some very fair side scenes, as presenting a room or street, or even a wood if necessary ... and all was really a neat little theatre in miniature.

One drawback was that the head-dresses of the actors were often knocked off by the beams of the deck above. Otherwise, James was generally impressed by the performances but found the young midshipmen playing ladies' parts only 'so so' and was critical of their costumes. They also had no idea what to do with their hands, 'not perfectly knowing the pretty actions which females employ their arms and hands in', and kept shifting 'an unfortunate handkerchief from one hand to the other till it was like a wisp of hay'.

The evening's entertainment continued with supper, a liberal supply of wine '& some excellent comic songs sung which detained us most agreeably till one in the morning'. James's copy of the playbill for the evening grandly announced the play as performed 'Under the patronage of Capt. Bowles, Theatre Royal, Aquilon'.

Soon after this excitement there was the ceremony of Crossing the Line. James, one of the uninitiated, was a victim:

> I was blindfolded & ... a lather prepared of oil paint & water colours was applied to my face & questions asked to make me open my mouth which however I took care not to do as infallibly the lather would have been thrust into it ... I was saluted with three or four Buckets of water & was declared free but by the laugh round I could understand I was a frightfull figure from the Black & Blew paint on my face ... The ceremony concluded with gingerbread & wine in the gunroom & double allowance of grog to the men who had passed the Line before.

It was St Patrick's day, however, and Cotter, the Purser, among others, was Irish; consequently, the celebrations continued with a bowl of punch, 'which was so good that many got pretty well on on it & did not separate till two in the morning'. James abstained from all this, played a 'sober game of whist' and went to bed at eleven.

Captain Maxwell, determined not to be outdone by *Aquilon,* allowed the theatrical crew of *Daedalus* to plan a return match – a performance of *Venice Preserved,*[14] with invitations to *Aquilon, Bridgewater* and *Princess Royal.* Encouraged by the success of that evening, the company planned another, even more ambitious, production. It was to be *Macbeth*, with James choosing to play the part of Banquo 'as having very little to do & soon being rid of his part'. It would undoubtedly be very difficult to stage, 'but there is a maxim on board ... nothing is impossible aboard a King's ship'. The members of the cast were responsible for making their own costumes; James had luckily packed his tartan plaid and 'with this I will form a kilt ... & with armour & a bonnet it will be my dress'.

It was now about halfway through the voyage and supplies were beginning to run out: 'Today (30 March) we found that Hot Rolls are stopped so that one of our little comforts is gone'. Tempers were daily getting shorter, and Cotter, the Purser, announced that in a man o' war passengers were nothing but 'great pests' to the officers in the gunroom. James was offended but kept his temper and changed the subject, making a note that he would avoid arguments with Cotter in future.

The Rock

In mid-February *Surrey* sailed into St Helena Roads.[15] There they had to wait, riding at anchor along with a large fleet whose passengers had already filled every vacant room in the capital, Jamestown. Rocking gently in the harbour in a climate described by Aleck as heavenly, Edward's spirits rose; he talked frequently of their return to Bengal and seemed unaware of the danger he was in. Aleck knew this reprieve could only be temporary: 'during the whole voyage, debility had increased ... and by the time we landed Edward could scarcely walk across a Room'.

14 A tragedy in blank verse by Thomas Otway (1652–85).

15 Sheltered water where ships can ride at anchor

> His mild fortitude is unparalleled. I never hear him complain; he never is peevish, however harassed by the Cough, and the difficulty of breathing. He talks of you, and all with wonted affection, and is considerate not to give any trouble he can avoid, as if in perfect health ... Selfish feelings of themselves are with me ... for he was the companion to whom I clung as my dearest and best friend, as my comfort and support, and consolation. He was formed by Nature to be happy himself, and a blessing to those intimate with him.

Although there must still be hope for this beloved brother, they must all prepare 'with meekness and resignation' for the worst. Aleck enclosed his letter to his parents in a note to Dr Robertson in Inverness, asking him to be with them when they opened it.

During this time a French Physician, M Gofer, said to be 'a man of great science and experience', examined Edward. He proved more optimistic than Mr Daun and produced some *Lichen Islandicus* – 'a plant celebrated for its nutritive and tonic qualities, and reckoned on the Continent the best medicine in pulmonary disorders'. Edward mixed its juice with milk.

On 17 February he was taken ashore in a chair. Aleck turned down the usual accommodation offered to passengers in Jamestown, 'seats of the most sordid penury and the most disgusting Filth'. The Governor, however, came to the rescue with 'the best rooms in town, airy and cheerful looking on the sea'. Their landlord was William Balcombe, 'an open-hearted liberal Englishman', who along with his wife Jane and their children had been on St Helena for six years. He was Superintendent of Public Sales for the East India Company, supplied ships en route to and from India and ran a brewery, an orchard and a spacious market garden. A large man, charming, handsome, fond of good food and wine, he kept a sharp eye out for any opportunity to increase his considerable fortune. He sailed pretty close to the wind but was generous and hospitable; his comfortable house in Jamestown was usually full of passengers in transit.

The savage appearance of the extinct volcano which is St Helena, battered with crashing waves and its soaring, jagged rockfaces slashed with deep gorges (see Plate XIV), belied not only the hospitality of the islanders but also the welcoming nature of an oasis in the heart of the island. Here Balcombe had his country house, The Briars (see Plate XV), along with a little pavilion built in the garden to host parties and a small cottage. This green, smiling valley, one of the few fertile areas of the island with its 'delicious climate and a perfect quiet', was sheltered from the constant strong wind.

It was here that he suggested the brothers should escape the heat and bustle of Jamestown. He offered them the cottage and Aleck rode up to it one day; he was delighted with its snug and secluded appearance:

> It is a pleasant little spot about 2 miles from this House, and in a medium climate between the heat of the valley, and the Cold of the summits of the Hills. It is indeed just like a nest placed in a little ledge, on a vast craggy mountain.

Edward was now very weary. Trusting neither Aleck nor the Jamestown doctor to tell him the truth, he asked Dr Desborough, 'a Bengal medical gentleman who lodges in this House, and has been very attentive in visiting, and comforting him' for his honest opinion. Dr Desborough willingly gave it: Edward was in great danger but there was still a possibility of recovery.

⁂

In the early morning of a fine, calm day with the sun just rising behind the mountains, Aleck climbed up the steep hill to the cottage with Edward in a hammock slung on oars and carried by four soldiers. In the cooler air things began to improve once more: although extremely weak, emaciated and wrapped in flannel from top to toe, Edward became more cheerful and easier to manage. He let Aleck read to him, enjoying 'passages of light entertaining books'. His appetite improved: he managed a fish for breakfast and a few figs, grapes or raisins during the day, while continuing with digitalis and *Lichen Islandicus* in milk. Although he now seemed to understand the seriousness of his condition, 'yet ... he is perfectly calm and composed on all occasions ... scarcely ever suffering any peevish expression to escape him, even to a servant'.

At this point the fleet at anchor in the bay sailed for home, taking with it Mr Wilton, who had frequently visited Edward, always producing 'something for our comfort and advantage'. Aleck asked his father to welcome Wilton, who undoubtedly would call at Moniack when he was in the Highlands.

After the fleet sailed Aleck felt isolated and terribly lonely. He was finding his responsibility increasingly hard to bear: it was difficult to obtain on the island all that was needed for Edward's care; the 'necessaries and comforts of life' were extremely expensive. He knew the seriousness of the situation but for Edward's sake had to convince his brother that he was slowly recovering. William and Aeneas Mackintosh both advised that 'I should endeavour to rouse his hopes and spirits to the last'.

In his constant care of Edward, Aleck had no time to explore the island; the little he saw of it did not impress him. But if the object of their coming there could be achieved, then 'I will even think it a Paradise'. Two years later, in October 1815, St Helena's most famous resident, Napoleon Bonaparte, was equally unimpressed and remained so during the six years of his captivity on the island. One of his soldiers described it as 'the most wretched and desolate spot in the habitable world'. The little island, approximately the size of Jersey, had nevertheless been an essential part of the East India Company's operations since they had claimed it in the middle of the seventeenth century. In 1815 the British Government took control, in order to supervise its illustrious prisoner.

In February 1813, however, Napoleon was still at large, licking his wounds after the disastrous retreat from Moscow. This news would have only just reached St Helena, as mail took ten weeks from London. The battle of Waterloo and the Emperor's subsequent capture were still in the future. There was no hint of the event that, a little over two years later, would engulf the island and its inhabitants and change things forever. There is, however, a tenuous link between Napoleon's story and that of Aleck and Edward. Their accommodation would be needed for Napoleon's entourage and was possibly the cottage used to imprison one of Napoleon's court, Count Emmanuel de Las Cases, who was charged with smuggling letters to supporters in London by sewing them into the waistcoat of his servant. From the leafy garden, across a jagged foreground of precipices and steep gorges, there was a distant view of Longwood, Napoleon's eventual residence.

But that was in the future, and in 1813 Aleck had little time to wonder about the mysterious house in the distance. When Edward was awake he never left his side. While he slept Aleck took the chance to write letters and keep up his journal. His loneliness was exacerbated by the thought that the family at home could not yet be aware of the seriousness of Edward's illness; the first inkling of the drama, in its early stages, might just now be reaching Scotland. Aleck wrote constantly, as if the sheer quantity of letters might somehow mean faster delivery. He shared with his parents every change in Edward's pulse and temperature, every grain of his medication and everything he ate, keeping records of the contents of each letter and when and by what means each had been sent. To make sure that some, at least, reached their destination, he dispersed them among homebound ships: five letters by *Surrey,* one by *Tigris* and five by *President.*

He longed for letters from home but was constantly disappointed. In the Master Attendant's Office there were 'Boxes containing some thousands of letters lying ... uncared for, there being not Post Office or Postmaster on the island'. Seton, writing to sympathise with Reelig over the lack of news of Edward, commented that 'opportunities of hearing from St Helena are very rare'.

⁂

In March there was another change for the better, and Aleck was more hopeful than for some time:

> His spirits are very good; and he is most careful, and attentive to the minutest directions of the Doctor. He sleeps very well at night ... his appetite is good, even to craving; but he does not indulge it beyond prudence ... He sits up to his meals and occasionally walks to the window, to enjoy the view of the green fields: an exertion he desired not, nor attempted to make in Town.

Aleck was so encouraged that he found the energy to write a long letter to Jane Anne for her birthday, 25 April 1813. Having left her, in 1808, as a child of eleven, he found it hard to imagine what might interest a young lady of sixteen. He talked to her of his life in India, his horses and servants, and then, inevitably, compared it with life at home:

> There are few opportunities of enjoying pleasant family society in India ... They never assemble in little parties of six or seven intimate friends to enjoy a cheerful evening. All our time is spent in formal large parties ... Often have I thought with longing and useless regret on the delightful evenings I have passed at Moniack with none near me, but those I loved dearly ... when you and George were the little

> ones of the House, and our delight and amusement. Our rambles in the woods, our projects in the Garden, our Pond and Pets, and all the innocent and gay and delightful diversions that marked our early life.

✼

In early April *Daedalus* passed by St Helena. Busy with preparations for his part in *Macbeth* and unaware of the real-life drama being played out in Mr Balcombe's idyllic cottage, James, his mind on his reunion with Edward, sailed tranquilly on towards Calcutta.

There soon came a time when Edward could not bear to let Aleck out of his sight for one minute – 'He seemed to have a presentiment that we were about to part'. Near midnight, on Sunday, 25 April 1813, Jane Anne's sixteenth birthday and a day before his own twenty-seventh, he died in Aleck's arms.

> On the night of the 25th April I witnessed the final separation of the soul – it took place about midnight – and I was the sole witness – for my servants, wearied by long watching, were asleep – & after my Brother had expired leaning upon me, I watched till morning – when assisted by my Christian servants I washed & dressed his body myself and shortly after saw it committed to the Dust.

That same day, there was sudden stormy weather in the South Atlantic after a deep calm. James, within sight of Tristan da Cunha, 'the furthest from any land of any island in the world' wrote:

> The vessel lurches & rolls heavily but we go on nobly ... at last we have some prospects of getting on towards India – tho I have not expressed it I have certainly felt much irksome weariness at the length of the voyage & tediousness of the passage – little relieved as it has been in any way. I do feel it most pitiably.

Brief respite

Two weeks later, *Daedalus* sailed into Simons Bay. James was enchanted with the scenery, which reminded him of the Torridon hills in Wester Ross. A party set off for Cape Town on miserable beasts which put him in mind of raggedy Irish ponies.

During their stay in Cape Town the tensions which had been simmering away beneath the surface in the mess suddenly bubbled up. The officers, insulted by Stewart's quibbling over costs, declared that they would not take a further penny from passengers Stewart, Uthoff and Fraser. The disagreement eventually reached such a pitch that Stewart took himself off in a rage to find another ship; James announced that he could only stay on *Daedalus* on exactly the same terms as before – as an honorary member of the Mess subject to all Mess expenses. This, Cotter said, was impossible: there could be no difference made between the passengers.

James and Uthoff spent the rest of the day hunting down the Captains of the other ships at anchor. The only ship which could accommodate them, most spaciously and comfortably, was *Lyon*, but her Captain would not commit himself until he had cleared the matter with Captain Maxwell.

Maxwell was astonished to hear that they wanted to quit his ship but felt confident that the matter could be resolved amicably. Eventually, after much heated discussion, it was agreed that James and Uthoff would continue in *Daedalus* on the same footing as before, paying their share of expenses. James, who had found the whole business most unpleasant, had been secretly hoping that he could escape to the comfort of *Lyon* and thus not have to face the hostile members of the Mess. However, he felt he owed it to himself and his friends in the ship to return '& peace was re-established'.

On the last night in Cape Town James attended a Subscription Ball. After a very elegant dinner James found himself standing next to Miss Maxwell. Presumably, he said hopefully, she was engaged for the next dance; but 'she assured me she was not ... I said I feared it was not according to rule for me to ask and that she was most likely to dance according to Etiquette but she said she knew no Etiquette in dancing and would be my partner with pleasure'.

By this time, however, the dance had started and, somewhat to James's relief, it seemed that they could not be fitted in. But unluckily for him, the ubiquitous Lady Hood happened to be in Cape Town and at hand. She was in organising mode and fixed them up with places almost at the top of the dance. They danced that one, and another, and then Miss Maxwell asked to be taken to her friend Mrs Alexander in the card room.

> I handed her there, helped her to a dish of tea and left her – but danced no more ... & kept myself disengaged till supper when I asked Miss Maxwell to allow me to hand her to supper what was granted but when we were just going Mr Alexander stepped in and I willingly assigned her to the better known member of rank.

Having done his duty by his Captain's sister, James then escaped to a smaller room, where he had another elegant supper 'with the chief delicacies of the season – strawberries were produced and pastries and jellies of the best kinds'. Reflecting later on the evening, he noted that there were few beauties and these were among the young ladies going out to India who still had their healthy pink and white complexions – 'good wholesome looks'.

After a shopping expedition, when James at the last minute succumbed to a lion's skin, he and Uthoff passed spent the final two evenings very happily at the establishment of a certain N D Skipps, who was easily persuaded on both nights to open a bottle of Constantia wine. They spent the days buying quantities of fruit and other luxuries for the next part of the voyage, then it was back to 'my old cot' on board.

The following day, James wondered how he was going to cope with 'the different people I am forced to coalesce with'. After the rumpus in the mess it was impossible to get back on to the earlier. trusting footing. There was an unpleasant atmosphere under the thin surface of camaraderie and with Cotter, in particular, James felt at odds.

Uncomfortable in every way in the mess, his thoughts naturally turned to the past and then to the future 'with its uncertainties as they dimly flit across the imagination tinged with hope, though sometimes blackened by fears and doubts'. Things were getting out of focus: his mind, usually so ordered and rational, seemed to have been affected by the recent trouble; he was having difficulty holding his thoughts long enough to put them down on paper. They were like 'the figures in a magic lantern and perhaps as wild and shapeless'. To counteract this worrying turn, he made every effort to return to a routine of study, journal writing and early bed.

Soon after setting sail, a man fell overboard; with the sea running high and the wind blowing hard the Captain 'very properly' forbade the lifeboat to be lowered. James was far more affected by this than he had been by previous similar incidents, grieving deeply for 'a young man hurried into eternity in a moment without the least previous warning'. The young man was a midshipman, 'much loved by his shipmates – perhaps the hopes of some mother who had but him ... this was his second voyage and here it is ended, his hopes and fears, his wishes for promotion now are sunk with him in the stormy wave'.

After this the days rolled tediously on, with James hardly speaking to anyone. He had troubling dreams: on the last day of May:

> I could not help ... thinking how sweet a season it now is in Scotland at my own Dear Home ... I never had so vivid a dream as last night thinking myself with my family and my sister with her cheerful smiles welcoming me as from a long journey ... I thought I had two other sisters ... one about Jane Anne's age, the other about 8 or 9 – the sweet smile of the young which gave me a feeling not easily expressed but inexpressibly sweet. Well! the old story – studied Hindoostanee till 12.

Retrospect

Aleck did not write to his father until two months after Edward's death. He sent the black-bordered letter via an old friend, Lieutenant Colonel Bowes, afraid that otherwise his mother or Jane Anne might open it before it reached his father:

> The appearance of this letter will too surely indicate the nature of its contents – Yet I write directly to yourself, trusting to your long and well tried fortitude to endure as a Man, and a Christian, the Shock of the Tidings I have to communicate. My Brother Edward is no more. His Death was peacefull, and cheered by a tranquillity and confidence of hope, I believe rarely equalled ... I never before witnessed the dissolution of the Soul and Body – it was awfully affecting – but without Terror ... I had at least the satisfaction, melancholy as it was, to perceive my Brother to the last moment, cheered by my presence.

One reason for the delay in writing was his reluctance to deliver the news; the other was that he had been trying to minister to the needs of Sandie Tytler and family. Sandie had arrived in St Helena, like Edward, to try to recover from consumption, and Aleck's first duty had been to break sad news to him: his adored father, Lord Woodhouselee, had died in January. He tried to persuade the little family to stay in the town but for reasons of economy they moved to a remote cottage, and Aleck, who had been looking forward to their company, now saw little of them.[16]

Several years later, Aleck, writing what he called his 'Legacy', looked back on his time in St Helena with some satisfaction: 'it is the only part of my life in which I can be said to have performed the duties required of me, with some degree of vigilance'. He had not summoned a priest to Edward's bedside because he did not believe in deathbed repentance: 'I believe his future felicity as well secured, as if Fifty Churchmen had prayed at his bedside'. He had no time for 'the mushroom Piety produced by a month of praying' but believed in 'the mature fruit of deliberate belief, and rational conscientious discharge of all the duties incumbent on a Christian'. His brother's life was innocent and virtuous: 'he possessed and exercised some of the most prized Christian virtues, and especially Charity, the chief of all'.

The months immediately following Edward's death were very difficult: Aleck had a horror of being alone and could concentrate on nothing. After a few weeks in the cottage, seeking any company 'however coarse', any diversion 'however frivolous', he moved back to Jamestown and lodged once more with the Balcombes.

Watching ships sailing for England, he longed to go home, but that would certainly cost him his job and possibly his position in the Service. He had to be content with the thought of a home trip in seven or eight years' time; meanwhile, he was lucky to have his profession and his life in India.

It was the custom for ships to wait off St Helena, often for months, until enough had collected to form a convoy. Houses in Jamestown accordingly filled to the brim with boarders patiently waiting for their ship to sail. Aleck discovered a store ship, *Pulteney*, bound for Bengal and immediately booked a passage, along with several others, including four young girls, three returning from school in England and one from St Helena going to visit friends in Bengal. They all lodged with Mr Balcombe while they waited. Desperate for companionship, Aleck made friends with the four lively girls; he lent them books and in return they played the piano and sang to him.

More ships arrived, more travellers crammed into the limited accommodation and there was much 'mirth and gayety'. Aleck threw himself into everything, confiding in anyone who would listen, drinking too much and staying up all night 'with an indifference and a carelessness that laid hold on me'. He went out in sun and rain without a hat, neglected his wet clothes and began to feel unwell. Meanwhile, his attention to the four young ladies had been observed: word went around that he was about to marry one of them, and the only way to scotch this rumour was to change his passage to another ship, *Batavia.*

Nearly four months after Edward's death, on 15 August, Aleck bade a final farewell to the island and set sail. He had left instructions for a stone to be put up in Edward's memory at St Paul's,[17] the quiet country church where he was buried.

16 Sandie died the following year, leaving his widow, Elizabeth, two sons and a daughter.

17 Now replaced by the Victorian St Paul's Cathedral.

Photo: Julie Ashdown

Edward's gravestone, now on the wall above the font in St Paul's Cathedral, St Helena.

As he was embarking, he wrote to his father about a young Captain Innes, whose mother lived near Forres in Morayshire. To him he had entrusted 'some memorials of my lost Brother' for delivery to Moniack.

The passage on *Batavia* did not work out well. Aleck was the only passenger, the Captain 'a fool and a knave, a miser and a tyrant' and the officers illiterate. After six weeks, weak, emaciated and depressed, his only hope was to plead illness and change ships yet again, to *Union*. Here he shared a large, comfortable cabin with Robert Wilson, a surgeon and part-owner of the ship, a lively companion who provided stimulating conversation and opposition at whist. Aleck consulted him on his health and with 'care, amusement and wholesome food' gradually recovered his strength.

⁂

By August the news of Edward's death had reached Moniack; Reelig was distraught. Reflecting on his loss, he felt compelled to revisit the reasons for sending his sons on 'foreign adventure'. Copies of his long letter to James, a form of apologia, were sent to William and Aleck.

His sole object had been their happiness but 'whether I took a right view of the nature of that happiness ... is a question by itself'. Had it been wise to try to elevate his sons 'into a status of greater opulence, of higher rank, or of more distinguished position' than that of their ancestors or indeed their father? He mused on his own early years: after schooldays at Charterhouse …

> … no-one had directed my pursuits ... my Scotch property afforded barely food and clothing and I had no capital nor had I any friends to take me up ... I had no advisor, no protector ... I had to furnish my House, stock and crop my farm, pay some debts.

> Thus it seemed to me that to live as a Country Gentleman decently and with moderate Hospitality, to rear my family and to educate them was the utmost I could do ... whatever might be the destination of my Children, I had no doubt that a most liberal Education would tend to their worldly advantage and I judged that the formation of their religious and moral principles, of their dispositions and tempers, of their manners and Habits, could nowhere be so anxiously and safely superintended as under the roof of their Parents – at any rate for some years.

He felt happy that this part of the plan had worked, but the next stage was more difficult. Should he send his children to 'foreign adventure' rather than keep them safely at home? The only objections that he could see then were the risk to health and his own sacrifice.

So, like parents before and since, he did what seemed right at the time and dispatched the very young James abroad; he realised now that it was 'far too early for securing his education as completely as I could have wished'. Now he felt he had made the wrong decision: the boys would surely have been better off at home, as farmers, in a 'comfortable life of Peace and Industry' with little in the way of status and wealth, but healthy and happy. But then, he argued to himself, farming seemed unprofitable at the time and he could not have contemplated 'so moderate a view for them; and, as it happened, James had turned out very well.

He had been misled about the prospects in Guyana and, in any case, Bonaparte 'arose and disturbed the world'; no one could have foreseen the changes consequently wrought in the British colonies. James and Edward had undoubtedly done all they possibly could in Berbice, 'but the sinister course of colonial concerns baffled their industry'.

He and Jane had had to sacrifice many years of the company of their children in the hope that they would return, independent, wealthy and successful, with families of their own, to be near their ageing parents. Edward' death had forced him, painfully, to rethink; he sadly concluded that his advice to his sons now would be never to let their children leave home in search of wealth.

> Farewell for the present, my dear James ... you are now on a new field; reap from it honestly what you can, but not at the expense of health. You are now your own Master ... but remember that we can always struggle in union and share each other's bannock.[18] I certainly hope that you may find a favourable career to early easy fortune; but I would not for any consideration have you or William or Aleck, risk Life and Health for mere fortune's sake.

When Aleck received his copy of this letter, 'as honourable to yourself as it is interesting to us', he was so horrified by the idea that they might all have been destined for farming that he spent some time composing a long reply. In his opinion, happiness would certainly not have been achieved by keeping the boys at home. In sending his sons abroad, his father had acted from nothing but affection and good judgement. The 'liberal' education

18 A round, flat, unleavened loaf in Scotland and the north of England.

Reelig had provided for his sons, wrote Aleck, had 'roused and stimulated ambition' and encouraged 'a love of rambling, of Enterprise, of everything new, surprising, improbable, romantic ... nothing can be more incompatible with the calm, sedate, steady application, the sleepless attention, the patient industry which are absolutely necessary to success in farming'. James was the only one of them who *might* have succeeded as a farmer, but 'take James's natural qualities ... a fine temper, warm imagination, strong sensibility and sanguine temperament' – were these likely to make a steady farmer?

If William had been a farmer he could not at the same time have been an honour to the family. Surely one letter telling of his honourable services to the East India Company was better than a year of his society? The Prodigal Son was, after all, more interesting to his father than his dutiful stay-at-home elder brother:

> Do you not enjoy his fame, his usefulness, his manly energy, his dignity among men, his vigorous intellect exercised in active service to his country? Is it not far better than to have him a clown,[19] cultivating a farm without an idea beyond the comparative profit of wheat or turnips? ... I am by no means convinced ... that the calm enjoyments of domestic life are the greatest sources of happiness ... I suspect that stronger passions are the greatest source.

William was a man of strong passions, which surely led to happiness; Aleck gave the example of Pitt 'successfully overthrowing the arguments of his antagonists' and Wellington 'arranging his troops for Battle'. These moments they would not have exchanged for 'years, nay ages, of domestic happiness'. If the brothers had all become Highland farmers what on earth would they have had to talk to their father about in the evenings around the hearth?

> That you could have derived happiness from being surrounded by a Family of Farmers is so totally repugnant to your nature and disposition that I can never believe it to have been possible. As it is, in some degree, we can all enter into your Ideas, participate in your feelings, discuss with you subjects of national and general interest.

He ended on what he hoped was a confident note:

> All I have to add is I trust and believe *James* need not long be withheld from you, *William* will some day return to cheer you, *George* will grow up to manhood. If I have luck I may see you ere long ... the fall of the tyrant Bonaparte will restore sunshine to thousands whom his overgrown power overshadowed and repressed – and even we may partake of the Beam.

This letter must have comforted Reelig: years later, copying Aleck's letters into a letterbook, he wrote in the margin, 'on my Family letter, preferring the actual disposal of our Family to any other'.

---

19 A rustic.

Farewell to Daedalus

In the Indian Ocean the weather was improving, but for James this could not compensate for the continued animosity of his messmates as manifested in various small slights – 'today at breakfast not a thing to eat but Biscuit and cocoa and in the forenoon almost all of them lunched and never asked us to partake ... I now doubly wish I was quit of this ship'.

James's thirtieth birthday on 10 June 1813 inevitably brought with it a review of his life:

> The period of my life is come, when if I were to be quietly settled in the land of my fathers, I should now be enjoying that state of Domestick peace and comfort I have during life sighed for – instead of which I am once more embarked in a long undertaking uncertain in its events & almost certainly productive of no quiet or hope of settled comfort ... at the age of 30 I am doing what I should have done at 15 so that 15 years of my life are lost.

His thoughts then turned to home and family; he wondered if Moniack was 'still our own – is the house of my forefathers still a refuge for their children?'

> Often do I now in dreams wander over our sweet walks, traverse every quarter of our woods ... I shall think of you all at Rebeg as the summer months sett in and view you enjoying the sweet walks of the Burn and be in spirit with you when far at sea or at length landing at Madras ... Never am I a hour, a moment without thinking – that is too weak a word – without dwelling on the memory of you all & those days that have passed never to return.

Luckily, these melancholy musings were interrupted by the appearance on the horizon of one of the Comoros Islands, Johanna as it was then called, or Nzwani (Anjouan) as it has been known since independence in 1975.

James was enchanted with Johanna. Its scenery and people reminded him of the West Indies; they poured on board *Daedalus,* laden with fruit and roots, making salaams and producing bundles of letters purporting to be certificates from visitors of influence. 'The best of the fun was that these grave Musselmen all had taken names from English noblemen': there was General Machin, Admiral Rodney, Commodore Blackett and all sorts of Dukes and Earls including the Duke of Buccleugh, who became James's companion and guide. The Duke, who spoke excellent English, offered to take James and his companions to see the King, His Majesty Sootan Allevi.

His Majesty was short and fat with squinting eyes 'and no eyebrows but in their stead Black paint is substituted'. He had a scraggy beard and his mouth and teeth were black from chewing betel nut. He wore a crown of gold foil, a black velvet robe embroidered with silver lace and was enveloped from head to foot in a long shawl.

Cotter opened the conversation: did His Majesty intend to come aboard *Daedalus*? But the King had just caught sight of James's gun. Intensely excited ...

> … he sprung from his seat with more activity than I suspected he had and came to examine it … many questions were asked regarding it – if there were many like it, if it was made in England, what it cost.

James obligingly fired it unloaded for his Majesty whose rapture, he reckoned, 'exceeded the bounds of Kingly dignity'; he was somewhat relieved when the Duke took them off to his own house for refreshment and a visit to the mosque. There they met an ancient 'Mufty'[20] who looked just like Moses. He had a deep interest in European affairs and was gratified by James's news that Bonaparte was 'completely beat … he seemed much rejoiced. He professed his love and veneration for the English who he seemed to think far the first people and said he would pray for us'.

He also wondered whether James could provide him with a pair of shoes and a knife, neither of which James could spare. There followed an ascent to the minaret, where 'many English who had been there had written their names on the walls'. James did not add his to their number.

Another Johanna character not to be missed was Bombay Jack, so called on account of his regular visits to that city. This 'most bustling, honest and intelligent man' knew exactly how to make British visitors off the ships feel at home:

> … we partook much to our satisfaction … and afterwards retired into the cool court, where we were treated with as fine a syllabub of milk &c as ever we had in England.

Bombay Jack was assisted in all this by his stalwart wife, 'quite a negress', who was the first woman of any consequence that they had seen in Johanna, since her husband, conforming to European manners, thought it 'foolish to confine his wife'. James was fascinated by the Muslim attitude to women: 'they are never seen except by their Husbands and Fathers; shut up in Dark apartments they do nothing and see nothing'. Mrs Maxwell and her sister were, however, admitted into the women's apartments at the Palace. When they met the Queen 'in a terribly dark sort of Dungeon' she ran up to them and shook their hands violently, saying, 'How do How do' very fast.

All this excitement gave James a bad headache and he retired to his hammock. Characteristically, though, he lost no time in recording every detail of all he had seen and learnt about Johanna – its geography, people, houses, resources, woodland, flora and fauna, mountains, hunting, fishing and produce. It would be a wonderful place for …

> … anyone who wishes to retire from the great world to bury himself and I should have no objection to try to bring some part of it into cultivation & civilisation … I am much pleased that I have seen this little monarchy. It is ludicrous to think that a negroe Prince should be the first royal presence I have been ushered into, but it is an interesting place and I shall think of the Comoro Islands with pleasure.

---

20 An expounder of Muslim law.

In mid-June *Daedalus* set sail again on the last leg of the journey. On 20 June James wrote to his mother:

> We now approach very near the place of our destination, Point de Galle in Ceylon ... and we are nearly sure that in one week ... we shall anchor in Madras Roads ... in the land of long promise, in the land of brothers, friends, relations – but in the land 15 thousand miles away from my nearer and dearer friends – mixed and troubled are these feelings ... and I am hardly master of myself when I think in 5 or 6 days I shall be ashore in India!

At last, on 1 July, land was sighted – Ceylon! Spirits rose and the passengers scanned the horizon for landmarks – they spotted the flagstaff and flag of the fort at Point de Galle, and Dondra Head, the southernmost point of the island, was just discernible as night closed in. The ship then headed east to keep well clear of the Basses, a sandstone reef 25 miles long lying dangerously close to the land. Relieved that the end of the voyage was at last in sight, James played a rubber of whist and went to bed.

Next morning, everyone was up early; James went on deck to enjoy the heart-warming sight of land on the port side as they sailed due north at the rate of eight knots. Just before eight bells he went below to the gunroom for breakfast; 'suddenly we felt a slight shock and a grating sensation as if the Vessell was running on a gravelly bottom'. Everyone rushed on deck, and it became instantly clear that the ship had hit the treacherous Basses. A signal was immediately sent to the Captain of the nearest ship, *Bridgewater*, to come to their aid. Various other ships sent their boats and Captain Nesbitt of *Essex* came on board. *Atlas*, in her eagerness to help, hit the reef herself but managed to sail on unscathed.

Initially, things did not seem too bad: the ship was soon clear of the rocks and the damage seemed small enough for her carpenter to repair. Soon, however, the cockpit and the bread room were under water, and orders were given to move all heavy equipment forward. Then, as the situation worsened, the guns were jettisoned. The sail makers treated a sail with tar and oakum 'to haul under her Bottom' and stop the leak, but in vain. Meanwhile, the ladies were sent on board *Bridgewater*; Mrs Maxwell, 'dreadfully agitated at leaving the ship', had to be urged over the side. People started to collect their possessions to transfer to the boats jostling for space around the stricken ship. James was almost too late – one trunk of clothes and drawing things was already underwater, but he managed to heave most of the rest of his belongings into any available boat – his guns, trunks of books and clothes, Black John's chest, their furniture and his precious lion's skin. As usual, he was observing every detail:

> Another sail was got ready to get under her – the people worked nobly and the Chain Pumps behaved admirably ... but the leak worked wider – the Carpenters found it but could not get at it to stop it – the ship was settling fast in the water ... all people were crowding up their trunks and boxes, the Captain's Stewart was sending away boatloads of the Captain's things, the launch was ordered alongside to carry the last of his things and I tossed in my Baggage and sent John in with it & followed myself quitting thus the *Daedalus* for ever!

Once safely on board *Bridgewater*, James was asked to look after the Captain's wife, who was …

> … perfectly composed apparently but wild with her eyes staring, and cold to the touch. I did not know what to say. I could give her no hopes of the ship, but she was far more terrified lest the Captain would not quit her – I tried to convince her he would be here in 4 hours at furthest if the ship could not be saved.

James stayed with her until she had composed herself and then hurried to the side of his dancing partner, Miss Maxwell, who was weeping copiously:

> Miss M did not so much fear for her brother as feel for his Distress – she wept for his agony and exclaimed 'Poor fellow what he is just now suffering' ... I could but tell her how he had done his Duty, how unmixed with any feeling of self-reproach his sorrow must be; and Begged her to Bear up against Distress and shew the strength of her mind in a trying situation – she could do little but Weep.

By 4 o'clock the Captain had ordered almost all the ship's company off; meanwhile, James, having had nothing to eat all day, was glad to join *Bridgewater*'s passengers for dinner. Everyone then watched the livestock being brought to safety 'and at last we saw the last boat ... and Capt. Maxwell quit the frigate ... I ran to inform Mrs Maxwell and then we ascended the Poop to see the noble Vessell go to her last abode'.

> To the ship I felt that kind of attachment one feels to a favourite animal or to a place of abode long lived in ... A noble ship was perishing ... she appeared settling forward and at every little heave of the sea she forged forward deepening in the water ... then keeping upright in awful Silence she majestically sunk deeper and deeper in the most gradual manner and in two minutes the finest frigate that ever swam, the noble *Daedalus* went to the bottom and was lost for ever ... For an hour after the water was in a foam when she went down. Her deck Blew up, and her Booms and spars all floated around – it was a most awfull grand and mournful sight & I will never forget it.

The Captain's conduct, James considered, was exemplary throughout: he was cool and collected, able to make swift decisions and implement them efficiently. Everyone on board had behaved with credit. 'Only one man, a Marine, was found drunk and that was from his being employed in the Gunroom helping in serving out refreshments, rather than from a wish to get intoxicated'. No lives had been lost and even all the livestock was saved, down to dogs, chickens and monkeys.

The crew and passengers of *Bridgewater* made every effort to help the refugees; a Major Fraser invited James to share his cabin and he accepted gratefully. Exhausted and suffering another of his bad headaches, he thankfully slung his hammock and went to bed early.

The next few days were spent sorting out the baggage on the various ships which had come to the rescue and assessing the damage to its contents. Mr Uthoff had lost his Persian dictionary. James's shirts and linen trousers were ruined and, more important to him, his drawing things were 'quite spoilt'. The weather, however, was cheering and they were progressing at a fine rate. The third lieutenant, Mr Woodly, knowing James would have recorded the disaster in minute detail, sensibly suggested that between them they should write an account for the Madras papers. James finished his contribution before dinner while Mr Woodly had only got as far as a carefully composed opening sentence, so it was James's version that was handed to Captain Maxwell and the ladies for their approval. The Captain drew on it when, faced with the inevitable court martial, he began his letter to Admiral Hood:[21]

> Honble Compys Ship *Bridgewater* Madras Roads July 7th 1813
> Sir
> It is with infinite concern I have to acquaint you with the loss of His Majesty's late ship *Daedalus* when under my command by striking on a shoal off the East Coast of Ceylon on the morning of the 2nd instant.

After a lengthy account of how his ship ran aground, the Captain described all that was done to try to save her until …

> … when I had fully ascertained that every Soul was removed from the Ship, I quitted her, with feelings, however painful, that were well supported by a sense of having done my duty, and five minutes afterwards her mastheads were below the surface of the water.

The Captain was acquitted at the court martial, the verdict being that the fault lay with the Master of the Ship, who had failed to take constant soundings on approaching the Basses; he was severely reprimanded.

The final part of this eventful voyage was on a *masoolah*, '… a boat of uncommon buoyancy and height – made of planks of light wood savagely painted white, red, yellow and blue and sewn together with coconut fibres.' This extraordinary vessel carried James safely through '… the tremendous surf of the Madras beach, which often breaks near a mile from the shore, rolling everything before it' (see Plate XV).

The surf-beaten Coromandel Coast was always dangerous …

> … but seldom is a life lost for there also in the highest most tremendous surf do the catamarans ply – 3 logs of light wood locked together and paddled by a couple of amphibian beings who ... live more in the water than on land – they attend the *masoolahs* in bad weather and never fail to pick up those who may be spilt by the violence of the surf.

Finally, on 7 July 1813, James stepped on to Indian soil in Madras.

21 National Maritime Museum Greenwich MKH/163.

8

1813–1815

MADRAS

James spent three months in Madras, where Lady Hood and her husband, Sir Samuel,[1] the one-armed Admiral, offered James accommodation and a secretarial post. He refused both – the job on the grounds that he would have to live in the '1st style' on a very small salary with no future prospects; the accommodation because he was already lodging with an agreeable family whose attractive daughter was a larger version of Jeanie Tytler. At Lady Hood's establishment there would be little peace, and her constant company 'might not altogether do'; this was confirmed by one 'who well knows what goes on there'. Undaunted, her ladyship thought James might like to accompany her to Trincomalee for the monsoon, 'but I came to work, not to go travelling'. What he wanted above all else was news of his brothers.

Often recognised by his likeness to William, he was generally encouraged by the stories circulating about this brother, now based north of Delhi at Panipat, who had the reputation of being the most active civil servant in India, albeit one of the most eccentric. The news that the other two were in St Helena threw James's feelings into turmoil – 'My heart sinks within me as I think what I may hear ... and bounds with the most eager hope at ... the unexpected blessing which may be in store.'

Meanwhile, enforced idleness was very tedious: he had no money for sightseeing, walking was not considered 'decorous' and he disliked the stuffiness of a palanquin. His day consisted of 'lounging' interspersed with billiards and chess, with the occasional outing in a gig.

> Most bitterly do I feel the want of pedestrian exercise ... to be as it were a prisoner to the house in the midst of a sweet & interesting country is a novel situation.

The searingly hot winds were impossible, and although he attended the odd ball it was strictly as a reluctant spectator:

> ... it is not pleasant to see a lady dancing down some twenty couples of a country dance exactly as if she had been dragged through a river all bloused and flushed and her eyes almost starting from her head.

1 1762–1814. After a distinguished naval career he arrived in Madras in 1812 as Commander-in-Chief of the East Indies and died there of malaria on 24 December 1814.

Calling hours were strictly 8.00 am to 11.00 am and there was endless debate about protocol and precedence; the whole social structure was pompous and wearing. Things improved a little when he found a *munshi*[2] to teach him Hindi every morning. During the late afternoon he sometimes took a palanquin along the Mount Road, 'perhaps the finest in the world', which was alive 'with all the beauty and fashion of Madras', rivalling even the Park in London and far excelling it in beauty of scenery. But most of the time he was alone, his thoughts continually on his brothers. There were also moments of longing for the active outdoor life of Berbice and regret at leaving 'my poor negroes ... whom I never can forget'.

One reason for prolonging his stay in Madras was his anxiety to meet Lord Moira, the new Governor General, soon to disembark from *Stirling Castle* along with his cousins, the Misses Ross, the elder of whom had charmed James in Raasay. When his Lordship and party eventually set foot on India, a sudden unexpected shower and breeze were seen as good omens. James pushed to the front of the jostling, cheering crowd trying, unsuccessfully, to catch the eye of Miss Ross or her sister.

William, far away in Panipat, was also wondering where his brothers were. There was no news from St Helena and no sign yet of James in Calcutta. He was still grudgingly acting as the family correspondent and losing patience with his mother's endless worry that he would forget his home. True happiness for a man, he wrote, lay in domesticity 'and an estate to live upon and improve'. Surely the day was not too far off when he would 'resume the spud'[3] and accompany his father around the estate?

In early August, James heard a rumour that Edward was still in St Helena; he was distraught. 'He was my best beloved & most anxiously wished for brother, to save him I would willingly give myself.' Two months later, on 12 October 1813, he arrived in Calcutta to be met with a packet of welcoming letters from William, 'very warm, but very flowery, much in the Persian style of diction, which cannot be wondered at, seeing he hardly ever speaks any language but Persian & Hindee'. His younger brothers were apparently still in St Helena, with Edward reputedly well on the way to recovery. He accordingly concentrated on making what he could of Calcutta life, based now with the ever hospitable Seton.

❋

Still hoping to attract Lord Moira's attention, James braved Government House, where he had a great welcome from the Ross sisters; he became their 'protector' and took it upon himself to warn them of all the pitfalls awaiting 'Griffins',[4] especially females. They made sure he was invited to all the parties, but like Aleck before him, he felt suffocated by the social life of Calcutta:

> There is no friendly familiar intercourse ... all stiff formal parties of from 30–50, expensive and disagreeable – no comfortable tea tables or chitchat parties. I fear it will be a long time ere I like Calcutta.

2 Indian secretary or language teacher.
3 Narrow spade for cutting roots, digging up trees etc.
4 Newcomers to Calcutta.

From all sides he heard of William's 'oddities', not least from Lady Nugent. She and her husband had been escorted on a tour by William. Concerned by his somewhat wild appearance, she had taken a motherly interest and got him to change his old shabby coat for a decent one, 'but no persuasion could induce him to part with his mustachios'. He had 'a little religious abhorrence to see a piece of roast beef sett before him, and had a great *tendre* for the Hindoos of course'. Otherwise she found him pleasant, warm-hearted and very attentive.

Almost everyone spoke with wonder of William's endurance. 'He is where no-one expects him or knows how he came in a moment'. It was usual for him to ride sixty or seventy miles 'without drawing breath', accompanied by 'a parcell of fellows from Skinners Horse a troop of native cavalry who flit about like the wind ... no man is accepted into them unless he can break a bottle at a hundred yards with his matchlock at full gallop'.

✲

In mid-November Aleck returned from St Helena – alone. James could now only look forward to the time when he and Edward might meet again 'in that better world where no moths corrupt, nor thieves break in to steal'. Knowing the effect Edward's death must be having on his mother, he tried to divert her with news of Aleck, whom he had last seen as a ten-year-old. He was 'certainly handsome and sometimes animated ... he has a good fresh colour & is very little brown'. He was brilliant in debate:

> Gifted with a strong mind with much clearness of head & quickness of apprehension, as well as a great power of language and facility of diction ... Aleck is disposed either cordially to agree or as decidedly to disapprove and his opinion being once formed he will not give up ... nor will he suffer the argument to drop ... till his adversary quits the field.

He was a strange mixture: 'ardent and romantic, brave and generous' but with a tendency to confess 'glaring defects to a great degree more than he actually possesses them partly from a love of sincerity & partly from a whimsical love of oddity & to cause opposition & astonishment'. His love of truth was so great that 'he would not violate it to save his life' but he lacked Edward's consideration of the feelings of others.

Aleck in turn described James's looks and character: in looks James was ...

> ... the Flower of your Family ... he has a flow of conversation; and in company delivers his sentiments extremely well. In private talks he sometimes proses a little ... He is almost as positive in argument as myself, which makes me resolve not to argue with him ... He is full of energy, enterprise, and a noble spirit of independence.

James's optimism was irritating:

> ... he goes with such extravagant hopes, as <u>cannot</u> possibly be fulfilled ... he is too credulous. Every general expression of politeness is by him construed into a serious assurance of support and friendship.

Aleck was also embarrassed by James's habit of holding forth, often on subjects of which he knew little, without noticing the effect on his yawning audience.

Aleck answered his mother's persistent questions about Edward as patiently as he could. What had become of Edward's belongings? Apart from the tin box entrusted to his friend Captain Innes to deliver to Moniack, he had himself kept two small seals and a pair of sleeve buttons belonging to David Gregoire; anything else would be in Delhi. Was his grave marked? It was, but Aleck had not yet been able to organise a stone or railing. There were 'friends there who will see my purpose properly executed ... but the island I will never revisit'.

The House of Becher and Fraser

In early 1814, James accepted a partnership with Mr Becher, an indigo merchant, and sat unwillingly hunched over a desk, scrutinising accounts and scribbling letters all day long. This, he gloomily reflected, would be his occupation for a long time, but if it achieved its end he would be satisfied. Aleck had reservations: he distrusted Becher who, although reputedly honest, was prone to 'haggling and shuffling and shilly shally mode of dealing'.

Although he disliked being stuck indoors juggling figures, James was, as usual, optimistic about the House of Becher and Fraser, envisaging a speedy fortune and a return home. Aleck was not so sure: James always harboured wildly unrealistic ideas – 'a dangerous tendency to a man engaged in mercantile transaction'. Warned of possible pitfalls ahead, James would answer irritatingly, 'Oh it may so happen and the sky may fall too.'

Although Becher's caution and experience might balance James, Aleck considered him narrow-minded, indecisive, conceited and pompous. For the moment, however, James was managing to cope with him, and the first consignment of indigo filled him with pride: 'I shall by this ship make about 80 or 100£ sterling and sweet is the first earnings of a new & serious enterprise – sweet is the promise of profit and speedy home'.

James's energy was amazing: it was hard to believe that he had spent so long in a tropical climate, but he attributed his good health to his vegetarian diet, exercise and temperance – drinking less than one glass of wine a day at a time when huge midday meals, washed down with numerous bottles of claret, were very much the norm among the British and exercise was not popular.

Aleck had joined James in Seton's house, where their host's kindness continued to astonish them. James told his mother that Seton would definitely visit them in Scotland when he got home and stressed Seton's desire not to be any trouble: if he thought that special food, or the best bed, had been prepared for him he would leave at once. 'If you wish to please him, make him one of the family ... don't mind his wonderfully polite and extravagantly courteous speeches ... he will be delighted and delight you all.'

The early months of their new relationship were very difficult for Aleck and James: they had looked forward to being three but were only two; they needed Edward. There was a draughty gap between them which he would have filled. He would have been the soothing, bonding link, always ready to laugh, conciliate and soothe, the brother they both knew well and loved best.

Neither was settled. Aleck, although not completely restored to health, was keen to get back to work in Delhi; James was still missing the freedom of his life in Berbice. Aleck was puzzled by this nostalgia but attributed it to the change in his situation: James had been 'absolute master of a little community and sole commander of the actions of a hundred and fifty of his fellow creatures'; now he was in an uncertain business of which he knew little, with a difficult partner and an unpredictable future.

James appreciated their friends, especially those who were a support to Aleck. 'Nicholson is a very sincere friend and admirer of Aleck's ... none can sway him and influence him as Nicholson can ... I believe Mackintosh would give half his fortune for Aleck's good'. Robert Wilton, Aleck's travelling companion to St Helena, was later to visit Moniack and describe Aeneas Mackintosh's attachment to Aleck as 'very uncommon indeed – like David's for Jonathan'. Aeneas had had a large portrait painted of Aleck on his return from St Helena, but no one thought of getting a copy made for Aleck's parents.

Meanwhile, Aleck's health was still causing concern, especially his eyes, of which the right had become useless. He was very thin and had a slight cough. Everyone was trying to persuade him to stay for a time, the hot winds of Delhi being considered dangerous for weak lungs, but there was little hope of a job in Calcutta. To recover his strength and spirits he took a trip to the country for a month, 'lived on milk, hunted and rambled' and came home feeling much restored.

LIONS AND TYGERS

After more than a year of struggling to write regularly home, William, busy as ever with his 'old jaunts and scampers', handed the task back to his brothers. When his parents complained, James leapt to William's defence: it was difficult for someone who 'dislikes his pen to sit and write a letter which is not indispensably necessary'; he had a large official correspondence to cope with and was often in places ...

> ... where for weeks he could not write if he would ... William would rather, in any weather, in any danger, ride a hundred miles, raised from his Bed at midnight, than write the shortest letter!

A few weeks later, a letter arrived from Jane Anne for William, the brother she had not seen for over fifteen years:

> We were much interested in James's accounts of you. I don't say *pleased* because in the first place I do not like ... *grave taciturn* people and hope James will put a little loquacity into you to suit my taste, and secondly because he says in figure you are as stout as *Raigmore* ... I wish also James would make you write us.

It was his feelings and thoughts, she sternly told him, that they wanted to hear about more than his appearance.

One of William's rare letters contained 'airy castles' about where he would live at home. As the second son he would inherit Rebeg but, he decided, Rebeg would suit Edward or Aleck and he would build his own house in 'the field where we used to go and see the hares and sometimes a roe sporting in the beautiful summer evenings and where so much bog myrtle and cotton grass grew'. The house would be called Rojkuh Farm. It would be designed 'in the Italian fashion' with the bedrooms above, breakfast parlour, dining room, drawing room, library, hall and billiard room on the ground floor and the kitchen in either one of the ornamental wings or in 'a sunk storey'. It would be a 'Batchelor's house with all the appendages, for ornament, of farmyard, garden etc. besides an ornamental bridge over the burn. [We] ought ... to make Moniack a little colony and the envy of the neighbourhood'. His thoughts then turned to his sister and brother at home:

> The last I recollect of George is seeing him rolling on the floor in long petticoats trying to lay hold of the bunch of keys ... and Jane Anne crying if she was not allowed to bring the toast rack in the morning from the kitchen to the parlour and indulged with the top of an egg for breakfast ... Tell all the old servants and their children that someday soon I mean to make them all dance, a merry dance that will ring through all the Aird.

When rumour of William's eccentricities reached the Highlands, Jane anxiously asked Aleck for reassurance. In his brother's defence he replied that although it had become the custom for Englishmen 'to speak to [natives] with haughtiness if men of Rank, with insolence, if inferior', that was definitely not William's way. 'William is feared, esteemed and loved by the numerous inhabitants of a country which he has improved, corrected and benefited.'

James agreed: Jane was not to listen to gossipmongers. If William 'wore whiskers' and refused to eat beef, it was because he wanted to identify better with the people he was serving: 'he does not eat Beef because that practice offends and disgusts our Hindoo subjects – the Cow is in their Eyes, sacred, and they look on the slaughtering and devouring of a cow in the same light as we regard the act and meal of a cannibal'.

There are titbits about William from his contemporaries. Charles Metcalfe confirmed that he 'would have no difficulty in dealing with the higher order of Natives, with some of whom he has been more intimate than most Europeans are'.[5] Much later, the young French botanist, Victor Jacquemont, summed him up:

> He is half Asiatic in his habits, but in other respects a Scotch Highlander, and an excellent man with great originality of thought, a metaphysician to boot, and enjoying the best reputation of being a country bear.[6]

5 *The Cornchest for Scotland: Scots in India* Alex M. Cain (1986) National Library of Scotland.
6 Ibid.

At that moment, the 'country bear' was having great fun with Lady Hood in north-west India. She had left her elderly husband in Madras and was off on an adventure of her own. 'What,' mused Aleck to his mother, 'will our Scotch Ladies think of her Ladyship's hardiness in venturing ... through some of the wildest parts of British India ... among a nation of semi-barbarians?' This and her exploits hunting lions with William would surely provide fodder for the tongue-waggers of Inverness-shire.

In early April, the pair were visiting a grotto between the Jumna to the west and the Ganges to the east, delighted with the highland flora and gathering bunches of 'common fern, brambles, mountain pine and some other Scotch remembrances'. William was completely bewitched – 'in raptures of her Ladyship; of the charms of her conversation; the affability of her manner; of her enthusiastic attachment to Scotland'. Her conversation was 'so very superior and so very different to that of any other woman I had seen in India'. He hoped that Aleck would meet her on her return to Calcutta.

Aleck hoped otherwise. He had already come across her Ladyship and found her 'masculine and yet frivolous ... totally different from my idea of what a woman ought to be'. She certainly had great strength of intellect, but this may have led her to be an unbeliever and worse, 'to boast of being a Freethinker'. He quite understood, however, why William was infatuated; after all, 'she hunted with him, and it is said, actually shot a Tyger, and she entered into all his fondness of enterprise and rambling'.

William had indeed taken her on shooting trips, and she allegedly shot a lion as well as a tiger 'and behaved like an Amazon ... She seems to me as a sister'. James told his parents that Lady Hood would be able to give them a wonderful first-hand picture of William when she reached Inverness-shire. Although 'few men could endure what Lady Hood has done & she has got enormously fat and large upon it', they would find her 'the same warmhearted and enthusiastic creature as ever'.

⁂

The brothers worried that William's irresistible expedition would damage his career prospects. He was out of Delhi just as he was about to be offered 'a very honourable and lucrative appointment' – Judge and Magistrate in the district of Cuttack. Aleck, however, doubted that he would accept the offer on account of his attachment to Delhi – 'yet ... the longer he stays it becomes more difficult and might in time be impossible, even to leave it for Scotland'.

When William turned the job down Aleck wondered whether he was no longer focussed on making enough money to get home quickly. William hotly denied this. The slightest hint that he had forgotten his country and family threw him into a passion. The truth was that William had his sights set on one of the 'few very great prizes', an eventual Residency, preferably in Delhi. The position in Cuttack would have been a cul-de-sac.

Aleck reluctantly explained to his dismayed parents that William had made the right decision: he would not have coped well with rules and regulations. William was perfectly aware that 'capacity and decision' were more his strengths than 'acumen and precision' and that he would make a better statesman than a lawyer. No wonder he refused to exchange a job where he was completely free to make his own decisions for one 'where ... he may be outshone by fifty laborious searchers of the regulations'.

It was when he was at full tilt with Lady Hood in March 1814 that William finally got confirmation of Edward's death; but he found time to write fully and bracingly to his father:

> You will not allow anything of this sort affect your health enjoyments or spirits ... Life is peculiarly precarious in this climate, and what has already removed one may remove others ... I entreat as the greatest comfort I can have you will have the portrait of our dear Edward which was done by Raeburn copied for me.

He also asked for miniatures 'by the first artists to be procured in Edinburgh or London' of his parents, Jane Anne and George – at his expense. A couple of weeks later, he wrote to James:

> At this moment Lady Hood is sitting at the same table as me. We are on a hunting party to kill lions ... Lady Hood orders me to give her love to you. See how you are honoured.

So who was this Lady Hood whose path so often crossed those of the Fraser brothers and of whom each had an opinion, however diverse? To Edward, who had met her in London, she had appeared 'a downright fright'; to Aleck, 'masculine and yet frivolous'; to their mother, potentially a 'delightful companion' for her sons; to James, 'very handsome'; and to William, the most interesting woman he had ever met.

She was exactly the same age as James, born Mary Elizabeth Frederica Mackenzie, the eldest of the six daughters of Francis Mackenzie, the deaf, and latterly dumb, Baron Seaforth of Brahan in Ross-shire. She married the Admiral, more than twenty years her senior, in 1804. In 1815, following the deaths of her husband and father, she succeeded to the family estate, her four brothers having predeceased her, thereby becoming the colourful chief of the Clan Mackenzie. Walter Scott described her as having 'the spirit of the chieftainness in every drop of her blood'.[7] She was also known as 'the hooded lassie', from a prediction by the seventeenth century prophet, the Brahan Seer, Kenneth Mackenzie.[8]

7 *Memoirs of the Life of Sir Walter Scott*, J G Lockhart (1837–8)

8 He foresaw that Lord Seaforth's possession would be inherited by 'a white hooded lassie from the East and she is to kill her sister'. Lady Hood returned to Brahan from India allegedly wearing the traditional Indian white coiffe of mourning to take up her inheritance. In 1823 she was driving her sister, Lady Caroline Mackenzie, through the grounds of Brahan. Something frightened the ponies, which bolted, overturning the carriage. Lady Caroline died of her injuries. *Ravens and Black Rain*, Elizabeth Sutherland (1985), Constable & Co. Ltd.

In answer to William's request, some coloured 'profiles', or silhouettes, were sent to India. On the whole, Aleck was irritated by them: George's likeness he considered well done but Jane Anne's was unrecognisable; his father looked like 'a starving attorney who has lost his cause'. James also disliked it:

> It has little benignity or kindness of expression without which it cannot be like him – I fear he was thinking of some abominable Berbice bill ... when it was taken. Aleck says he would not have known it.

James wanted a proper picture of his mother; both she and Jane Anne should be painted by Raeburn. 'All the rest are preserved in painting & I wish we had these two also to speak to other days & say what things *the Reelick family* were.'

Calcutta Mishap

The slightest hint of illness in his family always threw Aleck into a panic. In July 1814 he heard that his father had been unwell and immediately implored him to 'for once follow your own maxims' and go to London for medical advice, then Devon for the climate and Bath and Cheltenham for society and amusement with 'old Indians'. Money must be no obstacle – his sons would pay. He consulted Simon Nicholson, who stressed, 'it is of the first importance to keep the bowels open'. As usual, he seems to have forgotten that, by the time Reelig received this letter, something like a year would have elapsed since the onset of the ailment.

As far as his mother's health went, he was horrified to hear that she had suffered a shipwreck on the way to Bath: what on earth was his father doing allowing her to go to sea at all, or to Bath? Aleck disapproved of Bath, 'not from the expense incurred but by the unpleasantness of the unprotected state of my mother and her daughter in such a place and ... the great danger of great deterioration of the morals'. It was unwise 'to give the daughter of a country gentleman of moderate, nay small, means, the Education of a Dutchess'. Surely the country gentlemen of Inverness-shire would prefer Scotch airs to an Italian ditty; it was doubtful whether the Country Dance would be improved by 'Southern Steps'.

> Oh! I detest and dread that seat of vice, of frivolity, of idleness, that resort of Shattered Beaux, of unprincipled fortune hunters, of cunning scoundrels of every Caste ... I never read the word 'Bath' in your letters that I do not shiver; 'tis a vile Gossiping seducing sink of iniquity.

The visit to Bath was now presumably six months past but he advised his mother to ...

> ... set your force against late hours and thin clothing and prevent those sudden changes from heat to cold ... running from a crowded ballroom to a chair or carriage with scarce any defence from cold; and other trifling acts of carelessness often are the cause of untimely death ... the vivacity of young Girls is difficult to restrain.

Although inactivity was making him irritable, Aleck's own health was improving slowly. James was looking after him conscientiously and his friends rallied round, especially Molony who, a 'universal favourite', had been a rival at Hertford. It was strange, mused Aleck, how disagreeable schoolmates became great friends after 'years tossed on the Ocean of Life'.

Although the doctors, Nicholson or Russell, now had little fear for him, there was no immediate hope of resuming his career in Delhi. Things appeared to be improving, however, until one day in his room upstairs he was chasing boredom by fiddling around with chemicals, including a highly corrosive mixture of 'nitric acid with alcohol and silver'. It blew up in his face and he would have probably lost his sight had he not instantly bathed his eyes in cold water. His already weak eyesight was now further damaged, one eye being probably beyond repair. Simon Nicholson reckoned the other would eventually recover but at the moment it looked 'very ugly'. Meanwhile, he had to be kept in total darkness and deprived of reading, his only great amusement. 'Like most of my mishaps,' he ruefully told his mother, it was completely his own fault.

Kalanga

Meanwhile, having waved Lady Hood off back to Madras, William was feeling very flat. He soon, however, recovered his spirits, rambling from District to District, discussing farming concerns and village politics. He had recently become addicted to surveying and rode out with flags and theodolite to some high point to take bearings but, noted Aleck, rarely got round to recording his findings: 'He is very indolent in every business of the pen. I fancy in truth the excessive badness of his handwriting renders that employment irksome.'

He was keeping healthy on only one meal a day and never more than two glasses of Madeira. His recreations centred on horses, hawks and shooting from elephant-back. After his exploits with Lady Hood he would now, he announced, please his father and no longer hunt lions and tigers.

❁

Just around the corner, however, was something tailor-made to capture William's imagination. Border disputes in the North-West had been rumbling on for some time and Lord Moira, now Marquess of Hastings, was preparing to wage war[9] on the Gurkhas over their threat to the trade route to Tibet and China. The western divisions of the army were under the command of Major Generals Gillespie and Ochterlony.

Owing to the length of the Nepal border and the mountainous terrain, it was clearly going to be a very different kind of fighting from the skirmishes of the army on the plains. The regular Bengali troops were known to be intrepid, loyal, hardy soldiers but they had no experience of mountain warfare. Around a third of the Nepalese army, commanded by Amar Singh Thapa, were true Gurkhas. The rest were hill tribesmen, who might well be persuaded to desert to the British.

9 The Anglo-Nepal War of 1814–16, concluded by the Treaty of Sugauli, March 1816.

In order to reinstate chieftains displaced by the Gurkhas and to ascertain the mood of the inhabitants, Hastings appointed Political Agents in each division. William was chosen to serve under Major General Gillespie. Initially, his job was to communicate with the mountain people of north Garhwal and persuade them to cut off the retreat of the Nepalese army; he was then responsible for establishing the authority of the British government in newly won territories and setting up a police force and revenue system; he was to gather useful intelligence, but on no account was he to step over the line between civil and military duties.

Knowing William well, his superiors also told him firmly that he was not to 'assume any authority, separate or independent of that which must rest in Major-General Gillespie'. Hastings had rather unconvincingly assured Gillespie that he would find William cordial and obedient. Soon after his appointment, however, William was audacious enough to point out that it would have been more sensible to take immediate control of Srinagar, adding: 'I make this remark as matter of information ... not by any means suggesting it, which would be completely out of line of my duty, and deviating from the course of respectful and submissive deference'.[10]

Rollo Gillespie was a man after William's heart, glamorous and feisty, of Scots and Irish ancestry. In his youth he had killed a man in a duel; he had also eloped and then escaped a warrant for assault (on a man who refused to stand or remove his hat for the National Anthem) by disguising himself as a breastfeeding mother. He had survived a court martial, achieved many military successes in the West Indies and eventually taken himself overland to India where he played a major part in the suppression of the Mutiny at Vellore in 1806. William was delighted to be in his division. They were to move north 'to capture Dehra Dun, the valleys and passes of Garhwal and the land between the Jumna and the Ganges'.[11]After three unsuccessful attempts by Gillespie to capture Kalanga, a small hill fort which lay in his way, a fourth assault was planned for 30 October 1814. William, happily ignoring his civilian status, was at the forefront of the action.

Reinforcements had been summoned for a midday assault, but at first light the hot-headed Gillespie sprang into action and was killed instantly by a musket ball. His Political Agent, who should have been nowhere near the front line, then leapt into the fray, facing fire and a storm of arrows, one of which went through his neck. Despite this wound and a battering from heavy stones hurled by gallant women defenders of the fort, William, 'immediately and by express', wrote a report of the disastrous attempt to the Secretary to the Government. Some weeks later, James heard about the attack from Harrison, a comrade who had been at William's side:

> When they came to the stockades he threw off his jacket and tucked up his shirt sleeves and drew his *tulwar*[12] and he sprang over and pointing out the way cried

10 *A Special Corps: the Beginnings of Gurkha Service with the British*, A P Coleman (1999) Pentland Press.
11 Ibid. p. 81.
12 Sabre

> 'There's your mark Harrison' and on they went through a thick fire to the walls – William put his head into the wickets and instantly received the arrow through his throat.

Charles Grant had to break the news to Reelig that the 'Fraser Esquire' who was reported wounded had turned out to be 'W. Fraser, 1st Assistant'. Grant was furious with William for 'so unnecessarily exposing himself and the ... happiness of his family', but William received the 'most flattering public notice of his gallant conduct' from the Adjutant General:

> Sir,
> I am directed by the Right Honourable the Commander in Chief, to request you will bring to the particular notice of His Excellency the Governor General, the conduct of Mr William Fraser, First Assistant to the Resident at Delhi, and now attached in a political capacity to the British troops in Gurwhall; whose zeal for the service induced him to accompany the late Major General Gillespie to the assault of Kalanga on which occasion he was wounded by an arrow; while participating in the danger of the troops.

William naturally remained unrepentant. He wrote cryptically to James and Aleck, 'I am slightly wounded but able to write as you see' and added later that he had been determined 'to see and be at the head of one [assault] in my life'. He described the action to Aleck:

> The heat, impatience and impetuosity of poor Gillespie our General was the principal cause of our defeat ... General Gillespie was shot dead in the act of huzzaing to the men, waving his hat in his left hand and sword in his right hand; and yet not a man would follow him nor advance with him ... the Goorkhas fought most bravely and resolutely and if they fight as well in the field we shall have a tough campaign.

He was lucky that the arrow he had received was not barbed: 'it passed across my neck between the gullet and the windpipe avoiding on each side the arteries and large vessels'. On 10 November he wrote that the wound had healed up although he was still hoarse and had difficulty in swallowing.

Aleck tried to reassure his parents: 'He solemnly promises me, voluntarily, not to go upon another assault'. Later, James added his note of comfort: William had been involved in another assault on Kalanga but kept his promise and 'was not with the storming party'.

Hindsight

After an operation by Simon Nicholson, Aleck had regained full sight in one eye. At the end of 1814 he set off on a river trip with James, whose business, according to James, was now thriving. He had 'golden expectations and rich promise of profits', news which was to be taken with a pinch of salt and allowance for 'a warm imagination'.

James knew perfectly well that there was a long way to go before Aleck could be pronounced cured; Aleck, for his part, having witnessed every twist and turn of Edward's illness, was under no illusions about the likely outcome. He pretended, however, to believe that a river voyage would complete his recovery.

Cooped up on a boat, James found Aleck increasingly difficult but did his best to care for him. There were diversions in the friendly houses they stayed at, in shooting expeditions and in letters from Jeanie Tytler and home. On Aleck's better days they discussed everything from the theories of David Hume[13] to the poetry of Scott and Byron. But James was out of his depth when confronted with Aleck's daily mood swings. There were moments when Aleck announced that his recovery was unlikely and that he could see no difference between his state and Edward's, but James briskly dismissed this – the cases were 'widely differing'. He tried to convince himself that Aleck's sleeplessness was the problem and that his brother was getting stronger.

After just over two weeks on the river, however, Becher summoned James back to his desk. He set off at once, leaving Aleck to follow, and rejoined the party in Seton's house. On Christmas Day he took himself off to hear the new Bishop's[14] first sermon – 'a collection was made for the poor to which I was obliged to contribute, tho' poor myself, 8 rupees'. The Church in India was undergoing complete reorganisation and there was talk of converting the indigenous population to Christianity. James was sceptical: for a Hindu, it would mean giving up one's family. 'Why should they become outcasts from society, despised and abhorred by their only friends and companions?' Unless some great social change took place, he told his mother, 'there is no chance for any diffusion of Christ in the Eastern world'.

⁂

When Aleck reappeared Seton allotted him three large rooms, two of which opened on to a long verandah so that he had plenty of fresh air 'and in the hot winds we shut up house from top to bottom, early in the cool of the morning & enclose a body of cool air ... so that for an invalid we are in the best quarters'.

With one good eye, Aleck was trying to finish a kind of confession, his 'Legacy' he called it, that he had started in June 1814. In it he laid bare 'the principles or passions, that have chiefly influenced my actions'. It is a long document, looking far back to his early childhood and reliving his journey to St Helena and Edward's death. In the conclusion, written in Delhi in January 1816, he records that in his six years as Assistant in Delhi he was actually at work for only one year and five months. That time, and the months of his care of Edward are, he asserts, the only moments of his life that he can recall with any degree of satisfaction. The rest he considers 'a life useless to my Employers, burdensome to my friends and myself' and marked only by 'Pain and Illness; or worse, by Idleness'.

13 Scottish philosopher, economist and historian (1711–76).
14 Thomas Middleton (1769–1822), first Bishop of Calcutta, 1814–23.

Seton initially forbade all callers; when this was later relaxed, even visits from Aleck's friends sometimes failed to cheer him up. One day, James found Holt Mackenzie with him – 'a very pleasant young man' in his opinion, and he could not understand Aleck's hostility. He came to the conclusion that 'Aleck thinks and reflects more than I do ... he sees motives in Holt's conduct which he dislikes ... and he dislikes an image which he himself has made'.

Holt had recently lost a beloved brother; Aleck instantly sympathised and was generous enough to praise his old rival and admit his own faults:

> Although I do not personally like Holt Mackenzie, I am not so blind as to be unaware of his high talents, noble principles, and excellent heart ... The cause of this [disagreement] originated with him but continued by my fault[15] that is had I chosen to sacrifice some passions which you would probably call evil, I might have been intimate with him

Several of Aleck's friends, worried about his dire financial situation, promised to help. There was concern for him at higher levels, too: the Nugents, Edmonstones, Hastings and his wife 'were constant in their enquiries and presents'. They brought him flowers, fruit and his favourite strawberries. James, knowing Aleck's indifference to 'ladies in the high circles', was amazed at their attention to him considering that he had never bothered to call on them when he was well – 'a neglect a Calcutta Lady does not easily forgive'.

Escape

Now came a gleam of hope that James might get 'free from a most troublesome concern': Becher, intent on going home, was trying to create a new partnership with an Indian, Lolla Baboo, who would hold a quarter of the business; James would hold another quarter and Becher himself the rest. James, feeling that it was degrading to be put on the same footing 'with a native and one whose character was none of the best', disagreed with these terms. After long havering and wavering on Becher's part, and sleepless nights for James, he at last managed to disentangle himself from the partnership, which was then dissolved. On 20 January 1815, with Rs35,000 in his pocket, he finally shut the door on Becher and Fraser forever.

While aware that his father would be deeply disappointed by the apparent failure of the partnership, Aleck was not surprised at its demise: 'In the first place Becher knew nothing of business, James very little ... dealing more in the style of a Pedlar Jew than of a Gentleman Merchant.' Aleck acknowledged James's homesickness, but after a year at home his 'impatient spirit will again tire of home, and he will wander anew in search of adventure or in pursuit of mercantile speculation'. Reelig agreed: 'I entertain little hope of his sober unwearied exertions at home'.

James now had a choice: he could either go home, taking with him some good quality indigo and hoping to open up a market in Britain; or stay in India, still in hopes of a fortune round the corner, setting himself up as an agent for overseas trade. He took long

15 Here in the margin of Reelig's letterbook is a large exclamation mark in his hand.

walks chewing it all over with Seton: if he were to go home he must go at once as the indigo season would soon be over, in which case he would neither meet William again nor see Aleck completely recovered.

He next consulted John Palmer, a man of considerable standing in Calcutta, whose advice was quite clear: it was far too late in the season to take a consignment of indigo to Britain, so why not find William, see a bit of India and 'be assured of the health and life of Aleck'? He could then plan on returning home at the right time to take a cargo of indigo.

Thus was James's mind made up – a decision of great significance: he would join William's adventures and then would return home at the end of the year with a splendid cargo of indigo 'which I hope will pay my way most handsomely ... and then welcome Scotland forever'.

❊

Leaving Aleck in the good care of Archy Seton and Simon Nicholson, James began to prepare for his journey. He was advised to go by palanquin carried by four or six bearers, relays of whom would be posted at intervals along the way. This would be more expensive but faster than a river journey. It would also need careful planning, not James's forte, and Aleck foresaw all sorts of hitches 'owing to his extreme carelessness and inaccuracy of speaking, hearing and writing'.

And hitches there certainly were. The brothers spent their last night together reorganising the luggage, which was far too bulky. Having rejected many garments and four volumes of Gibbon, James declared himself ready to go, only to find that plans had already gone awry and there was not a bearer in sight. Aleck exploded again to his father:

> I never saw a man so improvident in the minor concerns of life ... he gives his servants the most vague and inaccurate order: and then is angry and surprised, that they are mistaken – precision in speaking, accuracy in writing, foresight and method in conducting business ... these are qualities which, I fear, James will never acquire.

Two days later the necessary bearers had been rounded up; James bade a hasty farewell to Aleck and set off on the first stage of his journey. He disliked travelling by palanquin, mainly because it was very difficult to see out, but he recorded as much as he could of the varying landscapes and was as excited as William had been at his first glimpse of the Indian hills. He wrote of the villages, crops, mud forts, temples, ruins, mosques, rivers and *nullahs*[16] that make up so much of the landscape of India. He ate too much fruit, which upset his stomach – not easy to cope with in a palanquin. His unplanned route took him to a river where there was no bridge, but he and his palanquin were taken across on an upturned wooden bedstead, balanced on six earthenware pots. 'These people have simple ingenuity and reserve, wonderfully useful and entertaining,' he wrote admiringly. But a week later, once again, there were no bearers.

16 Watercourse, sometimes dry.

In Lucknow things improved. The accommodating Resident, Major John Baillie, sent an elephant to bring James safely through the town, where the filthy streets were so narrow and the roofs so close that the elephant lumbering through 'disturbed the thatch'. Aleck had not thought Lucknow worth seeing, but James spent ten days exploring its wonders, so different from the Britishness of Calcutta: elephants wonderfully caparisoned, camels richly dressed, horsemen of all sorts gaily accoutred, the rich dresses and coloured robes of the Indians. He relished his elephant rides as the animal 'opens passage and [its] height gives full room for observation'– intriguing glimpses of lives being lived in shadowy upstairs rooms.

There were *nautch* evenings, breakfasts with the Nawab and an organised trip to Shahjehanpur, where he met Robert Home,[17] who had painted William in Indian dress. Home was now painting 'the Nawab in his Durbar ... surrounded by all his nobility and a number of Europeans – this will be a good picture to give them an idea at home of an Eastern court'.

This was the pivotal moment when James took up his pencil after so long and began tentatively to sketch, inspired by the magnificent Mughal architecture around him. His first attempt was a view of the Nawab's Palace from the top of the old Residency. He was not satisfied with it, 'but it will do for a memorial of Lucknow'.

Jaithak

Aleck remained convalescent in Calcutta. As self-appointed armchair war correspondent, he was keeping his parents informed of William's movements in the hills of what is now Himachal Pradesh. William had been waiting, with increasing impatience, for Major General Gabriel Martindell, who was to take over Gillespie's command. Meanwhile, he informed the Governor General that the underfed European troops were killing 'horned cattle' along the way to supplement their diet; this was no way to win the loyalty or respect of the Hindu hill tribes. He also suggested that he might start recruiting a force of irregular troops from the hill people who would be useful 'in a country so inaccessible, mountainous, and unknown'.

In November 1814, the Secretary to the Government, John Adam, replied to William: different arrangements would immediately be made for feeding the European troops. William's plan for raising irregular troops was approved and he was to proceed with this up to a corps of 1,500. In conclusion, Adam was ...

> ... directed to convey to you, the assurance of the Governor General; that he is happy to receive from you any suggestions that occur to your mind, relative to the conduct of the important *civilian*[18] branch of the public affairs with which your present labours are associated.

17 1752–1834. Court Painter of Nawab Ghazi-ud-din Haidar, for whom he also designed furniture and buildings.

18 My italics. The word 'civilian' was omitted from the copy Reelig made of these official documents ('Papers respecting the Nepaul War'). Was this a Freudian slip or a desire to portray William in a more compliant light?

William ignored this hint with another suggestion: an attack on a Nepalese position at Chamur.[19] He did, however, 'humbly' rely on the 'indulgent forgiveness of the Right Honourable Governor General for touching on subjects foreign to my situation, and duties apologising 'if I am led to hazard opinions which are obviously expressive of military subjects.'[20]

He revelled in his role as recruiting officer and was immensely impressed by the mountain peoples, their 'activity, enterprize, hardiness, patience and abstinence ... the knowledge they possess of the country ... their expertness in passing rivers not fordable.'[21] The native people of Nepal, especially the chieftains, were only too happy to join the British if it meant they could shake off the Gurkha yoke. Aleck had no doubt that William's work was absolutely vital and that it was through 'the great and fatal want' of information that the war had so far been unsuccessful. He was also impressed by the reputation of the enemy forces – 'brave, humane, honourable, enterprising and enduring cold, hunger and hardship incredibly'. He relayed to Jane Anne how a Gurkha chief took eighty-five prisoners and, apologising for not having enough food for them, sent them home after receiving their promise that they would not take any further action against his fort, though they were free to act against any other.

By April 1815 William's irregular force numbered over 6,000; as he had no official military rank, it was placed under the command of a Lieutenant Frederick Young, who was to become a close friend of both William and James. Later, the irregular force was divided into smaller bodies and the chieftains replaced by European officers. William was quick to point out that not any old officer would do. They had to be 'properly selected, with reference to the duties they are intended to discharge' and they needed to have a good knowledge of the 'Asiatick character ... An intemperate, hasty, boisterous person would do more harm than good.'[22] When the war was finally over many of these irregular troops were taken into the British army and the first two regiments were formed. William was thus one of the founders of the Gurkha regiments who have served Britain faithfully ever since.[23]

✣

The elderly Major General Martindell[24] eventually appeared; his military career had ended with resignation the previous year. However, finding no one else of suitable rank, Lord Moira gave him command of the 2nd field division of the Bengal army.

The 'lofty fortress of Jaithak' was Martindell's next obstacle. There were two unsuccessful attempts on it at the end of December, after which Martindell was only too happy to sit back and wait for reinforcements. This drove William to distraction:

19 Ibid. p. 93.
20 *A Special Corps: the Beginnings of Gurkha Service with the British*, A P Coleman (1999) Pentland Press.
21 Ibid. p. 92.
22 Ibid, p. 98.
23 *India Revealed*, p. 29.
24 1754/5–1831

> I cannot tell you how much General ... [Martindell]'s management is scorned and reviled by the army for indecision, want of promptness, energy and enterprise ... we might have been as safely and as far advanced a month ago as we are today.

The siege dragged on, the weather got colder and February 1815 found William still 2,000ft above the plain, in very wintry conditions. He was, however, happily engaged in drilling his bemused and shivering sepoys in the art of snowball fighting: 'I have been pelting snowballs and making new ones ... fighting the Sepoys and making them fight ... I suspect the Ghoorkas are just as unable to act in this weather, as we are.' A few sepoys and many bearers, used to the heat of the plains, had actually died of cold, but William's irregular forces had all survived 'taking much of the fag, without grumbling'. Despite his intense frustration he was finding the weather exhilarating:

> Every now and then I am forced to blow my fingers ... exercise and running about is delightfull, a cold damp tent and a sharp wind painful. My horses are kept warm with an inch and a half of snow on their Blankets ... Some sit with their tents shut up, and Candles. A preposterous arrangement for North Britons and Highlanders ... I do not like to see our Europeans petted and coaxed and the Native Infantry taking the hardest duty.

He was exasperated by James's plan to join him. 'What to do God knows,' he fumed to Aleck; why on earth was James 'hurrying and tearing on as if he came post haste to assume control of the Army'. He should have stayed to care for Aleck and saved the expense of such a wild-goose trip; he would, no doubt, 'expect a vivacious affection and incessant display of love for Home and Family' which William would not be able to provide, although his feelings for home were as fervent as any. He had, however, sent horses, tents, elephants, servants etc. to escort James to Kurnal.

Catching up

As James's palanquin moved slowly north towards William and the snow, the weather became noticeably colder and he had to sleep under three thick quilts while coping with 'a very execrable sett of Bearers'. He had written to Charles Metcalfe in Delhi asking him to send respectable bearers for the last part of the journey, but Metcalfe was out of town and yet again none materialised.

Worse was to come. Having rounded up bearers of sorts he set off again but woke to find they had all run away. 'I fumed, raved, fretted and swore and sent the *chokidar*[25]out for others'. Too impatient to wait, however, James found himself a pony with a piece of cloth for a saddle and a sling for a bridle, enlisted some female coolies to carry the bags and left the palanquin to follow as and when bearers could be procured.

Luckily, he found his way along the banks of the Jumna to the encampment of the 8th Light Dragoons where he chanced upon Edward's cabin-mate, John Fraser. By now he was

25 Watchman

half blinded by the glare of the unremitting sun, covered with dust and riding 'a miserable medium between a bad horse and a bad *tattoo*[26] with the bad qualities of each and the good qualities of neither'. The officers, astonished by the bedraggled apparition stumbling into their midst, were even more surprised to find he was none other than the elder brother of the hero of Kalanga; most of them knew William well. Their welcome and the stories they had to tell of his 'esteemed and valued' brother heartened James. More impatient than ever to find him, at the beginning of March he was off once more on his quest, this time to Delhi.

There were ghosts in Delhi. Everywhere James went he was treading in the footsteps of his three brothers:

> Here for many years my Brother William was in the plenitude of power and honour ... here also his Brother Aleck resided along with him ... and here our beloved Edward ... rapidly fell into the illness which deprived us of him forever – here now are none of all these – all are absent ... I tread these haunts with a feeling somewhat similar to that which I felt at Moniack when it was in danger – as if I were using as my own what had passed away to another.

His visit to William's bungalow was strange and disturbing. The current tenant showed James the room that held the belongings of his three brothers. William's curious collection amazed him: through the dusty gloom he could make out tiger skins, buffalo horns, old bows and arrows, matchlocks, armour, empty gun cases, Persian books and so on, 'all lying or standing in some sort of extraordinary order about the room'. Aleck's things he found 'in reasonably good order' but Edward's he could not bring himself to describe.

Charles Metcalfe welcomed James warmly to the Residency, where he enjoyed the stories of numerous old servants who appeared daily, with salaams and grapes, to salute William's brother.

Not to be outdone by William, James wangled an audience with a King – this time it was the Mughal Emperor Akbar Shah,[27] who had been on the Peacock Throne since Shah Alam's death in 1806. With other admirers James went through the usual formalities, although by now corners were being cut. With his shoes off and hat on he 'made three low bows or salaams', presented the King with his *nuzzur*[28] two gold *mohurs*,[29] and then was dressed in 'an abominably coarse muslin dress put on with a sort of shining silver jacket over it – a coarse sort of Turban or roll of cloth round our hats and a sort of clout round our necks'. After processing 'like a parcel of geese' back into the royal presence there were further low bows and then the party retired. The King was surrounded by numerous courtiers and 'many claimed acquaintance with me on account of my likeness to my Brother'.

> The farce certainly was ludicrous but worth going thro' for once, even for the novelty of the thing but when we conceded that the person to whom we were presented is the lineal descendant of the Grear Timour, the illustrious Akbar,

26 Native-bred pony
27 Akbar II (1760–1837)
28 Ceremonial gift
29 Coin worth about Rs15.

> Shahjehan and Aurangzeb and the son of the unfortunate Shah Allam, it was peculiarly interesting and perhaps affecting tho a shadow, a weak and miserable shadow, it was the vision of great things ... of majesty humbled with the dust.

With something of William's rapt attention to detail in Peshawar six years previously, he described the King 'clothed in a dress of pea green silk or satin very handsome but rather plain'.

> The vest was of yellow silk with gold, his cummerbund ... was an embroydered shawl and his turband was a curious thing, a rolled Blue shawl with a large tuft of fur at each side sticking out far and giving the whole a wonderfully broad foolish appearance like a Zanies or fools cap. On his two temples were stuck a patch of white paper, a plaister, I understand, of opium for the headache ... round his neck was a necklace of large Pearls, with some very valuable emeralds, one in particular of the size of a Pidgeon's egg ... he is very pensive but it does not appear to be from a sense of his degraded situation ... as from the effects of opium. His Eyes appeared possessed of a certain fire ... chiefly at the sight of the gold mohurs ... his person no-one could judge of as he sat cross-legged – but his portly paunch hung down with considerable dignity on his thighs. He seemed wonderfully alert at spooning the gold mohurs from one handkerchief to the attendant in waiting ... in the most decided business-like manner possible.

On his sightseeing tour through the interior of the Palace he bumped into the King's granddaughter:

> A fine little girl but miserably dirty in her dress – she appeared near four years of age, she was carried by a fellow like a common *kitmutgar*,[30] very dirty, across his hip, as the negro women carry their children. I shook the little thing's dirty paw ... her long hair tied up in a dirty brown rag ... only a dirty muslin frock or shift on and as dirty a cap.

On 10 March 1815, after only six days in the city, having raided Aleck's trunks for riding breeches, two volumes of Gibbon, 'the remains of a Persian dictionary', some shot, flints and 'an old fishing pocket book', James set off once more in search of William.

The elephants, bearers, horses and horsemen that William had sent to escort him to Kurnal were a heart-warming sight, but less welcome was a letter, addressed to Calcutta, that had finally caught up with him. William was adamant: it was pointless coming north to join him and he would be far better employed staying in Calcutta to look after Aleck. James was understandably hurt but, ignoring the letter, he rather nervously pushed on through the jungle towards Kurnal, reassuring himself by reflecting on the extravagant provision that William had made for the last stages of his journey (tents, servants, cooks, bearers, eight or ten of Skinners Horse, and four of his own most trusted servants). Surely this indicated a warm brotherly welcome at the journey's end?

30 Servant

Arriving in Kurnal, one of the best sporting stations in the area, he found that William had just that minute left and would be away for a few days. There was time to relax with a cricket match, a great deal of shooting in the jungle and a performance by *nautch* women. Too impatient to wait any longer, however, he then pushed on. By now he had reached the edge of the theatre of war at Nahan, 'perched like a Bird's nest overlooking the hills and plain at its feet'. He had had a difficult ascent through incredibly rugged and rocky country up roads worse than he had ever encountered, even in the Highlands of Scotland. Once again, William's tent was empty. He was marching higher into the snowfields with a hundred of his irregulars to join an assault on the fort of Chaupal. His hastily scribbled note assured James that his friends in Nahan would look after him until his return.

While waiting, James was happily diverted by the preparations for an assault on the fort of Jaithak (see Plate XVIII)`, another 1,500ft higher and clearly visible from Nahan. Shots were echoing in the hills all around, and he was fascinated by all the military activity. Enormous artillery pieces were being dragged uphill, 200 men to each gun. The guns were too clumsy to get round corners so the ascent was virtually perpendicular, often involving descents into gullies deep in thick jungle – 'I suppose no guns were ever drawn over such ground for such a distance since the world began'.

Elephants were being used for the smaller guns and the ammunition:

> Up this abominable path loaded Elephants find their way to the astonishment of all. These wonderfull animals find their way where a man can hardly go- slow by stepping by short steps and trying every stone and piece of soil with his trunk he gets along amazingly surely sometimes stopping for a quarter of an hour while a man digs a step for him.

The rumour was that the enemy were losing heart, that their Commander had 'a clouded countenance' and that his men were hungry. Several had deserted to the British. Things looked hopeful.

James now had time for both letters and sketching; he began to draw in earnest and regularly sent his sketches to Aleck. He described to his mother how he was ...

> ... taking sketches of the *fort* we are before, the *Ports* which surround it, the *hills* we are among, & some of the people we daily see ... when the Devil of Drawing broke loose there was no holding him.

Two days later, on 17 March about midday, while he was inspecting the batteries, came the moment James had been looking forward to every minute of his arduous journey of nearly four months, in fact ever since he had left Moniack at the end of 1812:

> A *chuprassee*[31] brought the news that the Burra Sahib[32] (William) was come. I left the Battery and halfway up the hill and near the Black hill, I met him – he had marched 12 miles that morning – it was an awkward place for a reencounter –

31 Messenger
32 Headman, master, boss

> surrounded by servants and officers... [from] rather a weak boy of 14, I now meet ... a large stocky strong man already famous & well known, having by his own exertions talents & activity gained a most respectable name.

✻

The brothers spent the rest of the afternoon watching the effect of their guns on the stockade and engaging in 'desultory chat'. A couple of weeks later, James sent his mother his first impressions of this thirty-one-year-old brother that he had not seen since they were boys. He had been prepared for a change, but he was not in the least like 'the picture he sent home to you[33] – and not till many days had familiarised his appearance to me could I trace out any resemblance to the picture of him by Raeburn'.

> Now I begin to do so – but I think he is much like my father ... and to that picture of my grandfather which used to stand in the lobby ... His person is nearly as large as my father – he is not so much fat as muscular – but this and much exposure has embrowned and enlarged his features ... and removed a sort of sleepyness which marks Raeburn's picture of him ... Business and the usual and necessary tone of command which he is obliged to keep up with the people in his charge – and a sternness he has contracted in the intercourse he has had with wild and vicious people whom he had to tame ... have tinged his face with these casts of expression, his eye varies very rapidly from soft to fiery as he smiles or scolds – he wears moustachios. This always alters the features and expression – his hair is just as grey as mine is.

He would try to 'steal a sketch of him' to give a better idea. Their meeting, surrounded by officers, soldiers and servants, had been stilted and 'you cannot suppose that much affectionate greeting could take place between us'. In any case, William now seemed so austere that a show of feeling was not to be expected.

James understood this reserve. William was in control of a very large, populous region with no assistants except 'native servants who are generally enough to destroy anyone's temper'. He had been deprived of family life for twelve years until Aleck and then Edward arrived in Delhi, and this had been cut short far too soon. His present plans were being thwarted by the dithering 'of an old man who will ruin the army in ... his charge & would tend to destroy the good will of the people who struck by our wavering conduct now waver themselves'. Was it surprising that he was sometimes 'thoughtful & abstracted ... & that the common charities & intercourse of private life are somewhat neglected by Disuse'?

Despite all this, James managed to turn William's attention ...

> ... to the Boyish Days when trifles pleased and vexed us when a fishing expedition interested as much as the fate of a fort or a Detachment & then I would recognise something of the Boy I once knew.

33 This is most likely the portrait by Robert Home of William in Indian dress

There was no more talk of William going home. It would be many years before he could save enough to enable him to live in Scotland, especially as he was now sending regular contributions to their father.

From now on James drew every day, starting immediately after breakfast and stopping only to see whether he could catch 'a Jelal trout as well as a Ness one'. He was also on the lookout for game: jungle fowl, quail, partridges and peacocks. He tried his luck for the pot with all except the last; William would object to a peacock being killed, 'they being sacred birds of the Hindoos'.

At this point, with 'shot ... playing over our heads quite briskly', a letter from his mother caught up with him. She was plotting again – this time for William. Wouldn't one of the two Misses Ross of Raasay, currently attending every ball in Calcutta, be just right for him? James disillusioned her: 'Your airy castles cannot be realised – in the first place both the Misses Ross are married – or about to be so'. William had never set eyes on either and was not likely to. Moreover, 'I do not think William will ever marry in India'.

This sent Jane off on a new worry: William must have fallen in love with an Indian woman and this attachment would keep him in India forever; she had heard rumours to this effect from Sandie Tytler. James had also heard tell of a ...

> ... connexion with a native woman ... Such a thing did once exist, but if it does now, or ever did, I am quite in the Dark as to *fact* but considering his roving life ... never stationary more than a month at a time ... it is not likely that any attachment could ever take place.

Of course, William was deeply attached to Delhi. Who would not be, in his position? He was ...

> ... the Lord paramount of a wide country ... where he may do good, prevent ill, reward merit & punish misconduct as he likes, where his word is law & his Presence like that of the Supreme Being – & where his justice has made him revered, his goodness loved, his courage & Bravery admired & feared.

His mother changed tack: what about a Congenial Personage for James? Was Jeanie Tytler perhaps still in the running? James was adamant: 'What I said "never could be" I meant then and now again say I mean "*never can be*".'

In any case, he was now older and wiser and rather than holding on to 'the Fairy vision of a youthful woman which must fade in a moment' he gave his mother permission to look out for someone 'of mild & quiet virtue, good humour, & the general social qualifications & accomplishments of life'. He would prefer moderate good looks, but more important was someone who could talk of something other than 'Balls, Dress, Puddings or Poultry ... and will at evening cheer the home with a song or a melody (she must sing or play) & cure all its ills by kindnesses & mild good humour'.

Meanwhile, Martindell was still lying low and William was frantic with frustration: 'I am quite sick of the business. A good General would have laid Jytuk in ashes before now'. But this gave James time to absorb the country around him: there were large forests of fir and cherry, apples, pears, mangoes, strawberries, raspberries and blackberries. He had invented a new breakfast of yellow raspberries, blackberries and yoghurt, almost as good as Scottish raspberries and cream; he sketched endlessly, watched the various battles exploding around him in the hills, wrote letters and kept a very detailed journal:

> Last night my Brother's Ghoorka company came in – such ragamuffins I have seldom seen – and such a sett of ugly faces never – they have the Chinese features, mixed with the tartars – strikingly ugly – their dirty sallow complexions is an admirable addition to their Dark shaggy hair ... shorn by the ears, and very Bushy – upon the head they wear a peculiar turban somewhat like the broad Scotch bonnet – their garments are filthy and they carry besides a *tulwar*, a short crooked knife in their cummerbund.

A few days later, there was a magnificent storm in the night. The sound of the thunder was so like 'a rolling piece of musquetry' that James leapt out of bed: the assault on Jaithak must surely have begun at last. But no, much to his disappointment, nothing was happening and 'Life is more like that of a Turnip'.

He was, however, collecting all sorts of 'curious and interesting things' to take home. William had managed to pick up for him the sword of a slain chief, Azumber Punt Qaree, one of the best Gurkha officers:

> ... along with his shield and a *cookery*[34] – this I prize highly and ... I shall hang up in the hall of Moniack as a relick of India and my first and last campaign.

❖

At the beginning of May 1815, driven to capitulation through hunger, the besieged population of Jaithak, almost 2,500 people, surrendered. A British force immediately occupied the fort, and it was obvious that its stockades would have been no defence against a vigorous attack, had one been attempted.

William, now appointed Commissioner for the affairs of Garhwal, could resume what he enjoyed most, penetrating the wilder parts of the area and dealing with the local people. His mandate was still to demonstrate British presence, to reconnoitre the northernmost Gurkha stronghold, the fort of Raeengurh, to persuade the petty chieftains to join forces with the British and to collect as much local intelligence as possible. With his extraordinary understanding of the locals and his knowledge of their languages, he was clearly well suited to the job. There was also no way that James was going to be left behind.

34 *Kukri* – a curved knife broadening towards a point used by Gurkhas.

9

1815–1818

LIVINGSTONE MANSE

Back in Scotland, fifteen-year-old George had finally untied himself from his mother's apron strings and gone off for his first 'collision with the world' at Livingstone Manse, a small school run by Revd Robertson, chosen for its proximity to Blackburn, the house near Edinburgh of Miss Jessie Fraser. A close friend of Jane Anne, she had bravely agreed to act *in loco parentis* to George, and he would spend days out and holidays with her.

On 18 July 1815 George set off in high spirits and reported on arrival, 'there are 12 of us and are all very happy'. His headmaster added:

> The first sight I had of George predisposed me in his favour. He has at once fallen into the ranks, and has already become one of us.

George's first letter to Jane Anne, however, showed a hint of homesickness:

> My Dear Sister
> I received your short though kind letter a few days ago but I think you might have written half a sheet at least. I thought I might as well write you and tell you a little about the place. Every day we go to the dancing and afterwards all the boys except me go to bathe I wish you very much to ask my father if he will allow me to bathe ... We were allowed to take a feed of gooseberries yesterday... The boys have got an ass and cart three of the boys and myself went to a little town about three miles of on a message for Mrs Robertson. I think I have said enough of this nonsense so goodbye ... give my love to ... Nanny Rose. Tell David [Gregoire] we went to fish twice and caught nothing tell him I would not give one day's fishing in the Ness for all the fishing here. Goodbye, my dear Jane Anne and believe me your affectionate Brother George J Fraser

His sister was missing him too, but her reply began in elder sister mode:

> Your letter of Aug 12 reached me a few days ago; it was most comfortable in all respects, but being rather too short; however, as you are only a young correspondent, I do not wish you to force yourself to write long letters ... I have been as happy as I can be without you ... rambling about a good deal ... All our pets are quite well ... The small fruit is nearly over, but the Plums are coming on well.

Reelig added news about his brothers: James was in Nepal with William who 'has been thrice wounded – and, I fear, runs more risks'. The word 'risks' reminded Reelig of a local tragedy which immediately led him into a litany of disasters for George to avoid:

> We are much shocked by an accident to Col. Rose Holm's only son ... he was killed by a Poney in the stable who kicked him on the Head and beat out his Brains. I need not remark to you on the dangers of approaching Horses ... caution is ever needed with all Horses – & all Guns.

There followed a list of people whose sons had been killed by horses or guns. Then there was fishing and the risk from wet clothes and feet, not to mention from the water itself. Bathing in fresh water was not safe at his age and, for salt water, 'I should like that you learned to swim.'

The Lord Provost of Glasgow, Henry Monteith,[1] had a son, also Henry, at the school, who invited George home for a few days. Jane flew into a panic:

> Let Face, Neck, hands and teeth be daily minutely attended to (the last ... using magnesia & a soft brush daily – & at *night* ... use *both* combs to your hair daily & afterwards the *hairbrush* – avoid *wet* and dirty shoes – both to prevent catching cold and dirtying the House – keep all your cloathes neat & in order and above all, avoid giving unnecessary trouble to *servants* – this last indeed you never was apt to do – except in not keeping your room in as exact order as I could wish.

She also reminded him that the younger Henry's pleasure must come first, and he was not to 'go off without him' on a more amusing ploy.

George also escaped to Edinburgh, following the well-worn path to Raeburn, with sittings between July 1815 and January 1816 (see Plate III). His portrait was said by the Tytler cousins to be very like him; it was certainly 'very like Aleck's and you say I am like him so as far as I can judge it will not be a bad likeness'.

Jane Anne was now eighteen and it was time to launch her into Highland society. At least Jane thought so; Reelig confided his mixed feelings to George:

> Your mother thinks there is a propriety in our going this year to the Northern Meeting with your sister – I do not object – perhaps it is prudent.

Jane Anne, however, 'trembles at the near approach of the [Northern] Meeting but resolves to enjoy it – she would gladly relinquish it for one day with you'. George would be there in spirit as Jane Anne danced her way through the week.

> Five nights you will be tripping on the light fantastick toe. I wonder whom you will dance with first. I suppose cousin William will have that honour before this reaches you you will be looking with delight over your dresses ... Give my love to all my friends in Inverness and to Nanny Rose and to Kate Martin remember me to James [pony boy] and the poneys and all the pets.

---

1 A very wealthy textile manufacturer who was twice Lord Provost of Glasgow, 1814–16 and 1818–20. He owned huge textile mills at Blantyre and made his fortune with the Turkey-red dye process.

A little later, in a letter to his father:

> Jane Anne will be pretty well tired of dancing by this time she ... must write me soon and tell me whom she danced with and if there were any matches made at it.

Jane Anne obliged a few days later: on the whole she had enjoyed it but it would have been much more fun with George or some of the Tytlers as companions – 'then what excellent fun we should have had. Some of the dancers were most ridiculous – we should have had fine fun laughing at some of the odd figures'. After the dinner parties there were songs, and neighbour Affleck Fraser's spirited rendering of 'Ca' the Ewes' was encored every night. Nanny Rose was highly excited by the whole thing 'and has already married me in consequence of supposed conquests'.

As far as Reelig was concerned it had been a success. Although he had attended reluctantly, partly to support his daughter and 'partly to support credit – and face difficulties', it had been 'all Harmony, and pleasantness' and the most brilliant Northern Meeting Ball for fifteen years, full of people of 'the best rank'. Jane Anne's behaviour had been 'dignified and natural' and everyone had admired her. She and her mother had been dressed 'as they ought to be – everything simple, in good taste'. No one had caught a cold or anything else.

✲

George's social life, his constant exeats and days off, soon soured his relationship with Mr Robertson, who complained to Reelig. This prompted a 'preachment': 'Give your attention *solely* to that in which you are engaged.'

But things continued to deteriorate. More complaints about absence and worse – insubordination, levity and defiance – arrived at Moniack. Reelig wrote much more harshly with a résumé of the shining qualities of George's elder brothers and a scathing attack on his 'self-conceit and arrogance'. What if he were expelled? What would his mother and brothers think? 'Unless you immediately and sincerely and respectfully return to your obedience and to your earnest duties I must despair of you.' George's reply to this tirade was a real cry from the heart:

> I do not attribute this to your being angry when you wrote it but to your great anxiety for my welfare but my dear Father (if it be allowed for a son to advise a father) you should remember as Burns said that to step aside is human. I have many a time since your letter found my pride and disgust rising but I then ... took a pill of reflection which soon chased all my pride away. You must know I am proud of three things which are my country, my family and my parents. I think this a proper pride ... Goodbye my dear Father your son is not so lost to virtue as you perhaps imagine. Believe me your affectionate dutifull though truly distressed son George John Fraser

Fortunately, release was just around the corner. Scarlet fever had reached the school and George escaped to the safety of Blackburn. He did not return to Livingstone Manse. Charles Grant was consulted and another school was found for him.

Off to the Hills

William and James set off north on 6 May 1815, taking with them a large band of irregular soldiers. There were Mewatties, Gujars, Sikhs and soldiers of fortune from the plains, many of them 'poor, old and ragged' and all in a great variety of dress; there were Pathans from Afghanistan, flags fluttering gaily from their spears, Gurkhas who had deserted, even more tattered and torn than the rest, and around thirty of Skinner's Horse, the 'Yellow Boys' in their bright yellow and scarlet uniforms. Altogether there were about six hundred people, including the usual ragtag camp followers, women and children, and porters. This motley crew straggled colourfully along the mountainside, 'winding in and out of the dark ravine among the black rocks' along paths hardly wide enough for even single file.

Although in the late eighteenth century Thomas and William Daniell had reached Srinagar, sketching all the way,[2] the Himalayas were virtually unknown to the British. The great Trigonometrical Survey of India had begun but it was not until 1835 that it reached Upper India.

James once more began to record everything in his Journal, a leather-bound volume of over six hundred closely written pages, secured with padlock and key. He was a man of his times, with an intellectual interest in everything, happily dipping in and out of geology, geography, botany, agriculture, mineralogy, flora and fauna, history, manufacture and anthropology. Sometimes he found words inadequate and, more and more as the journey progressed, he resorted to drawing.

He and William shared a tent ten feet square with beds of straw, cotton quilts, a table and two old chairs. They took with them wine, tea, coffee and sugar, but they had to depend on the locals for everything else.

To start with, their way followed 'sweet romantick' rivers, through thickets of roses and past cornfields full of peacocks. One of these days was 'far the most delightfull day's walk I have had in India – I could indeed have well forgot myself and felt in Scotland' – apart from the peacocks. But the terrain became increasingly difficult. Round every corner there were gloomy chasms 'of awful depth' and steep, jagged, narrow paths, often of polished marble and extremely slippery, sometimes obliging them to go on hands and knees. They groped their way through dripping tunnels clothed with mosses and ferns, emerging to views of wild villages clinging precariously to narrow ledges beneath towering crags. They crossed tumultuous rivers on terrifying rope bridges or single tree trunks, sometimes thrown across the river as they arrived. At one of these a *havildar*[3] – 'a willing active fellow and a good soldier' – insisted on carrying his wife with him in a *numlo* – a loop of rope suspended round his forehead. He fell, and both were dashed to pieces on the rocks below.

Sometimes communications broke down and they would arrive in the evening to find the tents pitched on the opposite side of the river. Often the going was so difficult that the rearguard did not catch up until the next morning. There were piercingly cold nights, dramatic thunderstorms, uncomfortably hot days and a fly 'with a yellow spotted head and shoulders, and grey speckled legs' whose bite caused intolerable itching and troublesome swelling.

---

2 Published in *Oriental Scenery* (1804).

3 Non-commissioned native officer.

Their way took them through 'deep and venerable' forests of oak, holly, yew, silver fir, rhododendron, horse chestnut and larch where the trees were the 'tallest, straightest and most magnificent I ever saw.' Some trees, James reckoned, were 25ft in girth, and he admired the 'fantastic forms of old trees ... blasted pines and withered oaks' worthy of 'the pencil of a Salvator'.[4]

Often, having negotiated a rocky tunnel or a 'wild and awful forest', they would come out into the sunlight and fragrance of a meadow of entrancing flowers. The list was endless: iris, lilies of the valley, roses and jasmine clambering over rocks and ancient stumps, orchids, buttercups, cowslips, polyanthus, columbines and 'thousands of other lovely flowers that sprang in rich confusions all around'. Occasionally they feasted on mulberries, apricots, pears and, favourite of all, wild strawberries; they made jam, too, while their sugar supply lasted.

The scenery constantly reminded James of Scotland. 'Asia was almost lost in our imagination ... a native of any part of the British Isles might have believed himself wandering among the lovely romantic scenes of his own country'. Comparing the mountain people with Highlanders at home, he noted that, although their morals were unusual, they were better clad and politer than their Scottish equivalents. Their houses were undoubtedly superior, well-constructed, more comfortable and far cleaner.

Most village houses were of three storeys: the cattle lived at ground level, stores were kept on the first floor and the family lived at the top, their living space often extended by a wooden balcony surrounding the house. There was no glass, so the few windows were small and closed against the elements with a piece of board. A plank of wood with rough steps cut into it served as a staircase, and there was little furniture in these 'remarkably snug, comfortable and clean dwellings'. Attached to the houses of the more affluent were towers to accommodate the various gods; in the houses of the 'vulgar' the gods had to be content with a niche in the wall.

The amount of land under cultivation was impressive. There was hardly any flat terrain, but somehow, with painfully hard work by men and women alike (harder, James felt, than the Highland crofter would have been inclined to), small fields and terraces had been hewn out of the rock. Sometimes the fields of wheat and barley 'had so highland an air, that it was difficult to believe it to be India'. There were fields of poppies for the opium trade and *bhang*,[5] very saleable in the plains.

In one village he was intrigued by the method of lulling children to sleep by violently whirling them round by the arms. The sleeping child was then wrapped up in a blanket and placed on the hillside with the crown of its head under a small spout of water from a stream directed through a hollow stick. Surprisingly, 'their sleep seemed sound and unruffled'.

In another village the brothers found themselves having to adjudicate in a marriage dispute. A twelve-year-old bride had been sold for Rs15 to a Gurkha on condition he stayed in her village. Now that the war was over he wanted to go home, taking his wife with him,

4 Salvator Rosa (1615–73), Italian baroque painter, poet, printmaker. One of the first to paint 'haunting landscapes, overgrown with vegetation, or jagged beaches, mountains and caves'.

5 Cannabis.

but her father objected and also refused to refund the money. James and William eventually hit on the solution of asking 'the lady' herself. She chose home, and her husband behaved very philosophically, admitting that more than losing a wife he regretted the loss of the Rs15.

James was intrigued by the character of the 'mountaineer', warped by 'the grinding tyranny of the Ghorka reign'. Where was the 'generous, free, enthusiastic spirit that commonly marks the highlander?' Now that 'they had been rescued by British power from the tyranny under which they groaned', perhaps things would improve.

> A British officer is looked upon almost as a supernatural being. From the rajah to the peasant there was not one who did not talk thus with confidence and enthusiasm ... 'Now we shall live and improve and be raised from beasts to men'. Such are the ideas, such the veneration entertained by these rude savages for the British name; and it is a proud and exulting feeling for a British subject to trace them so strongly in so remote a clime.

Sometimes the local chieftain came to pledge his allegiance. In Seran, the northernmost point of their journey, they pitched their tent quite near the palace in the shade of some trees in a cornfield. The chieftain, who was around seven years old, paid them a visit. He seemed overpowered by the strangers and 'continually made salaams and protestations to us', but after he had sat on James's knee for a bit he seemed more relaxed. They gave him several presents suited to his age and he went away happy.

The chieftain of Kotguru, their next visitor, was such a 'corpulent, sickly and ill-looking man' that he could not move and had to be 'pulled up the hills in a sort of litter by fifty men' (see Plate XIX). He lived in a curious many-towered house perched on a rock – an irresistible subject for James's pencil.

There were temples around every corner. James was especially impressed by the temple of Mangni.[6] Its interior was covered in the most intricate carving, which 'does honour to the mountain artist; and, considering his tools and materials, it is truly wonderful' (see Plate XVIII). He was amazed that the rich silver and gold adornments of the glittering idols had not been plundered, but it would take courage, even in a Gurkha officer, to rob such a sanctuary.

The only fort still holding out was Raeengurh, under the command of Runsoor Thappa. Part of William's mandate was to take possession of this fort. A message was accordingly sent to Runsoor Thappa informing him that the war was virtually over and offering him British service and protection; this was politely refused. Another message was sent pointing out that he was surrounded by irregulars only too eager to wreak vengeance on him for the tyranny they had suffered; still no surrender. Frustrated, but knowing that he could not hold out for much longer, the brothers decided to leave troops surrounding the fort and move further north. They were, in any case, ill-equipped to storm a fort, having neither ladders nor enough men, but were intrigued to hear the local plan for attack: a catapult fashioned from a large tree and some strong ropes, a force of between one and two hundred men and an enormous stone. James was amazed to find the '*catapulta* of the Romans in so remote

6 In Uttarkashi.

and savage a country'. While this was going on he had time to draw the fort on its great rock above the river Pabur.

He also had time to write to Jane Anne: the Pabur was 'murmuring within 10ft of the tent' and he was frustrated by his 'miserable want of Proficiency in drawing'.

> It cost me long and much trouble ere I could bring my eye & hand round to take an outline with tolerable accuracy which now I can do pretty rapidly – but colouring & finishing is a thing I can make no good hand of at all.

He tried to convey the difficulty of their journey: it was like climbing 'the Raven or Rebeg Rock at their steepest points for 5 or 6 miles & as steep a descent'.

A few days later, news reached them of the final surrender of the Gurkha commander, Amar Singh Thapa. Waiting for further instructions, they stayed put, James to work on his sketches and William to collect as much information as possible about the surrounding area.

They were struck by the abundance of superstitions, which seemed 'peculiarly natural to highland countries; such are the witches, spectres, and ghosts of the Scotch highlands' and by the stories of people being sold into slavery. Although in the plains James had come across slaves from the hills, he was nonetheless horrified by reports of the Gurkha regime selling the mountain people, especially their beautiful children. It was said that around 200,000 people had been taken in the last twelve years. This was slavery viewed from its raw end, and he listened to the villagers' stories with concern and sympathy. Indians were not usually cruel masters, but ...

> ... it is at all times dangerous and revolting to trust the liberty and person of one human being to the absolute disposal of another ... every well-wisher to humanity will join in hoping, that at no distant period, the trade and the existence of slavery may here and everywhere have an end.

Jumnotri and Gangotri

In mid-June 1815, at just about the moment that Napoleon's bid to dominate the world ended on the field of Waterloo, William received orders to return to Delhi. This was another pivotal moment for James: he wanted to continue the adventure, pushing deeper and higher into the mountains to reach the source of the great river Jumna and visit the holy pilgrimage places of Jumnotri[7] and Gangotri[8]. He had celebrated his thirty-second birthday by climbing a high peak from which he could see, to the east, the mountains guarding these fabled places. Now his imagination was alight.

He had read accounts of travellers to the region and knew that he would be faced with 'savage impracticable desertness of snow and rock', but in all probability the opportunity

7 Modern Yumunotri (10,804ft), the westernmost shrine in the Garhwal Himalayas.
8 Hindu pilgrim town near the source of the river Ganges (Gaumukh).

would never again come his way. He accordingly planned his route north along the Jumna to its source and, from there, to the source of the Ganges. He was typically upbeat: 'there was, in truth, not much real difficulty to be contemplated in the undertaking' – apart from, that is, his ignorance of the country, the lack of provisions and the little likelihood of his servants being able to withstand the conditions. He chose the best possible guides, in particular Kishen Singh, the favourite of a local Rajah, and the strongest servants, all keen to ensure the safety of their souls by such a pilgrimage. He packed a small bag of clothes, some food and wine and left his Journal in William's care. With these guides and servants, a small band of Gurkha officers and some porters, he set his face north towards mighty Bandarpunch,[9] the mountain which gave birth to the great rivers.

On the morning of 15 July, 'the wind blowing sharp and raw from the hills, down the glen of the river, like a cold winter's morning at home', the little party, together with the 'Jumnotri Pundit',[10] set off along the icy river, crossing and re-crossing it, then crept on hands and knees through jungle up a steep crag to the first shrine – 'extremely wild and gloomy, on the point of a rock overhanging the stream, which roars below'.

Eventually reaching Jumnotri, the nearest possible place to the union of the various small streams tumbling down the mountain, James, barefoot, approached the holy warm springs, 'bathed, was prayed over, and submitted to be marked by the sacred mud ... in the forehead like the rest'. He would have gladly dared a further ascent, but night was falling and there was a hazardous route down the rock face and across the rapidly rising river. James was assured that this sudden spate was a sign of favour from the goddess, but 'it was a most inconvenient mode of signifying it, for every time we crossed the stream now, it was at the imminent hazard of our lives.'

They struggled on, now heading east towards the Ganges and Gangotri. The terrain became wilder and more barren, very like 'the Scotch highland hills', and James found a type of white heather, 'this much loved and long-looked for remembrancer of the land of brown heat and shaggy wood ... I plucked it, and placed it in my hat, with a delight that I believe much amused my attendants'.

Villages were now scarce, and they often slept in caves, coping not only with extreme cold but with thick fog. Often it would clear at night, revealing 'the magnificent mountains by the light of the moon'. James was enchanted:

> ... there is something peculiarly awful and solemn in the sight of these huge masses and depths of snow by faint moonlight; a total lifelessness is shed over their calm chill features and the cold that emanates from then feels as it would freeze the soul itself.

By now serious altitude sickness, which they were not prepared for, was beginning to affect them. But James could not resist one final push to the source of the Ganges, struggling through a landscape ...

9 'Tail of the Monkey', the major peak (20,722ft) of the Garhwal division of the Himalayas.
10 Learned man.

> ... marked by features unspeakably more lofty, rugged, and inaccessible. There is even less of beauty, and more of horror; more to inspire dread, less to captivate ... an indefinite idea of desert solitude and helplessness steals over it: we are, as it were, shut out from the world, and feel our nothingness.

But he found a gooseberry bush, 'a plant I had long looked for without success'.

On 20 July, having bathed and been prayed over at various holy places along the way, they reached Gangotri – 'centre of the stupendous Himala ... the acknowledged source of that noble river, equally an object of veneration and a source of fertility, plenty, and opulence to Hindostan'. Immediately after bathing, the clouds parted and there was a breathtaking view of the sacred peaks[11] brooding over the five temples dedicated to Shiva. For the time of year this was most unusual and taken by the locals as another sign of the favour of the resident goddess. James was certain that he was the first European to have penetrated so far, but this was not a matter for boasting 'for no great danger had been braved, no extraordinary fatigues undergone ... but it was a matter of satisfaction to myself'.

❉

There was no choice now but to start for home; almost all the party were exhausted and affected by the altitude; their guide, Kishen Sing, had to be carried on a litter. Gradually, however, the way became easier, and soon the fearful chasms of the Jumna were replaced by gentle meadows embracing the river Bhagirathi.[12]

There was one more river to cross. The bridge was constructed for them as they waited – 'two small round sticks, extending from the one bank to a large rock in the middle; and from thence to the other side, three still smaller tied together ... on which a wild mountain stream was to be crossed by fifty or sixty persons, many of them heavily laden'. One unfortunate coolie missed his step, fell in and was carried away. He had been carrying in his load the property of the wife of a Gurkha recruit which included 'all her clothes and little trinkets, the savings of several years'. The lady loudly made her feelings known. James felt sorrier for the family of the coolie, who had been a very useful member of his family, and offered his brother some money in compensation. 'Means, too, were found subsequently, to restore the tranquillity of the poor Ghoorka wife, and make her forget the loss of her apparel and jewels'.

❉

Torrential rain made their journey south hazardous, but at last, on 27 July, they awoke to 'the cheering face of heaven; hills of a lovely green ... studded with villages and rich with cultivation'. Three days later they reached Saharanpur and were reunited with William.

James now admitted that he had hurt his leg in the trek to Gangotri and it needed complete rest. This gave him a few days to work at his sketches and he persuaded William to hire a native artist, practised in drawing figures, to help him depict the various characters

11 Kedarnath (11,755ft), Tungnath (12,070ft), Madmaheshwar (11,450ft), Rudranath (7,500ft) and Kalpeshwar (7,200ft).
12 One of the two headstreams of the Ganges.

that peopled his pictures. His subsequent paintings wonderfully illustrate his adventures, from the siege of Jaithak to the encounter with the hugely fat Rana of Kotguru, precarious rope bridges, forts, villages, temples and, above all, the mysterious majesty of the eternal snows of the great Himalaya.

Later, James offered his services for a future exploration of the source of the Sutlej River and even the Indus. Eventually, he was given permission for a tour deeper into the hills, the result of which 'may point the way to further researches of considerable value to Geography and general Science'. This irresistible adventure would be at the Government's expense, the date and details yet to be decided.

✻

In mid-August 1815 the brothers arrived at Shalimar, the country house of the Resident, about five miles from Delhi, where they found William's old friend, James Skinner (see Plate XVI). A friendship immediately blossomed between Skinner and James, and the great soldier assured James that, should he ever need the assistance of 'a native of Hindoostan', he must turn to 'Sekunder'.[13]

The last day of the tour was very exciting. The brothers were accompanied by a cavalcade of Gurkhas, Skinner's cavalrymen and their own servants and, as they approached the Delhi gates, hundreds of people came out to welcome them:

> ... the crowds and the noise of Beggars and singing of the village women and clattering of horses and bawling of the officials keeping the crowd under control, all together with the different gay costumes, made the procession very gay and whimsical.

It was something of a relief to get home to their own bungalow 'securely in Christian and pleasant society'.

James Skinner was to play a significant role in both brothers' lives. He was born in India in 1778, the grandson of a Provost of Montrose and the son of Hercules Skinner, who served in the army of the East India Company. His mother, Jeany, was the daughter of an Indian prince. When her son was twelve, unable to bear the sorrow of seeing her daughters being taken out of *purdah* and sent to boarding school, she took her own life. James and his brother were sent to an institution for children of mixed parentage. As a Eurasian he was disqualified from joining the British army, but his godfather found him a commission in the army of the Maratha chief, Scindia. He fought in various ways, especially in the taking of Delhi by the Marathas in 1798. When in 1803 Lord Arthur Wellesley defeated the Marathas and entered Delhi, Skinner accepted the command of a body of horsemen who had deserted from the Maratha army, on condition he would never have to fight against his old commander, Scindia.

At the head of his 'Yellow Boys' Skinner fought in numerous campaigns, earning the rank of lieutenant colonel, the order of Companion of the Bath and a grant of lands at Hansi, a few miles north of Delhi. There, loved and respected by his tenants, he lived in

13 Skinner's native name.

princely style and entertained on a lavish scale. He was brought up a Muslim, but the story goes that lying wounded on the battlefield he vowed that if he lived he would build a church, or, as some would have it, a mosque, a temple and a church. One result, at any rate, was St James's Church in Delhi, at a cost to Skinner of Rs90,000. On the day of its consecration he and three of his sons were confirmed, and he was buried there in 1841. He is said to have had sixteen wives or mistresses, five sons and several daughters.

Everything about this exotic figure appealed to William and in him he found a true soulmate. James was delighted to find himself included in this friendship, especially as William was much easier to get on with in Skinner's congenial company. While William identified with Skinner's ability to sit at ease astride two cultures (though Skinner himself found this less comfortable than he made out), his courage, both physical and mental, his skills of leadership, his sense of justice and his loyalty. James appreciated his patronage of native art, his conversational skills, his hospitality, the stories round the dinner table and his enthusiasm for exploring the environs of Delhi.

Entranced by the beauty of Moghul Delhi, James visited all the main monuments in the city, busily sketching domes, cupolas and minarets as he went. He was also intrigued by the nightlife, in particular the *nautch* girls, one of whom, Malaguire, was painted by Lallji, who also painted William (see Plate XXII).

The brothers continued to commission Indian artists to paint the local people they encountered. When James finally left Delhi for Calcutta, he asked William to extend this collection, partly because he knew the interest it would excite at home and partly because he would use the figures and their exotic costumes to people his landscapes. William accordingly took an artist with him on his expeditions and regularly sent portraits off to James in Calcutta, hoping that one day they would hang at Moniack. James was delighted:

> I have just received from William, a Portfolio of native Drawing, some old and valuable as being illustrative of native costume and feature; groups of Ghoorkhas, Sikhs, Patans, and Affghans, Bhuttees, Mewattees, Jats and Googers. Now these will illustrate anything I may have to show of these countries; and how valuable are these to me, as studies of costume, from which to fill in figures in my drawings [see Plate XVII]...

The news from Calcutta was that Aleck's condition was little better. His brothers thought he should go home, and James was perfectly prepared to accompany him. If Aleck refused, then James would stay with him but needed some pretext to 'give cohesion to the proceedings and not give him reason to believe he is in my way'.

But Aleck was already once more on the Ganges on his way to Delhi. His father had implored him to come home on sick leave, but he feared losing his place on the Company ladder. There would also be no hope of paying off his debt and he would thus be unlikely ever to be able to go home for good. After Edward's death, during the three terrible months in St Helena on his own, he had so nearly yielded to the longing for home but, had he done so, he would have 'sacrificed Duty to Indulgence'. He would leave the decision to Simon Nicholson, who eventually pronounced him not completely recovered but fit enough to travel. In late June Aleck once again embarked on the long tedious voyage upriver. After the usual adventures and mishaps he arrived safely on 22 September at Kanpur, where he lodged with Lieutenant Caulfield, Edward's shipmate on *Baring.*

TOGETHER AT LAST

By now James had had word that Aleck, in indifferent health, was on his way. He would meet him at Kanpur but first he wanted to explore the environs of Delhi. He and William spent five very pleasurable days scrambling 'over the wreck of former greatness', visiting Humayon's tomb, the great 237ft Qutb Minar[14] and the ruins of Tughlakabad.[15] He also visited Agra, where the 'incomparable beauty' of the Taj Mahal overwhelmed him. He returned to the Taj by moonlight, when it reminded him of moonlit snow in the Himalayas – 'the same motionless deathlike paleness and awfull yet beautiful majesty'.

In Agra he also visited an institution for the conversion of Indians to Christianity run by a converted Muslim and supported by Mr Cory, the local clergyman. James again pondered the question of mission: the Hindus seemed to have a good relationship with Christianity but feared loss of caste; if the Muslims had not effected conversion during the long centuries of their empire how could the British possibly expect it in so short a time? 'Only the wretches and the outcasts are the converts,' he concluded, watching 'a parcel of poor old women sitting spinning who were called Christians who get Rs2 per month from Mr Cory'.

On 23 September 1815 James reached Caulfield's house in Kanpur to find Aleck, weak and coughing. Caulfield, lucky fellow, had managed to find a Congenial Personage in a 'sweet good-humoured pleasant wife'.

✻

Aleck found no fewer than eleven letters from home waiting for him. There were still worries about the plantation. 'Sell it!' urged the clear-sighted Aleck:

> Cotton will every day be procured cheaper and better ... even here the improvements going on in the production, cleaning, packing &c of cotton will pour it at so cheap a rate into Britain, and the Continent, as to ruin every Plantation laboured by Negroes. Do then sell – sell while *something* can be got.

By this time he had become more argumentative than ever and turned the simplest conversation with James into a dispute 'so extreme and disagreeable ... that I dread even speaking to him'. Aleck was also feeling too weak to control the servants, several of whom had deserted and it was a great relief when the message came that William had sent ten *sowars*,[16] six *chuprassies*,[17] six camels, two horses and one elephant to meet them further along the route.

14 Twelfth century brick minaret.
15 Ruined fort now in the heart of New Delhi.
16 Indian cavalry soldier.
17 Messengers.

There was just one moment of relief, when 'a wonderfull report', several months old, brought the news that the Duke of Wellington had 'beat Buonaparte in person, with the loss of 300 pieces of cannon near Bruxelles'.

❀

One night in November, within about fifty miles of Delhi, they were camping near Moradabad when Aleck became seriously ill, giddy and spitting blood. Alarmed, James sent for a surgeon, whose prescription of more bleeding, purgatives and fasting left Aleck even weaker. James, despite a feeling of foreboding, surprised himself with his apparent ability to cope 'so coolly as I do'.

> I must act, not think and there is a cup preparing for me that I must not turn towards till it is forced on me – God grant me strength for that moment.

On the fourth day, cousin John Fraser, stationed further north at Meerut, once again came to the rescue, riding thirty-six miles on 'two miserable horses' without a saddle, bringing the rumour that Bonaparte was to be imprisoned at 'of all other places in the world, Fort George near Inverness!!!!!'

With great care they moved Aleck into a palanquin and gingerly set off again to Meerut, where William, alerted by James's alarming letter, rode sixty miles in two days to join them. Sixteen years since James' departure for St Vincent, the three brothers, now aged thirty-two, thirty-one and twenty-six respectively, were together at last, 'and it did us all good'. But these were 'scarce fleeting precious hours' – William had to leave almost immediately to resume his work.

Aleck and James stayed in Meerut with Colonel Stevenson for nearly a month. Aleck's mood and health continued to deteriorate; when friends came to dinner he roused himself but even then remained pretty silent unless the conversation turned to mathematics or 'some nicer point of Political Oecomony and Euclid'. James eventually took refuge in work on his map and journal. At times Aleck felt well enough to take an interest in what James was doing and reckoned that if he published his work ' he would rival in bulk at least Cicero ... his drawings are numerous & excellent and most interesting ... what the mass of his writings consists of I cannot imagine'.

They were all together in Delhi for Christmas, a 'very sober, rather melancholy' affair, with Aleck moody and tearful. William had reluctantly torn himself away from life under canvas, where he was living in great comfort. 'What,' asked James in his New Year letter to his mother, 'would Lord Wellington's Bivouacking army have said to tents 40ft. long, 26 broad, double all round with glass doors and fireplaces?' William's future was still uncertain, but soon the Rajah of Nepal would be restored to his throne and then, surely, he would be given the Residency of Kathmandu.

Resignation ... and Rejoicing

At New Year 1816 William returned to work and his brothers were left to days of 'great sameness'. James would sit with Aleck in the morning while working on his drawings or revising his Journal. He was hoping that his pictures would catch the public eye and bring in a tidy sum once they had had 'the advantage of a good engraver to correct their faults and shew the beauties of [the] country'.

There was no more argumentativeness. Now Aleck was keeping 'a listless silence apparently absorbed in his own dark reflexions', although he would still occasionally join the dinner table arguments about the treatment of Bonaparte by the Allies: some thought that he should have been treated as a king; James disagreed: the Allies had acted consistently in treating him as a 'captured General ... He should have every comfort consistent with strict security as a private individual but there should be no ridiculous state nor luxuries such as a king might look for'. The Tower of London was the proper place for him.

Occasionally, Aleck would agree to a jaunt in the buggy. Towards the end of January they rode out to Shalimar for a change of air. Quite soon after their arrival James had a dream which so affected him that he marked it with a large asterisk in his diary. He dreamt that he had returned to Scotland and found Jane Anne 'languid pale and thin':

> My mother told me that they feared she had received the seeds of a breast complaint ... My sister recognised me affectionately, but sadly and acknowledged her fears for herself. I remonstrated, why did they not move her to some more genial climate which they said they would do ... here distinctness ceased, and I soon woke ... but the final meeting with Jane Anne, her pale and melancholy face, I shall not easily forget ... it was so totally changed from the sprightly gleesome look it used to have.

James wrote constantly to his father, Seton and Mackintosh, keeping them in touch with Aleck's condition. William wrote a rare letter to his father from Skinner's farm at Hansi: Aleck was 'beyond the power of medicine or relief' and believed he had only a month or two to live; his father should 'argue [himself] into resignation'. After all, it was unlikely that he would ever again have seen Aleck whose debts would have imprisoned him in India.

James assured his mother that 'all that can be done is done, and has been done ... it cannot be supposed that I feel quite as calmly as I write on this subject, but I write as we should endeavour to feel'. Ultimately, he assured her, his own greatest wish was to return home 'and turn my attention to the improvement of land, for I am certain that it is the occupation I am best calculated for – and I would wish to marry as soon as possible after I returned'. Once again, however, he assured her that neither brother wanted to marry any of the 'glittering heartless butterflies' of Calcutta. Once again he stressed again that 'everything is perfectly at an end in the quarter you allude to': he considered himself disengaged and totally free.

He also confirmed that William's passion for Delhi and refusal of the position in Cuttack was not on account of 'any connexion of a domestic nature with a native ... it is a subject I do not like to write upon frequently but I have done it fully in two letters'.

Soon, however, Jane was diverted from the marriage prospects of her sons: Jane Anne's triumph at the Northern Meeting had borne fruit and she was to be married to Affleck Fraser of Culduthel. At first her parents had had reservations concerning a certain lack of 'Refinement and Education' but Aeneas Mackintosh thought the match 'in every way suitable' and William Tytler pointed out Affleck's many qualities including natural good sense. He had had a difficult childhood with a harsh-tempered father, consequently always played the role of peacemaker and was much loved by his own family. Reelig was soon persuaded:

> Few people exceed Affleck ... a very fine young man, the best Disposition & Temper & excellent Judgement – not greatly cultivated but a correct perfect Gentleman, Honourable and virtuous and not without information so that I believe he will do his part well in his new duties.

Affleck, who was ten years older than Jane Anne, had apparently been smitten for some time 'and at one time he had actually declared it but she, flurried and amazed, gave a refusal'. He persevered, however, and on his second application was accepted by both Reelig and his daughter.

Culduthel was a large estate between Inverness and Aldourie, and, his father having recently died, Affleck was now laird. The estate was free of debt, Affleck's mother was 'most handsomely provided for' and Reelig was delighted with 'the liberality' of his settlement on his future wife. They would begin their married life at Balloan, a small farmhouse not far from Inverness. Reelig dreaded the moment of the empty nest 'when we are left totally alone' but was cheered by the thought of their proximity. All this heart-warming news, of course, did not reach India until July that year.

JAKHAULI

On return from the hills William had asked for a military command. General Ochterlony, in the middle of negotiating peace in Nepal, wrote, 'I think there will be no call for your military services, my dear William, in any shape or form'. However, he was offered a commission as a major with Skinner's Horse which he unhesitatingly accepted, although it was not until two years later that Hastings gave him permission to join the corps. From then on William juggled an active military life in Skinner's Yellow Boys with his political duties in and around Delhi. At the moment he was in Haryana, north-west of Delhi, and very busy with projects that would occupy him for some time.

His mother was, of course, quite right in her suspicions: one of the chains that bound him to India was Amiban, a beautiful girl who lived in Rania, a small village in Haryana. She became his *bibi*[18] and favourite companion, although there were reputedly others. The French botanist, Victor Jacquemont, recorded, probably inaccurately, that William had 'six or seven legitimate wives, all living together near Delhi' and that 'he must have as many children as the King of Persia'.[19] In one painting of Amiban, who

18 Indian wife or mistress.
19 *India Revealed*, p18.

was also known as Surwen, by a local artist[20] she is portrayed alongside a small, pale-faced child (see Plate XX).

It had been common during the eighteenth century for East India Company servants to seek the company of such *bibis*, and 'countryborn' or mixed-race children were socially acceptable. Now, with shiploads of marriageable girls and missionaries docking regularly in Bombay or Calcutta, attitudes were changing, and William always took pains to put his parents off the scent.

⁂

Aleck was now fully dependent on laudanum. He was still able to express opinions but all his spirit had gone and 'he now never smiles but faintly ... muses or dozes whole hours and days'. He brightened up slightly when Skinner arrived, bringing with him 'a tolerable dish of the usual conversation relating battles and sieges and accidents'. Metcalfe was also a cheering dinner companion, regaling the company with a whole series of interesting facts: 'among the Bombay army ... many of the Sepoys are *Jews*'. Even more surprising was that 'a large part of the Madras native corps was composed of Christians' and it was generally accepted as true 'that the regiment which mutinied at Vellore was nearly entirely composed of Roman Catholics'. James was intrigued:

> A fine answer to those who pretend that this noted mutiny was in consequence of attacking their Hindoo prejudices ... but it is also a tolerably complete stopmouth to those Zealots who sing on about conversion to Christianity of the natives of India and pretend to make light of the moral obstacles ... What are they [the converted Christians]? A set of outcasts, employed in the lowest offices, and totally void of education or of the means of obtaining it – perfectly ignorant of the Principles of the faith they profess – they have not I believe a Bible – and if they had, none could read it – they know that the Cross is considered the symbol of Christianity – and they Bow and Salaam to a Church, and pay a blind adoration to the image of a saint.

Towards the end of February James himself began to feel unwell:

> I dawdled through 4½ hours of my Drawing working badly and unwillingly. I feel an oppression at the breast with some degree of pain ... anything with the appearance of attacking the breast cannot well fail to give alarm.

Not only did he now feel unable to cope properly with Aleck's care, but he found it increasingly difficult to concentrate on the corrections to his Journal and his mapmaking; this could well be the first stages of consumption.

There was then another blow: a letter from his father reported on the family's good health but its tone was 'very desponding' as Reelig revealed the extent of his present debt – £32,000. James was astonished:

20 Ibid., pp.18, 101.

> That the debt should have gone on as it were increasing instead of diminishing is beyond calculation when we consider the large sums that have been transmitted from India and I own that it is to me totally inexplicable.

Reelig reckoned that there was now no point in James coming home just yet; he had far better stay where he was until he had earned enough to return and live the life of a gentleman. Little did his father know how far he was from earning enough to live on in India, let alone sail home with a fortune in his pocket.

Little, in turn, did James know that his father had come up with an idea that might bring at least one of his sons home: he had decided to buy William a small estate, Dunchea, on the other side of Loch Ness not far from Aldourie. Reelig was extremely pleased with this extraordinary plan: after all, his ancestors had had lands close to it, the first land they possessed in the Highlands, having come originally from Tweeddale with 'Sir Simon of Rosline'; he had the charters still.

In June there was a family outing to see the place and Reelig and William Tytler rode around the boundaries. Reelig was immensely excited: there was an abundance of red deer, 'muirfowl' (grouse), ptarmigan, 100 acres of arable land, good sheep pasture, more 'improveable' land and a loch with 'a fine little Bay with a fine sandy Beach for Bathing'. There were fishing rights on at least three lochs and an isolated rock at the east end of Loch Ruthven which was 'the resort of Ravens and Falcons only, where they nestle & no man can disturb them'; it was paradise.

During the picnic he astounded the family by proposing William's health 'as Laird of Dunchea'. He mused in a letter on the appropriateness of the purchase: 'It is curious to see Balnain's[21] grandson and namesake acquire Property, bounding with that of the Heir Male,[22] and that of the Heir Female, of the Family – & with cousins, kindred & friends on every side.'

The only possible drawback to this plan, of which the future Laird of Dunchea was as yet unaware, was that £2,500 somehow had to be paid by November that year, but Reelig did not allow that to diminish his satisfaction; he had taken positive action to tempt William home.

❋

In the Delhi bungalow February dragged itself slowly into March and Aleck weakened daily, while James worried about his father's problems and his own health. By mid-March he was starting to cough, and they moved back to the Stevensons' house at Meerut to be near Dr Russell. The doctor was frank – James must take great care although he was in no immediate danger. Ironically, at this point a message came from John Adam, the Political Secretary, confirming Lord Hastings' permission for James to make an expedition further into the Himalayas. James was in despair: 'What a delightful order this would have been had it arrived when at all likely to take advantage of it but now, not only poor Aleck's situation shackles & detains me but health even deserts me'.

21 Jane's father, William Fraser of Balnain.
22 Heir male William Fraser Tytler; Heir Female Anne Fraser Tytler.

Aleck now managed a letter home: the good news was that, although the agreement signed at Segauli was in tatters, a new settlement was concluded at last with the Nepalese, defeated in two 'obstinate battles' by Ochterlony; the bad news was that Gardner, second assistant in the Residency and junior to William, was going to Kathmandu as Resident. Why not William? 'See the results of Lord's fine promises. William superseded by his Junior Assistant! Patience!'

The brothers discussed Aleck's wishes regarding his servants and his possessions. He trusted that his 'old horse', Eclipse, might never be sold and that his papers would be read before being burnt 'as they might contain much that the old folk would have wished to see'. For more than seven years he had always worn a little silver case on his arm containing 'a little trinket' that he had received from Isabella. He wanted this returned to her.

In April, Aeneas Mackintosh offered James a position in his Calcutta business with a salary of Rs800 a month and the prospect of becoming a partner – something James could not refuse. It would certainly be more lucrative than a venture into the hills, but would his health allow him to do more than return home?

April also brought William, not to leave again, James hoped, 'before the last distressing scene we have to witness'. His presence, however, was a mixed blessing: he would not leave Aleck's side and sat around 'melancholy & moping' or paced the room in silence. It was, for James, 'miserable fulfilment of all my once warm hopes of my Indian brothers – they are all lost for me & their country'. So the sad, dull days dragged on, the unbearably hot winds only just kept at bay by *tatties* (moistened screens) at all windows and doors.

❁

The early days of May brought cooling showers and the brothers were cheered by the sudden arrival of Skinner bringing Nawab Ahmad Baksh Khan of Firozpur, William's horse-dealing colleague – a 'very polite and pleasant native gentleman' – with whom he had bought 'a string of horses'. The Nawab and his family had become very close to William, and this friendship was to prove of great significance.

While accepting that William was now extremely knowledgeable about horses, James was worried about the expense:

> It is true he has no other extravagant passion but he has no oeconomy and is unbounded in the expense he puts himself in this & in dressing his troops: the Dress of his 50 troopers will be 4 or 5000Rs alone ... he is too much wedded to his own tastes and plans never to leave them while fit to enjoy them.

In mid-May the brothers returned to the heat of Delhi; knowing that William would soon have to return to his work in Panipat, thirty miles north, Aleck came up with a plan that would keep them all together: he and James would accompany William and camp nearby in the cool breezes off the river Jumna. 'With large tents and *tatties* we may keep the interior as cool – and perhaps enjoy the Evening air at times, a thing we cannot do in Delhi as the hot wind prevails all the night'.

Near midnight on 28 May 1816 James and Aleck got into their palanquins and William into his buggy and they set off through the dark towards Panipat. Next morning, they arrived at Jakhauli,[23] 'where the air was refreshingly cool and 'the morning was lovely & brought healing on its wings'. That night, William watched by Aleck's bed until James came to relieve him. The following night, James shared the watch with William but in the morning felt so ill that he stayed in bed; his pulse was racing, he was short of breath, had a high fever and a pain in his chest. When night fell he dragged himself out of bed to watch with William; soon after midnight Aleck died.

> William and myself closed our Brother's eyes – and washed his body – wrapping it up in sheets ... and a grave was dug under the tent itself, which was ready by Daylight – William stayed by the body for I was unable – about 6 o'clock we wrapt it up in a piece of bedding, and carried it ourselves to the grave where we deposited it and restored it to its native clay ... I cut off some of his hair and preserve with care the little articles he had on him when he left this world – may God have granted to him a happier life above than he enjoyed here below.

From the moment that the grave was closed William lay on the ground beside it 'weeping and groaning most bitterly'; James took up a position nearby. There the two remained all day till dark, when William went to his tent, calling to his servants for more laudanum. James, who had been unable to shed a tear, mused on the striking difference in their reactions to Aleck's death: people might think him unfeeling, but he would miss Aleck '... in every step of my dayly pursuits ... I shall have no-one to care about or tend ... the 4th June 1816 I shall never forget.'

William spent the night weeping and calling for larger doses of laudanum. In the morning he lay in his tent, refusing to move. James had no idea how to cope with the situation: dealing with death was one thing, but 'the obstinacy & Despondency of the patient united with a grief equal to a violent disease' was quite another.

Desperate to get back to Delhi to nurse his own illness in the comfort of the bungalow, James was equally sure that he could not leave William alone in his present state; William was adamant – it was not seemly to leave Aleck's grave for several days (see Plate XXI). In the end, it was Black John who saved the day; he came to James's bedside in tears, pleading with him not to die 'in this solitary place'. James sent him straight to William's tent with the same message and, after some resistance, William 'growlingly' agreed to go back to Delhi but in his own time. Reluctantly, James set off alone and arrived home on 6 June; William returned a couple of days later, still silent and unapproachable.

Four days later, on the other side of the world, on the eve of James's thirty-third birthday, Jane Anne, just nineteen, married the twenty-nine-year-old Affleck Fraser and became mistress of Culduthel.

✻

23 In Sonepat District about 25 miles north-west of Delhi.

Scott's Private Academy

The house in Castle Street was getting draughty: not only was Jane Anne about to become the possession of another but George was off again, this time to a small Rectory school at Gawcott, a village just outside Buckingham. The headmaster, Revd Thomas Scott, an Evangelical clergyman, was the son of another Thomas Scott, known as 'the Commentator' for having written a commentary on every verse in the Bible. This senior Thomas was also the founding secretary of the Church Missionary Society[24] and a member of the Clapham Sect, hence Charles Grant's recommendation. Jane Anne and Affleck were deputed to escort George to Gawcott at the start of their wedding journey.

Their marriage was a quiet affair. The ceremony took place in the house in Castle Street in the presence of Jane Anne's parents and George, with only four guests – Affleck's sailor brother John, William and Margaret Tytler and Miss Duff, the governess at Aldourie. George and John were the witnesses. The newly-weds and George set off almost immediately, first to Edinburgh for the young bride to sit to Raeburn (see Plate III), and thence to Ravenhead, Affleck's property near Liverpool, where there was to be a gathering of Culduthel Frasers.

George soon forgot his nerves in the excitement of travelling with Jane Anne and his brother-in-law, of whom he was already a devoted admirer. At Ravenhead he had a great deal of fun and fishing with Jane Anne's new family; having never been away from home before, Jane Anne was just as thrilled as her brother with all the sights.

In 1816 the clanking and whirring of the Industrial Revolution were still largely in the future, and George was very excited by their visit to a 'Pin Manufactury'. He gives a very accurate description of the process, similar to but somewhat wordier than that given by Adam Smith as his classic example of the division of labour.[25] In George's words and punctuation, or lack of it:

> ... we saw there the drawing of the wire to make it thinner which is done by a set of boys who cut it into the proper lengths it is then delivered to another set to be cut again the next stage is the giving the point to the lengths which is done by boys also, another boy puts the heads on they are then given to the women who boil them in a solution of the lees of port wine and tin they boil these for 4 hours then taken out put into bran well shaken scoured in another mixture the ingredients of which I could not learn taken out again put into bran and then delivered to twenty or thirty little girls who stick them into the papers with amazing agility each of these sheets contains so many thousand pins and 12 of these sheets make a parcel now they are delivered to a man and woman who make them into these parcels and pack them up for exportation. I have now given you the whole history of pin making to the best of my knowledge.

Nearing school, George's apprehension increased. They dined at the Inn in Buckingham, where 'I must say I felt a little uncomfortable at being so near the place of my destination' and then set off for Gawcott, about a mile away – 'the shortest mile I ever went'.

24 Founded 12 April 1799 with the aims of abolition of the slave trade, social reform and evangelism.
25 *Wealth of Nations* (1776), Ch. 1.

There they were welcomed by Revd Thomas Scott, 'a short fat funny looking man with a huge Corporation and a little marked with the Smallpox'.

Having waved goodbye to Jane Anne and Affleck, who set off back to Ravenhead, on their own for the first time, George found himself in 'Scott's Private Academy', a rambling red-brick rectory. Mr Scott, a keen amateur architect, had been given the living of Gawcott but no house; he accordingly designed and built himself a rectory and, to pay for it, took in pupils –'and now I should suppose,' said George proudly, 'that there is not a more comfortable or better school in this County'.

He found letters from home awaiting him. His father, missing the company of his two youngest children, was packing up all the belongings that George, or more likely Nanny Rose, had not been able to squeeze into his trunk. He sent a list of these along with, inevitably, a lengthy 'preachment' which concluded 'Knowledge is Power'. George might be able to trim a fly or be a good shot, but what use was that without a good education and a cultivated mind?

Jane was worried about George's health, as was Nanny Rose, 'who trembles for your getting cold' He was to make sure his clothes were well aired when he got them back from the washerwoman. The beloved family dog, Sappho, had died and George's friend, James the pony boy, was inconsolable. George was philosophical; he felt perhaps Affleck, whose generosity to Jane Anne over a new horse had impressed him, might replace Sappho 'out of his abundance'.

It was the middle of the summer holidays and there was only one boy in residence – 'a very odd sort of person ... his voice is between the croaking of a frog and the squeak of a cat in agony'. This companion, who was always 'singing psalms and talking nonsense', was also intent on study and proving to be not much fun. George had very little to do, nor was he getting much sleep: the Scotts had recently lost a child in a whooping cough epidemic, which was still raging in the family; George had 'the almost insupportable felicity of sleeping very near a couple of hooping brats who do nothing else all night'. One of the brats keeping George awake with his coughing was the three-year-old George Gilbert Scott.[26]

He was also always hungry, thinking longingly of the feasts of summer fruit at home. He did not rate the school meals highly; breakfast was 'very different from our good Scotch ones consisting of very *small* tea and bread and butter' and tea was simply bread 'frightened with butter'; dinner, with meat forbidden by his father, was just vegetables, to which he was not partial. He soon persuaded Mr Scott to tear up the diet sheet and write an explanatory letter to Reelig:

> [George is] in robust health & growing fat ... a confirmed eater of meat & drinker of malt liquor, while he has very little relish for pudding & vegetables ... It is not unlikely that the milder climate of the south may better admit of animal food in considerable quantities without producing inflammatory symptoms than the more bracing & stimulating breezes of the North.

26 1811–78, leading architect of the Gothic Revival, e.g. the Albert Memorial, St Pancras and the Foreign Office. Knighted 1872.

It was not only the climates that were different: there was also a significant variation in the way Latin and Greek were pronounced north and south of the border, and George's pronunciation made everyone laugh. George was also 'deficient in his knowledge of Quantity' and frustrated by the restrictions on his liberty:

> We are not allowed to go to Buckingm if there is any fun going on such [as] fairs of which there are eleven in the year we are not allowed to go to walk out of a certain field or go into the village to buy upon any account in these things I think we are to much restricted now what Mr S reasons are I do not know they may be for our good but certainly not for our comfort.

His father approved of the rules, especially where Fairs were concerned – 'really dangerous places for seducing youths'.

When the other boys returned, school life started in earnest and, along with it, the inevitable teasing about George's accent:

> They always ask me if I do or say anything out of the way if it is so said or done in Scotland this is done only when Mr S is out of the way I try to bear all this as well as I can but it is disagreeable.

Then he was introduced to cricket: 'all of us yesterday went to play at Cricket I for the first time I stood rather awkwardly and hit myself on the feet several times indeed from what I have seen I do not much like the game'. Mr Scott, with huge enthusiasm, joined in every game and 'you would be surprised to see a man of 17 stone run so well'. Six weeks later, however, 'we have given up Cricket I am sorry for it is a very fine game and we have marbles instead I lose a great many'.

Christmas holidays in London or at home were completely out of the question. None of the family friends would be in town and it was far too expensive to come home; besides 'we would not like to have so soon again to take leave of you'. George resigned himself to Christmas at Gawcott:

> I must say I do not feel much regret for home but I should like to be with you since Jane Anne is settled and though it must be a great comfort to you to see her well and happy yet you must be rather lonely and indeed home will never be the same home to me as when she was there she might be thoughtless and even extravagant from her carelessness but she was a good daughter and kind sister but I must now leave for I have filled my paper.

Parting of the Ways

For ten days after Aleck's death James remained ill and had to resort to mutton broth, jelly and laudanum, which left him 'dismally sunk'. William was not a cheering companion; his 'repulsive attachment to concealment and solitude frightened away those who would have lent their aid to comfort me'. By 11 June William had, however, pulled himself together sufficiently to write to his father:

> When you receive this letter, recollect that the event ... occurred only on the morning of the 4th, think how calmly I write to you. James is more calm ... I read in the papers on the same day, Sandy Tytler's death, we shall all do the same, and what signifies it when the event occurs.

James now came to the conclusion that it would be best for the brothers to go their different ways:

> I see now it is best we should separate for I could do no good by him having no influence ... we may be on friendly terms asunder ... but that tender affection I felt for one brother & wished to feel for all ... can only be given when it is received & that I fear I shall never feel for William.

Feeling somewhat recovered towards the end of June, he made an effort to cope with Aleck's belongings, hindered by William who refused to dispose of any of the clothes, even though Aleck wanted them to be shared among his servants. He agreed, however, that any articles of value should be sold, raising perhaps Rs4,000 against Aleck's debts of Rs25,000.

In the early morning of 27 June, in pouring rain, James set off for Meerut after bidding farewell to William 'perhaps never more to meet'. Shaking hands, he hoped at least they might communicate. 'Occasionally.' said William. 'You see the life I lead gives me little to say'.

> Whether he felt or no I have no means of saying – I did feel a sinking of the heart but William's conduct of late has stifled all the softer and kindlier emotions of affection that I once naturally felt for him – and now little remains save that general love & tenderness with which I cannot but look on any Brother, still sharpened by the recollections of our Boyish days and those scenes we shall never more see.

That evening, as he crossed the Jumna, he turned and looked back at Delhi. At that moment the sun came out from behind the storm clouds and gilded the minarets and domes of the ancient imperial city.

❊

At the top of Aleck's letter from Meerut in March 1816, received at Moniack eight months later, Reelig wrote, 'The last letter he wrote us ... Alexander died 4 June 1816'. There was, however, one more, 'the last letter he probably ever wrote', addressed to Caulfield in Kanpur and dated 20 April 1816:

> My dear Caulfield,
> These are the last lines I shall probably ever be able to write to you ... they are merely to bid you Farewell! And to thank you warmly for all the kindness you shewed me when I needed it most and when I was stranger to you.

> I send you as a little memorial, a Delhi imitation of a Highland Dirk ...
> You are half a Scotchman so do not despise the national weapon.
> To Mrs Caulfield I send ... a Feerozee, or Turquoise, Delhi sett, and rather rare
> I believe at home but which she will accept as a remembrance of One, who
> was sincerely grateful for her kind and unaffected reception of a troublesome
> Invalid; so unlike the stiff and revolting ways of too many Ladies in Bengal.
> My blessing on the young one, and success to you all ... Once more Farewell!

Letters poured into the Delhi bungalow after Aleck's death. Seton wrote a characteristically long one to James; he was not surprised to hear of William's hysterical reaction: 'where he loves, he loves ardently. When attached, he is attached with his very heart'; James must now return to Calcutta, where all his friends were expecting him, and immerse himself in business.

Four years later, William admitted to his father his despair over the deaths of his two brothers:

> The world was changed to me; all my views, delights, desires, were laid in the dust and a callosity of feeling and recklessness of life, operated to an extent which has not surprised myself, although it appears strange to others. James and I have always felt and acted differently in this course. He seeks to retrieve; I feel that the loss is immeasurable, and that nothing on earth can compensate, and nothing replace the shattered columns of the house.

With Aleck's death the rich source of letters dried up: letters full of Aleck's philosophy of life, his accounts of his brothers and their doings, his concern for his family and his deep longing for home; letters enriched with beautifully balanced sentences and illustrated by metaphor, classical allusions and Latin quotations. Now his parents would have to make do with James's infrequent letters, William's hasty illegible scrawls, as often as not scribbled on horseback, and George's inky schoolboy missives.

Realising the merit and importance of Aleck's letters, Reelig now copied them all neatly and legibly into letterbooks, four volumes in all. He numbered each page and occasionally added in the margin comments or exclamation marks; he annotated each letter with the place and date of its sending, the ship that carried it and the date of receipt at Moniack. The last volume contains Aleck's 'Legacy', written during his illness in the belief that he would not recover.

He started it in June 1814: in it he looks back over his life with regret for his extravagance, idleness, his 'coolness' of heart and what he considered his cowardice; he had gradually learnt that openness would win him friends. He reflects on some of them: Mr Jowett, inspired teacher of the Classics; Gisborne, 'much my superior'; Mackintosh, who treated him as a brother; Nicholson, whose house had always been home and who had cared for Aleck without payment; Daun, the young ship's surgeon ; Balcombe, who came to the rescue on the island; and Caulfield, the stalwart friend of his last months.

Aleck would have been amazed by the tribute written for the Calcutta newspaper by his old schoolfellow, Molony. It was unusual to eulogise someone who was not in the public eye, but surely an exception could be made in Aleck's case? Fate had, after all, halted what might well have been a long and distinguished career in the East India Company. He spoke of Aleck's 'firmness and independence of mind' and his intellect and clear judgement, both of which he continued to exercise even through his three years of illness; he touched on Aleck's distrust of his own talents and achievements; and he praised his eagerness 'to disclaim whatever merit he considered as unduly ascribed to him' and his scorn of 'false pretension, or disguise, or affectation'.

Feverish, coughing and with pain in his chest, James nevertheless started yet another long voyage down the Ganges. Arriving at Caulfield's bungalow in Kanpur, he handed over Aleck's bequests – the dirk, the *kukri* and the turquoise ring – and gratefully accepted Mrs Caulfield's care. Soon, however, something happened to divert him from his own concerns: the Caulfields' small son died and his mother collapsed and was taken into the care of a neighbour. James pulled himself together and took charge:

> I remained and saw that every proper thing was done to the child ... I cut from its little head part of its hair by Caulfield's desire for his wife.

Tactfully leaving the Caulfields to their grief, he moved to stay with Affleck's sister, Mrs Rose, and her husband. She had changed from the 'quick lively and delightful girl' that he had known to 'an attentive anxious excellent wife', and they enjoyed talking over past times, although he was now worrying about a swelling on his chest and difficulty in speaking.

Neither James nor Mrs Rose had yet any idea that Jane Anne had married Affleck in June that year, although the Roses knew of her engagement, which was news to James. He mused slightly gloomily:

> This is a match that is likely to be soberly happy – Jane Anne has strong feelings, a high mind and good acquirements – with these I fear like some others of her family, a tincture of romance – now I believe Affleck to be a young man of only moderate talents – a plain matter of fact person without a grain of Romance in his mind – but good-humoured – perhaps somewhat rough and unpolished – but of the best principles – his Estate will be only moderate – perhaps 12–1400 pa – little enough in these times – I take it that if the marriage does take place they will sink down into a sober couple a little above those who surround them but far inferior to what Jane Anne might have been had fortune given her a husband with finer tastes, more soul and perhaps romance – query – would she have been on the whole happier?

When the news was confirmed he wrote in elder brother mode trusting that she would be guided by her own good sense, mature judgement, prudence 'and watchful affection of those parents whom you are so fortunate to possess as advisers'. He sent two copies of the letter just to make sure.

After nearly a month in Kanpur James set off again. He found Benares 'notoriously Picturesque and romantic'. The jumble of *ghats*, towers, bastions, pagodas and many-storeyed houses that clambered untidily from the banks of the Ganges reminded him of the old town of Edinburgh. Riding through the narrow tangle of streets on an elephant once again gave him a glimpse through the windows of the upper rooms, where, he observed, 'European fashions are gradually creeping into use'.

Always concerned about the relationship between Europeans and Indians, which was undoubtedly changing, he had an interesting conversation with a Muslim nobleman in Benares; a keen hunter, he spoke nostalgically of 'the time when Europeans kept company with the natives and used to hunt & shoot & make parties with them'. He spoke sensibly but regretfully about 'the Dislike that now seems to reign among the Europeans and the present day native society'.

In mid-October James received a typically effusive letter from Seton welcoming him back to his old quarters in his house; on arrival he consulted Simon Nicholson, who pronounced him perfectly fit and well enough to start work with Messrs Mackintosh Fulton McClintock in November 1816.

Schoolboy

By September 1816 Jane Anne and Affleck were home again. Jane Anne reported on her new life to George: 'I am quietly seated at sweet little Balloan. I find a great deal to do in the way of settling things to rights but really less than I thought'. She was finding Affleck 'a capital helpmate. I am never at a loss.'

There was much going and coming between Balloan and Castle Street, especially as, with Affleck often away, Jane Anne was finding married life quite lonely. She was not happy about the new plan to let Moniack. Reelig had already advertised the property and, if he was successful in finding a tenant, 'they will be excluded from the Aird all the summer ... does not this seem extraordinary I mean the idea that they will have no house to go to in the Aird'. She was thankful that they would always have another home with her and that 'my dear kind Affleck' was mostly tolerant about his parents-in-law's visits, especially when he was away. He got on well with Reelig but was sometimes irritated by 'poor Mama'. But, added his wife, loyal to both, 'they get on wonderfully', and the piano at Balloan kept Jane happily out of her son-in-law's way.

Soon there was a honeymoon baby[27] on the way. This, and the glad tidings that the good Dr Robertson was now Provost of Inverness, were the only welcome items of news that Reelig had for James. He had had no word of William's feelings about owning a Highland property and was beginning to regret the purchase of Dunchea, trying to postpone paying the first instalment.

27 James, born February 1817.

No news of Aleck had yet reached home, but Reelig wrote to William in September 1816 assuming that Aleck was 'with his Creator'; he was comforted that each of his lost children had had the love and support of a family member when they died: the three-year-old Jane had had her father with her, Edward had stayed by Mary's side, Aleck had been with Edward and now, in his turn, had had the companionship of William and James.

Jane's letters were full of foreboding, looking forward 'with melancholy resignation to hear that he is in a Happier state'. George, trying to help, was philosophical: perhaps Affleck could fill the gap:

> My mother seems to despond very much of Aleck but if it please God to take him though Affleck is not so well read or so accomplished he has every bit as good open and generous a heart and in him you must always find comfort ... Our weather has for sometime back been rather better the Harvest has commenced.

There was no way, swiftly replied his mother, that Affleck, pleasant, good tempered and excellent husband as he was, could *ever* take the beloved Aleck's place although 'I trust you will – we look to James and you as our greatest comforts in life for dear William will be long ere he can return'. It was more important than ever to avoid catching colds 'which has proved fatal to your two Brothers'.

✼

When, eventually, letters arrived there was still no final news of Aleck, but James was ill with possible consumption. 'God avert this evil', prayed Reelig in a panic. 'He ought not to remain one hour in India'. George agreed but was rather more concerned about the fact that Mr Scott had started fining the boys for mistakes in grammar 'and many a penny comes from my purse for the misapplication of "will" and "shall"'. He was also still being teased but was trying to obey his father's dictum: 'Never irritate, never be too irritable – Bear and forbear'.

It was a sad time for Reelig and Jane; bowed down by anxieties about their sons, they hardly went out except to church, avoiding all society except for Jane Anne and Affleck and their closest friends. The stalwart Miss Murray had raced back from Redcastle, where she had been needed at the old laird's deathbed, to be as great a support as ever.

Three days before Christmas the news came via a letter from Aeneas to his brother Raigmore that Aleck had died on 4 June, that James was fighting illness himself and William's grief 'was beyond all bounds'. They had heard nothing from either William or James. Jane was distraught that she had had the final confirmation of Aleck's death from friends 'without one line from the poor survivors to give us one ray of comfort as to their situation'; it was another four weeks before she heard the news direct from them.

✼

At Gawcott, when the Christmas holidays came round, Mr Scott confirmed that he would be happy to have George, the only boy not going home, as a travelling companion on his visits to friends. George made the best of it, regretting, however, that he would miss the Christmas fare at home; always hoping to improve the school dinners, he mentioned to Mrs Scott that they had very good curry at home. 'Mrs S begged for my mother's receipt [recipe] as she had always failed in making it now send it me soon'.[28]

George had also made friends with Mr Scott's brother-in-law, a Mr King, who expressed a desire to taste 'the Highland Whisky ... and as you ask me if I wanted anything a few bottles of good real Whisky would be a delightful and very acceptable present for him'; he also promised to get some Scottish pebbles[29] for his new friend. The whisky eventually arrived and George happily reported that the smell was strong and his room was like 'a whiskey shop'.

Reelig sent the pebbles with news that poor old Noble, the gardener, had had a family tragedy: his son Hugh, aged twenty-two, for 'repeated crimes', had been tried for his life at Perth Assizes. Owing to the efforts of Patrick Tytler, his sentence of death had been commuted to transportation. Poor pony boy James was sent to break this news to Noble, who thanked God it was not a 'more dreadful sentence'. 'What agony,' wrote Jane, 'a Parent must have dreaded and endured when a sentence of Banishment for life is a blessing'. Hugh went on to lead an eventful life in Australia and named one of his daughters after Jane Anne, his childhood friend.

Reelig at sixty-six was beginning to feel his age: 'My years run on rapidly – and I decline in life towards its close'. He was not too old or decrepit, however, to oversee the works in the woodlands whenever he could escape from the Customs House: the walks were now complete and there were seats from which to observe the waterfalls and various favourite viewpoints. His latest money-making project involved manufacturing herring barrels from birchwood. Later, he reported that he had '8 pr of sawyers at work' cutting 8,000ft per week of wood which would apparently fetch 9 shillings per 100ft. 'Calculate hence the weekly return', he wrote to George, who had just started Arithmetic and Algebra and was having problems; he could see no point in muddling numbers with letters.

Despite Reelig's expectations it was a time of deep anxiety in the Highlands: rents were not coming in owing to a terrible season with unsaleable produce and cattle at Beauly market were selling for less than half the price of previous years. The Moniack creditors were pushing and the yields from Guyana were not enough for the interest of the debt, not to mention the instalments due for Dunchea, the purchase of which William Tytler considered 'a most infatuated proceeding'. Soon, presumably, there would be Aleck's debts as well. One of the family's most valued and faithful advisers, he had the interests of Moniack at heart and was constantly worrying about the situation. Surely the only answer was to sell, like everyone else, and as soon as possible.

28 The first curry recipe appeared in *The Art of Cookery made Plain and Easy*, Hannah Glasse, 1747.

29 Nineteenth century term for the agate nodules readily available on many Scottish beaches. A huge collection is in the Museum of Scotland in Edinburgh.

That summer, George at last managed to wangle permission to go home for the holidays. He arrived in high spirits after a sea voyage of nine days and over a year's absence. He was 'very tall & thin & ruddy brown – very like you [William] in many respects at your age'; he seemed to have benefited from his English education and was 'honest & prudent, in short very manly – you would love him very much'.

Soon, however, it was clear that George was not wholly worthy of this glowing account. Mr Scott, among other things an amateur apothecary, had appointed him his assistant in the mixing of lotions and potions for the poor of his parish. George valued these sessions in the kitchen, normally out of bounds, but had taken advantage of the privilege. He and his friend Davidson, whose idea it was, had persuaded one of the kitchen servants to obtain and hide for them 'a magazine of wine & spirits'. The servant had been sacked, taking along with him his fiancée, the school cook of nine years, and poor Mr Scott was in despair – 'quite unsettled at a time when in this county it is very difficult to get servants particularly such as we want'.

Hating confrontation, Scott passed the buck to Reelig:

> I think you will agree with me that this is a matter which ought not to be concealed from you as a parent, and I trust that you will make it the ground of such parental admonition as may tend to fortify the mind of your Son against such seducing acts in future.

However Jane and Reelig coped with this, the tone of a letter from George, in London on his way back to school, is in no way chastened. The only clue that there had been discussion of any sort on the subject is the fact that he had spent a guinea on a present for Mr Scott 'with which he seems pleased besides it will soften down the looked for lecture'.

His journey by sea from Cromarty to London Bridge cost £4.8.6. Exactly a year later, John Keats was to make the same voyage and described the experience to his brother:[30] not being able to stomach the porridge provided for the passengers, Keats ate beef the whole way, fare which would have pleased George who took back to school Jane Anne's homemade biscuits and some tongue. He had also enlisted Nanny Rose's help in securing a supply of brandy; this was kept locked, but Nanny 'in her zeal for my stomach' broke into the cupboard.

Mr Scott did not deliver 'the looked for lecture' but he no longer asked George to be his 'Compounder of medicines'. George was resentful: since his return, Mr Scott had done nothing 'but call me names and find fault with me so you may conceive how very comfortable I am'. Jane loosed off a long lecture, trembling to think 'what that young man might have seduced you into and thank God it was discovered'.

George, having eventually untangled his mother's 'pothooks and hangers', decided she had been too severe: all he wanted, he said, was a chance to plead his case with Mr Scott who, he reckoned had behaved 'both measly and shabby'. He said darkly that there was more to it than met the eye and that Jane Anne would know what he was referring to. 'NB I wish that this subject to be dropped as soon as convenient'.

30 *The Letters of John Keats; To George and Georgiana Keats, Oct 1818* (ed. Forman), OUP 1952.

The subject was dropped and things returned to normal: Mr Scott found a new cupboard, outside the kitchen, for his mixtures and George got his job back; he reported happily to his mother that he was 'as good friends as ever' with Mr Scott, that 'an odd sort of feller' had replaced Davidson and cheerfully returned to the tricky question of his financial affairs. His purse was empty and he had had to ask Mr Scott for money for the servants 'and other things that might happen'.

One of the things that happened was the death of Princess Charlotte and her baby son.[31] Several months later, in Calcutta, James wrote in his diary:

> A more distressing event either private or public I have not heard of in latter time short of the great convulsions of the Continent – a fine sweet young creature just entered on the important part of life in a Character of the greatest consequence in society – with all that was likely to make her happy, respectable, useful and beloved, thus cut off with her infant from all these blessings – the hope of a nation gone, & plunged into the deepest gloom ... sad – I have not been for a long time more lowered in spirits than I have been from hearing it.

George recovered quickly from the sad news but it posed a practical problem for him:

> I do not think I ever before said so much about the Royal family in one letter as in this but it leads to something more nearly connected with myself which is this whether I should get my suit of Clothes made of Black I myself would much rather not have them of that colour but the question is this whether it will be proper or not however this is sure that I must get some sort of Clothes at Christmas for my Black ones begin to look very shabby now I hope to get them made at Bath as I would rather go without them for some time than have them made at Buckingham.

Home to Moniack

George spent his next Christmas, 1817, in fashionable Clifton with Affleck's Fraser relations; he thought the area beautiful but, unused to southern social life, found the 'continual going out and in' very tedious. The highlight of his visit was that Jane Anne and Affleck were expected in mid-January; they had left home in November, leaving the grandparents, with Miss Murray's support, babysitting the nine-month-old Master James, 'who is now a very diverting and intelligent fellow and as strong as a Poney'.

Miss Murray, however, was terminally ill with cancer: 'She suffers with Patience and Resignation but daily and hourly prays to God to *take* her to himself'. Reelig and Jane were determined to look after her till the end; this would afford them 'a satisfaction far surpassing all ordinary pleasures'. They were meanwhile babysitting 'dear little Jemmy', who was delightfully time-consuming and an antidote to their sad care of Miss Murray, who 'does indeed exhibit the Picture of a Dying Christian looking forward with joy and hope to

31 Princess Charlotte of Wales (1796–1817), only child of George IV and Queen Caroline. Married Leopold of Saxe-Coburg-Saalfeld and died in childbirth. Her son was stillborn. The tragedy set off tremendous national mourning as she had been a sign of hope and a contrast to her unpopular father and mad grandfather.

a better country'. James, writing from Calcutta, remembered her 'in youth & beauty, and delighting everyone with her lovely voice and sweet manners and amiable temper'.

⁂

Three weeks after the beginning of term, Mr Scott wrote to Reelig wondering where George could be. George, as usual, had an excuse: Jane Anne, having suffered a miscarriage en route, had arrived later than expected, and after their long separation she and George were so happy in each other's company that time had sped by; in any case, there was much mending and altering of George's shirts for Jane Anne to do as they were 'to short and small the frills sleeves and collars much to scanty'. He finally arrived back at school bringing with him some risqué jokes picked up in Clifton and explained to his father how hard it was 'to return to a school in the first instance with the expectation of a rowing and lastly to people who you know are not very fond of you'.

Reelig remained calm, but George must now make the best use of his final months at Gawcott. Meanwhile, he and Jane were much enjoying their grandson, 'a roaring Lion – and a very fine fellow'.

Only ten days later, Reelig wrote to George with tragic news: the very fine fellow, James, a month off his first birthday, had died on 22 February after a week's illness. His grandfather had 'no time and no spirits to write more – your mother is deeply afflicted – the dear angel had entwined itself around our Hearts – and was very attractive and intelligent'. Little James was buried at Culduthel two days later.

Jane followed this up with her own account:

> He suffered so distressingly that it was a great relief to agony – when the sweet angel breathed his last – I was able to remain with him to the last moment.

She was thankful that Jane Anne and Affleck were spared the anguish of seeing their baby die but distraught that the news could not reach them till 1 March at the earliest. On a practical note, she ended that there was no need to buy new mourning; George should use what he had worn for Princess Charlotte.

George wrote his sister as comforting a letter as he could, pointing out how much worse it would have been to lose Affleck and wondering if she knew how much longer he was to stay at school. She replied in March:

> You may believe my dear Boy this was an unlooked for & severe blow... Poor dear Affleck exerted himself to conceal his keen feelings from me & support me when he required it himself, but his natural Piety came to his aid ... You have as yet my dearest Brother known little misfortune nor have I either till this blow, but when you do you will then feel the consolations of religion. It enables me to say my beloved child is only removed a little sooner than I am myself from this world. God has taken him while he was innocent as an angel & therefore his Happiness is certain ... I am indeed blest with such a Husband, & as you say, what would my state have been had I lost him instead of my poor sweet Baby.

She urged George to make the most of his remaining time at Gawcott, to 'keep as free of disputes' as possible and to stay on the right side of Mr Scott; he was not to upset his father, who was 'much shook by the Death of his poor little Playfellow who was a great Pet of his'.

With no little Jemmy to amuse her, Jane was spending 'many melancholy and lonely hours' with Miss Murray, now suffering eight to ten hours a day of severe agony: ' I will never will quit her – many a month and year has she spent with us – in sorrow and sadness'. At the end of March Reelig wrote, 'This day I have carried to the grave our dear friend, Miss Murray who, after months of agony, is now at rest'. In her will her Christian name is at last revealed, Anna; it also becomes clear why she spent her days propping up the four or five families in the area: her mother was still alive and living with her nephew, Allen Cameron, and his wife at the old Cameron family house, Clune, about two miles from Moniack. Thus Anna had been able to keep an eye on her mother while offering care and consolation to others in their hours of need. In one of her infrequent letters to James she had confessed:

> I lead the same wandering kind of life – more from necessity than choice – a permanent home would be welcome however humble & to that, if Heaven permit I still look forward.

It was a very cold spring that year, 1818, following two hard winters 'severe beyond the Memory of Man ... there never was so heavy or so reiterated a succession of falls of snow in the Highlands – the sheep die innumerably – the people are ruined'. Many lairds were resuming their lands from necessity, including Reelig, who, despite no rents, remained busy and optimistic: his planting, farming, gardening and birchwood manufacture kept him occupied at Moniack whenever his Customs House duties allowed. In the absence of a tenant they planned to move back for the summer.

On 7 June, 'one of the hottest days I ever felt', Jane, home again, wrote that everything was in the 'greatest beauty'. They sat outside till eleven at night being deafened by the cuckoos, blackbirds, thrushes and doves, with the roebuck and owl joining in the chorus and scents of birch and lilac wafting into the house. She was happily expecting the usual summer flood of visitors, with an overflow at Rebeg; it was sure to be fun for George, who was pleasantly employed in his last few months of school with his friends brewing beer – ginger and spruce. He carefully copied out the recipes for his mother so that she would have a good supply ready for his return.

Reelig was less enthusiastic about the imminent social life and gloomily agreed that the constant invitations 'must at last be yielded to'. He was aching to retire from the Customs House and bury himself in his ploys at Moniack. Now perhaps it was time to 'resign office & the £180 & be free & healthfull and vigilate over my concerns at Moniack'; he was needed to run the farms that were being abandoned by bankrupt tenants. Could he manage all that had to be done at Moniack single-handed? He was feeling the want of a strong young son, and not only as an extra pair of hands. Soon, however, George would be home again.

10

1818–1820

Chinnery and Havell

One lonely evening in Calcutta, after a year of hard graft in Aeneas Mackintosh's House of Agency, James wrote in his diary:

> It is a mortifying idea to think that should I die suddenly & this book, not meant for the eyes of others, be opened to their inspection, nothing would present itself save a barren mass of uninteresting narrative ... no modes of thinking or history of ideas – a barren mind would be seen and a map of broken resolutions & lost occasions.

His life went on 'in a quiet jogtrot ... I fear that some day I shall break out and run away'. His only hope was a partnership: a fifth or sixth share in the firm would bring him around Rs50,000 annually 'so that a very short period would clear our family affairs'. Fulton and Mackintosh were both going home in the next two years and then there might be a chance for James, but 'delicacy will not permit me to enquire, or to gain information by even the remotest hints'. Yet these years were pivotal for James.

Outwardly little was happening to further his career or eventual return home; most of the time he was in the Customs House or godowns[1] handling paperwork for shipments of indigo or saltpetre; the work was underpaid and boring but it left him time and energy for the editing of his journal, the completion of his map and, most important of all, his painting.

He had had the good fortune to coincide in Calcutta with the renowned painter, the flamboyant George Chinnery,[2] to whom he went every Sunday for breakfast and a painting lesson (see Plate XVI). A later pupil described Chinnery as 'a droll genius'; he was also a comic actor, one of the ugliest men alive, short-tempered and 'particularly disagreeable at breakfast'. James loved him and looked forward throughout each tedious week to Sunday. Another eminent artist in Calcutta at the time was Charles D'Oyly,[3] who kept open house for anyone, European or Indian, who was interested in the arts. James was often to be found there, not least because Mrs D'Oyly was the former Miss Elizabeth Ross, who had captivated him all those years ago on the island of Raasay with 'one of the sweetest lullabies ever heard'; in her Calcutta drawing room 'she enchanted me with some of the old things she then first played to me'.

1 Warehouses.
2 1774–1852.
3 1781–1845. Public official and painter. Collector of Dacca 1808–17.

Life fell easily into a routine: from Monday to Saturday James painted for two or three hours before going to work. Evenings were devoted to his journal, map and more painting. Sundays were set aside for Chinnery or D'Oyly, often followed by a night at the Fultons' riverside house, where 'females and children give a domestic and happy look to a house that reminds one of home.'

Chinnery revelled in his role as the 'Master': 'it is a great thing to have you thus far in harness – a *very great thing*!' Sometimes James sent him a half-finished picture for his comments. They were occasionally favourable: 'there are parts *very admirable*' or 'it's a d----d clever Drawing ... as a whole it is thoroughly bang up!'; sometimes highly critical: 'I do not know what to say about this Drawing – that I do not like it is certain' and often encouraging and with hints of how to improve.

The main thrust of his advice was always to make a 'study' first, that is, 'the grey stage'. The only possible excuse was that 'a thing must be sometimes done quickly'. Of one of James's bigger pictures he wrote:

> So voluminous a thing cannot be brought under the eye, on the enlarged scale this is – you need not be ashamed of this for Turner himself could not do it without a study – the plan of it though is quite capital & does you all kinds of credit – we will take half an hour over it when we meet.

James's picture of Government House (see Plate XXIII) was, according to Chinnery, his best work so far – 'there is an *altogetherness* which is famous'; he recommended fewer figures, but 'the Foliage to the right is – like Foliage'. If James had gone about twenty yards back in the road it would have been better, 'but in this Drawing there is great merit'.

Sometimes Chinnery sent James diagrams in an attempt to clarify the lesson. He emphasised the importance of quick sketches, especially of figures, James's weak point, and sketched a group of figures with bullocks entitled 'Every little helps – one minute'.

From time to time James had to tear himself away from his easel and pay attention to Calcutta society. There were balls to attend, including one where there was...

> ... nothing remarkable save the shameful undress of Mrs Wilkinson and her sister who came in gowns cut down to the small of the back and below the Breast if they had any – their shoulders quite uncovered – very disgusting.

When he heard of the arrival in Calcutta of William Havell[4] James wasted no time in contacting him. Havell, probably the most talented member of the famous family of artists, engravers and publishers, had adopted a new style much influenced by the great Turner; James was thrilled by the vivid colour and minute detail of his drawings –'even the Blackberries on the Bushes are to be seen'.

Chinnery, on the other hand, was extremely jittery about the appearance of this renowned artist with his newfangled ideas. 'I have heard of the approach of Mr Havell,' he

4 1782–1857. Founding member of the Society of Painters in Water Colours. In India 1817–25.

remarked suspiciously, 'what his merits are I do not know at all.' Somewhat unconvincingly, he continued, 'Nothing will delight me so much as finding him as having *real* ability – if he is thus & a good gentlemanly liberal Fellow I shall be much happy.'

James bravely persuaded Havell to show his work to the Master. When Havell's pictures had duly been inspected and he had gone home, Chinnery put on an extraordinary show of glee and relief, grabbing James and dancing with him round the room until he 'rolled on the ground & committed all sorts of anticks'. At last, when he could speak, he declared 'with many oaths & many bursts of laughter that he was not 40th rate instead of firstrate'. He had heard so much praise of Havell that he was genuinely afraid he would lose his place as Calcutta's most prominent painter; having seen his work, however, he felt confident that 'he was as far above him as possible'. Amused but rather alarmed by this extravaganza, James was glad to escape to the sanity of the Fulton family.

From now on James was struggling to get his Himalayan portfolio ready for an imminent passage home. Some of the pictures, 'Crossing the Touse', for example, show Havell's influence in the detail of the foreground (see Plate XIX). Chinnery had been discouraging about this difficult painting but James had persevered, having persuaded Chinnery to give him a lesson on 'landscape with figures'. This lesson took place on a painting outing with D'Oyly; the subject chosen was the *ghat*[5] at Chitpore, just outside Calcutta – a very boring subject, in James's opinion, until he saw how the colourful groups scattered about made it picturesque. Chinnery 'proved the usual observation that frequently the least interesting object to general observers makes to a painter his finest studies'.

The Himalayan pictures and journal were finally entrusted to the vessel *Westmoreland* on 24 January 1818, followed soon after by the copy of his great map on *Richard*. Now he had to wait for news of their safe arrival and their reception in London and Edinburgh.

⁂

On New Year's Day 1818, James had cast his customary critical look over his shoulder at the past year. He had not read a single book but at least he had completed twenty-four pictures. He reviewed the family:

> William seems more or less lost to us – my father and mother still further decline into the vale of years ... when I think of us young things all playing in the Moniack courtyard ... that exquisite feeling that the sight of a prosperous happy family gives rise to – and now to think how lonely these places are, that this can never be again ... We will however not despair but fight the good fight even unto the last.

Soon there was reason for optimism: the plantation in Berbice had been sold. The Moniack debt was thereby reduced to around £13,000, so perhaps James could look forward to going home in 1821. He had also had a letter from Jeanie Tytler which he had not yet had the courage to read. Every time he mentioned Jeanie or marriage in letters home, his father marked the reference in the margin.

5 Landing or bathing place.

James's thirty-fifth birthday, 11 June 1818, was recorded in his Journal, again with despondency, not least because he spent the whole day confined to his room by painful boils on his leg. He looked back on a year of 'thinly sprinkled happiness': he had good friends 'but this is not the life for me – I love it not & again I repeat my resolution to spend my 40th birthday – please God to keep me in life – in Great Britain and at Moniack'. He now set himself the task of completing his pictures of Calcutta; writing up his journal only intermittently when there was something significant to report.

There was soon more good news in his parents' letters, 'so cheerful and comfortable that they spread a perfect gleam of sunshine on me here'. Reelig had at last retired from the Customs House with honour and a pension of £200 per annum. He and Jane would be able to pack up in Castle Street and concentrate on affairs at Moniack, where they would be 'fixed', probably never to leave again. Jane Anne was well and expecting again. James felt a glow of happiness for several days and even felt relaxed enough about money to buy himself a pony and buggy.

With his precious cargo on the high seas, James worked harder than ever: completing his Calcutta views, accepting commissions to paint his friends' houses, reproducing some of his watercolours in oils and still breakfasting with Chinnery most Sundays.

Poor Chinnery. In a series of moves from country to country to escape creditors he had borrowed money from everyone possible, including Indians who charged up to 48 per cent interest. James, appalled at this, approached in vain various influential people on his friend's behalf. A couple of years later, still bankrupt, Chinnery escaped to Serampore, a Danish settlement where English law did not apply, and later to Macau where, welcomed by the expatriate community, he continued to paint until he died in 1852.[6]

BUNDELKHUND AND BACK

William was not given the Residency of Lucknow. James considered this a glaring injustice, but William was unperturbed: he was perfectly happy where he was, in the wild, mountainous country north-west of Delhi:

> I have the option now at all times to live in a climate like Scotland. All the hills ... from Paneeput to Bursut, are ours. Those awful snowy peaks, and enormous masses, which exceed our imagination, are now within the British dominions. I can go, and lie down under the Oak, Birch, Larch, Elm, and gather strawberries and raspberries, as at home.

James was assured that the Residency of Jaipur was reserved for William but he remained suspicious that his brother's interests were not the priority of those in power: 'Thank God I am independent of great men, and spend my time better than dancing attendance on them'.

The truth was that Charles Metcalfe, Resident in Delhi from 1811 until 1819, was desperate to find William a job as far as away as possible. The two men, roughly the same

6 *The Flamboyant Mr Chinnery*, Patrick O'Connor (2011), River Books Co. Ltd.

age, had had a tricky relationship since 1806, when Metcalfe was made First Assistant in Delhi. Metcalfe had been sensitive enough to realise that this was a great blow to William and tried to compensate, treading very carefully. The result was that William had become 'the most uncontrolled officer in the Company's service'.

When Metcalfe was appointed Resident, with William as his First Assistant, the situation became more delicate. The tolerant Metcalfe made even greater efforts not to offend William – 'the fear of hurting his feelings tied my tongue'. William accordingly took less and less notice of his superior and in 1817, when he took charge of the Revenue Office, he apparently thought it unnecessary to pay the slightest attention to him. Metcalfe was despairing: there was little semblance of any control over the Revenue Office.

Eventually, William broke off all relations with his Resident except on public matters, when communication was through a third party. Added to this there was a dispute over the bungalow in the grounds of Shalimar, the Resident's country house, that Metcalfe wanted to use when he retired. William had constantly used the bungalow and, rightly or wrongly, considered himself its owner. How did the bungalow dispute end? William certainly gave way on some matter – probably 'for his own convenience' was Metcalfe's opinion – but whether he agreed to give up or sell the place to Metcalfe is not clear. It was around now that he was buying land and planning his house on the hill above Delhi.[7]

By 1818 the two men were back on speaking terms but then William refused yet another appointment, to the Residency of Holkar's Court, on grounds of the effect that the climate there would have on his health. Metcalfe was again in despair. He was prepared to offer William any job within his gift, 'anything in short but my Assistant'.

In the summer of 1818, to everyone's amazement and Metcalfe's relief, William accepted the Political Agency of Bundelkhund, an area south-east of Delhi, 'a post of very great consequence and trust, with a noble salary (Rs50,000 a year) and much respectability'. His parents were ecstatic: at last William would be settled and able to save towards his homecoming. Reelig, of course, had a list of questions: where was the nearest town? Was the job diplomatic, military or judicial? Would he be involved with native rulers? What was the population of the place? Where were the nearest Europeans? What he did not know was that William had only accepted the job on condition that if he did not like it he could return to Delhi as Resident.

Without waiting for an answer to this demand, William headed south for Bundelkhund. The authorities, however, did not take kindly to this interference in their patronage and, in any case, Ochterlony had already asked for a second term as Resident in Delhi. They discouraged 'in a very decided manner his hope of succeeding to Delhi as a matter of right' and rejected the condition. William reached Bundelkhund, 'flew off at a tangent', refused the offer, declaring that it in no way reflected his 'merits, talents or services', and turned his horse for Delhi and home.

7 This still stands. It was bought after William's death for Rs 20,000 by Hindu Rao and was heavily damaged in the Indian Mutiny of 1857. It then became a hospital and has remained so ever since. See Sylvia Shorto, *British Houses in Late Mughal Delhi* (Boydell & Brewer, 2016), especially Chapter 4.

Reelig considered the refusal unfortunate. Like Jane, he correctly suspected that 'it proves an attachment to Delhi so strong as to lead to ... more desperate ties than I had imagined'. William, however, would 'look back with satisfaction on the act of refusal to the last day of my life'. He had rejected one of 'the most lucrative situations in the service', but he would not give up his independence 'for all the wealth in India'. As to his attachment to Delhi, was it surprising? The city was one of 'the liveliest, most frequented and most civilised stations, having a large society ... & being within a morning's ride of one of ten most agreeable stations in the country – Meeruth'. He had, moreover, completed his hilltop house just outside Delhi. He still looked forward, however, to spending 'the mild Autumn of life' at Moniack on all the things he had delighted in as a boy: 'road makings, walks, plantations, jungle work, gardening etc'.

It was not until a year later that the paths of the two men at last diverged: Metcalfe went to Calcutta as secretary to the Governor General and thence in late 1820 to the Residency of Hyderabad. William, in the same year, was recommended by Holt Mackenzie for the post of Deputy Superintendent of the Delhi territory. When they saw William coming the authorities changed the conditions of this position: he was to be 'put on a footing of complete subordination to the Resident'. Even so, it was one step nearer to where he wanted to be, and there was a sigh of relief all round when he accepted the job.

Farewells

Throughout these productive years in Calcutta James was often coping with bouts of illness. From his symptoms and the mention of 'an angry mosquito', it appears he had malaria. Furthermore, he was worrying about Seton who, also unwell for some time, had been advised to go home and was completely unsettled by the idea. Eventually, the doctors were unanimous: Seton must sail without delay, in fact in two days' time on *Wellington*.

His many friends assembled to work through the night and get his packing done. There were countless books to be inventoried, a turmoil of papers to be sorted and not nearly enough trunks to accommodate everything. An urgent message was sent to hold the ship and eventually, amid 'Bustle and Confusion', Seton, totally exhausted, embarked on the pilot vessel that would take him down the Hoogly.

> Thus rapidly was Archibald Seton, a man who had been thirty years in India, and scarcely even a day ill, and had held the highest stations of trust and honour, hurried from the family under the influence of a disease that threatened the most dangerous consequences.

After all the rush, the sailing of this pilot vessel was considerably delayed and there was now time to spare. James took it upon himself to stay on board with Seton until he reached *Wellington* and he daily made the doctors' prescription of porridge, boiled eggs and bread and milk for 'the Laird'. There was a tricky moment when Seton's servant Tom, taking Black John with him, indulged in one last evening ashore carousing with his friends. Tom was firmly left behind and Black John, much the worse for wear, was severely reprimanded.

As it happened, Seton had to make do with the inferior accommodation on another vessel, *Sophia.* Here James said his final farewell but with a promise to see him again in the morning in order 'to spare him the pain of leavetaking – So we waved a last adieu to him ... may he see and love again his own dear native land he has sacrificed so much for'.

William, in a rare letter home, hoped Seton would visit Moniack and that Reelig would spend some time with him at his beloved Touch. These wishes were not to be granted. In March the following year, the news arrived that Seton had died on board *Sophia.*

There were other farewells that year. Havell, 'disgusted with India, with the people and climate', was going home. He had failed to get Lord Hastings' patronage and felt confident that he would find far greater rewards in England.

James was extremely sad to see him go: he had had great fun with Havell 'but more than all I owe to him the opening my Eyes fully and feelingly to the beauties of nature'. James now looked with completely different eyes at 'this great Book':

> Each tree & shrub, every glimpse of landscape gives me a sensation which before I saw his pictures and heard his conversation I did not experience. Instead of now attempting to make strange and unnatural things under the name of landscape, I endeavour to avail myself of what passes before me, and imitate the beauty that I see abroad and the tints that are so delightful in nature.

From Madras on his way home Havell kept up a spirited correspondence with James, who was by now seriously experimenting in oils. This delighted Havell, although he hoped that it was not at the expense of 'the mantle of light & air, space and truth' which James so competently achieved in his watercolours.

James would miss Havell greatly although he was suspicious of his habit of altering other people's work:

> [I] saw him alter much a picture which I had bestowed great pains on & considered as finished – perhaps he was right – I think not & doubt that the thing was better after he touched it than before ... indeed I doubt much if even a superior artist can touch with success the picture of an inferior unless he could exactly enter into his feelings & occupy the original ideas which gave birth to the first drawing.

A few months later, James lost another friend. Aeneas Mackintosh was told to go home, also for reasons of health. At first, he also stoutly refused to budge, but in November 1818 he agreed to embark on the same ship that took Fulton's wife and family home, leaving James 'solitary and melancholy'; he would miss both Aeneas and the domesticity of the Fultons. 'We unmarried folks of the house are all thrown adrift. Formerly there was a sort of rallying point which is now lost to us.'

At this point James found himself 'a small tenement' in the Chowringhee area of Calcutta 'where I can be quiet, and enjoy myself in my own way'. He kept his old room in Fulton's Garden House for Sunday nights; the house was now dull without the noise and bustle of a family, but Fulton needed his company.

HOME TO MONIACK FOR GOOD

Home once more that September, this time, she trusted, for good, Jane was her old self – throwing herself into preparations for a full house with her former energy. Reelig, who had taken over the farms himself, found the visiting hordes expensive and time-consuming but was prepared to put up with them for Jane's sake.

In the 'most glorious weather and season ever known' there was abundance everywhere: flowers and soft fruit, the dairy overflowing, a good harvest, plenty of honey, apples and pears. The buildings and fences were gradually being repaired and the woods were becoming valuable. Nanny Rose was 'tottling about' rather ineffectually, and Reelig had a manservant who could turn his hand to anything even if he did nothing well. There were a few fine farmhands, and old Noble crept around the gardens always finding something to do. All that was missing was a handful of responsible farm tenants.

George, released at last from school, had had a good sporting season at home and had also much enjoyed his first Northern Meeting; he was proving a popular fellow with 'a large share of good sense and good humour'. In the late autumn he reluctantly departed for Edinburgh, where he enrolled at the College for courses in Latin, Greek and Mathematics. At night he was earning 'threepences' working as a clerk in a lawyer's office, closely supervised by a Mr Hotchkiss. He attended as many balls and concerts as he could and was taking dancing lessons: quadrilles were 'troublesome ... my head which was never very clear for study [is] now crammed full of Turn out your Toes for God Sake'.

He lodged with Mr and Mrs Lindsay of 30 Hanover Street, 'where the dirt is most abominable'. As usual, the catering was not to his liking, especially the 'execrable butter', and he sent a plea to his mother:

> Your long letter I have at length completely deciphered ... I have a request and here it comes ... send by sea a keg or jar of your salt butter if it can be spared a couple of your cheeses, if you can a few bottles of what you call your bad gooseberry wine and fill the crevices with what you please jam jelly or any other good thing ... anything else you may think of nuts apples but recollect the wine the gooseberry wine.

❊

The New Year, 1819, started off well for the family. Affleck was busy improving the house and grounds at Culduthel, where Jane and Reelig spent several months after Jane Anne's daughter, Jane, was born on 25 January. They stayed for the child's baptism in March, after which they returned to Moniack for the summer 'with thankful hearts to be enabled to do so – but feeling lonely & desolate after so long a stay with our dear Jane Anne'.

Jane was astonished that Jane Anne found her husband's company perfectly congenial – 'It shews how much the heart will accommodate itself to all situations'. To Jane's mind, Affleck left a lot to be desired: he had no conversation apart from field sports and 'he requires always some stimulus to revive him'. But he seemed sensible and judicious in the management of his affairs, and 'Jane Anne & he are devoted to each other & she is quite happy. Can we wish for more.'

While Jane was, according to her husband, 'the most active person of her time of life I ever saw & looks more young than most women at 40', and he was, on the whole, sprightly, the two old people were lonely: 'We eat alone, we walk alone, we read & write alone ... we play picquet and wonder at ourselves'. They wrote constantly to the boys and re-read their past letters. Reelig sent William a good deal of chitchat about the neighbourhood and musings on the state of the world. Belladrum was making great improvements to his great house just down the road – squares of offices, gardens and hothouses. The country 'seems quite reviving and general prosperity in prospect', contrary to the gloomy pronouncements of Parliament. He reflected on the political situation in India, assuming that all was now quiet and that 'little more now, except regulation, remains to be done'.

There was news of the Grant family: young Charles was now Secretary for Ireland, his brother Robert[8] was an established Member of Parliament and their sister, Sophia, had married her cousin, the young laird of Redcastle. Raeburn's portrait of Charles Grant had been presented to the County Courthouse (see Plate V).[9]

Thomas Telford's great canal 'which may, or may not, be extensively useful' was progressing, and the fine roads that Telford was constructing across the Highlands were 'like gravelled walks'[10] so that 'no place is out of reach for comfort'.

There were exciting improvements at home too. The Mill was at last ready to start grinding and there was a new road to replace 'the old ragged road' from the farmyard, past the Mill and on up to Rebeg. The lawn in front of the house had been extended and edged with clumps of trees.

Whether William replied or not, his father would continue to send him 'constant knowledge of your family'. He no longer mentioned marriage but urged William never to forget Moniack: 'it will not be exactly the same home when we are going – or gone – but it will be the best home (if preserved) that any man could ever retreat to'. Later, he wrote with a heavy heart that he would stop describing the delights and improvements of Dunchea 'as you do not seem to care much about them'.

Now in his seventieth year, Reelig was faced with an unending search for tenants. Most of the land was still in hand which meant keeping 'a larger farm establishment' than was economically viable or suitable for a man of his age. But what could he do? The question was becoming daily more urgent, and an unwelcome idea was dawning: perhaps it would be best to let the whole property complete with employees; that way the servants would be taken care of and the land protected for James when he came home with the fortune that was needed to put the old place on its feet again.

Panipat

That spring, just as his parents were happily settling back to Moniack life, James's relative peace of mind was shattered by an alarming letter from Metcalfe: William had been attacked and wounded at Panipat on 18 March but was recovering.

8 He wrote the hymn 'O Worship the King'.

9 Now in Inverness Library.

10 Thomas Telford (1757–1837), Scottish engineer, architect and stonemason, known as 'the Colossus of Roads', was building the great Caledonian canal, bridges and roads in the Highlands.

William subsequently gave James a long, vivid account of this incident. He had been out since daybreak shooting tigers and, on returning to his camp in the cool of the evening, sat in his office tent hearing petitions. There was a larger crowd than usual, four to five hundred people, agog to see the three tigers that had been killed. When darkness fell, William strode out towards his dining tent, stopping on the way to prescribe medicines for some waiting patients:

> The crowd pressed so close had squeezed behind and separated me from the *Chuprassies*, two Orderly troopers & two Orderly Ghoorkas who usually attend me. I had advanced within 15 paces of the ropes of my tents, and about 20 from the Office tent ... when I noticed a man ... standing about 7 or 8 paces off ... his left hand holding his sword by the scabberd below the hilt stuck in his Kummerbund. His appearance and attitude immediately struck me as insolent and threatening, but I had not a moment to remark him when he drew his sword, and ... leaped two paces to my left & his own right where the crowd was not so thick. That moment I knew what was to happen.

Having nothing with which to protect himself, William turned to look for help, but the instant the fellow drew his sword, the crowd, including his orderlies and *chuprassies*, vanished into the jungle. The man struck and felled William with a wound to his head.

William parried the next blow with his foot, luckily encased in a stout boot. The fellow danced around to try again, and this time William defended his head with his hand, receiving cuts to his fingers. The would-be assassin was just positioning himself for a third and potentially fatal blow when a favourite servant, young Ummeechund, who 'had been holding the inkstand to me in the office', realised what was happening, dropped his inkstand and rushed into action. Without so much as a stick in his hand he grappled the fellow to the ground, whereupon the orderlies reappeared. Ummeechund's father got hold of the assassin's sword, but the orderlies 'were however such awkward operators that instead of cutting the fellow one of them cut poor Ummeechund across the hand, & the Assassin was unhurt'. They then all rushed to William's aid, and the assassin would have got away if a Gurkha had not appeared to finish him off. Wanting to find out who he was, William tried to halt the *coup de grace* but found himself temporarily unable to speak.

Staggering back to his tent, he bound up his wounds, made his will, sent for some leeches and a servant to bleed him, took a 'good dose of salts' and slept for two hours. His loss of speech proved temporary, and although the wound to his head was serious it had not injured his brain. No one seemed to know the identity of the assailant, although he had been noticed recently performing the Hindu rites required before going into battle. He was assumed to be either an employed assassin or a religious fanatic. William concluded his letter:

> My articulation is now almost perfect ... but I still feel a slight defect in enunciation of hard words ... I have given up wine, tobacco and meat, I am thereby reduced to a moderate & genteel size. I was before much too fat & gross. PS You remember

> Ummeechund, he was with us in the hills & with me at Kalunga, a lad then of 19 or 20. Tall & goodlooking. I now owe my life to him & shall take care to have his life made a comfortable one.

Ummeechund had been caught cattle rustling, aged fourteen, and William had given him the choice of gaol or service in his irregular army. The boy had chosen the latter and was currently, aged twenty-two, William's head servant. Now William had a splendid portrait painted of him in the uniform of Skinner's Horse, inscribed 'Ummee Chund the son of Oodey Ram by birth a Jath ... the man who saved my life when an assassin cut me down tho' unarmed himself' (see Plate XXII). Later, George and his cousins spent some time in Edinburgh choosing a sash in Fraser tartan for Umeechund. George hoped that he would like it as it was 'handsome though not gaudy'.

✻

The news of William's narrow escape reached Moniack on 1 November 1819. Jane was too distraught to go to church that day. Instead she read one of Venn's sermons on the Vanity of Life and went to bed with thanksgiving for William's life 'tho still much agitated'.

Charles Grant added his shock and astonishment. In all his acquaintance with India he could not remember another similar attack and felt it must have been motivated by personal revenge. William certainly had 'too great a leaning to the Natives' – perhaps he would learn from the experience.

Until his long account of the drama there had been a deep silence from William. His parents longed for descriptions of his travels, but if he sat in his tent writing letters and journals, he said, when thousands of people were queuing outside for justice, 'I must have a heart of stone'. Even writing to Jane Anne he now considered pointless: 'I fancy that Mrs Fraser Culduthel is now as happy as our nature will allow us to be, a happy wife, a happy mother ... what can I say to her that she cannot imagine?'

It was useless trying to explain to anyone the sort of life he was leading: 'It is certainly a very different life from that of a Scotch Laird ... but not without its pleasures. Domestic society is the want, the blank of Indian life'. To his mother's persistent nagging he answered, 'I think there is much greater chance of my being buried, than married, in India. So much the better for Mrs Fraser Culduthel. The old Indian uncle will surely leave all his fortune to the second son'.

Jane still worried about the matrimonial prospects of both sons; 'when I see Affleck & Jane Anne together and their smiling little babe – I think what would I give to see a Son of yours or James's climbing our knees'. She could not resist recommending to William one of Affleck's sisters, a pretty seventeen-year-old, who was going out to India to keep her sister Lilly, Mrs Rose, company. Or what about his cousin Mary, Dr Fraser's ladylike daughter, a great friend of Jane Anne's who was also on her way to India? Later, when the amiable Mary had married someone else, Jane thought that her younger sister, Elizabeth, would fit the bill, although she was worried about her 'extreme delicacy'.

Like Reelig, she was beginning to accept, however, that William would never come home, his debts, not including Aleck's, now being well over £10,000. In any case, his passionate desire for the Residency of Delhi would keep him in India. As for Dunchea, which was regularly emptying the coffers, William never mentioned it.

He was still commissioning local artists[11] to paint groups of native people for James to use in his pictures: 'the natives are minutely accurate in outline and figure, although they do not understand perspective and effect. He had sent James around forty paintings of figures to send home. 'Some years hence I shall con[12] them at Moniack with recollections that can never leave my heart'. James confirmed this, hoping that 'this may turn out to account one day ... you must contrive for me a painting room at home'.

THE DIE IS CAST

That same spring, 1819, after some tricky negotiations, James was offered a proper position in his firm, to start in May. It could not be a true partnership, as he was not prepared to stay in India long enough to merit it, but he would be a partner in name with a liberal monthly allowance and the promise of £5,000 to his credit when he went home. This was too good an offer to turn down. On 1 May he was 'recognised in all the public parts as a partner of Mackintosh & Co. & congratulated accordingly'. He confided wistfully, however, to his journal:

> [Fate seems] determined that never anything splendid or really magnificent shall ever occur to me – probably perhaps my own fault – and certainly so in this case ... the probability is that I shall go home to an income of 700 per annum little enough, and a situation that will call forth all the energies I may possess.

Preparation for his new job as debt collector took up so much time that James took to sleeping in the office, returning to his house for breakfast and squeezing in his painting before going back to work. In September 1819, however, a new partner, Gordon, was taken on over James's head. Aeneas Mackintosh and the other partners had come to the conclusion that James undervalued the business and was merely 'riding' it or 'quitting' it as it suited him. A partner had to commit himself to at least ten years with the firm.

This would prove to be another pivotal moment for James: unable to make such a commitment, he wasted no time in planning his escape. The seeds of the idea of an overland return had been sown in his mind, jokingly, by Aleck's old schoolfellow, Melville. James's debt-collecting duties would involve travelling westwards, far 'up-country', and it seemed sensible just to keep going. The journey home overland would cost about the same as a sea voyage, would take only a little longer and, said he airily, the risk would be little or nothing. Melville, however, thought better of it.

---

11 These artists produced a series of groups of natives annotated in William's hand. They are thought to be the work of the well known Delhi artist Ghulam Ali Khan and members of his family. The collection, known as the Fraser Album, which came home to Moniack but now is dispersed worldwide, is accepted as one of the finest groups of Company pictures yet known (*India Revealed*, Archer and Falk, p. 42).

12 Study attentively.

Undaunted, James packed up his books to send home and employed a *munshi* to teach him Persian. Sometimes he had cold feet but he easily persuaded himself that this was the right moment: although he was no nearer the elusive fortune, he was better off than he had ever been; his parents were getting older and his father was not in good health; mercantile careers often failed and it was better to go while the going was good; many died before they could get home or were too late to enjoy an active life in Britain; he had no interest in 'the weariness of dry routine ... there is here no domestic circle to fly to after the cares of the day are over, no amusement beyond the dull routine of a dinner party'; he missed 'the sweet influence which the society of females sheds on European circles'.

He tried to explain his reasons in an extremely long letter to his father on 4 October 1819. After several convoluted paragraphs about the duty of every man to increase his value, he came to the point. He was perfectly fit enough to undertake such a journey and, when he reached Scotland, they would be welcoming not a 'washy, if not withered, Indian, but one able and willing, as ever, to encounter the air and exercise, that formerly gave pleasure and health'.

In November James wrote:

> I already look on myself as no longer of this country; and have all those delightful startlings and thrillings at the idea, that not only shall I leave a place I do not like, but I shall soon be in the way of reaching by a delightful route, the only place I can wish to live in, in which I wish to end my days.

He was not planning in detail, just to right or left as 'the curious or remarkable' presented itself. Black John was an essential part of the plan but there had been another drinking incident which had ended in fisticuffs. James was loath to part with him …

> … having brought him to this country ... & considering the scenes we have passed through together but if he persists he will be worse than lost to me & I fear we must separate.

Meanwhile, he gave Black John a final warning and packed him off upriver to Delhi with the advance luggage.

He pored over guidebooks and pestered his friends, especially William and Skinner, for advice and information. Then he had a brainwave: he would take William home too to divert him from the 'mad attachment to the situation he holds & the country about Dehlee'. He would never quit the country of his own accord, but surely an overland trip would appeal to his adventurous spirit.

William's valuable collection of horses and his vast house with its extensive grounds could be sold to settle his debts. Completely forgetting their inability to live together comfortably, James let his imagination soar as he dwelt on the 'mutual delight' they would have as travelling companions across the world. If he came, they would have the comfort of tents and elephants. William's career prospects had been weakened by his consistent refusal of promising appointments; maybe he should be out of the way for a time. He could always return to Delhi when his parents had had their fill of him.

William, in fact, still sometimes talked of going home and had mentioned the adventure of an overland journey as 'the most interesting and delightfull which could be traced out upon the Globe'. But, unsurprisingly, he refused the invitation. James should go home for his father's sake, 'on his own account, and on the account of every member of the family; and I therefore rejoice that he will be once more restored to yet happy Moniack'.

William was extremely well, 'still wandering in deserts and wild ... but I am now indifferent about the favour, or the countenance of men who think the world is filled by their importance'. All was now quiet in India: 'Cashmeer at last is reunited to India. The Ufghans are completely broken up; and the Sikhs occupy both banks of the Indus'. As for his own eventual return, he assured his parents that he looked on it as 'an event too great for contemplation, but upon which the eye should ever fix and the mind be ever intent ... none know me who do not think I hold home a step to Heaven; a Heaven in itself'.

James sent his parents a comforting list of all the people who could help him along the way, assuring them that he would 'delightedly plunge into the straitened strait I know to await me at home'. He looked forward to helping to turn the dairy and the garden into going concerns. Marriage was very much part of his plan if he could find 'a companion to think like me and to consent to share unpretending comfort'.

In Edinburgh at the same time, Jeanie Tytler was composing a long, complicated, effusive letter to James: apparently marriage was very much part of *her* plan too. She complained of her uncertainty about his movements and 'what I *ought* to wish with regard to them'. James's last letter revealed that his feelings, 'clogged and choked by weight of business', had been aroused by her previous one which had cleared away 'the rubbish and allowed the crushed branches to extend to the genial influence of Nature'. She continued in this vein for several pages written in tiny writing and 'tartanised'[13], making it very difficult to make out what she actually wanted to say. Her confidence, she declared, had been destroyed for 'surely nothing is more dreadful to the pride & feelings of a woman than to have her affections courted one moment and capriciously trampled upon the next but all that is forgiven'.

She appreciated the openness with which they could now both write, but how it would be when they eventually met she could not tell. Much would depend upon James: 'If you are communicative & unreserved with regard to your own feelings & opinions that will lead to the development of mine, there is not I think a cloud that could cross my brow'.

In a shop in Edinburgh, her eye had chanced upon ...

> ... a Magnificent Portfolio with Specimen's of *Fraser's Views in the Himala Mountains*. You may think with what a proud heart I opened them. There were 3 coloured Paintings on good Elephant paper in the style of Salt's view – they looked very well indeed.

She shuddered, however, at the newspapers with their 'dreadful list of Deaths from India'.

❊

13 Written from left to right and then crossed from bottom to top.

James was still tidying up the loose ends of his brothers' affairs. He sent home with his friend Dr Rankine a lock of Aleck's hair and 'his last cloaths' along with Edward's watch and gold wafer stamp, David Gregoire's sleeve buttons, given to Edward by Aunt Gregoire, the arrowhead that wounded William at the siege of Kalanga, a length of *puttoo*[14] – capital for socks and to line boots with 'some more shawls and some wine'. He hoped that the woollen material and shawls would not be locked up in a cupboard, prey to worm and moth, but would be worn and enjoyed. Later Reelig wrote that the *puttoo* was his 'constant companion'. Dr Rankine had also been given the task of taking to St Helena a black marble slab to mark Edward's grave.[15]

In March 1820 he sent his father an inventory of all that was to go home by sea, eight packages in all, insured for £2,000: clothes, books, tiger and lion skins, prints, sketches, drawings and paintings, shawls and woollens, painting materials, Aleck's desk and gun cases. There was also a small portfolio 'containing a most valuable collection of native portraits and costumes ... one, in itself a treasure; a Portrait of the favourite Elephant of the great Akbar, by his own painter, signed by his own seal, and approved by his own hand'.

By May 1820 James had completed around thirty views of Calcutta and its surroundings. He had made his will and was now ready to pack up his paints and finalise things for his departure.

❊

Then came a thunderbolt – the package of letters which made 15 May 'memorable to me for the misery it has produced to me': his parents were completely aghast at his plans and both had seized their pens to persuade him to stay put.

His mother's ten-page letter dwelt on the respect, confidence and esteem with which he was looked upon by the other partners. Being within a very few years of 'a comfortable independence' it would be 'the Height of Madness' to throw it all up.' If you do not remit yearly what will pay the *interest* of the debt – we should be overwhelmed!' She concluded:

> I do think I may as well have done – for if you are not *already* convinced of the necessity of the case by all I have said and still more by what your Father has already written & sent – *nothing* I can add will have any effect – at the same time I could weep – for being obliged to write as I do & my heart sinks as much at lengthening the period of your stay as yours can do.

His father reckoned James was 'casting away a proferred fortune'. Mackintosh had recently opened a London branch where perhaps there would eventually be a position for him; if he came home now he would be excluded from this office, which would only take partners from Calcutta.

Charles Grant was no comfort. Reelig copied his letter and included it in the package:

> It is the most surprising instance ... I have ever heard of a man of sense ... He has

14 Presumably woollen cloth.

15 This slab was moved when St Paul's Church was altered and is now fixed inside the Church above the font. It reads 'Sacred to the Memory of EDW. S. FRASER Third son of EDW.S. FRASER of Reelick in Scotland Died APl.25th 1813 Aged 27 years'.

> now the fairest prospect a man could desire for attaining an independence which may make the family also independent and if he renounces it before it can be of any material use to him, upon any account except bad health or some other overpowering cause, I am persuaded he will never cease to repent it.

Reelig frankly admitted to James that the family failing was 'want of pecuniary prudence and perhaps the tendency to decline great advantage, from our yielding too extremely to feeling' and enclosed a note of his present, deteriorating financial position. The interest payments were weighty; there were no rents on account of crop failure; it was costly to find new tenants and for him to farm all the land would be 'problematical, precarious, slavish'. His threefold wish was to save Moniack, to see James independent and to 'advance George *without the risk of health*'. With typical generosity, however, he concluded:

> Should you nevertheless on full consideration decide on return immediately, and pull the Oar at home, in whatever way you can, compatibly with your own happiness, we shall approve all, join in all, confirm to all, and bless you.

⁂

James read the letters again and again. It was there in black and white – the debt remained at £21,000 and his father needed at least £1,000 a year from him to pay the interest. His thoughts whirled endlessly. How on earth could he manage that? How was the principal debt to be liquidated? All his plans and hopes for the future were vanishing into smoke. Everything seemed to rest on his shoulders: William, who was in debt to the tune of Rs50,000, could not be counted on; Aleck and Edward were dead, and George must on no account follow their fatal footsteps to India. Who else was there? Where else could he turn? Burdened with responsibility and racked with guilt, he lay awake all night.

In the early light of dawn, he dragged himself out of bed with the shadow of an idea forming. If he could get his job back maybe he could go home on leave to assess the true position at Moniack, find a wife and return to India for the requisite number of years, before going home for good. Heartened by this decision, he dressed, called for his buggy and hurried hopefully to the office to present this plan to Gordon.

Gordon was not sanguine but agreed to talk to Fulton and Calder. Calder was adamant – it could not be done. There was no way they would take him back on any terms. They had, in any case, already taken on someone else in his place; James was far too attached to literature and the arts, his health was not good and his desire to go home was so great that he could not give proper attention to business. James was astonished: his old friend Fulton, now 'testy and peevish', had never mentioned any of this before. But now he had no choice left.

> Thus then the die is cast & I return to Scotland, to poverty & probably to ruin – ruin which is caused by the unhappy error in which I was involved by calculating, perhaps too sanguinely and securely, on the statements I received from home.

The £5,000 promised on his return would keep him going for a bit, and he hoped his drawings would help him 'to rub on for a while'. Meanwhile, there was no point wallowing in regret; action was the thing, and he went to bed determined to face the future positively.

He wrote to his father: 'though I have reflected & turned the subject in every direction I see little more to be done than pursue the course before me'. He sent Jeanie Tytler an 'offhand' letter giving her 'a good many strong reasons tho not all, for my apparently extraordinary determination'. He asked Aeneas Mackintosh to look out for a job in Britain – he was ready to do anything to relieve 'the false step I have made & the family affairs'. He composed notes to his colleagues to be delivered after his departure 'saving myself farewell visits'.

He was cheered by a letter from Jane Anne. She hoped very much that James would get rich soon but she was tired of the constant talk about money:

> Oh that torment of the world, *money* well may we say it is the root of all evil. I wish ... we could learn to live without it but alas! We are far too much the slaves of opinion ... that foolish idea that we must be *neighbourlike* & do as other people do, I believe ruins half the world. If people had only the urge to think & act for themselves & not mind what Tattlers and busy Ladies say of them they would be much happier I think.

Having got that off her chest she chatted on about the baby, Jane, who was a 'sweet lively child but *not* pretty tho being like her Father She has very small eyes & a little *pug* nose & very large *teeth* but a pretty skin & hair'.

A week later, on 23 May 1820, James left Calcutta. He spent the day dealing with servants who came for recommendations and favours and suffering 'the constrained looks & action which one keeps with those with whom you are about to part'. At nine in the evening he paid off his bearers and other servants and, lonelier than he had ever felt, climbed into his palanquin 'to quit Calcutta, I hope forever. The natural sinking of the heart at the quitting scenes so long known & friends so highly valued was not relieved by any alleviating circumstance.'

HIMALAYAN DRAWINGS AND JOURNAL

The precious consignment of drawings, journal and map had arrived safely at Moniack; before sending it off to Edinburgh, Reelig was instructed to 'correct the style & errors and cut out what may be thought too prolix or like repetition'. Nervous that the printers would spoil the original, he was laboriously copying the whole thing, working from six to nine every morning. He reported to James:

> The work I have myself corrected and modelled (adding nothing) but shading, softening & omitting, as I have judged prudent and generally correcting orthography & composition where obviously needed. I had little to do except in the Ghoorka war part ... thought the best way was to correct by transcribing the whole ... and at the same time imbuing myself, more perfectly with the work which indeed has interested me far beyond what I expected.

William Havell in Madras had alerted his uncle, Robert Havell,[16] to the arrival of the Himalayan portfolio. Later, the publishers Rodwell and Martin employed Robert to engrave the watercolours, certain that they would appeal to the public appetite for the 'Picturesque and the Sublime'. Robert Havell considered that the drawings 'will be the finest collection of views that ever were published in England'. Various artists, including 'the famous Turner', admired the pictures. William Tytler was amazed: 'Certainly the first sight of your Drawings was a greater astonishment to me than anything I ever met with – you are a surprising fellow.' 'If James chose to follow up his taste as an artist,' wrote his proud father to William, 'he would soon be the first perhaps in Europe. The first now in Britain talk in this way, after seeing his Drawings'. On 1 June 1820 *Views in the Himala Mountains by J.B.Fraser Esq* was published by Messrs Rodwell & Martin, Bond Street.

Walter Scott and William Tytler discussed how best to get the Journal and map 'exhibited to the world'. Tytler proposed to present the Journal as a paper to the Royal Society of Edinburgh; he went over it four times before he got it down to a reasonable length, then extracted two parts to read, reporting later:

> The paper went off with great éclat – it was heard by a most numerous & intelligent audience – in fact almost all the distinguished men of Edinburgh – and excited very strong interest ... I am convinced that no paper read before the Royal Society for a very long time has been so successful.

It was later received enthusiastically at the Geological Society of London, and Murray's publishing house offered around £800 for the Journal and map; although he would have liked the whole project to be sold together, James declared himself content.

In October 1820 a twenty-eight-page article on James's Journal appeared in *The Quarterly Review*. The reviewer lamented the fact that James had not been equipped with scientific instruments to measure temperature, atmospheric pressure or the height of the mountains; these scientific deficiencies were 'provoking enough', but worse was 'the total want of arrangement of the matter which he has collected, the perplexing mixture of camps and campaigns and military movements with manners'. After struggling through what he called 'a minute detail of uninteresting matter', he finally decided that the work was 'highly worthy of public notice, and encouragement' and that 'a kind of witchery hovered over the pages which brought before us those holy haunts of superstition, where, enthroned on the lofty and snow-capt pinnacles of the Himalaya, the divine Mahadeo sat and surveyed the fertile plains of Hindostan'.[17]

George, like Jeanie, had spotted James's pictures displayed in a bookseller's and told all his friends to go and admire them:

> I have just been looking at three of James's drawings sent down as a specimen they are not published yet they are lying at one of the Booksellers ... upon the largest Elephant papers engraved by Havell & Son I should think the expense must be enormous.

16 1769–1832. Expert in aquatint engraving and colouring, founder of Havell & Son.
17 Art IV *The Quarterly Review*, Oct 1820, 24, 47, British Periodicals p. 102.

Private collection

The title page of James's *Views In The Himala Mountains.*

GEORGE'S FUTURE

In the dark, dusty lawyer's office in Edinburgh George was often at work from six in the morning until midnight. He had, however, found time for the recently founded Celtic Society[18], the object of which was 'to bring together as many of the Gentlemen of Highland birth ... as they can twice a year and likewise to keep up if possible the old Highland dress'. He was very excited by the prospect of a dinner on 3 March 1820 for which full Highland dress was compulsory; could his father send his 'Highland purse and dirk and *my* own steel Pistol'? Reelig thoroughly disapproved of the whole idea – it was far too extravagant, and much too soon for George to become a member of any club or society. Too late – George had already joined. 'It really is a respectable society,' he assured his father, 'and has many members of some note.' Walter Scott, no less, was to be in the chair on 3 March. Reelig still grumbled that George should have asked him or James Tytler first. Jane, however, persuaded him to send the purse and dirk by return.

The dinner was a great success: seventy-two people 'plaided and plumed in their tartan array' assembled at 5 o'clock and sat down to dinner, followed by dancing. George was ecstatic:

> I never saw a finer sight every person looked proudly well and enthusiastically happy even Walter Scott with his lame leg after going home attempted to show his family one or two of the most singular reel steps ... he left us at 11 o'clock highly delighted and after giving us some brilliant and appropriate speeches there was some tolerable singing a great deal of talking and very little drinking the

18 Founded to promote interest in the history, traditions, language and arts of the Highlands and Western Islands and encourage the traditional and correct wear of Highland dress.

meeting broke up at half past three. I went home at that hour as cool as if I had never been there thus ended the dinner and *miserabile dictu* without a single dirk being drawn.

During the spring of 1820 there was a list of commissions for George: Jane Anne needed new dresses and a bonnet; Affleck needed a new servant; Jane needed spectacles, books, shoes, a gown, caps and a 'Butter Kit'. Sometimes Jane's odder demands defeated everyone: even James Tytler had never heard of 'lactometers' or 'graduated cast iron milk dishes'. She also wanted a copy of the Baskerville Bible.[19] George queried the sense of this, reckoning that she might prefer a 'fine Newfoundland dog' or a mastiff, either of which he could easily procure. All through George's time in Edinburgh, the knotty question of his finances constantly worried his father. George obliged with fairly detailed accounts and was better at controlling his belongings and money than Aleck had been. There was, however, always the problem of mourning; he had again outgrown his mourning attire and so, when Mrs Hotchkiss suddenly and painfully expired in May 1820, her death cost George 'some sorrow and a black coat'. He might have earned a few more threepences, however, as 'we are all busy writing funeral letters for Mr. Hotchkiss'.

It was time to find out whether George felt suited to a life as a Writer to the Signet;[20] he declared he did not care what profession he followed as long as he had enough to live on. The chief object of all the family was to free Moniack; if that could be achieved he would be perfectly happy 'living the rest of my life in the Bothy at Killin'. However, he had worked out that to qualify as a lawyer he would have 'a long look forward – seven years of hard labour before I can practise for myself'. He also observed that the expense of becoming a WS was £430–£440 'which is awfull and also about £8 for dinners which last sum is optional but must be given'. Later, he was still less enthusiastic, considering a career as a WS 'a dreary outlook'. He now had a better idea.

During his first winter in Edinburgh the town had been 'all in a bustle' as the Yeomanry marched off to Glasgow, where there was a rumour of an uprising. In their absence, Edinburgh Castle was being guarded by volunteers, a calling that greatly appealed to George; he did not yet have time for such a commitment, but the seeds were sown. The idea of a career in the army grew daily more appealing, although he kept it from his parents.

He arrived home in July and enthusiastically whirled into Highland social life and goings-on at home. Jane Anne's third baby, another James, had made his appearance; there was a stream of visitors at Moniack to see James's paintings; Jane had all the activity around her that she could possibly want and was consequently in fine health and spirits.

19 Printed in Birmingham by John Baskerville, 1769.
20 A senior solicitor in Scotland.

A last look at Delhi

As Aleck had complained years earlier, James was incapable of properly planning any journey. He was travelling by palanquin with two basket carriers for his baggage. Otherwise, arrangements were pretty vague: if no bearers appeared then he would get coolies to carry the palanquin while he rode a pony; he hoped to find shelter in villages or *serais*, the buildings scattered along the way to accommodate travellers with pack animals.

Often their path wound along 'dismally sloppy and slippery roads', sometimes no more than narrow ridges between fields, and across roaring rivers with no bridges. He frequently had to make long, tedious detours, and more than once he and his palanquin crossed a river on a raft, now familiar, hurriedly made of old beds and upturned pots. Bearers were as unpredictable as ever: they came and went as they pleased and were rarely available in sufficient numbers; he wasted a lot of precious time waiting for them to appear.

At each stage, that most elusive of men, the *Munshi* of the *Dak*, or organiser of bearers, was nowhere to be found. June was the wedding season, and James found that not only were all the bearers happily employed at weddings but the bungalow that was usually available for travelling Company servants was overflowing with merrymaking locals.

The weather alternated between intense heat and thunderous rain. He walked most of the first stages, often knee deep in water, alongside the bearers carrying the heavy palanquin for his night-time accommodation. They sometimes arrived in villages too poor to provide food or drink, and James had to survive on the food he had brought with him: gingerbread and '4 or 5 biscuits about the size of a dollar, with a gulp of milk, a dish of tea and perhaps a head of corn'; sometimes he lived on mangoes. There was the added complication of not being able to leave his possessions unattended while he sought help.

He was dependent on the goodwill of his bearers, especially when he could find no one else willing or able to help with directions or provisions. Often the locals knew nothing of life beyond their own village; indeed, 'I know nothing about it' was the usual answer to his enquiries. Like the *Munshi* of the *Dak*, the local *thakur* (landowner) was 'anywhere but at home'.

Characteristically, he managed to fit in some sketching and make notes on every aspect of the country through which he was travelling. There were also occasional visits to old friends along the way, where he could at last wash, change his clothes and dine well.

William was as irritated about James's impractical planning as Aleck had been: it was ludicrous to think of travelling without tents & comforts 'when such can be taken just as easily as they are abandoned'. When James came to Hansi he could fit him up with everything in three days – elephants, camels and riding horses. James had asked for sextants and other instruments for surveying, but William was scornful: what was the point of bothering with all that when 'we have now all India open and surveyed & nothing new is to be now done in that department'.

James had always wanted to see Gwalior. William could not imagine why and had crossly warned James that 'Gwalior is the most villainous & wretched place in India. There is not a single attractive point about it.' But James loved Gwalior. It afforded him endless opportunities for pictures and, much to his bearers' relief, he stayed longer than planned to draw the gigantic figures cut into the Rock of Gwalior, wonders which he understood had not yet been shown to the world at large.

⁂

Another wonder was Scindia, the Maharajah of Gwalior,[21] 'Great King over Kings of the Brave, the Exalted Dignity'. James had hoped for an audience, but the Maharajah was in mourning for his favourite daughter. He found ...

> ... a man seated on the ground, wrapt partly in an old dirty white *chuddah*,[22] ... a small slovenly red turban of the Mahratta fashion on his head, & his seat was a horsecloth or two with a back & two side cushions covered with an old shawl – this was the Maharajah – thus seated as it were in the dust – for there was no cloth around him to cover the floor.

Like William, James was deeply affected by the fate of the great Mughal princes of India and very moved by the sorrow of the old man as he wept for his daughter.

Agra provided James with irresistible sketching material and, most magical of all, there was once more the Taj by moonlight. At Fatehpur Sikri he was horrified to learn that the Government had given permission for the stones of the ancient city to be sold '& thus in all probability the whole of this fine ruin will in time be carried away'. Admiring the delicate ornamentation of the pillars and doorpost festooned with clusters of grapes, pomegranates, apples and pears, he reflected that 'of all this beauty a few years will perhaps not leave a vestige'.

At the beginning of October 1820 he reached Delhi and William:

> I found him in the best health – our meeting was kind in appearance and kinder in feeling tho nothing further than the shake of the hand exemplified or expressed it.

William was eager to show off his magnificent new house. He rarely mentioned this project in his letters home, but other travellers commented on it: Victor Jacquemont, for example, with some exaggeration, later spoke of 'Mr Fraser's immense house, which is a kind of Gothic fortress, built by himself, at an immense expense where Timour ... once pitched his tent when he laid siege to Delhi'.[23] James thought it suited William admirably:

> It is a fine [house] in an extraordinary situation – like himself – rough about, pleasant and comfortable inside – it commands a noble view, but he ... means to leave it nearly in a state of nature even close to the doors.

William himself was more incomprehensible than ever – 'I do not think that ... I have met with a character so extraordinary as that of my brother William'. He was generous and warm-hearted to a fault but regarded as 'trifling and commonplace' actions which in others

21 1779–1827. Maratha chief defeated by the British in the Third Mahratta War, 1818.
22 Sheet or square piece of cloth.
23 *Letters from India*, Vol. II , Victor Jacquemont, 26 Dec 1831. Asian Educational Services.

would seem 'magnificent and splendid'. He was impulsive and demanding, and his every whim required instant gratification. He was now drinking heavily and suffered periods of deep depression. Edward's arrival in Delhi all those years ago had restored William to some sort of normality and he had relaxed in the company of his sunny younger brother, but Edward's death in 1813 'threw him back into despondency'; Aleck's fatal illness three years later 'threw a gloom on his spirits which I fear will never leave him'.

The evenings cloistered alone with William were very trying. William refused most invitations and James did not like to press him. Things improved, however, when they rode out to Hansi, Skinner's farm forty miles north-west of Delhi, where William had a bungalow. He was now a recognised major in the Yellow Boys and recently had been, briefly, in the reserve army under Ochterlony when the North-West had been 'all in a flame'. At long last, his military prowess was being recognised.

The brothers got on better in the company of Skinner, who eased the tension and acted as a mediator. At night he entertained them with stories of his various campaigns; by day he showed them over his farm and they attended a parade of two hundred of the Corps. Here they witnessed the famous manoeuvre in which a man on horseback galloped at a tent peg hammered firmly into the iron-hard ground and attempted to carry it off with his spear – 'a very severe thing on the horse and the arm, the shock alone at full speed is great', so much so that Skinner allowed neither horse nor man to attempt it too often.

One companionable evening at the end of October 1820, James summoned his courage and touched on the subject of William's children. He had already met them at Hansi – a girl of about four and two boys, the elder about one-and-a-half and the other about nine months old. 'The girl is rather pretty, but I think the features are somewhat Tartar like'. The youngest child, on the other hand, was as white as a European, with fair hair and blue eyes. How William reacted James does not relate; they agreed, however, that the children's existence should be kept from their parents: knowing that Indian letters were public property for family and friends, William would enclose a second letter addressed to his parents when he sent James news of the children.

James was relieved that the subject had been aired. He had known for some time that at least one of William's relationships had produced children, and it was inevitable that he would eventually meet them at Hansi. In the relaxed Eurasian ambience of Skinner's home, there need be no secrets; it was a safe retreat, where William could gather his children, assured of their welcome and happiness. Skinner, whose own mixed racial background had been such a drawback to his early career, and who still felt not wholly accepted by either community, understood William's need for a safe haven for his family and trusted that one day his own children would be welcome at Moniack.

Not only were there Skinner's children to play with, there were also, from time to time, those of William's horse-dealing partner, Ahmad Baksh Khan, recently made Nawab of Firozpur (see Plate XXIV). His eldest son, Shams-ud-din, was an attractive twelve-year-old of whom William was especially fond and who called him 'Uncle'. This boy would enter the story again much later with dramatic consequences.

❋

It was now time to return to Delhi and prepare for the next stage of James's adventure. Ahmad Baksh Shah was to escort him to Firozpur, sixty miles south of Delhi. William confounded James with his excessive generosity: '20 camels, 1 elephant, 3 horses for me and I believe 5 for the people!! What a *sowaree*[24] for a poor man!!!' William was determined that James should not be put to any expense and arranged to pay the servants six months' wages and all costs to Bombay. James was embarrassed: 'This is like him but it vexes me. I had no wish by my visit to put him to such cost, but without offending & hurting him I cannot [refuse] it'.

He paid a farewell visit to the riverside bungalow which held so many memories, climbed up to William's house to take a final look at the city and dined with Skinner – 'the last time I shall probably see this excellent man'. He asked Skinner to let him know how William was bearing up 'for tho it is not death he knows as well as I do too, how many chances there are of our ever again meeting'. Skinner loaded him with presents, including a suit of chain armour, and arranged the best possible farewell party for him – a *nautch* evening with the delectable Malaguire, who had so entranced him five years earlier on his return from the hills. He then took leave of all his friends:

> 'God Bless you' said Skinner '& remember old Sekunder'. These were his last words to me – I think I am not likely to forget such a man ... This is the way of the world – when we have found a thing we can value, we are forced to leave it or part with it – it has been so with me ever since childhood.

Then he squeezed in a last visit to the Qutb Minar, where he camped for the night and was up early for a last sketch. William joined him there for breakfast, and there was still just time for a discussion of their futures: William reckoned he would be out of debt in five years' time and home in ten. Then came the final moment – the horses were saddled and Ahmad Baksh Kahn was at the door of the tent.

> William is not a man to shew his feelings however keen – nor to give way to the common forms on such occasions – we got up – he gave me his hand & said 'Well Good Bye – take care of yourself" – gripping it hard – but I did not speak – I did not trust myself – I took one look – probably I shall see him no more – & quitted the tent.

Turning his back on the brother that he would never fully understand, he resolutely set his face to the west and the future.

24 Cavalcade of mounted attendants.

James Fraser, 12th Laird of Reelig, was an eminent collector of Sanskrit manuscripts. He built 'a pretty box' at Moniack, roomy enough to entertain eight Highland chieftains at one sitting. The bay window extension is Victorian.

Edward Satchwell Fraser, the 14th Laird of Reelig. His wife, Jane, was the daughter of William Fraser of Balnain.

Private collection

James Baillie Fraser, aged twenty-six, by Henry Raeburn.

Metropolitan Museum of Art, New York, USA, Robert Lehman Collection

William Fraser, aged sixteen, by Henry Raeburn.

Courtesy of the Taft Museum of Art, Cincinnati, Ohio, Bequest of Charles Phelps and Anne Sinton Taft. Photo: Tony Walsh

Edward Satchwell Fraser Jnr, aged seventeen, by Henry Raeburn.

Private collection

Alexander Charles Fraser, aged fourteen; a carbon print (1897) from the original painting by Henry Raeburn.

Philadelphia Museum of Art, USA, Gift of Mr and Mrs Wharton Sinkler, 1963

Jane Anne Fraser, aged nineteen, by Henry Raeburn, painted for her marriage.

Private collection

George John Fraser, aged fifteen, by Henry Raeburn.

Private collection

Rebeg Cottage, a much loved house on the hill, where the family lived when Moniack was let. Jane Anne chose to stay here the night before her marriage.

© Charles W Traylen; originally published Ackermann, 1816.

'Charter House from the Play Ground', the school for 'Decayed Merchants Sons', where Edward Fraser's passion for education was developed.

Private collection

'Sweet Aldourie', the lochside house of the Tytler cousins, was a beloved home-from-home for the Moniack family.

By Henry Raeburn; courtesy Highland Council and Inverness Library. Photo: Ewen Weatherspoon

Courtesy St George's Bloomsbury. Photo: Stephanie Lord

Charles Grant, Director of the East India Company and MP for Inverness-shire, played a significant role in the lives of the Fraser family. His monument in St George's Church, Bloomsbury, records he was 'the prime mover of those noble works which have changed the face of the Scottish Highlands' – notably the Caledonian Canal and the road system.

Courtesy Hertford Town Council

Hertford Castle was the temporary home of the East India Company College until the foundation of Haileybury. Charles Grant was influential in both curriculum design and in the appointment of teaching staff, modelling his vision on Oxford and Cambridge Colleges. In the grounds two students are talking to a Persian 'munshi' or teacher.

Private collection

Alexander Tytler, Lord Woodhouselee, was a significant figure in the academic and literary circles of Edinburgh and 'the sun and centre of his family'.

by Henry Raeburn. Courtesy Brooklyn Museum, NY, USA

Lady Woodhouselee, a much admired aunt who, though mean in small concerns, 'in matters of moment ... had an open hand that freely obeyed the dictates of a warm heart'.

Courtesy of Lady Erskine

Woodhouselee, 'romantically situated on the eastern slope of the Pentland Hills', six miles from Edinburgh. Lord Woodhouselee's daughters would light a candle in the window of his library at the top of the tower to welcome him home at night.

© Sir Henry Wade. Courtesy Royal College of Surgeons, Edinburgh, Licensor www.rcahms.gov.uk

The dining room at Woodhouselee in 1804 painted by Isabella and portraying a family of 'the most perfect social happiness'. From left to right Jane (Jeanie), Isabella, Aunt Christy (Aunt Woodhouselee's spinster sister), Annie, Patrick (Peter), James, Willliam, Aunt Woodhouselee, Sandy and, close to the fire, Uncle Woodhouselee.

Photo: MKF

The Rectory, Little Dunham, Norfolk, where the Revd Henry Jowett provided seven teenage boys with a rigorous classical education.

East India House, Leadenhall Street, London, c. 1820, where the passages to India were given the go-ahead, was demolished in 1861. The Lloyds Building now occupies the site.

An East Indiaman. William's ship, Comet, the second ship of that name, weighed 529 tons, was 120 ft long, 32 ft wide and had three decks with sometimes a mere 5ft between them.

Private collection

William in Indian dress, attributed to Robert Home, which William sent home to his mother. She much preferred the Raeburn portrait.

Courtesy of the Taft Museum of Art, Cincinnati, Ohio, USA. Bequest of Charles Phelps and Anne Sinton Taft. Photo: Tony Walsh

Jeanie Tytler, first cousin and wife of James Baillie Fraser, by Henry Raeburn, c. 1810.

Private collection

William Tytler, Sheriff of Inverness, was a first cousin of the Moniack family to whom he was a faithful and trusted adviser.

Courtesy of Lady Erskine

Margaret Tytler, née Grant, wife of William Tytler, was a great friend of Jane Anne and a constant source of support to the Moniack family.

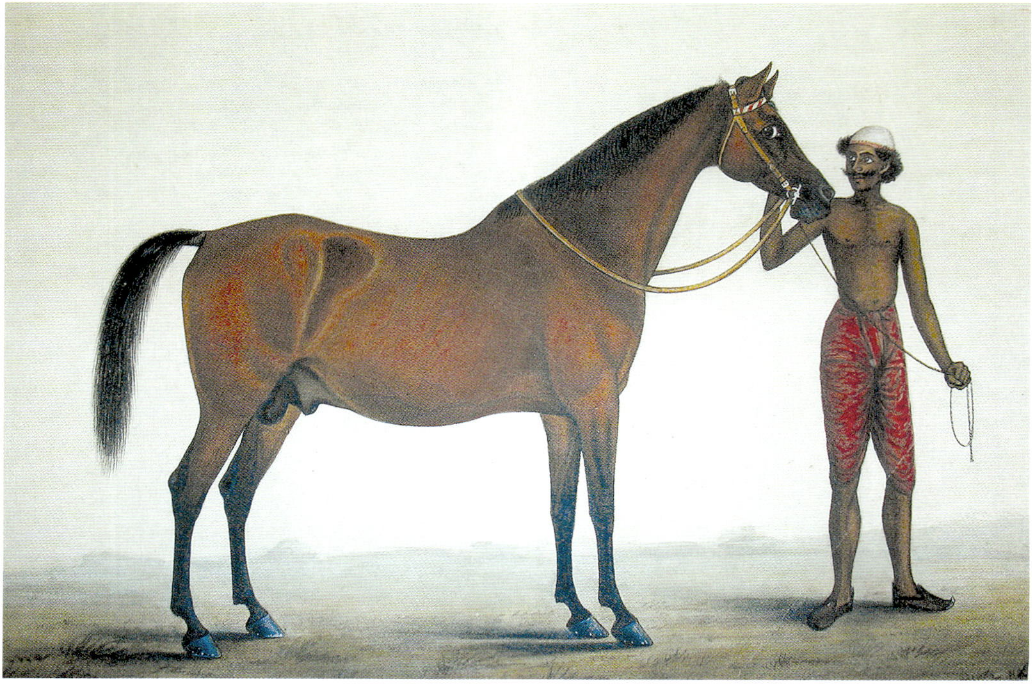

Private collection

Eclipse, Alexander's horse, was bought for him by William at the Hardwar Horse Fair. The horse, 'which has not his parallel in India for viciousness, and goodness', accompanied Aleck on his journeys between Calcutta and Dehli and assisted in the killing of numerous wild boar, in the end being too badly wounded to hunt again.

Yale Center for British Art, Paul Mellon Collection USA/Bridgeman Images

James's picture of the 17th century Writers' Buildings (behind the Black Hole Monument). Here the junior servants, or Writers, of the East India Company were accommodated. According to William the institution was 'a very bad place for the restless and impatient, the unsteady or animated'. St Andrews, the 'Scotch Church' is in the distance.

Private collection

Archibald Seton of Touch, 'a most excellent, worthy and well known character', was a fellow Scot who took the Fraser boys and their problems to his heart.

Collection of William Dalrymple

Archy on a hot day engrossed in composing one of his wonderfully effusive letters. Perhaps the picture on the wall is of Touch.

Indian School (19th Century) British Library UK/Bridgeman Images

Sir David Ochterlony lived magnificently in the style of a Mughal nobleman. Here he is in Indian dress, smoking a hookah, in the company of his thirteen wives. Tradition has it that he paraded them, each on her own elephant, around Delhi of an evening.

by George J Stodart after William Henry Pickersgill. © National Portrait Gallery

Mountstuart Elphinstone, 'the most romantic of the Empire builders' was the leader of the mission to Kabul to enlist the support of Shah Shuja against the apparent Franco-Russian threat.

Courtesy of the Council of the National Army Museum, London

Shah Shuja, King of Kabul – 'Absolute Monarch of the North'. During an audience with Shah Shuja, William was filled with 'romantic Oriental awe'.

Arthur William Devis: Scottish National Portrait Gallery

General Sir David Ochterlony commanded one of the western divisions of the Nepal War and successfully brought it to an end in 1816. Like William, he saw the benefit of recruiting Gurkha troops into the Bengal army.

Samuel William Reynolds Senior after Thomas Lawrence: Courtesy of Fortrose Town Hall

Lady Hood, who, according to Sir Walter Scott, had 'the spirit of the chieftainness in every drop of her blood'. William, taking her with him on his lion hunts, was 'in raptures of her ladyship'.

Collection of William Dalrymple

William Fraser, officers and ladies at dinner. The artist has painted William, the most important person present, as enormous while the humble servant in the foreground is tiny. William is apparently wearing the same hat as in his portrait on Plate IX.

Courtesy of the Council of the National Army Museum, London

Sir George Nugent, Colonel of His Majesty's 6th Regiment of Foot, was appointed Commander-in-Chief of India in 1811. He and his wife sailed on the same ship as Edward who, to please his mother, spent much of the voyage trying to attract their attention.

George Chinnery: © National Portrait Gallery

Charles Theophilus Metcalfe was always one rung ahead of William on the ladder of promotion and made every effort to compensate, treading very carefully.

French School 19th Century Bibliotheque Nationale, Paris, France/Bridgeman Images

The island of St Helena, a towering, jagged inhospitable rock, reputedly had 'the finest climate in the world for Phthisical Patients'.

'Napoleon facing The Briars' – home of the Balcombe family on St Helena. It was situated in a lush valley, an oasis in the island where, two years earlier, Aleck and Edward had found refuge in a cottage.

Engraving after Major Ludovick Stewart. Private Collection/Bridgeman Images

'Madras Landing'. An East Indiaman can be seen in the distance while the 'masoolahs' riding the surf bring the top-hatted, frock-coated, crinolined passengers ashore. In the foreground catamarans wait for the summons to rescue any unfortunates from the waves.

Acquatint engraved by C Hunt; Ackerman & Co (1856)/Bridgeman Images.

© National Portrait Gallery

George Chinnery (a self-portrait) was James's much-admired painting master. A comic actor and 'one of the ugliest men alive', he was particularly disagreeable at breakfast.

Courtesy of the Council of the National Army Museum, London

Colonel James Skinner was a great friend to both James and William. His farm at Hansi was a refuge for William's mixed-race children; his own children were made welcome at Moniack.

Private collection

'Palanquin Bearers Resting' by George Chinnery in 1806. James found palanquin travel uncomfortable and tedious as he could not see out well enough for detailed observation.

Courtesy of Sothebys.

William employed an artist from Delhi to paint groups of local people. These, among others, are known as the Company Drawings. Here William's 'Moonshee' (teacher) and 'Deewan' (secretary) are seated with a group of villagers. The Deewan, with his spectacles on his nose, is writing in a book, surrounded by more books and pen-boxes.

Courtesy of the Trustees of the National Gurkha Museum

Eight Gurkhas, Haryana c. 1815–16. Not satisfied with his own efforts to draw local people, James got 'the native artist my brother hired to take the likenesses of several of the Ghorkas which will assist me much'. He described 'their dark shaggy hair, shorn about the ears' and their headgear 'like the broad Scotch bonnet'.

Private collection

The ridge and fort of Jaithak, where William fretted and fumed over General Martindell's dithering and 'the Devil of Drawing broke loose' in James. This and the next three paintings are from James's Himalayan portfolio.

Private collection

The Temple of Mangni. James admired the intricate carvings of its interior. The brothers' tent can be seen on the left.

Private collection

Crossing the Touse in a numlo – a loop of rope suspended round one's forehead – and often with someone in one's lap.

Private collection

The House of Rana where the chief had to be dragged up the hills in 'a sort of litter'. His 'curious many-towered house' can be seen perched on its rock in the middle foreground.

Courtesy of Sotheby's

Salabat Bhatti and villagers at Rania c 1816. The girl on the left is identified in William's writing on the back of the painting as Amiban, or Surwen, his bibi or 'chosen one'. The child is their daughter, Shaman, (later Amy who, later still, took the name of Surwen). This and the next two paintings are from those commissioned by William by native artists.

Courtesy of Sotheby's

The Village of Rania c 1816 where Amiban lived. The beautiful girl seated on the left and the child behind her could be Amiban and her daughter.

Courtesy of Sotheby's

Six villagers standing on a hillside. The child on the left is possibly one of William's children.

Private collection

A watercolour sent home to Moniack of Aleck's handsome tomb erected by William at Jakhauli, about 24 miles from Delhi. It is now demolished but a remaining sandstone post was found in 2013 by Sebastian Mills with the help of BACSA (British Association for Cemeteries in South Asia) and a local farmer.

Courtesy of Sotheby's

Malaguire in her nautch dress – a favourite dancer who entranced James in Delhi. Skinner engaged her to dance again for James at his farewell party in 1820.

Courtesy of Sotheby's

Ummeechund in the uniform of Skinner's Horse, Haryana, May 1819. It is inscribed in William's hand: 'The man who saved my life when an assassin cut me down by seizing him tho' unarmed himself'.

Courtesy of the Council of the National Army Museum, London

The 1st Regiment of Skinner's Horse returning from a General Review. William Fraser is riding with Col Skinner in the centre of the picture. Skinner gave him the rank of Major, 2nd in command of his corps and wrote 'a better soldier than William never drew cold steel in the world'.

Government House, Calcutta, painted by James. Chinnery said of the picture 'there is an altogetherness which is famous'. He recommended fewer figures and a viewpoint from twenty yards further back but reckoned that 'the Foliage to the right is - like Foliage'.

James's picture of St Andrew's, 'the Scotch Church', with Writers' Buildings in the distance.

William enjoying a hookah and the company of his great friend and horse-dealing partner, Ahmad Baksh Khan, Nawab of Firozpur, and father of Shams-ud-Din, William's protégé and nemesis.

Top: South-east view of St James's Church, Delhi, by Ghulam Ali Khan, c 1836. Built by James Skinner reputedly in gratitude for recovering from wounds sustained in battle. On the day of its consecration he and three of his sons were confirmed there and he was buried there in 1841.

Bottom: William was buried in this magnificent tomb, built for him by Skinner. It is just visible in the churchyard (*top*) to the left of the Church. The tomb was destroyed in the Mutiny in 1857. The sandstone base survives and one of the larger marble panels, beautifully inlaid, is set into the floor of the Church.

Private collection

A caravanserai. Sketch no. 37 from James's Persian sketchbook.

Private collection

Sketch no 52. The Jehan Numa at Farrahbad, 3 May 1822.

Private collection

Sketch no 69. The tomb of Sayed Quwam ud Din at Amol, May 1822.

Private collection

Sketch no 15. Tomb of Saadi at Shiraz.

Private collection

Sketch no 36. Tomb at Tus, 22 July 1822.

Private collection

Sketch no 40. The shrine of Imam Reza at Mashhad – one of the greatest sites of pilgrimage for the majority of Shia Muslims and one of the world's largest mosques.

Private collection

Sketch no 25. The road through the mountains to Kohrud, between Tehran and Amol.

The Persian Princes, by John Partridge, 1836. The Prince is, presumably, seated, Timour in the middle adopts a charmingly nonchalant pose and the Wali, quite different, stands in the background. James was presented with one of the best of the early sketches.

Photo: Sorrel Bentinck

George's tomb in the Christian cemetery in Aurangabad was discovered by Sorrel Bentinck in 2015 with the help of Praise-the-Lord Peter Pawar, Graveyard Caretaker. The inscription reads: Sacred to the memory of Captain George John Fraser of the 1st Regimt Bengal Cavalry. Assistant to the Resident at the Court of Nagpore who departed this life on the 27 August 1840.

Private collection

George's profile, done in 1814 at William's request, along with those of his parents and Jane Anne. Aleck considered George's likeness 'well done'

Private collection

Reelig House c 1920, just as James designed it, apart from the Victorian conservatory on the left of the house. Ben Wyvis looms in the background.

Photo: MKF

Photo: Mary Lewis

Walks along the burn: Jane's walk (left) is on the eastern side; Alexander's walk (right) is on the western side.

Photo: Mary Lewis

The tall trees of the glen, which is now owned by the Forestry Commission.

William and James collected Indian miniatures, beautifully decorated, almost exclusively of people. Is it fanciful to think that this, a very different image, entitled 'Dippers by a Stream' (c. 1860) reminded them of the dippers in the burn of their childhood?

11

1820–1822

En route

On 6 September 1820, just before James left Delhi, the family at Moniack drank a birthday toast to William. All were 'tolerably merry' and, after songs from Affleck and George, Jane scrawled a birthday greeting with yet another reminder of marriage and a plea for letters:

> Whoever you make choice of will be acceptable to us – we are much amused by George's sentiments on this subject – he is not only *always* in love which is natural to his time of life but constantly says had he but 500 a year he would set his brothers an example of marrying! Poor fellow I wish he had any prospect of making even so slender a fortune as 500 ... The memory of your youthful days are so delightful that I often dwell upon them 'til I forget the lapse of time & cannot imagine why you are in a manner so distant from me that I do not know what you are doing – what are your tastes, your pleasures & why you do not write to tell me all those things! ... again, I beg, my dearest William, you will remember that henceforth we have no means of hearing of you but by your own Pen.

Meanwhile, Reelig, confident that both his sons would be home in July the following year, was anxiously poring over his globe and plotting James's route:

> I allow you a month to saunter to Bagdat, & to reach Aleppo 1 Feb, to loiter a month in Syria to 1 March and whether you go southward to Egypt or by Asia Minor & Greece; or whether you go by Cyprus & Rhodes to Europe, I cannot know ... [the] arrangement of our lands and the decision for George await your coming.

✲

The weather in the Highlands that December was unseasonal. The evenings brought the family round the fireside but outside it was 'summer warm'. Everyone seemed cheerful, busy with the corn mill and sawmill, both now working well; George was happily becoming 'quite a Miller'. But in their hearts there was winter chill: the end of life at Moniack, as they had known it for nearly forty years, was on the horizon.

A few days earlier, Affleck and Edward Fraser, a neighbour from Gorthleck, came to a business dinner during which Jane and Reelig learnt with dismay 'that we should quit the place ... as soon as possible'. Affleck and Jane Anne were thinking of going to live in Bordeaux for a few years: travel had become fashionable among the young and they wanted to experience it while they had only three children. It would also make economic sense since life in France was cheap; surely the whole family, including James and possibly William, could be reunited in France?

Jane and Reelig sat long over the fire digesting this and discussing George's future. He had firmly turned his back on the law but had only recently plucked up courage to announce his hopes of a military career. However, he agreed to wait for James's return before making a final decision; the only alternative future that might tempt him would be a business venture at home with James. His parents had to be content with that.

At first, Jane found the whole French idea impossible: how could they, at their time of life, uproot themselves from their home, extended family, friends and neighbours for transplant in a country of which neither spoke the language? But a worse prospect would be life at Moniack without Jane Anne or George. Gradually, she began to accept the notion of a temporary exile to France; after all, it would be for a limited time and at least they would be with the grandchildren. Preparations were put in hand: the management of Moniack would be left to Edward Fraser Gorthleck and an agent, John Edwards; already corn merchants were jostling to rent the Mill. Older servants would be retired on 'a moderate subsistence', tenants would be sought for the lands and other employees dismissed. The house and gardens would be let, the crops and livestock sold and Nanny Rose would live in 'Noble's house' in charge of all the belongings stored in the loft.

The immediate plan was to go to St Omer in March and settle near Jane's sister, Catherine Gregoire, and her family. Northern France had become popular with the British, of whom there was such a large community in St Omer that it was known as *La Petite Angleterre*. It was also 'as near the London Post Office as we could wish' and easy for James to reach; they would wait there for him and the Culduthel family to arrive, by July at the latest. James and George would then face the future together, while the rest of the family headed further south to the sun. They could live quite happily in France on £200 a year (around £14,000 today) in a small house which would preclude the expense of entertaining. It was hard for James, declared his mother, to realise how expensive a spacious house could be: 'You, East & West Indian Nabobs,[1] ruin poor country gentlemen like us, by your example, compelling us to live as we had rather not.'

Health was another factor. Reelig suffered badly from colds and gout, and there was hope that he would thrive in the sunny south. But paramount was the truth that, faced with losing the Culduthel family, 'the only Bairns we have within hold', to the sun, Reelig and Jane were not inclined to be left alone in northern climes.

⁂

1 'Anglo-Indians' who returned with fortunes from the East.

James and William had to be told, but Reelig waited until the sales and most of the letting were behind them; then there would be no going back.:

> I shall say nothing on the subject of leaving Moniack and Culduthel – the thing was right, and therefore done – and my affairs are managed by a friendly knot of disinterested and able persons ... the House stands furnished for any offering Tenant. The Lands are all let, and fairly ... We shall sell Dunchea, whenever a fair offer invites.

He ended his letter to James on an optimistic note:

> Meantime ... I may say that a more beautiful residence ... can hardly be. I have done a great deal ... but there is at least enough for you, when opulent, to do, to complete [the place] to perfection.

Having made the decision, they found it hard to keep cheerful during the ensuing winter months. They had lost the company of William Tytler's family, who had finally let Aldourie and moved about thirty-five miles east to Sanquhar, Margaret Tytler's family home. Reelig spent the long winter evenings sorting James's collection of books and Indian articles and rereading the letters of all the boys. These he arranged 'distinctly & correctly', copying them in his careful writing, so that William, George and Jane Anne might one day 'have the delight of perusing these family treasures'. Jane busied herself, emptied the shelves of jam and marmalade and packed the jars off to William. George continued his social life, trying to take his mind off the partings to come.

Jane just had time to dangle yet another a marriageable girl in front of William: 'Now do not laugh at my Castle, William, and Blow it in the air'. This time it was 'comely' Miss Jane Mackenzie, whose father, brother to Sir Hector Mackenzie of Gairloch, 'has taken infinite pains to cultivate her!' She was not beautiful but had been 'carefully educated in a quiet domestic manner'. What was more, she played the piano and excelled at Highland airs.

William, however, was adamant: he was not going to consider marriage till he got home. 'I have never seen a woman in this country whom I could marry. I am, thank God much out of the way of spinsters.' James, according to the grapevine, was almost certain to marry Jeanie Tytler when he came home, an idea that Jane still could not accept: 'I cannot believe it ... certainly his cousin is not the woman we should wish ... even were there no other objection their nearness in blood & in years is a great one'. But, she wisely concluded, 'parents should never set their hearts on the marriage of a son no more than on a Profession for him – in either case they will probably be disappointed'.

On Saturday, 14 April 1821, an unusually warm evening, after months of 'constant fagging & much distress and anxieties', they shut the door of Moniack behind them and set off. It had been a difficult week, with a stream of friends and neighbours calling to take their leave. George, who as the day approached had become increasingly upset, could not bear to hang around till evening but left early, walking the twelve miles or so to Culduthel.

Parting with the old retainers was distressing: 'still,' said Jane 'it was with the Hope of one day returning to them ... & reoccupying the place'. Nanny Rose was heartbroken: not only was she losing her beloved Jane Anne and her children, but George, she knew, was longing to follow his brothers' footsteps to the other side of the world.

They stayed two weeks at Culduthel, where Jane spent every moment with her grandchildren; perhaps she and Reelig might be of use as babysitters in France. George, more cheerful now that the actual moment of leaving Moniack was past, caught up with his friends in Inverness while Reelig finalised estate details with his agent. They had not yet found a tenant for Moniack, 'but it is so much the rage or fashion for English people to take Scotch residence that we have no doubt we shall ultimately succeed'.

Reelig was full of praise for Affleck, 'who is all energy in our cause [and] superintends the respective roups[2] at Dunchea & Moniack'. He had throughout acted 'like a respectful affectionate supporting son ... he is a firm, manly, clearsighted & judicious man'. Perhaps travelling and meeting different people 'may help to rub off some of the asperities of the Rough Diamond as his mother calls him'.

The Rough Diamond was now the Secretary of the Northern Meeting. Recently, a bitter row between two factions of local businessmen, including the rival newspapers *Inverness Journal* and *Inverness Courier*, had rocked the foundations of the Northern Meeting Committee. It resulted in a General Meeting, one of the 'stormiest and uncomfortable ever held',[3] and the consequent search for a Secretary with no fingers in local politics or business led to Affleck. He eventually became first Convenor of the Meeting, held the post for thirty years and was generally considered to have served faithfully and efficiently.

❊

The next stop was Sanquhar, where the huge Tytler family welcomed them and they felt 'as at home & contented to enjoy ourselves'. Thereafter, it was inevitable that they would feel despondent on the coach journey south, but the *Caledonian*, a new coach, was quite comfortable, and their evening at Bridge of Carr was enlivened, at any rate for Jane, by a 'Country Teacher of Church Music' who sang them many unknown Psalm tunes. She was excited by her first voyage in a steamboat across the Firth of Forth to Newhaven, and they finally arrived at the Tytler house, 108 Princes Street, on 19 May.

---

2 Sales

3 *The Northern Meeting*, Angus Fairrie.

Leaving the Shores of India

In the springtime of 1821, as his parents were turning their backs on Britain, James, in Bombay, was preparing to leave India. Inevitably, his journey from Delhi took far longer than anticipated; he could not resist exploring each ancient site, eliciting stories and legends from the locals with the help of a *munshi*, following every interesting byway, probing the family trees and histories of each Rajah he came across – and all the way he sketched.

A week after parting from William in November 1820, James and Ahmad Baksh Khan, along with a company of Yellow Boys, a small band of servants and Black John, had reached Ahmad's mud fort in Alwar. This was the parting of the ways with Ahmad, who had entertained James along the way with endless praise of William and tales of his own heroic exploits.

Entering the deserts of Rajasthan, the party proceeded on camels. James was entranced by the wonders of Amber and of Jaipur: 'I have no hesitation in saying that [Jaipur] is far superior in its way to anything I have seen in India'; Delhi and Agra were scattered with ruins, 'but here all is in order ... this and Amber present a good specimen of Hindoo taste & style in building'.

Pacing slowly on through the 'waste of sand in waves', they visited Ajmer and then headed due west on a detour to Jodhpur, where they had a great welcome from the Rajah; he demanded a private conversation, at the end of which James could hardly walk after sitting cross-legged for so long. He was given but refused 'an animal with four legs called a horse', and was then offered its price, Rs250; again he declined but was told that 'Tod ... had agreed so I could not refuse'. The next Rajah along the route sent a message that all James's wants should be supplied 'as if I was Capt Tod himself'.

Who was this great Tod[4] of whom he heard so much? A year older than James, Captain James Tod had had a brilliant career in India culminating in five years, 1818–23, as the Company's political agent in the western Rajput states, where he restored peace, confidence and prosperity to the area ravaged by the Maratha raiders. He was so successful in this mission that he became loved by rich and poor alike, but above all by the princely families of Rajasthan.

Tod was stationed at Mirta, where James, relieved to be in European company once more, stayed for two weeks. He wanted to elicit as much information as possible from the great Captain, especially the details of 'the taking of Oodepore & Jhoudpore' by the British. This proved difficult:

> I find Captain Tod pleasant enough though tolerably important and vain but he seems most confoundedly reserved on subjects connected with the country and to antiquities & history ... he hummed and hawed a good deal.

This was not surprising. Tod had, after all, spent over ten years recording the history of the country, and one can only guess that he did not feel inclined to hand his findings, gratis,

4 1782–1835. Collected coins, MSS and antiquities. Commissioned first pictures of Rajasthan. Returned to England in 1823. Librarian of Royal Asiatic Society in London. Wrote *Annals and Antiquities of Rajasthan* (1829–32) and *Travels in Western India* (1839).

to this arty, itinerant journalist from Calcutta who was likely to reach the London publishers long before he did. James had been anticipating companionable evenings gathering Tod's stories of the Ranas and their family histories, legends of the area and details of its flora, fauna and geology; he reluctantly had to content himself with general information on the ancient sites he hoped to visit on the way to Bombay.

However, James found much to delight his 'Painter's eye' in Udaipur, where Captain Tod took him to an audience with the Rajah, who thought himself superior to any other Rajput; James considered him 'a mere machine in Tod's hands'. He was known as the most generous monarch in the world but was also very vague: 'he will today give a village to one person and the next day forgetting his gift present it to another'. Captain Tod had had to take control of the disposal of Royal property, villages and all; no gift was made without his sanction, for which the Rajah was humbly grateful. He was the scruffiest Rajah James had yet encountered: he sported no jewels and his trousers were 'far from splendid & not very clean'. James wanted to add the family tree of this Prince to the others he had collected, but 'Tod has cast such a spell around me that neither I nor my people can get a single word of information regarding the family or the antiquities of the place'.

On 10 January one of James's favourite old servants, Man Sing, died very suddenly. Two days later, he felt a moment of deep depression: 'Poor Man Sing's death, no doubt, has its part in it and I am I confess far from easy with regard to the great retardation in my journey & the time that must evidently relapse before I can get to its end.'

Moving on southwards, he reached the great cave temples of Dhoomnar. He kept a notebook to record local fables and jot down details of places visited; there are over sixteen pages of close writing in the notebook on Dhoomnar, a vast rambling warren of cave temples. By now he was an expert on Hindu temples and at Dhoomnar he was frustrated that the original marble carvings had been restored with *chunam*, the local lime plaster:

> The elephant ears of Ganesh, as well as many parts of his body are certainly only of *chunam*, but the elephant trunk & part of his big belly as certainly seem to be of the original stone.

At Mhow he stayed for nearly three weeks with General Sir John Baillie who, to his relief, was 'no man of mystery like my friend Capt Tod' but was perfectly willing to provide anecdotes, 'numberless, unceasing & excellent', even at breakfast. He gave James unlimited access to all his writings, his history of the area and his public and private letters, so that James had to get up at 4.00 am to read and write; there was little time for sightseeing, but he left with bulging notebooks.

Although it was already the end of February and time to head for Bombay, he could not resist squeezing in a search for the ruined ghost-town and great mosque of Mandu. Struggling over jungly plains and through 'ravines furrowing the sides of the mountainous wall ... down which in the rains precipitous cataracts fall', they stumbled into a mighty chasm. On a square plateau in the centre stood the mosque – 'a scene ... wonderfully singular, romantic & almost savage'.

Throughout his journey James carried with him various instruments to take astronomical observations. At Mandu he 'took two Southern & one Northern star for Latitude before I went to bed & at 12 o'clock at night in spite of weariness'. He had no instrument for establishing heights so took 'a large and sensible thermometer to ascertain the boiling point of water in different situations'. After nearly a week at Mandu scrambling into every ghostly corner and gloomy crevice, and thirty-four pages of description in the journal, they set off south again.

Arriving in Bombay, James found a swinging social life, for which he did not have the right clothes; life was more formal than in Calcutta and no one left their house without a coat, but he was surprised 'to find everything so rare and the place so very bare & behindhand in the common comforts & necessities of life':

> There is no good watchmaker in all Bombay & still less anyone sensitive enough ... to take the rate of a chronometer & put it in order – there is not a mechanic that can make or mend brasswork, a gun lock, or a shoe maker ... or even European Taylor ... the whole place is a century behind Calcutta.

The few ladies he came across met with his approval, 'but I have chiefly seen the most agreeable'. The Bombay bungalows also found favour with him:

> I delight in the greenness, the foliage, the variety of Bombay, the houses half hid in trees sparkling from among them like woodbined cottages. Many of them have an infinity of shrubs and flowers in pots & in parterres around & before them, with arbours, trellis works & all the adornments we hear of Italian gardens.

The one-storey houses, reflecting the influence of the early Portuguese settlers, were far preferable to the splendid houses of Calcutta 'with their colonnaded verandahs, 3 stories & bare parched compounds'.

Now that they had reached the edge of India, his entourage were getting restive. When, at the beginning of April, another servant died, throwing a gloom over the party and 'incurring their desire to be off & mine to dismiss them', it was time to part company:

> I dismissed Bhujoo and *all* my Delhi servants whom I shall almost certainly see no more – the pain I suffered for this dismissal and parting was not trifling – and it afflicted my spirits more than I hoped it would – I think they are far easier depressed now than should be the case, or than they used to be ... the elasticity of youth is gone by – the Bowstring is somewhat slack.

This was his last link with Delhi and all the 'interesting & affecting recollections'; the next day it was the turn of Skinner's Yellow Boys:

> Last evening I saw the last of my good friend and fellow traveller Narsing & his party – the last I shall see of Skinner's Yellow Boys! Well everything has an end – it will not be the last or the worst farewell forever I shall have.

Two days later, however, came the cheering news that Dr Jukes, who was to accompany him to Persia, had arrived in town. Andrew Jukes[5] was a Scottish surgeon who had had a very successful career in Persia and was well versed in Persian customs, geography and language. His arrival put James 'on the figets'; it was the signal for him to leave the country with which he had had such a tricky relationship, the country which had taken the lives of two of his brothers, cast a spell over a third and, with George plotting to follow his brothers' footsteps, might well enchant another.

Now that James was about to leave India forever, he could confide to his journal his true feelings about her. India was a country of 60 million people, one of the oldest civilisations in the world, which had survived a succession of conquerors with its constitution intact. How could such a country be subjected to the rule of a handful of strangers …

> … who not only substitute their own rules & regulations and keep everything jealously to themselves … who govern the country, not for its political or civil advantage *but for their own*, who have extirpated the nobility & middle classes from the society leaving but the cultivation of the ground & the mercantile classes … that such a state of things should exist seems almost incredible … we talk of the uprightness of the British administration, the strict adherence to the pledge of Government – the attention paid to Police, in short, the great attention paid to making the people happy – was there ever a more complete fallacy – to what does all this lead but to the security of our Indian empire, to the filling of our own Treasury.

This extraordinary country was, under the British, 'a mass of flesh without bones'; if the British were to withdraw now, the mass would fall to pieces:

> We have reduced them to such a state that they cannot govern without us. Yet we govern them with no view to their advantage but to our own … we are thus in a dilemma – we have committed a great crime – probably drawn into it unintentionally – which is still going on & which we cannot discontinue even if we wished it without a consummation that must be deprecated as the melancholy end of this criminal course.

⁂

James spent his final two days in India sketching 'one of the most varied loveliest views I have ever seen' – the view of Bombay and the bay laid out before him like a map from the top of Malabar Hill – and fitting in a quick visit to the caves at Elephanta. On 14 May 1821, he and Dr Jukes boarded *Francis Warden* for a two-month voyage to the Gulf of Oman and Muscat.

5 East India Company surgeon and political agent 1774–1821. Selected by the Governor of Bombay, Mountstuart Elphinstone, to negotiate with the Persian Government terms for stationing British troops on Qeshm island and eliminating piracy in the Persian Gulf.

St Omer

Meanwhile, in Edinburgh, Jane and her elder sister Anne, Lady Woodhouselee, met for the first time for four years, and the next ten days passed 'in ... a hurry & Bustle' of final shopping and social calls. Jane found time to go to the New Chapel[6] on Sunday and Reelig tried to hear the famous Thomas Chalmers[7] preach at the Canongate Church, but the crowds were such that he could not get in. Very early on 1 June Anne gave them coffee and saw them off on the coach to London.

Jane was enchanted with the beauty of the Borders, where their travelling companion from Inverness, Revd Brown, a new tenant at Aldourie, joined them and pointed out the various 'Gentleman's seats' that they passed, along with relevant gossip. George was busy on top making friends with a Frenchman and picking his brains about life in France. Jane and Mr Brown attended a service in York Minster which was too 'high' for Jane's taste; at the end Mr Brown said, 'Now let us really go to a church & worship God for I do not feel that I have been in a church today.'

In London there was a whirlwind tour of St Paul's before they boarded the Dover coach. Jane deeply regretted not having time to see Canterbury Cathedral but cheered up on reaching Dover, where the sea was 'calm & clear as a Lake'.

Once safely on French soil, 'where we are determined to view all things *couleur de rose*', and through the complicated Customs, they brandished their introduction to the Hotel Maurice, where they found comfortable apartments and an excellent dinner.

The next day was disappointing in its lack of 'foreignness', but their spirits rose at the distinctive skyline of St Omer – the ruins of the seventh century L'Abbaye Saint-Bertin and the tower of the magnificent Gothic Cathedral rising from the marshland surrounding the little town. They arrived exactly a week after leaving Edinburgh, 'without exertion or fatigue' according to the indefatigable Jane, who reckoned that at sixty (more accurately, sixty-four) and seventy they had done well to arrive unscathed. For the twenty-one-year-old George the whole venture was 'only play and amusement'.

At 53 rue de l'Arbaleté they found Jane's sister, Catherine, who, like Anne, had changed little. Her elusive husband, David, was 'the same kind indolent being as ever – totally idle & spending most of his time at the Coffee House'. Daughters Eliza, Emilia, and Caroline, despite having 'lost their youthful bloom', were healthy, pleasant and contented young ladies of thirty-three, thirty-one and twenty-four respectively, agog to meet their cousin George, whom they had last seen as a boy of ten.

The Gregoires had found them a comfortable furnished house nearby, 123 Rue de Dunkerque, for 50 francs per month, consisting of a salon, a sitting room, two bedrooms, a kitchen and a lumber room, and also Goton, 'a tolerable cook and market woman', for 18 francs a month. For another 10 francs a month a valet would come daily to clean clothes, shoes and cutlery.

6 Almost certainly the Cowgate Chapel with its minister, Revd Archibald Allison.

7 1780–1847. Divine, writer and giant of the Scottish Church. Enrolled at St Andrews University at the age of eleven. 1823 Chair of Moral Philosophy at St Andrews. 1828 Chair of Theology in Edinburgh. 1834 Leader of the evangelical section of the Scottish Church in the General Assembly. Head of the party in the Church of Scotland which stood for 'non-intrusionism', the principle that no minister should be appointed to a parish against the will of the congregation which led to the Disruption of 1843 when 470 clergy withdrew from the General Assembly and constituted themselves the Free Church of Scotland, with Chalmers as Moderator.

The next day, a Sunday, Jane found comfort in a very good sermon at the 'English Chapel', while George lost no time making friends with a young Englishman, Frank Lyon, whom he found fishing on the river. Frank was lodging with M. Dassie, the doctor – a useful, even essential, contact. George soon found his way to Dassie's house, where he regularly played cards late into the night, worrying his parents, who insisted on sitting up till he came in.

❊

During her time in St Omer Jane wrote a very detailed diary, the main source of information about this period, in which she always referred to her husband as 'Mr F'. Since Reelig is now exiled from his Highland property it seems appropriate to mark his change of status and, for the moment, call him 'Mr F' along with Jane. Their lives had certainly changed radically: after years spent bringing up their family and struggling to keep Moniack going, they now had to get used to having almost nothing to do. With a small townhouse and no garden, no friends yet and no business to attend to, daily life dwindled to a dreary routine of walks around the town and visits to the Gregoires. Mr F discovered a Reading Room, where he scoured the English newspapers for news of ships which might bear letters from James or, better still, James himself. Their visits to the Gregoires were sometimes tricky. Catherine swung unpredictably from high spirits to the depths of depression, and Jane found both extremes hard to handle. Mr F coped better and was often to be found at his sister-in-law's, leaving Jane alone and disgruntled.

They longed for news of Jane Anne's plans and James's whereabouts. From now on, their lives revolved round Thursdays and Saturdays when the English mail arrived and they were constantly disappointed. Still, they kept reminding themselves, it was only for a few months.

There were hundreds of British in St Omer at that time, but the Frasers shunned society to avoid the expense of entertaining. Jane tried other ways to pass the time: she attended everything on offer in the Cathedral – any baptism, wedding or funeral. She attempted to learn French in order to communicate with Goton but soon left the task to Mr F and George, apparently never getting much beyond 'Samedi', which she wrote occasionally in her diary. She and Mr F often wandered along the old ramparts of the town and eventually discovered a path along the River Aa to a pretty little village called Arque.[8] The weather was unusually cold and wet, with constant north-east winds, and often they awoke to the gloom of a fog swirling in from the marshland. Jane looked forward to a move 'to some more genial clime' the moment the Culduthel family joined them, which surely must be any day soon.

George also did his best to fill his days. He grabbed any chance of social life that came his way, took French lessons at the local College, fencing lessons, flute lessons, 'attitude & carriage' instruction from a sergeant, piano tuition from Caroline Gregoire and mathematics from a neighbour. Two hours daily were spent practising French with his cousins '& all of this his own choice & arrangement'. Mr F struggled to recover his

8 Now totally taken over by La Verrerrie Cristallerie, a huge glassware factory, founded 1825 to make demijohns for Bordeaux winemakers and, with 11,000 shift workers, the largest employer in the North Pas-de-Calais.

The house with the scooter parked in front is almost certainly 53 rue de l'Arbaletè, St Omer, the home of the Gregoire family, often visited by the Frasers who lived a street away in a similar, but smaller, house.

schoolboy French but was frustrated that his grasp of the colloquial language was slow and insufficient for conversation.

⁂

In a very chilly July, far colder than the Highlands, the news reached St Omer of Napoleon's death on St Helena. Jane spent the whole day 'in melancholy remembrances of our beloved Edward – from our thoughts being turned to the Death of Buonaparte at St Helena & his wish to be buried there & the contrast with the Character of that mild Gentle being who's beloved remains rest there'. Mr F reported to William:

> The death of Bonaparte seems to create no sensation here – nor as I am led to expect will it produce any in France. The retreat from Russia and the day of Waterloo are now turned up against him & he will soon be almost forgotten except in History. I do not find that even the officers who served under him ... respect him much. They admitt the grasp of his mind as a daring Statesman & General but they are aware of his great errors in both capacities.

Thinking of Edward, he noted 'the Levelling power of death when the most ambitious mortal & one who had transcended most conquerors in success in extent of power & dominion ... now reposes almost by the side of one of the mildest & most unassuming of human beings'.

Not surprisingly, Jane soon succumbed to illness – both rheumatism and 'my old complaint'. M. Dassie prescribed the inevitable calomel, which she supplemented with laudanum.

⁂

The monotony was briefly relieved for Jane in mid-July when she was invited to join the Gregoires and their friends on an outing to a farm for Sunday lunch. The only thing that blighted this jaunt was Mr. F's refusal to accompany her. It was a lovely day and they all set off 'in a kind of Covered Cart – 9 of us – a miserable equipage and wretched Horse but all in high spirits'. It took two hours to reach the farm, 'where we were most Hospitably received by the Farmer & his Wife who had prepared an excellent dinner for us'. They had soup, turkey, pigeons and veal cutlets, followed by 'excellent Pancakes called Goffres ... plenty of excellent Beer w/ spirits & liqueurs of various sorts'. They digested all this with an invigorating walk and returned for 'a Gout of a kind of Cream – very rich ... & a fresh supply of Goffres '. They rumbled home through a brilliant sunset reflected in the river. That night, Jane slept better, undisturbed by her usual uneasy dreams about Jane Anne.

Mr F's account of the expedition was short and to the point – 'This day she is gone with George & the Gregoires & some Frenchmen in a wagon'. In his letters he always reported on their health; she felt, with good reason, that he 'often boasts more of mine' than was accurate. In truth, she had never felt really well since their arrival in France.

⁂

On 19 July the weather suddenly changed and became intolerably hot. Jane sat in the salon, hitherto freezing, with all the doors and windows open. It was the George IV's Coronation Day[9] and the British community were giving a dinner and a ball. The Gregoire girls attended and M Dassie invited George, but 'his Father did not subscribe to it' so he declined. Inevitably, there was a brawl at the ball, with two English gentlemen behaving in a way that was 'a disgrace to the English'; Jane was kept awake all night by the revellers

She was now becoming resigned to the idea of a military career for George and was consoled by the fact that, once more, two of her sons would be together. William disagreed:

> I think he can do nothing worse; but if he will put his neck into a halter, it should have one end tied to a horse; that is he should come out in the cavalry.

Just as Mr F had described Aleck to William, Jane now introduced George, 'that interesting infant you left in the 01' who had now become 'an equally interesting youth of 21'. He was a mixture of all his brothers. He looked like James, with strong features; he had his father's sound principles but, like Aleck, 'he is inflexible in his opinions too much for his years'; he had William's fearlessness and 'total want of caution as to society or its dangers would make me tremble for his being led astray ... in India'; and like Edward, he was 'also of a convivial bent fond of society & really captivating in his manner in company'.

Cholera: Büshehr and Shiraz

The two months' voyage from Bombay on *Francis Warden* was something of a nightmare for James, who felt consistently unwell. Among the crew there was 'more bustle, more noise ... less of that beautiful order which is so observable on a well regulated Indiaman'. For much of the time the ship was frustratingly becalmed. His great consolation was the company of Dr Jukes, whom he pumped for information about Persia. The best part of the day was the evening ...

9 Notable for its splendour and extravagance and the fact that the King's estranged Queen Caroline was excluded.

> … we issue from our cabins like bats from our holes & walk for half an hour till teatime when we sit on the poop for an hour or two & talk conversation, the chessboard then employs us till past 9 when ... we go to our nests.

Once they reached land there began an extraordinary journey packed with danger, hardship and untoward events. Landing on the strategically important island of Qeshm, they found the small force there decimated by a cholera epidemic. Moving swiftly on, they reached Büshehr in early August where they camped in extreme heat and discomfort on the beach and, to James's amazement, 'two English gentlemen come overland from England' suddenly appeared. One turned out to be none other than the Mr Wilton who had befriended Edward and Aleck on the voyage to St Helena and subsequently visited Moniack.

At night, James and Mr Wilton, who was now engaged in a secret government mission, talked into the small hours. James gleaned everything possible about Wilton's journey and, of course, every detail of the situation at home. Wilton confirmed what James had long suspected about Moniack – that there was 'a want of sound business talent in the house'. However, Jane was reported to be 'a very stout hale old lady' and Reelig, though less strong, was good for several years yet.

The cholera was creeping up on Büshehr and the baggage muleteers were unwilling to move. Jukes, reluctant to be a carrier of the disease to Shiraz, feared that, in any case, they might not be allowed into the town and wanted to stay put. James was in a quandary: already long behind schedule he was loath to spend a moment longer 'on a barren sand or shore without a single object of interest'; on the other hand there were the undoubted advantages of travelling with Jukes, who spoke the language, knew the area, had immediate access to all the important people and places along the way and was saluted with gunfire wherever he arrived. James agreed to stay one week longer.

He hoped to move in the middle of August, but there was a further delay when the muleteers refused to take one step on the thirteenth day of the Muslim month, considered by some unlucky. They pointed to James's becalmed voyage from Bombay and subsequent tricky journey from Muscat, both started on the fateful thirteenth. James had no choice but to sit on the beach and sketch the mules.

They finally set off by the light of a full moon on 11 September. After a hazardous journey leading their mounts though the narrow, rocky defiles of the mountain range between Büshehr and Shiraz they reached Kazerun, where they discovered that, in Shiraz, the cholera epidemic had reached such proportions that the Prince was camping outside the walls. Many of the Royal harem were dead and there was deep mourning for the Queen Mother.

The Prince was clearly in no position to give Dr Jukes the necessary audience during the long period of mourning. Once more there was a dilemma for James: should he just continue alone? He had already sacrificed much time by being attached to Jukes's mission; maybe a lone individual would find it easier to slip in and out of the towns along the way.

On 23 September 1821, he reluctantly set off with a pony and four mules, hoping that Jukes might eventually catch him up. He had had the greatest difficulty finding servants and it was only after much argument and the promise of extra wages and sheepskin coats on arrival that James had persuaded four servants to accompany him and Black John. It was not an easy journey: there were more desolate mountain passes to be negotiated, it was bitterly cold and they ran out of food. They avoided the caravanserais, where they could have rested, as they were moving through the area inhabited by the dreaded Eels[10] and needed to be inconspicuous. The servants were 'grumbling and growling' and spirits generally were low. All the way they passed parties of people fleeing the disease in Shiraz. On 25 September the weary, hungry little party finally found refuge outside the mud walls of the town in the gardens of the Jehan Numa, the usual accommodation for European travellers, where James was overjoyed to find Claudius Rich.

The brilliant young Rich,[11] who for some years had been the East India Company's Resident in Baghdad and was now based in Basra, had come to Shiraz with his doctor friend, another Tod, to explore Persepolis. On account of the fighting between the Turks and the Persians, James had been advised to consult Rich about his further route home and had long been hoping to meet him.

Waiting for James

In sultry St Omer Jane and Mr F were also worrying about the conflict between the Turks and the Persians. Even discussing James's whereabouts agitated Jane so much that she had to retire to compose herself. It was now too hot to walk far and her only consolation was immersing herself in *Ivanhoe*,[12] followed by *The Life of Buonaparte*, in the mercifully cool salon.

Mr F's spirits were not much better. He was often 'languid & fatigued' or 'silent & sad' and very crotchety with George, who was usually home later than his father considered appropriate. However, despite his gloom, he wrote positively to William about life in St Omer: George was 'on the floor breaking apricot stones for flavouring Brandy – your mother making tea – we live easily – and cheaply and comfortably'. There were diversions:

> Plenty of fetes and all manner of gorgeous processions – religious ceremonies and Gaiety & Idleness all mingled ... the people courteous & well behaved & comfortable but I fear that the Priesthood will recover & have recovered too much of their former ascendancy – & that the Government & Nation are rapidly reverting to the old regime – to probably a source of some serious disturbance before too long.

He maintained he had no problem 'in accommodating the French living – but we have no society except the Gregoires, who have very few acquaintances from a necessary attention to expence'.

---

10 Lawless tribes.
11 1787–1821
12 Novel by Sir Walter Scott, published 1819.

The sultry days gave way to cooler weather at the end of August, forcing Mr F into his winter clothes, and the monotony was temporarily relieved by a move to more permanent accommodation nearby at 101 Rue de Dunquerque. The new house, tall and narrow like the others in the street, was clean, comfortable and pleasant, and a new maid, Josephine, replaced Goton.

A letter from Jane Anne, however, dashed Jane's hopes: there was now no possibility of their arriving until after the Northern Meeting week in October, in which Affleck would be heavily involved as Secretary. Jane resorted to laudanum again, was troubled by uneasy dreams and made even more miserable by constant bickering between George and Mr F. The situation was compounded by Josephine's departure to look after her father and an argument with Mr F over Catherine Gregoire's erratic behaviour.

Two events towards the end of the month cheered her up. First the King visited St Omer, and although she saw him 'but imperfectly (from a window)' and was not, on the whole, impressed by his manner – 'not very gracious' – her spirits were lifted by the excitement of the occasion. Then, better still, the Polsons, 'an amiable & interesting family', arrived in St Omer; at last there was the promise of some society and something useful to do.

Mr F and George immediately helped Mr Polson to find accommodation, while Jane took his wife under her wing and introduced her to St Omer life. The two families met every day and, when one of the Polsons fell ill, Jane was a constant support. Although Jane found the sight of Mrs Polson surrounded by a large happy family somewhat unsettling, she was delighted when Edwin, one of the sons, came to play chess with her.

In early October a letter announced that Jane Anne was expecting again and would not now be able to travel for some time. Jane accordingly felt 'pains in her limbs' and restlessness, followed by a bad bilious attack. By now she was taking laudanum regularly and her sleep was still interrupted by anxious dreams. On 14 October a letter from Affleck confirmed that, owing to his commitments and Jane Anne's pregnancy, they had finally abandoned all hopes of coming to France. This was followed four days later by James's news that he would not be home till February 1822. Jane's spirits plummeted.

The weather was now as cold as in Scotland and there seemed even less point in being in France. Mr F was out most of the day leaving Jane alone. At least Josephine had reappeared and George was sometimes persuaded to stay at home playing the flute to his mother. Then came his sudden announcement that he could wait no longer for James and was planning to go to London to arrange a passage to India – 'a most distressing circumstance'. Mr F told him of 'the folly & impropriety of such a step' in no uncertain terms which brought on such a battle of wills that Mr F stamped out and Jane retired in tears. George, undaunted, went shooting with Dassie.

The year wore drearily on. Jane let her diary lapse apart from remarking that for the first time she had persuaded George to play picquet. They were, however, heartened by the news of Jane Anne's next baby, Edward, and of William's appointment as Deputy Superintendent of the Delhi Territory. George, with the blessing of both Affleck and Charles Grant, was planning to set off as soon as he could. His mother, although now resigned, was dreading the parting; he had been 'the stay & comfort since we have been in St Omer' but, by the time they had to say goodbye to George, then surely James would be home.

At the news of William's new job his mother was already envisaging 'that joyful day when we may once more embrace my Dearest William & even if it please God bless his children ere we die'. Surely after all his exciting exploits he would settle down to life at home in the company, she trusted, of 'a Northern damsel' who would be happy with 'our Highland Hills'.

Marriage was in the air in St Omer as Emilia Gregoire had for some time been walking out with Benjamin Vaneechout, 'a very respectable & pleasant man about her own age – 31 – a Capt. Of Engineers a native of the place'. Mr F thought him 'very intelligent & superior'. Jane Anne, knowing her father's extravagant generosity, hoped that the wedding was not imminent: 'I pray ... the marriage may *not* take place till our folk are away ... for it must cost them something & dear Papa's liberal spirit will never do'. When it eventually took place, a Roman Catholic rite in the Vaneechouts' town house followed by the Protestant ceremony at the Gregoires', Mr F acted as a witness.

Christmas was a difficult time, although George danced at every ball he could find. Mrs Polson was ill, and over the festive season Jane trudged daily through the icy streets between her sister and the Polson household, happy to combat 'a feeling of loneliness unavoidable in a foreign country' at Christmastime. Lying in bed on 31 December listening to the noisy New Year celebrations outside, she hoped fervently that 1822 would bring the return of James.

Shiraz to Mashhad

James spent that Christmas on the first stage of his journey from Teheran to Mashhad. His autumn in Shiraz had been eventful. Cholera was raging and there were various rumours abroad as to its cause. One suspect was the water supply, the little stream that ran through the Jehan Numa gardens where James was staying; some of the *mullahs* held the disease was a judgement from heaven on those who drank alcohol. Fired with religious indignation, their followers rampaged through the town breaking into the houses of Jews and Christians and smashing every bottle they could find.

James was anxious to be on his way, but the servants were reluctant to move a yard further. On arrival they had demanded, and received, a cloth coat each as well as the promised sheepskin jacket, but James could not rely on them to stay with him. He was unwilling to run the risk of being abandoned in unknown territory, with inadequate command of the language and the possibility of wild Eels lurking round every rock. Once again, perplexed as to his next move, he resorted to his sketchbook and journal, wrote a detailed account of Shiraz and extracted information from Claudius Rich, a pleasant and stimulating companion.

His decision to stay longer was propitious. On 5 October, Rich was suddenly taken ill and twelve hours later, with James and Dr Tod by his side, he died.

> It is impossible not to dwell with melancholy pain on the catastrophe we have just witnessed ... to see a man so highly endowed, who has distinguished himself in so many places – to whom science was in all probability soon to be indebted for information & observations of the most interesting nature – to see all this brought to an end in a dog hole like this ... it is too melancholy & depressing.

There was no time, however, to dwell on melancholy scenes since the burial had to take place quickly. James and Dr Tod applied for permission to bury Rich in the Armenian Christian burial ground, but no corpse was allowed to be brought in from outside the walls. Not even the Queen Mother had been allowed this privilege during the epidemic. The only hope was the garden where they were staying – at least this would not attract notice and might be safe from future desecration.

They went to bed anxious and exhausted; at three in the morning they were woken by the sounds of horses at the gate to find to their intense relief none other than the eminently capable Dr Jukes. 'We felt we had acquired a friend in a land of strangers, almost of enemies, at the moment we most needed such a blessing.'

With Jukes's help, James chose a quiet spot in the garden, gathered the Armenian clergy of Shiraz, persuaded all the servants to attend and arranged for the Anglican burial service to be read over the grave. 'On the top we placed a slab of Tabreez marble, on which was engraved his name, and the date of his decease'.

After a visit to Persepolis, which he sketched from every angle but left unrecorded in his journal as it had been described so often, James was impatient to leave Shiraz. There was a further delay: yet again Jukes wanted an audience with the Prince, whose whereabouts were a mystery.

Eventually, the Prince sent a message: he would see Jukes but only in the Palace, as a meeting in his camp would deprive him of 'the state and pomp so essential to the gratification of Persian vanity'. It was a strange audience. With the court in disarray and so many courtiers dead or vanished, the Prince, unable to do anything without 'unnecessary affectation of state', had to summon crowds of 'cringing slaves and ragged troops from their peaceable occupations, to stand in mock array'. They were awkward and unrehearsed, and the 'tinsel tawdriness of the show' was laughable. However, it counted as an audience and Jukes and James were allowed to proceed to Isfahan.

It was now October 1821. In the steep, rocky passes between Shiraz and Isfahan they had to grope through dust storms, battle through whirlwinds and endure the bitter cold which numbed their hands and feet and froze their moustaches and beards. They passed ghost towns and villages deserted on account of either the cholera epidemic or the practice of '*soorsaut*'.[13]

13 The custom, practised by 'all great men, or messengers travelling on the part of the king', of demanding free food and lodging, often way beyond what a village could afford or provide. To escape these demands villagers often left their homes to find shelter off the beaten track.

In early November they reached Mayar, some twenty miles south of Isfahan. Dr Jukes was showing alarming signs of fever and James sent for a litter to carry him to the town. The bearers enthusiastically led the party on a sightseeing tour through interminable winding lanes, murky alleys and wonderful bazaars, until Jukes testily remarked that he had often seen the sights of Isfahan before and asked them to get him to the palace without further delay. On arrival, James wrote to Mr Willock, 'Charge d'Affaires to his Britannic Majesty', in Teheran and to Dr John MacNeill,[14] the Residency doctor, informing them of Jukes's illness. Despite the dubious attentions and placebos of a Persian quack doctor, to whom he was unfailingly polite and grateful, Jukes died on 10 November.

James was now alone. Once again there was no time for melancholy reflection: dead bodies had to be removed the same day. Jukes's servants having vanished, James left Black John watching over the body and sprang into action. Making sure first of all that all Jukes's valuables and diplomatic papers were locked away, he once again recruited the Armenian Christians, hoping that there would also be a fitting presence of respected Muslims to honour 'the ambassador of a great and friendly nation'. The Armenian Archbishop read the funeral service, which James followed with that of the Church of England. He retired to bed wondering how long he himself would escape the cholera and who would perform these final services for him.

There was too much to do to give way to these feelings. Having travelled for six months with Jukes, James not only knew a great deal about his mission, but also realised that he had to be seen to be totally in control – 'I assumed as it were the authority and importance of an envoy'. He had to keep one step ahead.

His actions now belied his lack of confidence. Sending for the authorities, he announced that he was now in charge of the mission and demanded a meeting with the relevant minister. He went through all Jukes's papers, made inventories and packed everything up as if nothing unusual had happened. He breakfasted with the minister and expressed his dissatisfaction with the lack of respect that had been shown to the late envoy. The minister heard him politely and promised a return visit.

Once more help appeared just when most needed, in the shape of Dr John MacNeill from Teheran, who had received James's message and ridden for nearly four days without stopping, arriving too late to save Jukes but in time to share the burden of responsibility. He and James liked one another instantly, and thus began a very long friendship. After a further meeting with the minister, James, with Black John, his *munshi* and one other trusted servant, set off for Teheran, leaving his other servants to follow with the baggage.

Crossing the valley of Kashan and skirting the Great Salt Desert, they glimpsed the far off Elburz Mountains and the golden dome of Qom glittering in the early sunshine. Here James was permitted to enter the inner sanctum of a holy shrine, the tomb of Fatima Masumeh, probably the first European to do so. His identity, however, was questioned and, one by one, the *mullahs* emerged suspiciously from the gloom holding their lanterns

14 1795–1883. Diplomat and surgeon. Born on the island of Colonsay, Argyll. 1820–35 attached to EIC legation in Teheran, at first in medical charge and latterly as political assistant to the envoy. 1836 Envoy and Minister-Plenipotentiary in Teheran. Knighted 1839.

high to examine his face. When their murmurings grew a little too loud for comfort James gathered up his sketching things and left. The *munshi* calmed the protesters, explaining with some truth that James was interested in the 'Mahometan faith'.

On the tract of salt desert between Qom and Teheran they rode into a storm and a piercing north wind that first soaked and then froze them through layers of clothing, in James's case a flannel waistcoat, a woollen waistcoat, a cloth jacket, a great coat and a cloak. They lost their way in the snowy darkness and wandered for hours, narrowly avoiding falling into steep gullies. Later, James heard that on that night a royal servant had been carried by his horse into a caravanserai, frozen to death in the saddle. Mr Willock met the weary little group on the outskirts of Teheran, and James sank with relief into the warmth and comfort of his hospitality and the welcome of a 'decent breakfast table'.

James spent a month in Teheran, visiting every Prince and anyone else in authority to find out as much as he could about relations between Persia, Turkey and Russia. The principal point of the alliance between Great Britain and Persia had been to baffle the schemes of France and Russia to invade India. Now that the French threat was over, British attention was turned to the ambitions of Russia. Eager to visit the hitherto unexplored area east of Mashhad, James set his sights on Bokhara and Samarkand. He had employed a new servant, more of a companion, one Mirza Abdul Reza, 'of some rank and very good character', who was admirably suited to the job, speaking Arabic, Turkish and Persian and being very fond of travel. The rest of the party included a horseman, a groom, a cook and Black John. On 19 December they left Teheran with James disguised, convincingly he hoped, as a Persian merchant. He carried as little baggage as possible – suitable merchandise, his astronomical instruments and a supply of medicines.

To start with, the servants kept giving away their master's true identity. Matters were further complicated by the interest evoked by his instruments and medicines. Wherever they stopped, the sick appeared, with ailments ranging from obesity through rheumatism and infertility to gunshot wounds. James resorted to common sense, homemade pills of bread flavoured with peppermint and advice about diet and physical exercise. One patient was so grateful that he reappeared with a chicken under his arm which duly provided James with a fresh egg for breakfast every day.

A vast desert lies between Teheran and Mashhad, roamed then by hordes of plundering horsemen from (modern day) Turkmenistan, rendering it far too dangerous to cross unescorted. At every town there was a frustrating delay while they waited for a caravan to assemble. If there was the slightest rumour of an attack ahead, the servants refused to move a step further until they were reassured that the way was safe again. Sometimes the leaders of caravans refused to take James and his party along, maintaining that this mysterious stranger would attract too much attention. The caravans tended to travel at night, allowing the camels to graze by day, and as they only moved at two and a half miles per hour it was a slow, frustrating business.

No one much was taken in by James's disguise and there were some unpleasant incidents of stone throwing and insults. On one occasion James was uncharacteristically provoked into a fight with a youth who had hurled abuse at him. Black John, hearing the fracas, rushed 'like a lion upon the assailant & beat him to the ground'.

On 21 January they reached Neyshabur, where James managed to fit in several sketches and a visit to the famous turquoise mines, described in detail in his journal. Then they rode through sleet and wind over the hills towards Mashhad and glimpsed 'the lofty gilded dome of the shrine ... glimmering dimly through the storm'.

James made a sketch of the 'magnificent cluster of domes and minarets' of the mausoleum of Imam Reza (see Plate XXVIII). He also managed, once again, to get permission to enter the Shrine. For two wonderful days he was allowed to sit high up under the arches and sketch unattended. When some boys, however, started stoning him and chanting, 'A Jew. A Christian!' the attendant came to his rescue just in time. He was advised by Mirza[15] Abdul Reza not to visit any other shrines.

He was interested in the different reactions of the *mullahs* to his presence. Some simply considered it unimportant, while others felt honoured by his interest in their religion and welcomed him as a brother. There were zealots who tested him on the more difficult tenets of their faith, and others who believed his story implicitly. Some, thinking he was a convert, questioned him in great detail about Christianity. Floundering for an explanation of the Trinity, he was interrupted by the Vizier, who helpfully described it as a cord made of three strands which, when twisted together, became one.

Having achieved his aim of seeing the holy shrine he was impatient to be off, but the usual delays and disappointments forced him to spend another frustrating month in Mashhad. With news of fighting on the borders of (modern day) Uzbekistan and Turkmenistan, on his projected route to Samarkand, it was essential to wait for returning caravans to report on the situation. He needed a written 'safe-conduct' from someone in authority, but although 'everything was promised' nothing materialised. He also needed an armed escort. The only person who could provide this was 'Killidge Khan', who had gone off north with several hundred horsemen to escort a caravan home and was likely to be away for some time.

People were losing interest in James. The hitherto useful Abdul Reza was becoming inefficient and vague. Two of the Mirzas who had supported him had left Mashhad. There were more spitting and stone-throwing incidents and even rumours of plots to stone him to death, poison him or sell him to the Turkomans. Worse still, James was running alarmingly short of money and was obliged to sell some of the precious artefacts he had so carefully collected. To add to his difficulties, the weather was terrible and, apart from a visit to the ruins of the ancient city of Tus, he was stuck alone in his lodging, 'brooding over reflections which were as gloomy as the weather'. He longed for someone trustworthy to talk to, but the very air seemed infected with deception. His servants were in a constant state of alarm and it was unlikely that any would agree to accompany him.

---

15 Title of respect placed before the name of a distinguished man and after the name of a prince.

Still hoping, however, that he might reach the 'furthest goal' of his wishes and see Bokhara and Samarkand, James wrote to William. Disappointed with Persia so far, he tried to dissuade William from going home that way. The country was 'a dreary waste of sand and rock' and there was hardly a trace of the ancient cities that he had hoped to see. William's 'Indian Persian' would be as useless to him as Latin in modern Italy. Hindi had served James well as far as Isfahan, but thereafter he had been forced 'to fight my way in Persian'. Black John, however, was doing his best:

> You would laugh to hear John at the Persian, he has no idea of grammar & the only part of any verb he knows is the imperative ... yet he manages to make himself understood & we get on very well. Love to Skinner & would I had his 10 yellow boys here.

It was now March 1822 and time was running out. The safest season to travel in these dangerous regions was winter. With the coming of spring the wandering tribes of the desert were once more on the prowl and James would be unwelcome in any caravan: an apparently rich European was a great attraction to marauding Turkomans.

At last, with great reluctance, James gave up his dream of seeing Samarkand and, much to the relief of his servants, set his face west again. His last day in Mashhad was spent ministering to patients queueing at his door for one final prescription of peppermint pills. On 11 March, with an armed escort and the necessary letters of introduction, he was on his way once more. The moment they rode through the gates of Mashhad and into open country his spirits rose. It was a beautiful, balmy spring day and there was evidence of new life and movement all around. The dry brown grass was softening into green, the birds were tumbling in the warm sunshine, early spring flowers were glowing among the stones and there were picturesque crowds of people moving their flocks and herds to higher pastures. After the lonely weeks of waiting in his dreary lodgings, he was glad to be on the move again.

Impatient to be off

In Scotland, Jane Anne was also enjoying the coming of spring. She and her family were now living at Moniack, still unlet while Culduthel had a tenant, and she was revelling in being back in her childhood home, 'in the loveliest April weather I can remember' although, as she told George:

> I feel myself quite a usurper in this place & more so every day when I see many things growing so lovely round me I have never mentioned to Mamma any of these feelings or ever spoke of the beauty of the place to her as it would only awaken regrets & painful remembrances ... I dreamt last night I saw my dear Mother again & cried for joy I soon woke & behold it was but a dream!!! But oh what wd I give for even *one* day spent with you all now.

It was convenient to have Nanny Rose's willing babysitting services; Affleck was often away on business and becoming increasingly prominent in local affairs, so the couple were more in demand socially. But Jane Anne was often content to let him go while she stayed at home with her children. The three-year-old Jane was her 'chief companion', already quite a conversationalist, while James was more forward for his age and 'holds a chat with me too after his fashion & really very intelligibly for not quite 2'. Edward was 'a merry little sprite ... the best child I have yet had'.

She had also had to supervise the cleaning of Culduthel between tenants. It 'was in such a mess of Filth *literally not to be spoken of or described* ... Dirt and nastiness of *all* kinds' that Affleck had decided not to risk another English tenant. 'I am really quite disheartened at seeing the new dirt that springs up daily under my eyes ... we have now been 4 days at it and it looks dirty yet'. Her next task was to rummage in the loft at Moniack, under Nanny Rose's eagle eye, to find towels and shirts for George to take to India. George, meanwhile, had asked her to send another flute but 'I grieve no say no such thing as a *Flute* could I find in any of the boxes I opened in the Loft'.

William Tytler was making interesting plans to take his whole family, except the baby, to live in the south of France at Pau,[16] where life was 'cheap in every respect except house rent which however is only the same as hereabouts'. Jane Anne was unsettled by this news, partly because she would miss them but mainly because 'I wish every day our Plans were settled a little'.

✻

At the end of March George left for London to seek a passage to India, armed with a Book of Instructions from his father and bundles of letters to dispatch. That evening, Jane went to bed early 'taking medicine & very unwell'. She felt unable to go out next day, but gradually the ceremonies and services of Holy Week diverted her. On 'Samedi 6' she was woken very early by the noise of the market carts in the street, 'a great inconvenience in this House'. At Moniack she had been used to waking to the sounds of birdsong and a household moving about its early morning tasks; now she woke to the rumble of vehicles on the cobbles and cheerful shouts between traders. On that Easter Saturday a short note arrived from George. He was safely in London, after a rough passage, but his 'plans for oeconomy' were already sadly awry. He had got through Customs safely with his gloves hidden in his hat but had had to pay duty on his new boots and shoes. On 14 April there was a longer letter, 'very overpowering indeed', requesting his parents' permission to embark for India immediately. His mother was distraught: 'Mr F perfectly calm while my agitations & misery were very great.'

Mr F replied the same day. He had never approved of the idea of George going to India at all, let alone as a soldier. However, as George had the support of Affleck, Jane Anne and William Tytler, not to mention Charles Grant, he felt outnumbered and had merely advised George to wait and consult James before making his final decision. Now he

16 City on the northern edge of the Pyrenees especially recommended for health owing to its altitude and popular with the Scots, who built the first Continental golf course there in 1856 (*The Smell of the Continent*, Mullen, Pan, 2009).

accepted the idea, but with reservations: 'How you are to be enabled to pay your passage, money and your equipment, I know not. This, however, I know, that I cannot contribute one shilling'.

George replied by return. He was hoping to get permission from the directors of the East India Company to embark on a ship bound for Bengal on 8 June. He would have felt happier and easier if he had his father's 'unqualified and unlimited approbation ... but go I must'. Affleck and his other friends had told him to get on with it:

> They saw me idle and getting on in years ... they saw a situation open for me, they knew that my inclination pointed that way – when I proposed the plan they approved of it and gave me their advice – that advice and my own inclination has most unhappily for all parties been at variance with yours.

But the moment he heard of a plan involving William or James in Britain in which he might join, or if his health failed, he promised he would board the next available ship and head for home.

Affleck added a postscript to one of Jane Anne's letters to George. He was investigating passages and George should return to St Omer and await word. 'It is not just impossible,' he added, 'that I may come for you & ask your Daddy & Mummy how they are for a day or so.' Jane Anne, knowing her husband well, begged her parents not to expect Affleck 'for fear you may be disappointed. I fear so much he may not make it out tho he would have all the will in the world.'

For the next six weeks tensions ran high in 101 Rue de Dunquerque. George was impatient to be off but dreading the parting; he was also well aware of his parents' feelings as the moment approached when they would be left alone in France.

In the middle of June things suddenly became clearer. George had definitely been accepted for a military posting and needed to be in London as soon as possible. He accordingly spent a few days going the rounds of his friends, while Jane packed his trunk in the thundery heat with a heavy heart and a bad cold. She confided the parting to her diary:

> George had gone down to his aunt's early in the evg to say Farewell ... I had then gone up to my own room & then he came to take leave of me ... which he did under much agitation – I was not so much overcome as I had dreaded tho in much anguish of heart – he then ran downstairs to take leave of his Father ... but did not stay a moment but rushed out of the house ... on coming in to his Father I found him much agitated & dreaded the consequence but in a moment perceiving George had left his Pocket Book his Father instantly snatched up his hat & went after him ... he thus saw George again but on returning – seeing also he had left his Gloves & Handkerchief he set out once more & just caught the Carriage ... that little incident was perhaps of use diverting for a moment the pang of parting.

The next day, the neighbours came round to offer comfort. Then the usual routine started again, but on 20 June the news arrived that Moniack was at last let for three years and that Affleck was in London. What was more, the sailing had been delayed and so, rather than waste time and money hanging around London, George was on his way back to St Omer bringing Affleck with him! He lost no time introducing Affleck to all his friends and favourite haunts and taking him to every party and cricket match, while his parents somehow got through the next few steamy days.

On Sunday, 30 June they had to endure parting all over again. All day long, friends called until …

> … Mr F Affleck George & myself remained alone – till 11 – when the Carriage drove up to the Door & in a few minutes George & Affleck drove off – this indeed our last parting with that Dear Boy! He was less overcome at this time than the former & I think so was I but his Father fully more! – soon after he went away Mr F & myself went upstairs & to bed about 12. God knows if we shall ever see him again!'

Dark days followed. For a week Jane had been suffering from a sprained ankle, for which Dassie prescribed leeches. A leech bite poisoned her ankle, which became badly inflamed, and Josephine had to carry her up and down stairs. Mr F, as dismissive of her ailments as ever, reckoned that it would probably be merely 'a temporary confinement' and took over George's room, where he buried himself in his letterbooks.

By 26 July news came that George was at last at Portsmouth and waiting on board the East Indiaman *Sir Edward Paget*. Mr F hastened to send him a last letter: everything depended on James; when he appeared a decision would be made whether they would stay in France or move to England. 'To Scotland I will not return. If I fix in France, it will not be here – I will assuredly join the Tytlers – & I hope Jane Anne & hers' All that had kept him in St Omer so far was 'pecuniary uncertainty'. A short preaching followed: 'Cultivate Temper as much as possible. I know no Shield of better proof – it wards off cutting weapons ... I know of no honest cover under which Reasons can so securely & effectually play, as Temper'.

George was finding it hard to cultivate temper. He had spent twelve hours on the coach to Portsmouth in constant fear of missing the ship, only to find that she had been delayed by strong winds on her voyage from Gravesend. On board he found a state of confusion and thirty-six passengers. 'Just conceive,' he told his father gloomily, '... the delightful state we shall be in with the thermometer 96, 36 passengers a hot dinner and not a breath of air.' His own cabin-mate, Hugh Fraser, was 'long thin and gentleman like ... 6'2" in height ... who I daresay will be an agreeable companion'. There were also nine ladies on board, most of them married and four on honeymoon.

He tried to be optimistic and was eager to get going, partly because he was already running out of money. But the wind was contrary and *Sir Edward Paget* did not weigh anchor until 8 August. That day Jane wrote in her diary, 'and now for 12 months Farewell to all hopes of hearing from him'.

12

1822–1823

RASHT: NARROW ESCAPE

In mid March James reached Quchan where he heard of the existence of some pages of a magnificent and enormous Qur'an[1]. He was astounded by what he found in the Imamzadeh, or Saint's Shrine – 'leaves [which] when opened out, measure from ten to twelve feet long, by seven or eight broad'. The vast letters of the majestic script were 'finely formed apparently with a single stroke of an immense pen' and the 'marginal and other ornaments are emblazoned in azure and gold'. This was one of the most breathtaking moments of his journey and he was certainly the first European to wonder at these tremendous pages.

On 15 April he got his first distant glimpse of the Caspian Sea. Approaching Gorgan, they rode over gentle hills, along winding paths, past streams, through woods of oak, beech, elm, alder and cherry, where cuckoos called and doves cooed, and over carpets of primroses, violets, lilies and hyacinths. It reminded James of home and was paradise compared to the terrain he had recently crossed.

Travelling along the great causeway of Shah Abbas,[2] however, they got the alarming news that Henry Willock, Dr MacNeill and every other Englishman at Teheran and Tabriz had unaccountably been sent home; there was nothing for it but to push doggedly on with 'a confident demeanour and inoffensive conduct'.

By mid-May they reached the Caspian and cantered along the beach, much to the alarm of their Arab horses, who had never seen the sea; they were equally spooked by the furious boiling of the formidable Safid Rud torrent, which roared down from the mountains, and by the boat they were expected to board – a rickety, flat-bottomed craft rowed by inexperienced locals; James covered the eyes of the horses and manoeuvred them, snorting, stamping and tossing, on to this 'frail and most awkward machine', which brought them, miraculously, safe to shore.

He did not plan to spend more than a day in Rasht, which they reached on 25 May, but torrential rain and a swollen river made his departure impossible. The next fine day was

1 This Qur'an, considered to be one of the earliest, was made for Timur (1336–1405) and probably intended for an enormous marble lectern of the same dimensions in Bibi-Khanym, his great Friday Mosque, in Samarkand. Local legend has it that the pages were removed from Timur's tomb by the soldiers of Nadir Shah (1688–1747) and that some were later collected and housed in Quchan. James's guess at the measurements appears somewhat overestimated.

2 1571–1629. 'Abbas the Great' rid Persia of Ottoman and Uzbek troops, created a standing army, made Isfahan his capital, fostered commerce and built the celebrated stone causeway along the swampy shores of the Caspian Sea.

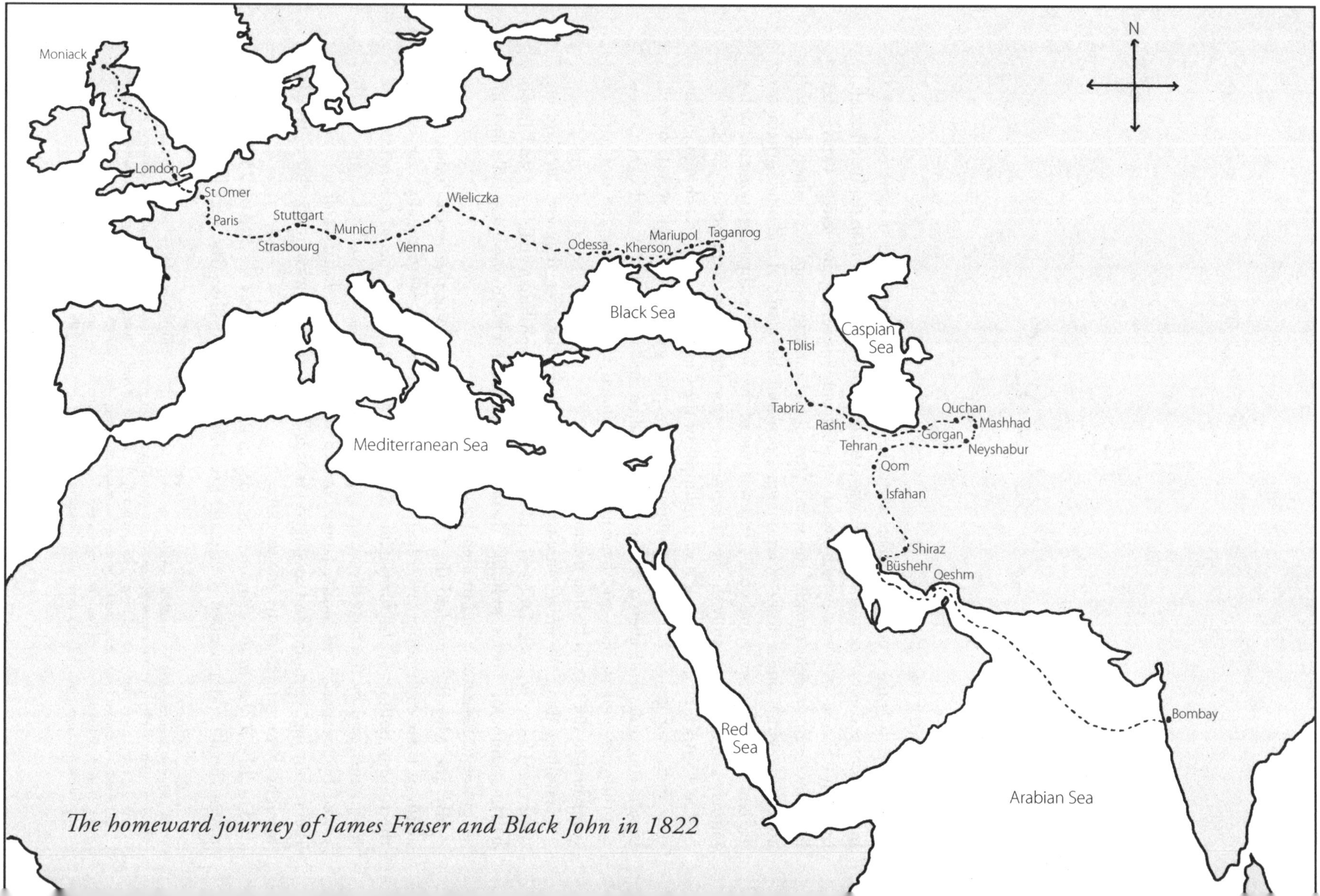

The homeward journey of James Fraser and Black John in 1822

Private collection

James's sketch No 71: '... the night bivouak on 13th May 1822', en route to Rasht.

a Monday, which some of the servants declared unlucky for a journey. By the end of the month, however, the rain had stopped and they were on their way again.

They were threading their way through the bazaar when a mud-bespattered rider galloped past them towards the Governor's palace; not long afterwards a messenger rode up: they were to proceed to the palace immediately. There they were informed of an order from Teheran that they were to delay their departure. Appalled, James remonstrated, but the minister was adamant. Apparently, a rumour was circulating in Teheran that a Russian envoy had arrived in Rasht, and the King, surprised that he had been told nothing of it, had summoned his son, Mahomed Reza Mirza, Governor of Rasht, for an explanation; the Prince had declared his ignorance of the matter and ordered the suspect to be detained until he returned to Rasht in two weeks.

James was furious: he could not be detained for a day, let alone two weeks, against his will; he was a British subject with passports from all the right people, a harmless traveller who had committed no fault in Persia. He rose to leave. The minister begged him to sit down and patiently explained that he had no choice. James lost his temper, declared, '*Khodah Hafiz*' ('May God protect you') and left the room; he got no further than his horse.

There was nothing for it but to submit to house arrest. His horses were removed but he was allowed to wander around the town and along the river, although he was constantly watched. A younger Prince, educated in England, sympathetically lent him his copies of Milton's poems and Pope's *Homer*, which he read from end to end, and he was also kept busy in his role as town quack: there was a daily queue at his door, and his peppermint pill stock fell dangerously low.

Most of the time he spent miserably tossing back and forth the possible reasons for his arrest: perhaps the King knew of his visit to the Shrine at Mashhad and his plans to go further east? Had the departure of Willock and MacNeill from Teheran got anything to do with it? Racking his brains for means of escape, and not knowing whom to trust, he sent Black John to try to retrieve two of his horses under the pretence of checking their condition. The guards, however, had been tipped off by an inside informer and had hidden the horses. Devastated to discover such betrayal among his servants, James was in despair.

At last he decided to escape on foot, taking with him Sayyid Ali, the one Persian servant he considered trustworthy. It was the festival of Ramadan when, at noon, everyone went to the mosque to pray for three hours. At midday he mingled with the crowds, sauntering along as though going for his usual walk along the river. He had given Black John a cover story with instructions to prepare dinner and keep the lights burning, as if expecting him home. He took with him his remaining medicines, his journal and sketchbook, pen and ink, a pistol and dagger, some money and the bread left over from breakfast. Passing the palace gates, the customs house and the police station unchecked, they reached the walls, then open country: 'I felt a sensation of security and joy when a turn in the road shut the town and its inhabitants out from our view.' They headed north in the general direction of Ardabil, about fifty miles away, on the western shore of the Caspian Sea.

They soon got lost. After three days of floundering in flooded rice fields, stumbling through tangled jungle, crossing and re-crossing torrential rivers, following vague directions from villagers and often finding themselves retracing their tracks, they struggled through a snowy mountain pass down to the village of Dees. Here they spent the night, hungry, wet and frozen, huddling together for warmth on the roof of an obliging muleteer.

Woken by voices, they found themselves surrounded by a group of rough-looking armed men jostling to arrest 'the Russian prisoner who has escaped'. These were wild Talish highlanders sent by their terrible chief, Mahomed Khan. James surrendered, well aware that they were just as ready to carry out the bloodthirsty orders of their master as the clansmen of any Highland chieftain.

Tying their captives' arms tightly behind them, the ruffians separated them, taking Sayyid Ali ahead and dragging James over the rough, stony ground; if he stumbled or fell he was punched and beaten. With difficulty they forded a river and then reached easier terrain, a lonely desert of sand dunes.

James prepared himself for death. He reasoned that if the authorities in Rasht had wanted him back they would have sent their own people to apprehend him; it was far more probable that they believed he had collected too much vital intelligence. The easiest way to rid themselves of the troublesome fellow was to have him executed in a faraway desert; no one would know what had happened to him and his remains would probably never be found.

Facing these uncomfortable facts, he was bundled behind a sand dune and robbed of all his possessions except his journal, sketchbook and papers. Attempts to reason with the ruffians only met with more blows, and he was thrown to the ground. One of them, drawing his knife, announced that he would cut off his head and leave it for the birds. James's thoughts 'glanced rapidly homewards, and to all I had left; and then ... to the awful presence I was about to enter'. The ruffian, enjoying his terror, shouted with laughter, sheathed his knife and resorted to more blows accompanied by oaths and insults. His colleagues joined in this entertainment, vying with each other for the coarsest language and doubling up with amusement at their own wit.

At length they caught up with Sayyid Ali and his guards. They were dragged through more wild mountain passes, across further torrential rivers, to the camp of the chief where a messenger from Rasht demanded James's immediate return. Bruised and battered, exhausted after three sleepless nights, they battled through wind and rain on the long road back to Rasht.

On the way, James learned what had happened the night he escaped: his absence had been noted and Black John had forgotten his cover story. The alarm was raised and the order sent out to recapture the fugitives. The search party, despite Black John's violent protestations, took James's fine Arab horses which, totally unused to the mountainous terrain, collapsed, leaving the searchers to continue on foot, eventually enlisting the help of the Talish highlanders to guide them through the maze of perilous mountain paths.

On 20 June the prisoners reached Rasht, where their bruised and bedraggled appearance aroused great interest and much sympathy, especially from James's erstwhile patients. 'Half the rabble' of Rasht accompanied him to the Vizier's house, where he was soundly upbraided for causing such trouble. The Prince was within a day's journey of Rasht, and if James had waited just a little longer, scolded the Vizier, he would have been allowed to continue on his way.

The Prince eventually rode into town three days later bringing with him Mirza Taqi, who had been on intimate terms with the English at Teheran. James told him the whole sorry tale and the Mirza asked the Prince for amends to be made. The Prince regretted the affair but James must forgive and forget as his province had been very unsettled in his absence; he promised to provide James with the letters necessary for him to resume his journey.

The following day, James was delighted to be reunited with his stolen possessions, albeit rather the worse for wear. At sunrise on 2 July 1822 he took his leave of Rasht and started on the road to Tabriz where, after encountering no more adventures than usual, he arrived on 12 July to a warm welcome from Henry Willock's brother, Captain George Willock.

❁

Sinking back once more into the comfortable company of English people, James spent six enjoyable and restorative weeks in Tabriz, the capital of Azerbaijan, then the most important province of Persia, and resumed his exploration of ancient sites.

Towards the end of July, cholera broke out in Tabriz and the panic-stricken inhabitants were encouraged to find temporary sanctuary in the country. Once again, James and the other English visitors were given accommodation in a garden outside the town. Having regretfully decided that it was impossible to take the direct route through Turkey on account of fighting between Persians and Turks, James set off north towards Teflis (Tbilisi) on 29 August. From there, he told William, he would make his way to France, where 'from some stray letters I have picked up I have some idea our folks may be'.

Distraction in St Omer

In France, Jane was facing up to another winter in St Omer, this time without George's company. She missed him 'every day & every hour', her ankle was still painful and her spirits low. When Mr F surprisingly announced that William Balcombe,[3] from St Helena, had come to live in St Omer her feelings were mixed: 'How many sensations does his very name call up to me & the memory of those who are gone.' But she cheered up when Mr Balcombe eventually visited and spent some time 'calling to mind every particular relative to our dear departed Boys Edward & Aleck'. The Balcombes were in St Omer apparently for health reasons and had brought with them their whole family, including their recently married younger daughter Betsy, formerly Napoleon's teasing playmate.[4] Her husband, Edward Abell, claimed to have known William in Nepal, another connection which made the family 'sacred and interesting to us'. Mrs Balcombe soon became firm friends with Jane, who often looked after the three young Balcombe boys when their mother was ill or their father away.

Meanwhile, Margaret Tytler sent Jane a glowing account of life in a sunny chateau just outside Pau. Although prices had recently risen, owing to the influx of English, everything was still far cheaper than in Scotland. Margaret was doubtful, however, whether Pau would suit Jane and Mr F: there was no English doctor nearer than Toulouse, the local French one being 'in no repute', and it was so far from London. As for Jane Anne and family, Margaret thought Pau would suit them apart from 'a want of sport of *every* kind – neither Shooting or Fishing ... Affleck would find the time hang heavy', while James, if he appeared in Pau, 'would soon be off again to explore the mountains.'.

⁂

On 6 September, William's thirty-ninth birthday, Jane wrote him a long, frustrated letter: Mr F kept assuring his sons that 'everything was pleasant & comfort with us' when, for her, things were far from being either pleasant or comfortable; they had no idea where William was and she was languishing 'day after day & month after month absent from Jane Anne, her interesting children & all that rendered life desirable'; her ankle had been painful for ten weeks and she could not take the walks which were her only enjoyment.

3 The background to the Balcombes' appearance in St Omer and the rest of their intriguing story appears in *The Emperor's Shadow: Bonaparte, Betsy and the Balcombes*, Anne Whitehead, Allen and Unwin, 2015.

4 The relationship between Napoleon and Betsy Balcombe is the subject of her memoir *To Befriend an Emperor*, Ravenhall Books, 2005.

September thus dragged by with the two of them 'silent & dull' or 'very low indeed', Jane resorting more and more to laudanum and Mr F writing and 'looking over his letter Bks'. October was shrouded in fog. The candles were lit by six and they had fires morning and evening. The few entries in Jane's diary were shakily written and related mostly to another new friend, Mrs Harrison, who was nearing the end of her tenth pregnancy. Towards the end of the month she was so unwell that a nurse was sent for and when Jane went to help she found Mrs Harrison in labour, which resulted in a stillborn son. She then sat up all night with her, the nurse having 'been taken with a Hysterical affliction & obliged to be put to Bed'.

Mr F dealt with the burial of the baby and Jane divided her time between her two friends, Mrs Polson, 'poorly & much agitated', and Mrs Harrison, who was hovering between life and death. She rarely got home before ten or eleven and often spent the night in Mrs Harrison's room, taking turns with the three Harrison daughters, Laura, Fanny and Maria, and Mrs Caillol, 'the Pastry Cook'. The five smaller children were looked after by neighbours. On 2 November, appropriately 'All Souls' Day' as Jane noted, their mother died.

The Frasers' maid, Josephine, was now called upon to help Jane perform 'the last Duties to this Lamented Mother & Wife', none of the daughters feeling able to cope. There followed 'a scene Mr Fraser said he never could forget': the doctor decreed that the body must be moved from the bed to a board on trestles; this proved something of a struggle with 'Laura supporting her beloved Mother's head & ... Maria & Fanny with myself & one of the women the Body'.

Mr F was chief mourner and 'never was a Funeral more numerously ... attended'. Afterwards, the Harrison family returned to Tunbridge Wells where, they assured Jane and Mr F, there would always be a welcome for them.

Diversion in Vienna

Late at night, on the last day of August, James and his escort glimpsed the Armenian Highlands, 'which terminated in [Mt] Ararat ... we now neared him and could see him by the light of a brilliant, almost full, moon becoming more and more distinct'. The next day, he sketched the snow-capped mountain in the glories of the sunrise. They rode on through villages which reminded him of the worst hamlets in the Highlands; there was an abundance of good-looking girls, but ...

> ... they have the same fault I find with all Persian women – they have no bosoms – they have either hanging leather bottles or nothing but a nipple ... no fine form or fullness which constitutes the beauty of a fine bosom.

On 4 September they reached a Russian outpost: they were now in Georgia. Suddenly there was a European air about everything: smart soldiers in grey greatcoats and small caps 'stepping about', horse-drawn carts and farming activities going on 'with rapidity & perseverance'. James felt a great sense of security – 'Now [I] have done with Persia, please heaven'. At last he was in a region where 'Europeans & Christians were at least the ascending powers'. In Tbilisi the kindly Colonel Wright and several Generals offered him hospitality.

It was just over twenty years since Russia had annexed Georgia; Tbilisi now boasted fine public offices, new caravanserais and bazaars and a spacious public square, although the interiors of the buildings were disappointingly plain and functional. The population was fast increasing, trade was reviving and the city was becoming something of a resort.

After the dull streets of Persian towns, James was enchanted to see women mixing happily with men in public, 'letting a fine shape & a beautiful complexion ... appear'; what a contrast with Yerevan, the last Persian town he had visited, where women were only spotted 'flitting around in sheets'. There everything was stationary, here all was improvement & rapid advance. He was greatly heartened and unpacked his sketchbook.

There was the usual delay in leaving – the Russian working day finished at noon, and on the next day, the Tsar's birthday, nothing could be done. James passed the time happily sketching views of the town and its significant buildings, gathering information about the army and admiring the women.

Russian soldiers were paid a quarter of an English soldier's wages but each was provided with good clothes, food and three days a week 'to work for himself'; everything was done by soldiers, from building and constructing furniture to shoemaking. Although there was stll a regrettable lack of 'firm bosoms', the women were statuesque, with beautiful, fair, natural complexions, regular features, large noses, well formed mouths with coral-red lips, large deep-set black eyes and exquisitely arched eyebrows.

At last the luggage was loaded, papers checked and a guide found. James took leave of his new friends, 'tenderly kissing & embracing after the Russian fashion'. They were loaded with bread and pies 'enough for a whole army' and were off by 5.00 am, heading due north for the majestic cliffs and spires of the Caucasus Mountains.

Taganrog, a busy port on the north shore of the Sea of Azov and later the birthplace of Anton Chekhov,[5] was full of English traders, one of whom brought James news of home: Walter Scott was apparently to be ennobled 'by the title of Lord Abbotsford', which was inaccurate, and Castlereagh had committed suicide, which was true. From Taganrog James moved west to Mariupol, thence across the plain to Kherson and round the tip of the Black Sea to Odessa,[6] a city packed with merchants from all over the world.

Here the Consul took him to see *The Barber of Seville*. Feeling himself now well and truly in Europe, he was astounded to find that Vienna was still 1,300 miles away. Hurrying on through Ukraine and into Poland, James noted the contrast with Russia: here everything was 'neatness and comfort' and Polish women were very enticing, with strong healthy faces and colourful handkerchiefs wound round their heads and adorned with flowers.

In mid-November, having bypassed Krakow, they stopped at Wieliczka, where a French-speaking gentleman offered to show them the famous salt mines,[7] and they descended, at James's guess, about 500ft down a wooden staircase. Nervously asking how often it was

5 1860–1904. Russian dramatist.

6 A relatively new city founded by Catherine the Great in 1794 and the fourth largest in imperial Russia.

7 Worked until 2007, 190 miles long, 1,073 ft deep and known as 'The Underground Salt Cathedral of Poland'. The chapel is said to have the best acoustics in Europe. Now a UNESCO World Heritage Site.

replaced, he was told that it would last forever, being impregnated with salt which rendered it incorruptible. For an hour they wandered through passages, chambers and galleries cut out of the solid salt. The highlight of the visit was the chapel with its salt sculptures – 'saints & crucifixes without end ... many of the figures really wonderful ... the whole put me in mind of some of the Indian caves'. He discovered that the workmen were paid well, had good working conditions and that it was considered a privilege to be a miner.

With his interest in gemstones, James was disappointed by the grey drabness of the salt, which he had expected to sparkle and glow. He was amazed that the roofs of the vast chambers supported 'the immense superstructure of the earth' without falling in. Everywhere there were ancient carvings: 'when the Emperor Alexander passed this way they cut his name & titles on a slab in one of the passages where it will probably remain as long as the mines or the world'.

They left as the sun was lighting the snow on the Carpathian tops to the south. Things were improving every day: now there was always good coffee and a soft feather bed; the architecture of the towns, each with its central square and well, was pleasingly influenced by Spain and Portugal. The women were attractive, dressed in red stockings, buckled shoes, skirts with blue and red borders and short jackets; the men wore red waistcoats and large-brimmed hats decorated with flowers on Sundays. Well wooded hills, hedgerows and copses, snug white villages, each with their church spire – all gave an air of population and prosperity.

On 16 November, cresting the brow of a hill, they could just make out the enticing spires of Vienna; there they were delayed for seven weeks while James waited for money to be credited to his account.

✽

That winter Vienna was alight with gaiety and James was captivated; everyone who was anyone in Austria and beyond was there: Princes and Princesses, Counts and Countesses, Barons and Baronesses appeared round every corner and, along with numerous English people, filled the theatres, the opera, balls and parties; it suited James perfectly.

The first night, having delivered his despatches, he went to a ballet of *Hamlet*, which turned out to be a sort of pantomime; he especially enjoyed the moment when the ghost of Hamlet's father descended from the clouds but disapproved of 'the style in which the women lifted their legs on a level with the horizon'. With a production of *King Lear* a week later he 'had never been more gratified in my life': the scene where Lear kneels to Cordelia and begs her forgiveness 'was too much to bear ... all the house was in a ferment ... I never saw anything so feeling & forcible – not even Mrs Siddons'.[8]

News soon got around of his arrival, and there were pressing invitations to bring his portfolio to parties. At one such occasion – 'a truly alarming assemblage of ladies & gentlemen including Princes & Princesses, Counts & Countesses' – there was 'such a talking and babbling' while he attempted to explain his paintings that he had to shout. He was 'most perfectly tired of it' pretty soon. Some of the ladies were vulgar and noisy,

8 Sarah Siddons (1755–1831), the best-known tragedienne of the period.

including a Polish Princess who climbed on chairs to see better and waved her arms around – a mixture of ploughman and Wapping landlady, James reckoned.

The Emperor's brother, the Archduke Maximilian, also demanded to see James's sketchbook (see Plates XXVI, XXVII, XXVIII). His thrifty Royal Highness kept his rooms at a low temperature and, while he examined every sketch 'very minutely almost with the eye of a connoisseur', James shivered, longing for the end of this flattering but freezing engagement.

On Christmas Day, at midnight mass in St Stephen's Cathedral, he mingled with 'all that was noble and respectable of Vienna ... there was nothing but stars, ribbons & orders, Princes, Counts and Nobles' with a large sprinkling of Esterhazys and Lichtensteins.

Two days later, James was in particularly high spirits: the young Russian Countess Ivanowska had asked to see his pictures.

> I found her just got out of bed and she received me in tying the strings of her gown yet very kindly & frankly. She is a charming woman with a degree of witchery in her smile which I have seldom met with, speaks enough of English to be extremely interesting. She is separated from her husband who is a Pole I believe.

Still glowing after this delightful morning, he was brought down to earth by an unusually stern letter from Jane Anne:

> I know my Father so well that I fear he has not pressed your return ... I therefore write in Affleck's name as well as my own, to conjure you, my dear Brother, as soon as you receive this *to lose not one hour* in setting off for home ... [take] the shortest route you can ... to St. Omer & do not remain even *there* after seeing our dear Father & Mother for it is <u>here</u> at Culduthell that you are so urgently wanted. Both Father & Mother are well but you must of course look for a great change in their appearance & you will be shocked at the first look of Papa. We have all undergone great anxiety of late but I hope your presence will make all right. Affleck and I too are well and our dear children, *Jane*, *James* & *Edward*, but you will find in me an elderly staid matron instead of the girl you left 10 years ago.

Disappointed that he would have to forego a glimpse of Italy, James started to prepare to leave. First, however, there was an engagement at Countess Valentine Esterhazy's, a very pleasant evening with much singing and many pretty Polish and French dances 'as well as the waltz in which my little favourite Madame Ivanoska distinguished herself'. The following evening, at a recital of Lord Byron's poetry, there she was again: 'the little Countess has a most flexible sweet ... voice and her delightful manners would go far to turn a man's brain – it is well to fly her'. The next day he called on her in bed, and the following day she interrupted his packing on the pretext of showing his pictures to a friend: 'the little lady was as fascinating as ever'. New Year's Day 1823 brought a party consisting of games with forfeits 'in which the little Countess was the life of the party and much amusement was produced in redeeming the forfeits'.

On 2 January he made a determined attempt to get going. In return for taking despatches to Paris he obtained a Courier Pass 'which will expedite my journey much & save me something in turnpikes'. That evening, however, the bewitching Countess persuaded him to read her 'The Prisoner of Chillon'[9] in French, a tall order 'but I got through it assisted by her vivacity'. The following morning, he made a valiant effort to take leave of her but she poured out the story of her unhappy marriage: her husband had rendered her so miserable that her friends advised her to leave him: 'she had suffered much, so much that a calm relief from suffering was all she wished & hoped for as her prospects in life were all faded'. He concluded:

> The little Countess is something of a coquette but still has an openness & naivete quite charming – I took leave of her kindly & with all good wishes for her future happiness & some wish to see her more in future.

With that, he trusted, satisfactorily concluded, he had dinner with the French Ambassador, enjoyed one final evening at the Opera in the Rothschild box and went to collect the precious dispatches; but they were still not ready for him. This further delay was extremely annoying, 'but I always find something to do'.

The next day indeed there was something to do: a message arrived from the little Countess demanding to see him before he left. 'She received me with great joy and we commenced an animated but very strange conversation ... I declare I did not give the tone to this, it seemed her own curiosity alone'. The conversation moved from his travels to the different moral codes relating to the sexes in various countries and 'the innate feelings of right & wrong on which we are supposed to act – in short it became a sort of half physical, half I don't know what, sort of a dialogue'. She then asked to whom James meant to dedicate his works 'and after a variety of little blushings and circumlocutions it came out that ... she wishes me to dedicate it *to her*'.

Taken aback, James hedged: although extremely flattered, he had to consult his parents and his friends; he assured her, however, that 'if her name was not there that of no other woman should be'.

> She took the half denial graciously enough & after much more of the same I took my leave, kissed her hand (I believe I might have kissed her lips) & departed ... I think that what with her own natural warmth & tendresse and flattering her weakness anything might have been done with her but this was not for me for many reasons – had I remained at Vienna I know not what follies I might have been tempted to commit.

The despatches were at last ready and, with mixed feelings, he bade 'adieu to Vienna & all its allurements' and set off into the darkness of a bitterly cold evening, 6 Jan 1823.

Munich, Ulm, Stuttgart, Karlsruhe, Strasbourg – all flashed by in a flurry of snow, and there was little sleep on the way for James and Black John in their crowded carriage; then

9 A 392-line narrative poem written in 1816 by Byron.

through deep snowdrifts past Luneville and Chalons-sur-Marne and on towards Paris, 'the postilions ... drove absolutely like mad people almost at the gallop which on a good road would have been delightful'.

Home

In St Omer it was colder than ever and there was a fire in the bedroom for the first time. Mr F was gloomily certain that if he was to live much longer he needed a warmer climate. They were convinced that something must have happened to James but had been cheered by two unexpected letters from George at the Cape, in good health and spirits. Mr F had found a new book, 'a Voice from St Helena by O'Meara',[10] in which he buried himself, intrigued by the references to the Balcombes.

On 13 January everything changed: James was in Vienna and could be with them in a week to ten days. Jane could settle to nothing but once more took the letter on the rounds of her friends. The next day, she started packing.

James and Black John arrived in Paris on 14 January and made straight for the Embassy, where James delivered his despatches. His father had sent word that Annie Tytler was in Paris and that James should bring her to St Omer; the first hotel James tried provided him with a small, freezing room but, no matter, by lucky chance Annie had already booked in:

> She did not know me until I spoke but when I went up & addressed her she came forward & embraced me – it was a joyful recognition ... she is certainly far older looking – the crowsfoots are making sad havoc in her countenance but I should I think have known her.

Thankful that James was so near, Jane nevertheless suspected that there still might be some hitch in her plan to accompany him across the Channel. Indeed there was: a letter made it perfectly plain that he was not going to take his parents home; they were to stay 'quietly at St Omer' until he returned from Scotland. His strongminded mother then produced another idea to which Mr F reluctantly agreed: they would accompany James at least as far as Tunbridge Wells to join the Harrisons; she still had to persuade James, however, and spent the next few days in a state of agitation, unable to rest, expecting him every night.

There was little in James's journal now but hurried scribbles: he discovered a coach that went every other day to St Omer, but there was still time to meet the Persian Envoy, see the contemporary paintings at the Luxembourg Palace and fit in a second visit to the Louvre before boarding the coach with Annie on 24 January, another very cold night with a bitter wind. They rattled on their way, squashed uncomfortably among people 'of great dimentions' and unable to see through the windows, arriving in St Omer early on Sunday, 26 January.

'Early in the morning James arrived'. That was all. After the long months of waiting, after the switchback of hopes and disappointments, Jane was unable to confide more than that to

---

10 *Napoleon in Exile; or A Voice from St Helena* (1822) by Barry Edward O'Meara, Napoleon's physician on St Helena.

her diary. James, however, described the meeting in detail: his parents had been sitting up all night '& received me in their arms as I entered': he was horrified by his father's condition, toothless, shrunk and pale; his mother he found little changed.

They talked all day; he soon heard the plan to accompany him to England, and reckoned that there was nothing for it but to acquiesce. The moment eventually came for the inevitable discussion of his father's finances: James was astounded to hear that the debt was in still in excess of £30,000:

> This strikes cold on me & proves in a miserable way the mismanagement that has taken place in the affairs ... all that I can command to meet this is almost nothing! And what is to be done I really cannot yet determine.

That first night he was unable to sleep.

❧

Three days later, having made all their farewells, with just Caroline to wave them off, to Jane's considerable relief, they were away:

> Thus did we take our leave of St Omer after 18 months stay dreary & uncomfortable to me from a thousand circumstances & from which I considered it a relief as from a Prison to be released.

In Dover James took charge: having 'stowed the party' he went through customs, where his argument that all his treasures were imported for scientific purposes worked wonders; only his books, paints and a few prints were taxed, and a picture 'of the Pretender as a child' was confiscated. The warmth and good cheer of the Union Hotel soon restored them all and, on the last day of January, Jane 'went early to a Comfortable Bed ... rejoicing to sleep on English Land!'

The confiscated picture belonged to George. Various details such as the *Cordon Bleu* and the King Charles spaniel were considered proof that it portrayed Bonnie Prince Charlie as an infant. It had originally hung in the English College in St Omer where, according to Mr F, 'some furious Whig had thrust through the Child's Heart', damage later repaired. During the Revolution it was acquired 'by an old Gentleman of eccentric modes of life' who collected flowers and paintings. When George admired the picture, he presented it to him.

For the journey home Mr F rolled it round his umbrella, ostensibly 'to keep it from cracking the varnish', but an eagle-eyed Excise Officer spotted it. Mr F thought it should be given to the King, since he had heard that His Majesty collected 'reliques of that Family'. 'On no account,' he told James, 'could we afford to pay the Duties – they would be too high for us'.

Leaving the Pretender to his fate, the parents set off for Tunbridge Wells where, after a joyful reunion with the Harrisons, they rented a cottage for three months. Meanwhile, James, Annie and Black John arrived in London, where James booked rooms for himself and Black John at the Tavistock Hotel. Next day, he called on Aeneas Mackintosh to discuss his father's affairs. Aeneas advised him not to entangle himself in them in any way but to let things take their course; James had certainly not got enough money to make any difference. After a week of looking up old friends and going to as many art exhibitions as he could, he set off for the north.

⁂

The old couple stayed near Tunbridge Wells until the middle of May. There was a general feeling of anti-climax and life fell into its former routine: Mr F went out after breakfast each day in search of letters and then to the Reading Room, while Jane visited the Harrisons and their friends. In mid-March she sprained her ankle again and was confined to the house; all the old anxiety returned and she resorted to laudanum. She was further cast down when the Harrisons moved to Brighton.

Mr F, as ever, was copying and writing letters. On 2 April 1823 he wrote to William: his mother's ankle was 'vexatious and has been painful – it is however doing perfectly well'. He himself was looking forward to permanent residence somewhere in the south of England, where he would 'hope to occupy myself in some degree usefully in James's literary pursuits ... I require nothing but quiet and warmth ... my own family is all in all whether present or absent – my pen and my Books my recreation'.

He was optimistic about Britain in general. With manufacturing on the rise and 'the consumer growing opulent again', he hoped that 'demand upon the production of the agriculturalists' would return. 'Farmers therefore will be enabled to pay labourers – and the consumption thereby also increase – rents can be paid – and Landlords again do well.'

⁂

James having reached Moniack at last, was far from optimistic. He had had a terrible journey: at Newcastle he found that the road was blocked by snow 'as high as the top of the carriage' and the snow-clearing teams were on strike. As usual, he made the best of things, booking a room, getting *Kenilworth*[11] out of the library and settling himself comfortably by the fire until it was time to go the theatre to see *King John.* The next day, he wrote to Jeanie Tytler and explored the town, but heavy snow soon drove him back to his book. The following day was no better: the Duke of Northumberland had provided 200 men to clear the road, but they had managed less than a mile. He decided to take the Carlisle route to Edinburgh, in a coach that jolted and shook its way through the night, until the sight of Arthur's Seat by starlight raised his spirits. At last he was home in a '*pays de connaissance*'. With great relief he booked into the Black Bull on Leith Walk.

Early next morning, he made his way to 108 Princes Street, where everyone was in still in bed; he wandered through the well remembered rooms, noting with satisfaction that nothing had changed. Jeanie was first to come down, and 'the meeting I need not describe'; she was soon followed by Aunt Woodhouselee and Isabella. His aunt seemed little changed,

11 Historical novel by Walter Scott published in 1821.

but the appearance of the girls was worrying: Jeanie was pale and thin – her 'fine skin has felt the effects of time & anxiety'. Isabella was a shadow and very haggard. Affleck, visiting his old mother in Edinburgh, James Tytler and Elizabeth, Sandie's widow, completed the party. It was a sweet but sad meeting: two principal players from past scenes were absent, and 'the past cannot be forgotten and the future promises not much'.

He had an excellent excuse to stay for a couple of weeks: William Tytler, whom he was anxious to see, was not due in Edinburgh till early March. James spent time catching up with friends, sightseeing, painting a picture for Jeanie, attending the brilliant sermons of Mr Allison and enjoying to the full the company of a family so close to his heart:

> Why should it be denied to me to pass my day thus with those I perhaps love best in the world; certainly the calm enjoyment of this would be preferable to the more fevered pleasure attending on large societies & greater fortunes, or even than the success of a struggle like that in which I am about to engage for an Estate which is already more than lost.

Much as he would have liked to, he could not wholly turn his back on his father's debts; so much was owed to friends and relatives 'who have so disinterestedly united to keep him above water', confident that the sons in India would, sooner or later, repay them. 'Thus are the miserable effects of the Parent's mistakes and imprudence entailed inevitably on his children'. One thing was painfully clear: he could not possibly consider marriage. 'How can I expect that any woman will attach herself to me on the apparently hopeless state of my affairs?' What would anyone see in him except 'the disqualifying properties of Poverty and the want of youth'? And yet:

> The nature of my connexion with - - - - - - - is very extraordinary – there is a tenderness ... and an exclusive sort of attachment which seems to be all that can be wanting between two persons of opposite sexes to form the closest tye.

But perhaps it was too late:

> I know too much of the effect of these late marriages to enter on the misery that attends them – continual illness perhaps Death from change of constitution at too late a period – a miserable prospect – and yet so much congeniality of mind is hardly to be looked for again and a disposition to overlook so much of disqualification in favour of the good, real or supposed, which I may possess.

Perhaps Jeanie's tenderness towards him was simply because she knew their relationship could go no further. Thus he argued with himself, back and forth, until at last he assured his journal that he was doing the right thing 'in not seeking or proposing the connexion'.

On his last day in Edinburgh he was invited to the Royal Society[12] to be introduced to Sir Walter Scott and other eminences of the literary world. He and Affleck then set off for the north. They arrived at Culduthel two days later in the evening; Jane Anne, who was expecting her fifth child in August, had been waiting up for them but had fallen asleep on the sofa and awoke in a daze of bewilderment. Apart from being slightly larger she had not changed: 'the face was quite the same with beauties & defects & the heart evidently as warm as ever'. She was also just as untidy: 'The room was in no great order – things lay scattered here & there on chairs & on the floor.'

> This meeting is the only one I looked forward to with *almost* unmixed pleasure & it has not disappointed me ... *almost* unmixed happiness I said for there is a selfish feeling of pain in the being deprived of the first right to her love and society by the right of a husband ... yet ... Affleck is most perfectly good & kind to her & is ... far from fettering or constraining her.

Then he was taken up to the nursery, where Nanny Rose still reigned, to meet his niece and nephews.

They took a postchaise to Moniack the next day. Nearing the entrance, James was impressed by the attractive new bridge that Telford had thrown over the burn where the ford had been; they left the chaise there and walked up to the house:

> No-one welcomed us. The farmyard and all about was as desolate as a deserted city – there were the marks of solitaryness though not of decay ... there is an old woman living in one of the outhouses to air it, and keep it clean – all the rest is deserted.

There was no time to explore every corner and it was no use recalling the former life of the place, the 'gorgeous noise of infancy and the kindly feelings of parental love' and the glow of hospitality he remembered so well.

In the garden all the fruit trees, including the old cherry trees, and vegetable plots had vanished. The cedars and laurels were 'venerable with age', imbuing him with a sense of decay and time passed. He was glad to see that his father's new garden and orchard were in good order, although the deer were gone from the park in front of the house.

> I may say that a visit of more unmixed pain I have not paid for long. All, though not in dilapidation, bears marks of the want of a master – the woods are thinned & the planting which my father delighted in is much destroyed – I miss many old friends.

At Noble's house they found the old man in the act of making himself decent 'for the Laird's son'. After this distressing meeting they climbed up to the the loft, where the various packages from India had been deposited. They spent the rest of the day sorting them all and then went with relief to Achnagairn for the night.

With advice from all sides on his father's affairs, James made a list: Aeneas Mackintosh told him to steer clear of his father's entanglement; the Tytler brothers reckoned that the

12 Scotland's National Academy of Science and Letters.

estate was a lost concern and should be given to the creditors unless William, who was now in a good situation in India, chose to come to the rescue; Affleck agreed that James should let it be known that his father's debts were not his concern. Perhaps William could be persuaded to buy the estate, or at least repay Affleck and the Tytlers and then contribute £2,000 annually. All were agreed that Dunchea should be sold as soon as possible, although getting the necessary permission and signatures from William would be a hurdle. For the moment, Affleck would stay in charge of Moniack while James was to write to William and find a job in London.

On the way back to London James and Black John stayed again in Edinburgh, where there was an expedition to Mount Eske with Jeanie; it was a beautiful day, clouded only by the knowledge of the parting to come:

> That feeling is dayly more painful to me – it is distressing that we cannot live in the society we love ... but I must let matters take the course Providence shapes out for them & not speculate idly on the future.

From Mount Eske they went to Mavisbank,[13] where he and Jeanie sowed seeds of mignonette. 'The drive was charming & I shall probably remember it always'. It was time to work out what his feelings for Jeanie really meant: 'The beauty once there has fled & withered', but it was the beauty of her mind that counted and he could not imagine any woman who would make him happier. But did the obstacles outweigh the advantages?

How could he marry in such a state of uncertainty about his future? How could he be sure of offering an appropriate home to a wife? How could Jeanie possibly leave her family, especially her widowed mother and the fragile Isabella? What were the chances of a woman of her age (thirty-seven) dying, or becoming an invalid, through childbirth? Last but not least, his parents disapproved of the match, and 'I could not bear to give them uneasiness tho it certainly is my affair not theirs'.

There were compelling advantages, however: Jeanie's 'strength of mind, tenderness & delicacy of feeling, soundness of judgement & general accomplishment' were such that, at his age, he would never find them in any other woman. When his mother was no longer there, Jeanie would ably step into her shoes as the pivot of the family. If he did not marry her he would probably remain single. He at last concluded: 'at present I can do nothing ... I resolve then to leave matters to their Fate – let Providence decide what is to be best for us'.

After a night of tossing and turning it was time for a last embrace, and he hurried away:

> ... from the bright drawing room to the cheerless dark coach, from the kindly looks of friends to the coarse jests and rude tongues of coachmen & grooms ... hurrying away from those I loved best.

13 Designed by William Adam and built 1723–7. One of Scotland's most important country houses, but suffered neglect in the twentieth century, its interior gutted by fire in 1973

Things were not improved by his travelling companion – 'the most disagreeable man I was ever was in a coach with 'who hawked and spat ... not *out* but inside the carriage'. He then began to eat oranges and biscuits, which 'he spit & spattered about the carriage [to] the annoyance of my cloaths', and refused to have the window open. James, hot and depressed, with his feelings in total disarray, got no sleep. A night spent at York was no better, but when his companion disappeared in search of a shave and missed the coach, his spirits rose. In vain. A mile or two down the road, 'the gaunt figure appeared by the wayside' and stopped the coach.

At last this difficult traveller departed, to be replaced, most serendipitously, by Mr Arbuthnot, a customs official, to whom James related the story of the picture of the Pretender confiscated at Dover. If he called at 12 Downing Street, Mr Arbuthnot would see what he could do. Despite having allegedly been 'rolled round a Parasol ... apparently for the purpose of deception', the picture was restored to James a few weeks later.

Househunting

After two weeks of tramping the streets of London, James had found suitable lodgings in Argyle Street, 'on pretty moderate terms in a decent reputable street'. Later that month, he nervously opened a letter from Jeanie:

> Indeed I could not write to you at first ... the divested Library, even the very drawing room was wretched! People came out & in and I cared not, the door bell rang but it could not be you!

Her letter was full of ifs and buts, whys and wherefores and contradictions; maybe she was worried, with good reason, that he would find it impossible to settle down; maybe she was afraid of yet another disappointment. The letter rambles on until she eventually returns to the matter in hand and demands to know where they stand. James was in a panic:

> ... What can I reply but that I never intended it should lead so far as it has and now that it has gone on I can only let matters take their course ... God knows I should be happier always with her if the thing were advisable & possible.

All the obstacles were still there, and he had no idea how to answer her.

*

Deciding that the London area could provide as good a home for his parents as any, he again immersed himself in house-hunting, while debating his answer to Jeanie. He was also meeting as many painters as possible, including Samuel March-Phillips,[14] husband of William's old heartthrob, Charemile Grant; at their house he met the eminent Wilkie[15] and admired his famous but uncompleted picture of John Knox preaching.

14 (1780–1862), legal writer and civil servant. James was perhaps expecting to meet Thomas Phillips (1770–1845), a noted portrait painter.

15 Sir David Wilkie (1785–1841), Scottish painter of genre, historical subjects and portraits. Painter in ordinary to George IV. Knighted 1836. The unfinished picture, 'Preaching of Knox before the Lords of the Congregation', was begun in 1823.

He also had an introduction to 'the great Turner' at his house in St Anne's Street, off Cavendish Square. After the initial embarrassment of mistaking the painter for a servant, he asked if he could see his new gallery. Not surprisingly, because it was still unfinished, it was with 'with some grumbling and difficulty' that Turner agreed:

> We talked the bear however into something like good humour and on the whole I hope made ourselves agreeable. I would wish to cultivate the acquaintance, however rude & bearish, on account of the talents. Turner is a most poor looking mean creature very little & ugly & certainly as far from the appearance of a man of Genius as well can be imagined.

James saw, among others, *The Destruction and Building of Carthage*, *The Passage of Hannibal over the Alps* and Turner's picture of Richmond but, disappointingly, no watercolours.

Around this time he wrote to a friend in Vienna, asking for news; it was not until October that the reply came: the town was dull and empty after the season and 'I am not acquainted with the Countess Ivanowska of whom you enquire'.

❊

James considered 13 Edwardes Square, 'warm, dry, airy, near Gardens, & field', in the village of Kensington, perfect for his parents. It had two rooms on each floor and would be ready in mid-May; once again,the old couple set about packing, leaving Tunbridge Wells with considerable regret 'after a three months stay on Mount Ephraim in our opinion the pleasantest spot there & the country now with great beauty'.

After saying goodbye to yet another group of friends, they set off for Kensington via several 'Beautiful Gentlemen's Seats' and along roads 'like a Gravel walk' with little of the usual dust. Nearing London, they were struck by how 'the Buildings rose so incessant that it appears one incessant street' and they were quite bewildered by the continual procession of villages. They finally arrived at their destination on the evening of 17 May and Jane found their new lodgings 'most agreeable & commodious':

> Oh what a change from the two last dull listless summers in St Omer where the sight of a shady walk (the ramparts excepted) never greeted our eye but the tall grey house on the opposite side of the way was all we had to contemplate – where the noise of the carts on the market days was straining our ears ... since we must not return to our own dear house I really do not know where we could be more pleasantly situated.

For Mr F it was going to take time to find 'the true points of the Compass of this place'. He 'felt as if dropped from the clouds knowing not a creature & bewildered among new & magnificent buildings trying to recognise that London which he had formerly been acquainted with'.

James was now only a few miles away and his father wasted no time in hunting down his lodgings. He walked what turned out to be four miles, through Kensington, Hyde Park and Piccadilly to Argyle Street, where he found James painting. Jane was looking forward to many such expeditions but she slipped and again hurt an ankle. Mr F was unsympathetic, merely irritated by her carelessness, and she lay on the sofa frustrated by this further hindrance to her pleasure.

Life in the elegant house in Edwardes Square gradually fell into a familiar pattern: Mr F was often out immediately after breakfast, sometimes walking until early afternoon; Jane, left alone, resumed her letter writing, walked in the Square Gardens, ankle permitting, and hoped that someone would call. It was difficult to get hold of books, but Mr Coxedge, the young owner of No 13, invited them to his house, showed them his prize tulips and told them they could borrow any of his books. Jane chose *The Life of Mahomet*, 'an oldfashioned book but one that I had often wished to see'.

They found themselves a church, St Mary Abbots, 'handsome tho plain & seemingly a very respectable congregation'. The first day, they heard a thirty-minute sermon upon 'the Christian Faith – Doctrine & Practice'. The organist performed to Jane's satisfaction and she came away happy to be once more a member of a congregation.

Mr F took to long walks in search of his past: he visited the 'noble College' at Chelsea,[16] where he met a veteran from the War of American Independence; they spent a happy afternoon exchanging recollections. As Jane's ankle improved she extended her walks from the Square to Kensington Gardens, which provided shade and easy walking, but the 'stiffness & formality' of the layout was uninteresting; there was also the danger, on Sundays, of running into 'a number of the lower orders returning many of them somewhat in liquor from their Sunday's excursions'. Still in ignorance of James's dilemma, they hoped every day for a letter from him or, better still, a visit.

Resolution

Jeanie's letter still lay unanswered. At last James decided to seek advice from Aeneas Mackintosh, who was frank: James had gone too far to withdraw and must consider himself 'in point of fact the betrothed of that lady' who was undoubtedly expecting a proposal. He had hit on the one thing that would push James into a decision – his desire to behave honourably. James left the breakfast table resolved to write proposing marriage; but first he must write to his father.

When the letter 'by the twopenny post'[17] arrived, Mr F burst from his room shouting, 'It is just as I expected. James is resolved to marry his cousin'. At first, Jane refused to believe it: in a puff of smoke all her 'airy Castles' vanished. There would be no rosy-cheeked, plump, smiling Highland lass, docile yet intelligent, young and strong enough to bear James a quiverful of children. All she could do was hope that his father's reply would change James's mind.

16 Royal Hospital, Chelsea, founded by Charles II as a retirement and nursing home for soldiers. Designed by Sir Christopher Wren and completed in 1692.

17 Service started in 1801 for deliveries within London.

Mr F had always suspected that 'the thing would happen' but he could not understand James's belief that it was the only honourable thing to do. He thought Jeanie might well have devised a plan to draw a net around James on his return:

> Blind I am not. Candid I would be – therefore I do not conceal to you how I feel. I do not see, in all you write to me, one argument, to require your honor ... to form this engagement.

Nevertheless, generous as ever, Mr F added:

> ... if your heart beats decidedly for it, I am too solicitous for your happiness, to hesitate a moment to sanction *whatever* you decidedly & deliberately consider, as essential to it. My Love and Blessings you will ever have my dearest James.

Jane slept badly that night, 'feeling every plan & project I had formed for future comfort in James's society demolished!' At the same time, she acknowledged that all they could do was 'silently regret ... He is his own Master and has a right to do as he likes.'

Nervous about James's reaction, the next day they diverted themselves with a long excursion through Hammersmith and down to the river at Chiswick, where the church bells were ringing to commemorate the day of the Restoration and the birthday of King Charles II.[18] By this time they were hot and tired and Jane's ankle was aching, so they took a boat, 'the river like glass & the rowing delightful', back to the village of Fulham and a pleasant wander home through the meadows.

That evening, the twopenny post brought James's reply. His father's letter had had no effect. Jane confided to her diary:

> This finishes this month & the first fortnight of our residence at Kensington – begun with very different hopes & expectations as to James & future prospects – however disappointing the marriage he contemplates making – may be to us – the motives from which he makes the connection are highly Honourable to himself ... may he be rewarded by the Happiness he looks for in the connection he means to form & which the Purity of his motives *will* entitle him to – spite of our disapprobation!

❁

Meanwhile, James was temporarily distracted by a new anxiety: Black John was missing. He had arrived in London in a very weak condition and had been referred immediately to St George's Hospital. With directions from James, he had set off through the unfamiliar streets and vanished. Two days later, a nurse from the Middlesex Hospital reported that John had collapsed at the Hospital door and had been admitted. Going straight to John's bedside, James found him very confused 'and wandering in his mind but not I thought in an immediately dangerous state'. He knew James and spoke about his usual occupations,

18 Known as Oak Apple Day, the day when Charles II entered London after nineteen years in exile

worrying about not having taken James's clothes to the wash. James encouraged him to rest, gave orders that he should have everything he wanted and left the hospital.

✻

Before Jane had time to post her letter to him, James arrived to breakfast and his mother leapt into the fray, using 'very strong and indeed intemperate language'.

> We argued long & toughly ... she talked of the matter being likely to put an end to our intercourse & even ... of going abroad away from the possibility of being disturbed by seeing this hated union.

They then went upstairs to continue the conversation with Mr F who lost his temper to such an extent that Jane had to intervene. Mr F was still unable to accept that marriage was inevitable: James needed time to look round and find employment; he must establish exactly what William was prepared to do for Moniack and to ascertain if he had enough money to support a wife. This should take at least a year, but he suspected that James would reply, perfectly reasonably:

> That you are a young man, under 40 years of age.
> That you have ten thousand pounds in your pocket.
> That you have a sound and excellent constitution.
> That you have travelled much, and seen various countries and nations.
> That you have conducted business, as a Partner, in two Commercial Houses, and must have attained considerable experience in Trade.
> That you possess a Talent of Pen & Pencil, which has already proved productive, in even your first efforts.
> That you are unembarrassed by our Family affairs, and profess to be irresponsible for them.
> That you have some address & appearance, and a well grounded reputation.

These, indeed, were all advantages but surely they gave him the right 'to expect a most respectable and fortunate match, in Goodness, in accomplishments, in Fortune, in Youth, in good connexions'. He could not believe that James was weak enough to be trapped into marriage by someone who had once rejected him, had undoubtedly done the rounds of others 'and now comes round to you' again. But, he concluded, James was old enough to make up his own mind and 'any Lady presented as your wife, will be kindly received by us'.

They eventually agreed that the subject should be dropped for the moment, and James, anxious to visit Black John, left at midday to walk to the Middlesex Hospital. His parents accompanied him as far as Hyde Park, after which Jane lay all afternoon on the sofa 'badly worn out with the agitation of the day'.

A further letter from James convinced her that she must now support him 'in the Connection he was determined to make'. Any parent who was not moved by the letter he had written 'does not deserve such a son!' She begged his forgiveness 'for the distress I so unwillingly gave you yesterday ... [I] shall not be easy unless I have a line from your own hand saying you feel as ever for your distressed & affectionate Mother'.

⁂

James's next letter, however, brought news that, for a moment, distracted them: three hours after James's visit to the Middlesex Hospital, Black John had died.

> Thus closes the scene over my poor and faithful John – a more attached servant none ever had – his manners were unpleasing to those who knew him not ... but to those who knew his worth, their harshness was nothing. I believe him to have been most seriously attached & faithful to me ... he has followed me all over the world, has attended me in peril – saved my life perhaps – has been with me in all the most unlucky scenes ... and now he dies unexpectedly in a sick ward of Middlesex Hospital. I would it could have been otherwise – but it was so willed – his memory long will live with me and much shall I miss his faithful service.

Jane and Mr F were equally affected: Black John had shadowed their eldest son's adventurous footsteps from Guyana to Scotland, thence to India and home overland, but not to the comfortable retirement that James had planned for him. 'Poor John,' wrote Jane, '... his attached service will ever be cherished in the memory of us all with affectionate regard'. He was buried quietly in 'the churchyard near Paddington beyond the Regent's Park' in the presence of James. 'Little recks the fellow now of any parade that might be made, even of the grief which the few who knew him do & will pay to his memory.'

The next day, Mr F capitulated: everyone had had their say and it was best to allow the subject to drop. He returned to editing William's letters and his day-long walks into London, while James took refuge in his drawing by day and writing at night.

⁂

On 6 June James heard from Jeanie: she found his proposal unsatisfactory. He had clearly written very practically and unemotionally, no doubt mentioning duty and honour; she needed something more romantic. She should, he felt, have understood that he loved her sufficiently to ask her to marry him; the time was past for 'the strong sensations that once had place'. James felt he needed Aeneas to stiffen his resolve and, finding him out of town, took himself off to the opera, where he heard 'some of my favourite Vienna airs, those of the Countess Ivanowska'.

Aeneas was firm: nothing was to be done about the parental objections, but James must be entirely frank to Jeanie about his own financial situation and the privations she might have to undergo if she accepted his offer: 'proceed as you have commenced my dear James to make honourable principle the rule of your conduct through this trying occasion'.

James accordingly tried again: if he had not expressed his feelings adequately it was because he had had to rein them in for so long. Jeanie had known them before he left Scotland but had given him no reason to hope. He had been taken aback by the strength of her feelings when at last they met again. Now it was up to her and, to help her to come to a decision, he would explain how their life together might be as far as he could foretell.

They could, at a pinch, live in London on the money he had; it was desirable to stay there for a couple of years for 'frequent reference to literary men & establishments'. He knew it would be hard for Jeanie to leave her family and doubly hard for her mother if she brought a sister with her to London for company. He hoped that they would be able to entertain friends in a quiet, inexpensive way, 'but it would not be Princes Street or Mount Eske'. As his pictures and books became more widely known, there was a chance that he might become more of a public figure. Could she cope with that?

> All this my dearest Jane you may deem too cold and calculating to be compatible with a warm & sincere love but it is not so. I can bear disappointment for I am used to it but I could not bear to see one whom I tenderly love placed by my means in a situation of distress, & pining for the society & comforts she has been ever used to & which I might be unable to afford her.

She must take as long as she liked to decide, but if it was 'yes' then he wanted to get married as soon as possible. A week later he had Jeanie's answer 'which concludes the negotiations favourably – my aunt has given her consent & now all that remains is the where & when'.

Engagement

James was doing his best to finish his Persian pictures and had already written about 250 pages of his book on Persia, taking Sundays off for lunch in Edwardes Square. He was planning to go north in mid-August to fit in with the plans of William Tytler, who was to give his sister away.

One summer Sunday in St Mary Abbots his parents heard an excellent sermon from the vicar, Mr Rennell, on 'mutual submission and forbearance to one another'; Jane, much impressed, resolved to act accordingly but her resolution wavered when a letter from Jane Anne revealed that she was 'quite overwhelmed' at the news of James's proposed marriage and had written to him to say so: Jeanie had always been 'the kindest and warmest of friends' to her and she appreciated her many qualities, but 'Pardon me my dearest James if I appear presumptuous or impertinent to my elder brother when I add that we <u>did</u> think it imprudent'.

As ever, however, Jane Anne's common sense prevailed: it was important to remember that men were happier married. Although she was perfectly aware of her parents' feelings on the matter and, in some respects, agreed with them, there was nothing anyone could do:

> Our blessings and prayers for your happiness dear James (whether quite prudent or not) you surely have ... *Here dear* James you and your wife will be welcome, joyfully welcome, & surely you will stay as long as possible with us?

The subject was now taboo in Edwardes Square, and the talk after Sunday lunch inevitably turned instead to the old couple's possible return to Moniack; there seemed little prospect

The house in Edwardes Square, 'most agreeable & commodious' where Reelig and Jane lived for over eight years.

of this, however, and the topic always caused Jane sleepless nights and resort to laudanum. Their social life, however, was expanding. By now they knew all the other residents in the Square; more and more of their Scottish friends were dropping in, the Chambers family were living opposite and the Harrisons had taken a cottage in Hammersmith.

During this time Jeanie wrote frequently to James. Her letters, in a careful, tiny hand, were long and rambling. She was not in the least surprised by the reaction of James's parents; her family also considered the marriage imprudent. Was James concentrating on finding them somewhere suitable to live? They would need one servant in lodgings but two in a small house; a house would avoid the expense of laundry as the washing could be done at home. She might persuade Isabella to join them; if not, she said firmly, James would require training in his wife's maintenance before he could be of any use. James was no doubt spending too much money and she wished she could be there to control him. He was to have her letter in front of him when he answered 'for I have asked a world of questions which I expect you to reply to'.

Raeburn was dead. 'Poor Raeburn the Painter. We felt his death like an old friend'. He had died on 8 July soon after an excursion, 'a very merry party', to Fife with a group of old friends including Sir Walter Scott. Jeanie was thankful he had been able to paint 'so many of those I love ... Often did I look at your Picture at Inverness ... but now I am quite disposed to be content with the living substitute'.

By the end of July the date of the marriage was still not fixed, and William Tytler, who was to give Jeanie away, was still in Pau. James was not to come north too early as he would get under everyone's feet and make 'my little mother more active & fidgety than ever'.

The visitors who flocked to congratulate Jeanie would scare James 'into the woods'. Well into August there was still no date and many changes of mind from Jeanie:

> You may shake your head and think me as changeable as any of my sex but what can I do when I cannot get my own way. I did wish for a few quiet weeks after the bother of driving out & in to Town about my things was over and all my plaguey letters written (not those to you my love) to recruit myself and feel that it was all true and that I was happy, but I find there can be no quiet here now.

She loaded James with commissions. She wanted, from Cavendish House, Wigmore Street, '2 doz long white kid ladies gloves, ½ doz short white kid ditto, 1 doz gents pale yellow kid ditto and ½ doz short ditto for maidservants'. From the Soho Bazaar she required 'a little Italian iron for doing up ruffles' and 'wreaths for the hair made of *brown feathers* in the form of leaves or acorns'. She was mindful of his wardrobe as well: knowing he was absentminded and uninterested in his appearance, she hoped his mother was getting him 'nice neckclothes, pocket handkerchiefs, shirts because I do like to see gentlemen with nice white fine linen – but if she has not I shall see about that when I have a right to do so'.

She was nervous about the 'oddness of the time' when they would at last be alone together, but they would have a piano and books 'and when you weary of me you will be more at liberty to amuse yourself and when I find you troublesome I can always go to Jane Anne'.

Jeanie's lawyer brother James was dealing with the knotty problem of the marriage settlement. James showed his father the draft and asked for his opinion, which was given in no uncertain terms: 'I must say that I do not by any means approve the terms which even you propose; far less those proposed by him.' He objected to almost all James Tytler's clauses, considering that they were more suited to 'families of high rank and great fortune'. He especially disliked the power given to Jeanie to bequeath her part of the marriage settlement to her own family, should there be no children – 'a most unheard of privilege'. James wanted everything to be as simple as possible and, for once, Jeanie agreed; she disliked fuss and ceremony as much as he did. His aversion to 'display and racketing' was more important to her than any money, and she looked forward to evenings spent by their fireside with 'you reading to me whilst I work or I reading to you whilst you draw or singing to you some of your favourite melodies'.

❊

The moment the engagement was announced, the Tytler family had declared to the world that James's affairs were completely separate from those of his father. Jane was deeply offended and wrote to George: 'Isn't it natural that parents should feel a little mortified I may even say indignant at a connection that renders this necessary separation of interest?' Mr F was so upset he refused to talk about it,'so that on you my dearest George falls all my lamentations'.

George, now settled into army life in India, later reported to William on this letter, 'rather of the grumbling order ... She harps on James's marriage as if he had committed a deadly sin. I have the benefit of all this for, if she does mention the matter to you, you have the advantage of not being able to read her hand'; his mother's 'pothooks & hangers' were becoming increasingly illegible. William eventually commented that he would say nothing: he himself was not a marrying man and, by the age of forty, James should know what was best for him.

Those whom God hath joined together

On a particularly gloomy, drizzly day in mid-August James set off for the north on a steam packet, leaving his parents in extremely low spirits. For diversion and a change of scene they braved the weather and went in search of Betsy Abell, daughter of the Balcombes. William Balcombe, still in France, had asked the Frasers to visit the ill-fated Betsy who, abandoned by her scoundrel of a husband, was living in penury with her little girl in Blackfriars, then a less than respectable area. She was soon to join her parents in St Omer; the whole family were then to set off for New South Wales, where William Balcombe had secured a good job.

It was a depressing visit. Betsy, now 'a tall handsome elegant looking young woman with an amiable & pleasing countenance', poured out the story of her disastrous marriage, in rather too much detail for the fastidious Jane. Betsy was very grateful, however, both for their visit and for the kindness they had shown to her parents in St Omer. Glad to have done their duty, they took their leave.

Finding themselves in the City, the old couple wandered 'through many extraordinary streets & lanes & turnings' to Aldersgate and thence by many 'well remembered' ways to the Charter House, Mr F's old school.

> Mr F showed me the House he had inhabited ... the schoolroom where he had been taught the Cellar or Cloister through wh he had to *run* every morning to the schoolroom from where he was boarded the Park & Play Gardens where the Boys amused themselves – in short every spot sacred in his memory & interesting as such to me! And after having more than an hour in this curious & interesting seminary we ... walked home much gratified w/ our day's excursion but myself somewhat fatigued & not well.

James reached Edinburgh to find Jeanie exhausted, even thinner and paler than before and suffering from a feverish cold. Next day, he met his lawyer cousin in his chambers in Frederick Street to settle the marriage contract: £3,000 was to be transferred to Jeanie's trustees.

William Tytler eventually appeared, hoping that the marriage would take place quickly as he was longing to get back to his family in France. Jeanie, however, won the day:

she would countenance no time but early September and no one but her eldest brother to give her away. At last the date was fixed for 4 September and preparations began in earnest: notes of invitation were sent out, a chaise booked, a tea urn bought. Jeanie seemed in better spirits and James relaxed. There were the usual pre-wedding hitches: the carriage booked turned out to be a rattle-trap, so James and Patrick Tytler went into town to sort it out and after encountering several shady characters got a very decent vehicle at 35/- per day from a Mrs Smith – 'a curious original specimen of the old Scotch wife – about 25 stone in weight – with a great Beard but frank, honest & plain dealing as plain looking'.

The night before the wedding, Jeanie slept well and rose 'tolerably prepared for the formidable business of the day'. James felt nervous and emotional – 'I really could not rest in any one place the whole morning'. At eleven precisely all was ready, the company were assembled in the drawing room and the servants summoned. Mr Allison was imposingly in his place and in came the bride on her brother's arm. She 'trembled sore' throughout the 'awful & severe' ceremony but managed the responses with self possession. James reckoned he and Jeanie were the most composed of the family, many of whom were in tears. He was not sure if he had got the kissing right:

> I – don't know if there was any mistake about kissing. Did not kiss the Bride & only afterwards the Bridesmaids & sisters ... & then we all went into the dining room & there was fruit cake &c &c of which the rest partook but we very little. After a while of compliments & congratulations we both went & changed our cloaths, and soon after took an affectionate leave of all our friends & getting into the carriage drove off .

On 8 September the news of Jane Anne's new daughter, Millicent, reached the house in Edwardes Square, and next day there was a letter from James announcing he and his wife were now embarked on their 'Highland Tour'. Mr F went out alone for a ramble round the Park and that night Jane took laudanum again for the first time for several weeks.

❊

Towards the end of the month, a letter from Jane caught up with James; she was still finding fault, speaking scornfully of Jeanie's pre-wedding nerves and her sister's distress at the loss of a daughter while she had lost a son. James, restraining his irritation with difficulty, tried to reassure her: Jeanie would surely perform the role of 'an affectionate & attached daughter' and, more importantly, she understood her husband completely. 'In short, I am satisfied; I hope you will be too.'

Mr F was resigned. All he could repeat was that they had loved James's wife before she became his wife and 'that we shall receive her as such with kindness; and that we think there can be no more said on these points, but to leave the future to the future'.

13

1823–1833

Faithful steward of Moniack

James now had his work cut out to cope with the demands on him: he was eager to push on with publication of his pictures and books and desperate to continue his painting and writing; he had to set Moniack on its feet; he had to keep an eye on his ageing parents in Kensington; and he had to make Jeanie happy.

He divided his time between Moniack and London, where he was hoping to bring out his Persian travel book the following year. His father was delighted to be asked to edit the manuscript. 'Dear man,' said his daughter-in-law fondly, 'he was always better at advising than acting'. Mr F observed of the newly-weds, 'I do not hear of any chance of his having a family by her – which does not surprise me'. Jeanie touched on this in a letter to her mother-in-law:

> Our expenses alas have no prospect of increasing. Had it been the will of Heaven to bless us with a family I think I could have worked with my poor little hands for such a blessing – but, as it is I am teaching myself to be reconciled and ... I have now the more need to be a cheerful and contented companion to the kindest husband a woman was ever blessed with.

Jane Anne now had four children and was as busy as her brother; the house was always bursting, beds stowed in every corner. Not only was she constantly paying and receiving visits and giving parties, she was also 'Purveyor General to all the sporting parties' around – exactly like her mother. Affleck took a leading part in all this, but when he was away she took over with great charm, efficiency and enthusiasm. Mr F wrote proudly to William:

> I cannot withhold from you the repetition of how delightful a creature Jane Anne is – and accordingly all the Northern world sounds her praises – she is deservedly one of the most popular heads of family in the Highlands.

❋

Moniack was now let to Affleck's mother at an annual rent of £150, which would enable James to get the house in order without burdening the estate. He was taking difficult decisions, sacking some of the old estate workers and making do with day labour. The incessant October rain had caused expensive problems when the burn burst its banks and threatened the house, though Jeanie and James high up on the hill at Rebeg were 'snug in our nest on the rock. We heard the crash of the stones & rocks going down, grinding against each other.' Many good trees had been washed away and the low-lying fields were flooded.

Relieved that his father was not there to witness the neglect, James still harboured a hope that the old couple would eventually come home. His father, however, had vowed never to return, partly because he feared the Scottish climate and partly, James suspected, because he did not want to see the changes wrought during his absence.

In December 1824 a rare letter from William arrived. He repaid the estate's obligation to James of £2,000 and declared his resolution 'to save every pyce'[1] to pay off the whole Moniack debt so that the old parents could go and live there '& you too!' The condition was that all he remitted, including the price of Dunchea, for which, so far, there were no offers, should be secured in his name only.

> You have married, I never will, and if you like I will make a will in favour of you and your sons after the demise of our parents or my death ... something should be done in a legal way about Moniack, the Estate secured against further debt; its rents secured to pay interest of debt. After 40, I cannot go on without some way of settling for a chance misfortune and, although I care not about money, I like certainty and security ... how do you secure Moniack against further debt? I think every debt on the estate should be ascertained and ... transferred to me ... and then I could see my way, which at present I certainly do not, for it has been getting darker for twenty years, and there is no light yet.

James, who had also been almost entirely in the dark, was relieved to hear what William thought. In reply he attempted an explanation of the financial situation up to Michaelmas 1824, a complicated state of affairs not helped by 'the loose tho ... zealous management' of Affleck, who was no accountant. All the small debts were now paid but the sum of £31,000 was still outstanding; the 'Northern Tenantry' was in a bad state with rents yielding only £650–£700 a year, while the interest on the debt was more like £800; the only remaining asset was Dunchea.

Reviewing expenditure was a depressing exercise: James had had to spend extensively on the Mill, the banks of the burn, the roads, the enclosures and on labour. They had to employ an extra boy, Hector, and buy a horse for their little phaeton. Journeys up and down the country and residence in London were expensive. Jeanie insisted on having one or other of her sisters to keep her company in London which added to the cost. Sir Henry Steuart was, moreover, understandably demanding repayment of Archy Seton's £6,000. From now on the plan was to retrench: Jeanie would stay with her family in Edinburgh while James

1 Usually 'pice' (Hindi), a small copper coin of very little value.

was in London, where he would lodge with his parents. At Moniack the improvements for the year would be restricted to planting trees to beautify the approach and screen the house from the farm buildings.

He had also taken a major decision: William had too long been called upon 'for indefinite sacrifices upon vague and uncertain grounds'. He should be repaid and the only way that James could see to achieve this was to hand the estate over to him, debts and all, 'for all I have in the world would not redeem enough of its debt to enable me to keep it even if I could live on nothing'. He would harbour no grudge; his own efforts to preserve the property had failed, and he would happily live at Moniack, doing his best for the true owner until he came home. It only remained for William to put pen to paper and officially agree to become laird of Moniack.

⁂

The following summer, Moniack was let to 'the Stewarts of Bombay'. Mrs Stewart was the former Jamesina Fraser of neighbouring Fanellan and an erstwhile playmate of the boys. They turned out to be less than ideal tenants, neglecting the garden and allowing cows to feed among the Portuguese Laurel plantation, Mr F's pride and the admiration of the county. What was more, their geese made a terrible mess of the circular lawn and gravel in front of the house. Mrs Stewart was a very different tenant from Affleck's mother. According to Jeanie, 'the one was a lady and the other is not'; but then, as Nanny Rose darkly pointed out, 'what could we expect from a Fanellan! They were aye queer folk and none of them should ever have gotten Moniack.'

Rebeg was refurbished for James and Jeanie, and they had found a knowledgeable new gardener:

> [He] comes up rubbing his hands perfectly delighted with the discoveries & precious things he finds in the woods, rocks & mosses – and the rare trees & shrubs here ... he says there's trees about this place the like o' which is no' to be seen in all the country.

He reckoned Mr Murray of the Botanic Gardens in Glasgow would give £1,000 for the Stone Pine in the garden.

When in July 1825 Jane Anne produced her fifth child, Mary, Jeanie was there to help. Jane Anne rarely had any problems giving birth and maintained that if she felt weak it was only because everyone insisted on keeping her in bed. Jeanie marvelled that 'anything could have been so easy' and reported on the children to their exiled grandmother: Jane, now six, was a great favourite with her aunt Jeanie; Ned, aged three, was off and out the moment the nursery door was open, and finding him was like looking 'for a needle in a bundle of straw'. The two-year-old Millicent was very pleased with her new sister, a birthday present for brother James, who was just five.

There was as yet no clue as to William's thoughts; James was optimistic, but when at last a letter did appear it threw him into confused exasperation. Firstly, to the news that Dunchea had at last been sold, reducing the debt considerably, William declared that he wished it had been kept; next he announced that if he were to take on Moniack it would only be for his parents' sake, not for his own:

> My object is to put it in the power of my father and mother to return when they like to Moniack free & to have it rent free for their use for their lives.

After some calculations, based on William's income and recent sale of horses and property, James reckoned that the plan could succeed. But would saving Moniack prevent William's homecoming during his parents' lifetime? James doubted whether they would ever return. His father 'took his farewell of it when he left it for France ... the great pang has long since been over'. His mother would certainly regret it but would rather see a prosperous William home again. As for James and Jeanie, they could be happy anywhere but if they thought that William was imprisoned in India 'our happiness would be poisoned'.

So it was up to William: he had to decide whether, after paying his own debts and the £22,000 still hanging over Moniack, he would have enough to live on in India and, eventually, at home. If not, then the estate must be sold. James asked again: 'If you are *determined* to save Moniack and can do it, tell me so in plain terms'.

A month later, James was still in a miserable state of uncertainty, worrying that William might accept out of a sense of duty; he would, after all, receive no advantage from being laird of Moniack. Would it not be better to leave the place to its fate and get William home sooner? Supposing an accident should befall him – what would happen then?

Meanwhile, at Rebeg he was painting all morning, writing all evening and in between times supervising the levelling of the rough ground around Moniack and at the entrance, 'which now has a more polished air and looks like an approach'. The next task was the front of the house, where evergreens were planned 'for the angles of the lawn'. Jeanie was as enthusiastic as James, finding the place 'a constant source of occupation, interest & delight'.

⁂

In the autumn of 1825 Jeanie played her part in trying to help William make up his mind, but more deviously than James. She dwelt on her happy walks through the glen, especially along William's walk, and the pleasure she and James took in restoring the place. She described the flourishing planting around the Raven's Rock, the ivy 'climbing over the little bridges & the ferns, wild geraniums and heath your father planted all getting up their heads again'. She talked about the fun of having so many nieces and nephews around. If she had a Fairy gift she would free Moniack from debt, bring the old couple home, enlarge Rebeg for James and herself ...

> ... and surround it with smiling children ... (Dear William the tears are in my eyes while I write the words) and I would have you and George rich enough to come home.

William and Margaret Tytler would willingly let her and James adopt one of their numerous children …

> … but it must be a Fraser bairn that I would have and if you will not marry, dear William, you must make George do so and send home his bairns to me and I will be as good to them as if they were my own and teach them to love Moniack as much as you all did.

While Sanquhar was being improved, Margaret and William were renting Thornhill, a house in Morayshire, a county which Margaret found 'the most stupid unsociable place possible', very different from the Highlands. '*Style* has so increased in this neighbourhood that ease & hospitality are banished ... I hope we shall have firmness enough to withstand the folly of *three* courses in the country'. At Christmas they relaxed with relief into the homely festivities at Moniack. Margaret sent a New Year letter to Edwardes Square: 'if dear Jeanie's neatness & hospitality & kind attention to everyone could bring back Moniack to what it once was she leaves no effort unperformed'. Old Nanny Rose was keeping the house 'nicely clean', and Jane Anne was looking well and happy.

The abnormally hot summer of 1826 produced a serious drought: almost all the trees James had planted were dead, the vegetables in the garden were scorched and the tenants, with failed crops, were unable to pay rents. The soft fruit, however, was in great profusion, and Nanny Rose, now bent with rheumatism but still toddling about, was once more put to work; twenty-two pots of jam and four bottles of raspberry vinegar were sent off to Edwardes Square. Jeanie was having trouble with her cook, confusingly called Jean; she was not as clean as she might be, knew nothing whatsoever about cooking, and Jeanie was having to instruct her from *The Cook's Oracle*.[2] 'A most active little elf' called Hannah was a new addition to the household. She was extremely bright, just the thing for the school in Kirkhill that Jeanie and some neighbours were planning.

Affleck's mother, now tenant again, was delighted with the changes since her previous visit, in particular the new kitchen grate on which now 'it is possible to cook a dinner'; Nanny Rose tartly informed her that 'many a good dinner was cooked in the old one'.

There was still no word from William and Jeanie, far more attached to the place than she had anticipated, dreaded his next letter:

> Oh my dear Aunt we are both I fear getting too much welded to this place and looking at it in all its beauty I feel my heart so sad to think what these expected letters may bring ... I cannot think William will have courage to order it to be sold ... Yet ... he seems to grudge even the very necessary limited outlay ... Would to heaven our little all could save it.

2 A cookery book by William Kitchiner (1775–1827), whose name was a household word in Britain and America during the nineteenth century. Unlike most food writers of the time he cooked the food himself and travelled around with a folding cabinet of his mustards and sauces.

There was nothing for it but to hope that William would somehow make the fortune that had been eluding him for so long and that George would marry and send his children home 'to range about yet in the woods and glens of Moniack'. That summer, however, two excited children were climbing trees and splashing about in the burn – the Skinner boys had arrived for a holiday from Edinburgh.

⁂

A couple of years earlier, James Skinner had sent his sons to be educated near Edinburgh hoping James and Jeanie might keep an eye on his 'poor Black Boys'. They had excused themselves, giving pressure of business as their reason, but the truth was that Jeanie wanted nothing to do with 'half-caste' children. When Skinner got wind of this, his letter to James barely concealed his disappointment in his old friend. He quite saw, he said, that James was far too busy to visit the children 'particularly when they are *native* born', knowing that James was not '[his] own master' and that there was family prejudice where such children were concerned. He then dropped the slightly offended tone, ending on a warmer note: 'By your not seeing my Children I can assure you that our friendship cannot lessen in my Heart.'

William was furious with James and scribbled a tirade:

> Why did you not see his children, one my godson ... You should treat them as your own children and now as you have a wife of your own to look after the house you can when in Scotland see after them & have them often with you.

Eventually, James persuaded Jeanie to change her mind: they visited the children, sent their father an encouraging account of their progress and invited them to stay at Rebeg in August, although it would be a squash. The two boys slept in 'one pigeon hole above ... for either man or maidservant we have not a hole' and had a wonderful time running free with whichever of Jane Anne's children happened to be visiting, wasting the lad Hector's time and fishing the burn with James. The elder, thirteen-year-old Hercules, terrified everyone by taking off on his own to Inverness, walking the eighteen miles there and back. Jeanie gave him 'a lecture, his dinner, and some wine & some water' and sent him to bed. Having waved them off at the end of their stay, Jeanie wrote to Jane:

> Poor boys they seemed very sorry to go and said they had been quite happy – but they had got too fond of Hector our lad and were forever either in the kitchen or the stables with him which we did not like.

Revealingly, she added, 'They are fine boys ... I only wish for our credit in the country they were white bairns'. James reported that they had been badly in need of Highland air and food, but 'oh! Hercules is dark'.

In gratitude, Skinner sent Jeanie 'a beautiful tartan scarf made at Cashmere ... which I hope she will accept from your Black friend who considers the whole family as his own relations'; there was also a white shawl for Jane from 'your Indian son whose heart flows with gratitude towards you & your noble family'.

⁂

Towards the end of the year, James and Jeanie moved back to Moniack and shook 'the proper collection of filth' out of the door in preparation for Christmas. The house was full again, ringing with noise and laughter as in the old days. Jane Anne and Affleck brought their family to stay and Nanny Rose was in her element, bustling about and giving orders to the nursery maid. Jean the cook was now working wonders and Hector, 'tho not an elegant youth serves a table very well now'; all went smoothly, although James found it impossible to do any work. Affleck, demanding constant entertainment with a gun, got bored if he could not talk about the day's sport. Much to James's relief, he went home the moment he could. Jeanie reckoned that 'in the kindly intercourse of relations he is greatly wanting'; at Culduthel Jane Anne was only allowed to invite 'who Affleck pleases' and visits there were no longer so enjoyable. 'But that cannot be helped,' concluded Jeanie briskly, 'and as Jane Anne really seems to enjoy us much more at Moniack than she does there she shall ever feel that she and all that belongs to her will be welcome to us at all times.'

Jeanie updated Jane on the progress of her grandchildren. Even though it was Christmas, Jane Anne insisted on lessons for the elder ones every morning; in the afternoon they were all together, with Millicent established on Uncle James's knee, Mary on Jeanie's and 'the rampaging Master Affleck' on his mother's. Then Jane Anne played the piano while the children danced. Millicent sang from morning to night, while Mary was 'getting very pretty again – like your own dear Mary'. The boys, however, were not yet 'as good looking as Reelicks'.

Although he had enjoyed having the old house full of children James was melancholy: 'I do not feel the same joyous spirit which once used to be shed over our Christmas festivities – the youthful sunshine is gone.'

There was still silence from William. Meanwhile, he was not yet confident that his pictures would sell, although he had had one or two successes at exhibitions. He was also finding publishers hard to pin down. All round him estates were being sold – Belladrum had gone, and William Tytler was worried about the future of Sanquhar.

But James was enjoying Moniack: he loved planting and beautifying the grounds; he had become passionate about trees and was researching what he called 'the ornamental approach'. The lime, 25ft high, that he had transplanted to adorn the entrance, looked as if it had been there for twenty-five years. The cottage at the entrance had grandly become the 'Porter's Lodge', with a neat porch and old Mrs Noble and her granddaughter installed as porteresses. He found the daily grind of a landlord irksome, however, and hoped he would soon be able to employ a factor to cope 'with all these wretched bodies about their bills & their rents'.

Meanwhile, William, getting wind of these changes, at last roused himself enough to complain to George 'that Kate Martin's old house at the Gean Tree was away'. Later, William was 'boggling' at touching any part of Moniack, which he wanted to see just as he left it: 'if I had my will, I would be as bad as old Noble, and complain of the removal of even nettles ... I want to find in the same places the stones I used to turn up for worms, the old stumps, stocks, holes and ditches, barns, buildings'. Jeanie hoped he would not object to the bow windows planned for the drawing room and the library.

At last William made up his mind: in March 1827 the 'Estate of Reelick' was passed by Disposition to William Fraser Esquire.

Surveyor in Saharanpur

In 1827, after the Anglo-Burmese war,[3] military establishments were drastically cut and George was transferred to the Revenue Surveying Department. According to William, he was endowed with 'Fraser obstinacy ... lazy, idle and happy only when whistling his old Scotch tunes'; he was bored by regimental life and often in trouble for insubordination.

In the end, William had intervened on his behalf and George was now at last doing something he enjoyed: measuring villages, fixing boundaries and gathering information 'for Collectors to make assessments of rent and revenue'. He was about to move to a remote station north-west of Delhi:

> I am quite alone and shall be so till the month of May – grilling May – when I go to Meerut and until that time I shall not speak a word of English.

His establishment as a junior surveyor was considerable:

> I have two men carry my guns — a flock of sheep and fowls to give me limbs and milk for my tea there being no cream in this warm climate when a man is marching – two cows for butter – horses, monkeys, fowls, pets – soldiers and tents bring up my rearguard. When I arrive at my ground my breakfast and my appetite are generally ready together.

After each day's work he sat through long lonely evenings with only wine and walnuts for company. 'I go out to my work in the morning ... and return to my solitary dinner. Having no-one to speak my own language to I must perforce converse with myself.' Meanwhile, he was grateful for two large boxes of books from home, enough to last until he was within reach of the London libraries. He unpacked the boxes and then 'crept to my bed with two dogs to keep me warm, a candle and *The Chelsea Pensioners*'.[4] Another parcel from his mother contained four handkerchiefs, two combs and 'a long admonition on the strict performance of the duties of the toilette'. His friend, Peter Grant, being 'a neatly dressy man', coveted one of the combs, which George handed over as a present; he wished she had included razors 'for it is only in the Jungle I am an Esau and when I return to cantonment I am obliged to be as smooth as other people'.

Like Edward before him, George longed for music. His mother had sent him sheet music but his flute had cracked in the heat and he was having to resort to whistling: 'I have never forgotten a single Irish melody that James whistled or Jane Anne played'. He amused himself by whistling tunes to test his friend Snodgrass, 'a masterly hand on

3 1824–6, the longest and most expensive war in British/Indian history with huge casualty numbers on both sides. The high financial cost to India (£13m) led to the severe economic crisis of 1833.

4 Colburn's Standard Novels.

the violin', who could name almost every Scots or Irish tune. George remembered hearing the great Niel Gow[5] when at school near Edinburgh 'and the notes are yet in my ears'. He thought nostalgically of those days and of another, less eminent, fiddler:

> Were I ever to come home as a man of easy fortune, I should certainly keep a fiddler ... like an old drunken friend of mine to whose music I have often danced and cried, and who played just equally feelingly and charmingly drunk or sober – John Nimmo – blind from 5 years old ... he used to come to [school] to play to us – those days never can come back.

In between surveying expeditions George was based, rent-free, in William's house in Delhi and was now earning enough to save towards a three-year furlough at home planned for 1833. Maybe he would find a wife when he was on leave; on the other hand, he might have to choose between marriage and an early retirement, as marriage would sink him further into debt.

The mention of marriage elicited an immediate response from his father: nothing could give his parents greater happiness 'but I do not think it unreasonable to guard you thus early from a choice which would wholly poison that happiness, I mean, its falling on a *cousin*'.

The family grapevine had revealed, alarmingly, that George was corresponding with his cousin, another Jane, the daughter of William Tytler. It was more than his parents could bear to see him fall into the same trap as James, entangled 'in a connexion which has ever since been and ever must be poignantly felt by us'. George was their last hope of another generation through the male line and here he was, like James, apparently setting his cap at a cousin. His father had to some extent been proved right in his fears for James – 'they have no family – nor do I wish they should'. Children of cousins were, he reckoned, usually defective in mind or body or both.

Although it was difficult to tell a man of thirty what he ought to do, he felt that, at eighty, he was entitled to tell George what he ought <u>not</u> to do. As long as 'loveliness of mind and of person' existed, neither nationality nor rank mattered; fortune, however, and a family of genuine worth, certainly were important; George must ensure that whoever he married had no hereditary malady in the family such as 'Insanity, Epilepsy, Consumption, Scrofula or other such miseries'. Above all, he must be on his guard against 'sudden attachment to any Inferior Object'; what he needed was 'a Person of comely and interesting figure and form, feature and expression – one of superior natural gifts and endowments, of education and accomplishments of a sterling and ornate character, of connexions to be rationally gratified by and of fair competent fortune'. His father followed this letter with a copy six weeks later.

He was still writing copiously and legibly but Jane noted, 'he takes longer now to compose what he writes & cannot now as he used to do write when people are talking round him'.

5 1727–1807. The most famous Scottish fiddler of the 18th century.

In April 1828 George was in Saharanpur, north of Delhi, where he had been conducting a survey of about 170 villages. He had enjoyed the work:

> The season is fast advancing to harvest and the fields are waving with heavy produce – a fine cheerful sight and prospect of great plenty – the people are on the whole happy.

He concluded, however, that the Government did not do enough for 'the cultivators of the soil'. The great Akbar, one of the wisest princes that ever sat on a throne, had decreed that the rents of those who improved the land and increased produce should not be raised; it was a wise and liberal law which had long fallen into disuse.

William was still disappointed in George: though he worked conscientiously, he never considered anything 'out of the sphere of common exertion' and, like his elder brother, was self-willed. He did not seek out the kind of people who would help him to improve his mind and was not likely to become 'a great Hero or a great Philosopher'. If he wanted a political appointment he needed either 'great talents, or great interest'; if he had talents he was keeping them to himself, and apparently his only hobby was watch making.

When William was in Delhi, George, Peter Grant and the rest of his lodgers, saw little of him; he worked at his desk all day, then drove to his Court in the city, returning home around nine, sometimes joining the others after dinner. The talk invariably turned to home and the cost of living there; William reckoned he would need a large income to keep himself in the manner to which he was accustomed. He was now relying on George to be the family newscaster; for five years there were no more scrawls to his parents, although he kept in touch intermittently with James.

Peter Grant, who had a job with the Palace Guard, 'a pleasant and easy position from all accounts', was planning to go home soon with a healthy bank balance. George thought that he might apply for the vacancy. When, however, he approached the new Governor General, Lord William Bentinck,[6] known as the 'Clipping Dutchman' for his cutbacks, he was politely refused – 'Economy is the fashion'.

The clipping continued, and there was little prospect of a return to his Regiment. He was not sure, in any case, whether he wanted to return to being 'a parade drudge'; there was much discontent in the army, who cursed 'Lord B ... from the bottom of their souls with grinding teeth and indrawn breath ... in these clipping days no man's appointment is safe for an hour'. Since Aleck's old sparring partner, Holt Mackenzie, now 'a man of weight', was wholly in favour of the surveys, George felt his job might survive. If not, there was a rumour that he might be transferred to the Great Trigonometrical Survey under Colonel George Everest.[7]

6 1774–1839. Second son of the 3rd Duke of Portland and Governor General of Bengal (1828–33). His principal concern was to turn around the loss-making East India Company so that its charter would be renewed. Known for his ruthless financial efficiency, social reforms including the abolition of sati (suttee), and introduction of English as sole official language.

7 1790–1866. 1823 Superintendent of the Great Trigonometrical Survey of India. 1830 Surveyor General of India. Returned home in 1843. Peak XV, a mountain he had never seen, was named for him, after much argument, in 1856.

He had had enough of worrying about his future and reckoned that he should have been allowed to learn a trade. It was wrong that tradespeople were held in contempt by professionals and stuck at the bottom of the employment ladder. It was all a question of education: if a bookseller, for example, were properly educated he would look 'beyond the bindings of the volumes':

> My favourite trade watch making requires a man of high attainments in science to conduct that business properly and so do many other mechanical and chemical callings ... Now to these employments properly educated would I put my sons nor feel the slightest shame at seeing them stand behind a counter – they might leave it when they have made their fortunes.

If he had sons and was planning their future, he crossly told his mother, he would draw his pen through the whole continent of India.

He was proud, however, of the maps and reports that his survey had produced, but 'you would think that the Government might say something encouraging to us, and express their satisfaction at our progress; sweet words cost nothing and are ... pleasant to receive. The only morsel of praise we ever had bestowed on us was this "that our progress was satisfactory".'

On Holt Mackenzie's suggestion, George and his colleague had spent considerable time and trouble teaching six native assistants to calculate decimals 'in the English mode' and to write the English alphabet so that they recorded the names of the villages 'very prettily' – all in five months. The field books were sent to Calcutta but, once more, the message was disappointing: 'The Government considers the results satisfactory'. Like William, George lived in hope of a trump card – something just round the corner to render life more interesting and fulfilling.

Small dark stranger

The summer of 1828 at Moniack was as full of social activity as ever. Aeneas Mackintosh had been to stay and visited Belladrum, where preparations were being made for its new owners, the erstwhile tenants of Moniack, the Stewarts of Bombay; they had snatched it from under the nose of Lord Lovat, who was reputedly late with his offer. Belladrum was no longer so beautiful, the garden now 'a map of disorder and neglect'. Claudius Rich's widow, Mary, also came to stay and there was a dinner party for fourteen – 'too much for our cook and butler the god-like Hector'.

Their most eccentric guest was Edward's old friend, Mrs Fraser, late of Belladrum: she slept with eight pillows under five blankets and was 'dumb till 2 o'clock to save her lungs and blind all the evening to save her eyes'. When she emerged from the pillows and blankets, she lay on the sofa with her eyes tight shut, chatting nonstop with Jane Anne and Jeanie.

In July James wrote to his mother with a surprising revelation concerning an acquaintance of Peter Grant, Mrs Grant of Auchterblair, who lived in Nairn. She had a large house and a warm heart and welcomed 'young ladies from India meaning thereby young ladies of European parents'. Many women, especially those in reduced circumstances, offered this service to European children, often as young as four, who were sent home to avoid the fatal illnesses of India. Major Frederick Young, who had fought alongside William at Jaithak, was apparently looking for a respectable establishment for his daughter, Amy; William had recommended Mrs Grant. When the little girl, who was about twelve, arrived in Nairn, Mrs Grant was not a little taken aback to find she was of mixed race and very dark; there was nothing for it, however, but to welcome her and she turned out to be so amiable and docile that the Grant family grew very fond of her.

William had asked James to report on the child's progress; James and Jeanie accordingly invited Amy and Matilda Grant, her contemporary, to stay at Moniack for a few days. It was a great success – Amy was 'sweet tempered, mild, of good disposition and very truthful' – and from then on there were regular visits. Jane Anne's children were in and out of Moniack all that summer as their mother was expecting again, and nine-year-old Jane got on famously with Amy and Matilda: 'it was strange to see her wreathing her little white arm about Amy's olive coloured neck on the green before the house and all playing uproariously together'. After their lessons the children were free to ramble along the burn gathering wild strawberries – 'a joyous liberty after the streets of Nairn'. James and Jeanie enjoyed their visits and he did not retire to his den nearly as much as usual.

One of the happiest days was the clearing out of 'Noble's loft'. All the artefacts from India, all the household equipment not needed for tenants, all George's belongings and much else had been dumped here over the years. There were trunks full of moth which all had to be smoked with juniper: what 'a clearing, burning, brushing & washing we had at that Noble depository of confusion'. Throughout her life Amy would remember the happiness of her days at Moniack.

❖

Jeanie continued to report to Jane on the progress of the Culduthel family: Jane Anne was still extremely firm about the children's diet: meat only every other day and nothing stronger than milk or water to drink. Affleck, now known as 'Adoo', 'a noble bluff independent funny fellow' and ludicrously like his father, spent his time chasing the ducks with Nanny Rose panting in hot pursuit. Jeanie reckoned that Adoo was spoilt by his mother – he got away with everything, including 'riding my poor old sofa cushions and bridling the stools and chairs'. But she loved them all and enjoyed their different personalities and looks. Ned was 'quite a Reelick & tho not handsome very like his grandfather. He and Mary are the only two Reelicks – the others are all Culduthels in looks'. Mary took after the aunt for whom she was named and not only in looks; she was very engaging ...

> ... with a good spice of obstinacy & wilfulness which must be corrected ... even Uncle James's grave look & imposing voice does not daunt her ... she has the very sweetest voice and the sweetest smile possible and I think will be very pretty ... Oh I shall miss their dear little tongues when they go.

The new baby, born in December 1828, was called William despite Jane Anne's vote for George after her best loved brother; 'if it had been a girl no-one would have prevented her calling it Georgina,' pronounced Jeanie with foresight. She worried that Jane Anne never seemed to have time for herself. Her figure was 'prodigious' and it was impossible to have a proper conversation with her as she was 'so driven from pillar to post with all the different demands on her time' and was too much in the society of 'uncultivated sportsmen'. However, 'she seizes all the happiness of life & flings away its troubles, does her duty admirably as a wife, and a mother, knows no anxiety and anticipates no evil.'

The following year, 1829, brought to the Highlands 'a sweet cheerful quiet summer ... no hurry or worry but all peace & sunshine' – and Lady Woodhouselee. She was at last persuaded to make the journey north and she and Isabella spent the summer at Moniack; they both gained in health and strength which was gratifying to Jeanie:

> The blessing of seeing my dear mother perfectly happy & content reading her book, working her stocking or wandering about the garden enjoying the beauty of the trees & flowers ... the greatest delight to me.

Jeanie was also thriving at Moniack: she had never had to take 'so much as a pinch of rhubarb[8] since ever I came north & am fatter & stouter than I have been for years' and she rarely got so much as a cold.

The next two years, 1830 and 1831, followed a pattern: James and Jeanie divided their time between Moniack and Edinburgh. James found it easier to write in Edinburgh without the distractions of home. Taking over the old library at 108 Princes Street, he often wrote till one in the morning. His new book was a biography of Genghis Khan and he was finding it much more difficult writing from life than composing 'from my own brain'. He was enjoying the literary companionship of brother-in-law Patrick, who had been commissioned to write the history of Scotland – 'fame to him but no money yet – the *lives* are the potboilers – we neither of us go out much finding that company & work are scarcely compatible'.

James also spent time in London, leaving Jeanie in Edinburgh to help Isabella look after their indomitable, and increasingly difficult, mother. Lady Woodhouselee could read the smallest print of the newspaper without spectacles but never went out; she demanded constant attention, having 'no notion of being a moment left to her own resources'. James's few social engagements included a notable dinner with the erstwhile Lady Hood and her new husband, James Stewart. They had a 'long chat ... travelling over all the fields of India again ... she has grown very coarse in person but her fine voice and captivating manners still remain'.

8 Used for medicinal purposes since ancient China, especially for the treatment of intestinal and liver problems.

They returned as usual to Moniack for the summers, where they had little Mary to stay during Jane Anne's next pregnancy: her eighth child put in his appearance in September 1830, and Jane Anne was once again not allowed to name him George; he was baptised Alexander but always known as Alister.

At last, in June 1831, there is the first hint from Jeanie that the old couple might be coming home: 'By this time next year if it please God to preserve us all you will perhaps be walking about in your own sweet garden again.' George was delighted and visualised his own return:

> I have ever since your letter came thought of nothing else than how I am to make the selfsame trip. I have already pictured my reception among my friends, my taking my possession of my own room where I shall dispose my multifarious collections of guns, fishing tackle etc ... my visits to all my old acquaintances and my old haunts, my walks, the old servants tottering about and I assure you I have begun to look forward to the good fresh herring and speldings[9] and green hams at breakfast.

Exiles return

After over eight years in Edwardes Square, Reelig and Jane closed the door for the last time on 6 August 1831 and sailed from London to Aberdeen, where they arrived three days later. Going straight to the Tytlers at Sanquhar, they stayed for nearly three weeks to recover. It had all been difficult and exhausting, and Reelig, now over eighty, was recovering from a long illness. Then came a joyful reunion with Jane Anne at Culduthel, where they at last set eyes on their latest grandchildren.

They stayed at Culduthel until early March, braving the 'sweet higeldy pigeldy mess' in which Jane Anne always lived. All the children were musical and the house was full of singing and whistling which Jane found 'perhaps more than cheerful – rather at times noisy'. Reelig, still very weak, was confined to his room. Jane was full of praise for the care shown not only by Jane Anne and the grandchildren, who vied with the servants to wait upon Grandpapa, with Adoo and Willie, four and three, competing to take him breakfast in bed, but also by Affleck, 'a man so little used to sickness'; he had shown unabated kindness and thought of all he could to interest and amuse his father-in-law.

At last, on 8 March, after an absence of almost twelve years, they reached Moniack. Neither was very well: Reelig was still suffering badly from gout and the effects of his illness, while Jane was living on 'Blue pills' and fairly regular doses of laudanum. But at home again Reelig soon regained his health: 'he has not the slightest appearance of an aged or infirm man – no person will believe he is in his 82nd year'. He still took pleasure from the natural world:

9 Split, dried haddocks.

> I am just now delightfully deafened by a mavis[10] of extraordinary powers, pouring forth its evening song from the very top of the old silver fir opposite to my mother's chamber window – I believe she is teaching her nestlings their first notes.

Sometimes he would accompany James to town and then Jane would be alone all day, deep in Patrick Tytler's *History of Scotland*, just out and highly acclaimed. There was the delight of occasional babysitting and walks with the children, although when they had had the six elder ones for the day they were quite glad when they went home. Sometimes the six-year-old Mary came on her own, to Jane's delight, singing and dancing the evening away. She was often on her way from Beaufort, where she was a great favourite and a playmate of little Simon, Master of Lovat; the house seemed very dull when she had danced off home.

One day, Jane plucked up courage to walk once more through the woods and along the paths that were so much part of their past; the wood was 'beautifully grown up but the walk recalled many feelings of days long past which were at once pleasing & painful'. Another day, she ventured up to the family burial ground at the top of the hill behind the church; she had not been there since the day of Mary's funeral twenty-five years ago:

> The day was lovely & the prospect from our burial ground looking over the river Beauly truly beautiful & inspired soothing thoughts – may the remainder of the time I have to spend in this world fit me for the change when I shall be laid in that peaceful spot.

It was a beautiful spring, and Reelig was out from morning till dusk pottering about the place, resuming all his old ploys: 'I amuse myself much in my old ways and, without costing the Estate one shilling, constantly do something towards its embellishment and improvement'. William had told him to act 'just as if the property was yours', and this is what he intended to do, but it could cause difficulties. Jane confided to the diary – in which she was still writing illegibly – that she had had a talk with James 'relative to the work his Father is carrying on – quite in good humour tho not all!'.

Although he revelled in the place, Reelig privately felt the two of them could live far more cheaply if they moved into town; but 'to quit Moniack and his Rooftree' might hurt James's feelings. He appreciated James's care of the old place but suspected that James's true preference was for London and the society of artists and writers:

> His tastes for rural scenery and rural pursuits are merely those of a landscape painter, not those of a landscape gardener and ... all rural exertions are with him merely those of duty and brotherly affection and otherwise are all against the grain and a Bore.

James had just finished *The Highland Smugglers*, which brought him recognition as a novelist, and was embarking on a short History of Persia.

10 Songthrush.

William's satisfaction with his parents' return was tempered with warnings to James:

> My return depends on your management – I have saved for the last 2 years my yearly income; when by my continued saving the debt of Moniack is discharged & the place free, then I depart from this & not until then.

James was not to keep a gardener ...

> ... unless the garden repays ... what is it to me, gasping in India, whether the shrubbery at Moniack have flowers in it or weeds? Mere prevention of loss, is what I want ... Grieves,[11] Foresters, Gardeners &c &c unless necessary to make or save, discharge.

He gave orders that a comfortable carriage and good horses were to be bought for his parents at his expense – 'this request I expect will be complied with'. It was not. As Reelig explained to George, they did not need a carriage and horses, being firm in their resolve not to dine or sleep away from home except at Culduthel:

> I am no longer *locomotive*. I never stir from Moniack. Your mother seldom goes from home, when she does so ... James drives her in his carriage which is a very comfortable open one ... My main object and your mother's is to see William home – and to this effect to avoid every expence to William.

The following year, 1832, Jane did grandmotherly duty looking after Adoo and his younger brother Willie while Jane Anne produced her tenth child and fourth daughter, Georgina. At the end of the year they all attended a concert at which little Jane, now twelve, was playing for the first time under the auspices of Jane Anne's old master, Mr Thomson, who had taught Aunt Mary all those years ago. At Hogmanay there was a large party; Grandmamma Jane's diary recorded, 'all merry & happy & myself contrasting this Happy Anniversary ... from that of [18]21 when we were preparing to leave the country'.

Trump cards in India

A couple of years previously, William had bought a bungalow in Mussoorie, a beautiful hill station with a delicious climate; here he installed his children. But things were changing: all the Residency staff were new, Frederick Young and Skinner were now his only 'landmarks' and he felt lonely and depressed. Sketching out for James his plans for an eventual departure from India, he finally admitted how difficult this would be:

> I shall transport everything I wish to take with me; and leave myself for the last year or two completely naked so that I may mount my camel, and cross to Persia; and leave India, not for an everlasting adieu, but as I would leave Delhi for Kurnal. I dread the pain of being torn up by the roots; and I know the best way to escape it is to set off home, with an intention of wandering again, if it be necessary, from feeling or retrospect; but with a hope; that what is in Europe will be too fascinating, to let me think of India again.

11 Farm foremen.

Botanist and geologist Victor Jacquemont (1801–1832).

There was, however, time for one more great friendship, with Victor Jacquemont.[12] The tall, tousle-headed young French botanist, commissioned by his Government to undertake a scientific mission in Tibet, Lahore and Kashmir, had arrived in Delhi in 1831. Throughout his time in India he dashed off charming and amusing letters home, full of information about the Indian way of life and the characters he came across. On their first meeting William 'pleased me extremely and I pleased him no less';[13] they immediately agreed to travel together.

Jacquemont, aware of William's misanthropic reputation, found him 'the most sociable person in the world. He is a thinker, who finds nothing but isolation in the intercourse of words without ideas, miscalled conversation by the society here, which he therefore very seldom frequents.'[14] He was amazed by William's personal courage but 'Mr Fraser is the most pacific of men. You would take him for a quaker, notwithstanding his large black beard.'[15]

William badly wanted to accompany Jacquemont to Lahore but his application for leave was not granted. A year later, however, Jacquemont was back in Delhi to spend six weeks with William 'and, thanks to his kindness, Delhi will remain one of my happiest

12 1801–32. French botanist and geologist. Wrote *Letters from India: India, Tibet, Lahore and Cashmere, 1828, 1829, 1830, 1831.*

13 *Letters from India*, Vol. 1.

14 Ibid.

15 Ibid.

recollections of India'.[16] In Firozpur he received a lavish welcome from William's protégé, the wealthy young Nawab, Shams-ud-din, son of Ahmad Baksh Khan who had died in 1827.

William was enchanted with Jacquemont, travelling with him often and more than once neglecting his duties in consequence. Inevitably, the moment came when Jacquemont's mission would take him too far from Delhi for William to accompany him. They parted company with a silent handshake and Jacquemont rode out to camp alone at the Qutb Minar. During the night, a messenger came with a note from William: he was prepared to risk censure for the joy of a few more days in his friend's company and would catch him up. Unable to believe this, Jacquemont dejectedly continued on his way but in camp at Gurgaon that evening saw a familiar figure hurrying towards him across the plain. They walked on together for several days until one morning Jacquemont woke to find William gone, but 'he will come one day to see me at Paris'. A month later, Jacquemont was taken ill; he died in Bombay in December 1832.

In his first letter to his parents for five years, and his last,[17] William wrote of his desolation. Jacquemont was 'by far the best man I have met in India, to visit whom in Europe was my greatest solace in anticipation ... one of the most amiable person I ever yet met with'. He greatly admired 'people of this stamp ... men whose reason has subdued feeling which is the conquest all should endeavour to achieve, if they wish to be happy'.

This same, prophetic, letter expresses an underlying weariness and disillusionment: 'this service is really now, not only disagreeable, but precarious'. He refers to his own death: 'I hope when I make my Exit, it may be standing, or walking, or sleeping, or riding, and alone. Certainly, for myself, I should say, the sooner the better ... as long as life lasts its scenes are interesting; but who does not say to himself, what is it all, and what follows.'

That same year, 1832, William at long last achieved his passionate desire: he was made Resident, or as it was now termed, Civil Commissioner of Delhi and agent to the Governor General. The role was a complex one. To quote from Sir John Kaye's biography of Charles Metcalfe,[18] Resident in 1811–18 and 1825–27:

> The Delhi Resident was at once a diplomatist and an administrator. It was his duty not only to superintend the affairs of the pensioned Mughal and his family, but to manage the political relations of the British Government ... it was his duty, too, to superintend the internal government of all the Delhi territory – to preside over the machinery of revenue collection and the administration of Justice, and to promote by all possible means the development of the resources of the country and the industry and happiness of the people.

16 Ibid.

17 In his father's letterbook, after this final letter, the next few pages are all ruled with neat red margins in anticipation of the next communication.

18 *Life and Correspondence of Charles, Lord Metcalfe*, J W Kaye (1854).

With his love of India and its people, his respect for the Mughal dynasty, his extensive knowledge of the Delhi area and the far-flung villages, together with his talents for negotiation and communication, William was surely the man for the job; but as it turned out, his tenure of the position he had so long craved was to be cut short.

⁂

That same year, the trump card turned up for George, too: he was offered a transfer to the Great Trigonometrical Survey under Colonel Everest. The only drawback was that he was entitled to imminent furlough, but Everest agreed to keep the job open and George started planning: he would need two weeks in London to buy some new clothes, organise his finances and then make for home, at last 'my own master in my own country'.

But none of this happened. The transfer to Everest's team was cancelled in July. Fate had intervened in the shape of Miss Wilhelmina Moore from Liverpool.

⁂

There is no mention of Mina, as she was known, in George's letters until March 1833, although they were married in Delhi in September 1832. According to Peter Grant, she was the daughter of a Colonel Moore, commanding a regiment in Allahabad, and had come to India with her sister the previous summer. They were reportedly 'very fine girls, very young & rather little but very pretty & accomplished – they are very well connected in England'. When Jane eventually heard of the marriage, she trusted it was not 'an imprudent step – tho seemingly very speedily resolved upon'. Reelig felt, 'if it is for his happiness poor fellow I am satisfied & he shall have my blessing'. They were disappointed that it would mean the postponement of his furlough, but both wrote Mina welcoming letters and Jane hoped that 'we shall find in her an amiable addition to our family circle ... she must do much to recompense your Father and me for thus detaining him in India – tho I trust that will only be for a short time'.

Soon after their marriage George took Mina off to camp in Bareilly, about a hundred miles east of Delhi. In March he wrote home that they were leading a 'calm and satisfying life', Mina not being one for parties and late nights.

George had another reason to be thankful for Mina. Unbelievably, in the disastrous Indian economic crisis of 1833, the great financial houses of Calcutta crashed, the firm of Aeneas Mackintosh among them, and countless East India Company servants went bankrupt. Everyone was affected: James lost his precious Indian nest egg but pointed out that:

> ... had I, as most of my friends conceived would have been for my good, *remained* in the Calcutta House ... instead of withdrawing and coming home, I should now have been a beggar after a 20 year residence in India.

William had suffered great losses but 'bears them like a man – meekly and cheerfully' and continued to save 'with his eyes and his heart unchangingly turned to his home as his ultimate resting place'.

If George had gone home before the crash, he would have drawn out the Rs5,000 he had saved and returned to India penniless, unable to borrow more as his agent, Colvin, had stopped trading. Instead, he had drawn it all out for his marriage, 'regretting that it was not more to have enabled me to make a little nest egg for the wife in case of accidents'. But together with his pay it was enough for their needs. The Revenue Survey had survived the cutbacks and he had been promoted to full surveyor, with an assistant and corresponding increase in pay.

He and Mina, who was twenty-one, twelve years younger than her husband, were very happy in their comfortable little house. She accompanied him on his surveying expeditions whenever possible, often being the only woman in the cantonment. She ticked almost all Reelig's boxes: she was practical, cheerful, unaffected and resilient; she shared George's interests, was prepared to tolerate discomfort, heat and isolation and loved helping him in his work; she had a warm heart and was in no way a doormat, well able to hold her own with her strong-minded husband; and she enjoyed informal entertaining with commendable economy. Things were changing: it was no longer the fashion to entertain on a large scale and keep open house. This suited them both; they were perfectly happy with their own company or that of a few good friends.

Mina had looked forward to inheriting a fortune from the fond bachelor uncle for whom she had kept house in London, but soon after their marriage they heard that 'our hopes had flown away on the wings of the marriage bells at his wedding'. Luckily, George had never counted on this windfall. They had just enough money and all they had to do was keep free of debt and save to go home.

There were problems to begin with where housekeeping was concerned: Mina's experience had been with her pernickety uncle and she had to work hard to persuade George out of his untidy, carefree, bachelor ways, but they reached a compromise to which George gave in 'with a tolerably good grace'.

❋

At the same time, James and Jeanie had found comfortable lodgings at 72 Piccadilly along with Lady Woodhouselee, Annie and Isabella. It was noisy, but James took over a room at the back where he could write and entertain his literary circle, while his mother-in-law sat at the front window keeping a sharp eye on the teeming life of the street. They had two maids and a cook, and seven guineas a week covered everything except fires in the bedrooms.

James immediately took himself off to Guildford to interview Mina's uncle, who showed him her portrait: 'If she is like that picture she is a very lovely girl – the hair is brown & she is fair ... the expression was sweet & intelligent so all this is very nice'. Jeanie was equally impressed with Mina's good-looking brother Robert. 'So,' wrote Jeanie briskly to Jane, 'you must be content with this'.

But while George and Mina were settling into married life in India, Jeanie was having to face a long separation from James.

'Heaven preserve my patience'

Early in 1833, Lord Palmerston, the Foreign Secretary, asked James to go back to Persia on an intelligence mission: he explained with some understatement that there were 'two or three points regarding which Government wished to have correct & full information principally connected with the progress of Russian influence'. It was highly confidential and for the moment James was to tell no one but Jeanie; he was to go incognito as a private individual, an author ostensibly collecting material for his next book.

James now had to come to terms with leaving Moniack, Jeanie and his parents for what was likely to be a year. Charles Grant had decreed that James should be ready to go at a moment's notice; hence the house in Piccadilly. With his knowledge of Persia and his taste for adventure, not to mention his urgent need for an income, James was both gratified and excited by the prospect.

The background to Palmerston's move was complicated. For nearly a century, and especially since Elphinstone's abortive embassy to Kabul in 1808, London and Calcutta had been struggling with the question of how to defend India from France and Russia, and who should be their ally in this cause. The obvious answer was Persia, strategically placed and needing support in her conflicts with Turkey and Russia. Various treaties were accordingly drawn up and training given to the Persian army, but there were always too many apparently more important events nearer home to allow much attention to be given to the issue. When, however, the terms of the Treaty of Turkmenchay between Russia and Persia in 1828 revealed Russia's expansionist aims, minds in London became a shade more concentrated. The Duke of Wellington, now Prime Minister, and Lord Ellenborough, who had taken over the Board of Control, saw clearly that Russia's new relationship with Persia could well threaten British India. Lord Bentinck, India's Governor General, agreed: if Russia took it into her head to invade India, a close alliance with Persia would be her first step.

Persia in 1833 was far from stable. The sixty-three-year-old Fath Ali Shah, once a vigorous and highly intelligent ruler, now indolently divided his time between his treasury and his concubines, leaving the country for the most part in the hands of his second son and heir, Abbas Mirza. As James had recorded in the account of his Persian adventures, the Shah had about fifty sons and a hundred daughters; fourteen of these sons and four grandsons, several with their eye on the crown, were now governing provinces and running their own expensive establishments. It was a tinder-dry situation, and the moment the Shah died civil war might flare.

This complex situation led to what became known as the 'Great Game' between Britain and Russia, in which James was invited to become a player, a shadowy world of intrigue, espionage, alliance and counter-alliance.

He was by no means the only player. From early in the nineteenth century adventurous young men of various nationalities were drawn to the lonely passes and deserts of Central

Asia, eager to serve as intelligence agents. Often in disguise, as holy men, merchants or horse dealers, they slipped in and out of the shadows and haunted the bazaars. Some suffered cruel deaths, like Stoddart and Connolly, beheaded in the great square of Bokhara after months of imprisonment in an underground, rat-infested room. The young Polish aristocrat, Captain Yan Vitkevich, playing the Game for Russia, took his own life in a boarding house in St Petersburg. Others died in action or were struck down by fever.

Not surprisingly, Jeanie was horrified at the idea that James was to leave her for such a risky venture:

> When it was first proposed my whole heart turned against it so much that he said if it was to cost me so much pain he would give it up at once; but even then I saw he felt it very gratifying and in many ways advantageous to him.

Her conscience, however, was clear: 'it was not born of our seeking – it was no restlessness or ambition of his which sought it'; it was God's will 'but I do not know how I can bear it'. She thought of going too, but Charles Grant advised against it on account of danger, cost and the publicity her presence would attract. 'So,' she concluded, 'I shall return to Moniack. I thank God I have so kind and sweet a home to go to. It is there I will feel less separate from him than in any other place.'

James had left Moniack in the care of an agent, James Wilson, and farm manager Gair; William and Margaret Tytler, now temporarily renting Achnagairn, would keep an eye on the old couple and Nanny Rose. Inevitably, every letter from Moniack brought a new complaint: Nanny Rose, 'very dottled', had forgotten that the drawing room candles were now kept in the storeroom; no one understood oil lamps, and supplies of tea had not been ordered. Reelig was badly missing James and frustrated because he was not feeling well enough for his old ploys outdoors. Jane, on the other hand, he reported, was 'charmingly well and gay as a lark'.

James wrote bracingly that there was no alternative to his leaving them for a time: 'Alas the matter becomes imperative when we contemplate the great reduction of income from Indian losses & the further that may happen'. Jeanie would return to look after them 'with the most dutiful & affectionate tenderness & care' and they were surrounded by friends and relations. His mother was not convinced: 'It is too great a sacrifice but they are best judges of their own affairs & what constitutes their happiness. I only feel for being left without any one of my sons in your Father's very advanced period of life.'

In May James was still in London waiting for instructions. By June there was a rumour that he would set off at the start of July. Relieved that he would be thus be well advanced in his journey before the desperate privations of a Tartar winter, he and Jeanie hurried north for a few days. Leaving Jeanie at Moniack, James then returned to London, based himself at the Athenaeum Club in Pall Mall and waited. July came and went still with no word. He passed the dreary days as best he could, occasionally visiting his parents' numerous friends in Edwardes Square where, apparently, the Square society had been declining ever since the couple moved north.

While James was hanging around London, Jeanie, at Moniack, blamed the 'undecided & dilatory' Charles Grant for the delay. The thought of over a year apart was bad enough without this extra separation: 'I feel as if I should be quite an old woman when you see me again ... My heart is all your own and hangs on you alone for all its happiness in this world ... I can only wish you to be off now'. He was to go to church and read his Bible and trust, as she did, in his heavenly Father.

There were more problems at Moniack: Reelig had returned to all his old ploys in the woods, giving orders and countermanding those of Wilson and Gair. He was planning to enclose a field with a dyke and use three men to make a road – 'a very useless work but quite in his usual style, dear man,' commented Jeanie through clenched teeth. One or two of the lazier workmen were only too pleased to return to the old ways, complaining of the severity of their new masters. Eventually, Reelig wrote a petulant letter to Wilson with a copy to James, and Jane joined the fray: 'your father is most annoyed at the idea of not being at liberty to give any directions relative to the management of the place particularly the woods'.

Reelig was furious that Gair was planning to cut down trees near the house; Jane thought he should be allowed the veto 'rather than that his feelings (which he cannot control) should be so hurt considering the very short time he may have to interfere'. The trouble was, she said, that his memory was going and he kept forgetting the details of the new regime; he had to be excused on the grounds of age and mental infirmity. Meanwhile, according to her husband, she was in superb health and 'sweeps round the Burn walks once a day at least – up one side & home the other from the Raven Rock'.

Longing for harmony, Jeanie kept out of the dispute, managing to stay on good terms with the old gentleman, of whom she was very fond. In the end, James, who reckoned that 'the old gentleman's qualification of his original *non-interference* prohibition is worthy of a Diplomatist' wrote a careful and conciliatory letter to his father explaining everything all over again; Reelig, feeling flattered and important, took it very well, although Jane retorted that 'old people do not like to be lectured to ... even by their own children'.

Although admitting to being 'just a bit rickety', with joints that were neither pliable nor elastic so 'accordingly I make few experiments on their powers', in his letters to William Reelig showed little sign of 'mental infirmity'. He was still keeping abreast of national and international news and was very much in support of the Reform Bill of 1832,[19] of which he reckoned that 'the effect on public credit at home & abroad has been very favourable'. He also had views on what was happening in India, especially in the light of the advanced age of the great Lion of the Punjab, the Sikh leader, Ranjit Singh, ruler of the last strategically placed part of India not yet under British rule:

19 Proposed by Earl Grey and the Whigs, it disenfranchised 57 rotten boroughs, redistributed seats in Parliament to the new industrial cities and increased the electorate from around 400,000 to 650,000, allowing a sixth of the male population the vote.

James Baillie Fraser, October 1833. A portrait by William Brockedon (1787–1854).

> Should Runjeet die as he must, ere long – and a confused struggle follow – will not our usual practice be put in force of interfering and taking steps for *defensive* extension of frontiers?

⁂

In September, the passing of the India Bill[20] diverted the Government from affairs in the East which, James reckoned, were 'assuming a complexion which calls imperatively for attention'. The London season over, he was almost alone in his Club – 'this great magnificent house'– with just the odd passer-by joining him for breakfast and two or three round the fire of an evening.

In October, daily trudging between the Athenaeum and the Foreign Office, James spent some of the time sitting for a portrait by William Brockedon. There were mixed reactions to the crayon sketch: Jeanie disliked 'the cock of the eye' but considered it 'far more like and gentlemanly than Raeburn's ... in short I like the picture and so does your mother – your father not so much'. Amy approved and so did Nanny Rose. A retired retainer, Sandy the elder, commented, 'Oh it's very nice! So very like but it's but a picture! It's no himsel! Oh you should no hae let him awa frae ye!' Jane Anne declared, '[I] just love to look at its smiling face ... Oh this house is sad without you'.

By November almost everything was in place but there was a further delay because Charles Grant, needed for the final details, was ill in Paris and the King, whose signature was essential, was in Brighton. Jeanie wrote constantly, desperate to reach James while she still could. Her letters were full of love and advice, as well as furious reproach for neither answering her questions nor sympathising with his father on his recent illness; he was now better and poring over maps, trying to work out James's possible route. Jeanie was reading all she could find about Turkey and Persia but she was 'groping in the dark' and often frightening herself unnecessarily. She hoped that James was revising his Persian, polishing up 'all the flattery hyperbole & oriental flowers you can possibly muster to ensure your reception'. If this adventure did not satisfy his wanderlust, then next time 'you must take me with you for I never will consent to be so defrauded again'.

She would find it hard to forgive Charles Grant for the past eleven months of unnecessary separation, but at least James had used the time latterly for valuable talks with Alexander Burnes,[21] the brilliant young son of the Provost of Montrose. Burnes had recently returned to a hero's welcome in London after his hazardous survey of the Indus and the Oxus, an expedition for which James had been Lord Ellenborough's first choice but had declined the offer.[22] Burnes and James met at Charles Grant's dinner party, where the guests included Palmerston, the Lord Chancellor and Thomas Babington

20 The Government of India Act redesignated the Governor General of Bengal as Governor General of all India, ended the commercial activities of the East India Company and vested St Helena in the monarchy.

21 Sir Alexander Burnes (1805–1841), political officer in India and explorer. His linguistic abilities, self confidence, charm and diplomatic guile fitted him for intelligence missions concerning Russian expansion in central Asia. Sent to Kabul in 1836, he took part in the restoration of Shah Shuja to the throne of Afghanistan but was murdered in 1841 by a vengeful mob (*DNB*).

22 Possibly because he was fully occupied with Moniack and writing his books.

Macaulay.[23] James was delighted to find that Burnes knew William and urged him to call at Moniack.

Another dinner party consisted of a menagerie of lions, hyenas and bears and 'a most strange heterogeneous set' of guests. James described the ladies in details from 'the old white, fat, half smiling, half ghastly unshapely wreck of Lady Charlotte Bury' to some girls who 'do shew so much of shoulder & bosom!'

Three days later he went to see Palmerston who discussed the mission 'with, seemingly, a very tolerable notion of what he was talking about – which is saying a great deal for him'. Financial matters, he trusted, were arranged but James later found 'that all was by no means arranged ... the amount to be advanced and the amount of the allowance (two tolerably important items) seemed still unfixed'. Eventually he heard that he would receive £700 for lost time and £1200 a year with expenses.

At last all was settled. On the evening of 11 December James took a final look round the Athenaeum and his 'neat little room with its snug French bed' and saw the 'great folding doors of the Club-house close behind me upon its gorgeous apartments and delightful library'. Wrapped in his old travelling cloak, he made his way to Downing Street, where there followed 'a long bustling hour or two of sealing and directing papers, and packing of white sheepskin bags' during which he sat by the last coal fire he might see for some time. By one in the morning all was ready, the postchaise was at the door and off they went, tearing over Westminster Bridge through a tempest of wind and rain. Seven hours later, he was on the Dover packet-boat bound for Calais.

His mandate was considerable: among other things he was instructed to report on the extent of Russia's influence and trade in Persia, to gauge whether Abbas Mirza could capture the strategically important Herat and, in the event of the Shah's death, obtain the throne without foreign assistance. He was also to assess the state of affairs at Baghdad and 'sedulously to avoid all appearance of being invested with any diplomatic character of mission whatsoever'. Thus were the dice thrown for James's turn at the Great Game.

23 (1800–1859). British historian and politician. Played a major role in India and introduced English as the medium for education.

14

1833–1835

London to Constantinople

James's journey started badly, with an ancient, rickety carriage and no fewer than seven delays for repairs before they reached Vienna. He remained calm, however, admired the pretty girls and congratulated himself on having a good fur cloak, a bag for his feet and 'one of the greatest comforts ... that has been of late bestowed upon travellers ... the air-pillow of India rubber cloth made by Messrs Mackintosh and Co'.

Throughout his journey he wrote short letters to Jeanie and kept a journal, also addressed to her and minutely detailed, often with humorous accounts of the extraordinary characters encountered along the way. The closely written pages of this journal were sent home whenever a safe courier was found and eventually published in two volumes entitled *A Winter's Journey (Tatar) from Constantinople to Tehran*. It is too long for more than a sprinkling of its more telling incidents to appear in this story.

⁂

In Vienna there was business to be done but also time for concerts and theatres. He wrote to Jeanie, wishing she could enjoy 'the busy scene – busy with the vanity of folly':

> Vienna may be compared to a fine peach, all softness, sweetness, richness & beauty without – but deep in the core of this delicious exterior lies the bitter kernel of deep calculating politics, full of a sort of Prussic acid which only a few privileged & powerful statesmen can stomach or digest.

He reassured her that absence was making his heart grow fonder and that he was not planning a reunion with the little Countess.

From here everything deteriorated. The smart Austrian postilions 'with their gallant silver-laced cocked hats and badges, their red-laced jackets, and their tasselled French horns' were replaced by 'an aged man, clad in a ragged wrapper as grey and old as himself, his grey head covered with a grey felt wig, and that with a grey felt hat'; this decrepit fellow, who confessed he was eighty-five, shot off at a surprising pace. When his hat consequently blew off he spent a long time wondering whether it was worth saving, finally creaking down into the mud to retrieve it. The next postilion was a deaf hunchback, who overturned the carriage into the 'thick fat mud-porridge', which after two months of continual rain covered the country. While they waited for help James arranged himself in the hood of the vehicle, lit a candle and 'noted out the incidents of the night'.

On went the carriage, jolting, rocking and hurtling from one accident to another, with the quality of horses, accommodation and fare all deteriorating daily. There were moments of enjoyment: in a Hungarian village they were entertained by a group of gypsy musicians who played dances and waltzes of which one 'was neither more nor less than a good Scottish reel ... worthy to be placed in any lady's collection'.

In Turkey the real challenge, the Tatar[1] journey, began. At the border, James was received by the Dragoman (interpreter):

> 'Now,' said he, 'you have done with the other side; you are one of us; there is no return yonder'. It was the breaking the last slender link that united me to the habits and people of Europe, and I almost felt the mysterious sort of spell which separated us.

James was then kitted out with *shulwars* or riding trousers, 'a petticoat of the most prodigious dimensions with the bottom sewed up, leaving two holes for the legs to go through'. These 'inexpressibles' were very inconvenient for walking or mounting a horse but extremely efficient protection against cold. There were also warm Tatar stockings, to be worn three pairs at a time inside stout Tatar boots, a sword and a knife. While James was struggling with the cords and tapes that held it all together, his Tatar guide, Mehmet Aga, appeared. He was the most beautiful man James had ever seen: his face was 'an almost faultless oval' and his exquisite mustachios 'shrouded the upper lip of an equally beautiful mouth' full of perfect teeth; his nose was the best of Grecian and Roman and his eyes were full, dark and sleepy. Silks and velvets clothed this Adonis and, on top of *shulwars* and shawls, a scarlet jacket embroidered with gold and lined with fur.

The Tatar horses were like 'Cinderella's mice', so tiny that when James managed to mount and stow away 'the interminable quantity of broadcloth that enveloped my lower man', there was nothing to be seen of the horse save his ears, tail and hoofs. Two *Sorajees* (guides and grooms) rode ahead in charge of the baggage horses, and then up leapt Mehmet Aga with a shout of '*Yahullah* and a bound that shakes his little steed to its very marrow'; the fascinated bystanders all responded with the same shout 'and away we go dashing through the thick mud and mire'.

A survival from the great days of the Turkish Empire, posting houses were placed along the main roads for government officials and later for anyone prepared to pay. A *cahwajee* (brewer of coffee) would hand travellers a cup of strong Turkish coffee the moment they dismounted, and sometimes food was produced – eggs fried in butter or scrawny old hens, 'torn joint from joint by the paws of a Tatar, and cut in pieces by the rusty, greasy knife of a Sorajee'. At other times, the Tatar guide would produce, from deep in the folds of

1 Tatars were tribes composed of Mongols and Turks who, under Genghis Khan, conquered much of Asia and Eastern Europe in the early 13th century. Tatars were their descendants and a Tatar journey was a journey on horseback through the historical Tartar region in Eastern Europe and Asia.

his clothes, large lumps of raw meat wrapped in a filthy handkerchief and kept close to his body to protect them from freezing. These were then cooked on the fire in the stable; gathered around it in the thick, smoky dark would be a barely distinguishable assortment of travellers, some huddled, odorous and snoring on filthy rotting mats.

It was now New Year and the snow had begun in earnest; often the road was lost in drifts and there were fierce arguments between Mehmet Aga and the *Sorajees* as to the way forward. Mehmet liked to prove his mettle by leading the little train of horses at a breakneck gallop into the towns, whisking through gateways and tearing along narrow streets 'until at length, with a shower of fire-sparks and an explosion of mud ... we all brought up sharp at the entrance of the post-house'. In one town Mehmet took James to a Turkish bath, where he spent three luxurious hours divesting himself of a fortnight's dirt.

On they went through mud, snow and wind, always cold and wet, always hungry, until at last they came in sight of the domes and minarets of Constantinople, where James presented his credentials to the Consul, Mr Cartwright. He had travelled the 750 miles across European Turkey in just over eight days – 'pretty well I think you will allow, for a gentleman of a certain age, who had not crossed a horse a dozen times during the preceding dozen years'. The Consul was understandably surprised at the apparition on his doorstep:

> Covered with mud from head to foot ... bedabbled with dirt and rain; my eye and the whole side of my face black, blue and green from the effects of the kick of a horse, and my person girt with sundry nondescript appendages required on the journey ... his eye glanced rather waggishly at my figure; upon which I laughed and then he laughed, and we became excellent friends in a moment.

James was to look back on the ten days of comfort with the Cartwrights amid the wonders of Constantinople 'as a bright light shining for a moment [which] deepens the darkness that succeeds'.

Constantinople to Teheran

For the first few months of James's absence Jeanie tried to stay cheerful:

> No longer does Nanny's little fat hand draw out your dear letters from the post bag and bring them to my bedside ... I have promised to you & to my own mind that I will keep up my spirits ... I do not allow myself to droop.

After New Year 1834 she dispatched her parents-in-law to Culduthel and sneaked off to Edinburgh to see her mother and sisters and catch up with friends. She found them all gripped by a craze for a new game – backgammon; her mother liked to hear the rattle of the dice and clink of the counters, 'for this town is like a deserted village since they have macadamised Princes Street. I never hear a carriage sound. I think it no improvement but very dull.'

Jane Anne, meanwhile, was pregnant yet again, and Affleck was worrying about his financial position, having sunk into debt like everyone else. With the turn of the year, Jeanie was counting the months to James's homecoming:

> Oh I had such a sweet dream the other night of your return – so vivid – I felt your warm soft lips when I awoke just as if they had actually pressed mine. Gracious how I will enjoy that blessed moment that gives you back to me.

He had said he would be away ten months, so she would generously give him till the end of October. Everyone was complaining, 'Oh when will Mr Fraser be home again – it's bad for everyone when he is away'.

Reelig, meanwhile, was writing to James regularly, still glorying in his natural surroundings. It was a very cold spring that year, 'however the mavis gives us a song ... & snowdrops are abundant as well as other spring flowers – but they all shiver while they smile'.

❋

Throughout the next stage of his journey, undertaken at the worst possible time of year and through wild country, James kept up his journal in minute detail, sparing the reader not a step of the way, not a moment of discomfort or extreme exhaustion. The following passage, written on arrival in Teheran over three months after leaving London, is from the end of Volume II of *A Winter's Journey*:

> We have been wading night and day through interminable wastes of deep snow, exposed to all the violence of storm, and drift, and wind, with the thermometer frequently from 15 to 20 under zero. Our clothes and face and beards, were clotted into stiff mats of ice; our boots, hard as iron, frozen to the stirrup, and our limbs tortured with pain, or chilled into insensibility by intense cold. We were mounted on wretched carrion, which it was our daily and hourly task to whip and beat to the end of their stage, to dig out of the snow-wreaths into which they had sunk, or drag with their loads from the bottom of ravines down which they had rolled. Far from having the means of shifting when comfort of cleanliness required it ... we continued riding for weeks without a change, though wet through once a day at least by the melting ice that hung upon our clothes, or the snow that fell on them; and rest, when we halted from necessity, was banished, not oftener by the swarms of vermin and the foul air which infested our squalid quarters, than by the cold, which, in spite of our furs, would strike from our thawing clothes or the frozen floor to our very marrow.
>
> But worse even than corporeal sufferings was the anxiety of mind inseparable from the responsibility that rested on me, and the moral effort required not only to judge what should be done under circumstances of great embarrassment, but to force myself, day after day, and night after night, and oblige others, also to face the physical suffering and consequences which that decision might involve. To know that the lives of many men and animals, as well as your own, rest upon your judgement and discretion, is a consideration that may well make a man pause before he acts and the impulses of mere humanity and self-preservation must be greatly heightened ... by the recollection, that with you must perish all you may

have done, and must terminate your efforts to do more – for to little end have been all your exertions, if, by one false step on your part, the fruits of them are to lie buried with yourself under a wreath of snow.

I know no consideration upon earth, short of absolute and imperative duty, which would induce me to undertake such another journey at such a season.

Summer in Scotland

In the Highlands that summer of 1834, a brilliant sun shone every day – a 'hissing hot July' Reelig called it. James had sent Jeanie some seeds from Persia which were 'watched over by good Macallum whose broad unlovely face glowed with delight when I told him you had gathered them'. She once more reminded James that his allotted ten months were drawing to a close and he was not on any account to risk another journey through the snow. She was busy overseeing Nanny Rose and the making of the raspberry jelly and jam, especially James's favourite *white* raspberry jam, and the cherry brandy.

Reelig was up to his old tricks, 'prowling about the burn' with his partner in crime, James McQueen, and quarrelling with Wilson and Gair. Jane called it 'doing many little jobs about the place', while Jeanie reluctantly took the view that Reelig and McQueen could 'daunder & meander together' harmlessly. 'It is good, dear old man, that he can thus amuse himself ... if it keeps him happy it is well & we must be content with that.'

In August Jane Anne gave birth to her fifth daughter and eleventh child, Frances Elizabeth. At the same time she saw her eldest daughter, Jane, off to Miss Gibson's school in Essex. She had wanted to keep all her children under her wing, with a governess if necessary, but life at Culduthel was chaotic and no governess lasted for long. Jane Anne missed this fourteen-year-old companion very much:

> ... such a big person makes a gap in the family and Papa and I are sitting down to our tete a tete dinner instead of our round table that we were used to for so long.

She reassured Jane that she was looking after her little garden, bursting with hollyhocks, roses and carnations, and sent her news of the new sister:

> I am very sleepy for Miss Frances Elizabeth chose to *dance* last night instead of sleeping & as she is my companion at night, it did not suit me so well.

There was a big change in Amy's life, too: she had stayed happily with Mrs Grant in Nairn until she was considered mature enough to stretch her wings a little. Now about seventeen, she moved to live with the respectable Johnstone family in Keith, Aberdeenshire, where there were two other boarders, both 'charming & very carefully educated'. By now she was 'rather improved in appearance', still very dark but with a good figure and even 'sometimes rather goodlooking'.

Amy was very sad at leaving Moniack, and Jeanie thought that perhaps, one day, they could have her with them, 'but at present that would never do'. The secret of her real identity was still safe – she was introduced to Mr Johnstone as 'a ward of William's'. Her grandmother, who had so far met her only twice, remained determined she was nothing but 'a plain black lassie' although pleasing and amiable. Jeanie suspected that Jane knew perfectly well who Amy really was but was determined not to say so 'for she insists on referring all to Col. Frederick Young & thinks him a very heartless extraordinary person never to ... thank us for all our care of his child'.

Jeanie, despite her earlier prejudice, shared by her mother-in-law, had become very fond of Amy, whom she considered 'sensible, modest, amiable and most correct in all her ideas as far as I can judge'; her only fault was laziness. Mrs Grant had been economical in providing clothes for the girl, so Jeanie was busy choosing things for her from her own wardrobe as well as 'any stray books', since she was very fond of reading.

Tabriz to Teheran

That October, the whole family pored over a long letter from James in Mashhad on his fifty-first birthday in June. He was still daydreaming of home:

> But I scare away the blue fiends as best I may ... & find in motion & in business and in a conviction that I am doing my duty ... a cure for low spirits ... & when I get into my saddle by the glimmering of a pearly dawn & with the sky flush gradually till the glorious sun himself arises to enlighten my path I feel how vain have been my nightly fancies.

The second part of his journey, through spring and summer, was marginally less dangerous and arduous than the first but, nonetheless, had its fair share of delays, setbacks and dangers. It also had its interesting moments: before leaving Teheran, James had had an audience with the Shah for which he had to find a full-dress coat and red stockings. Accounts of audiences with the King of Persia were fairly common, but James reckoned Jeanie would never forgive him if he passed over the interview 'in utter silence'.

Arriving at the hall of audience, he could barely make out the aged and frail Shah sitting hunched in the middle of 'glittering frippery'. He started bowing before entering, advanced halfway towards the hall, bowed again, took off his slippers and advanced in his red stockings, stopped, bowed again and then advanced to the hall steps, bowed again, entered, bowed again and then stood erect in the presence of 'The Point of the World's Adoration'. Fath Ali Shah Qajar was glad to hear of James's book on his earlier travels in Persia but more interested in the news that a detachment of British officers had recently ridden into Teheran declaring 'they are English men and all the English are good', on which optimistic note the audience was terminated. Later he gave orders that James should be provided with a reliable guide and the necessary letters of introduction.

James set off for Mashhad with five horses and five mules, a horse-keeper, a cook and several servants. He had also engaged a young Persian as a travelling companion to teach him more Persian and to write letters for him; whether he could trust any of them was another matter: 'It is now that I miss my faithful [Black] John, who was so capital a hand on a march, and who used to look after so much which I now must see to myself, whether weary or not.'

There were moments of stunning beauty on the way: in one mountain pass he came upon 'hundreds, both of red and yellow tulips, with hyacinths and geraniums, all bursting into flower amongst thickets of wild almond-bushes all rich in blossom; it was exceedingly beautiful'. He recognised landmarks from his previous journey, most of which were in a more ruinous state than before, although one remained untouched by the events of the past twelve years, a magnificent *chinar* or sycamore tree, 19ft in girth and 90ft high, which James guessed dated from the era of Shah Abbas. He was delighted to come across this old friend again; it reminded him of the big ash tree at Rebeg.

He spent ten days in Mashhad having audiences with the Vizier and the Governor, looking up old acquaintances and hearing their stories. Everywhere things were 'like the country itself, crumbling into decay', and at every corner there were beggars and starving children; they came from the surrounding villages earlier destroyed by Persian soldiers, who descended like a flight of locusts, leaving a desert behind them. In the *Sahn*, or great square, all the beautiful tiling and gilding which had made the place like a jewel had vanished, leaving but 'a patched and shabby-looking ruin'.

He had hoped to travel far north of his former route in order to get a glimpse of the 'curious though dangerous' Turkomans and ascertain their feelings towards Europeans. One reason for abandoning this plan was the rumour that Shah Shuja, the exiled King of Afghanistan, William's old friend, was planning, with the assistance of the British, to reclaim his throne and had already taken Kandahar. Since Persia reckoned Kandahar belonged to her, the authorities were alarmed by the part Britain was said to be playing; even the Vizier in Mashhad believed that the English had taken Kabul and were on their way to meet the Russians. None of this was true, but it was clearly not the moment to take on anything more hazardous. James reassured Jeanie, 'I ... shall do nothing that a due regard to duty and prudence may forbid; so, dear, have no dread for me.'

Before he left Mashhad, however, things got a little too warm for comfort. The Vizier announced to a guide: 'Here is an English gentleman who wishes to go and see the Toorkomans to take account of the ... passes and the roads, where guns can go, and by which an army may come, that the English may come and take the country – what say you.'

As taken aback as the guide, James assured the Vizier that he was travelling 'entirely from curiosity' but would willingly return the way he had come.

'Only joking', or the equivalent, said the Vizier.

Two friends, the only ones James almost trusted, agreed that he should not enter Turkoman territory; there was neither chief nor government, they would cut a throat for four farthings 'and if they take in into their heads that you are a spy, they will show you no mercy'. Very reluctantly, he abandoned, probably forever, the chance of seeing the famous fortress of Khelaat [Qual'at], bade farewell to Mashhad with relief, turned his back on the east and set his face north.

He was now at his furthest point from Britain and every step would take him nearer home. On one hand he was longing for the adventure to be over, but 'How shall I brook the change from this bustling life of journeying and excitement, among kings, and princes, and ministers, and khans, and caravanserais, and palaces, by turns, to the quiet retirement of [home] if it pleases God I ever do return there.'

He promised Jeanie he would take no risks on the way and was looking forward to talking of it all by the Moniack fireside during the long winter evenings. Usually forced to write his letters squatting on the ground after a long day's march, he was amused by the possibility of Jeanie's company on his next adventure and visualised her 'bumping after me upon a Tatar saddle – no no – if you should ... accompany me it must be at leisure and in comfort ... but I trust that our fate may rather be cast at home – for I have enough of wandering.'

It was now almost impossible to find food for his men, let alone his horses. On his earlier trip he had met with ready hospitality in this area. Now, after all the destruction and extortion by the military, the mere glimpse of a stranger made the villagers hide their possessions and head for the hills. James had to resort to catching fish with a branch for a rod, his own precious fishing gear having been stolen in Mashhad. He was relieved to meet a detachment of the Persian army and become a temporary camp follower, picking up important information along the way. There were no regular rations; the men were permitted to obtain food in any way they wanted, with spear, sword or fire. Horses were tethered in the corn, trees were stripped of fruit and branches, houses were pulled down for firewood. This, he concluded, was the approved Qajar policy:

> They destroy instead of conciliating the old families; they depopulate district after district and then call it quiet – pacificated. They make a desert and call it peace.[2]

There were, as usual, diversions. On the very first night James was startled to hear a sort of regimental band playing familiar music:

> Think of my sensations on recognising 'Cease, rude Boreas', the Scotch trumpet tune, and several reels and quicksteps played by Persian fifers ... within sight of the great Toorkoman Desert, and being wakened every morning by the reveillez of the cavalry bugles!

There were also the usual camp annoyances – the nightly braying of mules, and appalling insects; far more terrifying than any wild Turkoman to the arachnophobic James were the 'camel stingers', huge, hairy, yellow and black spiders, which managed to crawl up his wide Persian trousers as he was dressing in the morning and slither down his neck as he sat at dinner.

Reluctantly leaving the protection of the camp, he set out with two guides towards the 'vast and dreary wastes' of the desert bordered by the river Atrak, which lay between him and the Caspian Sea. This country was so dangerous that the local governor provided him with an escort of thirty horsemen; one delightedly recognised James from his previous travels, so 'I had special service enough for the rest of my journey'. The struggle across

2 Echoing the description of Roman imperial policy by the Caledonian chieftain Calgacus, as reported by Tacitus.

the utter desolation of the desert, through the grim, grey rocks and brown plains, was rewarded by suddenly coming on a scene of 'inexpressible fertility and richness'. It was as if a magician had waved his wand to reveal 'a park of nature's own cunning handiwork, on the most magnificent scale, a park such as no nobleman on earth can boast of possessing – such oaks, such limes, such elms, such sycamore ... it was a sight to put even old Windsor to shame, with all its ancestral magnificence'.

Longing to reach the Caspian Sea and Asterabad, where he had business, James was frustrated at having to move inland again because the area was in a ferment after another rumour of the Shah's death. He therefore resigned himself to a futher uncomfortable, but safer, trek through the mountains. Far from assistance of any kind he had proof that some of his servants were plotting to rob him. Worse still, the local ruler was apparently hostile to the heir apparent to the Shah and, knowing that the British were well disposed to that particular prince, he might detain James if the Shah were indeed dead. He thus decided to head straight for the safety of Teheran, where he believed he would find his friend MacNeill and others. He had, after all, finished his survey of 'that turbulent and restless province Khorasan and have, thank God, possessed myself of all the information Government can desire regarding it'.

Along the way he checked, whenever he could, that the English mission was still in Teheran, but the nearer he rode the deeper were his forebodings. He rode faster and faster, covering 176 miles in two days, only to find his fears realised: he arrived at a locked Residency to find that *all* the English had left a month before. At this news, exhausted and emaciated, too tired even to read a packet of letters from home, James most uncharacteristically collapsed with fever. He was ill for several days, during which no one came near him and he missed Black John more than ever. He had run out of money to pay his servants, and promised funds did not materialise. Although he had Persian friends in high places they did not immediately respond to his pleas; in the present climate it would not do to befriend a European. He felt lonelier than ever before, 'far from all who care for or would assist me'. He did what he could to self-medicate (antimonial powder and opium), 'swallowed my impatience and bore the blue devils as best I could'. By the evening of the fourth day he was better and thankful to receive a visit from his old friend Mirza Mahomed Ali, who produced some money and trustworthy servants.

On 17 August he was on his way again, faced with traversing 'the hottest regions of Persia at this burning season of the year', then struggling up and round the great volcanic cone of the 'mighty Demawund', one of the highest mountains of the great Elburz range.

After a great deal more scrambling and sliding, slipping and stumbling over great rocks, along 'a nose like promontory sharp as a knife' and down to stony river beds, always leading the horses, often carrying the baggage themselves, they reached the jungle of Mazanderan.

The jungle bred flies:

> Flies, said I? Winged imps rather ... which ... with infinite fury, settled on every part of horse and man, and wherever they struck their fangs the blood spirted out as from a lancet wound.

There was nothing for it but to ride as fast as possible for Amol, where he was in familiar territory, although the well remembered streets were now thick jungle and the houses roofless.

At Rud Sar, on the western shore of the Caspian Sea, they found the beach crowded with groups of peasantry dressed in colourful holiday garb, for it was a fair-day 'and all the world was flocking to it'. James was enchanted: forgetting for a moment his exhaustion and emaciated condition, he threw himself into the bustle and excitement, noting it all down in colourful detail for Jeanie. He was amused to see that while most of the women, riding with veils lifted for air, would 'hurry it down' when they saw a stranger approaching, '*sometimes* the young and pretty would experience some difficulty in adjusting this shroud, so as to let a pair of bright eyes, or a pretty mouth be seen'.

Rasht, the scene of his house arrest on his previous adventure, was a ghost of its former prosperous self, the population diminished from 60,000 to less than 20,000. Here his cook fell ill and was replaced by a Negro, 'a real black jewel by his own account ... tall and thin enough to make a spare fishing rod but in the meantime he concocts my pillaw'.

James was nervous in Rasht, always looking over his shoulder for something that would prevent him, once again, from leaving. But all was well, and they set forth on the same path along which he had escaped, 'through bush and brake, and swamp and pool' and a terrific thunderstorm. He even recognised 'the very spot ... to which the ruffians dragged me to rob, and, as I then verily believed, to murder me'.

By now the servants were taking it in turns to succumb to jungle fever, and at Turkomanchai James decided to leave them behind, the cook 'shaking like an earthquake, and roaring like a bull under a pile of great coats', to push on alone with a guide and send them help from Tabriz. There was still, however, one more obstacle to surmount: a three-day quarantine requirement. James talked and bribed his way out of this, and on 14 September 'at length the town *was* won, the gates *were* passed ... the English Jack, waving from the staff, pointed the way' and he arrived at the Consulate in Tabriz just in time for lunch 'with *tables* and *chairs,* and *knives* and *forks,* and *spoons,* instead of carpets and fingers.' At last he was among friends and countrymen and above all people he could trust. He was handed a bulging packet of letters from home and found that 'all was well'

Waiting for James once more

In truth, everything at Moniack was at a standstill waiting for James's return – everything, that is, but Reelig who was more active than ever.

> The dear old man is stronger in health, weaker in mind ... he thinks things ought to be under *his* management ... & will submit to none but yourself. He cordially hates Gair & is cold to Wilson.

Up to now, Reelig's letters to James had shown no sign of senility, but his November letter was more shakily written than usual. As ever, he gave news of his wanderings around the estate, observing that if you do not plant oaks, woodpigeons will: 'We yesterday found a dead Gourmand who had, I think, been choked by his Greediness, having no less than 45 acorns in his crop.' He was still intrigued by politics but 'my mind runs more upon what *fixed* ultimate employment you may reasonably expect to await you at home'.

The next letter from James brought disappointing news: there was no way he could be in London before March owing to the pressing need for him to obtain 'information in other quarters'. Jeanie had to reconcile herself to another long dark winter of waiting, but the prospect of spending it alone with her parents-in-law was too much; she fled once more to her family in Edinburgh, where she found John MacNeill and his wife, who had been with James in Tabriz. She was cheered by the MacNeills, who pronounced James the picture of health.

Her only real worry in leaving Moniack was abandoning her father-in-law who understood her disappointment about James's delay, but replied bracingly. She should remain calm for her health's sake: ' James is as well in Persia as he would be here. Trust MacNeill.' He added a postscript: on his doctor's advice, he and Jane had finally quitted Moniack and taken lodgings in Inverness.

He had suddenly gone downhill. The doctor considered that the old couple should not be alone and Reelig should be removed from the temptation 'to go out & overlook things at Moniack'. Jane Anne had accordingly found them rooms above Tait's shop, where she suspected her father would end his days. They had gone off in style 'in good Mrs Mackintosh's carriage', with Nanny Rose and a housemaid to settle them in. There would be no more interfering with Gair in the management of the woods.

Jeanie was horrified. She had suspected something of the sort might happen the moment she turned her back; it would have been much better to let the old man potter out his remaining time at Moniack. If he had fallen ill while she was there, she assured Jane Anne, she would never have left him: 'I always loved your Father and shall love him to the last.' She turned to practical matters: it was a pity that Reelig's new bedroom was so dark – she would have chosen lodgings with cheerful, airy bedrooms. The old couple should send their washing back to Moniack once a fortnight to give the remaining servants there something to do; they should get candles, soap and sugar from Moniack and butter from the estate cow; turkeys and fowls, honey and preserves ('only take care of the pots as they are precious to fill again') would be sent to Inverness as needed.

Jane Anne was glad to have her parents near at hand: she was still missing her daughter, her brother James was goodness knows where and Jeanie, 'my best & dearest friend & constant adviser,' was in Edinburgh; having her parents in Inverness would be good both for company and convenience. It was, after all, more than an hour's drive from Culduthel to Moniack. She still had seven children at home, including the baby Fanny. Somehow she juggled their lessons so effectively that Mary and Adoo could now write and read very well, could translate a little French and were improved in music; they were all progressing in arithmetic and the girls in 'work'; Geography, English Grammar, reading, hymns and prayers were also squeezed in somehow. In the evening they all practised their reading and then, if there was time, they could play. The only time she had for writing her copious and surprisingly legible letters was after nine o'clock at night.

A MATTER OF TIME

At Christmas, Jeanie, her mother and sisters took themselves off to 44 Western Road, Brighton, hoping the sea air might strengthen the fragile Isabella. There were walks through the cold sunshine to 'enjoy the sight of all the Fashion & wealth of the Aristocracy for the Court is still here'. The gay dresses of the ladies on the Esplanade were 'a bed of tulips', but Jeanie's Scottish frugality was scandalised by the vanity and extravagance. Babies were 'fluttering' in silks and even their nurses were tricked out like fine ladies carrying infants sleeping under lace veils. 'It is indeed Vanity Fair but very amusing withal!'

> The number of splendid equipages are beyond anything; carriage and four as common as blackberries ... the very infants of 4 years old gallop about as if they had been born on horseback whilst others drive in little fancy carriages, drawn by goats in full harness. How Smout [Mary's nickname] would be enchanted with them!

She was intrigued by the Royal Family, with whom they sometimes rubbed shoulders: 'I walked *cheek by jowl* with Adelaide & Cumberland[3] the other day on the cliff for half an hour'. The Queen was 'a sweet enough quiet lady but no great look for a Queen'.

❈

At the end of January 1835, Jeanie was back in Princes Street, brandishing a long delayed letter from Pest in Hungary, where James had been in perfect health and excellent spirits. She also enjoyed an Edinburgh Ball, where she saw 'all the world' including the bogus 'Prince Charles Edward Stuart[4] with all his flowing ringlets, tartan orders & nonsense'.

The following month, she went to London to wait for James at 45 Manchester Street, where there was also room for her mother with her companion. She was still pestered with complaints from the north: the cook and Nanny Rose, by now back at Moniack, were discontented with not enough to do; the new 'Porteress', Mrs McQueen, wanted to have a little shop at the Gate Lodge; this was briskly dealt with: 'She was placed there with her own consent to keep the Lodge & not to keep a shop & bring idle people about the place ... James I feel assuredly never would consent to it.'

3 Queen Adelaide (1792–1849) and the Duke of Cumberland (1771–1851), respectively wife and brother of King William IV.

4 Charles Manning Allen, who with his brother, John Carter Allen, claimed to be descended from the Stuart kings. Charles called himself 'Charles Edward Stuart'; John was 'John Sobieski Stuart'. They assumed Highland dress, converted to Catholicism and were given a shooting lodge, Eilean Aigas, near Beauly, by Lord Lovat.

By March, Jeanie was spending as much time as she could in the cheering company of the MacNeills. That same month, an event took place in India which shook Delhi to its Mughal foundations and would have far-reaching effects at Moniack. Long before this news could reach them, however, the family had to face the tragic death of Rachel Tytler, the beautiful and popular wife of Jeanie's literary brother, Patrick. Everything had been done to save her, including moving the whole family to the island of Bute, considered to be free from east winds, but in vain: she died of tuberculosis, leaving three small children.

In May James's letter from Baghdad was straight from *The Arabian Nights*: 'grave Turks strutting by, wild Arabs galloping steeds along streets, herds of camels grunting and roaring, bazaars and mosques & minarets and muftis & muezzins & Jews & Armenians & date trees & orange trees and the Plague and the Tigris all around us'. The plague had carried off 100,000 inhabitants 'and the river came in one fine day very *politely* & swept off all the empty houses & so Baghdad is in a pretty pickle'.

Meanwhile, there was diverting news of Amy: contrary to expectation she was finding Keith anything but dull.. Her exotic looks had soon attracted admiring attention, and John Forsyth, 'one of the best informed well doing young men there', wasted no time in proposing marriage. Amy, however, was firm: she could go no further in the matter without the approval of James and Jeanie, who wrote:

> On receiving this letter dear James I as usual felt the want of you but ... they should have some time to know their own minds and we further knowledge of the young man's family situation & means of supporting her.

It would be good for Amy to have a 'protector before William comes home'; meanwhile, William must be asked for consent and a contribution to the marriage. The obliging Peter Grant, who was home and settled at Tannochy, near Forres, went to Keith to inspect John and gave his approval – 'a steady and excellent young man'. Amy paid another visit to Moniack and Jeanie reported her looking well and happy: 'Jack Forsyth ... is well spoken of by everyone so I think it is a blessing indeed'. As there had been complete silence from William for many months, James considered that there was no need to wait for his agreement.

The marriage took place in Keith on 1 August 1835, with Peter Grant giving the bride away. John and Amy set up house and started happily producing a large family. We have a glimpse of Amy ten years later, now aware of her true identity and proudly calling herself Amy Surwen (after her mother) Fraser Forsyth, when she took her two small daughters, Jane and Amy, on one of their visits to Grandmamma at Moniack.

Mission now accomplished, James was safely through the warlike Kurds and heading for home, once again through the worst months of the winter. He was desperate to get to London to debrief to Sir Henry Ellis, who was soon to leave for Persia as Ambassador, ostensibly to offer the King's condolences on the death, in October 1834, of the old Shah and to welcome the new one. The moment Lord Ponsonby, Ambassador in Constantinople, gave the go-ahead, it would be 'Hey for old England!', and James hoped to reach London on 10 May, although, he warned his father, he would long be detained there for debriefing meetings. He thought longingly of his reunion with Jeanie:

> How often do I speculate the time, the place, the mode of our meeting, how often anticipate that blessed day, if God grant it to us ... I trust I find news of you waiting me at the Athenaeum ... will you know me? I shall be such a wild looking wretch, so thin and lank & brown but I must not speculate or haver more.

Knowing her husband's infinite optimism and unreliable planning, however, Jeanie took his date of 10 May with a pinch of salt:

> I shall be thankful if even the 8th June sees you in my arms, wild, brown & lank as you may be, oh! How welcome! We shall not quarrel with each other's looks – mine, alas, are none of the best at this moment!

A little later he wrote, 'My dearest love – expect me 25th or 26th ... I can scarce believe myself that that blessed time is so near at hand.' Nor could Jeanie:

> My head like his own is in a whirl at the thought and now I can as little sleep for joy as I did before for anxiety ... I cannot know the hour but shall be watching every carriage – but hope you will not drive up early when I am in bed in the room with Annie and Isa for that would put me in such a state to get on my clothes!

At last, on 25 May, 'He is come! Our beloved James is actually here *in the body*!' Jeanie was in bed reading the 91st Psalm and had just reached the comforting verse 11, 'For he shall give his angels charge over thee, to keep thee in all thy ways', when she heard a carriage at the door and, rushing to the window, 'the first object I saw was James in his red cap & mustachios'. She shouted to her sisters to stay upstairs 'and the next moment I was in his arms in the room alone with him'. He had to leave immediately for the Foreign Office to deliver his despatches but that night 'snored most musically ... it sounded to my ears sweeter than the nightingale. I never closed my eyes but often looked at the whiskered Turk I had beside me so unlike my rosy James.' He was the colour of mahogany and looked ten years older but the next morning 'he sacrificed the mustachios to me and I began to trace my James again'.

⁂

Meanwhile, in the small apartment above Tait's shop in Inverness, Jane and Jane Anne were preparing themselves for the worst. Reelig was sleeping his life away. He was totally confined to bed, no longer took any interest in what was going on around him and hardly spoke when Jane Anne visited. Jane wrote in her diary, 'Myself in much sadness & restless agitation all alone' but she was still able to find comfort 'from the promise of Scripture of support in the Hour of trial'.

Shocked to find Jeanie looking so thin and worn, James was even more worried to hear that his father was now fast failing. He wanted to jump on the first coach north, but the young Charles Grant, now Lord Glenelg and recently appointed Secretary of State for War and the Colonies, although perfectly aware of Reelig's frail state, was adamant that James must first submit his full report to the Foreign Office. Henry Ellis's forthcoming mission to Persia had been held up long enough 'at great expense and inconvenience' waiting for James's intelligence: 'until this is despatched, *I cannot move*'.

He was very gratified by his reception in London – meetings with three Cabinet Ministers and dinners with Lords Glenelg and Grey[5] – but assured his father that it was the hope of being useful and not the desire for honour that led him to cultivate 'these stars of the Political firmament'. He was not motivated by ambition and would be perfectly happy to return to obscurity.

Desperate to get James home in time, Jane sent him regular accounts of his father's frailty and her anxiety – in a way 'that goes straight to his heart,' said the irritated Jeanie, 'but what can he do'?! Reelig would be the first to tell James to stay where he was and do his duty. They had moved to 17 Montague Square, lent to them by Aeneas Mackintosh, where James was at his desk at dawn every morning compiling his reports. There was pressure from every side on him, and Jeanie grumbled, 'As yet I have not got an hour alone with him.' He breakfasted each day with Aeneas and then hurried off 'before I have got my ideas collected', to return only to dress for dinner, either out 'or here with Gentlemen friends'. Aeneas, the MacNeills and Mrs Rich were constant visitors; with them, at least, he could talk 'unfettered'.

Palmerston, now back in the Foreign Office, was proving difficult to pin down: he had cancelled three appointments with James because of the turbulent politics of France and Spain – 'Consul Sebastiani[6] [is] a greater man than James Fraser so I am forced to smother my impatience'. Henry Ellis was also desperate to get going and John MacNeill was on tenterhooks, not knowing whether he was to accompany him or not.

In his frustration James wondered whether ministers would ever realise 'when Russia is pressing on in all directions and specially eastward that all our interests do not lie in Europe and America'. The part he had played in this he knew was small but 'as one link or part of a link in a great chain it is of importance'. At the end of June he tried again to convey to the Foreign Office the urgency of his need to get home; John Backhouse, one of the Under Secretaries, gave Palmerston's answer:

> I must see Mr Fraser. I am sorry for the inconvenience I have put him to but I cannot create additional hours to the Four and Twenty. I will try to see Mr Fraser on Saturday between 2 and 3 unless there should be a Cabinet.

Then a levee, at which James was presented to the King, kept him in London. He was introduced by Palmerston as 'James Baillie Fraser Esq on his return from a journey to Persia on His Majesty's service'. There was some discussion as to whether James had been on a 'journey' or a 'mission', but it was decided that 'mission' was too much of a giveaway.

5 Earl Grey, Prime Minister 1830–4.
6 Horace Sebastiani de la Porta (1771–1851), French Ambassador to Great Britain 1835–40.

Sir John MacNeill from the Island of Colonsay, doctor and diplomat, who held, along with several of James's correspondents, the belief that Russia planned to use Afghanistan as a base from which to attack India.

At last, James saw a chance to get north; he would have to miss MacNeill's interview with Palmerston, on which 'hangs much of the fate of poor Persia whether it is to be the prey of Russia or effectually protected by England' but he made the decision and boarded the steamer to Aberdeen on 6 July.

Jane's diary records James's arrival and his father's last day. On 1 July she thought it impossible that the old man could hold out till James got home: he was scarcely speaking or eating and became distressed when she left the room. A few days later, to her great comfort, Margaret Tytler, summoned by Jane Anne who was coping with a family recovering from measles, including herself, came to keep her company. On 7 July James at last arrived and his mother described the moment:

> I heard a little bustle in the passage. When I stepped out & was ... told that he was actually come ... having been seen descending in the coach & at that moment at the Hotel I was much agitated but Margaret entreated me to compose myself ... it was joy that agitated & overwhelmed me – the sound of his voice & seeing [him] once more near me at such a moment.

When the doctor, preparing Reelig for the surprise, gently told him that he had some good news; the old man muttered, 'I wish for no news but to hear of my son James's arrival'. Jane was so concerned about the effect of the reunion that she dared not witness it. Reelig remained calm, and James merely said he was sorry to see him so unwell and hoped he would be better soon. He then reverted to his journey and his difficulties in London. 'Soon it was thought right James should leave him & take some refreshment as he had not slept on the steam boat'.

James spent five days in Inverness, seeing his father alone for short times every day but unable to hold anything of a conversation with him. Reelig seemed placid and composed and his 'marble pale features' were beautiful. The day after James left, 12 July, he continued to sink, with Jane in constant attendance day and night. Two nights later, Jane was advised to leave the room, 'yet I could not prevail upon myself to do so'. She once more took up her place on the bed beside him:

> Such was the stillness & composure I fell asleep & actually slept for more than an hour ... and it was nearing 2 in the morning & daylight commenced when I awoke [unaware] for the first few minutes where I was or the cause of the extreme stillness around me on seeing a number of anxious faces around me fixed on one object – I still felt the beloved hand in mine ... his breathing then was soft ... he did not seem to suffer in any way whatever ... & in this manner he continued to breathe on ... till the moment the blessed spirit fled & returned to his creator – during the whole of that time from my awaking I continued in the same position leaning over him & holding the hand next to me I neither sighed nor sobbed or even shed a tear.

Three days later, the thirteen-year-old Ned wrote to his sister Jane. He and his father and brother James had been to view Grandpapa's body: 'I should never have known him, he was so changed.' He was taken home to Moniack that day and buried the next day, Saturday, 18 July, in the family graveyard above Kirkhill. Grandson James described how he had suffered: his back was 'one continued sore from his shoulders down to the end of the backbone with continually lying in the same position & at the time of his death he was so wasted that he was nothing but skin and bone ... Grandmamma is wonderfully composed'.

Grandmamma was also firm: she would return to Moniack for the rest of her days. James, who had not returned from London for the funeral, agreed, assuring her that he would resume the management of the place whether he were there or not. He had told both George and William of their father's death and suggested that William should contribute £100 a year towards his mother's keep. Jeanie had been ill, but niece Jane, on holiday from school, had risen to the occasion and moved in to cope with Uncle James's breakfast and minister to her aunt.

To occupy herself in London, Jeanie had taken over the care of fifteen-year-old Jane and had managed to persuade Jane Anne and Affleck to move her from Miss Gibson's establishment in Essex, which Jeanie considered 'an underbred school'. She had discovered that the twenty-seven girls were only allowed to wash their feet, with a change of stockings, once a fortnight and their hands once a day. This was all bad enough for the fastidious Jeanie but, worse still, Jane seemed to have got into a set of girls 'whose aim seems to be to get over their lessons & wearisome tasks & plot against the mistresses'. If Affleck could afford another year of education for Jane then she must move to a better school.

Camden House in Kensington was chosen. Jeanie had interviewed the headmistress: Jane was to make friends only with girls who were 'anxious about their improvement'. She had checked that the music was up to standard, arranged for drawing lessons and made sure that Jane would have private tuition and a bed to herself. Jane settled in happily for one more year's schooling, partly paid for by Uncle James. Released from school at last, aged sixteen, she was allowed to go to the Northern Meeting Ball, 'very prettily dressed & the picture of youthful spirits & gaiety' according to Margaret Tytler.

James was still mingling with the great in London, in particular Lord William Bentinck, who 'talked much about William in the highest terms ... an honourable upright & a most zealous public servant'. He was delighted to meet the brother 'of a Bengal civilian whom he much regards & respects'. He kept coming back to the subject of William which was most gratifying, especially as there was still a mysterious silence from India.

Buying dogs in Delhi

By the end of July Jane was home again, with Margaret Tytler still for company. Early on the morning of 24 August, her neighbour from Newton brought three letters for Moniack: two were from India. Jane, heartened at hearing from her sons at last, sat up in bed and opened one in what looked like William's impossible writing. The address was 'Hansi' – it must therefore be from Skinner. Then the words 'a calamity' caught her eye. Was someone dead? She read on, saw that it was from Skinner to Reelig, and the three words 'your noble son' told her the truth: 'William was gone'. As the letter dropped from her hand another sheet fell out: William had been killed 'by the blow of an assassin on the evening of the 22nd March last returning from a visit in Delhi to his own house with but a single attendant!' All other information was unnecessary and all comfort in vain: 'In those few words William was "no more" was summed up the greatest calamity myself or my family could know.'

The same post had brought the news to the 'Public Prints' of Inverness, and Gair reported on the 'grief and lament' caused by the news. Jane and Margaret remained alone all that day; the evening brought Jane Anne, but she could not stay the night. She came back a couple of days later with the two little girls, Georgy and Fanny, to cheer their grandmother.

The following days were dark for Jane. Longing for more details and for a word from James, she kept to her room, emerging only to be polite to the stream of commiserating visitors. Sunday, 6 September, William's birthday, was an especially bad day – 'now a blank forever or only to be remembered with anguish'. So the sad autumn dragged on for Jane, surrounded by kindly neighbours yet bereft and alone.

Jeanie was not well enough to go north, and in any case James still had to be available to the Foreign Office, where he hoped, more urgently now, that he would be kept on the payroll. Meanwhile, to give Jane something to divert her, there were various articles needed from Moniack which Jeanie hoped she would manage to send: James was missing his black merino coats and would like six pairs of 'poor Mrs Noble's blue worsted stockings'; she wanted her little Indian jackets, some pots of jam and also hams; James ate nothing but ham for breakfast. There were also instructions about the servants, one or two of whom were to be paid off during the winter. Jane could keep three women in the house, and three men would help Gair run the property.

❖

Charles Metcalfe's brother, Thomas Theophilus,[7] was working in Delhi at the time of William's death. His daughter Emily spent the first four years of her life in Metcalfe House, a splendid mansion on the Jumna, and later wrote reminiscences of her life in India:

> It was Sunday evening, March 22nd 1835 ... The whole house was still and hushed as only an Indian house can be, when suddenly there were sounds of great stir among the servants, and my Father came hurriedly into the room ... and announced Mr Fraser's death, and that he was going out at once to enquire into the murder. How well I remember clinging to my Mother, and her horror at the news – and our childlike fears for our Father's safety, because if Mr Fraser had been murdered, perhaps Papa would be killed too! ... I shall remember that day I think as long as I live.[8]

The next day, 23 March, Emily's father wrote to George, who was in camp near Bareilly:

> I trust that you are *quite alone*, and that you will constrain yourself to receive with as much composure as possible the intelligence of the death of a very near and dear relative. You have been suddenly deprived of your brother William and under circumstances which will add a deeper poignancy to the grief you would naturally have felt on such an occasion.

There follows a detailed description of the murder, which was committed with 'a Blunderbuss loaded with three balls or slugs two of which have been extracted'. It was clear to all that 'from the calm serenity of his countenance ... his suffering could have been but momentary'. A reward of Rs2,000 was immediately offered by the Government for the apprehension of the assassin, together with a further Rs10,000 from others.

George, aware neither of his father's death nor of Skinner's impulsive letter to Reelig, immediately wrote to Affleck begging him to break the news to his parents as gently as he could. At the same time he resolved to go straight to Delhi to investigate William's affairs, about which he knew very little. He was puzzled by his own reaction:

> My state of mind is unnatural. I have lost a brother to whom I was attached and whose character I highly esteemed – yet I have scarce shed a tear – these signs of grief find no place in me. I am sometimes thankful I am collected enough to write as I do and at others think myself brutally devoid of feeling.

The murder rocked Delhi. Like everyone else, George was convinced that William had been killed by a hired assassin – who else would murder a man 'so generally beloved

7 1795–1853. Political Agent Delhi 1835–53. Commissioned local artists to compile *Reminiscences of Imperial Delhi*, known as 'the Delhi book', now in the British Library.

8 *The Golden Calm*, ed. M M Kaye (1980) Webb & Bower Ltd.

in the city and the country ... as he was?' His own course was plain: he stoutly and somewhat unrealistically declared that he would take on the role of supporting his parents and saving Moniack.

James felt paralysed but characteristically pulled himself together to write immediately to his mother: they must look forward to George's return 'as the cheering event of our latter days' and remember that Jane Anne and her children would ever provide a source of interest. Now he would have to double his efforts to preserve that for which William had sacrificed so much. He could not come home to comfort his mother, for there was still too much to be done and, in any case, Jeanie was not yet well enough to travel.

The accounts of William's last moments differ in their details. George's emotional black-bordered letter to his father describes William, in the evening of the fateful day, riding home from visiting the Rajah of Kishangarh, accompanied by a boy on horseback and two grooms on foot. The Rajah had offered two escorts, which William declined. Leaving the city, he rode up the hill to his house and was just about to enter the gates when one of the grooms noticed a horseman, his face concealed in a cloak, riding slowly just ahead. Waiting until William drew almost level, the rider turned in the saddle, fired his sawn-off blunderbuss, put his heels to his horse and disappeared at full speed.

> William fell to the ground & never breathed or spoke – death was instantaneous – his body was carried to his house and medical aid called in but in vain – life had departed with the report of the carabine.

Three months earlier, Skinner had warned William of reports of a murderous plot by a nobleman, but William had laughed it off 'as improbable and scarcely worth a thought'. Early in March, an old Indian friend had advised him to abandon his habit of going about unattended and unarmed: there were now louder rumours that a nobleman had employed a potential assassin. Again William was scornful and there was no investigation; such reports came 'in vague forms from doubtful quarters' and were impossible to trace round the shadowy corners of the bazaars or through the sinister alleys of Delhi.

The funeral, with full military honours, took place the following day, with Charles Metcalfe conducting the service. It was attended by every European in the city and 'almost all the populace and better classes of Delhi'. Skinner erected a handsome tomb of white marble in the grounds of his church, St James's (see Plate XXV); it was almost completely destroyed in the Mutiny and only the sandstone base remains, along with a piece of inlaid work, now in the church, and an inscription written by Skinner.

Evidence started coming in slowly but steadily. Large sums of money poured in from all sides, from the old King of Delhi down to the local people, including, to put people off the scent, the instigator of the crime himself. In September, James had word that, owing to the perseverance of Metcalfe and Magistrate Simon Fraser, aided by young John Lawrence, a hitherto unknown district officer and an extraordinarily able sleuth, a certain Karim Khan had been arrested after fifty volunteers of Skinner's Yellow Boys had searched the area in disguise. Karim Khan's accomplice then turned King's evidence

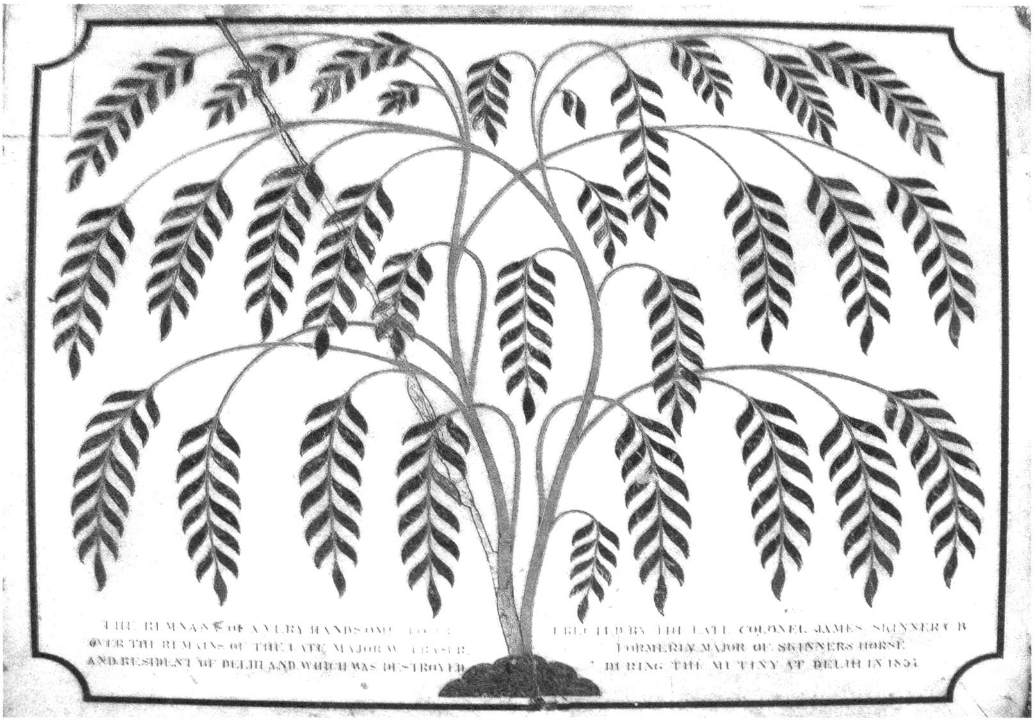

Photo: MKF

One of the beautifully inlaid marble panels from William›s tomb saved from the destruction of the Mutiny and now set into the floor or St James's Church.

and incriminated Shams-ud-Din of Firozpur, son of William's great friend, Ahmad Baksh Khan; this was the childhood playmate of William's children, the charming boy who had called William 'Uncle'. According to William Sleeman,[9] he was 'a handsome young man, and an extremely agreeable companion; but a most unprincipled and licentious character'. He was also a man with a motive.

After Ahmad's death in 1827 Shams-ud-Din and his two younger brothers became involved in a lengthy and complex dispute about their inheritance in which William, in his new position as Commissioner for Delhi, had to arbitrate. Shams-ud-Din assumed the suit would be decided in his favour and was angered by William's attempts to be fair to all three. He was further enraged by William's refusal to receive him in his house because of his apparently dissolute, and even murderous, behaviour in his principality of Firozpur:

> Mr Fraser became so disgusted with his conduct, that he would not admit him into his house when he came to Delhi, though he had ... brought him up as a child of his own; indeed he had been as fond of him as he could be of a child of his own; and the boy used to spend the greater part of his time with him.[10]

9 Sir William Sleeman (1788–1856), army officer in the East India Company and administrator in India. 1839–42 head of commission for the suppression of thuggee and dacoity, which had virtually ceased by 1848. Resident in Gwalior 1843–9 and in Lucknow 1848–54. Author of *Rambles and Recollections of an Indian Official*, Vols I & II.

10 *Rambles and Recollections of an Indian Official* (Vol II p.49) William H Sleeman (2012) General Books, Memphis, USA.

In September 1834 the humiliated and infuriated young Nawab plotted his revenge. He hired a sharpshooter, Karim Khan, instructed him to observe William's daily habits and concocted an elaborate method of communication using the 'purchase of dogs' as code for the murder. For months they were frustrated – William either took a different route home or rode attended by guards – until, late on 22 March, the right moment came, the dogs were purchased and 'the chivalrous and wayward genius of the Delhi area lay dead'.[11]

Tributes flowed in from all sides, including a letter to James from the Governor General, Lord William Bentinck: he waxed eloquent on William's virtues, in particular 'the romantic nobleness and kindness of his character' and his deep interest in and knowledge of the Delhi territory. Although this passion had ...

> ... woven a net round his life and actions from which ... he never in my opinion would have been able to extricate himself, still in imagination his whole heart was in Scotland and his family, his home and his native hills formed the promised land full of all his future happiness.

William died intestate, which complicated matters. To begin with, George was not allowed to administer William's estate as the law decreed that his personal property reverted to his father, who was still alive at the time of the murder. After Reelig's death, the right of administering the Indian estate passed to Jane, who now had to authorise George to act in her name. This was not sorted out until November, eight months after William's death. Meanwhile, there was the knotty question of whether the family would receive any compensation. The Company had confiscated the estates of the murderer and agreed to allow Jane a pension of £200 a year: James had applied to the Court of Directors of the East India Company for £5,000, although he felt £10,000 would have been fairer.

> May I not hope that the rulers of India will, under all the circumstances, decide that something more is due to the memory and services of their old & faithful servant than a pension of £200 a year to a woman of 81? That something out of the immense revenue derived from the estate of his murderer may be spared to the brother whom that murder has ruined?

William Tytler supported James's bid for compensation. ' Is it possible,' he demanded of Lord Glenelg, ' ... that in the circumstances of so distinguished a servant of the Company terminating a career of 34 years in India by a death so awful something might be done for his family in lieu of that pension which he so richly earned?'

Knowing how slowly the wheels of such things turned, James felt he could not leave London until the matter was settled, and in any case his work on Persia was not yet completed.

He was still stunned but, to his mother, declared himself determined to preserve Moniack all costs not just because it was 'the house of my youth endeared by a thousand recollections' but also as 'a rallying place for the scattered reliques of our family' and a

11 Ibid.

place where he could spend the evening of his life with those he loved best.

While they waited for news of William's estate, James was facing the fact that his income was, for the moment, 'the *only* thing which the remaining branches of the family – yourself, my wife, myself, George in case of sickness, has to depend upon for subsistence'. He had a three-part plan: to follow up the question of compensation, continue to work for the Foreign Office, and instruct the factor at Moniack, James Wilson, to save every shilling. Meanwhile, they must look forward to George's homecoming – 'the bright spot in our evening sky'.

A few weeks later he felt strong enough to renew his suit with Palmerston: all he needed to know was whether there was a job for him or not. The foundations on which he had built his plan for Moniack were so shaken that he was prepared to take anything on offer: 'there is no sacrifice ... which I am not disposed to make for the preservation of Moniack ... I am omitting nothing that may forward this great object'. But Palmerston was not easily pinned down. One day James got home at 10 pm after another fruitless day with the Foreign Secretary:

> Well all I have gathered from nearly a full hour's talk with Palmerston is this – that he *now* permits MacNeill to draw out those suggestions with regard to our policy in Persia which we had offered to do *6 weeks ago* & has ordered us to have them ready when he returns to town ... he is to be absent for 8–10 days.

To James's direct question about another job Palmerston replied,'Well Mr Fraser when I return we shall talk over this but you well know that this is no time for Government to be put to any expence.'

Jeanie proudly told Jane Anne that everyone in the Foreign Office was aware of the abilities of both MacNeill and James, but 'the home politics so engrosses all here as to make Eastern matters a secondary consideration'. She would not mind being tied to London for a year or two if it meant rescuing Moniack, but they could not let the place until James's future was more certain.

Jane had at last gone to stay at Culduthel, where she found the children much improved and Jane Anne 'the same affectionate kind child that she ever was!' She had been very downhearted at leaving Moniack, and Margaret Tytler had the unenviable task of breaking the news to her that a future there might no longer be possible. Margaret gently suggested that Jane might spend the summers at Rebeg and the winters at Sanquhar or Culduthel; it would be a great relief to James to know that she was not lonely. Jane stoutly declared that she was not in the least lonely and, if she was, she could find a companion; she was used to being left to her own devices at Culduthel, as Jane Anne was always so busy; she was determined to keep a home for James at Moniack. In any case, she argued, rents were now so low that letting it would not be worth the trouble. When Margaret pointed out that William, with his ample salary, had not saved the estate on which there was still £20,000 owing, Jane at last reluctantly agreed that there might be no alternative to letting or selling; in that case, she was sure she would somehow bear up.

Jeanie and James were now comfortably established in Hampstead, sharing a house with Jeanie's mother, sisters, brother Patrick and his three motherless children who kept them all amused. Little Tom sang all his songs to Uncle James, while Mary and Alexander 'are darling children full of fun & spirits'. Jeanie approved of their governess, who 'delights in fresh air & exercise', and she loved Hampstead, revelling in the freedom of walks on the heath and through the fields.

For the winter they all moved back into London to 22 Wimpole Street, a house big enough for the whole extended family. Jeanie and James had a bedroom and a sitting room, with a bed in a dressing room for niece Jane's school holidays. Peter had 'a good library room with a bookcase bed', while Lady Woodhouselee had the best front bedroom. She sat all day in the bow window keeping, as ever, an eagle eye on the goings on outside. Annie, Isabella, Peter's three children and their governess were all in the attics. They had taken the house till the end of April. After that, 'all depends on my Lord Palmerston who keeps us in profound ignorance of all but the present', but meanwhile James would spend every morning at the Foreign Office. He was also trying to complete his travel writing while it was still fresh in his memory.

December brought news of the trial and conviction of Shams-ud-Din and the assassin. On 3 October they had both been hanged outside the Kashmir Gate, near the spot where William fell. For his execution the handsome Shams-ud-Din chose 'an extremely rich and beautiful dress of light green, the colours which martyrs wear' although, according to some accounts, he had to make do with a simple white outfit. He was horrified to find that an outcast, a sweeper, was to put the rope round his neck 'but he soon mastered his feelings and submitted with a good grace to his fate'. The only people who really mourned him were the prostitutes and dancing girls of Delhi, on whom he had squandered his money.[12]

There was no news from George, and the uncertainty was beginning to tell; there were frayed nerves at Culduthel as well as in Wimpole Street. To one of his mother's complaints James told her snappily to accept that everyone was striving 'to save you from as much annoyance as possible; in short if you will only believe that our feelings towards you are those of sincere love & affection it would save a great deal of pain to both parties'. He could not write more often as he was never in bed before 2.00 am and spent most of his time either at the Foreign Office or the India House, hoping for the compensation on which, he reckoned, the future of Moniack depended.

He was also being pestered by his mother to write 'a memorial to William's character', but he refused: 'Were it done & <u>well</u> done I should rejoice'. But whether it were done or not, William had left behind him 'a name that I am persuaded that will live in the hearts & remembrance of the natives of Upper India after the ferment which the circumstances of his death have caused shall have ceased'. It was a name that would claim a place in the history of British India.

12 *Rambles and Recollections of an Indian Official* William H Sleeman (2012) General Books, Memphis, USA.

15

1836–1837

The Persian Princes

Early in 1836 'a new and singular duty' fell into James's lap. He was asked by Palmerston to take charge of three young Persian princes who were on their way to England to seek protection and support. Mohammad Mirza, grandson of Fath Ali Shah, had been recognised as Shah by both Britain and Russia 'but not by his myriad uncles and cousins'. The crown of Persia was currently 'the property of the sharpest sword and strongest arm' of the countless princes scattered over the country. As each ruled supreme in his own Province, chaos swiftly ensued, and various claimants found their properties confiscated and their families facing exile or worse. One such was the uncle of the new Shah, the Firmaun Firma, powerful Governor of the important province of Fars. Holed up at Shiraz, he summoned his numerous sons to protect him.

The vast forces of Mohammad Mirza, however, laid siege to Shiraz. The Firman Farma[1] and his sons narrowly escaped, six sons fleeing to the mountains, where letters from their father reached them advising them to make for England:

> Throw yourself on the generosity of its sovereign, and, with your hands upon his skirt, implore his protection and assistance. The English have always been my friends, they are powerful and generous, and your appeal to them will not be made in vain.

In Baghdad they were welcomed by the British Consul and encouraged to continue their journey to Damascus where they received further hospitality and an interpreter, Assad Khayat, to accompany them.

After overcoming various terrifying hazards and refusing tempting offers of protection, three of the sons made it to Beirut. They were Reza Quli Mirza, the eldest son, Vice Governor of Fars and known as 'the Prince', Najaf Quli Mirza, known as 'the Wali', and Timour Mirza (see Plate XXIX).

The eldest and youngest, the Prince and Timour, had the same aristocratic mother. The thirty-two-year-old Prince took his responsibilities very seriously, having always been his father's right hand, or more: 'the title was with my father, the rule with me'. He was tall, good-looking, charming and courteous.

1 Literally 'the man who gives the order' (usually royal).

His twenty-six-year-old brother Timour was 'fearless, reckless, joyous ... a young soldier' with an eye that 'could melt in love as well as kindle in war'. He cared for little but hunting and weaponry and 'those feasts where the wine cup circulates freely'. High spirited and passionate, he was a warm admirer of female beauty and had been given the title 'Sword of State' by his grandfather for killing a lion. During his flight from Shiraz he had escaped death from a musket ball, which was stopped by three thick slices of bread hidden in his clothing for the journey. His reaction to this near miss was irritation that one slice was now inedible.

The middle brother, the Wali, was the odd one out, the son of a slave girl. Completely different in looks from his brothers, he was shy, awkward and uncouth with a rough, deep voice. But he was a forceful character, shrewd and intelligent. His brothers depended on him as their negotiator.

Arriving in Beirut, the three young men realised to their horror that they would have to face a sea journey. At that time Europe was like the moon to Persians, who rarely travelled anywhere, except to visit Mecca, and, being true hydrophobists, certainly never by water. There was, however, nothing for it but to board a British naval vessel and brave the sea from Beirut to Falmouth via Malta. There was a slight respite at Gibraltar, where they attended a ball and 'for the first time in their lives beheld an assembly of females unveiled ... dancing with persons of the other sex'. Their worst fears, however, were realised during a storm in the Bay of Biscay, and they reached England vowing they would never again set foot on board ship.

The princes sensibly booked themselves into a hotel in Bath to recover from the journey and establish their chances of a warm reception in the capital. The Wali was deputed to travel ahead to London with letters for Palmerston announcing their arrival and took with him Assad Khayat, their interpreter.

All three brothers were naïvely hopeful that the British Government would immediately effect the restoration of their provinces. Luckily, the Wali arrived on 27 May, the day before John MacNeill left London, and so was received by the one man who could, with sensitivity, disabuse the Wali of 'his towering pretensions' and persuade him to be grateful for anything offered by the Government. The Wali booked rooms in Mivart's Hotel[2] in Brook Street and summoned his brothers and their three servants.

Two days later, James called on the Wali to introduce himself as the princes' guide and mentor in London. He was intrigued by the task ahead, impressed by the courage and resilience of the young men 'who had thus broken the ice of intercourse between central Asia & England by so spirited an enterprise'. He knew well the perils and discomfort they had encountered on their journey and the cultural difficulties and homesickness they now faced. He took on the job with his usual energy and commitment as well as relief that he now had something lucrative to do.

2 Now Claridge's. In 1812 James Mivart started a hotel for long-stay visitors at 51 Brook Street. By 1838 he had five properties in Brook St and knocked through to create one building. No 49 was another hotel owned by Mr and Mrs Claridge, who bought Mivarts in 1854.

He had reported to Palmerston that the cost of the princes' apartments, a carriage, two footmen and accommodation for their servants would be around £60 a week, 'which considering the season, & the shortness of time for preparation, I trust your Lordship will think moderate'. He was given carte blanche for their entertainment as long as he kept within 'the narrowest limits consistent with the suitable reception of the Princes as guests of his Majesty'. First, however, he had to gain their confidence, hear their story, gather general information about Persia and assess whether they would serve any political purpose.

Meanwhile, the Prince had sent his appeal to the British Government which James followed up with a long memorandum to Palmerston. He was convinced that life for the fugitives should be made as comfortable as possible, not only because he was sympathetic to their plight, but also because he was pretty sure they could be useful politically and diplomatically. They were, James explained, of the 'highest blood' of Persia, grandsons of the late Shah, first cousins of the present Shah and sons of the powerful Governor of Fars. In obedience to their father, all three had made a long and arduous journey, ignoring bribes along the way, straight to London. The custom in Persia was to treat fugitive princes as royalty, and to offer hospitality grudgingly, or not at all, would be regarded as disgraceful.

The Shah, James pointed out, had already pardoned other princes and was likely eventually to show friendship to Britain by forgiving the fugitive three; if he refused them pardons then British influence in Persia would be clearly at a very low ebb and Russia might have a foot in the door already; if that were the case, Britain could take advantage of the happy fact that the princes were in Britain and not in Russia. Other countries, much less rich and powerful than Britain, had welcomed fugitive Persian princes, and, in any case, if the Shah chose to ignore the princes, should the British Government simply abandon them to starve? If Britain's delicate relationship with Persia were to deteriorate the princes could be very useful: the Prince could raise 'a formidable band of followers', while Timour, who had a huge fan club, was a national hero.

He summed up: to refuse to offer the princes a permanent home could be throwing away an opportunity and playing into the hands of Russia:

> And motives of policy apart, will England send from her shores to misery and want, three Princes and their families – the first from Asia that ever put her hospitality to the test – who have spent their last shilling in seeking her protection, in the hope of a liberal provision from a rich and powerful and a generous people?

In his evening chats with the princes James discovered what was happening in the rest of Persia. He was especially interested to hear about other princes still at large 'who might give trouble'. He made a careful note of the most turbulent and powerful chiefs and the number of families that each controlled: all useful stuff for the Foreign Office. But now, how to entertain the young men?

LIFE IN LONDON

It was the start of the London season so there was no shortage of entertainment, and the princes soon found their names at the top of every invitation list. At parties the Prince found the excited attention distasteful and preferred to retreat to an anteroom with a few select companions, while Timour, in stumbling English, joyfully set about choosing his friends from among the prettiest girls and the Wali watched suspiciously from behind a pillar. At the Caledonian Ball, for which James donned Persian dress, they were reduced to tears by the strains of the bagpipes, which reminded them of their own martial music.

Interpreting was sometimes tricky: Timour was inclined to ask crude questions of his lady friends which had to be communicated without offending delicate sensibilities. His compliments were always 'in the most flowery style of the East'. How could he not be happy when he was surrounded by angels of paradise? At one point his chosen companion was a French belle so James had to manage three languages at once, feeling rather like 'a fine lady chaperoning a set of uneducated country misses'. All the English Timour could manage so far was 'You very purty'.

In reply to the continual questions about polygamy the Prince had the answer: one English woman, in education and accomplishment, was worth ten Persian women, so 'we take quantity to make up for quality'. Even the Wali was skilful at fielding such questions, especially when he had had a drink or two. Asked about the custom of veiling women, he replied: 'we only veil those who are not worth looking at but who would ever think of veiling such fair creatures as we see here?' His questioner pointed out that every Persian woman was veiled; surely the Wali would veil every woman in London if he could?

> 'And if we did,' replied he, 'the resplendence of their beauty, like the brightness of the sun, would shine forth through all veils. We have a Persian proverb which says, there are two things which cannot be hid – transcendent beauty and true love – tell her that,' said he, giving me [James] a push in the side, as much as to say, 'That will surely please her.'

They were invited to dinner with Lord Palmerston. Elegant dinner parties had James on tenterhooks because of the wide cultural differences: in Persia dining took place on the floor in total silence, with everyone urgently helping themselves with their hands as they felt inclined, from a communal dish, and expressing their appreciation at the end of the meal with a loud burp. The young men quickly learnt to use a knife and fork but Timour remained prone to shouting from one end of the table to the other or suddenly leaving the room spouting poetry or humming soulfully to himself. Sometimes he would empty the whole dish of something he fancied on to his plate; but then, seeing the 'blank faces' around him 'would quietly rise and empty from his own plate into theirs two-thirds of what he had taken'. To Persians it was a distinction to receive food 'from the plate of a great man'.

When it came to escorting ladies into dinner, James was amused by the way in which each performed this duty. The Prince simply offered his arm with charm and courtesy; Timour claimed his partner with joy and enthusiasm 'like a gallant soldier claiming the mistress he has won by deed of arms'; while the Wali, always clumsy and awkward, clutched his companion by the upper arm 'as if it was the handle of a teapot or mug'. However, he was something of a poet and able to write verses to order – an excellent way to pass the time at parties. He would find a comfortable sofa in a quiet corner and cover sheet after sheet with verses, handing them out to the queue of delighted women, who then flew to James for translation. 'Your lips are as a cup,' he would scribble, 'and the words that flow from them is the wine thereof; their sweetness is its intoxication and delights my soul.'

James took the trio to the Zoo, to a military display on the anniversary of the Battle of Waterloo at which Timour became very overexcited, to the London Diorama and to the Opera. They refused to go anywhere without him, so it was hard work. They also had no idea of time: often he would arrive to collect them only to discover them still in bed. He got into the habit of calling for them an hour in advance of the appointed time. 'Ah,' would say the Prince, hearing James's footstep, 'here is Saheb Fraser, sword in hand, to push us out of our holes, desperate tyrant that he is.' As the hot, dusty summer season wore on, the princes' energy waned and they spent more time in their hotel; only Timour would sometimes sneak out to the gunsmith's.

They were overjoyed to receive a huge bundle of letters with news that their wives and children had been liberated by the Shah. Far from losing heads, eyes, ears or even noses, all they had been relieved of was money. Two of Timour's daughters had died; on reading this news he merely remarked that one had been as beautiful as the full moon. The letters contained 'a variety of interesting particulars relative to the state of Persia' which James painstakingly copied for the Foreign Office.

Tiring of the heat, noise and dust of London the princes always relished a trip to the countryside, especially to Putney and Richmond, but when kind hosts inevitably offered a boat trip the Wali replied in alarm, 'No no no good. I no boat, no more boat, no Biscay!' They were, however, eventually persuaded to brave the Thames and were awestruck by the opening of Hammersmith suspension bridge.

The Wali and Timour were so excited by Madame Tussaud's waxworks that they decided to play a practical joke on the Prince, who had stayed at home in bed. They told him they were all to be officially presented to Princess Victoria and returned to the waxworks; Faced with her waxen Royal Highness and, totally taken in, the Prince was just about to perform his most graceful bow when James intervened saying enough was enough. Luckily the Prince joined in the laughter.

Knowing the Persian love of outward appearances of power and greatness, James took them to Windsor Castle. King William was otherwise engaged, but Queen Adelaide and Princess Victoria appeared as if by chance and graciously conversed with the princes.

Queen Adelaide. In Jeanie's opinion she was 'a sweet enough quiet lady but no great look for a Queen'.

Later, they were again received by Princess Victoria and her mother, the Duchess of Kent, at Kensington Palace. The Prince wrote some verses to enclose in his thank-you letter and in true Persian fashion exclaimed ecstatically, 'nothing ever was or will be written like them. Nothing so happy was ever produced. They are truly admirable.' When it was explained to him that this was called blowing his own trumpet, he replied that it was the truth; why should he not express it? Such boasting, James agreed, was common in Persia and accepted as the expression of an opinion.

A visit to an evening military review at Woolwich left the brothers speechless with amazement. They were especially impressed with the exercise in which, with perfect discipline, a gun carriage was taken to bits, reassembled, loaded and fired in less than a minute. They wanted to see what the soldiers kept in their knapsacks; James was relieved to find a Bible was included in each – evidence of regard for the religion that was so little paraded compared to that of the princes. The Prince approved: 'Very good, very good'.

By mid-July, exhausted by the pace of London social life, they were refusing most invitations that dropped daily into Mivart's Hotel and asked instead to be taken to 'useful' institutions. Accordingly, James took them to some prisons, the Penitentiary and to Bedlam, or Bethlem Hospital, where they were impressed by the clemency shown to James Hadfield,[3] the man who had taken a pot shot at George III. He also took them to India House, where they were excited to see some Persian MSS and recognised their uncles and father in a picture of the late Shah and his sons.

3 1771–1841. Attempted to assassinate George III in the Theatre Royal Drury Lane 15 May 1800. Declared insane and committed to indefinite detention, the Criminal Lunatics Act having been hastily passed. Died in Bethlem Royal Hospital of TB.

The former ambassador to Teheran, Sir Gore Ouseley, invited them for a day to his beautiful house and grounds, Hall Barn, near Beaconsfield. The Wali, suffering from having eaten too many cucumbers and 'other indigestible substances', stayed at home; the other two revelled in the escape to the fresh air of the country, Timour, in the wildest of spirits, running about 'like a young kid trying to catch the pheasant chicks'.

A welcome relief to their growing ennui was sitting to the artist John Partridge.[4] His studio was just along the street from Mivart's Hotel so they could wander at their leisure to their sessions and they enjoyed the whole experience. James considered the early sketches 'excellently characteristic and spirited' and was very honoured to be given the best of them.

At the beginning of August, the princes had a private audience with the King who assured them of the interest he took in 'personages who had so frankly put their trust in the royal generosity and protection'; the Prince expressed his gratitude for the hospitality they had received ever since seeing the British flag flying at Gibraltar. It was, he considered, the omen of a happy future and, *Inshallah,* God willing ,all would now go well for them.

The London season now danced itself wearily to a close; the town was thinning and many friends and acquaintances had departed to the country. The princes stayed for the most part in their hotel, behaving as they pleased and eating when they liked, sometimes rousing the house at midnight to get a snack. At first, the Persian disregard for time or routine had greatly upset the cook. Such was the charm of the three, however, the good manners of the Prince, the happy go lucky friendliness of Timour and even the inoffensiveness of the Wali, who had spent at least half his time in bed, that they had become firm favourites with the hotel servants.

They were very picky eaters, initially suspicious of everything and firmly refusing to eat turtle or lobster; even oysters were off limits at first, but once tasted they were ordered every night they dined in. The Wali's favourite pudding was Charlotte Russe and he amused himself making numerous puns about its 'sweetness and fairness', comparing it with the Charlottes of his acquaintance. One of their Persian servants, Taqi the cook, was allowed in the kitchen to help prepare Persian dishes.

'AND AWAY WE WENT'

At last another fat packet of letters arrived from Persia: the Shah was ready to forgive his three cousins and it was safe for them to join their families in Baghdad. The bundle contained letters from powerful chiefs all over Persia urging their return '& detailing a variety of interesting particulars relative to the state of Persia' which James again copied for the Foreign Office.

There was no way the princes would consider another encounter with the Bay of Biscay, so after long deliberation it was reluctantly agreed they should go home by the longer and

4 1789–1872 . Scottish artist, briefly 'portrait-painter extraordinary' to Queen Victoria and painted many of the notable figures of the time.

costlier overland route. The Wali had to be shown a map to persuade him that as Britain was an island, he could not escape the Channel. Obviously, they needed a guide, at least as far as Constantinople, and clearly that man should be James. He now knew them well, had become fond of them despite the problems they presented and was familiar with the arduous journey through Europe. On 23 August Palmerston wrote:

> His Majesty having been pleased to signify his acquiescence in the wish expressed by the Persian Princes to be accompanied on their return to Asia by some person on the part of His Majesty, I have acquainted their Royal Highnesses that you have been selected for this service.

This would be no light charge as they were 'little else than great spoilt children, wayward & capricious, as much from habit & education as from utter ignorance of the world'. But James had become deeply interested in 'these homeless wanderers' and felt a strong desire to help them to find their families. They were to progress as fast as possible to avoid winter but James should allow them to sightsee along the way. Once safely at Constantinople the British Ambassador to Turkey, Lord Ponsonby, would advise on the next move.

There were several exchanges between James and the Foreign Office about arrangements for the journey, including for the interpreter, Assad, who was to have one guinea per day and £50 at the end. James also had to negotiate the payment of debts incurred by the princes in Bath, where, with no money, they had unsuccessfully tried to pay with jewellery. The Prince, terrified that a bad impression at this stage might stand in the way of their departure, begged James not to tell Palmerston of these embarrassing obligations. Inevitably the preparations took some time and a period of low spirits followed. James wrote to John Backhouse at the Foreign Office:

> I do not like teazing Lord Palmerston about these poor Princes but really if his Lordship saw how unhappy they are I am sure he would take pity on them ... they can now enjoy nothing but mope all day in their chambers ... the constant theme of their conversation with me is 'When, when are we to be off?'

He pointed out that they were costing the country a great deal of money and that it would be best to leave while they were still enjoying Britain. He thought up interesting ways to fill their remaining days, taking them to the home of Ibrahim Mirza, a tutor at Haileybury, where they examined more Persian MSS and ate too many green apples in Ibrahim's garden. The Wali and Timour attended the State Opening of Parliament, where Timour, unable to stifle his giggles at the Lord Chancellor's wig, almost had to be escorted out. The Prince had declined the invitation, afraid that the seats allocated to them would be in a position degrading to his rank.

❊

In July, Jeanie wrote an excited letter to Jane Anne. She was to be allowed to go too! 'I feel very queer about this & can scarcely take in the fact that I may be at Constantinople'. But travelling had always agreed with her – better than any medicine. She would pay her own way and would take her sister Annie as companion. They were to have a carriage to themselves with another for the princes, Assad and one servant. The other Persian servants, along with the luggage, would have to brave the sea voyage from Falmouth.

By the beginning of September all was ready. At the last moment there was a delay when two Persian servants decided against it: Taqi, the cook, wanted to stay within easy reach of English ale and the tailor had fallen in love. All night long the Princes and the servants argued until at last handsome bribes appeared to persuade them. Even then there was a farce with the coach at the door: as fast as one was bundled in the near door the other shot out of the far door and ran off – 'like buckets in a well,' said the infuriated James. Not until he had let fly a stream of Persian abuse did they manage to get both men into the coach at once and slam the door.

After yet another delay, with both Timour and the Wali laid low as a result of 'excesses', very early on 3 September, the coaches were once more at the door in a scene 'fit for a novel'. Everyone in the hotel turned out to see them off, and the neighbours, who had watched their comings and goings with interest for three months, thronged the street outside. People hung out of windows and friends of the princes gathered for a last farewell. There were tears and even hysterics from certain ladies and the princes, from excitement and sympathy, were almost as bad:

> It was a most moving business. But all things must have an end; the last hand was shaken; the last – no perhaps not *last* tear was shed; with difficulty we forced our way through the crowd that had thickened round the carriages. In got the Princes – the door was shut – adieu, adieu! And away we went.

James sat back with a profound sigh of relief.

London to Vienna

They spent the first night at the George Inn in Sittingbourne and the next at the Ship Inn in Dover where it was blowing a gale. Unfortunately, the Wali's windows looked out to sea and he sat up all night gazing out and moaning with dread. The Prince stayed in his carriage for the voyage while Timour and the Wali, 'determined from the first to be sick', stumbled below with Assad, who 'shouted and roared and ejaculated for mercy in all languages'. After nearly three hours 'of bitter misery we were duly ejected from our aquatic prison upon the quay of Calais and soon well lodged in Monsieur Dessein's most comfortable hotel'.

Jeanie had begun her diary at Sittingbourne and was enchanted by the Prince. With such a sweet and benevolent expression she found it hard to believe that he could cut off noses or pluck out eyes.

> He said to me, 'Now that Mrs Fraser is come with us, all will go well'. Prince Reza Kolee handed me to table, and sat next to me during dinner! I felt at first as if I would rather we had dined alone; but ere half the dinner was over, we were all quite at ease. They are so frank and sweet with their little English phrases; and between Mr F and the interpreter we get on finely.

She was amused by Timour's hearty appetite. At breakfast in Dover, despite complaining of feeling unwell, he ate mutton chops, an omelette, chicken and rice mixed together with lemon squeezed liberally over it. 'They devour lemons; no wonder he is ill; the wonder will be if he is not worse.' They were all in good spirits and even 'melancholy Jacques', the Wali, very nearly laughed at Jeanie's attempts to speak Persian. Once safely across the water, the three pleaded with Jeanie to persuade James never to put them on another ship: 'You – Saheb Fraser – no go ship – no go sea – no go black sea –no no ship – ship no good – carriage good – you tell Saheb Fraser – go carriage.'

The journey through Europe started badly. The first night James was woken at 4.00 am by a great commotion in the princes' room where he found them all, including a pretty chambermaid and a waiter, clustered round the Wali who lay groaning from the after-effects of seasickness. There was nothing for it but to brace him up and get going. At Lille he was still suffering and James called a doctor who ordered him into a warm bath which worked wonders for a time. In Brussels repairs to the carriage gave him time to recover while the others visited the Cathedral; Timour was not impressed with the representation of God. 'The Almighty!' he shouted, 'Paint the Almighty! And under what likeness? That of an old man with a beard! Why not paint the wind? You can see it as well as the Almighty. Where is it and where is he?'

For some distance through Germany they travelled in the wake of a Russian prince, who, by the time they arrived, had always taken the best rooms and all the horses. The princes, suspicious of the catering in third-rate accommodation, decided to buy food along the way and store it in the carriage, their 'very goot leetle house', which soon became a wonderful mess of bread and cheese, roast chicken, onions, lemons and fruit on which they snacked all day. This rotting 'hodge podge' was accompanied by an unhousetrained dog, bought by Timour, who shared the carriage with them. Their servant was in despair.

Whenever they could they left the carriages and walked, the Prince beaming with delight, the Wali 'grunting out his joy' and Timour singing like a bird as he gambolled and leapt and 'flew up to the top of every height'. They picked bouquets of wild flowers for Jeanie and Annie; they gathered berries and squeezed the juice to make sherbet – 'never was good housewife more earnest about the manufacture of her jams and jellies ... than they are about that of their sherbet'. The Wali, who drank gallons of it, declared it was far better than 'the medicine of your Feringee[5] doctors'.

5 Foreign.

The further they travelled the more the Prince worried about the lack of attention paid to his rank. James warned him that this would be the norm from now on but reassured him that he would do all in his power to secure every possible comfort for his charges.

By the time they reached Frankfurt the princes and their female fellow travellers knew each other so well that James had no fear of leaving them in each other's care. The princes were delighted to be able to practise their English on Jeanie and Annie with stories about their families: Timour would dance around the room singing his wild music, 'much like an old Highland *croon* ... between signs and words we got on wonderfully'. When spirits drooped Timour would cheer them up with insider gossip about the Royal ménage. The Prince, however, had moments of doubt and depression: would the Shah ever restore to them their lands and possessions? If not, maybe he would cut off his long locks and become a hermit.

In one inn the Wali's room was unfortunately hung with seascapes which reminded him that they were facing a voyage down the Black Sea to Constantinople; there was no way he would countenance this: he would find a way to go by land. An argument ensued and the Prince had to divert the Wali, still growling his determination to avoid the sea, by showing everyone how to make apple sherbet.

In Würzburg Jeanie was ecstatic at the magnificence of the buildings: 'nothing descriptive in the Arabian Nights was ever more glitteringly splendid'. Timour nosed out the Royal roundabout, the King of Bavaria's entertainment for his children. Jeanie was electrified to find him 'flying through the air on a magnificent horse flourishing a sabre which he was slashing about in a grand style – his attitude was perfectly beautiful – suddenly he attacked a mounted warrior and with one stroke severed his head from his body'. Noses, legs and arms flew in all directions and Jeanie reflected that this must have brought him many happy memories.

They were still eating lemons all day long and Timour was worryingly yellow. James told him that, with that colour, no London lassie would have looked at him twice, whereupon Timour appealed to Jeanie: 'Me very pretty eh lady? You say Timour very pretty?'

'No,' replied Jeanie firmly. 'Timour pretty in London. Timour no pretty here. Lemons ... make Timour ugly'. She found Timour's cheeky charm irresistible.

Vienna to Bucharest

They arrived in Vienna on 24 September and put up at the excellent Hotel de Londres where James had time to research the next stage of their journey. The plague was raging near Constantinople and there was thus no alternative to the Black Sea. He sternly pointed out that the British Government had already deferred to the wishes of the princes in allowing them, so far, an expensive journey overland.

Their stay in Vienna was marred by the ensuing dispute: Timour announced that he would die if he set eyes on the Black Sea, and the Wali suddenly remembered that the Black Sea was known to be the home of the Malak-al-Maut, the Angel of Death, who arranged shipwrecks. The Prince, tired of his brothers' obstinacy, took James's side. After 'as unpleasant discussion and dispute as I ever had in my life' there was deadlock. Just as James was wondering how it could be resolved along came a *deus ex machina* in the shape of a traveller, just arrived from Persia, who reported a calm passage on the Black Sea and scorned the plan to go by road through a plague-ridden country.

When they left Vienna the two younger princes were still sulking and Timour bought another dog 'to the no small discomfiture of our already disgusted servant and, I believe, of his own brothers.' There followed a nightmare journey through Hungary: a desert and a hurricane meant that often all the horses were needed to drag one carriage at a time through the sand, so that progress was slow. The accommodation left much to be desired; fleas and mosquitoes abounded and the Wali and Timour resorted to eating nothing but huge quantities of grapes and pears. Jeanie reckoned they 'manage their stomachs in a wild way'. With great relief they crossed the border into Transylvania.

At Szarvas, the hungry princes, despairing at the food provided by The Two Pistols, took over the kitchen to make themselves a pilau, to the great dismay of the poor hostess 'who ran about wringing her hands'. Next day they came upon a Viennese banker who described to James the best route across the Transylvanian Alps via Walachia; he also agreed to send notice of their approach to the British Consul in Bucharest and arranged for horses to meet them at their next stop.

The Wali was still growling and shaking his head about the Black Sea, and the Prince was worrying again – this time about how he would be received in Constantinople. He had many friends there so he needed splendid apartments and servants to receive them. If he went to call on the Sultan he would need an appropriate train. James was again bracing – he had no idea what attention the Sultan might feel disposed to pay but he would write to Lord Ponsonby to alert him of the Prince's concerns.

The journey across the mountains was arduous. The 'arrangements' made for them by the Viennese banker turned out to be a band of Walachian peasants, very colourfully dressed in 'wide breeches or longtailed skirts, sandals or boots, or bits of either, and an hundred other rags and tatters'. These fellows produced small, wild, shaggy ponies 'with manes, tails, forelocks and fetlocks, matted into solid masses with the burrs of the pasture in which they had just been caught'. Twenty-two of these were duly harnessed together with a complicated and fragile-looking structure of branches. The horsemen, officially mounted police, were no less wild, ten to each carriage and one on foot at each door clutching a rope tied to the roof to prevent the vehicle overturning. Off they went along a river on a road often cut into the edge of the mountain and constructed of logs, with the water boiling below visible through the chinks. But 'the scenery was splendid throughout and ... amply compensated for the rudeness of the road,' wrote the resilient James.

As they climbed higher, oxen were added to the train of ponies. These were attached simply by a long pole and a wooden peg on which the whole perilous contraption depended, but, as usual, for James there were compensations: 'the mountains reared their heads fantastically out of a sea of mist that filled the valleys like a lake'. There were tantalising glimpses into beautiful wild glens which made James long for his pencil, but there was no time for such amusement and on they struggled.

On the outskirts of Bucharest they were met by police and Cossacks who, much to the Prince's satisfaction, identified the carriage carrying the Royal personages, surrounded it like a cloud 'and away they scoured, like hey-go-mad, leaving us to follow as we might'. They eventually skidded to a halt at the house of Mr Colquhoun, the British Consul. Prince Ghika, ruler of Walachia, had arranged accommodation for the princes with a guard of honour to attend them. The second stage of the journey was now complete. It was 29 October, thirty-nine days since they had left London.

Bucharest to Constantinople

For a few days the Prince's head was in danger of being turned by the brilliancy of their reception. Prince Ghika sent his own carriage to convey the princes to his palace, where he received them most graciously and made a return visit in great state; he then forgot them. The Prince was deeply offended by this neglect which was compensated for, to some extent, by the unvarying kindness and friendship shown to them all by the Consul and his sister, an example, James was quick to point out, of the 'steady nature of English friendship'.

On hearing that the plague was daily strengthening its hold on Constantinople and creeping towards them, the terrified princes announced that not one step further would they take. How could they travel by land, demanded the despairing Prince?

> I cannot touch a mat, or bit of old rag, that may lie on the road by accident, but, *tchick*, I have the plague. *Ai wahi, ai wahi,* what a fortune is mine! ... On one side my way is bounded by the wide sea; on the other cut off by the plague!

No amount of persuasion would make them change their minds until James agreed to write to Lord Ponsonby for advice, provided that, when it came, they would take it.

Lord Ponsonby was comforting: there was no need to worry. The Sultan had arranged accommodation for the princes at Yeni Köy, some way out of the city on the Bosphorus, beyond the reach of the plague. While they waited for the next steamer the Wali terrified them all by one night waking up covered in blood. He had been treated with leeches for a sore throat and the bandages had not stopped the bleeding. He appeared in his brothers' room 'steeped with gore ... his arms outspread like a reanimated corpse, yelling: "*Ai, Ai* ... help, I am dying, all my blood is spilt".' A little rum came to his rescue, while a nurse was called to dress the wounds.

For the princes this was one of the lowest moments of the journey. Terrified by the prospect of the Black Sea, uncertain of their future, overcome with boredom while they waited, they had time to reflect.

> And now came apologies without number for past follies and petulance; entreaties for forgiveness and promises to sin no more; and acknowledgements of the great trouble they had given, and the exertions that had been made for their comfort. 'We are ashamed when we look you in the face, Saheb Fraser,' declared the Prince, 'your words were always right; and as for me I will never slight your advice again, nor dispute your words, whatever they may be.'

They had now been in Bucharest for more than a month. When James told the princes that he had decided to leave the women with the Consul and his sister and accompany them to Constantinople alone, they were distraught. Jeanie and Annie were equally distressed. Jeanie described their last dinner together:

> The dinner was sad enough; Timour declared that, whenever he looked round the table at us all, a lump rose in his throat and he could not eat ... the Prince was sweet and grave ... he bade James tell me, that if ever he had offended me, or been unreasonable or troublesome, he now desired my forgiveness, and begged me to remember that he had been spoiled in his youth ... 'I had been used to much attendance; I had twenty women to make my bed; so pray forgive me'. I told him ... no cloud had ever come between us and that the remembrance of the time we had passed together would ever be pleasant to me.

If, as he said, he wanted to give his son an English education, Jeanie would 'act a mother's part to him, and teach him to be good'. She presented them with gifts, including one for the Prince's chief wife; then came the parting:

> The prince, when he saw me overcome, had tears in his own eyes: he took my hand and pressed it to his heart, saying 'Don't cry, lady; I will send Saheb Fraser soon back to you, and I will watch over him that no harm come near him; I will be a father and a brother to him, so help me, God.'

Their trials were not yet over. In Galatz (modern Galati) near the mouth of the Danube which, drowning in an ocean of mud, reminded James of Starbroek in Guyana, they found that their steamer had been diverted to Trebizond. They stayed in the house of Mr Cunningham, the Vice Consul, but Galatz had little to offer and there was no easy means of negotiating the thick porridge of mud that invaded every corner. Even Mr Cunningham's servants had given up the unequal task of keeping the house free of mud, what with the comings and goings of the doctor and the activities of Timour's dogs.

Both James and the Prince were ill; James recovered fairly quickly, but the Prince alarmed them all with a high fever and a bad cough, which worsened daily. His brothers attended him most tenderly and in between times they slept or nostalgically groaned, '*Ai* London *ai* Mivart's'. The doctor seemed unable to help, and James began to fear for the Prince's life:

> It was only now, in this extremity of danger, that the restlessness of my own mind and the sinking of my own heart, rendered me sensible of how much I truly loved the Prince – how much, in spite of all petty causes of vexation, his mild and amiable manners and real goodness of heart had won upon my own affections... the loss of a brother would scarcely, I think have cost me a severer pang.

But after two weeks of real anxiety the Prince recovered enough to lie on Mr Cunningham's sofa. It was now a race between the arrival of the steamer and the Prince's struggle to regain strength enough for the voyage; winter was round the corner, threatening to cover the river with ice.

At the beginning of December the steamer arrived; although he was still very weak, the news was like a tonic to the Prince. Even the Wali, who had pestered James to ask the captain to keep near to the shore, 'for when I see the land ... I feel as if the danger were less', went on board without a murmur and soon the three of them were enjoying a good meal.

As they proceeded down the Danube towards the Black Sea they could see the Cossack quarantine guards on the northern Russian bank follow the progress of the steamer, narrowly watching for any hint of landing. A day later, they arrived at the dreaded Black Sea, 'and little did it deserve its black name for a more smiling sea I never sailed upon'. But James spoke too soon. The next day, the wind rose and soon 'sounds of woe began to issue from the aftercabin ... we heard the Wali groaning, Timour retching and the Prince *ai-wahi*-ing; as for Assad he was worst of all'. Even James succumbed. By the time the wind had dropped, people had emerged from their cabins and the decks had been sluiced down, they were passing the castles at the entrance to the Bosphorus. 'Need I attempt to express the joy and gratitude with which I perceived ahead the village of Therapia, the flagstaff of the English embassy, and the English colours themselves floating from the mizzen-peak of his Majesty's frigate *Volage*?'

Parting

James was invited to stay with his friends, Lord and Lady Ponsonby, who gave him his old room in the Embassy where there was peace and congenial company. The princes were less pleased with their accommodation at Yeni Köy and the lack of food. James pointed out that they had arrived in the middle of Ramadan, when fasting is the order of the day, and that everything is scarce in a plague-ridden country. He visited them often, going either by boat or over the hills, armed with a pole to ward off possible plague victims. The princes had nervously put themselves into a type of self-imposed quarantine, inventing a smoking box to fumigate their garments and allowing no one in without permission.

Relieved that the princes were for the moment safe, James took himself into the hills to relax and paint. At a particularly good vantage point he was about to enter a little hut when a shout from a guard alerted him to stop: it was full of 'poor plague-smitten Armenians' sent out from the city to die in isolation, proof that the tentacles of the plague were creeping nearer.

Waiting for news of the next stage of their journey, the princes were dismayed by a decree from the Sultan of Baghdad that there were now too many Persian princes of the blood in his city and they should choose somewhere else as their destination. But their wives and families, along with servants, mothers, aunts, sisters – some 200 to 300 people – were awaiting them in Baghdad. Where else could they go? James could not resist reminding them that if they had gone by sea they would by now be safely in Baghdad. Lord Ponsonby, however, took up their case with the Sultan, remonstrating with him on grounds of common humanity and his previous promises. Eventually, the 'firm and decided tone' of his Lordship won the day and consent was grudgingly given for the princes to go to Baghdad but not necessarily to settle there. The Prince gloomily suspected that this was all some plot to deliver them into the hands of the Shah but Timour cheered up and took himself off to shoot waterfowl to augment their skimpy fare.

They were invited to a farewell dinner at the Embassy and the Prince lamented that it was the last English dinner that he would enjoy. 'And these the last of such ladies I shall behold. Woe's me! Woe's me! Tell her ladyship that my heart turns to water at thinking I shall never see her more.' England and the English had risen in their estimation with every step they had taken from her shores. They had come to respect English habits and now preferred knives and forks to their fingers. They promised to visit James in Scotland where Timour would shoot grouse and the Wali would look up a certain Scottish lady friend. The prince talked seriously of sending his favourite son to school in England and into James's care, even working out how much it would cost.

'Turks do not move with rapidity', and it was only on 17 January 1837 that they got word that they could proceed to Baghdad with a *mehmandar*[6] but not till mid-February. Meanwhile their servant and the faithful interpreter, Assad, could wait no longer and departed, leaving the princes to make shift as best they could. Next day, James found them peeling walnuts, picking raisins and wondering how to make a stew; they cut up the waterfowl provided by Timour 'with their own princely hands'. James was touched by this but there was nothing to be done – patience was the only hope. The Prince's patience was long since exhausted: 'Oh God, for freedom, for freedom only! Let us but go, and we will travel barefoot; we want neither *mehmandar*, nor money ... all we want is to be put free upon the hillside, and to make our way as best we can.'

Early in the morning of 14 February James was woken with the news that the princes were leaving in an hour; if he did not come at once he would not see them again. He jumped into a boat and rowed for the last time to Yeni Köy. He found them in high spirits, which fell when the moment came to part:

> I hate such scenes and cannot describe them; they were affected sincerely I believe; and the elder prince turned away to conceal an emotion which I certainly participated in myself ... they embraced me à *la mode de Perse*, commended me to the care of God, received from me a like and very sincere adieu, and I left them.

6 An official courier appointed to escort an important traveller.

That same month, MacNeill wrote from Teheran with the news that the Shah had given the princes a full pardon and a welcome to Persia 'with full security and favour'. There was no doubt that James was thankful to be relieved of his charges but these three young men had wound themselves around his heart and such ties, he wrote, 'must give pain when snapped'. He had developed almost paternal feelings towards them:

> The mild dignity and affectionate kindness of the elder prince, the rough but kindly oddity of the Wali ... and the frank and openhearted warmth of the gallant Timour ... were all present to my mind and a lump, I do confess it, rose in my throat as I thought 'I shall see them all no more!'[7]

He turned his thoughts firmly towards Jeanie and Annie and headed for Bucharest. Hiring a Tatar guide, Ali Aga, he set off up the Black Sea coast. Each day they rose at 2.00 am and rode as far and fast as they could, often sleeping under the stars and at times having to travel in a bullock-cart when no horses were available. It was yet another difficult, uncomfortable journey and he was often reminded of his youthful adventures:

> Strange how our feelings alter with advancing life, yet leave behind a savour of the past! I remember well with what keenness I enjoyed full many a wild expedition in the forests and savannahs of Guiana and on the moon-lit seas of the West Indies. I still recall with delight my long and various Indian travels, and ... many a toilsome and dangerous night-march in Khorasan.

But would he willingly expose himself once more to such discomfort and risk? 'I fear me, no; duty alone – imperative duty – would now start me afresh and that with no good will'.

On they dashed to the shores of the Danube where they hired a rowing boat and reached the Romanian quarantine station at Calarasi – 'Oh how I rejoiced – there was rest for me at length'. He and Ali Aga were assigned two small rooms and remained locked up for twenty-one days. James was perfectly happy writing his journal and working up pictures of the Bosphorus and Constantinople. At the end of March he reached Bucharest and was reunited with Jeanie and Annie who had been hospitably entertained by the Colquhouns for five months – 'a serious intrusion on any family ... no relatives could have watched over them with more solicitude than the kind consul and his most amiable sister.'

On 3 April 1837 Jeanie wrote a long letter to Jane Anne describing the thrill of coming home to the Colquhouns' house one day and finding James waiting for her in the salon. The next day, armed with a large hamper of provisions from their kind hostess, they set off to brave the journey back over the Transylvanian Alps, now rendered far more hazardous by the ravages of the snows and frosts of winter and the swollen rivers. Rather than face the danger and jolting of the carriage as it lurched its way over the familiar 'wooden shelves'

7 They eventually settled in Baghdad with a small pension from the British Government, which refused to hand them over to Muhammad Shah (*The English amongst the Persians*, Denis Wright, 1977).

precariously fixed to the rocky precipices overhanging the torrents, the two women often got out of the carriage and walked: 'Our bones could not have stood it even if we had not been afraid ... the boards were shook from the books we were reading and our watches have been so confounded they have never gone since'. Two oxen had to be added to the twelve horses and several nights were spent sleeping in the carriage. However, the weather was fine, the scenery magnificent and they eventually arrived safely at the next 'lazaretto' or quarantine station.

There they were entirely surrounded by towering snow-capped mountains so that the sun barely reached them and the raging river 'brawls through the rocks making melancholy music against our prison walls'. Inside their 'queer little prison in the mountains', however, there was merriment, singing and laughter. Annie welcomed the enforced inactivity to continue with a book she was writing.[8] They made their own beds, did some cooking to supplement what was sent in each day from the local inn, kept up the fires and washed up the tea things ' which we fortunately brought with us'. There were two rooms for the three of them and a stable for their servant and the guard who attended them. A doctor came daily to inspect them for signs of the plague: 'All we had to do was bare one arm & he smiled & was satisfied'. All their clothes were strung on pegs round the walls for fumigation: the chemises and velvet gowns, the pantaloons and waistcoats 'most tastefully interspersed with ... caps, veils and ribands' reminded Jeanie of the pawnbroker's shop in St Mary's Wynde in Edinburgh. They were allowed a walk a day within bounds, accompanied by a 'Guardian Angel' smoking, smelling of garlic and brandishing a large stick to frighten off any unwitting passers-by.

On their release they hoped to reach Vienna in ten days by a route that avoided the terrible sands of Hungary and to continue via Salzburg, Strasbourg and Paris:

> I am sure I shall feel quite satisfied with continental travelling by the time we return & willingly confine myself and James to what our own little island affords for the rest of our lives – too happy if he is permitted to sit quietly in London to do the work of the Foreign Office for a few years longer.

Their thoughts were returning to Moniack. They had been away so long and were anxious to take up the reins but Jeanie would always regret that she would never again feel the warmth of Reelig's 'gracious and benignant smile' as he stood at the front door with open arms to welcome her home.

8 *Mary and Florence or Grave and Gay* (1835). Ann Fraser Tytler wrote several children's books including *Leila* and *Leila at Home* which sold numerous editions in England and America.

16

1836–1846

NAGPUR: RUMBLES OF WAR

In January 1836 George was appointed Assistant to the Hon. Richard Cavendish, the Resident of Nagpur, a town about 400 miles south of Delhi. The Resident was welcoming but Mina had reservations: he certainly did not rank 'with the Malcolms, Baillies, Elphinstones or Frasers, the ornaments of this country' and he had an insatiable appetite for flattery and entertaining. They were not likely to get on intimate terms with him but he was upright and pleasant.

Nagpur was a healthy area, popular for rest and recreation, so there was a fairly regular stream of visitors. Here, for the first time since he arrived in India, George surprisingly became ill. He put this down to too little exercise, too much social life, too much food and a very changeable climate. Mina rose admirably to the occasion and George was proud of her:

> I had a nurse in Mina who certainly did as much as the medicine ... by rousing my energies, cheering my spirits and keeping me in order, and within due bounds when recovering ... a more gentle tender more attentive or kinder nurse could not have been found for me.

With growing confidence, she also coped with the greater social demands of their new situation: they had to attend weekly formal dinners at the Residency, 'stale, flat and unprofitable' affairs, which George reckoned less interesting than the Pigeon Club in Delhi.

They also had to repay hospitality regularly. George proudly described to his pernickety mother a dinner they gave for ten friends, including the Resident, to celebrate their fifth wedding anniversary:

> I flatter myself that even you, who criticised the dinners given by every person within miles of us with so nice and correct a taste and eye, would have been pleased to satisfy the manner in which the table was laid out, the dinner served and the dishes cooked. Yet all this without expense, merely the result of ... Mina's good taste and knack (I can't find a better word) of making good things and arranging them ... we broke up at 10 at night having got through our parts as Host and Hostess without a single mistake or contretemps.

Knowing his mother's passion for entertaining, he sent her a detailed description of the menu for one informal dinner party: soup 'for which we are noted', then 'a fine fat fowl for which we are equally noted' on one side of the table and a 'ham from our own curing' on the other; a leg of lamb at the foot of the table and a boiled rabbit at the top, with a pigeon pie in the centre and vegetables, 'croquets' and lamb chops *en papillotte* at the corners. There followed the customary curry and rice, then 'a beautiful pudding of Mina's manufacture' and cheese but 'music we have none as it is difficult to keep a piano in tune'.

They gave a dinner like this for their friends every ten days and soon got the reputation for giving very good parties. If they were better off and had more room, no doubt Mina would add 'elegance to neatness'. In between parties they amused themselves by riding in the country or taking long walks. From time to time they had copies of the *Inverness Courier* to keep them *au fait* with Highland goings on. Mina, who had never been to Scotland, was hungry for information about the Highlands and when George's childhood friend, Hugh Inglis of Kingsmills, appeared, Mina took to him immediately and loved hearing the stories of their boyhood in and around Inverness.

George was always keeping an eye out for promotion and, remembering William's advice, had conceived the idea of compiling a political history of the State of Nagpur in the hope that it would catch the eye of the authorities in Calcutta; they eventually pronounced it 'creditable to his industry and Knowledge'.[1] There was also a favourable report from the Resident:

> I deem it my duty to report for the information of the Rt. Hon. The Governor General of India in Council that my assistant, Mr Fraser, has conducted the duties of his offices with zeal and ability, and to my entire satisfaction; that he speaks the Hindoostanee language with great fluency and precision and is a very good Persian scholar. But the most important of all points is a kindly feeling for the natives – and Mr Fraser is eminently distinguished for his mild and conciliatory manner and language.[2]

The Resident was rumoured to be moving to Hyderabad and George hoped that his successor would not be 'so insatiably hospitable'. Meanwhile, there was an audience at the Palace, to which he was summoned; they would have to 'squat on their ends for a full hour much to the detriment of tight pantaloons'.

⁂

The following year, the rumbles of war reached them. Despite John MacNeill's attempts to dissuade the new Shah, a Persian army with Russian backing had besieged Herat in northern Afghanistan, considered the gateway to India. In London James was bombarded with letters from John MacNeill in Teheran and his assistant, Captain Justin Shiel, who assumed he still had the ear of the Foreign Office:

1 British Library L/MIL/10/25-27 Aug 1841.

2 Extract of letter from the Hon R. Cavendish, Resident at Nagpur, to the Secretary to the Government of India, 10 Feb 1837. British Library L/MIL/10/25–27.

> What can be the occasion that the English Government tolerates so evident an advance of Russian projects towards India for no one can help feeling that by the capture of Herat by Persia Russia has made a step in the invasion of India ... does anyone anticipate that the Persians will halt at Herat, you of course who know them do not.

James must urge the authorities 'to assume an appearance of a quality we seem to have taken farewell of – vigour ... England is getting old, I fear, and timid ... Russia is in her youth and daily gaining strength. We, I fear, are in our declining years and as rapidly losing it'. 'The good old King' had been interested in Eastern affairs but the new young Queen Victoria seemed not required to immerse herself in such things. Although the Shah was gallant in his attitude to the Queen, nevertheless 'there is that lingering feeling that a female Government must be weak'.

James, however, apparently looked with favour on the young Queen, who had been on the throne for a matter of months. Lord Ponsonby in Constantinople wrote to him:

> What you say of our Queen is most pleasant to hear. The fate of Empires and of the world may depend on the qualities of the young girl. I hear from other persons ... that the Queen is full of sense and *modesty* & capable of great application to business & state secrecy.

By December 1837 Shiel reported to James: 'We have arrived at a point when the Government will be forced *nolens volens* to take a decided course.' A Russian emissary was thought to have orders to induce Dost Mohammad, the King of Afghanistan, to accept Persia's protection, 'so there are Persia and Russia acting in concert versus us in Afghanistan almost on our very frontier'. The only safe course for Britain was to secure Afghanistan at all costs.

Later, Henry Rawlinson,[3] also part of the British team in Teheran, added his frustration: the siege of Herat was still at stalemate, but the Shah, with a passionate desire to capture the city, felt his crown depended on victory; Russia was doing all she could to further the siege and promising financial support. What was needed was a show of force.

At last in April 1838 British troops landed on Kharg Island, just off the Persian coast. After endless delays and broken promises, the Shah eventually backed down and withdrew his forces. Meanwhile, the moment had come to put into action a plan that had long been lurking in the heads of Westminster and Calcutta.

Dost Mohammad, considered to be hand in glove with the Russians, was to be deposed, and his brother Shah Shuja, still in exile in India under British protection, restored to his throne with the backing of Ranjit Singh, the wily old leader of the Sikhs. There were, however, grave warnings from MacNeill and Burnes, who had been negotiating in Kabul: the forceful and popular Dost Mohammad, provided he could be won over, would be a far better ally than the weak Shuja to lead a strong and united Afghanistan. But Palmerston

3 GCB 1810–95, EIC army, served in Persia 1833–8, Afghanistan and India 1839–43. Resident Baghdad 1843–55. MP 1858 & 1865–8

and Auckland[4] had the bit between their teeth and were determined that the time had come for Afghanistan to be made a British dependency. The Army of the Indus, as it was called, had been gathering during the siege of Herat, and now it was given the order to march, eventually entering Afghanistan through the Bolan Pass in early 1839.

George described the troops mustering for the great march to Kandahar, reckoning that the ineffectual Shah Shuja, if restored, would be 'like feather ... betwixt the wall and heavy brunt of cannon ball'. None of this was likely, as yet, to affect George far south in Nagpur, but how William would have welcomed this second chance to see Afghanistan, not to mention the chance of a battle:

> How joyfully would he have hailed the approaching expedition to the countries he so ardently desired to explore and how highly would his liberal views, extensive information and highly talented mind have come into notice – he would have been Lord Auckland's right hand and chief adviser but, as an ardent admirer of William's and a friend of my own wrote me some time ago 'alas, alas, that weapon of war is broken'.

To George's relief, as an intelligent officer 'acquainted with surveying', he was given a timely job far from the expedition: to superintend repairs to the road between Nagpur and Raipur, 180 miles east, which would mean about three months travelling. Mina was delighted at the prospect of 'a pleasant ramble for three months through the country'; it would be conducive to good health and, as they would be leaving on in early December, they would miss 'all the stupid parties' of the cold weather.

They started their journey in a state of exhaustion, Mina worn out by the Resident's constant entertaining and George thin and weak from his illness. The moment they got on the road, however, their spirits lifted and their health improved. They covered six to ten miles every day, with Mina gamely striding alongside her husband until weariness forced her on to horseback. For four happy months they travelled through 'a plentiful fruitful country', where living was cheaper and healthy while 'thousands of the natives of Upper India are dying of famine, cholera and smallpox'.

Back in Nagpur, the report had to be written up, and here again Mina proved herself a worthy wife. While George was writing she spent hours on her knees, with bits of the map spread out on the floor, working on 'the pasting of the pieces together, the cleaning of it and clipping of it, heart and soul'. Their joint effort resulted in two letters from the Government 'very gratifying to us as highly approving what I have done'. He sent extracts to his mother 'not to be blazoned abroad' but for her own information and pleasure.

❈

Throughout these years Jane, lonely and bored at Moniack, wrote constantly to George. They were still arguing about handwriting: with failing eyesight, she asked George to write more often and adopt a bolder, better spaced hand. He complied: it used nearly double the time

4 1784–1849. George Eden, first and last Earl of Auckland, Governor General of India 1836–42.

and paper but he supposed that was better than causing her eyes and patience to suffer. All day he was writing, and it was hard in the evening 'with a hand cramped and an eye fatigued to sit down by candlelight' and write home. Anyway, her own letters were increasingly illegible and he usually had to read them at least twice with his spectacles on; if only his mother could put more distance between the lines he would find them easier to decipher. It was very frustrating when he could not make out important pieces of information, like who had married whom. He was now keeping his letters under control, all carefully bound in red ribbon and marked outside with the date 'in true lawyer style'.

Most of Jane's letters brought news of the death of a neighbour or two. If he ever got home he would be more familiar with 'monuments and epitaphs' than with the living. At least Nanny Rose was still going strong; it would be a dark day indeed when she shuffled off her mortal coil. He sent his mother £116, asking that Nanny Rose and his old nurse should be given £5 each with his love. In 1838 news came of the deaths of both his aunts: Aunt Gregoire he remembered, for all her problems, as being very good with the young, and Aunt Woodhouselee, though mean in small concerns, 'in matters of moment ... had an open hand that freely obeyed the dictates of a warm heart'. She had died peacefully in the arms of her beloved son Patrick.

Jane sent George a copy of his father's memoir of his early life and description of his grandfather's character, both of which documents he treasured. He was disappointed, however, in the length of the memoir and regretted not having talked more to his father about his adolescence in England. Just think – it took up to eight hours then to travel from London to Cheshunt 'and we can now travel at the rate of twenty miles per hour'.[5] But were people now any happier? George doubted it: 'I lament over those happy old times and would rather have lived from 1740 to the present time.'

Jane also sent him a copy of Henry Thornton's prayers which he received with mixed feelings, doubting whether prayer was necessary and believing that the important thing was to follow the simple rules and precepts of Christ. There was certainly no need to understand the whole Bible – the Gospels and the Acts of the Apostles were all that were required :

> For though I admire the Epistles and reverence them as the productions of men who associated with our saviour and generally speaking were inspired when they wrote I see beyond a doubt that their human nature frequently influenced them – and that they could not always agree on doctrinal points.

In this he had been greatly influenced by his old schoolmaster, Revd Thomas Scott, who tempered the rigid narrow beliefs of his fierce Calvinist father with 'the milk of human kindness and a forgiving nature'. The moral precepts and principles he taught had stood George in good stead.

Jane, having admitted she knew Amy's true identity, now got wind of her two younger brothers and asked George for news of them; reluctantly, he told her that William's friends had helped him find them jobs in Government offices, and for some time the elder boy, Charles,

5 In 1825 the first steam train from Stockton to Darlington travelled at 20mph.

had done well, though he was now in a less promising situation in the Trigonometrical Survey Office: 'I shall keep my eye upon him and I shall do my best to assist him if I find him deserving'.

The younger boy, William, was a different story – 'radically bad and I fear unretrievably vicious'. He was dishonest, addicted to drinking and gambling with friends of 'the lowest and worst company both male and female'. George had lost touch with the boy but still had a faint hope that shame would retrieve him.

A year later, the news came that Charles was doing well and that William 'has taken a step which may prove his salvation or his ruin'. He had applied to both Skinner and George for money to clear his debts because he had got married; George reckoned this was a mistake in view of his youth and lack of a permanent job but all they could do was hope that marriage would bring him to his senses.

Waiting for the Ambassador

In 1837, James, still hovering on the steps of the Foreign Office hoping for a job, sent his book on the mission to Persia to William Fox Strangeways, Under Secretary for Foreign Affairs. Fox Strangeways thought it far too long, but it contained nothing to which Palmerston objected 'unless it were mention of Russia's outwitting us in Europe, which it is as well not to admit & which I have scratched out'. He recommended sending an article to the *Edinburgh Quarterly* or *Blackwood's Magazine* and advised that the milder the language 'the more weight will the subject have with the best class of readers'. He confirmed that Palmerston had great pleasure in agreeing that the book be dedicated to him 'if there is nothing political in the work' and gave James permission to leave London for two months that summer.

James was desperate to get home: he was in the middle of plans to make extensive alterations to Moniack, pulling down the disintegrating School and Nursery wings and replacing them with a more imposing front, designed by a notable local architect, William Robertson. To pay for all this he was depending on his Persian book and was finalising his *Narrative of the Residence of the Persian Princes in London*, in two volumes, published by Richard Bentley early in 1838. Its success exceeded all expectations.

William's affairs were at last sorted out: his debts amounted to £39,000 and his assets to £27,000. His house was to be sold for £2,000. At the same time Affleck enquired, somewhat hungrily, about Reelig's marriage settlement for Jane Anne. James managed to scrape up £700 with £1,300 promised on his death. At least there was news from East India House: compensation of £5000 for William's murder had finally been awarded to the family.

The building work began in the winter, but there were inevitably delays, leaving Jane shivering in a house of which much was open to the winter winds. James had done his best to persuade her to spend winters at Culduthel or Sanquhar but she had adamantly refused to move. Now she suddenly announced that she would be moving into an unfurnished rented cottage and 'setting up a separate establishment'; she would not be at Moniack next summer. James, who had reluctantly kept the house unlet to suit her, answered irritably, 'Strange that I was the last to hear of your new plans'. He was pretty sure that the moment he was home she would want to be there too and, in any case, if she changed her mind, the house would be habitable by the summer.

Meanwhile, torn between the need to be at Moniack to supervise the works and the desire to be in London with a job, James again wrote to Palmerston asking if the Foreign Office needed him further. Backhouse replied:

> Sir, Having laid before Viscount Palmerston your letter of the 15th June I am directed by his Lordship to express to you his entire satisfaction with your conduct during the period you have been employed under the directions of this office but his Lordship desires me to add that he regrets that he has no means of affording you further employment.

That was unless the Persian Ambassador, Hussain Khan, appeared in London for Queen Victoria's Coronation, due to take place in June 1838, in which case James would be needed as an escort and guide. In mid-January he was told to be in London as soon as possible, at a daily allowance of three guineas to cover all expenses except journeys. He accordingly set out, stopping in Edinburgh, where another letter caught up with him – the Ambassador had gone to Vienna, so there was no hurry to come; he replied that he was on his way and continued his journey. In February the news came that it would be an indefinite time before his services were required and he would not be paid the daily allowance of three guineas until Hussain Khan appeared.

At this point Jeanie lost patience and joined him in London, living 'a most quiet life' since James spent every day working in the British Library or enjoying the company of 'such men as he meets at the Athenaeum Club'. If only these *literati* could be transplanted to Moniack as easily as the flowers she collected in London! She had left niece Jane in charge of Moniack and plied her with anxious notes: was 'Bab' better at serving at table? Does she keep the plate and glass clean ... does she rub up the furniture & keep the tables bright? Keep an eye on all this mistress Jane and it will prepare you for your own house'. She was also worried that the masons and carpenters would be making 'blunders in our absence'; if it was not for 'the filthy lucre' she and James would hurry home to superintend the works.

It was not till mid-June the following year that James was finally summoned to attend a private conference with the Persian Ambassador – the very next day. After the meeting, James, who had as usual recorded everything, sent an account of it to Palmerston. At the bottom of the twelve pages Palmerston wrote, 'This is a very correct report of the substance of a conversation which lasted more than three hours.'

At last, in July 1839, James was free. His five-year employment at the Foreign Office was at an end and henceforth he would depend on his pen for an income. But, Jeanie proudly announced to Jane Anne, they had saved £6,000 and he was making roughly £1,000 a year from writing. He would now divide his time between London, where he would work in the British Library, and Moniack – but not until it was painted and papered and everything in its right place.

Heigh for home!

George had promotion: he had been appointed Superintendent of the Road which meant an allowance of Rs300 a month and at least five months every year in the open air. This appointment was likely to last three years, after which he and Mina would go home for good. By January 1843 he would be nearly forty-three and would have completed twenty years' service; although rumour had it that a married man needed £1,000–£2,000 a year to retire in Britain, he reckoned that if they were careful they would have enough to live on. They spent many an evening daydreaming of home, but at the moment, because of the turbulence in the North-West, all army leave was stopped.

Meanwhile, he and Mina were happily living under canvas again, walking through pretty country where George was turning his hand to designing stone bridges. In December 1839 he was commended for 'the prompt and effectual manner in which he has executed the work on the Raepore Road'. His progress was considered 'extremely satisfactory ... and his exertions highly commended'.[6]

Mr Cavendish had departed for England in January 1839, leaving the Residency in such a filthy state that George had to warn the incoming Resident of the need for much cleaning and redecoration. The supervision was assigned to Mina 'and certainly she has wrought a most wonderful change and has not rested until she made it a pleasant cheerful House with everything in it as clean as humans could make them'. She had also made their own house so attractive that everyone remarked on it. 'This is all due to Mina. My habits are still like those of my countrymen – "I canna be fashed".'[7]

The new Resident, Major Wilkinson of the Bengal Cavalry, forty-four years old and sixteen stone, arrived in March; to start with, George approved almost wholeheartedly of his new boss: not only was he plain and unaffected, a man with 'a clear head, sound judgement and unswerving principles', but he was also amiable, cheerful and generous.

Mina managed such a welcoming breakfast party for the Major that he came back to dinner that night and the night after. They then had to arrange a State Dinner, and 'we gave him thanks to Mina's care, good taste and management an entertainment such as he will not often see equalled'. She made no attempt at display or ostentation but all was 'comfort and good taste'. She also masterminded a dinner for fifty before the Resident's first Ball. It took a week's preparation, but she surmounted all the difficulties with great cheerfulness, and the result gained the approbation of both hosts and guests. She then astonished everyone by dancing the first reel.

In 1839 in the North-West things seemed to be settling down. By August Shah Shuja had been restored to his throne, Dost Mohammad had surrendered and British troops were safely in the great fortress-palace of the Bala Hissar in Kabul. It appeared that the Army of the Indus had achieved its aim. The troops had accordingly summoned their families to join

6 British Library L/MIL/10/25-27.
7 'I can't be bothered.'

them and continued life as if they were in India, with cricket matches, hunting parties, horse races and amateur theatricals. But unrest was simmering below the surface. The following year saw tension increase owing to the unpopularity of the restored King, the behaviour of the British, especially towards the beautiful Afghan women, and the appearance on the scene of the favourite son of Dost Mahommed. Central India was quiet but needed constant watchfulness: there were 'few times more interesting than the present'. George was convinced that it was the beginning of something much bigger.

Officers' leave was still forbidden except on health grounds. George and Mina reckoned it was best to stay where they were until the conflict was over and there was no danger of being called up, then 'Heigh for home!' Apparently, nothing could stop them making for Bombay in February 1843, and Jane could at last let herself look forward to welcoming them home. Mina's health was excellent and, although George suffered occasional recurrences of his former illness, he did not feel justified in using ill health as an escape route. Any hint of serious illness, however, and 'I shall not swither as they say at home but post for old Scotland'. As his mother would say, it was always good to build airy castles.

⁂

The airy castles continued into 1840 and George's thoughts focussed daily more on Scotland. Most of their good friends had now gone home or been posted elsewhere, and the honeymoon period with the new Resident was over. Major Wilkinson enjoyed nothing better than camping and often took off with his great friend, Dr Ludlow, leaving George in charge of the Residency without a doctor on hand.

George daydreamed of life on one of the Moniack farms – Knockbain or Drumreach would suit him well, and 'nothing would please me more than to poke about looking after the trees and crops with a dog at my heels and a gun on my shoulder for the partridges'. He would never be able to afford to keep a horse, so walking everywhere would keep him fit. Mina might not take immediately to farm and dairy work, far from her friends and family in the south, so they would probably do some travelling before finally settling down to country life. They had just celebrated their eighth wedding anniversary: 'If the rest of our married life passes so pleasantly and as free from annoyance, though we have had our troubles, as these 8 years have done, I shall be well pleased'.

Jane, worried that George would be disappointed to find Moniack changed, wrote of her distress at the alterations to the old house, although James had been reassuring:

> I can fancy ... your feelings in the pulling down of the wings etc of the House but this is an alteration which would have been made many years ago had it been practicable ... and if the wings were about to come down themselves why it is better they should be taken down.

George would still miss the old nursery and schoolroom but not nearly so much as he would miss 'old Tom the wright, Sandy the wright, James Cumming and many others'.

In any case, he trusted James to spend his money judiciously and 'the grand features of nature will continue unaltered':

> Woods, Burns, Hills and Moors remain ... if it be my lot to see my own old house once more though there may be many changes there will be still enough of all that I once enjoyed to gaze on and ramble over to delight me.

Jane Anne, meanwhile had produced two more children. John Donald was born in February 1838, after which Jeanie fervently hoped that 'God will allow her to rest from adding to her family'. John survived just two months and was replaced early in 1840 by Jane Anne's thirteenth and final child, Catherine Amelia, 'a little fat pretty thing and very like Papa', according to her eldest sister, Jane. Her birth coincided with the departure to India of her eldest brother, James, now twenty; Affleck accompanied him to London and left Jane Anne feeling desolate: 'I feel myself really getting on apace in years. Even Baby cannot beguile me into feeling young'.

All the children were nostalgic about the 'many romps' in the old wings of Moniack but glad that Grandmamma would now have a large airy room with a view of the firth; Nanny Rose would be happy to be released from her 'little dark room in the wing'. By the end of 1841 most of the house was 'delightful and comfortable', much to the relief of James and Jeanie, still shivering up the hill at Rebeg.

✻

In 1841 George was offered a better job as Assistant in charge of Nimar,[8] but with his eyes now firmly fixed on Scotland he refused it.[9] There was still, however, the dreaded chance that his Regiment could be called up to relieve the second Cavalry Regiment and uncertainty ruled the day. Two of his friends had already been killed in action at Kabul.

Late in 1841, an insurrection in Kabul led by Akbar Khan, son of Dost Mohammad, resulted in the overthrow of Shah Shuja and the murders of the British envoy, Sir William Macnaghten[10] and his deputy, Sir Alexander Burnes. The British forces subsequently capitulated, and 17,000 Europeans, including 12,000 wives, children and civil servants, were assured safe passage out of Afghanistan. The retreat began just after New Year 1842. Once out of Kabul, however, they were ambushed and slaughtered; just a hundred survived to be taken prisoner and only one, the Scottish Company Assistant Surgeon, Dr Brydon, famously reached safety at Jalalabad. The situation remained ominous, with the other garrisons stationed in Afghanistan in great danger.

In April 1842 the dreaded call came: Captain Fraser was required to rejoin his Regiment to be 'placed at the disposal of the Commander in Chief'. In despair he and Mina saw all their plans vanishing into thin air. However, George, who had fallen ill again, now requested the long overdue furlough to which he was entitled and was granted sixteen

8 South-western region of Madhya Pradesh
9 British Library L/MIL/10/25-27
10 1793–1841. Responsible for the decision to invade Afghanistan.

months' leave. 'Nothing but a sick certificate could have prevented his obligation to join his Corps,' declared Mina. For convalescence, before the long voyage from Bombay, the doctor recommended a three-month journey to Ootacamund in the Nilgiri Hills, the summer capital of the Madras Presidency and later known as'Queen of Hill Stations', where soldiers often went to recuperate,

George and Mina, however, were not destined to see the Nilgiri Hills. They reached Achalpur, about seventy miles west of Nagpur, before George became too weak to continue. Captain and Mrs Ward, complete strangers, came to the rescue and did what they could to help, including sitting up all night with George to relieve Mina.

When George seemed to be on the mend they set off again for Bombay, still several hundred miles away. About halfway, nearing Aurangabad, George again became too ill to go further; once again they had to throw themselves on the mercy of total strangers, this time Captain and Mrs Strange. There, *The Times* of 24 November 1842 baldly states, George died on 27 August.

Mina managed to write to her mother-in-law in November: George had been in great pain in the final stages of his journey but, a few days before he died, was still expressing hopes of recovery; he then succumbed to a high fever and lost the power of speech.

> His end was peaceful ... I closed his eyes and held up his mouth until it was proper I should leave the room.

She was overwhelmed by her loss, declaring she had no wish to live any longer – 'all my joy in this world is gone'. She was only thankful that George had not died on the road but in the comfort of Captain Strange's home. His patience and resignation from the first day of his illness had been 'beyond belief ... I adored my Husband & ... Every person who knew him became attached to him'.

Captain Strange undertook to arrange a tombstone for George; meanwhile, Mina daily wept and prayed 'over the spot in which his dear body lies'. Her plan was to return to Nagpur to collect her possessions, sell the house and then return to Aurangabad to see the finished tombstone, before leaving for Scotland (see Plate XXX). Aware that he was dying, George had told Mina to go straight home to his mother at Moniack. 'He was perfectly resigned to his Maker's will but he had no wish to die – his desire was to get home – to Moniack.'

She wrote again from Nagpur on Christmas Eve that year: she longed to leave India, but George's affairs were not yet settled. Everything reminded her of George and their happiness together. Letters from Jane, still in ignorance and 'speaking of my beloved George as if he were still in existence' added to her distress, and now, four months later, she still found it hard to believe she would never see him or hear his voice again.

The best laid plans

Throughout that autumn the family at home were worrying, once again, about silence from India. Knowing that George had been ill and hearing that he had leave of absence, they continued to wait for the mail with 'sickening suspence'. By November they had had confirmation of his death and James heard from Aeneas Mackintosh that 'the Indian papers lament his death as a loss to the service ... well may you and the poor widow mourn your bereavement'. He added a postscript reporting Holt Mackenzie's opinion of what was going on in Afghanistan: there was a hawkish desire in India House to 'conduct with rage and cruelty a war begun in fear and folly. We ought rather to humble ourselves in repentance from a most unjust aggression on innocent people.'

The same month, Amy's husband, John Forsyth, wrote a sensitive letter of commiseration to James. Amy was especially concerned for Jane, knowing from her visits with her two little girls to Moniack, that her grandmother had long looked forward to George's homecoming 'as the last & greatest happiness she could expect in this world'. Jane, now eighty-five, was bearing up but, according to James, was 'wild & hard ... I hope she will soon be more softened & composed than at present'. All she could do was hang on to the bitter-sweet expectation of Mina's arrival at Moniack, 'where she will find a welcome and a resting place and we shall have all that remains of him'. James himself was desolate, mourning 'the last of our family – the last of a band of brothers such as seldom leave their home to lay their bones in a foreign land'.

Jane Anne was too worried about her mother to consider her own grief – she took her customary comfort in her faith and her belief that such trials were 'dealings from God to bring him to himself & to look to heaven only as our rest'. She was not able to be with her mother because Affleck was ill and needed hot drinks throughout the night and a fire kept burning in his room. The ten-year-old Georgy, 'such a tender little nurse & so sensible', was dispatched to cheer up Grandmamma. Jane Anne, worn out by the stream of commiserating callers, was also supervising the cleaning of Culduthel, 'rooting out the dirt & trash of 11 years accumulating'; Affleck, deeper than ever in debt, had reluctantly taken the decision to sell.

In February the following year, Major Brown, Edward's shipmate wrote to James: he counted both William and George among his closest friends 'and I shall ever deplore their deaths as my own brothers'; how often they had all talked of going home and now he had lost all desire to leave India without them. He had been doing his best to hurry the process of probate so that Mina could go home as soon as possible. 'She feels her loss very much particularly in being thrown among strangers and she is very anxious to join you.' However, there was still confusion about George's pay and it was unlikely that Mina would get home in the near future.

The Major had news of William's sons: he knew Charles well and spoke highly of him; he was working in the Customs Department and was soon to get promotion. William was said to be now doing well in Allahabad. He knew that Amy had corresponded with her brothers and had witnessed Charles's pleasure at receiving a letter from his sister.

There are five further letters from Mina to Jane. The first two, in June and October1843, were full of nervous indecision about the future. The next brought news of their friend from Nagpur days, Hugh Inglis, now Major, who had promised to visit her and might even escort her home. He and George had been very fond of each other since childhood and 'he still seems deeply interested & affected when I speak of our departed one which I often do to him'. He was 'a good & very intelligent officer' and was likely to get the command of a cavalry division. They had not met for nearly six years and she was apprehensive:

> I was then a gay thoughtless young woman & a wife, now I am a poor solitary widow & whatever my age may be in appearance I am ... haggard.

Despite her fears, Hugh Inglis was clearly not put off by her looks; on Christmas Eve 1843 Mina told Jane that she had 'consented to become the property of Hugh Inglis' and was married. She deeply regretted that she had not managed to get home to meet George's family, but Hugh talked of taking her to Scotland. They were living a quiet and easy life in a very small station, and her husband seemed surprisingly content despite his earlier love of society.

For Jane this was indeed bitter: she had set her heart on welcoming Mina. Jane Anne understood: she had suspected something of the kind might happen but was not prepared for it 'so very soon ... we are all greatly shocked but for you only do we feel and mourn your disappointment, hopes & insulted feelings'. She urged her not to let Mina know her hurt but 'let her feel that you are not so entirely dependent on her but have many others to love and care for you'. Jane Anne herself had other worries: Affleck had been ill for some time and she had accepted that his life was 'precarious'; they were still in the process of the sale of Culduthel and she hated the arduous business of having to keep the house tidy for potential buyers. Her great friend Eliza Kerr thought it a great pity that Affleck's extravagance had led to its loss and advised Jane Anne to 'take the subject to your God'.

Sale

With George's death, the rich stream of letters which had been flowing between Scotland and India for nearly half a century finally dries up. From now on it becomes more difficult to draw anything but a hazy picture of the family. There are countless notes from Jane Anne to her mother about day-to-day affairs and minor illnesses but most are undated with no address. There are also regular letters from Jane Anne to her children, which give news of the goings on at home, again undated. By now envelopes were in use but often, with their informative addresses and postmarks, they are missing. So the last part of the story must needs be something of a patchwork.

The year 1844 started badly for the family. Faced with leaving her beloved home, Jane Anne wrote to Affleck, who had been unwell for some time and was consulting doctors in London: 'I wish it were over & we away from it: it is misery to me to be longer here now.' She could hardly bear to see 'my poor sweet little garden looking so gay and smiling'. Affleck seemed merely to be relieved at the prospect of being free of his worries.

As well as the cleaning and packing up, Jane Anne was bearing the brunt of the search for a house to rent. Affleck would not settle for any of the country houses she suggested; in desperation, she took a house in Church Street, Inverness, opposite the Episcopal Chapel, St Johns. It was 'very airy & cheerful & convenient' with a view over the hills and a garden bordering the river. It was not, of course, quite big enough for the whole family and it would be a jigsaw to fit everyone in when the elder boys were home from school. Affleck would undoubtedly realise his loss when he was cooped up in Inverness with nothing to do but walk up and down the street.

His illness became so worrying that Jane Anne joined him in London to consult Dr Chambers; Jeanie took over the care of Georgy, now twelve, Fanny, nine and Catherine four, and put the house in Church Street to rights. The sale of Culduthel was concluded, for £53,000, on 24 Feb 1844, and James Evan Baillie took possession three months later.

James was also ill in Edinburgh, with pain in his side and throat, staying with the MacNeills in Queen Street and planning to escape the east winds of April by recuperating on the island of Bute. His health did not improve, however, and Jeanie joined him at 7 Church Row, Hampstead, for the summer months. Although they would have then preferred to go home and spend two weeks taking the waters at Strathpeffer, they eventually took advice and embarked on a tour of the Continent.

> With poor George's case before us and also the knowledge that his grandfather died at 42 of a liver complaint, I cannot but think [Dr] Fraser right in taking precautions.

They found it difficult to get good cheap accommodation as there were now so many tourists: the English 'ruin everything ... and swarm like bees!' Many of the tourists were young, with excellent French, and Jeanie urged Millicent and Mary to work at their languages as 'who is it that does not go abroad now?'

The trip did them both good, although Jeanie spent much of the time scribbling instructions to the gardener about painting the greenhouse; to the housemaid Isobel about laying the dust in the house with damp turnip and carrot leaves and to the dairymaid Peggy about selling her butter a penny a pound cheaper than the market. James was irritated as ever by news of his mother's erratic behaviour: 'pretty much in her usual way – endeavouring to impress people with an idea of how ill she is but going to dinner at Newton, into Inverness, to Aldourie & here & there & everywhere in a manner that disproves the force of her complaints'. By now Jane was eighty-seven and living more or less alone at Moniack, so it is not surprising that she had a few aches and pains and swollen feet or that she was 'very fidgety'. She continued to write a daily diary, totally illegibly, on scraps of paper.

Her granddaughters took it in turns to keep Grandmamma company whenever they could. Luckily, Georgy and Fanny were there when she set her bedroom curtains on fire; they raised the alarm, but 'ten seconds more and all was over'. She had already had another near fatal accident when she had set her cap alight while reading at night, badly burning her forehead and right hand. Mary, now seventeen, liked being 'walking stick ... when she goes to the Glen' and sighed from school, 'What would I give for a wander up by the side of the Burn with Grandmamma & Caesar'. Jane was generous to all her grandchildren, contributing to the boys' education and buying the girls new dresses for their balls. With no money of their own, they gratefully accepted her presents and pocketed the handouts.

The end of an era

On 11 March 1844, in Dehra Dun, William Fraser junior sharpened his pencil and sat down to write a careful, legible letter to his grandmother. He explained that he had written to his uncle James asking for assistance 'as I am in want of my daily bread', but in vain. His office having shut down, he had decided to become self-employed and 'carry on a small trade', for which he needed money:

> I therefore crave that for the sake of your deceased son William Fraser whose offspring I am [you] take the trouble of interceding of my behalf to your eldest son, J B Fraser, and persuade him to assist me with 700 or 800 Rupees by which means I will carry on some trade & support myself, an aged mother and a wife.

Several of his father's friends had helped him, suggesting that he approach his uncle for further assistance. He would have written to his grandmother often but did not know where in Scotland she lived. He hopefully addressed his letter to 'Mrs Fraser care of J.B.Fraser, Scotland'. He would write more 'but ... as you are in the dotage of your life it would be tedious for you to peruse the letter'; he ended by sending her granddaughter-in-law's best respects, remaining 'my dearest grandmother your affectionate grandson William Fraser'. Uncle James intercepted the letter and annotated it:

> William Fraser to Mrs Fraser senior not fit to be delivered to her & therefore retained, the young man by his conduct having forfeited all claim to attention.

It never reached its intended recipient.

✲

The following year, Jane Anne found a permanent home for the family at Laggan, just south of Inverness on the road to Aldourie 'in the blessed country once more'. It was not nearly as convenient as the Church Street house, being much further from Moniack and Grandmamma, 'whose time is short', but it was 'a sweet place' and the right size for the slowly diminishing family. She felt bereft as each child left home: 'People laugh when I say I am lonely but I miss every child & would rather all were at home'. She wrote to them all constantly, usually till one or two in the morning, criticising their handwriting and answering their requests: 'I will on no account consent to having your hair cut'; their desire for stiff petticoats was 'absolute nonsense'. Grandmamma was now in her ninetieth year, but with a healthy appetite and still able to get about with the help of an arm or a stick; she had daily doses of laudanum and, although confused, irritable and constantly restless, her mind had not completely gone. On her ninetieth birthday she wrote a note to Jane Anne and though it was illegible there was 'still strength in the hand that wrote this'.

James and Jeanie were often in London; 'railway mania' had gripped the country and, in between sessions in the British Library, he was fashionably dabbling in railway shares.[11] Jeanie was shopping and hunting for governesses for Jane Anne's remaining little girls – not easy, as a London governess was expensive and, not prepared to go to the north of Scotland for '£40 and her washing'. In exchange, Jane Anne was looking out for a manservant for Moniack who would ease 'the fatigue and bother of detail when we have company & who understands how to manage with company a little in the modern fashion'.

They were all home again in the autumn of 1847. For the first time since the splendid alterations, Moniack was once more full to the brim, bursting with merriment and laughter, Nanny Rose still gamely tottering on the edge of things. It was a happy housewarming party and Grandmamma loved every moment. Afterwards, Margaret Tytler wrote to her hoping that, once the visitors had gone home, she and James and Jeanie would give Moniack a rest and come and spend a quiet winter at Sanquhar.

It was not to be. Having joined in the fun of the autumn, with its poignant echoes of happy long ago days, Jane, with Jane Anne and James at her side, died in December. A friend wrote to Jane Anne:

> Her trials in so lengthened a pilgrimage have been many ... yet her final hour was blessed with the care & attention of a most affectionate daughter and the presence of that son ... in whose distinguished talents & abilities she must have felt great pride. I admired your mother greatly and I was peculiarly struck by the cheerfulness of her conversation and of the extreme & appropriate elegance of her manner & appearance.

Jane Anne wrote, 'there is an awful stillness in the chamber of death, to which the living can hardly reconcile their ... feelings'. It was the end of an era, undoubtedly, but not quite the end of the story.

11 In 1844 people realised that the railways were a medium of speculation. That year 48 Railway Bills were passed with around 220 more ready for the following session. In 1845 the bubble burst but speculation continued and thousands of miles of railway were constructed before the end of the decade.

EPILOGUE

For some time now Jane Anne's elder children have been at my elbow jostling and pleading for a proper place in the book. I have resisted them so far as this is the story of their grandparents, uncles and aunts, and it's quite long enough as it is. But, as they keep reminding me, they are the future and, in any case, readers might want to know what became of them. So I have given in on condition they share the Epilogue with James and Jeanie.

⁂

In early 1840 a letter had arrived for George from Madras addressing him as 'Dear Uncle'. It took him a moment to remember that this was James, Jane Anne's eldest son, now embarked on an Indian career and living in Madras. Doing his avuncular duty he sent James four letters of introduction to 'the best society male and female, civil and military at Madras' ...and let me tell you, sister mine, that there are few advantages of greater consequence to a young man than being well introduced in society'. Not having any idea what this young James was like, he hoped he was not being patronising in warning him against gambling, field sports and late hours.

A year later news came that nephew James was doing very well, had been mentioned in the Madras Government Gazette and won Rs3,500. He was also, he told his sister Jane, courting Miss Emma Gray although to his sister's irritation he had not said whether she was pretty. He described a sallow complexion, coal ('or to use a more elegant expression jet') black hair and 'a peculiar heaviness about her eyes that injures her appearance a good deal; but they are not *pigs eyes* for all that ... now I have been particular enough! But to say the truth when I find a person agreeable & ladylike & to crown all musical I never think for a moment whether they are pretty or not'. The liaison did not please Jane Anne and her correspondence with James became increasingly strained until she tried 'as much as possible to banish the subject from my thoughts'. From her London school Mary wrote to her mother that they had 'prayed for dear James that your letters might reach him in time to stop his marriage'. By October 1841 he was engaged to Miss Gray and married her on 29 December.

In 1843 Mina had news for Jane. Emma had had a baby, a daughter called Mary Emma.

> I can't say that the event gives me much pleasure as I highly disapprove of the connexion he formed – he certainly had a right to please himself in a matter where his own future happiness was so steeply at stake & I trust the lady has not disappointed his expectations but surely he might have made a more judicious choice or at least have selected a girl of *pure* blood for his wife. I don't like half-castes.

Emma was probably the victim of a rumour going around India on account of her black hair and sallow complexion which may account for Jane Anne's dislike of the match. James certainly took great pains to reassure his mother of her English and Irish antecedents; her grainy photograph is indecisive.

❁

The year that James and Emma got married, 1841, a distant cousin, Hugh Fraser of Balnain, was planning some shooting in his ancestral lands along Loch Ness. The Culduthel girls were agog to meet this new relation: 'I hear Hugh Balnain is positively coming north' wrote Jane to her sister Mary. 'I really have a great curiosity to see the man but don't say so to anyone. Millicent told me he is hideous'. Five days after meeting Jane, Hugh expressed his interest and, despite Jane Anne's warning that Mary was the eldest of a huge family and 'a *portionless* girl', he persuaded her to become engaged. Early the following year she married him. Jeanie was very excited about the marriage of her favourite niece and organised the cake to be sent from Edinburgh. She tried hard to point the bride's untidy mother in the direction of some suitable clothes – ' a ruby or green velvet dress … would make a countess of you for life'. It would cost £12 or £13 – far too much, probably, for the thrifty Jane Anne, who had inherited none of her mother's passion for the latest fashion, and never had the slightest interest in what she wore. After a European tour along with a King Charles Spaniel, the young couple sailed for Bombay in 1843.

After Jane and Hugh had left Jane Anne wrote to the boys:

> It was a sad sad parting. Poor Papa who had been so cheerful all along wept bitterly and so did Jane, the little girls too & all the servants who were all up & looking out at the dining room window were crying & blessing Jane ... Hugh poor fellow could say nothing but looked quite pale & the tears in his eyes when he said God bless you all. What a sad long day Wednesday was ... we dined in the drawing room for I could not have borne the dining room after having seen such merry happy faces there but 2 days before.

To add to their despondency, there was terrible news from India that week:

> The people at Cabal have revolted & massacred a fearful number of our troops, both men & officers, & the whole is at yet not known.[1]

Jane Anne, writing as usual in the small hours, was determined to be up early that day '& busy ourselves all day, the only way to keep off sadness'.

Poor Hugh Fraser of Balnain. He was one of the many who survived only a few months after arriving in India. He left a pregnant young wife, married for less than a year, who immediately set sail for home. She arrived at Culduthel just in time to have the baby, a little girl. For two years, however, the baby's health declined; she and her mother spent much

1 Massacre at Kabul during the 1st Anglo-Afghan War, 1839-1842, during which Alexander Burnes was among the many killed.

time at Moniack where Great Grandmother became deeply attached to the baby and was heartbroken when she died aged just over two.

✻

When Jane arrived at Culduthel, just about to give birth, Jane Anne had her hands full getting Mary and Millicent ready for the Northern Meeting Balls, Millicent in plain white with a Fraser tartan sash fastened to her shoulder and a head-dress of the Fraser badge 'with yew and a few hollyhocks to enliven it'. She reckoned the waltzing 'was more racing than anything else, as fast as possible, and there were several tumbles'. Jane Anne reckoned it 'a most merry ball' but was heartily glad when it was over. Afterwards she quizzed her daughters about their partners but 'like any other young girl in the room, they couldn't or wouldn't say'. Their cunning mother discovered that they had waltzed with at least 'three or four Lords if that is anything'.

✻

When, in 1844, Culduthel was sold, Jane Anne's elder children were distraught. The fourteen-year-old Alister, at Addiscombe Military College, wondered where his home was to be. Uncle James wrote bracingly:

> Unhappily the sacrifice was unavoidable – the heavy expence of a very large family with other serious drains & losses left your father no alternative but to dispose of his estate – & his anxiety to provide for his family, especially your sisters, who have no means of helping themselves, may be judged by the pain he has incurred by submitting to this sacrifice.

As to home, 'next to Culduthel Moniack I think must always be regarded by you as your true home ... so pluck up your spirits and take care of your health'.

Mary's nineteen-year-old sensibilities were badly wounded: 'the very idea of being *asked to dine at Culduthell*' she exploded, further infuriated that her father was pretending that 'he didn't care a straw about it'. She wrote to Affleck 'Oh Adoo, it is perhaps wrong pride but I feel so *ashamed* to hear Papa call[ed] Culduthell and all of us the same ... .when really we have no business with the name'.

She was the next daughter to leave home. She had always been the most difficult child of the Culduthel family, often crossing swords with her mother and recording in her diary 'a very unhappy day for I was out of favour with mama' and another day 'mama very cross'. She rebelled at Mrs Teed's school in London where her headmistress reported her 'most troublesome', (and Millicent 'sweet as honey'), earning a stiff letter from her mother who threatened not to have her home unless she improved: 'I could not bear to fight over these points in you ... instead of loving and trusting you as I hoped to do'. Mary latterly chose to find herself employment as a companion in other families rather than hang around at home. In 1847, however, she found herself a most suitable husband, the musical John Macdonald with a posting as a doctor in the East India Company.

John Macdonald, an only child, with few cousins, was totally unprepared for the family tears and outpouring of affection for Mary when the time came to leave after their wedding in January 1848. Unable to cope, he lost his temper, was rude to Jane Anne and the happy couple set off for their honeymoon in stony silence. Mary, however, was equal to this, took it calmly in her stride, told him what she thought of him and got him to write an apologetic letter to her mother from Southampton, before sailing.

She loved her life as a doctor's wife in India. By early 1849 they had settled on a farm outside Lucknow and she sent very detailed letters to 'Darling Mummy and Daddy' of her daily doings, their house and the surrounding area. Her first baby, Margaret Mary Jane, born in late 1848, was 'a v. pretty little button' and Mina came to help her. Just like her mother she had had no problem with the birth. John, who astonished the servants by being such 'a capital nurse', wrote to his mother in law of 'my own beloved Mary presenting me yesterday morning with such a dear little girl ... if it were not for the baby lying beside her you would never fancy she had been ill and God bless her she did bear it all *so well*.' Jeanie, the baby's godmother, sent her a travelling cap of tartan.

They managed to meet up with James and Emma on a boat trip and were concerned by Emma's flighty ways. It was not very sensible to sing to gentlemen on deck after dark: it occasioned gossip. Emma was always talking about 'that nice young man ... or her friend Mr ...' James seemed impervious to 'her odd ways' and was clearly very fond of his wife but how could he be so blind? The marriage lasted, however, and resulted in seven children.

Mary also caught up in India with brother Willie – 'very fat and popular because of his everlasting good humour'. 'Dear provoking Willie' his headmaster had called him. He was backward for his age but was the universal favourite 'always ready to oblige anybody'. All he ever wanted to do was fish. His letters from school were so badly written and lacking in information that he resorted to drawing, much to his mother's fury. 'Learn to write as if you were chatting to us ... pray write plain English and until you can *really* draw, don't favour us with any more such sketches'. Poor Willie. He had been sent down from Addiscombe Military Academy in disgrace and packed off to India. He had always been idle and had the great charm and easygoing nature of his Uncle Edward. Mary reckoned he might have married six times over but he was so mean that 'he looks at a rupee twice before he gives half of it'. In India his careless lifestyle probably contributed to his early death in March 1850. Ned also died young. He joined his brothers in India 'with a good character & great hopes', married in 1848 and was dead by June 1849.

'Sweet as honey' Millicent, the sister between Jane and Mary, danced her way through every ball possible and kept everyone happy. She ran Moniack during the alterations in the absence of Jeanie and James. 'I did not dine out once as Granny would have been alone and that would not do'. She was a godsend to Jane and her frail baby accompanying them on health promoting visits to Nairn. She managed her parents' household while they were in London seeking medical advice for Affleck. In October 1849 we hear of her heart being broken by 'these abominable selfish <u>he</u> creatures' and she remained unmarried; she lived latterly at Rebeg and was probably one of the 'old aunts' who used to steal down the hill to

Moniack, clamber up to the loft where the bundles of letters were stored and peel off the saleable stamps.

Two of the three little girls at the end of the family, Georgy and Amelia, were no doubt complicit in this venture too as they also died unmarried. Their sister Fanny, whose brightness and sweetness of temperament had always cheered everyone up, especially Grandmamma, married Montague White when she was eighteen and had two sons and a daughter.

And Amy Fraser Forsyth? By 1851 she had eight children and was living in a roomy comfortable house in Keith with three servants. By 1861 another four children had appeared but, by then, their two eldest daughters, Jane and Amy, aged 16 and 14, had died of consumption. Five of the nine boys were named William, James Baillie, Edward, Alexander and George while the one surviving daughter was Millicent. In 1836 John Forsyth, delighted with his first son, had written to say that he was to be called William in memory of Amy's 'departed parent'.

Amy's story should have a happy ending but, after 1861, something went badly wrong and she and John were divorced. In 1871 she is found living alone in one room in Keith, an 'annuitant'. John's will of 1877 makes handsome provision for his children, grandchildren, servants and his illegitimate daughter but 'by decree of divorce passed against my then wife and mother of these children she thereby forfeited all her claims and rights, whether by ordinary law or deed'. So the end of Amy's story remains a mystery for the moment.

After Jane's death James and Jeanie were mostly at Moniack, taking part in local life. There is a delightful snapshot of them sitting in 'the English Chapel', St John's in Church Street.

> One of the two gallery pews immediately below the organ was occupied by the aristocratic-looking Sheriff Tytler of Aldourie, and the other by the venerable and accomplished Mr James Baillie Fraser of Relig, the author of a number of books illustrative of Persian life and manners. The crimson rays from the stained glass window gleaned on many a Christmas and Easter day on the long silvery locks of the old Sheriff as they flowed over his drab overcoat, [see Plate IX] and on the pleasant face, white hair, and striped brown and yellow waistcoat of Relig as he sat by the side of his equally venerable-looking wife in her close satin bonnet and soft shawl.[2]

There were still visits for literary purposes to London. By 1844 James had published his four travel books[3], several romances and historical novels based on his adventures.[4]

2 *Inverness before the Railways*, Isobel Anderson, 1885, p. 108.

3 Journal of a Tour through part of the snowy range of the Himala Mountains 1820; Travels and Adventures in the Persian Provinces 1826; Narrative of a Journey into Khorasan, 1825; A Winter's Journey from Constantinople to Tehran, 1838; Narrative of the Residence of the Persian Princes in London, in 1835 and 1836 with an account of their journey from Persia, and subsequent adventures.

4 The Kuzzilibash, 1828; The Persian Adventurer, 1830; The Highland Smugglers, 1832; Tales of the Caravanserai, 1833; Ailee Nimroo, 1842; The Dark falcon, 1844.

This monument was erected in the garden by Jane in memory of William, Edward, Alexander and George. Her inscription ends with the words: *The aged mother trusts to be reunited with her children beloved in life and honoured in the dust*. Jeanie added to it to commemorate James and ended with a poem:

O weep not for the holy dead
His trials are past
His suffering o'er
And she he loved
The path will tread
And Death will join
To part no more.

Now he turned his pen to biography and the next years were devoted to recounting the story of James Skinner; he based his book on conversations remembered and on Skinner's own journal. This was challenging and he consulted many of his friends for their memories of Skinner and advice on how to go about it. Not everyone was encouraging. One publisher considered that, even though it would be under James's name, it 'does not possess that present interest which would render the publication desirable ... it might not pay its expenses'. Others thought it was likely to be far too long and James was advised to leave out many of the characters and events of the early nineteenth century. As Mountstuart Elphinstone had been told when writing his great *Account of the Kingdom of Caubul*, 'Cut out one half and let some other person cut off another half and the fourth will be read'. In June 1848 his former publishers, Smith Elder & Co., recommended that he write instead 'a work of fiction of stirring interest' based on Skinner's life. A month later they changed their mind and agreed to publish 500 copies, in two volumes, if James would contribute £100; it was published in March 1851 – *The Military Memoir of Lt. Col. James Skinner, CB*. There were over fifty presentation copies including over thirty to various magazines and reviews and three to Hercules Skinner. By the beginning of June there was not a single copy left.

⁂

James died at Moniack on 23 January 1856 aged 73. He was buried in the family enclosure in the churchyard high in Kirkhill with a view over the river Beauly and away to the hills of the west. Jeanie added his name to the monument in the garden at Moniack which commemorates his four brothers; it stands today shaded by the cedar trees he planted.

Once his last literary project had been achieved, for his remaining five years, James was able to indulge his passion for planting; he introduced many exotic species, including pines grown from seeds sent by MacNeill during the siege of Herat, and followed the landscape gardening ideas of the time by building romantic bridges and grottos in the Glen. One bridge is reputed to be a copy of a bridge in Ravenna; the grotto beside it, called the Chapter House, might have grown, if the story of his plan is to be believed, into a ruined Franciscan monastery. He was intent on creating a beautiful natural garden in this miniature glen, full of interest and places to sit and dream. Some of the conifers he planted along the burn are now among the loftiest in Britain, towering majestically above those who walk beneath.

And, today, down through the enchanting Glen, under the Ravenna bridge, past the foot of the tallest tree, heedless of the dog walkers, the joggers, the teenagers rapt in their world of mobiles and music, the photographers by day and the rustlings and callings of the night, unmindful, too, of the echoes of children's voices from long ago, the burn runs on to the sea.

Jane Anne's grandson, Philip Affleck Fraser, by the grotto and bridge built by James in the glen.

Acknowledgements

Through the long years of writing this book many friends have supported me in all sorts of generous ways and I ask forgiveness if I have left out any of your names.

My first thanks must be to the late Toby Falk, his wife, Gael, and the late Mildred Archer who helped us to understand the importance of the Fraser of Reelig archive discovered in the 1980s. Their beautiful book, *India Revealed*, which tells the story of James and William Fraser, their art and adventures, has been an invaluable help to me.

The enthusiasm and guidance of Anthony Chamier, also sadly no longer here, encouraged me in the early days and many people have since generously shared their expertise with me: David Alston (slavery), Rachel and Garth Armstrong (St Helena), Libby Brown (Lady Hood's portrait), Robin Campbell (Latin), Ted Dinsdale-Young (ships), Stephen Foster (Guyana), Jamie Gaukroger and colleagues (Highland Archive Centre), Chris Hillman (St Helena), Alexey Krichtal (cotton plantations), Daniel Leunens (St Omer), the late Raymond Salisbury-Jones (Charterhouse), Sylvia Shorto (buildings in Delhi), Antony Wakeham (Gurkhas), Bruce Wannell (Persia) and Anne Whitehead (St Helena, the Balcombe family and ever willing authorial help). Vee Bellars, Sue Duke and Mary Miers pointed me towards potential publishers and David Alderson, Sorrel Bentinck, Mary Lewis and others took photographs for me.

I am very grateful to Lavinia Horsbrugh-Porter for enthusiastically driving me to relevant places in England. Thanks to Diana Don who arranged for us to visit the Old Rectory in Little Dunham, Ed Grimsdale who spent a day guiding us around Gawcott and Toby Parker, archivist, who showed us Haileybury.

Various supporters have read bits, some sensibly reorganising my commas: Letty Buxton, Elizabeth Marshall, Juliet McCracken, Chen Miers, David Ogden, Simone and John Richards and Barbara Wallis. Kind friends found pictures for me including Clare Sorensen who also directed me to the various Fraser-Tytler locations around Edinburgh. Cousin Catherine Baines has given constant practical help while my brother, Ned Lyttelton, and sister Lavinia Northrop have listened tirelessly and encouragingly throughout. My thanks to you all.

Thanks to William Dalrymple for his more than generous Foreword. George Chamier has been a most understanding and painstaking editor and Charlie Gore did a wonderful job creating a map of the local houses. I am greatly indebted to the Alexander family: to Pen for her constant interest, support and encouragement, to Helen for her skilful maps and, above all, to Nick for his generosity, untiring tolerance and beautiful and creative design of the book. Thanks to all of them and to Mark Lawson for his help and advice.

My family, near and extended, has been supportive in many ways throughout and to all of them I say thank you, especially to Malcolm, for his willing advice and for his forbearance and understanding through the recent years of my preoccupation and neglect.

Kathy Fraser
Reelig House, November 2015

Short Bibliography

Throughout the text, where I have quoted from or referred to a book, it is described in the footnotes. I have dipped in and out of numerous books but the following is a selection of those that I have read from cover to cover, more or less, and found informative or entertaining and often both.

Anderson, Isobel (1885) *Inverness before the Railways.* A & W Mackenzie. Republished Charles Leakey, Inverness, (1984).

Archer, Mildred and Falk,Toby (1989) *India Revealed.* Cassell.

Balcombe, Betsy (Introduction by J David Markham (2005), *To Befriend an Emperor.* Ravenhall Books, Linden Publishing Ltd.

Dalrymple, William (2002) *White Mughals.* Harper Collins.

Dalrymple, William (2006) *The Last Mughal.* Bloomsbury Publishing plc.

Dalrymple, William (2013) *The Return of a King.* Bloomsbury Publishing plc.

Devine, T.M. (2003), *Scotland's Empire 1600-1815.* Allen Lane.

Grant of Rothiemurchus, Elizabeth, (1898), *Memoirs of a Highland Lady (*ed Lady Strachey) London: John Murray

Holman, Dennis (1961) *Sikander Sahib.* London, Heinemann.

Hopkirk, Peter, (1990) *The Great Game.* Oxford, OUP.

Ingram, Edward (1979 *The Beginning of the Great Game in Asia 1828-1834*: Clarendon Press, Oxford.

Mason, Philip (1985) *The Men who Ruled India.* Pan Books, Jonathan Cape Ltd.

Morris, Henry (1903) *The Life of Charles Grant.* London, John Murray.

Nenadic, Stana (2007) *Lairds & Luxury. The Highland Gentry in Eighteenth Century Scotland.* John Donald.

Raza, Rosemary (2006) *In Their Own Words, Women Writers and India 1740-1857.* Oxford, OUP.

Spear, Percival (1973) *Twilight of the Mughals:* Pakistan, OUP.

Wright, Denis (1977) *The English among the Persians:* William Heinemann Ltd.

SELECTED INDEX